Java Programming:
From Problem Analysis
To Program Design

Java Programming: From Problem Analysis To Program Design

D.S. Malik
P.S. Nair

THOMSON

COURSE TECHNOLOGY

Australia • Canada • Mexico • Singapore • Spain • United Kingdom • United States

THOMSON

™

COURSE TECHNOLOGY

Java Programming: From Problem Analysis to Program Design

by D.S. Malik and P.S. Nair

Senior Editor:
Jennifer Muroff

Executive Editor:
Jennifer Locke

Development Editor:
Deb Kaufmann

Associate Product Manager:
Janet Aras

Editorial Assistant:
Christy Urban

Production Editor:
Aimee Poirier

Associate Product Marketing Manager:
Angie Laughlin

Cover Designer:
Steve Deschene

Compositor:
GEX Publishing Services

Manufacturing Coordinator:
Laura Burns

TO
Our Daughters

Shelly Malik

and

Meera Nair

BRIEF
Contents

TABLE OF Contents

6. Graphical User Interface (GUI) and Object-Oriented Design (OOD)   263

Preface

Welcome to *Java Programming: From Problem Analysis to Program Design*. Designed for a first Computer Science (CS1) Java course, this text will provide a breath of fresh air to you and your students. The CS1 course serves as the cornerstone of the Computer Science curriculum. Our primary goal is to motivate and excite all programming students, regardless of their level. Motivation breeds excitement for learning. Motivation and excitement are critical factors that lead to the success of the programming student. This text is a culmination and development of our classroom notes throughout more than fifty semesters of teaching successful programming.

Java Programming: From Problem Analysis to Program Design started as a collection of brief examples, exercises, and lengthy programming examples. It soon turned into a collection large enough to develop into a text. *The approach taken in this book to present the material is, in fact, driven by the students' demand for clarity and readability.* Most of the examples in this book resulted from student interaction in the classroom.

As with any profession, practice is essential. Cooking students practice their recipes. Budding violinists practice their scales. New programmers must practice solving problems and writing code. This is not a Java cookbook. We do not simply list the Java syntax followed by an example, we dissect the "why" behind all concepts. The crucial question of "Why?" is answered for every topic when first introduced. This technique offers a bridge to learning Java. Students must understand the "Why?" in order to be motivated to learn.

Traditionally, a Java programming neophyte needed a working knowledge of another programming language. This book assumes no prior programming experience. However, some adequate mathematics background such as college algebra is required.

APPROACH

Once conceived as a Web programming language, Java is slowly but surely finding its way into classrooms in the computer science curriculum. Numerous colleges and universities now teach their first programming language course (CS1) using Java. Java is a combination of traditional style programming—programming with a nongraphical user interface—and modern style programming with a graphical user interface (GUI). This book introduces you to both styles of programming. After giving a brief description of each chapter, we discuss how to read this book.

Chapter 1 briefly reviews the history of computers and programming languages. The reader can quickly skim and become familiar with some of the hardware and software components of the computer. This chapter also describes how a Java program is processed. The two basic problem-solving techniques, structured programming and object-oriented design, are also presented.

After completing Chapter 2, students become familiar with the basics of Java and are ready to write programs that are complicated enough to do some computations. This chapter introduces some terms that you will encounter throughout the book: primitive type variables, reference variables, and objects. Chapter 3 makes clear distinctions between these terms and sets the tone for the rest of the book. An object is a fundamental entity in an object-oriented programming language. This chapter further explains how an object works. Because input/output is fundamental to any programming language, it is introduced early, and is covered in detail in Chapter 3. Chapters 4 and 5 introduce control structures used to alter the sequential flow of execution.

Java is equipped with powerful yet easy-to-use graphical user interface (GUI) components to create user-friendly graphical programs. Chapter 6 introduces various GUI components and gives examples of how to use these components in Java application programs. Because Java is an object-oriented programming language, the second part of Chapter 6 discusses and gives examples of how to solve various problems using object-oriented design methodology.

Chapter 7 discusses user-defined methods. Parameter passing is a fundamental concept in any programming language. Several examples, including visual diagrams, help readers understand this concept. To pass primitive type values as objects, we use several classes introduced in Chapter 6. (Appendix D gives more detail about these classes and how to use them in Java programs. Because Chapter 6 is not a prerequisite for Chapter 7, you can review these classes in Appendix D if necessary.) It is recommended that readers with no prior programming background spend extra time on this.

Chapter 8 discusses user-defined classes. In Java, a class is an important and widely used element. It is used to create Java programs, group related operations, and it allows users to create their own data types. This chapter uses extensive visual diagrams to illustrate how objects of classes manipulate data.

Chapter 9 describes arrays. Searching and sorting algorithms are studied in Chapter 10.

Inheritance is an important principle of object-oriented design. It encourages code reuse. Chapter 11 discusses inheritance, and gives various examples to illustrate how classes are derived from existing classes. In addition, this chapter also discusses abstract classes, inner classes, and composition.

An occurrence of an undesirable situation that can be detected during program execution is called an exception. For example, division by zero is an exception. Java provides extensive support for handing exceptions. Chapter 12 shows how to handle exceptions in a program. Chapter 12 also discusses event handling, which was introduced in Chapter 6.

Chapter 13 picks up the discussion of GUI components started in Chapter 6. This chapter introduces additional GUI components and discusses how to create applets.

Chapter 14 introduces recursion. Several examples illustrate how recursive methods execute.

Appendix A lists the reserved words in Java. Appendix B shows the precedence and associativity of the Java operators. Appendix C lists the ASCII (American Standard Code for Information Interchange) portion of the Unicode character set as well as the EBCDIC (Extended Binary Code Decimal Interchange) character set. Appendix D shows how to use user-defined classes in a Java program. Appendix E describes the Java classes used in this book. Appendix F gives the answers to selected exercises in the text.

HOW TO USE THIS BOOK

Java is a complex and very powerful language. In addition to traditional (non-GUI) programming, Java provides extensive support for creating programs that use a graphical user interface (GUI). Chapter 3 introduces graphical input and output dialog boxes. Chapter 6 introduces most commonly used GUI components such as labels, buttons, and text fields. More extensive coverage of GUI components is provided in Chapter 13.

This book can be used in two ways. One is an integrated approach in which readers learn how to write both non-GUI and GUI programs as they learn basic programming concepts and skills. The other approach focuses on illustrating fundamental programming concepts with non-GUI programming first, and later incorporating GUI components. The recommended chapter sequence for each of these approaches is as follows:

- **Integrated approach:** Study all chapters in sequence.

- **Non-GUI first, then GUI:** Study Chapters 1–5 in sequence. Then study Chapters 7–12 and Chapter 14. This approach initially skips Chapters 6 and 13, the primary GUI chapters. After studying Chapters 1–5, 7–12, and 14, the reader can come back to study Chapters 6 and 13, the GUI chapters.

If you choose the second approach, it should also be noted that the Programming Examples in Chapters 8 and 11 are developed first without any GUI components, and then the programs are extended to incorporate GUI components. Also, if Chapter 6 is skipped, the reader can skip the event handling part of Chapter 12. Chapter 14 (recursion) contains two Programming Examples: one creates a non-GUI application program, while the other creates a program that uses GUI. If you skip Chapters 6 and 13, you can skip the GUI part of the Programming Examples in Chapters 8, 11, 12, and 14. Once you have studied Chapter 6 and 13, you can study the GUI part of the Programming Examples of Chapters 8, 11, 12, and 14.

Figure 1 shows a chapter dependency diagram for this book. Solid arrows indicate that the chapter at the beginning of the arrow is required before studying the chapter at the end of the arrow. A dotted arrow indicates that the chapter at the beginning of the arrow is not essential to studying the chapter at the end of the dotted arrow.

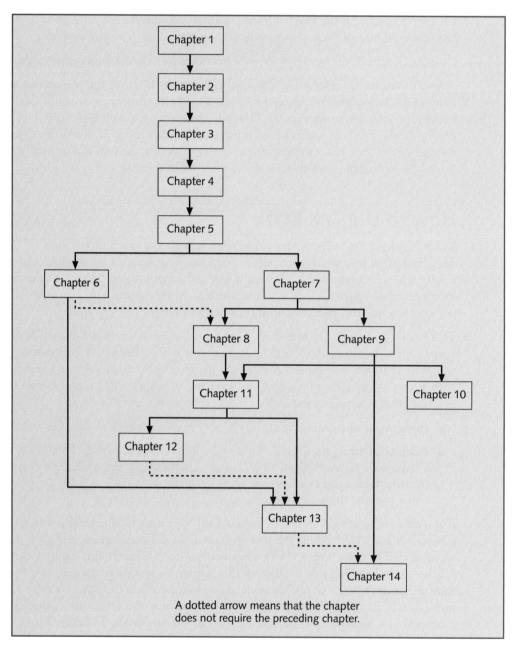

Figure 1   Chapter dependency diagram

FEATURES

Every chapter in this book includes the following features. These features are conducive to learning and enable students to learn the material at their own pace.

- Four-color interior design shows accurate Java code and related comments.

- *Learning Objectives* offer an outline of the Java programming concepts discussed in detail in the chapter.

- *Notes* highlight important facts about the concepts introduced in the chapter.

- More than 200 visual diagrams, both extensive and exhaustive, illustrate difficult concepts.

- Numbered *Examples* illustrate the key concepts with their relevant code. The programming code in these examples is numbered for easy reference, and is followed by a Sample Run. An explanation then follows that describes what each line in the code does.

- *Programming Examples* are complete programs featured at the end of each chapter. These examples include the accurate, concrete stages of Input, Output, Problem Analysis and Algorithm Design, and a Complete Program Listing.

- *Quick Review* offers a summary of the concepts covered in the chapter.

- *Exercises* further reinforce learning and ensure that students have, in fact, learned the material.

- *Programming Exercises* challenge students to write Java programs with a specified outcome.

From beginning to end, the concepts are introduced at a pace that is conducive to learning. The writing style of this book is simple and straightforward, and it parallels the teaching style of a classroom. Before introducing a key concept, we explain why certain elements are necessary. The concepts introduced are then described using examples and small programs.

Each chapter has two types of programs. The first type are small programs that are part of the numbered Examples (*e.g.*, Example 4-1), and are used to explain key concepts. In these examples, each line of the programming code is numbered. The program, illustrated through a Sample Run, is then explained line-by-line. The rationale behind each line is discussed in detail.

This book also features numerous case studies called Programming Examples. These Programming Examples form the backbone of the book and are highlighted with an icon in the margin like the one shown here.

The programs are designed to be methodical and user-friendly. Each Programming Example starts with a Problem Analysis, and is then followed by the Algorithm Design. Every step of the algorithm is then coded in Java. In addition to teaching problem-solving techniques, these detailed programs show the user how to implement concepts in an actual Java program. We strongly recommend that students study the Programming Examples very carefully in order to learn Java effectively.

Quick Review sections at the end of each chapter reinforce learning. After reading the chapter, students can quickly walk through the highlights of the chapter and then test themselves using the ensuing Exercises. Many readers refer to the Quick Review as an easy way to review the chapter before an exam.

All source code and solutions have been written, compiled, and quality assurance tested with Sun Java JDK 1.4.

INSTRUCTOR RESOURCES

The following supplemental materials are available when this book is used in a classroom setting. All of the teaching tools available with this book are provided to the instructor on a single CD-ROM.

Electronic Instructor's Manual. The Instructor's Manual that accompanies this textbook includes:

- Additional instructional material to assist in class preparation, including suggestions for lecture topics.

- Solutions to all the end-of-chapter materials, including the Programming Exercises.

ExamView®. This textbook is accompanied by ExamView, a powerful testing software package that allows instructors to create and administer printed, computer (LAN-based), and Internet exams. ExamView includes hundreds of questions that correspond to the topics covered in this text, enabling students to generate detailed study guides that include page references for further review. These computer-based and Internet testing components allow students to take exams at their computers, and save the instructor time because each exam is graded automatically.

PowerPoint Presentations. This book comes with Microsoft PowerPoint slides for each chapter. These are included as a teaching aid for classroom presentations, either to make available to students on the network for chapter review, or to be printed for classroom distribution. Instructors can add their own slides for additional topics that they introduce to the class.

Distance Learning. Course Technology is proud to offer online courses in WebCT and Blackboard, as well as at MyCourse.com, Course Technology's own course enhancement tool, to provide the most complete and dynamic learning experience possible. When you add online content to one of your courses, you're adding a lot: self-tests, links, glossaries, and—most of all—a gateway to the 21st century's most important information resource. We hope that you will make the most of your course, both online and offline. For more information on how to bring distance learning to your course, contact your local Course Technology sales representative.

Source Code. The source code is available at **www.course.com**, and is also available on the Teaching Tools CD-ROM. The input files needed to run some of the programs are also included with the source code. However, the input files should first be stored on a floppy disk in drive **A:**.

Solution files. The solution files for all programming exercises, are available at www.course.com, and is also available on the Teaching Tools CD-ROM. The input files needed to run some of the programming exercises are also included with the solution files. However, the input files should first be stored on a floppy disk in drive A:.

ACKNOWLEDGMENTS

There are many people that we must thank who, one way or another, contributed to the success of this book. We owe a great deal to the following reviewers who patiently read each page of every chapter of the current version and made critical comments to improve on the book: Dr. C. Michael Allen, University of North Carolina, Charlotte; Dr. Barbara Doyle, Jacksonville University; Khaled Mansour, Washtenaw Community College; Craig Murray, Indiana University; and Jennifer Stewart, Indiana University as well as proposal reviewer Michael Mick, Purdue University, Calumet. The reviewers will recognize that their criticisms have not been overlooked and, in fact, made this a better book. Thanks to Development Editor Deb Kaufmann for carefully editing and promptly returning each chapter. All this would not have been possible without the planning of Senior Editor Jennifer Muroff. We extend our sincere thanks to Jennifer, as well as to Production Editor, Aimee Poirier, and also to the QA department of Course Technology for carefully testing the code.

We are thankful to our parents for their blessings.

Finally, we are thankful to the support of our wives Sadhana and Suseela and especially our daughters Shelly and Meera, to whom this book is dedicated. They cheered us up whenever we were overwhelmed during the writing of this book.

We welcome any comments concerning the text. Comments may be forwarded to the following e-mail addresses: malik@creighton.edu or psnair@creighton.edu.

D.S. Malik

P.S. Nair

1

AN OVERVIEW OF COMPUTERS AND PROGRAMMING LANGUAGES

In this chapter, you will:

♦ Learn about different types of computers

♦ Explore the hardware and software components of a computer system

♦ Learn about the language of a computer

♦ Learn about the evolution of programming languages

♦ Examine high-level programming languages

♦ Discover what a compiler is and what it does

♦ Examine how a Java program is processed

♦ Learn what an algorithm is and explore problem-solving techniques

♦ Become aware of structured and object-oriented programming design methodologies

INTRODUCTION

We live in an era when information is processed almost at the speed of light. Through computers, the technological revolution is drastically changing the way we live and communicate with one another. Terms such as "the Internet," which was unfamiliar just a few years ago, are now common. With the help of computers you can send letters to, and receive letters from, loved ones within seconds. You no longer need to send a résumé by mail to apply for a job; in many cases you can simply submit your job application via the Internet. You can watch how stocks perform in real time, and instantly buy and sell them. Kids in elementary school regularly "surf" the Internet and use computers to design their classroom projects. Students no longer type their papers on typewriters or write them by hand. Instead, they use powerful word-processing software to complete their term papers. Many people maintain and balance their checkbooks on computers.

These are some of the ways that computers have greatly affected our daily lives. They are all made possible by the availability of different software, which are computer programs. For example, word-processing software is a program that enables you to write term papers, create impressive-looking résumés, and even write a book. This book, for example, was created with the help of a powerful word processor. Without software a computer is useless. Software is developed with the help of programming languages. The programming language Java is especially well suited for developing software to accomplish a specific task.

Until the early 1990s, at the beginning of a programming language course, instructors spent the first few weeks just teaching their students how to use computers. Today, by the time students graduate from high school, they know very well how to work with a computer. This book is not concerned with explaining how to use computers. Rather, it teaches you how to write programs in the Java programming language. It is useful, however, to understand some of the basic terminology and different components of a computer before you begin programming. This chapter briefly describes the main components of a computer system, the history and evolution of computer languages, and some fundamental ideas about how to solve problems with computer programming.

AN OVERVIEW OF THE HISTORY OF COMPUTERS

In the 1950s, computers were large devices accessible only to a very few people. All work—surgery, accounting, word processing, and calculations, among other tasks—was done without the aid of computers. In the 1960s, multimillion-dollar computers emerged, and only large companies could afford them. These computers were very large in size, and only computer experts were allowed to use them. During the mid-1970s, computers became cheaper and smaller. By the mid-1990s, people from all walks of life were able to afford them. During the late 1990s, small computers became even less expensive and much faster. Although there are several categories of computers, such as mainframe, midsize, and micro, all computers share some basic elements.

ELEMENTS OF A COMPUTER SYSTEM

A computer is an electronic device capable of performing commands. The basic commands that a computer performs are input (get data), output (display result), storage, and performance of arithmetic and logical operations.

In today's market, personal computers are sold with descriptions such as Pentium 4 Processor 2.5 GHz, 1 GB RAM, 80 GB HD, 19-inch SVGA monitor, and come with preloaded software such as operating systems, games, encyclopedias, and application software such as word processors or money-management programs. These descriptions represent two categories: hardware and software. Items such as "Pentium 4 Processor 2.5 GHz, 1 GB RAM, 80 GB HD, 19-inch SVGA monitor" fall into the hardware category. Items such as "operating systems, games, encyclopedias, and application software" fall into the software category. Let's look at the hardware first.

Hardware

Major hardware components include the following: central processing unit (CPU); main memory (MM), also called random access memory (RAM); input/output devices; and secondary storage. Some examples of input devices are the keyboard, mouse, and secondary storage. Examples of output devices are the monitor, printer, and secondary storage. Let's examine these components in more detail.

Central Processing Unit

The **central processing unit (CPU)** is the brain of the computer and the single most expensive piece of hardware in your personal computer. The more powerful the CPU, the faster the computer. The CPU contains several components, including the control unit (CU), program counter (PC), instruction register (IR), arithmetic logic unit (ALU), and accumulator (ACC). Figure 1-1 shows how certain components of the CPU fit together.

The CPU components shown in Figure 1-1 work as follows:

- The **control unit (CU)** is the brain of the CPU. It has three main functions: fetch and decode the instructions, control the flow of information (instruction or data) between the CPU and main memory, and control the operation of the CPU's internal components. The internal components are:

- The **program counter (PC)** points to the next instruction to be executed.

- The **instruction register (IR)** holds the instruction that is currently being executed.

- The **arithmetic logic unit (ALU)** carries out all arithmetic and logical operations.

- The **accumulator (ACC)** holds the results of the operations performed by the arithmetic logic unit.

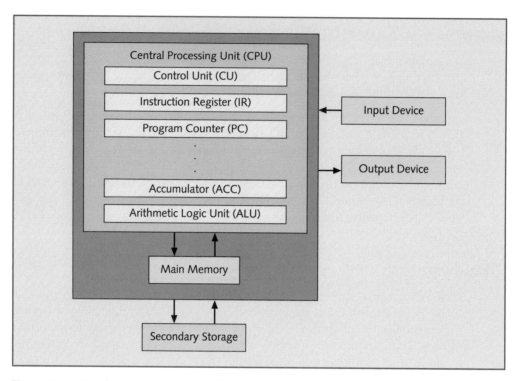

Figure 1-1   Hardware components of a computer

Main Memory

Main memory is directly connected to the CPU. All programs must be loaded into main memory before they can be executed. Similarly, all data must be brought into main memory before a program can manipulate it. When the computer is turned off, everything in main memory is lost for good.

Main memory is an ordered sequence of cells, called **memory cells**. Each cell has a unique location in main memory, called the **address** of the cell. These addresses help you access the information stored in the cell. Figure 1-2 shows main memory with 100 storage cells.

Today's computers come with main memory consisting of millions to billions of cells. Although Figure 1-2 shows data stored in cells, the content of a cell can be either a programming instruction or data.

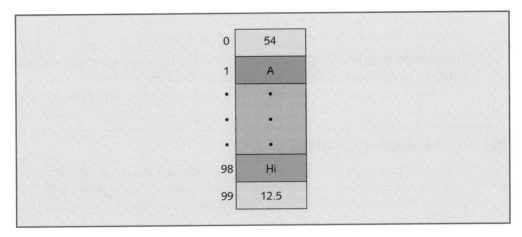

Figure 1-2   Main memory with 100 storage cells

Secondary Storage

Because programs and data must be stored in main memory before processing and because everything in main memory is lost when the computer is turned off, information stored in main memory must be transferred to some other device for permanent storage. The device that stores information permanently (unless the device becomes unusable or you change the information by rewriting it) is called **secondary storage**. To be able to transfer information from main memory to secondary storage, these components must be directly connected to each other. Examples of secondary storage are hard disks, floppy disks, ZIP disks, CD-ROMs, and tapes.

Input/Output Devices

For a computer to perform a useful task, it must be able to take in data and programs and display the results of calculations. The devices that feed data and programs into computers are called **input devices**. The keyboard, mouse, and secondary storage are examples of input devices. The devices that the computer uses to display results are called **output devices**. A monitor, printer, and secondary storage are examples of output devices.

Software

Software consists of programs written to perform specific tasks. For example, you use word-processing programs to write letters, papers, and even books. There are two types of programs: system programs and application programs.

System programs control the computer. The system program that loads first when you turn on your PC is called the **operating system**. Without an operating system, the computer is useless. The operating system monitors the overall activity of the computer and provides services. Some of these services include: memory management, input/output activities, and storage management. The operating system has a special program that organizes secondary storage so that you can conveniently access information. Moreover, operating systems are written in programming languages.

Application programs perform a specific task. Word processors, spreadsheets, and games are examples of application programs. All application programs are written using computer programming languages. The operating system is the program that runs application programs.

THE LANGUAGE OF A COMPUTER

When you press **A** on your keyboard and the computer displays **A** on the screen, have you ever wondered what is actually stored inside the computer's main memory? What is the language of the computer? How does it store whatever you type on the keyboard?

Remember that a computer is an electronic device. Electrical signals move along channels inside the computer. There are two types of electrical signals: analog and digital. **Analog signals** are continuous wave-forms used to represent things such as sound. Audio tapes, for example, store data in analog signals. **Digital signals** represent information with a sequence of 0s and 1s. A 0 represents a low voltage, and a 1 represents a high voltage. Digital signals are more reliable carriers of information than are analog signals and can be copied from one device to another with exact precision. Have you ever noticed that on an audio tape copy the sound quality is not as good as that on the original tape? Therefore, digital signals are used inside the computer.

Because digital signals are processed inside a computer, the language of a computer, called **machine language**, is a sequence of 0s and 1s. The digit 0 or 1 is called a **binary digit**, or **bit**. Sometimes a sequence of 0s and 1s is referred to as **binary code**.

Bit: A binary digit 0 or 1.

A sequence of eight bits is called a **byte**. Every letter, number, or special symbol (such as * or {) on your keyboard is encoded as a sequence of bits, each having a unique representation.

The most commonly used encoding scheme on personal computers is the seven-bit **American Standard Code for Information Interchange (ASCII)**. The ASCII data set consists of 128 characters numbered 0 through 127. That is, in the ASCII data set, the position of the first character is 0, the position of the second character is 1, and so on. In this scheme, **A** is encoded as 1000001. In fact, **A** is the 66th character in the ASCII character code, but its position is 65 because the position of the first character is 0. Furthermore, 1000001 is the binary representation of 65. The character 3 is encoded as 0110011. For a complete list of the printable ASCII character set, refer to Appendix C.

Inside the computer, every character is represented as a sequence of eight bits, that is, as a byte. Because ASCII is a seven-bit code, you must add 0 to the left of the ASCII encoding of a character. Hence, inside the computer, the character **A** is represented as 01000001, and the character 3 is represented as 00110011.

There are other encoding schemes, such as EBCDIC (used by IBM) and Unicode, which is a more recent development. EBCDIC consists of 256 characters; **Unicode** consists of

65,536 characters. To store a Unicode character, you need two bytes. Java uses the Unicode character set. Therefore, in Java, every character is represented as a sequence of 16 bits, that is, 2 bytes. The ASCII character set is a subset of Unicode; the first 128 characters of Unicode are the same as the characters in ASCII.

THE EVOLUTION OF PROGRAMMING LANGUAGES

The most basic computer language, machine language, provides program instructions in bits. Even though most computers perform the same kinds of operations, the designers of different CPUs sometimes choose different sets of binary codes to perform those operations. Therefore, the machine language of one computer is not necessarily the same as the machine language of another computer. The only consistency among computers is that in any computer, all data are stored and manipulated as binary codes.

Early computers were programmed in machine language. To see how instructions are written in machine language, suppose you want to use the equation:

```
wages = rate · hours
```

to calculate weekly wages. Assume that memory locations of `rate`, `hours`, and `wages` are `010001`, `010010`, and `010011`, respectively. Further suppose that the binary code `100100` stands for load, `100110` stands for multiplication, and `100010` stands for store. In machine language, you might need the following sequence of instructions to calculate weekly wages:

```
100100   010001
100110   010010
100010   010011
```

To represent the weekly wages equation in machine language, the programmer had to remember the machine language codes for various operations. Also, to manipulate data, the programmer had to remember the locations of the data in the main memory. Remembering specific codes made programming difficult and error-prone.

Assembly languages were developed to make the programmer's job easier. In **assembly language**, an instruction is an easy-to-remember form called a **mnemonic**. Table 1-1 shows some examples of instructions in assembly language and their corresponding machine language code.

Table 1-1 Examples of Instructions in Assembly Language and Machine Language

Assembly Language	Machine Language
LOAD	100100
STOR	100010
MULT	100110
ADD	100101
SUB	100011

Using assembly language instructions, you can write the equation to calculate the weekly wages as follows:

```
LOAD   rate
MULT   hours
STOR   wages
```

As you can see, it is much easier to write instructions in assembly language. However, a computer cannot execute assembly language instructions directly. The instructions first have to be translated into machine language. A program called an **assembler** translates the assembly language instructions into machine language.

Assembler: A program that translates a program written in assembly language into an equivalent program in machine language.

Moving from machine language to assembly language made programming easier, but a programmer was still forced to think in terms of individual machine instructions. The next step toward making programming easier was to devise **high-level languages** that were closer to spoken languages, such as English, French, German, and Spanish. Basic, FORTRAN, COBOL, Pascal, C, C++, and Java are all high-level languages. You will learn the high-level language Java in this book.

In Java, you write the weekly wages equation as follows:

```
wages = rate * hours;
```

The instruction written in Java is much easier to understand and is self-explanatory to a novice user who is familiar with basic arithmetic. As in the case of assembly language, however, the computer cannot directly execute instructions written in a high-level language. To run on a computer, these Java instructions first need to be translated into an intermediate language called **bytecode** and then interpreted into a particular machine language. A program called a **compiler** translates instructions written in Java into bytecode.

Compiler: A program that translates a program written in a high-level language into the equivalent machine language. (In the case of Java, this machine language is the bytecode.)

Recall that the computer understands only machine language. Moreover, different types of CPUs use different machine languages. To make Java programs **machine independent**, that is, able to run on many different types of computer platforms, the designers of Java introduced a hypothetical computer called the **Java Virtual Machine (JVM)**. In fact, bytecode is the machine language for the JVM.

PROCESSING A JAVA PROGRAM

There are two types of Java programs—applications and applets. Now that you have some understanding of machine language and high-level languages and recognize that the computer can understand only machine language, you are ready to review the steps required to execute programs written in Java.

You must carry out the following steps, as shown in Figure 1-3, to execute a program written in Java.

1. You use an editor to create (that is, type) a program in Java following the rules, or syntax, of the language. This program is called the **source program**. The program must be saved in a text file named `ClassName.java` where `ClassName` is the name of the Java class contained in the file. If a file contains a public class named `WelcomeAll`, then it must be saved in a text file named `WelcomeAll.java`. Otherwise an error will occur.

Source program: A program written in a high-level language.

2. You must verify that the program obeys the rules of the programming language— that is, the program must be syntactically correct—and translate the program into the equivalent bytecode. The compiler checks for correctness of syntax and translates the program into bytecode. That is, the compiler checks the source program for syntax errors and, if no error is found, translates the program into bytecode. The bytecode is saved in the file with the `.class` extension. For example, the bytecode for `WelcomeAll.java` is stored in the `WelcomeAll.class` file by the compiler.

3. To run a Java application, the `.class` file must be loaded into computer memory. To run a Java applet, you must use either a Web browser or an applet viewer, a stripped-down Web browser for running applets. The programs that you write in Java language are usually developed using a **software development kit (SDK)**. The SDK contains many programs that are useful in creating your program. For example, it contains the necessary code to display the results of the program and several mathematical functions to make the programmer's job somewhat easier. Therefore, if certain code is already available to you, you can use the available code rather than writing your own code. Once the program is developed and successfully compiled, you must still bring the code for the resources used from the SDK into your program to produce a final program that the computer can execute. This prewritten code resides in a place called the **library**. The Java library is organized into a set of packages, where each **package** contains a collection of related classes. A program called **linker** links the bytecode of your program with the necessary code residing in the library. This linking is done automatically and you need not be concerned with it.

Linker: A program that combines the bytecode with other programs provided by the SDK and used in the program to create the executable code.

4. The next step is to execute the Java program. First the bytecode of your Java program, linked with the library code used in the program, must be loaded in the main memory. When you give the execute command, a program called a **loader** automatically does this for you. Finally, a program called an **interpreter** translates each bytecode instruction into the machine language of your computer, and then executes it.

Loader: A program that loads an executable program into main memory.

Interpreter: A program that reads, translates each bytecode instruction into the machine language of your computer, and then executes it.

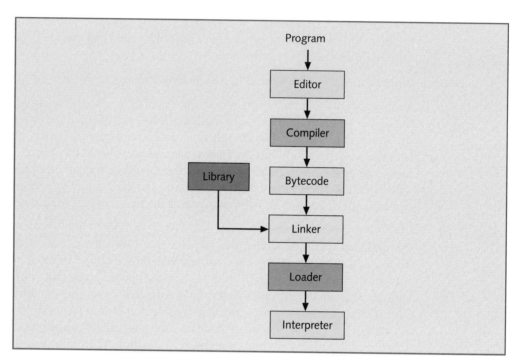

Figure 1-3   Processing a Java program

As a programmer, your primary concern is with Step 1. That is, you must learn, understand, and master the rules of the programming language to create source programs. As noted earlier, programs are developed using an SDK. Well-known SDKs used to create programs in the high-level language Java include Forte (from Sun), JBuilder (from Borland), and CodeWarrior (from Metrowerks). These SDKs contain an editor to create the program, a compiler to check the program for syntax errors, a program to link the object code with the resources used from the SDK, and a program to execute the program. These SDKs also are quite user friendly. When you compile your program, the compiler not only identifies the syntax errors, but also typically suggests how to correct them. Moreover, with just a simple command, the object code is linked with the resources used from the SDK. The command that does the linking in Forte is `Build`; in Java Builder, it is `Rebuild` or `Make`; and in CodeWarrior, it is `Make`. (For further clarification regarding the use of these commands, check the documentation of these SDKs.) If the program is not yet compiled, each of these commands first compiles the program and then links and produces the executable code.

In Chapter 2, after being introduced to some basic elements of Java, you will see how a Java program is processed. As a programmer, as noted above, you are still mainly concerned with the first step. That is, you must master the rules of Java to create the source program. The programs in this book are developed and tested using the Sun JDK version 1.4 as well as the SDKs mentioned above.

PROGRAMMING WITH THE PROBLEM ANALYSIS–CODING–EXECUTION CYCLE

Programming is a process of problem solving. Different people use different techniques to solve problems. Some techniques are nicely outlined and easy to follow; they solve the problem and give insight into how the solution was reached. Such problem-solving techniques can be easily modified if the domain of the problem changes.

To be a skillful problem solver and hence to become a skillful programmer, you must use good problem-solving techniques. One common problem-solving technique includes analyzing a problem, outlining the problem requirements, and designing steps, called an **algorithm**, to solve the problem.

Algorithm: A step-by-step problem-solving process in which a solution is arrived at in a finite amount of time.

In the programming environment, the problem-solving process requires the following steps:

1. Analyze the problem, outline the problem and its solution requirements, and design an algorithm to solve the problem.

2. Implement the algorithm in a programming language, such as Java, and verify that the algorithm works.

3. Maintain the program by using and modifying it if the problem domain changes.

Figure 1-4 summarizes this programming process. This figure shows only the main components of the problem analysis–coding–execution cycle. This figure does not show the linking and loading stages, shown earlier in Figure 1-3, which take place automatically.

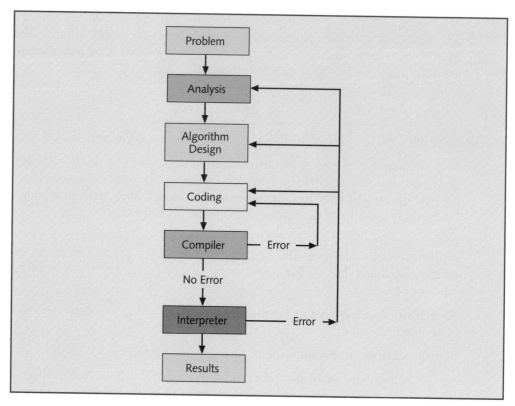

Figure 1-4 Problem analysis–coding–execution cycle

To develop a program to solve a problem, you start by analyzing the problem. You then design the algorithm; you write the program instructions in a high-level language, or code the program; and you enter the program into a computer system. Analyzing the problem is the first and most important step. This step requires that you do the following:

- Thoroughly understand the problem.

- Understand the problem requirements. Requirements can include whether the program requires interaction with the user, whether it manipulates data, whether it produces output, and what the output looks like. If the program manipulates data, the programmer must know what the data are and how they are represented. That is, you need to look at sample data.

- If the program produces output, you should know how the results should be generated and formatted. If the problem is complex, divide the problem into sub-problems and repeat Steps 1 and 2. That is, for complex problems, you need to analyze each subproblem and understand each subproblem's requirements.

After you carefully analyze the problem, the next step is to design an algorithm to solve the problem. If you broke the problem into subproblems, you need to design an algorithm for each subproblem. Once you design an algorithm, you need to check it for correctness. You can sometimes test an algorithm's correctness by using sample data. At other times, you might need to perform some mathematical analysis to test the algorithm's correctness.

Once you have designed the algorithm and verified its correctness, the next step is to convert the equivalent code into a high-level language. You use a text editor to enter the program into a computer. You must then make sure that the program follows the language's syntax. To verify the correctness of the syntax, you run the code through a compiler. If the compiler generates error messages, you must identify the errors in the code, remove them, and then run the code through the compiler again. When all syntax errors are removed, the compiler generates the machine code (bytecode in Java).

The final step is to execute the program. The compiler guarantees only that the program follows the language's syntax. It does not guarantee that the program will run correctly. During execution the program might terminate abnormally due to logical errors, such as division by zero. Even if the program terminates normally, it may still generate erroneous results. Under these circumstances, you may have to reexamine the code, the algorithm, or even the problem analysis.

Your overall programming experience will benefit if you spend enough time to thoroughly complete problem analysis before attempting to write programming instructions. Usually, you do this work on paper using a pen or pencil. Taking this careful approach to programming has a number of advantages. It is much easier to discover errors in a program that is well analyzed and well designed. Furthermore, a thoroughly analyzed and carefully designed program is much easier to follow and modify. Even the most experienced programmers spend a considerable amount of time analyzing a problem and designing an algorithm.

Throughout this book, you will not only learn the rules of writing programs in Java, but also learn problem-solving techniques. Each chapter discusses several programming problems, each of which is clearly marked as a Programming Example. These Programming Examples teach techniques to analyze and solve problems and also help you understand the concepts discussed in the chapter. To gain the full benefit of this book, we recommend that you work through the Programming Examples at the end of each chapter.

Example 1-1

In this example, we design an algorithm to find the perimeter and area of a rectangle.

To find the perimeter and area of a rectangle, you need to know the rectangle's length and width. The perimeter and area of the rectangle are then given by the following formulas:

```
perimeter = 2 · (length + width)
area = length · width
```

The algorithm to find the perimeter and area of the rectangle can be written as follows:

1. Get the length of the rectangle.

2. Get the width of the rectangle.

3. Find the perimeter using the following equation:

```
perimeter = 2 · (length + width)
```

4. Find the area using the following equation:

```
area = length · width
```

Example 1-2

In this example, we design an algorithm that calculates the monthly paycheck of a salesperson at a local department store.

Every salesperson has a base salary. The salesperson also receives a bonus at the end of each month based on the following criteria: If the salesperson has been with the store for five or fewer years, the bonus is $10 for each year that he or she has worked there. If the salesperson has been with the store for more than five years, the bonus is $20 for each year that he or she has worked there. The salesperson can earn an additional bonus as follows: If the salesperson's total sales for the month are more than $5000 but less than $10000, he or she receives a 3% commission on sales. If the salesperson's total sales for the month are at least $10000, he or she receives a 6% commission on sales.

To calculate a salesperson's monthly paycheck, you need to know the base salary, the number of years that the salesperson has been with the company, and the total sales made by the salesperson for that month. Suppose `baseSalary` denotes the base salary, `noOfServiceYears` denotes the number of years that the salesperson has been with the store, `bonus` denotes the bonus, `totalSale` denotes the salesperson's total sales for the month, and `additionalBonus` denotes the additional bonus.

You can determine the bonus as follows:

```
if(noOfServiceYears is less than or equal to five)
      bonus = 10 · noOfServiceYears
otherwise
      bonus = 20 · noOfServiceYears
```

Next you can determine the additional bonus of the salesperson as follows:

```
if(totalSale is less than 5000)
    additionalBonus = 0
otherwise
    if(totalSale is greater than or equal to 5000 and
              totalSale is less than 10000)
        additionalBonus = totalSale · (0.03)

    otherwise
        additionalBonus = totalSale · (0.06)
```

Using the preceeding information, you can now design the algorithm to calculate a salesperson's monthly paycheck.

1. Get `baseSalary`.

2. Get `noOfServiceYears`.

3. Calculate `bonus` using the following formula:

```
if(noOfServiceYears is less than or equal to five)
    bonus = 10 · noOfServiceYears
otherwise
        bonus = 20 · noOfServiceYears
```

4. Get `totalSale`.

5. Calculate `additionalBonus` using the following formula:

```
if(totalSale is less than 5000)
    additionalBonus = 0
otherwise
        if(totalSale is greater than or equal to 5000 and
                        totalSale is less than 10000)
            additionalBonus = totalSale · (0.03)
        otherwise
                additionalBonus = totalSale · (0.06)
```

6. Calculate `payCheck` using the equation:

```
payCheck = baseSalary + bonus + additionalBonus
```

 The type of coding used in Examples 1–1 and 1–2 is called **pseudocode**, which is an "outline" of a program that could be translated into actual code. Pseudocode is not written in a particular language, nor does it have syntax rules; it is mainly a shortcut to show the programming steps.

PROGRAMMING METHODOLOGIES

Two popular approaches to programming design are the structured approach and the object-oriented approach, which are outlined below.

Structured Programming

Dividing a problem into smaller subproblems is called **structured design**. Each subproblem is then analyzed, and a solution for the subproblem is obtained. The solutions of all subproblems are then combined to solve the overall problem. This process of implementing a structured design is called **structured programming**. The structured design approach is also known as **top-down design**, **stepwise refinement**, and **modular programming**.

Object-Oriented Programming

The previous section discussed the structured design programming methodology. This section briefly describes a widely used programming methodology called **object-oriented design (OOD)**.

In OOD, the first step in the problem-solving process is to identify components called **objects**, which form the basis of the solution, and determine how these objects interact with one another. For example, suppose you want to write a program that automates the video rental process for a local video store. The two main objects in this problem are the video and the customer.

After identifying the objects, the next step is to specify the relevant data for each object and possible operations to be performed on that data. For example, for a video object, the data might include the movie name, starring actors, producer, production company, and number of copies in stock. Some of the operations on a video object might include checking the name of the movie, reducing the number of copies in stock by one after a copy is rented, and incrementing the number of copies in stock by one after a customer returns a particular video.

This illustrates that each **object** consists of data and the operations on those data. An object combines data and operations on that data into a single unit. In OOD, the final program is a collection of interacting objects. A programming language that implements OOD is called an **object-oriented programming (OOP)** language. You learn about the many advantages of OOD in later chapters.

Because an object consists of data and operations on those data, before you can design and use objects, you need to learn how to represent data in computer memory, how to manipulate data, and how to implement operations. In Chapter 2, you will learn the basic data types of Java and discover how to represent and manipulate data in computer memory. Chapter 3 discusses how to input data into a Java program and output the results generated by a Java program.

To create operations, you write algorithms and implement them in a programming language. Because a data element in a complex program usually has many operations, to separate operations from each other and to use them effectively and in a convenient manner, you use **methods** to implement algorithms. After a brief introduction in Chapters 2 and 3, you will learn the details of methods in Chapter 7. Certain algorithms require that a program make decisions, a process called selection. Other algorithms might require that certain statements be repeated until certain conditions are met, a process called repetition. Still other algorithms might require both selection and repetition. You will learn about selection and repetition mechanisms, called control structures, in Chapters 4 and 5.

Finally, to work with objects, you need to know how to combine data and operations on that data into a single unit. In Java, the mechanism that allows you to combine data and operations on the data into a single unit is called a **class**. In Chapter 8, you will learn how to create your own classes.

In Chapter 9, using a mechanism called an array, you learn how to manipulate data when data items are of the same type, such as items in a list of sales figures. As you can see, you need to learn quite a few things before working with the OOD methodology.

For some problems, the structured approach to program design is very effective. Other problems are better addressed by OOD. For example, if a problem requires manipulating sets of numbers with mathematical functions, you might use the structured design approach and outline the steps required to obtain the solution. The Java library supplies a wealth of functions that you can use to effectively manipulate numbers. On the other hand, if you want to write a program that would make a candy machine operational, the OOD approach is more effective. Java was designed especially to implement OOD. Furthermore, OOD works well and is used in conjunction with structured design. Chapter 6 explains how to use an existing class to create a Graphical User Interface (GUI), and then gives several examples explaining how to solve problems using OOD concepts.

Both the structured design and OOD approaches require that you master the basic components of a programming language to be an effective programmer. In the next few chapters, you will learn the basic components of Java required by either approach to programming.

QUICK REVIEW

1. A computer is an electronic device capable of performing arithmetic and logical operations.

2. A computer system has two components: hardware and software.

3. The central processing unit (CPU) and the main memory are examples of hardware components.

4. The control unit (CU) controls a program's overall execution. It is one of several components of the CPU.

5. The arithmetic logic unit (ALU) is the CPU component that performs arithmetic and logical operations.

6. All programs must be brought into main memory before they can be executed.

7. When the power is switched off, everything in main memory is lost.

8. Secondary storage provides permanent storage for information. Hard disks, floppy disks, ZIP disks, CD-ROMs, and tapes are examples of secondary storage.

9. Input to the computer is done via an input device. Two common input devices are the keyboard and the mouse.

10. The computer sends its output to an output device such as the computer monitor.

11. Software are programs run by the computer.

12. The operating system monitors the overall activity of the computer and provides services.

13. The most basic language of a computer is a sequence of 0s and 1s called machine language. Every computer directly understands its own machine language.

14. A bit is a binary digit, 0 or 1.

15. A byte is a sequence of eight bits.

16. Assembly language uses easy-to-remember instructions called mnemonics.

17. Assemblers are programs that translate a program written in assembly language into machine language.

18. To run a Java program on a computer, the Java program first must be translated into an intermediate language called bytecode and then interpreted into a particular machine language.

19. To make Java programs machine independent, the designers of the Java language introduced a hypothetical computer called the Java Virtual Machine (JVM).

20. Bytecode is the machine language for the JVM.

21. Compilers are programs that translate a program written in a high-level language into an equivalent machine language. In the case of Java, this machine language is the bytecode.

22. A linker is a program that combines the bytecode with other programs provided by the SDK and used in the program to create the executable code.

23. In a high-level language, the necessary steps to execute a program are: edit, compile, link, load, and execute.

24. A loader transfers executable code into main memory.

25. An interpreter is a program that reads, translates each bytecode instruction into the machine language of your computer, and then executes it.

26. An algorithm is a step-by-step problem-solving process in which a solution is arrived at in a finite amount of time.

27. A problem-solving process has three steps: analyze the problem and design an algorithm, implement the algorithm in a programming language, and maintain the program.

28. There are two basic approaches to programming design: structured design and object-oriented design.

29. In structured design, a problem is divided into smaller subproblems. Each subproblem is solved, and the solutions of all subproblems are then combined to solve the problem.

30. In object-oriented design (OOD), the programmer identifies components called objects, which form the basis of the solution, and determines how these objects interact with one another. In OOD, a program is a collection of interacting objects.

31. An object consists of data and the operations on those data.

EXERCISES

1. Mark the following statements as true or false.

   a. Assembly language is the language that uses mnemonics for its instructions.

   b. The arithmetic logic unit performs arithmetic operations and, if an error is found, it outputs the logical errors.

c. A compiler is a program that translates a Java program into bytecode.

d. Bytecode is the machine language of the JVM.

e. The CPU functions under the control of the control unit.

f. RAM stands for readily available memory.

g. A program written in a high-level programming language is called a source program.

h. The operating system is the first program loaded into the computer when the power is turned on.

i. The first step in the problem-solving process is to analyze the problem.

2. Name some components of the central processing unit.

3. What is the function of the control unit?

4. Name two input devices.

5. Name two output devices.

6. Why is secondary storage needed?

7. Why do you need to translate a program written in a high-level language into machine language?

8. Why would you prefer to write a program in a high-level language rather than a machine language?

9. What are the advantages of problem analysis and algorithm design over directly writing a program in a high-level language?

10. Design an algorithm to find the weighted average of four test scores. The four test scores and their respective weights are given in the following format:

```
testscore1 weight1
...
```

For example, a sample data is as follows:

```
75 0.20
95 0.35
85 0.15
65 0.30
```

11. A salesperson leaves his home every Monday and returns every Friday. He travels by company car. Each day on the road, the salesperson records the amount of gasoline put in the car. Given the starting odometer reading (the odometer reading before he leaves on Monday) and the ending odometer reading (the odometer reading after he returns home on Friday), design an algorithm to find the average miles per gallon. A sample data is as follows:

```
68723 71289 15.75 16.30 10.95 20.65 30.00
```

2

BASIC ELEMENTS OF JAVA

In this chapter, you will:

♦ Become familiar with the basic components of a Java program, including methods, special symbols, and identifiers

♦ Explore primitive data types

♦ Discover how to use arithmetic operators

♦ Examine how a program evaluates arithmetic expressions

♦ Explore how mixed expressions are evaluated

♦ Learn about type casting

♦ Become familiar with the `String` type

♦ Learn what an assignment statement is and what it does

♦ Discover how to input data into memory by using input statements

♦ Become familiar with the use of increment and decrement operators

♦ Examine ways to output results using output statements

♦ Learn how to import packages and why they are necessary

♦ Discover how to create a Java application program

♦ Explore how to properly structure a program, including using comments to document a program

In this chapter, you will learn the basics of Java. As you begin to learn the Java programming language, two questions naturally arise: First, what is a computer program? Second, what is programming? A **computer program**, or a program, is a sequence of statements whose objective is to accomplish a task. **Programming** is a process of planning and creating a program. These two definitions tell the truth, but not the whole truth, about programming. It might take an entire book to give a satisfactory definition of programming. An analogy might help you gain a better grasp of the nature of programming, so we'll use a topic on which almost everyone has some knowledge—cooking. A recipe is also a program, and everyone with some cooking experience can agree on the following:

1. It is usually easier to follow a recipe than to create one.

2. There are good recipes and there are bad recipes.

3. Some recipes are easy to follow and some are difficult to follow.

4. Some recipes produce reliable results and some do not.

5. You must have some knowledge of how to use cooking tools to follow a recipe to completion.

6. To create good new recipes, you must have much knowledge and understanding of cooking.

These same six points can also be applied to programming. Let us take the cooking analogy one step further. Suppose you need to teach someone how to become a chef. How would you go about it? Would you introduce the person to good food, hoping the person develops a taste for good food? Would you have the person follow recipe after recipe in the hope that some of it rubs off? Or, would you first teach the use of tools, the nature of ingredients and foods and spices, and then explain how these subjects fit together?

Just as there are many ways to teach cooking, there are also different ways to teach programming. However, some fundamentals apply to programming, just as they do to cooking or music.

Learning a programming language is like learning to become a chef or learning to play a musical instrument. All three skills require direct interaction with the tools. You cannot become a good chef just by reading recipes. Similarly, you cannot become a musician by reading books about musical instruments. The same is true of programming. You must have a fundamental knowledge of the language, and you must test your programs on the computer to make sure that each program does what it is supposed to do.

THE BASICS OF A JAVA PROGRAM

There are two types of Java programs—Java applets and Java application programs. Java applets are programs designed to run on a Web browser. Java application programs are stand-alone programs. To introduce the basic Java components, in the next few chapters we develop Java application programs. Java applets are discussed in Chapter 13.

The program in Example 2-1 demonstrates a Java application program. At this point you don't need to be concerned with the details of the program.

Example 2-1

The following is a sample Java application program:

```java
public class Welcome
{
      public static void main(String[] args)
      {
          System.out.println("Welcome to Java Programming");
      }
}
```

If you execute this program, it will print the following line on the screen:

```
Welcome to Java Programming
```

If you have never seen a program written in a programming language, the Java program in Example 2-1 may look like a foreign language. To make meaningful sentences in any foreign language, you must learn its alphabet, words, and grammar. The same is true of a programming language. To write meaningful programs, you must learn the programming language's special symbols, words, and syntax rules. The **syntax rules** tell you which statements (instructions) are legal, or accepted by the programming language, and which are not. You must also learn **semantic rules**, which determine the meaning of the instructions. The programming language's rules, symbols, and special words enable you to write programs to solve problems. The syntax rules determine which instructions are valid.

Programming language: A set of rules, symbols, and special words.

In the remainder of this section, you will learn about some of the special symbols of a Java program. Other special symbols are introduced as other concepts are encountered in later chapters. Similarly, syntax and semantic rules are introduced and discussed throughout the book.

The smallest individual unit of a program written in any programming language is called a **token**. Java's tokens are divided into special symbols, word symbols, and identifiers.

Special Symbols

Following are some of the special symbols:

```
+       -       *       /

.       ;       ?       ,

<=      !=      ==      >=
```

The first row includes mathematical symbols for addition, subtraction, multiplication, and division. The second row consists of punctuation marks taken from English grammar. Note that the comma is a special symbol. In Java, commas are used to separate items in a list. Semicolons are used to end a Java statement. Note that a blank, which is not shown above, is also a special symbol. You create a blank symbol by pressing the space bar (only once) on the keyboard. The third row consists of tokens made up of two characters, but which are regarded as single symbols. No character can come between the two characters, not even a blank.

Word Symbols

A second category of tokens is word symbols. Some word symbols include the following:

```
int, float, double, char, void, public, static, throws, return
```

Word symbols are also called **reserved words**, or **keywords**. The letters in a reserved word are always lowercase. Like the special symbols, each word symbol is considered a single symbol. Furthermore, word symbols cannot be redefined within any program; that is, they cannot be used for anything other than their intended use. For a complete list of reserved words in Java, see Appendix A.

    Throughout this book, reserved words are shown in **blue**.

Identifiers

A third category of tokens is identifiers. **Identifiers** are names of things, such as variables, constants, and methods, that appear in programs. Some identifiers are predefined; others are defined by the user. All identifiers must obey Java's rules for identifiers.

Identifier: A Java identifier consists of letters, digits, the underscore character (_), and the dollar sign ($), and must begin with a letter, underscore, or the dollar sign.

Identifiers can be made of only letters, digits, the underscore character (_), and the dollar sign ($); no other symbols are permitted to form an identifier.

    Java is case sensitive—uppercase and lowercase letters are considered different. Thus, the identifier NUMBER is not the same as the identifier number. Similarly, the identifiers X and x are different.

In Java, identifiers can be any length. In actuality, however, some compilers may not distinguish between identifiers that differ only beyond that system's maximum significant number of characters. (Check your system's documentation for restrictions on the length of identifiers.) For example, if only the first seven characters of the following two identifiers were distinguishable, they would be regarded as the same:

```
program1
program2
```

Some predefined identifiers that you will encounter frequently are `print` and `println` which are used when generating output, and `readLine`, which is used to input data. Unlike reserved words, predefined identifiers can be redefined, but it would not be wise to do so.

Example 2-2

The following are legal identifiers in Java:

```
first
conversion
payRate
counter1
$Amount
```

Table 2-1 shows some illegal identifiers and explains why they are illegal.

Table 2-1 Examples of Illegal Identifiers

Identifier	Description
`employee Salary`	There can be no space between `employee` and `Salary`.
`Hello!`	The exclamation mark cannot be used in an identifier.
`one+two`	The symbol + cannot be used in an identifier.
`2nd`	An identifier cannot begin with a digit.

 Compiler vendors usually begin certain identifiers with an underscore (_). When the linker links the bytecode with the system resources provided by the Software Development Kit (SDK), certain errors could occur. Therefore, you should not begin identifiers in your program with an underscore (_).

DATA TYPES

The objective of a Java program is to manipulate data. Different programs manipulate different data. A program designed to calculate an employee's paycheck will add, subtract, multiply, and divide numbers; some of the numbers might represent hours worked and pay rate. Similarly, a program designed to alphabetize a class list will manipulate names. You wouldn't expect a cherry pie recipe to help you bake cookies. Similarly, you wouldn't manipulate alphabetic characters with a program designed to perform arithmetic calculations. Furthermore, you wouldn't multiply or subtract names. Reflecting such underlying differences, Java categorizes data into different types, and only certain operations can be performed on a particular type of data. At first it may seem confusing, but by being so type conscious, Java has built-in checks to guard against errors.

Data type: A set of values together with a set of operations.

Primitive Data Types

The primitive data types are the fundamental data types in Java. There are three categories of primitive data types:

- **Integral**, which is a data type that deals with integers, or numbers without a decimal part
- **Floating-point**, which is a data type that deals with decimal numbers
- **Boolean**, which is a data type that deals with logical values

Figure 2-1 illustrates these three data types.

Figure 2-1 Primitive Data Types

Integral data types are further classified into five categories, as shown in Figure 2-2.

Figure 2-2 Integral Data Types

Why are there so many categories of integral data types? Every data type has a different set of values associated with it. For example, the `char` data type is used to represent integers between 0 and 65535. The `int` data type is used to represent integers between −2147483648 and 2147483647. The data type `short` is used to represent integers between −32768 and 32767.

Which data type you use depends on how big a number your program needs to deal with. In the early days of programming, computers and main memory were very expensive. Only a small amount of memory was available to execute programs and manipulate data. As a result, programmers had to optimize the use of memory. Because writing and making a program work is already a complicated process, not having to worry about the size of the memory makes for one less thing to think about. To effectively use memory, a programmer can look at the type of data used in a program and figure out which data type to use.

Table 2-2 gives the range of possible values associated with the five integral data types and the size of memory allocated to manipulate these values.

Table 2-2 Values and Memory Allocation for Integral Data Types

Data Type	Values	Storage (in bytes)
char	0 to 65535	2 (16 bits)
byte	−128 to 127	1 (8 bits)
short	−32768 to 32767	2 (16 bits)
int	−2147483648 to 2147483647	4 (32 bits)
long	−9223372036854775808 to 9223372036854775807	8 (64 bits)

The most commonly used integral data types are `int` and `char` and are described next. Note that the discussion of `int` data also applies to the integral types `byte`, `short`, and `long`.

The `int` Data Type

This section describes the `int` data type, but this discussion also applies to other integral data types. Integers in Java, as in mathematics, are numbers such as the following:

−6728,   −67,   0,   78,   36782,   +763

Note the following two rules from these examples:

- Positive integers do not have to have a + sign in front of them.

- No commas are used within an integer. Recall that in Java, commas are used for separating items in a list. Thus, 36,782 is interpreted as two integers: 36 and 782.

The `char` Data Type

The `char` data type is used to represent single characters—that is, letters, digits, and special symbols. The `char` data type can represent any key on your keyboard. When using the `char` data type, you enclose each character represented within single quotation marks. Examples of values belonging to the `char` data type include the following:

'A', 'a', '0', '*', '+', '$', '&', ' '

Note that a blank space is a character and is written as ' ', with a space between the single quotation marks.

The data type `char` allows only one symbol to be placed between the single quotation marks. Thus, the value 'abc' is not of the type `char`. Furthermore, even though != and similar special symbols are considered to be one symbol, they are not regarded as possible values of the data type `char` when enclosed in single quotation marks. All the individual symbols located on the keyboard that are printable are considered possible values of the `char` data type.

Of the several different character data sets currently in use, Java uses the Unicode character set, which contains 65536 values numbered 0 to 65535. The position of the first character is 0, the position of the second character is 1, and so on. Other commonly used character data sets are American Standard Code for Information Interchange (ASCII) and Extended Binary-Coded Decimal Interchange Code (EBCDIC). The ASCII character set has 128 values. ASCII is a subset of Unicode. That is, the first 128 characters of Unicode are the same as the characters in ASCII. The EBCDIC character set has 256 values and was created by IBM. Both character sets are described in Appendix C.

Each of the 65536 values of the Unicode character set represents a different character. For example, the value **65** represents **'A'**, and the value **43** represents **'+'**. Thus, each character has a predefined ordering, which is called a **collating sequence**, in the set. The collating sequence is used when you compare characters. For example, the value representing **'B'** is **66**, so **'A'** is smaller than **'B'**. Similarly, **'+'** is smaller than **'A'** since **43** is smaller than **65**.

 The 14th character in the Unicode (and ASCII) character set is called the newline character and is represented as ' \n '. (Note that the position of the newline character in the Unicode and ASCII character sets is 13 because the position of the first character is 0.) Even though the newline character is a combination of two characters, it is treated as one character. Similarly, the horizontal tab character is represented in Java as ' \t ', and the null character is represented as ' \0 ' (backslash followed by zero). Furthermore, the first 32 characters in the Unicode and ASCII character sets are nonprintable. (See Appendix C for a list of these characters.)

The `boolean` Data Type

The data type **boolean** has only two values: **true** and **false**. Also, **true** and **false** are called the **logical (Boolean) values**. The central purpose of this data type is to manipulate logical (Boolean) expressions. An expression that evaluates to **true** or **false** is called a **logical (Boolean) expression**. Logical (Boolean) expressions are formally defined and discussed in detail in Chapter 4. In Java, **boolean**, **true**, and **false** are reserved words. The memory allocated for the **boolean** data type is 1 bit.

Floating-Point Data Types

To deal with decimal numbers, Java provides the floating-point data type, which we discuss in this section. To facilitate the discussion, we will review a concept from a high school or college algebra course.

You may be familiar with scientific notation. For example:

$43872918 = 4.3872918 * 10^7$ {10 to the power of seven}

$.0000265 = 2.65 * 10^{-5}$ {10 to the power of minus five}

$47.9832 = 4.7983 * 10^1$ {10 to the power of one}

To represent real numbers, Java uses a form of scientific notation called **floating-point notation**. Table 2-3 shows how Java might print a set of real numbers. In the Java floating-point notation, the letter E stands for the exponent.

Table 2-3 Examples of Real Numbers Printed in Java Floating-Point Notation

Real Number	Java Floating-Point Notation
75.924	7.592400E1
0.18	1.800000E-1
0.0000453	4.530000E-5
-1.482	-1.482000E0
7800.0	7.800000E3

Java provides two data types to manipulate decimal numbers: `float` and `double`. As in the case of integral data types, the data types `float` and `double` differ in the set of values. Figure 2-3 illustrates these data types.

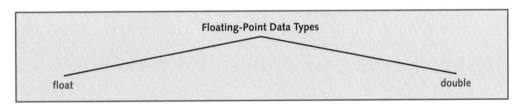

Figure 2-3   Floating-point data types

float: The data type `float` is used in Java to represent any real number between −3.4E+38 and 3.4E+38. The memory allocated for the `float` data type is 4 bytes.

double: The data type `double` is used in Java to represent any real number between −1.7E+308 and 1.7E+308. The memory allocated for the `double` data type is 8 bytes.

Other than the set of values, there is one more difference between the data types `float` and `double`. The maximum number of significant digits—that is, the number of decimal places—in `float` values is 6 or 7. The maximum number of significant digits in values belonging to the `double` type is 15. The maximum number of significant digits is called the **precision**. Sometimes `float` values are called **single precision**, and values of the type `double` are called **double precision**. If you are dealing with decimal numbers, for the most part you need only the `float` type; if you need accuracy to more than six or seven decimal places, you can use the `double` type.

If you use the data type `float` to manipulate floating-point numbers in a program, certain compilers might give you a warning message such as "truncation from double to float" or "possible loss of data". To avoid such warning messages, you should use the `double` data type. For illustration purposes and to avoid such warning messages in programming examples, this book mostly uses the data type `double` to manipulate floating-point numbers.

ARITHMETIC OPERATORS AND OPERATOR PRECEDENCE

One of the most important features of a computer is its ability to calculate. You can use standard arithmetic operators to manipulate integral and floating-point data types. There are five arithmetic operators:

+ addition

– subtraction

* multiplication

/ division

% mod (modulus) operator

You can use the operators +, –, *, and / with both integral and floating-point data types. You use % with only the integral data type to find the remainder in integer division. When you use / with the integral data type, it gives the quotient in integer division. That is, integral division truncates any fractional part; there is no rounding.

Since high school, you have probably worked with arithmetic expressions such as the following:

(i)   –5
(ii) 8 – 7
(iii) 3 + 4
(iv) 2 + 3 * 5
(v)   5.6 + 6.2 * 3
(vi) x + 2 * 5 + 6 / y

In expression (vi), **x** and **y** are some unknown numbers. Formally, an **arithmetic expression** is constructed by using arithmetic operators and numbers. The numbers in the expression are called **operands**. Moreover, the numbers used to evaluate an operator are called the operands for that operator.

In expression (i), the operator – (subtraction) is used to specify that the number **5** is negative. Moreover, in this expression – has only one operand. Operators that have only one operand are called **unary operators**.

In expression (ii), the symbol – is used to subtract 7 from 8. In this expression, – has two operands, 8 and 7. Operators that have two operands are called **binary operators**.

Unary operator: An operator that has only one operand.

Binary operator: An operator that has two operands.

In the expression (iii), 3 and 4 are the operands for the operator +. Because the operator + has two operands, in this expression, + is a binary operator. Now consider the following expression:

+27

In this expression, the operator + is used to indicate that the number 27 is positive. Here, because + has only one operand, it acts as a unary operator.

From the preceding discussion, it follows that – and + can be unary or binary arithmetic operators. However, the arithmetic operators *, /, and % are binary and must have two operands.

The following examples show how arithmetic operators—especially / and %—work with integral data types. As you can see from these examples, the operator / represents the quotient in ordinary division when used with integral data types.

Example 2-3

Arithmetic Expression	Result	Description
2 + 5	7	
13 + 89	102	
34 – 20	14	
45 – 90	–45	
2 * 7	14	
5 / 2	2	In the division 5 / 2, the quotient is 2 and the remainder is 1. Therefore, 5 / 2 with the integral operands evaluates to the quotient, which is 2.
14 / 7	2	
34 % 5	4	In the division 34 / 5, the quotient is 6 and the remainder is 4. Therefore, 34 % 5 evaluates to the remainder, which is 4.
–34 % 5	–4	In the division –34 / 5, the quotient is –6 and the remainder is –4. Therefore, –34 % 5 evaluates to the remainder, which is –4.
34 % –5	4	In the division 34 / –5, the quotient is –6 and the remainder is 4. Therefore, 34 % –5 evaluates to the remainder, which is 4.
–34 % –5	–4	In the division –34 / –5, the quotient is 6 and the remainder is –4. Therefore, –34 % –5 evaluates to the remainder, which is –4.

4 % 6

4   In the division 4 / 6, the quotient is 0 and the remainder is 4. Therefore, 4 % 6 evaluates to the remainder, which is 4.

Note that in the divisions 34 / 5 and -34 / -5, the quotients, which are 6, are the same, but the remainders are different. In the division 34 / 5, the remainder is 4; in the division -34 / -5, the remainder is -4.

The following expressions show how arithmetic operators work with floating-point numbers.

Example 2-4

Expression	**Result**
5.0 + 3.5	8.5
3.0 + 9.4	12.4
16.3 - 5.2	11.1
4.2 * 2.5	10.50
5.0 / 2.0	2.5

Order of Precedence

Consider the following expression:

3 + 4 * 5

Recall from a high school or a college algebra course that, in this expression, the operator * is evaluated first, and then the operator +. In other words, the operator * has higher **precedence** than the operator +.

When more than one arithmetic operator is used in an expression, Java uses operator precedence rules to determine the order in which operations are performed to evaluate the expression. According to the order of precedence rules for arithmetic operators,

*,   /,   %

have a higher level of precedence than

+,   -

Note that the operators *, /, and % have the same level of precedence. Similarly, the operators + and - have the same level of precedence.

When operators have the same level of precedence, operations are performed from left to right. To avoid confusion, you can use parentheses to group arithmetic expressions. For example, using the order of precedence rules,

3 * 7 - 6 + 2 * 5 / 4 + 6

means the following:

```
(3 * 7) - 6 + ( ( 2 * 5) / 4 ) + 6
= 21 - 6 + (10 / 4) + 6          (Evaluate *)
= 21 - 6 + 2 + 6                 (Evaluate /)
= 15 + 2 + 6                     (Evaluate -)
= 17 + 6                         (Evaluate first +)
= 23                             (Evaluate +)
```

Note that using parentheses in the preceding expression clarifies the order of precedence. You can also use parentheses to override the order of precedence rules (see Example 2-5).

Example 2-5

In the expression

```
3 + 4 * 5
```

* is evaluated before +. Therefore, the result of this expression is 23. On the other hand, in the expression

```
(3 + 4) * 5
```

+ is evaluated before * and the result of this expression is 35.

Because arithmetic operators are evaluated from left to right, unless parentheses are present, the **associativity** of arithmetic operators is said to be from left to right.

 Character arithmetic: Since the `char` data type is also an integral data type, Java allows you to perform arithmetic operations on `char` data. You should use this ability carefully. There is a difference between the character `'8'` and the integer 8. The integer value of 8 is 8. The integer value of `'8'` is 56, which is the Unicode collating sequence of the character `'8'`.

When evaluating arithmetic expressions, 8 + 7 = 15, `'8'` + `'7'` = 56 + 55, yields 111, and `'8'` + 7 = 56 + 7, yields 63. Furthermore, `'8'` * `'7'` = 56 * 55 = 3080.

These examples illustrate that many things can go wrong when you perform character arithmetic. If you must employ arithmetic operations on the `char` type data, do so with caution.

Expressions

To this point, we have discussed only arithmetic operators. In this section, we discuss arithmetic expressions in detail. (Arithmetic expressions were introduced in the last section.)

If all operands (that is, numbers) in an expression are integers, the expression is called an **integral expression**. If all operands in an expression are floating-point numbers, the expression is called a **floating-point** or **decimal expression**. An integral expression yields an integral result; a floating-point expression yields a floating-point result. Looking at some examples will help clarify these definitions.

Example 2-6

Consider the following Java integral expressions:

```
2 + 3 * 5
3 + x - y / 7
x + 2 * (y - z) + 18
```

In these expressions, **x**, **y**, and **z** represent variables of the integer type; that is, they can hold integer values. (Variables are discussed later in this chapter.)

Example 2-7

Consider the following Java floating-point expressions:

```
12.8 * 17.5 - 34.50
x * 10.5 + y - 16.2
```

Here, **x** and **y** represent variables of the floating-point type; that is, they can hold floating-point values. (Variables are discussed later in this chapter.)

Evaluating an integral or a floating-point expression is straightforward. As already noted, when operators have the same precedence, the expression is evaluated from left to right. To avoid confusion you can always use parentheses to group operands and operators.

Mixed Expressions

An expression that has operands of different data types is called a **mixed expression**. A mixed expression contains both integers and floating-point numbers. The following expressions are examples of mixed expressions:

```
2 + 3.5
6 / 4 + 3.9
5.4 * 2 - 13.6 + 18 / 2
```

In the first expression, the operand **+** has one integer operand and one floating-point operand. In the second expression, both operands for the operator **/** are integers; the first operand of **+** is the result of **6 / 4**, and the second operand of **+** is a floating-point number. The third example is a more complicated mix of integers and floating-point numbers. How does Java evaluate such mixed expressions?

Two rules apply when evaluating a mixed expression:

1. When evaluating an operator in a mixed expression:

   a. If the operator has the same types of operands (that is, both are integers or both are floating-point numbers), the operator is evaluated according to the type of the operand. Integer operands yield an integer result; floating-point numbers yield a floating-point number result.

b. If the operator has both types of operands (that is, one is an integer and the other is a floating-point number), during calculation the integer is changed to a floating-point number with the decimal part of zero, and then the operator is evaluated. The result is a floating-point number.

2. The entire expression is evaluated according to the precedence rules. The multiplication, division, and modulus operators are evaluated before the addition and subtraction operators. Operators having the same level of precedence are evaluated from left to right. Grouping is allowed for clarity.

Following these rules, when you evaluate a mixed expression, you concentrate on one operator at a time, using the rules of precedence. If the operator to be evaluated has operands of the same data type, evaluate the operator using Rule 1(a). That is, an operator with integer operands yields an integer result, and an operator with floating-point operands yields a floating-point result. If the operator to be evaluated has one integer operand and one floating-point operand, before evaluating this operator you convert the integer operand to a floating-point number with a decimal part of zero. Example 2-8 shows how to evaluate mixed expressions.

Example 2-8

Mixed Expression	Evaluation	Rule Applied
3 / 2 + 5.0	= 1 + 5.0	3 / 2 = 1 (integer division; Rule 1(a))
	= 6.0	(1 + 5.0 = 1.0 + 5.0 (Rule 1(b))
		= 6.0)
15.6 / 2 + 5	= 7.8 + 5	15.6 / 2 = 15.6 / 2.0 (Rule 1(b))
		= 7.8
	= 12.8	7.8 + 5 = 7.8 + 5.0 (Rule 1(b))
		= 12.8
4 * 3 + 7 / 5 - 25.6	= 12 + 7 / 5 - 25.6	4 * 3 = 12; (Rule 1(a))
	= 12 + 1 - 25.6	7 / 5 = 1 (integer division; Rule 1(a))
	= 13 - 25.6	12 + 1 = 13; (Rule 1(a))
	= -12.6	13 - 25.6 = 13.0 - 25.6 (Rule 1(b))
		= -12.6

These examples illustrate that an integer is not converted to a floating-point number unless the operator to be evaluated has one integer and one floating-point operand.

Consider the following examples. The values of these expressions were obtained from a Java program. In these expressions, x = 15, y = 23, and z = 3.75.

Expression	Value
x + y / z	21.1333
7 / 2 + 7.45	10.45
15 / 2 + 4 * 5 – 3.50	23.5
7 / 2 * 3.5 + 6	16.5
7.0 / 2 + 7.45	10.95

TYPE CONVERSION (CASTING)

In the previous section, you learned that when evaluating an arithmetic expression if the operator has mixed operands, the integer value is changed to a floating-point value with the zero decimal part. When a value of one data type is automatically changed to another data type, an **implicit type coercion** has occurred. As the examples in the preceding section illustrate, if you are not careful about data types, implicit type coercion can generate unexpected results.

To avoid implicit type coercion, Java provides for explicit type conversion through the use of a cast operator. The **cast operator**, also called the **type conversion** or **type casting**, takes the following form:

(dataTypeName) expression

First, the expression is evaluated. Its value is then converted to a value of the type specified by dataTypeName.

When using the cast operator to convert a floating-point (decimal) number to an integer, you simply drop the decimal part of the floating-point number. That is, the floating-point number is truncated. The following examples show how cast operators work. Be sure you understand why the last two expressions evaluate as they do.

Example 2-9

Expression	Evaluates to
(int)(7.9)	7
(int)(3.3)	3
(double)(25)	25.0
(double)(5 + 3)	= (double)(8) = 8.0
(double)(15)/ 2	= 15.0 / 2 (since (double)(15) = 15.0) = 15.0 / 2.0 = 7.5
(double)(15 / 2)	= (double)(7) (since 15 / 2 = 7) = 7.0
(int)(7.8 + (double)(15)/ 2)	= (int)(7.8 + 7.5) = (int)(15.3) = 15

```
(int)(7.8 + (double)(15/ 2))      = (int)(7.8 + 7.0)
                                  = (int)(14.8)
                                  = 14
```

Consider another series of examples. For these examples, x = 15, y = 23, and z = 3.75. A Java program generated the output of the following expressions.

Expression	Value
`(int)(7.9 + 6.7)`	14
`(int)(7.9) + (int)(6.7)`	13
`(double)(y / x) + z`	4.75
`(double)(y) / x + z`	5.28333

You can also use cast operators to explicitly convert **char** data values into **int** data values, and **int** data values into **char** data values. To convert **char** data values into **int** data values, you use a collating sequence. For example, in the Unicode character set, **(int)('A')** is 65 and **(int)('8')** is 56. Similarly, **(char)(65)** is **'A'** and **(char)(56)** is **'8'**.

Earlier in this chapter, you learned how arithmetic expressions are formed and evaluated in Java. If you want to use the value of one expression in another expression, you must first save the value of the expression. There are many reasons to save the value of an expression. Some expressions are complex and may require a considerable amount of computer time to evaluate. By calculating the values once and saving them for further use, you save computer time and create a program that executes more quickly, and you also avoid possible typographical errors. In Java, expressions are evaluated and if the value is not saved, it is lost. That is, to use the value of an expression in later calculations, it must be saved. In the section Saving and Using the Value of an Expression, later in this chapter, you will learn how to save the value of an expression and use it in subsequent calculations.

THE class String

In the preceding sections, we discussed primitive types to deal with data consisting of numbers and characters. What about data values such as a person's name? A person's name contains more than one character. Such values are called strings. More formally, a **string** is a sequence of zero or more characters. Strings in Java are enclosed in double quotation marks (not in single quotation marks, as are the **char** data types).

Most often we process strings as a single unit. To process strings effectively, Java provides the **class String**. The **class String** contains various operations to manipulate a string. You will see this class used throughout the book. Chapter 3 discusses various operations provided by the **class String**. Moreover, technically speaking, the **class String** is not a primitive type.

A string that contains no characters is called a **null** or **empty** string. The following are examples of strings. Note that " " is the empty string.

```
"William Jacob"
"Mickey"
" "
```

Every character in a string has a relative position in the string. The position of the first character is 0, the position of the second character is 1, and so on. The **length** of a string is the number of characters in it.

Example 2-10

String	Position of a Character in the String	Length of the String
"William Jacob"	Position of 'W' is 0.	13
	Position of the first 'i' is 1.	
	Position of ' ' (the space) is 7.	
	Position of 'J' is 8.	
	Position of 'b' is 12.	
"Mickey"	Position of 'M' is 0.	6
	Position of 'i' is 1.	
	Position of 'c' is 2.	
	Position of 'k' is 3.	
	Position of 'e' is 4.	
	Position of 'y' is 5.	

When determining the length of a string, you must also count the spaces if the string contains any spaces. For example, the length of the following string is 22.

```
"It is a beautiful day."
```

Parsing Numeric Strings

A string consisting of only integers or decimal numbers is called a **numeric string**. For example, the following are numeric strings:

```
"6723"
"-823"
"345.78"
"-782.873"
```

To process these strings as numbers for addition or multiplication we must first convert them into numeric form. Java provides special methods to convert numeric strings into their equivalent numeric form.

1. To convert a string consisting of an integer to a value of the type int, we use the following expression:

```
Integer.parseInt(strExpression)
```

For example,

```
Integer.parseInt("6723") = 6723
Integer.parseInt("-823") = -823
```

2. To convert a string consisting of a decimal number to a value of the type float, we use the following expression:

```
Float.parseFloat(strExpression)
```

For example,

```
Float.parseFloat("34.56") = 34.56
Float.parseFloat("-542.97") = -542.97
```

3. To convert a string consisting of a decimal number to a value of the type double, we use the following expression:

```
Double.parseDouble(strExpression)
```

For example,

```
Double.parseDouble("345.78") = 345.78
Double.parseDouble("-782.873") = -782.873
```

 You might be wondering why you need to know how to convert numeric strings into numbers. This is because Java only accepts strings and characters as *input* to a program. Even numeric data is input as strings. Therefore, to manipulate numeric data, after inputting it into the program as strings, you must convert it back into its proper form. For example, strings representing integers must be converted into integers. Similarly, strings representing decimal (floating-point) numbers must be converted into decimal numbers. The programming code necessary to convert numeric strings to their respective numeric formats is provided by the Java system; you only need to know how to use it. This is explained in the preceding examples.

Example 2-11

The following expression shows how numeric strings are converted to their equivalent numeric form.

1.

```
Integer.parseInt("34")        = 34
Integer.parseInt("-456")      = -456
Double.parseDouble("754.89")  = 754.89
```

2.

```
Integer.parseInt("34") + Integer.parseInt("75")  = 34 + 75 = 109
Integer.parseInt("87") + Integer.parseInt("-67") = 87 - 67 = 20
```

3.

```
Double.parseDouble("754.89") - Double.parseDouble("87.34")
= 754.89 - 87.34
= 667.55
```

INPUT

As noted earlier, the main objective of Java programs is to perform calculations and manipulate data. Recall that data must be loaded into main memory before it can be manipulated. In this section, you learn how to put data into the computer's memory. Storing data in the computer's memory is a two-step process:

1. Instruct the computer to allocate memory.

2. Include statements in the program to put data into the allocated memory.

Allocating Memory with Named Constants and Variables

When you instruct the computer to allocate memory, you tell it what names to use for each memory location, and what type of data to store in those memory locations. Knowing the location of data is essential because data stored in one memory location might be needed at several places in the program. As you learned earlier, knowing what data type you have is crucial for performing accurate calculations. It is also critical to know whether your data must remain fixed throughout program execution or whether it should change.

Some data must not be changed. For example, the pay rate might be the same for all part-time employees. The value in a conversion formula that converts inches into centimeters is fixed because 1 inch is always equal to **2.54** centimeters. When stored in memory, this type of data must be protected from accidental changes during program execution. In Java, you can use a **named constant** to instruct a program to mark those memory locations in which data is fixed throughout program execution.

Named constant: A memory location whose content is not allowed to change during program execution.

To allocate memory, we use Java's declaration statements. The syntax to declare a named constant is:

```
static final dataType IDENTIFIER = value;
```

In Java, **static** and **final** are reserved words. The reserved word **final** specifies that the value stored in the identifier is fixed and cannot be changed.

Notice that the reserved word **static** is shaded, that is, it may or may not appear when a named constant is declared. Also notice that the identifier for a named constant is in uppercase letters. The section Creating a Java Program, later in this chapter, explains when this reserved word might be required.

Example 2-12

Consider the following Java statements:

```
final double CONVERSION = 2.54;
final int NO_OF_STUDENTS = 20;
final char BLANK = ' ';
final double PAY_RATE = 15.75;
```

The first statement tells the compiler to allocate enough memory to store a value of type double, call this memory space CONVERSION, and store the value 2.54 in it. Throughout a program that uses this statement, whenever the conversion formula is needed, the memory space CONVERSION can be accessed. The other statements have similar meanings.

Using a named constant to store fixed data, rather than using the data value itself, has one major advantage. If the fixed data changes, you do not need to edit the entire program and change the old value to the new value. Instead, you can make the change at just one place, recompile the program, and execute it using the new value throughout. In addition, by storing a value and referring to that memory location whenever the value is needed, you avoid typing the same value again and again and you prevent typos. If you misspell the name of the location, the computer might warn you through an error message, but it will not warn you if the value is mistyped.

Certain data must be modified during program execution. For example, after each test, a student's average test score and the number of tests taken change. Similarly, after each pay increase, an employee's salary changes. This type of data must be stored in memory cells whose contents can be modified during program execution. In Java, memory cells whose contents can be modified during program execution are called **variables**.

Variable: A memory location whose content may change during program execution.

The syntax for declaring one variable or multiple variables is:

```
dataType identifier1, identifier2, . . ., identifierN;
```

Example 2-13

Consider the following statements:

```
double amountDue;
int    counter;
char   ch;
int    x,y;
```

The first statement tells the compiler to allocate enough memory to store a value of the type double and call it amountDue. Statements 2 and 3 have similar conventions. The fourth statement tells the compiler to allocate two different memory spaces, each large enough to store a value of the type int; name the first memory space **x**; and name the second memory space **y**.

From now on, when we say "variable," we mean a variable memory location.

 In Java, you must declare all identifiers before you can use them. If you refer to an identifier without declaring it, the compiler will generate an error message indicating that the identifier is not declared. Therefore, to use either a named constant or a variable, you must first declare it.

Putting Data into Variables

Now that you know how to declare variables, the next question is: How do you put data into those variables? In Java, you can place data into a variable in two ways:

1. Use an assignment statement.

2. Use input (read) statements.

The Assignment Statement

The assignment statement takes the following form:

```
variable = expression;
```

In an assignment statement, the value of the **expression** should match the data type of the **variable**. The expression on the right side is evaluated, and its value is assigned to the variable (and thus to a memory location) on the left side.

A variable is said to be **initialized** the first time a value is placed in the variable.

In Java, = (the equals sign) is called the **assignment operator**.

Example 2-14

Suppose you have the following variable declarations:

```
int i, j;
double sale;
char first;
String str;
```

Now consider the following assignment statements:

```
i = 4;
j = 4 * 5 - 11;
sale = 0.02 * 1000;
first = 'D';
str = "It is a sunny day.";
```

For each of these statements, the computer first evaluates the expression on the right and then stores that value in a memory location named by the identifier on the left. The first statement stores the value 4 in i, the second statement stores 9 in j, the third statement stores 20.00 in `sale`, and the fourth statement stores the character D in `first`. The fifth statement assigns the string "It is a sunny day." to the variable `str`.

2

A Java statement such as:

```
i = i + 2;
```

means "evaluate whatever is in i, add 2 to it, and assign the new value to the memory location i." The expression on the right side must be evaluated first; that value is then assigned to the memory location specified by the variable on the left side. Thus, the sequence of Java statements

```
i = 6;
i = i + 2;
```

and the statement

```
i = 8;
```

both assign 8 to i. Note that the statement i = i + 2 is meaningless if i has not been initialized.

The statement i = 5; is read as "i becomes 5" or "i gets 5." Each time a new value is assigned to i, the old value is erased.

Suppose that i, j, and k are int variables. The sequence of statements

```
i = 12;
i = i + 6;
j = i;
k = j / 2;
k = k / 3;
```

results in k storing the value 3.

Tracing values through a sequence of statements, called a **walk-through**, is a valuable skill to learn and practice. You will learn more about how to walk through a sequence of Java statements later in this chapter.

 The Java language is strongly typed, which means that you cannot assign a value to a variable that is not compatible with its data type. For example, a string cannot be stored in an int variable. If you try to store an incompatible value in a variable, an error is generated when you compile the program or during program execution. Therefore, in an assignment statement, the expression on the right side must evaluate to a value compatible with the data type of the variable on the left side.

Suppose that x, y, and z are **int** variables. The following is a legal statement in Java:

```
x = y = z;
```

In this statement, first the value of z is assigned to y, and then the new value of y is assigned to x. Because the assignment operator = is evaluated from right to left, the **associativity** of the **assignment operator** is said to be from right to left.

Saving and Using the Value of an Expression

Now that you know how to declare variables and put data into them, you can learn how to save the value of an expression. You can then use this value in a later expression without using the expression itself. To save the value of an expression and use it in a later expression, do the following:

1. Declare a variable of the appropriate data type. For example, if the result of the expression is an integer, declare an **int** variable.

2. Use the assignment statement to assign the value of the expression to the variable that was declared. This action saves the value of the expression into the variable.

3. Wherever the value of the expression is needed, use the variable holding the value.

Example 2-15 illustrates this concept.

Example 2-15

Suppose that you have the following declaration:

```
int a, b, c, d;
int x, y;
```

Further suppose that you want to evaluate the expressions

$-b + (b^2 - 4ac)$

and

$-b - (b^2 - 4ac)$

and assign the values of these expressions to x and y, respectively. As the expression $b^2 - 4ac$ appears in both expressions, you can first calculate the value of this expression and save its value in d. You can then use the value of d to evaluate the expressions, as shown in the following statements:

```
d = b * b - 4 * a * c;
x = -b + d;
y = -b - d;
```

Earlier, you learned that if a variable is used in an expression, the expression yields a meaningful value only if the variable has first been initialized. You also learned that after declaring a variable, you can use an assignment statement to initialize it. It is possible to initialize and declare variables at the same time. Before we discuss how to use an input (read) statement, we address this important issue.

Declaring and Initializing Variables

When a variable is declared, Java might not automatically put a meaningful value in it. In other words, Java might not automatically initialize all the variables you declare. For example, the `int` and `double` variables might not be initialized to 0, as happens in some programming languages.

If you declare a variable and then use it in an expression without first initializing it, when you compile the program you are likely to get an error. To avoid these pitfalls, Java allows you to initialize variables while they are being declared. Consider the following Java statements in which variables are first declared and then initialized:

```
int first, second;
char ch;
double x, y;

first = 13;
second = 10;
ch = ' ';
x = 12.6;
y = 123.456;
```

You can declare and initialize these variables at the same time using the following Java statements:

```
int first = 13, second = 10;
char ch = ' ';
double x = 12.6, y = 123.456;
```

The first Java statement declares two `int` variables, `first` and `second`, and stores 13 in `first` and 10 in `second`. The other statements have similar meanings.

 Not all variables are initialized during declaration. The nature of the program or the programmer's choice dictates which variables should be initialized during declaration.

Input (Read) Statement

In an earlier section, you learned how to put data into variables using the assignment statement. In this section, you learn how to put data into variables from the standard input device using Java's input (or read) statements.

 In most cases, the standard input device is the keyboard.

When the computer gets the data from the keyboard, the user is said to be acting interactively.

Putting data into variables from the standard input device is accomplished by using the **standard input stream object**, System.in. The data entered from the standard input device are characters, and the object System.in extracts data in the form of bytes from the input stream. Therefore, using System.in, we must first create another input stream object to read characters from the input stream.

To make input to the program easier, Java provides the necessary code. You only need to learn how to use it. To read characters from the input stream, you declare and initialize a variable as follows:

```
InputStreamReader charReader = new
                InputStreamReader(System.in);          //Line 1
```

After this statement executes, the variable charReader is initialized to the standard input device using the object System.in.

The variable charReader can read characters from the input stream, but only one character at a time. To read the entire line of characters you must declare and initialize another input stream variable as follows:

```
BufferedReader keyboard = new BufferedReader(charReader); //Line 2
```

After this statement executes, the variable keyboard is initialized to input data from the standard input device.

Just as the class String allows you to manipulate strings, BufferedReader and InputStreamReader are stream classes that provide the necessary operations for inputting data into a program.

Variables such as keyboard and charReader are called **input stream objects** of the classes InputStreamReader and BufferedReader, respectively.

Now that you know how to create input stream objects to input data from the keyboard, you next learn how to input data from the keyboard into a program.

Recall that Java accepts only strings and characters as input. We can, therefore, use a String variable to store the string containing the input. Suppose that you have the following declaration:

```
String inputStr;                                         //Line 3
```

The following statement reads and assigns the next line of characters to the String variable inputStr:

```
inputStr = keyboard.readLine();                          //Line 4
```

This statement uses the method readLine (of the class BufferedReader, designed to read a line of characters). At this time, you can think of a method as a set of instructions designed to accomplish a specific task. For example, the method readLine contains the code that is necessary to read a line of characters.

You can combine the statements in Lines 1 and 2, that is,

```
InputStreamReader charReader = new
        InputStreamReader(System.in);
BufferedReader keyboard = new BufferedReader(charReader);
```

into one statement as follows:

```
BufferedReader keyboard =
        new BufferedReader(new InputStreamReader(System.in));
```

Mostly, we will use this statement to create the input stream object, **keyboard**, to input data from the standard input device.

Inputting Numeric Data

You've seen how data can be input from the keyboard. Any data you enter from the keyboard (whether numbers or letters or spaces) is a sequence of characters. Therefore, the numeric data is also read as a sequence of characters. Using statements like Line 3 and Line 4 of the previous section, we can read numbers as a sequence of characters. We then parse the numeric string, as explained in the section Parsing Numeric Strings (earlier in this chapter), into an appropriate number. Example 2-16 illustrates how to convert a numeric string into a number.

Example 2-16

Consider the following statements:

```
String numString1 = "12345";            //Line 1
int intNum;                             //Line 2

intNum = Integer.parseInt(numString1);  //Line 3
```

After the statement in Line 3 executes, the value of the variable **intNum** is **12345**.

```
String numString2 = "765.43";           //Line 4
double doubleNum;                        //Line 5

doubleNum = Double.parseDouble(numString2);  //Line 6
```

After the statement in Line 6 executes, the value of the variable **doubleNum** is **765.43**.

We can now discuss how to read data from the standard input device. Consider the following statement, which creates the input stream object **keyboard** to input data from the standard input device:

```
BufferedReader keyboard =
        new BufferedReader(new InputStreamReader(System.in));
```

Suppose that **numString** is a **String** variable and **miles** is a variable of the data type **double**. Further suppose that the input is **73.65**. Consider the following statements:

```
numString = keyboard.readLine();
miles = Double.parseDouble(numString);
```

The first statement causes the computer to get the next string, which is "73.65", from the standard input device, and assigns it to numString. The second statement converts this string into a value of the type double, and stores it in the variable miles. After the second statement executes, the value of the variable miles is 73.65.

You can combine the preceding two statements into one statement, as follows:

```
miles = Double.parseDouble(keyboard.readLine());
```

This eliminates the declaration of the additional variable numString. We will use this form of input statement to input data from the standard input device.

Example 2-17 further explains how to input numeric data into a program.

Example 2-17

We assume that the input stream object keyboard has been created as before. Consider the following statements:

```
int feet;
int inches;
```

The following statement gets the next integer from the standard input device and places it into the variable feet:

```
feet = Integer.parseInt(keyboard.readLine());
```

Similarly, the following statement gets the next integer from the keyboard and places it into the variable inches:

```
inches = Integer.parseInt(keyboard.readLine());
```

Reading a Single Character

To read a single character, you can use the method read (associated with the class BufferedReader). The method read, in fact, returns the integer value of the character. For example, if you input A, it returns 65. You need to use the cast operator to convert this integer value into a char value. If ch is a char variable, the following statement inputs the next character (including the space and the newline character) from the keyboard.

```
ch = (char) keyboard.read();
```

where keyboard is as declared before.

 If your program requires more than one number, then enter each number in a separate line. If you input more than one number in the same line, the readLine method reads all numbers as one string. In Chapter 3 you will learn how to input more than one number in the same line.

Variable Initialization

Consider the following declaration:

```
int feet;
```

You can initialize the variable `feet` to a value of 35 either by using the assignment statement:

```
feet = 35;
```

or by executing the following statement and entering 35 during program execution:

```
feet = Integer.parseInt(keyboard.readLine());
```

If you use the assignment statement to initialize `feet`, then you are stuck with the same value each time the program runs unless you edit the source code, change the value, recompile, and run. By using an input statement, each time the program runs, you are prompted to enter a value, and the value entered is stored in `feet`. Therefore, a read statement is much more versatile than an assignment statement.

Sometimes it is necessary to initialize a variable by using an assignment statement. This is especially true if the variable is used only for internal calculation and not for reading and storing data.

 Recall that Java might not automatically initialize all the variables when they are declared. Some variables can be initialized when they are declared, whereas others must be initialized using either an assignment statement or a read statement. (Variable initialization is covered in more detail in Chapter 8.)

 Suppose you want to store a character into a `char` variable using an input statement. During program execution, when you input the character, you do not include the single quotation marks. Suppose that `ch` is a `char` variable. Consider the following input statement:

```
ch = (char) keyboard.read();
```

If you want to store K in `ch` using this statement, during program execution you type K without the single quotation marks. Similarly, if you want to store a string in a `String` variable using an input statement, during program execution you enter only the string without the double quotation marks.

When something goes wrong in a program and the results it generates are not what you expect, you should do a walk-through of the statements that assign values to your variables. Example 2-18 illustrates how to do a walk-through of your program. The walk-through is a very effective debugging technique.

Example 2-18

This example further illustrates how assignment statements and input statements manipulate variables. Consider the following declarations:

```
BufferedReader keyboard =
        new BufferedReader(new InputStreamReader(System.in));

int firstNum, secondNum;
char ch;
double z;
```

Also suppose that the following statements execute in the order given:

1. `firstNum = 4;`

2. `secondNum = 2 * firstNum + 6;`

3. `z = (firstNum + 1) / 2.0;`

4. `ch = 'A';`

5. `secondNum = Integer.parseInt(keyboard.readLine());`

6. `z = Double.parseDouble(keyboard.readLine());`

7. `firstNum = 2 * secondNum + (int)(z);`

8. `secondNum = secondNum + 1;`

9. `ch = (char) keyboard.read();`

10. `firstNum = firstNum + (int)(ch);`

11. `z = firstNum - z;`

In addition, suppose the input is:

```
8
16.3
D
```

Let's now determine the values of the declared variables after the last statement executes. To explicitly show how a particular statement changes the value of a variable, the values of the variables after each statement executes are shown. (In Figures 2-4 through 2-7, a question mark (?) in a box indicates that the value in the box is unknown.)

Before Statement 1 executes, all variables are uninitialized, as shown in Figure 2-4.

Figure 2-4   Variables before Statement 1 executes

Statement 1 stores **4** in the variable `firstNum`. After Statement 1 executes, the values of the variables are as shown in Figure 2-5.

Figure 2-5   Values of `firstNum, secondNum, z,` and `ch` after Statement 1 executes

Statement 2 first evaluates the expression `2 * firstNum + 6` (which evaluates to `14`) and then stores the value of the expression in `secondNum`. After Statement 2 executes, the values of the variables are as shown in Figure 2-6.

Figure 2-6   Values of `firstNum, secondNum, z,` and `ch` after Statement 2 executes

Statement 3 first evaluates the expression `(firstNum + 1) / 2.0` (which evaluates to `2.5`) and then stores the value of the expression in `z`. After Statement 3 executes, the values of the variables are as shown in Figure 2-7.

Figure 2-7   Values of `firstNum, secondNum, z,` and `ch` after Statement 3 executes

Statement 4 stores the character **'A'** into **ch**. After Statement 4 executes, the values of the variables are as shown in Figure 2-8.

Figure 2-8 Values of **firstNum**, **secondNum**, **z**, and **ch** after Statement 4 executes

Statement 5 reads a number (which is **8**) from the keyboard and stores the number **8** in **secondNum**. This statement replaces the old value of **secondNum** with this new value. After Statement 5 executes, the values of the variables are as shown in Figure 2-9.

Figure 2-9 Values of **firstNum**, **secondNum**, **z**, and **ch** after Statement 5 executes

Statement 6 reads a number (which is **16.3**) from the keyboard and stores the number in **z**. This statement replaces the old value of **z** with this new value. After Statement 6 executes, the values of the variables are as shown in Figure 2-10.

Figure 2-10 Values of **firstNum**, **secondNum**, **z**, and **ch** after Statement 6 executes

Statement 7 first evaluates the expression **2 * secondNum + (int)(z)**, (which evaluates to **32**), and then stores the value of the expression into **firstNum**. This statement replaces the old value of **firstNum** with the new value. After Statement 7 executes, the values of the variables are as shown in Figure 2-11.

Figure 2-11   Values of `firstNum`, `secondNum`, `z`, and `ch` after Statement 7 executes

Statement 8 first evaluates the expression `secondNum + 1` (which evaluates to **9**) and stores the value of this expression in `secondNum`. This statement updates the value of `secondNum` by incrementing the old value by **1**. After Statement 8 executes, the values of the variables are as shown in Figure 2-12.

Figure 2-12   Values of `firstNum`, `secondNum`, `z`, and `ch` after Statement 8 executes

Statement 9 reads the next input (which is `D`) from the keyboard and stores it in `ch`. This statement replaces the old value of `ch` with the new value. After Statement 9 executes, the values of the variables are as shown in Figure 2-13.

Figure 2-13   Values of `firstNum`, `secondNum`, `z`, and `ch` after Statement 9 executes

Statement 10 first evaluates the expression `firstNum + (int)(ch)`, which is `32 + (int)('D')`, which equals `32 + 68 = 100`. Here `(int)('D')` gives the collating sequence of the character `D` in the Unicode character data set, which is **68**. Statement 10 then stores the value of this expression in `firstNum`. This statement replaces the old value of `firstNum` with the new value. After Statement 10 executes, the values of the variables are as shown in Figure 2-14.

Figure 2-14 Values of firstNum, secondNum, z, and ch after Statement 10 executes

Finally, Statement 11 first evaluates the expression firstNum - z (which equals 100 - 16.3 = 100.0 - 16.3 = 83.7) and then stores the value of this expression in z. The values of the variables after the last statement executes are shown in Figure 2-15.

Figure 2-15 Values of firstNum, secondNum, z, and ch after Statement 11 executes

If you assign the value of an expression that evaluates to a floating-point value without using the cast operator to a variable of the type int, the fractional part is dropped. In this case, the compiler most likely will issue a warning message about the implicit type conversion.

INCREMENT AND DECREMENT OPERATORS

Now that you know how to declare a variable and enter data into a variable, in this section you learn about two more operators: the increment and decrement operators. These operators are used frequently by Java programmers and are useful programming tools.

Suppose count is an int variable. The statement

count = count + 1;

increments the value of count by 1. To execute this assignment statement, the computer first evaluates the expression on the right, which is count + 1. It then assigns this value to the variable on the left, which is count.

As you will see in later chapters, such statements are frequently used to keep track of how many times certain things have happened. To expedite the execution of such statements, Java provides the **increment operator**, ++, which increases the value of a variable by 1, and the

decrement operator, `--`, which decreases the value of a variable by 1. Increment and decrement operators each have two forms, pre and post. The syntax of the increment operator is:

```
Pre-increment:      ++variable
Post-increment:     variable++
```

The syntax of the decrement operator is:

```
Pre-decrement:      --variable
Post-decrement:     variable--
```

Let's look at some examples. The statement

```
++count;
```

or

```
count++;
```

increments the value of `count` by 1. Similarly, the statement

```
--count;
```

or

```
count--;
```

decrements the value of `count` by 1.

Because increment and decrement operators are built into Java, the value of a variable is quickly incremented or decremented without having to use the form of an assignment statement.

As you can see from these examples, both the pre- and post-increment operators increment the value of the variable by 1. Similarly, the pre- and post-decrement operators decrement the value of the variable by 1. What is the difference between the pre and post forms of these operators? The difference becomes apparent when the variable using these operators is employed in an expression.

Suppose that `x` is a variable of the type `int`. If `++x` is used in an expression, first the value of `x` is incremented by 1, and then the new value of `x` is used to evaluate the expression. On the other hand, if `x++` is used in an expression, first the current value of `x` is used in the expression, and then the value of `x` is incremented by 1. The following example clarifies the difference between the pre- and post-increment operators.

Suppose that `x` and `y` are `int` variables. Consider the following statements:

```
x = 5;
y = ++x;
```

The first statement assigns the value 5 to x. To evaluate the second statement, which uses the pre-increment operator, first the value of x is incremented to 6, and then this value, 6, is assigned to y. After the second statement executes, both x and y have the value 6.

Now consider the following statements:

```
x = 5;
y = x++;
```

As before, the first statement assigns 5 to x. In the second statement, the post-increment operator is applied to x. To execute the second statement, first the value of x, which is 5, is used to evaluate the expression, and then the value of x is incremented to 6. Finally, the value of the expression, which is 5, is stored in y. After the second statement executes, the value of x is 6, and the value of y is 5.

The following example further illustrates how the pre- and post- increment operators work.

Example 2-19

Suppose a and b are int variables and:

```
a = 5;
b = 2 + (++a);
```

The first statement assigns 5 to a. To execute the second statement, first the expression 2 + (++a) is evaluated. As the pre-increment operator is applied to a, first the value of a is incremented to 6. Then 2 is added to 6 to get 8, which is then assigned to b. Therefore, after the second statement executes, a is 6 and b is 8. On the other hand, after the execution of

```
a = 5;
b = 2 + (a++);
```

the value of a is 6 while the value of b is 7.

 This book most often uses the increment and decrement operators with a variable in a stand-alone statement. That is, the variable using the increment or decrement operator will not be part of any expression.

STRINGS AND THE OPERATOR +

One of the most common operations performed on strings is the concatenate operation, which allows a string to be appended at the end of another string. The operator + can be used to concatenate two strings, as well as a string and a numeric value or a character.

Consider the following statements, which illustrate how the operator + works with strings:

```
String str;

str = "Sunny";                          //Line 1
str = str + " Day";                     //Line 2
```

After the statement in Line 2 executes, the string assigned to `str` is

`"Sunny Day"`

Now consider the following statements:

```
str = "Amount Due = $" + 576.35;        //Line 3
```

When the operator + evaluates in Line 3, the numeric value `576.35` is converted to the string `"576.35"`, which is then concatenated with the string

`"Amount Due = $"`

Therefore, after the statement in Line 3 executes, the string assigned to `str` is

`"Amount Due = $576.35"`

Example 2-20 further explains how the operator + works with the `String` data type.

Example 2-20

Consider the following statements:

```
String str;
int num1, num2;

num1 = 12;
num2 = 26;

str = "The sum = " + num1 + num2;
```

After this statement executes, the string assigned to `str` is:

```
str = "The sum = 1226";
```

The string assigned to `str` is not what you might have expected. Rather than adding the values of `num1` and `num2`, the values of `num1` and `num2` are concatenated. This is because the associativity of the operator + is from left to right—the operator + is evaluated from left to right. The expression

`"The sum = " + num1 + num2`

is evaluated as follows:

```
"The sum = " + num1 + num2        = ("The sum = " + num1) + num2
                                  = ("The sum = " + 12) + num2
                                  = "The sum = 12" + num2
                                  = "The sum = 12" + 26
                                  = "The sum = 1226"
```

Now consider the following statement:

```
str = "The sum = " + (num1 + num2);
```

In this statement, because of the parentheses, you first evaluate `num1 + num2`. Because `num1` and `num2` are both `int` variables, `num1 + num2 = 12 + 26 = 38`. After this statement executes, the string assigned to `str` is:

```
str = "The sum = 38";
```

First the expression `(num1 + num2)` is evaluated, which results in 38. Therefore,

```
"The sum = " + 38
```

evaluates to

```
"The sum = 38"
```

Consider the statement:

```
str = num1 + num2 + " is the sum";
```

After this statement executes, the string assigned to `str` is `"38 is the sum"`. First `num1 + num2` is evaluated, which results in 38; then 38 is converted to `"38"`, which is then concatenated with the string `" is the sum"`.

For another example, consider the following statement:

```
str = "The sum of " + num1 + " and " + num2 + " = " + (num1 + num2);
```

Notice the parentheses around `num1 + num2`. After this statement executes, the string assigned to `str` is:

```
str = "The sum of 12 and 26 = 38";
```

OUTPUT

A program is of little use if it cannot display its results on an output device. Although you have seen how to put data into the computer's memory and how to manipulate that data, you have not yet learned how to make the program show the results.

The standard output device is usually the monitor.

2

In Java, output on the standard output device is accomplished by using the **standard output object** System.out. The object System.out has access to two methods, print and println, to output a string on the standard output device.

The syntax to use the object System.out and the methods print and println is:

```
System.out.print(stringExp);
System.out.println(stringExp);
```

These are **output statements**. The expression is evaluated, and its value is printed at the current insertion point on the output device. After outputting the stringExp, the method print leaves the insertion point after the last character of the stringExp, while the method println positions the insertion point at the beginning of the next line.

 On the screen, the insertion point is where the cursor is.

The next example illustrates how the output statements work. In an output statement, a string or an expression involving only one variable or a single value evaluates to itself.

When an output statement outputs char values, it outputs the character without the single quotation marks (unless the single quotation marks are part of the output statement). For example, suppose ch is a char variable and ch = 'A';. The statement

```
System.out.println(ch);
```

or

```
System.out.println('A');
```

outputs

A

Similarly, when an output statement outputs the value of a string, it outputs the string without the double quotation marks (unless you include double quotation marks as part of the string).

Example 2-21

Consider the following statements. The output is shown to the right of each statement.

	Statement	Output
1	`System.out.println(29 / 4);`	7
2	`System.out.println("Hello there.");`	Hello there.
3	`System.out.println(12);`	12
4	`System.out.println("4 + 7");`	4 + 7
5	`System.out.println(4 + 7);`	11
6	`System.out.println('A');`	A
7	`System.out.println("4 + 7 = " + (4 + 7));`	4 + 7 = 11
8	`System.out.println(2 + 3 * 5);`	17
9	`System.out.println("Hello \nthere.");`	Hello
		there.

Look at the output of Statement 9. Recall that in Java, the newline character is `'\n'`; it causes the insertion point to move to the beginning of the next line before printing. Therefore, when \n appears in a string in an output statement, it moves the insertion point to the beginning of the next line on the output device. This explains why `Hello` and `there.` are printed on separate lines.

 In Java, \ is called the **escape character** and \n is called the **newline escape sequence**.

Example 2-22

Consider the following statements. Assume that these statements are executed in the order given.

```
int a, b;
```

```
a = 65 ;                                     //Line 1
b = 78 ;                                     //Line 2

System.out.println(29 / 4);                  //Line 3
System.out.println(3.0 / 2);                 //Line 4
System.out.print("Hello there.\n");          //Line 5
System.out.println(7);                       //Line 6
System.out.println(3 + 5);                   //Line 7
System.out.print("3 + 5");                   //Line 8
System.out.println();                        //Line 9
System.out.println(2 + 3 * 6);               //Line 10
System.out.println("a");                     //Line 11
System.out.println(a);                       //Line 12
System.out.println(b);                       //Line 13
```

The output, which was generated by a Java program, appears as follows. The column marked "Output of Statement at" and the line numbers are not part of the output. The line numbers are shown to make it easy to see which output corresponds to which statement.

	Output of Statement at
7	Line 3
1.5	Line 4
Hello there.	Line 5
7	Line 6
8	Line 7
3 + 5	Line 8
20	Line 10
a	Line 11
65	Line 12
78	Line 13

For the most part, the output is straightforward. Look at the output of the statements in Lines 7, 8, 9, and 10. The statement in Line 7 outputs the result of 3 + 5, which is 8, and moves the insertion point to the beginning of the next line. The statement in Line 8 outputs the string 3 + 5. Note that the statement in Line 8 uses the method `print` to output the string 3 + 5. Therefore, after printing 3 + 5, the insertion point stays after 5; it does not move to the beginning of the next line.

The output statement in Line 9 uses the method `println`, which moves the insertion point to the beginning of the next line. Therefore, when the statement in Line 10 executes, the output starts at the beginning of the line. Note that in this output, the column "Output of Statement at" does not contain Line 9. This is because the statement in Line 9 does not produce any printable output. It simply moves the insertion point to the beginning of the next line. The statement in Line 10 outputs the result of the expression 2 + 3 * 6, which is 20.

Let's take a closer look at the newline character, `'\n'`. Consider the following Java statements:

```java
System.out.print("Hello there.");
System.out.print("My name is Goofy.");
```

If these statements are executed in sequence, the output is:

```
Hello there. My name is Goofy.
```

Consider the following **Java** statements:

```java
System.out.print("Hello there.\n");
System.out.print("My name is Goofy.");
```

The output of these Java statements is:

```
Hello there.
My name is Goofy.
```

When \n is encountered in the string, the insertion point is positioned at the beginning of the next line. Note also that \n may appear anywhere in the string. For example, the output of the statement

```
System.out.print("Hello \nthere. \nMy name is Goofy.");
```

is

```
Hello
there.
My name is Goofy.
```

Also note that the output of the statement

```
System.out.print("\n");
```

is the same as the output of the statement

```
System.out.println();
```

Thus, the output of the sequence of statements

```
System.out.print("Hello there.\n");
System.out.print("My name is Goofy.");
```

is equivalent to the output of the sequence of statements

```
System.out.println("Hello there.");
System.out.print("My name is Goofy.");
```

Example 2-23

Consider the following Java statements:

```
System.out.print("Hello there.\nMy name is Goofy.");
```

or

```
System.out.print("Hello there.");
System.out.print("\nMy name is Goofy.");
```

or

```
System.out.println("Hello there.");
System.out.print("My name is Goofy.");
```

In each case, the output of the statements is:

```
Hello there.
My name is Goofy.
```

Example 2-24

Suppose you want to output the following sentence in one line as part of a message:

`It is sunny, warm, and not a windy day. Let us go golfing.`

Obviously, you will use the methods `print` and/or `println` to produce this output. However, in the programming code, this statement may not fit in one line as part of the output statement. Of course, you can use more than one output statement, as follows:

```
System.out.print("It is sunny, warm, and not a windy day. ");
System.out.println("Let us go golfing.");
```

Two output statements are used to output the sentence in one line. You can also use the following statement to output this sentence:

```
System.out.println("It is sunny, warm, and not a windy day. " +
                   "Let us go golfing.");
```

In this statement, note that because there is no semicolon at the end of the first line, this output statement continues at the second line. Also, note that the first line is followed by the operator +, and there is a double quotation mark at the beginning of the second line. The string is broken into two strings, but both strings are part of the same output statement.

If a string appearing in an output statement is long and you want to output the string in one line, you can break the string by using either of the above two ways. However, the following statement using the **Enter** (or return) key would be incorrect:

```
System.out.println("It is sunny, warm, and not a windy day.
                   Let us go golfing.")
```

The **Enter** (or return) key on your keyboard cannot be part of the string—in programming code, a string *cannot* be broken into more than one line by using the **Enter** (return) key.

Recall that the newline character is \n, which moves the insertion point to the beginning of the next line. In Java, there are many other escape sequences which allow you to control the output. Table 2-4 lists some of the commonly used escape sequences.

Table 2-4 Commonly Used Escape Sequences

	Escape Sequence	Description
\n	Newline	Insertion point moves to the beginning of the next line
\t	Tab	Insertion point moves to the next tab stop
\ b	Backspace	Insertion point moves one space to the left
\r	Return	Insertion point moves to the beginning of the current line (*not* the next line)
\\	Backslash	Backslash is printed
\'	Single quotation	Single quotation mark is printed
\"	Double quotation	Double quotation mark is printed

Example 2-25 shows the effect of some of these escape sequences.

Example 2-25

The output of the statement

```
System.out.println("The newline escape sequence is \\n");
```

is

```
The new line escape sequence is \n
```

The output of the statement

```
System.out.println("The tab character is represented as \'\\t\'");
```

is

```
The tab character is represented as '\t'
```

The output of the statement

```
System.out.println("The string \"Sunny\" contains five characters");
```

is

```
The string "Sunny" contains five characters
```

The Method `flush`

In the preceding section, you learned how to use the methods `print` and `println` for outputting data. Recall that `println`, after outputting data, positions the insertion point at the beginning of the next line. Consider the following statement:

```
System.out.print("Enter a number: ");
```

When the computer executes this statement, you would expect to see the following line on the screen with the insertion point one space after the colon, as in the following:

```
Enter a number:
```

This might not happen because the output generated by the method `print` first goes into an area in the computer called a buffer. When the buffer is full, the output is sent to the output device. On the other hand, when the method `println` executes, the output goes to the output device even if the buffer is not full.

You can use the method `flush` associated with `System.out`, to empty the buffer even if it is not full. Unlike the method `println`, the method `flush` does not position the insertion point at the beginning of the next line; it simply empties the buffer and the output is sent to the output device. The preceding output statement can be written as follows:

```
System.out.print("Enter a number: ");
System.out.flush();
```

PACKAGES, CLASSES, METHODS, AND THE import STATEMENT

Only a small number of operations, such as arithmetic and assignment operations, are explicitly defined in Java. Many of the methods and identifiers needed to run a Java program are provided as a collection of libraries, called packages. A **package** is a collection of related classes. Moreover, every package has a name.

In Java, *class* is a broadly used term. The term **class** is used to create Java programs—either application or applet; it is used to group a set of related operations; and it is used to allow users to create their own data types. For example, there are various mathematical operations, such as determining the absolute value of a number, determining one number raised to the power of another number, and determining the logarithm of a number. Each of these operations is implemented using the Java mechanism of *methods*. Think of a **method** as a set of instructions designed to accomplish a specific task. For example, the name of the method implementing the operation of one number raised to the power of another number is `pow`. This and other mathematical methods are contained in the **class** Math. The name of the package containing the **class** Math is `java.lang`.

The package `java.io` contains classes for inputting data into a program and outputting the results of a program. For example, the **class** BufferedReader, contained in the `java.io` package, has the method `readLine` for reading a line of characters. We used this class and this method in this chapter's Input Statement section.

In the next section, you learn how class(es) are used to create a Java application program.

To make use of the existing classes, methods, and identifiers, you must tell the program which package contains the appropriate information. The `import` statement helps you do this.

The general syntax to import the contents of a package in a Java program is:

```
import packageName.*;
```

In Java, `import` is a reserved word. For example, the following statement imports the necessary classes from the package `java.io`:

```
import java.io.*;
```

To import a specific class from a package, you can specify the name of the class in place of the `*`. The following statement imports the `class BufferedReader` from the package `java.io`:

```
import java.io.BufferedReader;
```

 If you use the character `*` in the `import` statement, as in the statement

```
import java.io.*;
```

then the compiler determines the relevant class(es) used in the program.

 The primitive data types are directly part of the Java language, and do not require that any package be imported into the program. Also, the `class String` is contained in the package `java.lang`. You do not need to import classes from the package `java.lang`. The system automatically does it for you.

CREATING A JAVA APPLICATION PROGRAM

In previous sections, you learned enough Java concepts to write meaningful programs. In this section, you learn how to create a complete Java application program.

The basic unit of a Java program is called a class. A Java application program is, therefore, a collection of one or more classes. Roughly speaking, a class is a collection of methods and data members. As described in the previous section, a method is a set of instructions designed to accomplish a specific task. Some **predefined** or **standard** methods such as `parseInt`, `read`, `readLine`, `print`, and `println` are already written and are provided as part of the system. But to accomplish most tasks, programmers must learn to write their own methods.

One of the classes in a Java application program must have the method called `main`. Moreover, there can be only one method `main` in a Java program. If a Java application program has only one class, it *must* contain the method `main`. Until Chapter 6, other than using some predefined methods, you will mainly deal with Java application programs that have only one class.

Statements to declare memory spaces (named constants and variables), statements to create input stream objects, statements to manipulate data (such as assignments), and statements to input and output data will be placed within the class.

Statements to declare named constants and input stream objects are usually placed outside the method `main`, and statements to declare variables are usually placed within the method `main`. Statements to manipulate data, and input and output statements are placed within the method `main`.

The syntax of a class to create a Java application program is:

```
public   class ClassName
{
     classMembers
}
```

where `ClassName` is a user-defined Java identifier; `classMembers` consists of data members and methods (such as the method `main`). In Java, `public` and `class` are reserved words.

The general syntax of the method `main` is:

```
public static void main (String[] args) throws clause
{
     statement1
        .
        .
        .
     statementn
}
```

 In syntax examples, the shading indicates the part of the definition that is optional.

where `throws clause` consists of exceptions thrown by the method `main`. If there is more than one exception, they are separated by commas. An **exception** is an occurrence of an undesirable situation that can be detected during program execution (see the following Note). For example, division by zero is an exception. In Chapter 12, you will learn about exceptions in detail.

throws clause: During program execution, various things can happen. For example, division by zero or inputting a letter for a number are examples of events that sometimes occur. The system does not tolerate such cases, which are described by saying that an exception has occurred. If an exception occurs in a method, then either the method should handle the exception, or the method should *throw* it for the calling environment to handle. The methods `read` and `readLine` both throw the exception called `IOException`. Because these methods are used in the method `main` and they throw `IOException`, then the method `main` either handles this exception or throws this exception. For the next few chapters, we will not be concerned with handling the exceptions, we will simply throw the exceptions. Since we do not require the method `main` to handle I/O exceptions, we include a command in the heading of the method `main` to throw I/O exceptions. Therefore, if there is input to the program, the heading of the method `main` will be:

```
public static void main(String[] args) throws IOException
```

In Java, **throws** is a reserved word.

A Java application program might be using the resources provided by the SDK such as the necessary code to input data, which require your program to import certain packages. You can therefore, divide a Java application program into two parts: import statements and the program itself. The import statements tell the compiler which packages are used in the program. The program contains statements (placed in a class) that accomplish some meaningful results. Together, the import statements and the program statements constitute the Java **source code**. To be useful, this source code must be saved in a file, called a **source file**, that has the file extension `.java`. Moreover, the name of the class and the name of the file containing the Java program must be the same. For example, if the name of the class to create the Java program is `Welcome`, then the name of the source file must be `Welcome.java`.

Because the programming instructions are placed in the method `main`, let us elaborate on the method `main` a bit more.

The basic parts of the method `main` are the heading and the body. The first line of the method `main`,

```
public static void main(String[] args) throws clause
```

is called the **heading** of the method `main`.

The statements enclosed between curly braces (`{` and `}`) form the **body** of the method `main`. The body of the method `main` contains two types of statements:

- Declaration statements
- Executable statements

Declaration statements are used to declare things such as variables.

Executable statements perform calculations, manipulate data, create output, accept input, and so on.

In Java, variables or identifiers can be declared anywhere in the program, but they must be declared before they can be used.

Example 2-26

The following statements are examples of variable declarations:

```
int    a, b, c;
double    x, y;
```

Example 2-27

Some executable statements that you have encountered so far are the assignment, input, and output statements.

The following statements are examples of executable statements:

```
a = 4;                                          //assignment statement
b = Integer.parseInt(keyboard.readLine());  //input and
                                                //assignment statement
System.out.println(a + " " + b);             //output statement
```

In skeleton form, a Java application program looks like the following:

```
import statements if any

public class ClassName
{
declare named constants and/or stream objects


 public static void main(String[] args) throws IOException
 {
        variable declaration

        executable statements
 }
}
```

NOTE Notice that the heading of the method `main` contains the reserved word `static`. The statements to declare the named constants and the input stream objects are placed outside the definition of the method `main`. Therefore, Java requires that you declare the named constants and the input stream objects with the reserved word `static`. Example 2-28 illustrates this concept.

Example 2-28

The following is a simple Java application program showing where in a Java program import statements, the method **main**, and statements such as named constants, declarations, assignment statements, and input and output statements typically appear.

```
import java.io.*;                                              //Line 1

public class FirstJavaProgram                                 //Line 2
{                                                             //Line 3
    static final int NUMBER = 12;                            //Line 4

    static BufferedReader keyboard = new
          BufferedReader(new InputStreamReader(System.in));  //Line 5

    public static void main(String[] args) throws IOException //Line 6
    {                                                        //Line 7
        int firstNum;                                        //Line 8
        int secondNum;                                       //Line 9

        firstNum = 18;                                       //Line 10
        System.out.println("Line 11: firstNum = "
                           + firstNum);                      //Line 11
        System.out.print("Line 12: Enter an integer: ");     //Line 12
        secondNum = Integer.parseInt(keyboard.readLine());   //Line 13
        System.out.println();                                //Line 14
        System.out.println("Line 15: secondNum = "
                           + secondNum);                      //Line 15
        firstNum = firstNum  + NUMBER + 2 * secondNum;       //Line 16
        System.out.println("Line 17: The new value of " +
                           "firstNum = " + firstNum);        //Line 17
    }                                                        //Line 18
}                                                            //Line 19
```

Sample Run: In this sample run the user input is shaded.

```
Line 11: firstNum = 18
Line 12: Enter an integer: 15

Line 15: secondNum = 15
Line 17: The new value of firstNum = 60
```

The preceding program works as follows: The statement in Line 1 imports the **class** **BufferedReader** and other components required by the program. The statement in Line 2 names the **class** containing statements of the program as **FirstJavaProgram**. The left brace in Line 3 marks the beginning of the **class FirstJavaProgram**. The statement in Line 4 declares the named constant **NUMBER** and sets its value to 12. The statement in Line 5 declares and initializes **keyboard** to input data from the keyboard. The statement in Line 6 contains the heading of the method `main`, and the left brace in Line 7 marks the beginning of the method `main`. The statements in Lines 8 and 9 declare the variables `firstNum` and `secondNum`.

The statement in Line 10 sets the value of `firstNum` to `18`, and the statement in Line 11 outputs the value of `firstNum`. Next, the statement in Line 12 prompts the user to enter an integer. The statement in Line 13 reads and stores the integer into the variable `secondNum`, which is `15` in the sample run. The statement in Line 14 positions the insertion point on the screen at the beginning of the next line. The statement in Line 15 outputs the value of `secondNum`. The statement in Line 16 evaluates the expression

```
firstNum + NUMBER + 2 * secondNum
```

and assigns the value of this expression to the variable `firstNum`, which is `60` in the sample run. The statement in Line 17 outputs the new value of `firstNum`. The right brace in Line 18 marks the end of the method `main`, and the right brace in Line 19 marks the end of the `class FirstJavaProgram`.

PROGRAMMING STYLE AND FORM

In previous sections you learned how to create a Java application program. Here we describe the proper structure of a program. Using the proper structure makes a Java program easier to understand and modify. It is frustrating trying to follow, and perhaps modify, a program that is syntactically correct, but has no structure.

Every Java application program must satisfy certain language rules. It must also satisfy the syntax rules, which, like grammar rules, tell what is correct and what is incorrect, and what is legal and what is illegal in the language. Other rules give precise meaning to the language; that is, they support the language's semantics. The sections that follow are designed to help you learn how to put together the Java programming elements you have learned so far and create a functioning program. These sections cover syntax; the use of blanks; the use of semicolons, brackets, and commas; semantics; form and style; documentation, including comments and naming identifiers; and prompt lines.

Syntax

The syntax rules of a language tell what is legal and what is illegal. Errors in syntax are detected during compilation. Consider the following Java statements:

```
int x;          //Line 1
int y           //Line 2
double z;       //Line 3

y = w + x;      //Line 4
```

When these statements are compiled, a compilation error will occur at Line 2 because there is no semicolon after the declaration of the variable `y`. A second compilation error will occur at Line 4 because the identifier `w` is used but has not been declared.

As discussed in Chapter 1, you enter a program into the computer by using an editor. When a program is typed, errors are almost unavoidable. Therefore, when the program is compiled, you most likely will see syntax errors. It is possible that a syntax error at a particular place might lead to syntax errors in several subsequent statements. It is common for the omission of a single character to cause four or five error messages. However, when the first syntax error is removed and the program is recompiled, subsequent syntax errors caused by the first syntax error may disappear. Therefore, you should correct syntax errors in the order in which the compiler lists them. As you become more experienced with Java, you will learn how to quickly spot and fix syntax errors. Note that compilers not only discover syntax errors, but also provide hints and sometimes tell the user where the syntax errors are and how to fix them.

Use of Blanks

In Java, you use one or more blanks to separate numbers when data is input. Blanks are also used to separate reserved words and identifiers from each other and from other symbols. Blanks must never appear within a reserved word or identifier.

Use of Semicolons, Braces, and Commas

All Java statements must end with a semicolon. The semicolon is also called a **statement terminator**.

Note that braces, { and }, are not Java statements even though they often appear on a line with no other code. You might regard braces as delimiters because they enclose the body of a method and set it off from other parts of the program. (Braces have other uses, which will be explained in Chapter 4.)

Recall that commas are used to separate items in a list. For example, you use commas when you declare more than one variable following a data type.

Semantics

The set of rules that gives meaning to a language is called **semantics**. For example, the order-of-precedence rules for arithmetic operators are semantic rules.

If a program contains syntax errors, the compiler will warn you. What happens when a program contains semantic errors? It is quite possible to eradicate all syntax errors in a program and still not have it run. And if it runs, it may not do what you meant it to do. For example, the following two lines of code are both syntactically correct expressions, but they have different meanings:

```
2 + 3 * 5
```

and

```
(2 + 3) * 5
```

If you substitute one of these lines of code for the other in a program, you will not get the same results—even though the numbers are the same, the semantics are different. You will learn about semantics throughout this book.

Form and Style

You might think that Java has too many rules. However, in practice, the rules give Java a great degree of freedom. For example, consider the following two ways of declaring variables:

```
int feet, inch;
double x, y;
```

and

```
int feet,inches;double x,y;
```

The computer has no difficulty understanding either of these formats, but the first form is easier to read and follow.

What about blank spaces? Where are they significant and where are they meaningless?

Consider the following two statements:

```
int a,b,c;
```

and

```
int    a,   b,   c;
```

Both of these declarations mean the same thing. Here the blanks between the identifiers in the second statement are meaningless. On the other hand, consider the following statement:

```
inta,b,c;
```

This statement contains a syntax error. The lack of a blank between the `t` in `int` and the identifier `a` changes the reserved word `int` and the identifier `a` into a new identifier, `inta`.

The clarity of the rules of syntax and semantics frees you to adopt formats that are pleasing to you and easier to understand.

Documentation

The programs that you write should be clear not only to you, but also to anyone else. There-fore, you must properly document your programs. A well-documented program is easier to understand and modify, even a long time after you originally write it. You use comments to document programs. Comments should appear in a program to explain the purpose of the program, identify who wrote it, and explain the purpose of particular statements.

Comments

The two most commonly used types of comments in Java are: single line comments and multi-ple line comments. **Single line comments** begin with `//` and can be placed anywhere in the line. Everything encountered in that line after `//` is ignored by the compiler. **Multiple line comments** are enclosed between `/*` and `*/`. The compiler ignores anything that appears between `/*` and `*/`.

You can insert certain comments at the top of a program to briefly explain the program and give information about the programmer. You can also include comments before each key step to briefly describe what that step accomplishes.

 In this book, in the programming code, comments are shown in green.

Naming Identifiers

When naming identifiers, choose self-documenting names. Consider the following two sets of statements:

```
final double A = 2.54;   //conversion constant
double x;                //variable to hold centimeters
double y;                //variable to hold inches

x = y * A;
```

and

```
final double CONVERSION = 2.54;
double centimeters;
double inches;

centimeters = inches * CONVERSION;
```

As you can see, self-documenting identifiers can make comments less necessary.

Consider the self-documenting identifier `monthlypaycheck`. This identifier is called a **run-together-word**. When using self-documenting identifiers, you may inadvertently include run-together-words, which may lessen your documentation's clarity. You can make run-together-words easier to understand by either capitalizing the beginning of each new word or by inserting an underscore just before a new word. For example, you could use either `monthlyPayCheck` or `monthly_pay_check` to create a clearer identifier.

Traditionally, identifiers used by Java programmers to name named constants, variables, and classes follow these rules:

1. An identifier used to name a named constant is all uppercase. If the identifier is a run-together-word, then the words are separated with the underscore character. For example:

```
final double CONVERSION = 2.54;
final int INCHES_PER_FOOT = 12;
```

2. An identifier used to name a variable is lowercase. If the identifier is a run-together-word, then the first letter of each word, except the first word, is upper-case. For example:

```
double salary;
int firstNumber;
```

3. An identifier used to name a class is all lowercase with the first letter of each word in uppercase. For example, `Welcome` and `MakeChange`.

Prompt Lines

Part of good documentation is the use of clearly written prompts so that users will know what to do when they interact with a program. It is frustrating for a user to sit in front of a running program and not have the foggiest notion of whether to enter something, and if so, what to enter. **Prompt lines** are executable statements that inform the user what to do. Consider the following Java statements, in which `num` is an `int` variable:

```
System.out.println("Please enter a number between 1 and 10 and "
                  + "press Enter");
num = Integer.parseInt(keyboard.readLine());
```

When these two statements execute in the order given, first the output statement causes the following line of text to appear on the screen:

```
Please enter a number between 1 and 10 and press Enter
```

After seeing this line, an example of a prompt line, users know that they must enter a number and press the `Enter` key. If the program contained only the second statement, users would not know that they must enter a number, and the computer would wait indefinitely for the input. The preceding output statement is an example of a prompt line.

In a program, whenever users must provide input, you must include the necessary prompt lines. Furthermore, these prompt lines should include as much information as possible about what input is acceptable. For example, the preceding prompt line not only tells the user to input a number, but also informs the user that the number should be between 1 and 10.

MORE ON ASSIGNMENT STATEMENTS

The assignment statements you have seen so far are called **simple assignment statements**. In certain cases, you can use special assignment statements called **compound assignment statements** to write simple assignment statements using more concise notation.

Corresponding to the five arithmetic operators +, -, *, /, and %, Java provides five compound operators +=, -=, *=, /=, and %=, respectively. Consider the following simple assignment statement, where `x` and `y` are `int` variables:

```
x = x * y;
```

Using the compound operator `*=`, this statement can be written as:

```
x *= y;
```

In general, using the compound operator `*=`, you can rewrite the simple assignment statement

```
variable = variable * (expression);
```

as

```
variable *= expression;
```

Similar conventions apply to the other arithmetic compound operators. For example, using the compound operator `+=`, you can rewrite the simple assignment statement

```
variable = variable + (expression);
```

as

```
variable += expression;
```

Thus, the compound assignment statement lets you write simple assignment statements in a concise fashion by combining an arithmetic operator with an assignment operator.

Example 2-29

This example shows several compound assignment statements that are equivalent to simple assignment statements.

Simple Assignment Statement	Compound Assignment Statement
`i = i + 5;`	`i += 5;`
`counter = counter + 1;`	`counter += 1;`
`sum = sum + number;`	`sum += number;`
`amount = amount*(interest + 1);`	`amount *= interest + 1;`
`x = x / ( y + 5);`	`x /= y + 5;`

 Any compound assignment statement can be converted into a simple assignment statement. However, a simple assignment statement may not be (easily) converted to a compound assignment statement. Consider the following simple assignment statement:

```
x = x * y + z - 5;
```

To write this statement as a compound assignment statement, the variable x must be a common factor in the right side, which is not the case. Therefore, you cannot immediately convert this statement into a compound assignment statement. In fact, the equivalent compound assignment statement is

```
x *= y + (z - 5)/x;
```

which is more complicated than the simple assignment statement. Furthermore, in the preceding compound statement x cannot be zero. We recommend avoiding such compound expressions.

In programming code, this book typically uses only the compound operator +=. That is, statements such as a = a + b; are written as a += b;.

PROGRAMMING EXAMPLE: CONVERT LENGTH

Write a program that takes as input given lengths expressed in feet and inches. The program should then convert and output the lengths in centimeters. Assume that the given lengths in feet and inches are integers.

Input   Length in feet and inches

Output   Equivalent length in centimeters

Problem Analysis and Algorithm Design

The lengths are given in feet and inches, and you need to find the equivalent length in centimeters. One inch is equal to 2.54 centimeters. The first thing the program needs to do is convert the length given in feet and inches to all inches. Then you can use the conversion formula, 1 inch = 2.54 centimeters, to find the equivalent length in centimeters. To convert the length from feet and inches to inches, you multiply the number of feet by 12 (1 foot is equal to 12 inches), and add your answer to the given inches.

Suppose the input is 5 feet and 7 inches. You find the total inches as follows:

```
totalInches = (12 * feet) + inches
            = 12 * 5 + 7
            = 67
```

You can then apply the conversion formula, 1 inch = 2.54 centimeters, to find the length in centimeters.

```
centimeters = totalInches * 2.54
            = 67 * 2.54
            = 170.18
```

Based on this analysis, you can design an algorithm as follows:

1. Get the length in feet and inches.
2. Convert the length into total inches.
3. Convert total inches into centimeters.
4. Output centimeters.

Variables

The input for the program is two numbers: one for feet and one for inches. Thus, you need two variables: one to store feet and the other to store inches. Because the program will first convert the given length into inches, you need a third variable to store the total inches. You need a fourth variable to store the equivalent length in centimeters. In summary, you need the following variables:

```
int feet;          //variable to store feet
int inches;        //variable to store inches
int totalInches;   //variable to store total inches
double centimeters; //variable to store length in centimeters
```

Named Constant

Recall that to calculate the equivalent length in centimeters, you need to multiply the total inches by 2.54. Instead of using the value 2.54 directly in the program, you will declare this value as a named constant. Similarly, to find the total inches, you need to multiply the feet by 12 and add the inches. Instead of using 12 directly in the program, you will also declare this value as a named constant. Using named constants makes it easier to modify the program later. Because the named constants will be placed before the method main, you must use the modifier static to declare these named constants (see the section, Creating a Java Application Program).

```
static final double CONVERSION = 2.54;
static final int INCHES_PER_FOOT = 12;
```

Main Algorithm

In the preceding sections, we analyzed the problem and determined the formulas to do the calculations. We also determined the necessary variables and named constants. We can now expand the algorithm given in the section Problem Analysis and Algorithm Design to solve the problem given at the beginning of this programming example (converting feet and inches to centimeters).

1. Prompt the user for the input. (Without a prompt line, the user will stare at a blank screen and not know what to do.)
2. Get the data.
3. Echo the input—output what the program read as input. (Without this step, after the program has executed, you will not know what the input was.)
4. Find the length in inches.
5. Output the length in inches.
6. Convert the length to centimeters.
7. Output the length in centimeters.

Putting It Together

Now that the problem has been analyzed and the algorithm has been designed, the next step is to translate the algorithm into Java code. Because this is the first complete Java program you are writing, let's review the necessary steps in sequence.

The program will begin with comments that document its purpose and functionality. As there is both input to this program (the length in feet and inches) and output (the equivalent length in centimeters), you will use system resources for input/output. In other words, the program will use input statements to get data into the program and output statements to print the results. Because the data will be entered from the keyboard, the program must import the **class BufferedReader** from the package **java.io**. Thus, the first statement of the program, after the comments as described above, will be the **import** statement to import the **class BufferedReader** from the package **java.io**.

This program requires two types of memory locations for data manipulation: named constants and variables. Recall that named constants are usually placed before the method **main** so that they can be used throughout the program.

This program has only one class, which contains the method **main**. The method **main** will contain all of the programming instructions in its body. In addition, the program needs variables to manipulate data, and these variables will be declared in the body of the method **main**. (The reasons for declaring variables in the body of the method **main** are explained in Chapter 7.) The body of the method **main** will also contain the Java statements that implement the algorithm. Moreover, the program will use an input stream object, as described in this chapter, for inputting data and the method **main** will not handle I/O exceptions. Therefore, for this program, the definition of the method **main** has the following form:

```
public static void main(String[] args) throws IOException
{
    declare variables
    statements
}
```

To write the complete length conversion program, follow these steps:

1. Begin the program with comments for documentation.
2. Use **import** statements to import classes required by the program.
3. Declare named constants, if any.
4. Write the definition of the method **main**.

Complete Program Listing

```
//*****************************************************
//    Program Convert: This program converts measurements
// in feet and inches into centimeters using the
// formula that 1 inch is equal to 2.54
// centimeters.
//*****************************************************
```

```
import java.io.*;

public class Conversion
{
    static BufferedReader keyboard = new
                BufferedReader(new InputStreamReader(System.in));

    static final double CONVERSION = 2.54;
    static final int INCHES_PER_FOOT = 12;

    public static void main (String[] args) throws IOException
    {
            //declare variables
        int feet;
        int inches;
        int totalInches;
        double centimeters;

        System.out.print("Enter feet: ");                        //Step 1
        System.out.flush();
        feet = Integer.parseInt(keyboard.readLine());            //Step 2
        System.out.println();
        System.out.print("Enter inches: ");                      //Step 3
        System.out.flush();
        inches = Integer.parseInt(keyboard.readLine());          //Step 4
        System.out.println();
        System.out.println("The numbers you entered are "
                        + feet + " for feet and "
                        + inches + " for inches.");              //Step 5

        totalInches = INCHES_PER_FOOT * feet + inches;           //Step 6

        System.out.println();
        System.out.println("The total number of inches = "
                        + totalInches);                          //Step 7

        centimeters = totalInches * CONVERSION;                  //Step 8

        System.out.println("The number of centimeters = "
                        + centimeters);                          //Step 9

    }
}
```

Sample Run: In this sample run, the user input is shaded.

```
Enter feet: 15

Enter inches: 7

The numbers you entered are 15 for feet and 7 for inches.
```

```
The total number of inches = 187
The number of centimeters = 474.98
```

 The programming code of this program must be saved in the file `Conversion.java` because we named the `class` containing the method main Conversion.

 When you execute this program on your computer, depending on the SDK you are using, it is quite possible that after entering the values of feet and inches you might not see the output. This is because the program does the calculation extremely fast, displays the results, and the output window disappears. To make the output window stay open as long as you want, add the following statements after Step 9 (before the first right brace):

```
String key;

System.out.println("Press the ENTER key to continue");

key = keyboard.readLine();
```

The first statement declares the variable `key` of the type `String`. The second statement displays the following line of text:

```
Press the ENTER key to continue
```

When you press the ENTER key, the output window will disappear. You can include such statements in your programs to see the entire output.

PROGRAMMING EXAMPLE: MAKE CHANGE

Write a program that takes as input any change expressed in cents. It should then compute the number of half-dollars, quarters, dimes, nickels, and pennies to be returned, using as many half-dollars as possible, then quarters, dimes, nickels, and pennies, in that order. For example, 483 cents would be returned as 9 half-dollars, 1 quarter, 1 nickel, and 3 pennies.

Input   Change in cents

Output   Equivalent change in half-dollars, quarters, dimes, nickels, and pennies

Problem Analysis and Algorithm Design

Suppose the given change is 646 cents. To find the number of half-dollars, you divide 646 by 50, the value of a half-dollar, and find the quotient, which is 12, and the remainder, which is 46. The quotient, 12, is the number of half-dollars, and the remainder, 46, is the remaining change.

Next, divide the remaining change by 25, to find the number of quarters. The remaining change is 46, so division by 25 gives the quotient 1, which is the number of quarters, and a remainder of 21, which is the remaining change. This process continues for dimes and nickels. To calculate the remainder (pennies) in integer division, you use the mod operator, %.

Applying this discussion to 646 cents yields the following calculations:

1. Change = 646
2. Number of half-dollars = 646 / 50 = 12
3. Remaining change = 646 % 50 = 46
4. Number of quarters = 46 / 25 = 1
5. Remaining change = 46 % 25 = 21
6. Number of dimes = 21 / 10 = 2
7. Remaining change = 21 % 10 = 1
8. Number of nickels = 1 / 5 = 0
9. Number of pennies = remaining change = 1 % 5 = 1

This discussion translates into the following algorithm:

1. Get the change in cents.
2. Find the number of half-dollars.
3. Calculate the remaining change.
4. Find the number of quarters.
5. Calculate the remaining change.
6. Find the number of dimes.
7. Calculate the remaining change.
8. Find the number of nickels.
9. Calculate the remaining change.
10. The remaining change is the number of pennies.

Variables

From the previous discussion and algorithm, it appears that the program needs variables to hold the number of half-dollars, quarters, and so on. However, the numbers of half-dollars, quarters, and so on are not used in later calculations, so the program can simply output these values without saving them in variables. The only thing that keeps changing is the change, so the program needs only one variable:

```
int change;
```

Named Constants

The program performs calculations using the values of a half-dollar, 50; a quarter, 25; a dime, 10; and a nickel, 5. Because these data are special and the program uses these values more than once, it makes sense to declare them as named constants. (Using named constants also simplifies later modification of the program.)

```
static final int HALFDOLLAR = 50;
static final int QUARTER  = 25;
static final int DIME = 10;
static final int NICKEL = 5;
```

Main Algorithm

In the preceding sections, we analyzed the problem and determined the formulas to do the calculations. We also determined the necessary variables and named constants. We can now expand the algorithm given in the section Problem Analysis and Algorithm Design to solve the problem given at the beginning of this programming example (expressing change in cents).

1. Prompt the user for input.
2. Get input.
3. Echo the input by displaying the entered change on the screen.
4. Compute and print the number of half-dollars.
5. Calculate the remaining change.
6. Compute and print the number of quarters.
7. Calculate the remaining change.
8. Compute and print the number of dimes.
9. Calculate the remaining change.
10. Compute and print the number of nickels.
11. Calculate the remaining change.
12. Print the remaining change.

Complete Program Listing

```
// **************************************************
// Program Make Change: Given any amount of change
// expressed in cents, this program computes the number
// of half-dollars, quarters, dimes, nickels, and
// pennies to be returned, returning as many
// half-dollars as possible, then quarters, dimes,
// nickels, and pennies, in that order.
//**************************************************

import java.io.*;
```

```java
public class MakeChange
{
    static BufferedReader keyboard = new
          BufferedReader(new InputStreamReader(System.in));

    static final int HALFDOLLAR = 50;
    static final int QUARTER  = 25;
    static final int DIME = 10;
    static final int NICKEL = 5;

    public static void main (String[] args) throws IOException
    {
        //declare variables
        int change;

        //Statements: Step 1 - Step 12
        System.out.print("Enter the change in cents: ");    //Step 1
        System.out.flush();

        change = Integer.parseInt(keyboard.readLine());     //Step 2

        System.out.println();
        System.out.println("The change you entered is  "
                           + change);                       //Step 3

        System.out.println("The number of half dollars "
                      + "to be returned is "
                      + change / HALFDOLLAR);               //Step 4

        change = change % HALFDOLLAR;                       //Step 5

        System.out.println("The number of quarters to be "
                      + "returned is "
                      + change / QUARTER);                  //Step 6

        change = change % QUARTER;                          //Step 7

        System.out.println("The number of dimes to be "
                      + "returned is "
                      + change / DIME);                     //Step 8

        change = change % DIME;                             //Step 9

        System.out.println("The number of nickels to be "
                      + "returned is "
                      + change / NICKEL);                   //Step 10
```

```
        change = change % NICKEL;                          //Step 11

        System.out.println("The number of pennies to be "
                            + "returned are " + change);//Step 12

    }
}
```

Sample Run: In this sample run, the user input is shaded.

```
Enter the change in cents: 583

The change you entered is 583
The number of half dollars to be returned is 11
The number of quarters to be returned is 1
The number of dimes to be returned is 0
The number of nickels to be returned is 1
The number of pennies to be returned is 3
```

QUICK REVIEW

1. A Java program is a collection of classes.
2. Every Java application program has a method called `main`.
3. In Java, identifiers are names of things.
4. A Java identifier consists of letters, digits, the underscore character (_), and the dollar sign ($), and must begin with a letter, underscore, or the dollar sign.
5. Reserved words cannot be used as identifiers in a program.
6. All reserved words in Java consist of lowercase letters (see Appendix A).
7. A data type is a set of values with a set of operations.
8. The primitive data types are the fundamental data types in Java.
9. The three categories of primitive data types are integral, floating-point, and Boolean.
10. Integral data types are used to deal with integers.
11. There are five categories of integral data types—`char`, `byte`, `short`, `int`, and `long`.
12. The `char` data type is used to represent integers between 0 and 65535. The memory allocated for the `char` data type is 2 bytes.
13. The `int` data type is used to represent integers between -2147483648 and 2147483647. The memory allocated for the `int` data type is 4 bytes.
14. The data type `short` is used to represent integers between -32768 and 32767. The memory allocated for the `short` data type is 2 bytes.

15. Java uses the Unicode character set, which is a set of 65536 characters. The ASCII character set, which has 128 values, is a subset of Unicode. The first 128 characters of Unicode, 0–127, are the same as those of ASCII.

16. The collating sequence of a character is its preset number in the character data set.

17. The data types `float` and `double` are used to deal with floating-point numbers.

18. The data type `float` is used in Java to represent any real number between −3.4E+38 and 3.4E+38. The memory allocated for the `float` data type is 4 bytes.

19. The data type `double` is used in Java to represent any real number between −1.7E+308 and 1.7E+308. The memory allocated for the `double` data type is 8 bytes.

20. The maximum number of significant digits—that is, the number of decimal places—in `float` values is 6 or 7. The maximum number of significant digits in values belonging to the `double` type is 15. The maximum number of significant digits is called the precision.

21. Values of the type `float` are called single precision, and values of the type `double` are called double precision.

22. The arithmetic operators in Java are addition (+), subtraction (−), multiplication (*), division (/), and mod (%).

23. The mod operator, %, takes only integer operands.

24. Arithmetic expressions are evaluated using the precedence rules and the associativity of the arithmetic operators.

25. All operands in an integral expression, or integer expression, are integers, and all operands in a floating-point expression are decimal numbers.

26. A mixed expression is an expression that consists of both integers and decimal numbers.

27. When evaluating an operator in an expression, an integer is converted to a floating-point number, with a decimal part of zero, only if the operator has mixed operands.

28. You can use the cast operator to explicitly convert values from one data type to another.

29. The `class String` is used to manipulate strings.

30. A string is a sequence of zero or more characters.

31. Strings in Java are enclosed in double quotation marks.

32. A string containing no characters is called a null or empty string.

33. A numeric string consists of integers or decimal numbers.

34. To convert a numeric integer string into an integer, you use the expression

    `Integer.parseInt(strExpression)`

    where `strExpression` is an expression containing a numeric integer string.

35. To convert a numeric decimal string into a `double` value, you use the expression

    `Double.parseDouble(strExpression)`

    where `strExpression` is an expression containing a numeric string.

36. During program execution, the contents of a named constant cannot be changed.

37. A named constant is declared by using the reserved word `final`.

38. A named constant is initialized when it is declared.

39. All variables must be declared before they can be used.

40. Java may not automatically initialize all the variables you declare.

41. Every variable has a name, a value, a data type, and a size.

42. When a new value is assigned to a variable, the old value is destroyed.

43. Only an assignment statement or an input (read) statement can change the value of a variable.

44. Input from the standard input device is accomplished by using the standard input stream object `System.in`.

45. To read a line of characters, first you create an input stream object of the `class` `BufferedReader` and then use the method `readLine`.

46. When data is input in a program, the data items, such as numbers, are usually separated by blanks, lines, or tabs.

47. The increment operator, `++`, increments the value of its operand by 1.

48. The decrement operator, `--`, decrements the value of its operand by 1.

49. The operator `+` can be used to concatenate two strings.

50. Output of the program to the standard output device is accomplished by using the standard output object `System.out` and the methods `print` and `println`.

51. The character `\` is called the escape character.

52. The sequence `\n` is called the newline escape sequence.

53. A package is a collection of related classes. A class consists of methods, and a method is designed to accomplish a specific task.

54. The `import` statement is used to import the components of a package into a program. For example, the statement

```
import java.io.*;
```

imports the (components of the) `package java.io` into the program.

55. In Java, `import` is a reserved word.

56. Because the primitive data types and the `class String` are directly part of the Java language, they do not require any import statement to use them.

57. All Java statements end with a semicolon. The semicolon in Java is called the statement terminator.

58. A file containing a Java program usually ends with the extension `.java`.

59. A single line comment starts with the pair of symbols `//` anywhere in the line.

60. Multiple line comments are enclosed between `/*` and `*/`.

61. The compiler skips comments.

62. Prompt lines are executable statements that tell the user what to do.

63. Corresponding to five arithmetic operators +, -, *, /, and %, Java provides five compound operators +=, -=, *=, /=, and %=, respectively.

64. Using the compound operator *=, you can rewrite the simple assignment statement

```
variable = variable * (expression);
```

as

```
variable *= expression;
```

Similar conventions apply for the other arithmetic compound operators.

EXERCISES

1. Mark the following statements as true or false.

   a. An identifier can be any sequence of digits and letters.

   b. In Java, there is no difference between a reserved word and a predefined identifier.

   c. A Java identifier can start with a digit.

   d. The operands of the modulus operator must be integers.

   e. If the value of a is 4 and the value of b is 3, then after the statement a = b; the value of b is still 3.

   f. In an output statement, the newline character may be a part of the string.

   g. The following is a legal Java program:

   ```
   public class JavaProgram
   {
       public static void main(String[] args)
       {
       }
   }
   ```

   h. In a mixed expression, all operands are converted to floating-point numbers.

   i. Suppose x = 5. After the statement y = x++; executes, y is 5 and x is 6.

   j. Suppose a = 5. After the statement ++a; executes, the value of a is still 5 because the value of the expression is not saved in another variable.

2. Which of the following are valid Java identifiers?

   a. RS6S6

   b. MIX-UP

   c. STOP!

   d. exam1

   e. September1Lecture

   f. 2May

   g. Mike's

   h. First Exam

   i. J

   j. Three

3. Which of the following is a reserved word in Java?

   a. int

   b. INT

   c. Char

   d. CHAR

4. Circle the best answer.

   a. The value of 15 / 2 is:

      (i) 7   (ii) 7.5   (iii) 7¹/₂   (iv) 0.75   (v) none of these

   b. The value of 18 / 3 is:

      (i) 6   (ii) 0.167   (iii) 6.0   (iv) none of these

   c. The value of 22 % 7 is:

      (i) 3   (ii) 1   (iii) 3.142   (iv) 22/7

   d. The value of 5 % 7 is:

      (i) 0   (ii) 2   (iii) 5   (iv) undefined

   e. The value of 17.0 % 4 is:

      (i) 4   (ii) 4.25   (iii) 4¼   (iv) undefined

   f. The value of 5 - 3.0 + 2 is:

      (i) 0   (ii) 0.0   (iii) 4   (iv) 4.0

   g. The value of 7 - 5 * 2 + 1 is:

      (i) -2   (ii) 5   (iii) 6   (iv) none of these

   h. The value of 15.0 / 3.0 + 2.0 is:

      (i) 3   (ii) 3.0   (iii) 5   (iv) none of these

5. If `x = 5, y = 6, z = 4`, and `w = 3.5`, evaluate each of the following statements, if possible. If it is not possible, state the reason.

   a. `(x + z) % y`

   b. `(x + y) % w`

   c. `(y + w) % x`

   d. `(x + y ) * w`

   e. `(x % y) % z`

   f. `(y % z) % x`

   g. `(x * z) % y`

   h. `((x * y) * w) * z`

6. Given:

   ```
   int n, m, l;
   double x, y;
   ```

   which of the following assignments are valid? If an assignment is not valid, state the reason. When not noted, assume that each variable is declared.

   a. `n = m = 5;`

   b. `m = l = 2 * n;`

   c. `n = 5; m = 2 + 6; n = 6 / 3;`

   d. `m + n = l;`

   e. `x = 2 * n + 5.3;`

   f. `l + 1 = n;`

   g. `x / y = x * y;`

   h. `m = n % l;`

   i. `n = x % 5;`

   j. `x = x + 5;`

   k. `n = 3 + 4.6`

7. Do a walk-through to find the value assigned to **e**. Assume that all variables are properly declared.

   ```
   a = 3;
   b = 4;
   c = (a % b) * 6;
   d = c / b;
   e = (a + b + c + d)/ 4;
   ```

8. Which of the following variable declarations are correct? If a variable declaration is not correct, give the reason(s) and provide the correct variable declaration.

```
n = 12;                    //Line 1
char letter = ;            //Line 2
int one = 5, two;          //Line 3
double x, y, z;            //Line 4
```

9. Which of the following are valid Java assignment statements? Assume that i, x, and percent are double variables.

   a. i = i + 5;

   b. x + 2 = x;

   c. x = 2.5 * x;

   d. percent = 10%

10. Write Java statements that accomplish the following.

    a. Declare int variables x and y

    b. Initialize an int variable x to 10 and a char variable ch to 'B'

    c. Update the value of an int variable x by adding 5 to it

    d. Set the value of a double variable z to 25.3

    e. Copy the content of an int variable y into an int variable z

    f. Swap the contents of the int variables x and y (Declare additional variables, if necessary.)

    g. Output the content of a variable x and an expression 2 * x + 5 - y, where x and y are double variables

    h. Declare a char variable grade and sets the value of grade to 'A'

    i. Declare int variables to store four integers

    j. Copy the value of a double variable z to the nearest integer into an int variable x

11. Write each of the following as a Java expression.

    a. −10 times a

    b. The character that represents 8

    c. $(b^2 - 4ac)/ 2a$

    d. $(-b + (b^2 - 4ac)) / 2a$

12. Suppose x, y, z, and w are int variables. What value is assigned to each variable after the last statement executes?

```
x = 5; z = 3;
y = x - z;
z = 2 * y + 3;
w = x - 2 * y + z;
z = w - x;
w++;
```

13. Suppose x, y, and z are `int` variables and w and t are `double` variables. What value is assigned to each variable after the last statement executes?

```
x = 17;
y = 15;
x = x + y / 4;
z = x % 3 + 4;
w = 17 / 3 + 6.5;
t = x / 4.0 + 15 % 4 - 3.5;
```

14. Suppose x is an `int` variable and y is a `double` variable. What value is assigned to each variable after the last statement executes?

```
x = Integer.parseInt("875");
y = Double.parseDouble("374.98");
```

15. Suppose x, y, and z are `int` variables and x = 2, y = 5, and z = 6. What is the output of each of the following statements?

a. `System.out.println("x = " + x + ", y = " + y + ", z = " + z);`

b. `System.out.println("x + y = " + (x + y));`

c. `System.out.println("Sum of " + x + " and " + z + " is " + (x + z));`

d. `System.out.println("z / x = " + (z / x));`

e. `System.out.println(" 2 times " + x + " = " + (2 * x));`

16. What is the output of the following statements? Suppose a and b are `int` variables, c is a `double` variable, and a = 13, b = 5, and c = 17.5.

Output

a. `System.out.println(a + b - c);`   _____

b. `System.out.println(15 / 2 + c);`   _____

c. `System.out.println(a / (double)(b) + 2 * c);`   _____

d. `System.out.println(14 % 3 + 6.3 + b / a);`   _____

e. `System.out.println((int)(c)% 5 + a - b);`   _____

f. `System.out.println(13.5 / 2 + 4.0 * 3.5 + 18);` _____

17. How do you print the carriage return?

18. Which of the following are correct Java statements?

a. `System.out.println("Hello There!");`

b. `System.out.println("Hello");`
   `                 (" There!");`

c. `System.out.println("Hello" +`
   `                 " There!");`

d. `System.out.println('Hello There!');`

19. The following two programs have syntax mistakes. Correct them. On each successive
    line, assume that any preceding error has been corrected. After you have corrected the
    syntax errors, type in these programs to check if all errors have been found.

2

a.

```
public class ProgWithErrorsA
{
    static final int  PRIME = 11,213;
    static final RATE = 15.6
    public void main(String[] arg)
    {
        int i, x, y, w;
        x = 7;
        y = 3;
        x = x + w;
        PRIME = x + PRIME;
        System.out.println(PRIME);
        wages = rate * 36.75;
        System.out.println("Wages = "  wages);
    }
}
```

b.

```
public class ProgWithErrorsB
{
    static final char = BLANK = ' ';
    static final int  ONE 5;

    public static void main(String[] arg)
    {
        int a, b, cc;

        a = one + 5;
        b = a + BLANK;
        cc := a + ONE * 2;
        a + cc = b;
        ONE = b + c;
        System.out.println("a = " + a
                        + ", b = " + b
                        + ", cc = " + cc);
    }
}
```

20. Write equivalent compound statements if possible.

    a. x = 2 * x;

    b. x = x + y - 2;

    c. sum = sum + num;

    d. z = z * x + 2 * z;

    e. y = y / (x + 5);

21. Write the following compound statements as equivalent simple statements.

    a. x += 5 - z;

    b. y *= 2 * x + 5 - z;

    c. w += 2 * z + 4;

    d. x -= z + y - t;

    e. sum += num;

    f. x /= y - 2;

22. Suppose a, b, and c are int variables and a = 5 and b = 6. What value is assigned to each variable after each statement executes? If a variable is undefined at a particular statement, report UND (undefined).

```
                          a        b        c
a = (b++) + 3;          _____  _____  _____
c = 2 * a + (++b);      _____  _____  _____
b = 2 * (++c) - (a++);  _____  _____  _____
```

23. Suppose a, b, and sum are int variables and c is a double variable. What value is assigned to each variable after each statement executes? Suppose a = 3, b = 5, and c = 14.1.

```
                      a        b        c        sum
sum = a + b + c;    _____  _____  _____  _____
c /= a;             _____  _____  _____  _____
b += c - a;         _____  _____  _____  _____
a *= 2 * b + c;     _____  _____  _____  _____
```

24. What is printed by the following program? Suppose the input is:

```
20
15
```

```java
import java.io.*;
public class Mystery
{
    static BufferedReader keyboard = new
                BufferedReader(new InputStreamReader(System.in));

    static final int NUM = 10;
    static final double X = 20.5;

    public static void main(String[] arg) throws IOException
    {
        int a, b;
        double z;
        char grade;
        a = 25;
        System.out.println("a = " + a);
        System.out.print("Enter the first integers: ");
        System.out.flush();
```

```
        a = Integer.parseInt(keyboard.readLine());
        System.out.println();
        System.out.print("Enter the second integers: ");
        System.out.flush();
        b = Integer.parseInt(keyboard.readLine());
        System.out.println();
        System.out.println("The numbers you entered are "
                            + a + " and " + b);
        z = X + 2 * a - b;
        System.out.println("z = " + z);
        grade = 'A';
        System.out.println("Your grade is " + grade);

        a = 2 * NUM + (int)z;
        System.out.println("The value of a = " + a);
    }
}
```

25. What type of input does the following program require, and in what order must the input be provided?

```
import java.io.*;
public class Strange
{
    static BufferedReader keyboard = new
            BufferedReader(new InputStreamReader(System.in));
    public static void main(String[] arg) throws IOException
    {
        int x, y;
        String name;
        x = Integer.parseInt(keyboard.readLine());
        name = keyboard.readLine();
        y = Integer.parseInt(keyboard.readLine());
    }
}
```

PROGRAMMING EXERCISES

1. Write a program that produces the following output:

```
*********************************
*      Programming Assignment 1     *
*        Computer Programming I      *
*         Author: Duffy Ducky         *
*      Due Date: Thursday, Jan. 24   *
*********************************
```

2. Write a program that prints the following pattern:

```
    *
  * *
  * * *
```

3. Write a program that prints the following banner:

```
***************************
***************************
********  WELCOME  ********
===========================
===========================
********   HOME    ********
***************************
***************************
```

4. Write a program that prompts the user to input a decimal number and outputs the number rounded to the nearest integer.

5. Write a program that prompts the user to input the length and width of a rectangle and then prints the rectangle's area and perimeter.

6. Write a program that prompts the user to enter five test scores and then prints the average test score.

7. Write a program that prompts the user to input five decimal numbers. The program should then add the five decimal numbers, convert the sum to the nearest integer, and print the result.

8. Write a program that does the following:
   a. Prompts the user to input five decimal numbers
   b. Prints the five decimal numbers
   c. Converts each decimal number to the nearest integer
   d. Adds the five integers
   e. Prints the sum and average of the five integers

9. Write a program that prompts the user to input a four-digit positive integer. The program then outputs the digits of the number, one digit per line. For example, if the input is 3245, the output is:

```
3
2
4
5
```

10. Write a program that prompts the user to input a length expressed in centimeters. The program should convert the length to inches, to the nearest inch, and then output the length expressed in yards, feet, and inches, in that order. For example, 123 inches would be output as:

```
3 yard(s), 1 feet (foot), and 3 inch(es)
```

It should not be output as:

```
2 yard(s) 4 feet (foot) 3 inch(es)
```

or

```
10 feet (foot) 3 inch(es)
```

or

```
10.25 feet (foot)
```

CHAPTER 3

INTRODUCTION TO OBJECTS AND INPUT/OUTPUT

In this chapter, you will:

♦ Learn about objects and reference variables

♦ Explore how to use predefined methods in a program

♦ Become familiar with the `class` String

♦ Learn how to use input and output dialog boxes in a program

♦ Learn how to tokenize the input stream

♦ Explore how to format the output of decimal numbers with the `class` DecimalFormat

♦ Become familiar with file input and output

Chapter 2 introduced you to the basic elements of Java programs, including special symbols and identifiers, primitive data types, arithmetic operators, and the order of precedence of operators. You were briefly introduced to the `class String` for manipulating strings, and to the `class BufferedReader` for inputting data into a program, as well as general rules on programming style. In this chapter, you learn more about input and output and how to use predefined methods in your programs. You also learn, in some detail, how the `class String` is used to manipulate strings.

OBJECTS AND REFERENCE VARIABLES

Three terms that you will repeatedly encounter throughout this book are variables, reference variables, and objects. This section explicitly defines these terms early in the book so you will be familiar with them.

In Chapter 2, you learned the primitive data types such as `int`, `double`, `char`, and also worked with strings. We used `String` variables to manipulate or process strings. To convert integer numeric strings into their corresponding numeric form, we used the following expression:

`Integer.parseInt(strExpression)`

where `strExpression` is a string expression containing the integer. Similarly, we used the following expression to determine the equivalent form of decimal numeric strings:

`Double.parseDouble(strExpression)`

where `strExpression` is a string expression containing the number.

Just as `String` is a predefined Java `class` to process strings, `Integer` and `Double` are predefined Java `class`es designed, among other things, to manipulate numeric strings.

Consider the following statement:

`int x;`   `//Line 1`

This statement declares `x` to be an `int` variable. Just as you can declare primitive type variables, you can also declare an `Integer` variable. For example, consider the statement:

`Integer num;`   `//Line 2`

This statement declares `num` to be an `Integer` variable.

The statement in Line 1 allocates memory space to store an `int` value and calls the memory space `x`. The variable `x` can store an `int` value in its memory space. For example, the following statement stores `45` into `x`, as shown in Figure 3-1:

`x = 45;`   `//Line 3`

Figure 3-1   Variable x and its data

The statement in Line 2 allocates memory space for the variable **num**. However, unlike the variable **x**, the variable **num** *cannot* directly store data in its memory space. The variable **num** stores the memory location, that is, the address of the memory space where the actual data is stored. First we need to tell the system to allocate memory space to store data, in this case for an integer. This is accomplished by using the reserved word **new**, which you encountered in Chapter 2. In Java, in fact, **new** is an operator. We explain how the operator **new** works in the next section.

The Operator new

Consider the statement in Line 2:

```
Integer num;
```

This statement allocates memory only for the variable **num**, not for the actual data, which in this case is an integer. To allocate memory space for the data, Java provides the operator **new**. The statement

```
num = new Integer(78);          //Line 4
```

uses the operator **new** to allocate memory space to store an integer, the value **78** is stored into the allocated memory space, and the operator **new** returns the address of the allocated memory space. The assignment operator, **=**, stores the address, returned by the operator **new**, into **num**. Suppose that the address of the allocated memory space is **2500**. The effect of the statement could be shown graphically, as in Figure 3-2.

Figure 3-2   Variable num, its value, and the `Integer` object

The variable **num** stores **2500**, the address of the allocated memory space, and the memory space **2500** stores the value **78**. In Java, variables such as **num** are called **reference variables**. More formally, reference variables are variables that store the address of a memory space. In Java, any variable declared using a **class** (such as the variable **num**), is a reference variable. Because **num** is a reference variable declared using the **class Integer**, we say that **num** is a reference variable of **Integer** type.

The memory space **2500**, where the value **78** is stored, is called an **Integer object**. Moreover, we call **Integer** objects **instances** of the **class Integer**.

Because num is a reference variable of Integer type, num can store the address of any Integer object. In other words, num can point to or refer to any Integer object. We call the Integer object that num points to the object num.

Using the operator new to create a class object is called an **instantiation** of that class.

To emphasize that the Integer object at memory space 2500 is the object num, we can redraw Figure 3-2 as Figure 3-3.

Figure 3-3 Variable num and object num

To summarize the Java terminology used in the preceding paragraphs, especially the use of the terms *variable* and *object*: While working with classes, we declare a reference variable of a class type, and then using the operator new we instantiate an object of that class type and store the address of the object into the reference variable. For example, suppose that refVar is a reference variable of a class type. When we use the term *variable* refVar, we mean the value of refVar, that is, the address stored in refVar. When we use the term *object* refVar, we mean the object whose address is stored in refVar. The object to which refVar points can be accessed via the variable refVar.

The next obvious question is how can you change the value from 78 to, say, 50 in Figure 3-3? To do so, you must look at the class Integer and see if it provides a method that allows you to change the value from 78 to 50. Unfortunately, the class Integer does not provide any such method. You could execute another statement, similar to the statement in Line 4, with the value 50. Suppose that the following statement is executed:

```
num = new Integer(50);
```

The operator new again would allocate memory space to store an integer; 50 would be stored into the allocated memory space; and the address of the allocated memory space, returned by the operator new, would be stored in num. However, the address of the allocated memory space will be different than that in the first statement. To be specific, suppose that the address of the allocated memory space is 3800. Figure 3-4 illustrates the result.

Figure 3-4 Variable num, its value, and the object num

3

This is an important property of reference variables, objects, and the operator **new** and must be recognized and understood. Furthermore, it is especially important to know this property when we start comparing reference variables and objects.

To simplify Figure 3-4, we usually use the format in Figure 3-5.

Figure 3-5 Variable num and object num

In Figure 3-5, the arrow originating in the box **num** means that **num** contains an address. The arrow pointing to the memory space containing the value **50** means that the variable **num** contains the address of the object containing the value **50**. We will use this arrow notation to explain various examples.

You might ask: What happened to the memory space **2500** and the value **78** stored in it? If no other **Integer** variable refers to it, then sometimes during program execution, the Java system reclaims this memory space for later use. This is called **garbage collection**. If you do not want to depend on the system for garbage collection, then you can include the statement

```
System.gc();
```

in your program to instruct the computer to run the garbage collector.

We can now summarize the discussion of the preceding sections. You can declare two types of variables in Java—primitive type variables and reference variables, as shown in Figure 3-6. Primitive type variables directly store data into their memory space. Reference variables store the address of the object containing the data. An object is an instance of a **class** and the operator **new** is used to instantiate an object.

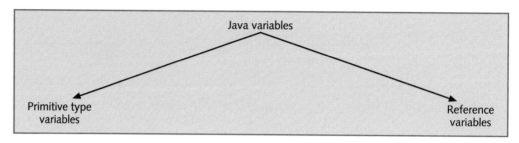

Figure 3-6 Java variables

Before discussing the **class String**, we first discuss how to use predefined methods in a program.

USING PREDEFINED CLASSES AND METHODS IN A PROGRAM

Recall that a **method** is a set of instructions. When a method executes, it accomplishes something. The method **main**, with which you worked in Chapter 2, executes automatically when you run a Java program. Other methods execute only when they are activated—that is, called. Java comes with a wealth of classes called **predefined classes**. In addition, every predefined **class** contains many useful **predefined methods**, which accomplish amazing results. In this section, you do not learn how to write your own methods, but you do learn how to use some of the predefined classes and methods that are provided by the Java system.

Recall from Chapter 2 that predefined classes are organized as a collection of packages, called **class libraries**. A particular **package** may contain several classes and each **class** may contain several methods. Therefore, to use a predefined **class** and/or a method, you need to know the name of the **package**, the name of the **class**, and the name of the method. To use a method, you also need to know a few other things, which are described shortly.

There are two types of methods in a **class**: **static** and non-**static**. A **static** method can be used, that is, called, using the name of the **class** containing the method.

The Java system contains the **class Math**, which in turn contains powerful and useful mathematical functions. The **class Math** is contained in the **package java.lang**. Every method of the **class Math** is a **static** method. Therefore, every method of the **class Math** can be used using the name of the **class**, which is **Math**.

The **class Math** contains a very useful method, **pow**, called the method **power**, which is used to calculate x^y in a program, that is, **Math.pow(x, y)** = x^y. For example, **Math.pow(2,3)** = 2^3 = 8 and **Math.pow(4, 0.5)** = $4^{0.5}$ = $\sqrt{4}$ = 2. The numbers **x** and **y** which are used in the method **pow** are called the **arguments** or **parameters** of the method **pow**. For example, in **Math.pow(2,3)**, the parameters are 2 and 3.

An expression such as Math.pow(2,3) is called a **method call**, and causes the code attached to the method pow to execute and, in this case, computes 2^3.

In general, to use a predefined method in a program:

1. You need to know the name of the class containing the method.

2. You need to know the name of the package containing the class, and import the class from the package in the program.

3. You need to know the name of the method. In addition, you need to know the number of parameters the method takes and the type of each parameter. You must also be aware of what the method is going to do.

For example, to use the method readLine, you include the package java.io.

 As noted in Chapter 2, the Java system automatically imports methods and classes from the package java.lang. Therefore, you do not need to explicitly import any contents of the package package java.lang. Because the class Math is contained in the package java.lang, to use the method pow, you need to know that the name of the method is pow, method pow has two parameters, both of which are numbers, and the method calculates the first parameter to the power of the second parameter.

The Dot Between Class (Object) Name and Class Member: A Precaution

In Chapter 2 you learned how to use the method parseInt of the class Integer to convert a numeric integer string into an integer. Similarly, you used the method readLine of the class BufferedReader, together with a BufferedReader variable, to get data into the program. In the preceding section, you learned how to use the method pow of the class Math.

Consider the following statement,

```
x = Integer.parseInt("75");
```

where x is a variable of the type int. In this statement, the method parseInt of the class Integer is used to convert the string "75" into the integer 75. Notice the dot between Integer and parseInt. The name of the class and the name of the method are separated by the dot.

In Java, the dot (.) is an operator called the **member access operator**.

Omitting the dot between Integer and parseInt results in a syntax error. In the statement

```
x = IntegerparseInt("75");
```

IntegerparseInt becomes a new identifier. If you used IntegerparseInt in a program, the compiler would try to resolve the undeclared identifier syntax error. Similarly, omitting parentheses, as in Integer.parseInt"75";, also results in a syntax error.

Usually, several methods and/or variables are associated with a particular **class**, each doing a specific job. In **dot notation**, the dot separates the **class** name from the member, or method, name.

Dot notation is also used when a **class** variable accesses a certain member of the **class**. For example, consider the following statement (assume that **keyboard** is a **BufferedReader** variable, initialized to the standard input device, and **str** is a **String** variable):

```
str = keyboard.readLine();
```

If you omit the dot between **keyboard** and **readLine**, this results in a syntax error such as an undeclared identifier. Similarly, missing or empty parentheses at the end also results in a syntax error.

THE class String

Recall that the **class String** is one of the most important classes in Java. You saw in Chapter 2 that each input to a program is a string. For example, if input to a program is numeric data, then the numeric data is read as strings of numbers. After reading numeric data into string form, the program converts strings into numbers for processing. In a similar manner, before numeric data is output, it is first converted into strings, which are then output.

Consider the following statement:

```
String name;              //Line 1
name = "Lisa Johnson";    //Line 2
```

The statement in Line 1 declares **name** to be a **String** variable. The statement in Line 2 creates the string **"Lisa Johnson"** and assigns it to **name**.

In reality, the statement in Line 2 is equivalent to the following statement:

```
name = new String("Lisa Johnson");
```

Therefore, to execute the statement in Line 2, during program execution memory space is allocated to store the string **"Lisa Johnson"**. That is, the **String** object with the value **"Lisa Johnson"** is instantiated. The location of the object where this string is stored is then stored to **name**. In other words, **name** contains the address of the **String** object where the string **"Lisa Johnson"** is stored. Figure 3-7 illustrates this concept.

Figure 3-7   **String** variable name, its value, and the **String** object

Here we assume that the string "Lisa Johnson" is stored in the String object at location 1500. Figure 3-7 can also be simplified, as shown in Figure 3-8.

Figure 3-8   String variable name, and the String object

 Some notes on terminology:

1. In the statement in Line 2, that is,

```
name = "Lisa Johnson";   //Line 2
```

we usually say that the string "Lisa Johnson" is assigned to the String variable name. In reality, as explained by Figure 3-8, a String *object* with the value "Lisa Johnson" is instantiated and the address of the object is stored in name. However, we will use the phrase "the string "Lisa Johnson" is assigned to the variable name" to explain statements such as in Line 2.

2. Whenever we use the term the string name, we are referring to the object containing the string name (see Figure 3-9). Similarly, when we use the terms variable name or String variable name, we simply mean name, whose value is an address.

Figure 3-9   String variable name, and the string name

You might wonder why we used the assignment operator to assign a string to a String variable. This is because the **class String** is so important in Java that it has defined the assignment operator for the **class String**. Therefore, while working with String variables and objects, you can eliminate the use of the operator **new** and use the assignment operator to instantiate a **String** object.

In the remainder of this section, we describe various features of the **class String**. In Chapter 2, you learned that two strings can be joined using the operator +. The **class**

`String` provides various methods that allow us to manipulate strings in various ways. For example, we can find the length of a string, extract part of a string, convert a string into uppercase or lowercase letters, find the position of a particular string in another string, convert a number into a string, or convert a numeric string into a number.

Each method associated with the `class` `String` implements a specific operation and has a specific name. For example, the method for determining the length of a string is named `length`, and the method for extracting a string from within another string is named `substring`.

As explained in the earlier section, Using Predefined Classes and Methods in a Program, in general, to use a method you must know the name of the `class` containing the method, the name of the `package` containing the `class`, you must import the `class`, and you must know the method name, its parameters, and what the method does.

Because the Java system automatically makes the `class` `String` available, you do not need to import this `class`. Therefore, in order to use a `String` method you need to know its name, parameters, and what the method does.

Recall that a string is a sequence of 0 or more characters, and strings are enclosed in double quotation marks. The **index** (the position) of the first character is 0, the index of the second character is 1, and so on. The length of a string is the number of characters in it.

Suppose that `str` is a `String` variable and we need to determine a substring in the string `str`. For the method `substring` to work, it must know the following:

1. The position of the first character of the substring being determined in the string `str`

2. The position of the last character of the substring being determined in the string `str`

That is, to use the method `substring`, you must know the starting and ending position of the `substring`. The general statement to use the method `substring` is:

`StringVariable.substring(startIndex, endIndex)`

This statement determines the substring in the string specified by `StringVariable` starting at the position indicated by `startIndex` until `endIndex-1`. For example, the statement

`str.substring(3, 8)`

determines the substring in the string `str`, starting at position 3 until the position, 8-1, that is, 7.

Example 3-1 illustrates how to use the method `substring`.

Example 3-1

Consider the following statements:

```
String sentence;
String str1;
String str2;

sentence = "It is cloudy and warm.";
```

Now consider the following expression:

```
sentence.substring(0,12)
```

This expression says, in the string **sentence**, determine the substring starting at position 0 and ending at position 12 − 1, that is, position 11. The character at position 0 is I and the character at position 11 is y. Therefore, the preceding expression returns the string "It is cloudy". Similarly, the expression

```
sentence.substring(3,5)
```

returns the string "is" because the character at position 3 is i and the character at position 5 − 1, that is, position 4, is s.

Example 3-2

Assume the declaration of Example 3–1, that is,

```
String sentence;
String str1;
String str2;

sentence = "It is cloudy and warm.";
```

The following statements show the effect of the method substring:

Statement	Effect
`System.out.println(sentence.substring(0,5));`	Outputs: It is
`System.out.println(sentence.substring(6,12));`	Outputs: cloudy
`System.out.println(sentence.substring(6,22));`	Outputs: cloudy and warm.
`System.out.println(sentence.substring(3,9));`	Outputs: is clo
`str1 = sentence.substring(0,8);`	str1 = "It is cl"
`str2 = sentence.substring(2,12);`	str2 = " is cloudy"

The program in Example 3–3 tests the preceding statements.

Example 3-3

```
//The substring function

public class SubstringMethod
{
    public static void main(String[] args)
    {
        String   sentence;
        String   str1;
        String   str2;

        sentence = "It is cloudy and warm.";                         //Line 1

        System.out.println("Line 2: "
                            + sentence.substring(0,5));              //Line 2
        System.out.println("Line 3: "
                            + sentence.substring(6,12));             //Line 3
        System.out.println("Line 4: "
                            + sentence.substring(6,22));             //Line 4
        System.out.println("Line 5: "
                            + sentence.substring(3,9));              //Line 5

        str1 = sentence.substring(0,8);                              //Line 6
        System.out.println("Line 7: str1 = \"" + str1 + "\"");      //Line 7

        str2 = sentence.substring(2,12);                            //Line 8
        System.out.println("Line 9: str2 = \"" + str2 + "\"");      //Line 9
    }
}
```

Output

```
Line 2: It is
Line 3: cloudy
Line 4: cloudy and warm.
Line 5: is clo
Line 7: str1 = "It is cl"
Line 9: str2 = " is cloudy"
```

Like the method **substring**, the **class String** contains various methods to manipulate a string. The methods associated with the **class String** are called **members** of the **class String**.

Table 3-1 lists some commonly used **String** methods. The table shows the method heading, the method name in bold, and parameters (if any). Comments explain the purpose of the method, show the return type, and give examples. Examples in Table 3-1 use the following statements:

```
String sentence;
sentence = "Programming with Java";
```

Table 3-1   Commonly Used String Methods

`String(String str)`
  `//Constructor: Creates a string object and initializes the string`
  `//object with characters specified by str`
  `//Example:`
  `//String myStr = new String(sentence);`
  `//        myStr is a String variable initialized using sentence`

`char charAt(int index)`
  `//Returns the character at the position specified by index`
  `//Example: sentence.charAt(3) returns 'g'`

`int indexOf(char ch)`
  `//Returns the index of the first occurrence of the character`
  `//specified by ch; If the character specified by ch does not`
  `//appear in the string, it returns -1`
  `//Example: sentence.indexOf('J') returns 17`
  `//        sentence.indexOf('a') returns 5`

`int indexOf(char ch, int pos)`
  `//Returns the index of the first occurrence of the character`
  `//specified by ch; The parameter pos specifies from where to begin`
  `//the search; If the character specified by ch does not`
  `//appear in the string, it returns -1`
  `//Example: sentence.indexOf('a', 10) returns 18`

`int indexOf(String str)`
  `//Returns the index of the first occurrence of the string`
  `//specified by str; If the string specified by str does not`
  `//appear in the string, it returns -1`
  `//Example: sentence.indexOf("with") returns 12`
  `//        sentence.indexOf("ing") returns 8`

`int indexOf(String str, int pos)`
  `//Returns the index of the first occurrence of the string`
  `//specified by str; The parameter pos specifies from where to begin`
  `//the search; If the string specified by str does not appear`
  `//in the string, it returns -1`

`int compareTo(String str)`
  `//Compares two strings character by character`
  `//Returns a negative value if this string is less than str`
  `//Returns 0 if this string is same as str`
  `//Returns a positive value if this string is greater than str`

Table 3-1 Commonly Used String Methods (continued)

```
String concat(String str)
   //Returns the string that is this string concatenated with str
   //Example: The expression
   //         sentence.concat(" is fun.")
   //         returns the string "Programming with Java is fun."
boolean equals(String str)
   //Returns true if this string is same as str
int length()
   //Returns the length of the string
   //Example: sentence.length() returns 21, the number of characters in
   //         "Programming with Java"
String replace(char charToBeReplaced, char charReplacedWith)
   //Returns the string in which every occurrence of
   //charToBeReplaced is replaced with charReplacedWith
   //Example: sentence.replace('a', '*') returns the string
   //         "Progr*mming with J*v*"
   //         Each occurrence of a is replaced with *
String substring(int startIndex, int endIndex)
   //Returns the string which is a substring of this string
   //starting at startIndex until endIndex - 1
String toLowerCase()
   //Returns the string that is same as this string except that
   //all uppercase letters of this string are replaced with
   //their equivalent lowercase letters
   //Example: sentence.toLowerCase() returns "programming with java"
String toUpperCase()
   //Returns the string that is same as this string except
   //that all lowercase letters of this string are replaced with
   //their equivalent uppercase letters
   //Example: sentence.toUpperCase() returns "PROGRAMMING WITH JAVA"
```

 1. Table 3-1 lists only some of the methods for string manipulation. Moreover, the table only gives the name of the method, the number of parameters, and the type of the method. See Appendix E for the complete heading of each method.

2. The `class String` contains the method `compareTo` for string comparison. Chapter 4 explains how this method works. All the methods associated with the `class String` are listed in Appendix E.

The general statement to use a `String` method, listed in Table 3-1, on a `String` variable is:

`StringVariable.StringMethodName(parameters)`

In this statement, the variable name and the method name are separated using the dot (`.`).

The program in Example 3-4 illustrates how to use some of the **String** methods shown in Table 3-1.

Example 3-4

```java
//Program to illustrate the effect of various String methods

public class VariousStringMethods
{
    public static void main(String[] args)
    {
        String sentence;
        String str1;
        String str2;
        String str3;
        int index;

        sentence = "Now is the time for the birthday party";    //Line 1

        System.out.println("Line 2: sentence = \""
                            + sentence + "\"");                  //Line 2
        System.out.println("Line 3: The length of sentence = "
                            + sentence.length());                //Line 3

        System.out.println("Line 4: The character at index 16 in "
                            + "sentence = "
                            + sentence.charAt(16));              //Line 4

        System.out.println("Line 5: The index of first t in "
                            + "sentence = "
                            + sentence.indexOf('t'));            //Line 5

        System.out.println("Line 6: The index of for in sentence "
                            + "= "
                            + sentence.indexOf("for"));          //Line 6

        System.out.println("Line 7: sentence in uppercase = \""
                            + sentence.toUpperCase() + "\"");    //Line 7

        index = sentence.indexOf("birthday");                    //Line 8
        str1 = sentence.substring(index, index + 14);            //Line 9
        System.out.println("Line 10: str1 = \"" + str1 + "\""); //Line 10

        str2 = "Super " + sentence.substring(index, index + 14);//Line 11
        System.out.println("Line 12: str2 = \"" + str2 + "\""); //Line 12

        str3 = sentence.replace('t', 'T');                       //Line 13
        System.out.println("Line 14: str3 = \"" + str3 + "\""); //Line 14
    }
}
```

Output

```
Line 2: sentence = "Now is the time for the birthday party"
Line 3: The length of sentence = 38
Line 4: The character at index 16 in sentence = f
Line 5: The index of first t in sentence = 7
Line 6: The index of for in sentence = 16
Line 7: sentence in uppercase = "NOW IS THE TIME FOR THE BIRTHDAY
PARTY"
Line 10: str1 = "birthday party"
Line 12: str2 = "Super birthday party"
Line 14: str3 = "Now is The Time for The birThday parTy"
```

The preceding program works as follows: The statement in Line 1 initializes the **String** object **sentence** to the string

```
"Now is the time for the birthday party"
```

The statement in Line 2 outputs the string **sentence**, and the statement in Line 3 outputs the length of the string **sentence**. Note that the output of the statement in Line 2 contains double quotation marks around the string because the print statement in Line 2 contains double quotation marks. The statement in Line 4 outputs the character at index 16, which is **f** in the string **sentence**. The statement in Line 5 outputs the first position (index) of the character **t** in the string **sentence**. Similarly, the statement in Line 6 outputs the index of the string **"for"** in the string **sentence**. The statement in Line 7 uses the method **toUpperCase** to output **sentence** in uppercase letters. The statement in Line 8 determines and stores the index of the string **"birthday"** in the string **sentence**. The statement in Line 9 determines the substring starting at the index specified by **index** until the index given by **index + 14 - 1**. The substring is assigned to the variable **str1**. The statement in Line 10 outputs **str**. The statement in Line 11 concatenates the string **"Super"** with the substring determined from the string **sentence**. Note that the string assigned to **str2** is **"Super birthday party"**. The statement in Line 12 outputs **str2**. The statement in Line 13 assigns to **str3** the same string in **sentence** except that lowercase **t** is replaced with uppercase **T**. The statement in Line 14 outputs **str3**.

To summarize the preceding discussion of the **class String**:

1. **String** variables are reference variables.

2. A string object is an instance of the **class String.**

3. The **class** String contains various methods to manipulate **strings**.

4. A **String** variable invokes a **String** method using the dot operator, the method name, and the set of arguments (if any) required by the method.

INPUT/OUTPUT

A program performs three basic operations: it gets data into the program, it manipulates the data, and it outputs the results. In Chapter 2, you learned how to manipulate numeric data using arithmetic operations. Because writing programs for input/output (I/O) is quite complex, Java offers extensive support for I/O operations by providing a substantial number of I/O classes such as the **class BufferedReader**. In the remainder of this chapter, you will:

- Learn other ways of inputting data and outputting results in Java.

- Learn how to break a string into meaningful pieces—**tokens**—a process called **tokenizing the string**.

- Learn how to format the output of decimal numbers to a specific number of decimal places.

- Learn how to instruct the program to read data from or write output to a file. If there is a large amount of data, inputting data from the keyboard every time you execute your program is not practical. Similarly, if the output is large or you want to save the output for later use, you must be able to save a program's output to a file.

Using Dialog Boxes for Input/Output

Recall that you have already used the **class BufferedReader** to input data into a program from the keyboard and you used the object **System.out** to output the results.

Another way to gather input and output results is to use a graphical user interface (GUI). Java provides the **class JOptionPane**, which allows the programmer to use GUI components for I/O. In this section, we describe how to use these facilities to make I/O more efficient and the program more attractive.

The **class JOptionPane** is contained in the **package javax.swing**. This **class** has two methods that we use here—**showInputDialog** and **showMessageDialog**. The method **showInputDialog** allows the user to input a string from the keyboard, and the method **showMessageDialog** allows the programmer to display results.

The syntax to use the method **showInputDialog** is

```
str = JOptionPane.showInputDialog(stringExpresson);
```

where **str** is a **String** variable and **stringExpression** is an expression evaluating to a string. When this statement executes, a dialog box containing the **stringExpression** appears on the screen prompting the user to enter data. The data entered is returned as a string and assigned to the variable **str**.

The **stringExpression** usually informs the user what to do.

Consider the following statement: (Suppose that `name` is a `String` variable.)

```
name = JOptionPane.showInputDialog("Enter your name and press OK");
```

When this statement executes, the dialog box shown in Figure 3-10 appears on the screen. (Note that the arrow and the words Text field are not part of the dialog box.)

Figure 3-10 Input dialog box prompting the user to input name

The user enters the name in the white area, called a **text field**, as shown in Figure 3-11.

Figure 3-11 Input dialog box with user input

After you enter a name and press the OK button, the dialog box disappears and the entered name is assigned to the variable `name`. In this case, the string `"Snow White"` is assigned to `name`.

Now that you know how to use an input dialog box, let's turn to the method `showMessageDialog` for output.

The syntax to use the method `showMessageDialog` is:

```
JOptionPane.showMessageDialog(parentComponent,
                              messageStringExpression,
                              boxTitleString, messageType);
```

The method `showMessageDialog` has four parameters, which are described in Table 3-2.

Table 3-2 Parameters for the Method `showMessageDialog`

Parameter	Description
`parentComponent`	This is an object that represents the parent of the dialog box. For now, we will specify the `parentComponent` to be `null`, in which case the program uses a default component that causes the dialog box to appear in the middle of the screen. Note that `null` is a reserved word in Java.
`messageStringExpression`	The `messageStringExpression` is evaluated and its value appears in the dialog box.
`boxTitleString`	The `boxTitleString` represents the title of the dialog box.
`messageType`	An `int` value representing the type of icon that will appear in the dialog box. Alternatively, you can use certain `JOptionPane` options described below.

Table 3-3 shows the options of the `class JOptionPane` that can be used with the parameter `messageType`. The option name is shown in bold. The table describes these options, and Examples 3-5 through 3-7 illustrate them.

Table 3-3 `JOptionPane` Options for the Parameter `messageType`

messageType	Description
`JOptionPane.ERROR_MESSAGE`	The error icon is displayed in the dialog box.
`JOptionPane.INFORMATION_MESSAGE`	The information icon is displayed in the dialog box.
`JOptionPane.PLAIN_MESSAGE`	No icon appears in the dialog box.
`JOptionPane.QUESTION_MESSAGE`	The question icon, question mark, is displayed in the dialog box.
`JOptionPane.WARNING_MESSAGE`	The warning icon, the exclamation point, is displayed in the dialog box.

Example 3-5

The output of the statement

```
JOptionPane.showMessageDialog(null, "Hello World!", "Greetings",
                    JOptionPane.INFORMATION_MESSAGE);
```

is shown in Figure 3-12.

Figure 3-12   Message dialog box showing its various components

After you press the OK button, the dialog box disappears. Notice the INFORMATION_MESSAGE icon to the left of Hello World!, and the word Greetings in the title bar of the dialog box.

Example 3-6

Figure 3-13 shows the output of the statement

```
JOptionPane.showMessageDialog(null, "Amount Due = $" + 500.45,
                    "Invoice", JOptionPane.PLAIN_MESSAGE);
```

Figure 3-13   Message dialog box without any icon

In the message dialog box in Figure 3-13, no icon appears to the left of the `messageStringExpression`. This is because the `messageType` is `JOptionPane.PLAIN_MESSAGE`.

Example 3-7

Consider the following statements:

```
String str;
int num1 = 45;
int num2 = 56;
int sum;

str = "The two numbers are: " + num1 + " and " + num2 + "\n";
sum = num1 + num2;

str = str + "The sum of the numbers is: " + sum  + "\n";
str =  str + "That is all for now!";
```

Figure 3-14 shows the output of the statement

```
JOptionPane.showMessageDialog(null, str, "Summing Numbers",
                    JOptionPane.ERROR_MESSAGE);
```

Figure 3-14   Message dialog box showing the output of the string `str`

The **class** `JOptionPane` is contained in the **package** `javax.swing`. Therefore, to use this **class** in a program, the program must import this **class** from the **package** `javax.swing`. The following statement illustrates how to import the **class** `JOptionPane`. (You can use either of the following statements.)

```
import javax.swing.JOptionPane;
```

or

```
import javax.swing.*;
```

The Statement `System.exit`

In order to use the input/output dialog box and properly terminate program execution, the program must include the following statement:

```
System.exit(0);
```

Example 3-8 shows a program that calculates the area and circumference of a circle and uses input/output dialog boxes.

Example 3-8 (Area and Circumference of a Circle)

The program in this example prompts the user to enter the radius of a circle. The program then outputs the radius, area, and circumference of the circle.

```
//Program to determine the area and circumference of a circle

import javax.swing.JOptionPane;

public class AreaAndCircumferenceProgram
{
    public static final double PI = 3.14;                      //Line 1

    public static void main(String[] args)                     //Line 2
    {
        double radius;                                         //Line 3
        double area;                                           //Line 4
        double circumference;                                  //Line 5
        String radiusString;                                   //Line 6
        String outputStr;                                      //Line 7

        radiusString =
            JOptionPane.showInputDialog("Enter the radius: ");  //Line 8

        radius = Double.parseDouble(radiusString);             //Line 9

        area = PI * radius * radius;                           //Line 10
        circumference = 2 * PI * radius;                       //Line 11

        outputStr = "Radius: " + radius + "\n" +
                    "Area: " + area + " square units\n" +
                    "Circumference: " + circumference +
                    " units";                                  //Line 12

        JOptionPane.showMessageDialog(null, outputStr, "Circle",
                    JOptionPane.INFORMATION_MESSAGE);          //Line 13

        System.exit(0);                                        //Line 14
    }
}
```

Sample Run Figure 3-15 shows a sample run of this program, with the input screen on top and the output on the bottom.

Figure 3-15   Sample run of program to calculate a circle's area and circumference

The preceding program works as follows. The statement in Line 1 declares and initializes the named constant `PI` to `3.14`. The statements in Lines 3 through 7 declare the appropriate variables to manipulate data.

The statement in Line 8 displays the input dialog box with the message `Enter the radius:` (in Figure 3-16, the entered value is 12.50).

Figure 3-16   Input dialog box to enter the radius

The string containing the input data is assigned to the **String** variable **radiusString**. The statement in Line 9 converts the string containing the radius into a value of the type **double** and stores it in the variable **radius**.

The statements in Lines 10 and 11 calculate the area and circumference of the circle and store them in the variables **area** and **circumference**, respectively. The statement in Line 12 constructs the string containing the radius, area, and circumference of the circle. The string is assigned to the variable **outputString**. The statement in Line 13 uses the message dialog box to display the radius, area, and circumference of the circle, as shown in Figure 3-17. The statement in Line 14 terminates the program.

Figure 3-17   Output dialog box showing radius, area, and circumference of the circle

 If the amount of input data is small and the output is small, dialog boxes are an effective and attractive way to build your application.

Tokenizing a String

In Chapter 2, we discussed how to input data into a program using the methods **read** and **readLine** and **BufferedReader** variables. (Recall from Chapter 2 that **BufferedReader** variables are commonly called input stream objects.) The method **read** reads the input character by character, and the method **readLine** reads the entire line. If you need to enter three numbers, you must enter them in separate lines, which is not very efficient. Suppose that you want to process the following two sets of data. For data set (a) you want to add the numbers to find their average. Data set (b) includes employees' names, IDs, and annual salary. You need to update the salary data.

a.

```
23 45 78 54 78 98 27
73 78 24
```

b.

```
William Smith        555-55-5555      76542.56
Lisa Jackson         444-44-4444      77654.78
```

If you use the method **readLine** to input data, then the entire line would be read as a string. However, we want the program to break each line into meaningful units of data called **tokens**. In (a) each token is a number. In (b) each line contains four tokens: the employee's first name, last name, employee ID, and annual salary. The **class BufferedReader** is not equipped to break each line into tokens.

Java contains the **class StringTokenizer**, which contains methods to tokenize a string. Tokens are usually delimited with **whitespace** characters. In Java, whitespace characters are: space, tab, newline character, and certain nonprintable characters. You can also specify the delimiting character.

In the remainder of this section, we describe how to use the **class StringTokenizer** to effectively process input.

The **class StringTokenizer** is contained in the **package java.util**. Therefore to use this **class**, the program must import this **class** from the **package java.util**. Table 3-4 describes some members of the **class StringTokenizer**.

Table 3-4 Members of the **class** **StringTokenizer**

Method/Description

public **StringTokenizer(String str)**
//This method is called a constructor.
//It executes when a StringTokenizer is instantiated. The instantiated
//object is initialized using the string specified by str.
//The delimiting characters are the default characters.

public **StringTokenizer(String str, String delimits)**
//This method is also a constructor.
//It executes when a StringTokenizer is instantiated. The instantiated
//object is initialized using the string specified by str. The string
//delimits specifies the delimiters.

Table 3-4 Members of the `class StringTokenizer` (continued)

Method/Description

`public StringTokenizer(String str, String delimits, boolean tokens)`
//This method is also a constructor.
//It executes when a StringTokenizer is instantiated. The instantiated
//object is initialized using the string specified by str. The string
//delimits specifies the delimiters.
//If the boolean variable tokens is true, the delimiters are treated
//as words.

`public int countTokens()` //Returns the number of tokens in the string

`public boolean hasMoreTokens()`
//Returns the value true if there are tokens left in the string;
//otherwise it returns the value false

`public String nextToken()` //Returns the next token in the string

`public String nextToken(String delimits)`
//Returns the next token in the string
//The string delimits specifies the delimiters.

To tokenize a string, you first need to create a `StringTokenizer` object and store the string in the created object. For example, consider the following statement:

`StringTokenizer tokenizer = new StringTokenizer("Hello there!");`

This statement creates the `StringTokenizer` object `tokenizer` and stores the string `"Hello there!"` in the object `tokenizer`. There are two tokens in the object `tokenizer`—Hello and there!.

You can now use the method `nextToken` with the object `tokenizer` to retrieve the next token from the string. Suppose that `str1` and `str2` are `String` variables. Consider the following statements:

```
str1 = tokenizer.nextToken();                    //Line 1
str2 = tokenizer.nextToken();                    //Line 2
```

After these two statements execute, the string assigned to `str1` is `"Hello"` and the string assigned to `str2` is `"there!"`.

Example 3-9

Suppose that we have the following input data:

`Mickey 97 158.50`

Also suppose that we have the following statements:

```
BufferedReader keyboard = new
        BufferedReader(new InputStreamReader(System.in));  //Line 1
StringTokenizer tokenizer;                                 //Line 2
String inputLine;                                          //Line 3
String name;                                               //Line 4
int num;                                                   //Line 5
double decNum;                                             //Line 6
```

The statement in Line 1 creates the input stream object **keyboard** to input data from the keyboard. The statement in Line 2 declares **tokenizer** to be a reference variable of the type **StringTokenizer**. The statements in Lines 3 and 4 declare the **String** variables **inputLine** and **name**. The statement in Line 5 declares the **int** variable **num** and the statement in Line 6 declares the **double** variable **decNum**.

Consider the following statements:

```
inputLine = keyboard.readline();                           //Line 7
tokenizer = new StringTokenizer(inputLine);                //Line 8
name = tokenizer.nextToken();                              //Line 9
num = Integer.parseInt(tokenizer.nextToken());            //Line 10
decNum = Double.parseDouble(tokenizer.nextToken());       //Line 11
```

The statement in Line 7 reads and assigns the string **"Mickey 97 158.50"** to **inputLine**. The statement in Line 8 instantiates the object **tokenizer** and stores the string **"Mickey 97 158.50"** in this object. Notice that the object **tokenizer** has three tokens in it. The statement in Line 9 retrieves the next token, which is the string **"Mickey"** and assigns this string to **name**. The next token in the object **tokenizer** is the integer numeric string **"97"**. The statement in Line 10 retrieves the integer 97 and stores it in **num**. Now the next token in the object **tokenizer** is the numeric string **"158.50"**. The statement in Line 11 retrieves this number and stores it in **decNum**.

Note that the statement in Lines 7 and 8 can be combined in one statement as follows:

```
tokenizer = new StringTokenizer(keyboard.readline());
```

This statement would eliminate the declaration of the variable **inputLine**.

 Suppose that **str** is a **String** variable. Suppose that the value of **str** is **null**, that is, **str** does not point to any **String** object. If you try to tokenize **str**, when you execute the program it will generate **NullPointerException**, and if the program does not handle this exception, the program will terminate. Therefore, you should be careful when you tokenize a string. Exception handling is discussed in detail in Chapter 12.

Formatting the Output of Decimal Numbers

The default output of decimal numbers of the type `float` is up to 6 decimal places. Similarly, the default output of decimal numbers of the type `double` is up to 15 decimal places. For example, consider the statements in Table 3-5 (the output is shown to the right).

Table 3-5 Statements and Output

Statement	Output
`System.out.println(22.0 / 7.0);`	3.142857142857143
`System.out.println(75.0 / 7.0);`	10.714285714285714
`System.out.println((float)(33.0 / 16.0));`	2.0625
`System.out.println((float)(22.0 / 7.0));`	3.142857

Sometimes floating-point numbers must be output in a specific way. For example, a paycheck must be printed to two decimal places, whereas the results of a scientific experiment might require the output of floating-point numbers to 6, 7, or perhaps even 10 decimal places.

Java provides the **class DecimalFormat** to format decimal numbers in a specific manner. The method **format** of the **class DecimalFormat** is applied to the decimal value being formatted. The following steps explain how to use these features to format decimal numbers:

1. Create a **DecimalFormat** object and initialize it to the specific format. Consider the following statement:

   `DecimalFormat twoDecimal = new DecimalFormat("0.00");`

   This statement creates the **DecimalFormat** object **twoDecimal** and initializes it to the string **"0.00"**. Each 0 in the string is a **format flag**. The string **"0.00"** specifies the formatting of the decimal number. This string indicates that the decimal number being formatted with the object **twoDecimal** will have at least one digit to the left of the decimal point and exactly two digits to the right of the decimal point. If the number being formatted does not meet the formatting requirement, that is, it does not have digits at the specified places, those places are automatically filled with 0. Moreover, suppose that you have the following statement:

   `DecimalFormat twoDigits = new DecimalFormat("0.##");`

   The object **twoDigits** can be used to format the number with two decimal places, but the **##** symbols indicate that trailing zeros will appear as spaces.

2. Next use the method **format** of the **class DecimalFormat**. (Assume the declaration of Step 1.) For example, the statement:

   `twoDecimal.format(56.379);`

formats the decimal number `56.379` as `56.38` (the decimal number is rounded). The method `format` returns the string containing the digits of the formatted number.

3. The `class DecimalFormat` is included in the `package java.text.` You must import this `class` into your program.

Example 3-10 illustrates how to format the output of decimal numbers.

Example 3-10

```java
//Program to illustrate how to format the outputting of decimal
//numbers

import java.text.DecimalFormat;

public class FormattingDecimalNum
{
    public static void main (String[] args)
    {
        double x = 15.674;                                   //Line 1
        double y = 235.73;                                   //Line 2
        double z = 9525.9864;                                //Line 3

        DecimalFormat twoDecimal =
                    new DecimalFormat("0.00");               //Line 4
        DecimalFormat threeDecimal =
                    new DecimalFormat("0.000");              //Line 5

        System.out.println("Line 6: Outputting the values of "
                    + "x, y, and z with two decimal "
                    + "places.");                            //Line 6
        System.out.println("Line 7: x = "
                    + twoDecimal.format(x));                 //Line 7
        System.out.println("Line 8: y = "
                    + twoDecimal.format(y));                 //Line 8
        System.out.println("Line 9: z = "
                    + twoDecimal.format(z));                 //Line 9

        System.out.println("Line 10: Outputting the values of "
                    + "x, y, and z with three decimal "
                    + "places.");                            //Line 10
        System.out.println("Line 11: x = "
                    + threeDecimal.format(x));               //Line 11
        System.out.println("Line 12: y = "
                    + threeDecimal.format(y));               //Line 12
        System.out.println("Line 13: z = "
                    + threeDecimal.format(z));               //Line 13

    }
}
```

Output

```
Line 6: Outputting the values of x, y, and z with two decimal places.
Line 7: x = 15.67
Line 8: y = 235.73
Line 9: z = 9525.99
Line 10: Outputting the values of x, y, and z with three decimal
places.
Line 11: x = 15.674
Line 12: y = 235.730
Line 13: z = 9525.986
```

The statements in Lines 1, 2, and 3 declare and initialize x, y, and z to 15.674, 235.73, and 9525.9864, respectively. The statement in Line 4 creates and initializes the DecimalFormat object twoDecimal to output decimal numbers to two decimal places. Similarly, the statement in Line 5 creates and initializes the DecimalFormat object threeDecimal to output decimal numbers with three decimal places.

The statements in Lines 7, 8, and 9 output the values of x, y, and z to two decimal places. Note that the printed values of x in Line 7 and z in Line 9 are rounded.

The statements in Lines 11, 12, and 13 output the values of x, y, and z to three decimal places. Note that the value of y in Line 11 is output to three decimal places. Because the number stored in y has only two decimal places, a 0 is printed as the third decimal place.

FILE INPUT/OUTPUT

The previous sections discussed in some detail how to get input from the keyboard (standard input device) and send output to the screen (standard output device). However, getting input from the keyboard and sending output to the screen has limitations. If the amount of input data is large, it is inefficient to type it at the keyboard each time you run a program. In addition to the inconvenience of typing large amounts of data, typing can generate errors, and unintentional typos cause erroneous results. Sending output to the screen works well if the amount of data is small (no larger than the size of the screen), but suppose you want to distribute the output in a printed format? The solution to these problems is to use an alternative form of input and output: files. By using a file as a source of input data, you can prepare the data before running a program, and the program can access the data each time it runs. Saving output to a file allows the output to be saved and distributed to others, and the output produced by one program can be used as input to other programs.

This section discusses how to obtain data from other input devices, such as a disk (that is, secondary storage), and how to save the output to a disk. Java allows a program to get data directly from, and save output directly to, secondary storage. A program can use the file I/O and read data from or write data to a file. Formally, a **file** is defined as follows:

File: An area in secondary storage used to hold information.

To input data from a file, you use the `class FileReader`, and to send output to a file, you use the `classes FileWriter` and `PrintWriter`. These classes contain appropriate methods to read data from a file and send the output of a program to a file. Both of these classes are contained in the `package java.io`.

Java file I/O is a four-step process:

3

1. Import necessary classes from the `package java.io` into the program.
2. Declare and associate appropriate variables with the input/output sources.
3. Use the appropriate methods associated with the variables created in Step 2 to input/output data.
4. Close the output file.

We will now describe these four steps in detail. A skeleton program then shows how the steps might appear in a program.

Step 1 requires that the necessary classes be imported from the `package java.io`. The following statement accomplishes this task:

```
import java.io.*;
```

Step 2 requires that you declare and associate appropriate `class` variables with the input/output sources. First, we'll describe how to declare and associate `class` variables for inputting data from a file.

Inputting (Reading) Data from a File

As noted above, to declare a variable for inputting data you must use the `class FileReader`. Assume that the input is stored in the file `prog.dat` and is stored on the floppy disk **A**. Consider the following statement:

```
FileReader inData = new FileReader("a:\\prog.dat");     //Line 1
```

This statement creates the `FileReader` object `inData` and initializes it with the file `prog.dat`.

 Notice that there are two \ after **a:** in Line 1. Recall from Chapter 2 that in Java \ is the escape character. Therefore, to produce a \ within a string you need \\.

The `class FileReader` contains the method **read** that can be used with **inData** to read data from the file **prog.dat**. However, the method **read** only reads character by character.

To read the entire line of characters you can create a `BufferedReader` object and initialize the object to the input source using **inData.** For example, consider the following statement (assume the declaration of the statement in Line 1):

```
BufferedReader inFile = new BufferedReader(inData);     //Line 2
```

This statement creates the `BufferedReader` object `inFile` and initializes it using `inData`. After the execution of this statement, you can use `inFile` and the method `read` to read data character by character or the method `readLine` to read the entire line of characters from the input file `prog.dat`.

The statements in Lines 1 and 2 can be combined into one statement as follows:

```
BufferedReader inFile = new
        BufferedReader(new FileReader("a:\\prog.dat"));     //Line 3
```

 If your Java program and the input file reside in the same directory, then you do not need to include a:\\ before the file name in statements such as in Lines 1 and 3.

If you need to tokenize the input line, then you can use a `StringTokenizer` object. In this case, you can read the line and assign it to a `String` variable and use the `String` variable to instantiate the `StringTokenizer` object as discussed earlier in this chapter.

Storing (Writing) Output to a File

To store output of a program in a file, you use the **class** `FileWriter`. First, declare a `FileWriter` variable and associate this variable with the destination, that is, with the file where the output will be stored. Suppose that the output is to be stored in the file `prog.out` on floppy disk **A**. Consider the following statement:

```
FileWriter outData = new FileWriter("a:\\prog.out");     //Line 4
```

This statement creates the `FileWriter` object `outData` and associates it with the file `prog.out` on the floppy disk **A**.

Next, to utilize the methods `print`, `println`, and `flush` to output data, we create a `PrintWriter` object and initialize this variable using `outData`. The following statement accomplishes this:

```
PrintWriter outFile = new PrintWriter(outData);     //Line 5
```

You can now use the methods `print`, `println`, and `flush` with `outFile` just the same way they have been used with the object `System.out`.

For example, the statement

```
outFile.println("The paycheck is: $" + pay);
```

stores the output—The paycheck is: $565.78—in the file `prog.out`. This statement assumes that the value of the variable `pay` is `565.78`.

Of course, you can combine the statements in Lines 4 and 5 into one statement, as follows:

```
PrintWriter outFile = new PrintWriter(new
                    FileWriter("a:\\prog.out"));
```

Once the output is completed, Step 4 requires closing the file. You close the output file by using the method `close`. For example, assuming the declarations listed in Steps 2 and 3, the statement to close `outFile` is:

```
outFile.close();
```

Closing the output file ensures that the buffer holding the output will be emptied, that is, the entire output generated by the program will be sent to the output file.

Step 3 requires that you create appropriate objects for file I/O. In the case of an input file, the file must exist before the program executes. If the input file does not exist, then the statement to associate the object with the input file fails and it `throws` a `FileNotFoundException` exception. At this time, we will not require the program to handle this exception, so the method `main` will also throw this exception. Therefore, the heading of the method `main` will contain an appropriate command to throw a `FileNotFoundException`.

An output file does not have to exist before it is opened; if the output file does not exist, the computer prepares an empty file for output. If the designated output file already exists, by default the old contents are erased when the file is opened.

In skeleton form, a program that uses file I/O is usually of the following form:

```
import java.io;

//Add additional packages as needed

class ClassName
{
     //Declare appropriate variables
   public static void main(String[] args) throws
                                   FileNotFoundException,
                                   IOException
   {
       //Create and associate stream objects
       BufferedReader inFile =
                 new BufferedReader(new
                 FileReader("a:\\prog.dat"));
       PrintWriter outFile =
                 new PrintWriter(new FileWriter("a:\\prog.out"));

       //Code for data manipulation


       //Close file
       outFile.close();
   }
}
```

In the remainder of this chapter, we give two programming examples—one illustrating dialog boxes for input/output and the other illustrating file input/output.

PROGRAMMING EXAMPLE: MOVIE TICKET SALE AND DONATION TO CHARITY

A movie in a local theater is in great demand. The theater owner has decided to donate to a local charity a portion of the gross amount generated from the movie. This example designs and implements a program that prompts the user to input the movie name, adult ticket price, child ticket price, number of adult tickets sold, number of child tickets sold, and percentage of the gross amount to be donated to the charity. The output of the program is shown in Figure 3-18.

Figure 3-18 Output of movie ticket sales program

Note that the decimal numbers are output with two decimal places.

Input The input to the program consists of the movie name, adult ticket price, child ticket price, number of adult tickets sold, number of child tickets sold, and percentage of the gross amount to be donated to the charity.

Output The output is as shown in Figure 3-18.

Problem Analysis and Algorithm Design

To calculate the amount donated to the local charity and the net sale, you first need to determine the gross amount. To calculate the gross amount, you multiply the number of adult tickets sold by the price of an adult ticket, multiply the number of child tickets sold by the price of a child ticket, and then add these two numbers:

```
grossAmount = adultTicketPrice * noOfAdultTicketsSold
            + childTicketPrice * noOfChildTicketsSold;
```

Next you determine the percentage of the amount donated to the charity, and then calculate the net sale amount by subtracting the amount donated from the gross amount. The formulas to calculate the amount donated and the net sale amount are given below. This analysis leads to the following algorithm:

1. Get the movie name.
2. Get the price of an adult ticket.
3. Get the price of a child ticket.
4. Get the number of adult tickets sold.
5. Get the number of child tickets sold.
6. Get the percentage of the gross amount donated to the charity.
7. Calculate the gross amount using the following formula:

```
grossAmount = adultTicketPrice * noOfAdultTicketsSold
            + childTicketPrice * noOfChildTicketsSold;
```

8. Calculate the amount donated to the charity using the following formula:

```
amountDonated = grossAmount * percentDonation / 100;
```

9. Calculate the net sale amount using the following formula:

```
netSale = grossAmount - amountDonated;
```

Variables

From the preceding discussion, it follows that you need variables to store the movie name, adult ticket price, child ticket price, number of adult tickets sold, number of child tickets sold, percentage of the gross amount donated to the charity, gross amount, amount donated, and net sale amount. In addition, you also need a variable to get the string containing sales data and a string to form the output. Moreover, you need a `DecimalFormat` object to format the output of decimal numbers to two decimal places. Therefore, the following variables are needed:

```
String  movieName;
String  inputStr;
String  outputStr;
double  adultTicketPrice;
double  childTicketPrice;
int     noOfAdultTicketsSold;
int     noOfChildTicketsSold;
double  percentDonation;
double  grossAmount;
double  amountDonated;
double  netSaleAmount;

DecimalFormat twoDigits = new DecimalFormat("0.00");
```

Since the program uses the **class** `DecimalFormat`, you must include the **package** `java.text` in the program. Therefore, the following statement is needed:

```
import java.text.DecimalFormat;
```

Formatting Output

To show the desired output, you first create the string consisting of the strings and the values required. The following string accomplishes this:

```
outputStr = "Movie Name: " + movieName + "\n"
            + "Number of Tickets Sold: "
            + (noOfAdultTicketsSold +
               noOfChildTicketsSold) + "\n"
            + "Gross Amount: $"
            + twoDigits.format(grossAmount) + "\n"
            + "Percentage of Gross Amount Donated: "
            + twoDigits.format(percentDonation) + "%\n"
            + "Amount Donated: $"
            + twoDigits.format(amountDonated) + "\n"
            + "Net Sale: $"
            + twoDigits.format(netSaleAmount);
```

Main Algorithm

In the preceding sections, we analyzed the problem and determined the formulas to do the calculations. We also determined the necessary variables and the output string. We can now expand the algorithm given in the section Problem Analysis and Algorithm Design to solve the problem given at the beginning of this programming example.

1. Declare the variables.
2. Set the output of the floating-point numbers to two decimal places in a fixed decimal format with a decimal point and trailing zeros.
3. Display the input dialog box to enter a movie name and retrieve the movie name.
4. Display the input dialog box to enter the price of an adult ticket.
5. Retrieve the price of an adult ticket.
6. Display the input dialog box to enter the price of a child ticket.
7. Retrieve the price of a child ticket.
8. Display the input dialog box to enter the number of adult tickets sold.
9. Retrieve the number of adult tickets sold.
10. Display the input dialog box to enter the number of child tickets sold.
11. Retrieve the number of child tickets sold.
12. Display the input dialog box to enter the percentage of the gross amount donated.
13. Retrieve the percentage of the gross amount donated.
14. Calculate the gross amount.
15. Calculate the amount donated.
16. Calculate the net sale amount.
17. Format the output string.
18. Display the message dialog box to show the output.
19. Terminate the program.

Complete Program Listing

```java
//Program: Movie Ticket Sale and Donation to Charity

import javax.swing.JOptionPane;
import java.text.DecimalFormat;

public class MovieTicketSale
{
   public static void main(String[] args)
   {
           //Step 1
       String movieName;
       String inputStr;
       String outputStr;
       double adultTicketPrice;
       double childTicketPrice;
       int noOfAdultTicketsSold;
       int noOfChildTicketsSold;
       double percentDonation;
       double grossAmount;
       double amountDonated;
       double netSaleAmount;

       DecimalFormat twoDigits = new DecimalFormat("0.00");//Step 2

       movieName = JOptionPane.showInputDialog
                   ("Enter the movie name");              //Step 3

       inputStr = JOptionPane.showInputDialog
                   ("Enter the price of an adult ticket"); //Step 4
       adultTicketPrice = Double.parseDouble(inputStr);    //Step 5

       inputStr = JOptionPane.showInputDialog
                   ("Enter the price of a child ticket");  //Step 6
       childTicketPrice = Double.parseDouble(inputStr);    //Step 7

       inputStr = JOptionPane.showInputDialog
                   ("Enter number of adult tickets sold"); //Step 8
       noOfAdultTicketsSold = Integer.parseInt(inputStr);  //Step 9

       inputStr = JOptionPane.showInputDialog
                   ("Enter number of child tickets sold"); //Step 10
       noOfChildTicketsSold = Integer.parseInt(inputStr);  //Step 11

       inputStr = JOptionPane.showInputDialog
                   ("Enter the percentage of donation");   //Step 12
       percentDonation = Double.parseDouble(inputStr);     //Step 13
```

```
       grossAmount = adultTicketPrice * noOfAdultTicketsSold +
             childTicketPrice * noOfChildTicketsSold;    //Step 14

       amountDonated = grossAmount * percentDonation / 100;//Step 15
       netSaleAmount = grossAmount - amountDonated;         //Step 16

       outputStr = "Movie Name: " + movieName + "\n"
                  + "Number of Tickets Sold: "
                  + (noOfAdultTicketsSold +
                    noOfChildTicketsSold) + "\n"
                  + "Gross Amount: $"
                  + twoDigits.format(grossAmount) + "\n"
                  + "Percentage of Gross Amount Donated: "
                  + twoDigits.format(percentDonation) + "%\n"
                  + "Amount Donated: $"
                  + twoDigits.format(amountDonated) + "\n"
                  + "Net Sale: $"
                  + twoDigits.format(netSaleAmount);        //Step 17

    JOptionPane.showMessageDialog(null, outputStr,
                  "Theater Sales Data",
                  JOptionPane.INFORMATION_MESSAGE); //Step 18
    System.exit(0);                                    //Step 19
   }
}
```

Sample Run   In this sample run, the user input is in the input dialog boxes.

Figure 3-19   Sample run of movie sales program

In this output, the first six dialog boxes (from left to right) get the necessary data to generate the Theater Sales Data dialog box.

PROGRAMMING EXAMPLE: STUDENT GRADE

Write a program that reads a student's first and last name followed by five test scores. The program should output the student's first name, last name, the five test scores, and the average test score. Output the average test score with two decimal places.

The data to be read is stored in a file named `test.txt`, and the file is stored on a floppy disk in drive **A**. The output should be stored in a file named `testavg.out`, and the output file should be stored on the floppy disk in drive **A**.

Input A file containing the student's first name, last name, and the five test scores

Output The student's first name, last name, the five test scores, and the average of the five test scores, saved to a file

Problem Analysis and Algorithm Design

To find the average of the five test scores, you add the five test scores and divide the sum by **5**. The input data is in the following form: the student's first name, followed by the last name, followed by the five test scores. Therefore, we first read the line and tokenize it. Then we retrieve the student's first name, last name, and the five test scores. This problem analysis translates into the following algorithm:

1. Read and tokenize the input line.
2. Get the student's first name, last name, and the five test scores.
3. Output the student's first name, last name, and the five test scores.
4. Calculate the average.
5. Output the average.

You output the average test score in the fixed decimal format with two decimal places.

Variables

The program needs to read a student's first name, last name, and five test scores. Therefore, you need two variables to store the student's first name and last name, and five variables to store the five test scores. To find the average, you must add the five test scores and then divide the sum by **5**. Thus, you also need a variable to store the average test score. Furthermore, because the input data is in a file and output is to be stored in a file, you must declare and initialize appropriate variables. To tokenize the input line, we also need a `StringTokenizer` object. The program needs at least the following variables:

```
double test1, test2, test3, test4, test5; //variables to
                            //store five test scores
double average;      //variable to store average test score
String firstName;    //variable to store the first name
String lastName;     //variable to store the last name
```

```
StringTokenizer tokenizer;

BufferedReader inFile = new
        BufferedReader(new FileReader("a:\\test.txt"));

PrintWriter outFile = new
        PrintWriter(new FileWriter("a:\\testavg.out"));
```

Main Algorithm

In the preceding sections, we analyzed the problem and determined the formulas to do the calculations. We also determined the necessary variables. Now we can expand the algorithm given in the Problem Analysis and Algorithm Design section to solve the Student Grade problem given at the beginning of this programming example.

1. Declare the variables.
2. Create a `BufferedReader` object and associate it with the input source.
3. Create a `PrintWriter` object and associate it with the output source.
4. To output the floating-point numbers to two decimal places, create the appropriate `DecimalFormat` object.
5. Read and tokenize the input line.
6. Get the student's first name and last name.
7. Output the student's first name and last name.
8. Read the five test scores.
9. Output the five test scores.
10. Find the average test score.
11. Output the average test score.
12. Close the output file.

This program reads data from a file and outputs data to a file, so it must import the necessary classes from the `package java.io`. Also, the program tokenizes the input line. Therefore, the program must import the `class StreamTokenizer` from the `package java.util`. The program outputs the average test score to two decimal places., so you need to create an appropriate `DecimalFormat object`. The `class DecimalFormat` is contained in the `package java.text`, so import this `class` from the `package java.text` into the program.

Complete Program Listing

```
//Program to calculate average test score

import java.io.*;
import java.text.DecimalFormat;
```

```java
public class StudentGrade
{
   public static void main (String[] args) throws IOException,
                                           FileNotFoundException
   {

           //Declare and initialize variables        //Step 1
       double test1, test2, test3, test4, test5;
       double average;
       String firstName;
       String lastName;
       StringTokenizer tokenizer;

       BufferedReader inFile = new
          BufferedReader(new FileReader("a:\\test.txt")); //Step 2

       PrintWriter outFile = new
          PrintWriter(new FileWriter("a:\\testavg.out")); //Step 3

       DecimalFormat twoDecimal =
                   new DecimalFormat("0.00");             //Step 4

       tokenizer =
             new StringTokenizer(inFile.readLine());   //Step 5
       firstName = tokenizer.nextToken();              //Step 6
       lastName = tokenizer.nextToken();               //Step 6
       outFile.println("Student Name: "
                   + firstName + " " + lastName);      //Step 7

            //Step 8—Retrieve five test scores
       test1 = Double.parseDouble(tokenizer.nextToken());
       test2 = Double.parseDouble(tokenizer.nextToken());
       test3 = Double.parseDouble(tokenizer.nextToken());
       test4 = Double.parseDouble(tokenizer.nextToken());
       test5 = Double.parseDouble(tokenizer.nextToken());

       outFile.println("Test scores: "
                   + twoDecimal.format(test1) + " "
                   + twoDecimal.format(test2) + " "
                   + twoDecimal.format(test3) + " "
                   + twoDecimal.format(test4) + " "
                   + twoDecimal.format(test5));          //Step 9

       average = (test1 + test2 + test3 + test4
              + test5) / 5.0;                            //Step 10
       outFile.println("Average test score: "
                   + twoDecimal.format(average));        //Step 11
```

```
        outFile.close();                                    //Step 12
    }
}
```

Sample Run

Input File (contents of the file `test.txt`):

Mickey Mousey 87.5 89.00 65 37.5 98.0

Output File (contents of the file `testavg.out`):

```
Student Name: Mickey Mousey
Test scores: 87.50 89.00 65.00 37.50 98.00
Average test score: 75.40
```

3

QUICK REVIEW

1. A reference variable is a variable that stores the address of a memory space.

2. In Java, all variables declared using a `class` are reference variables.

3. A reference variable does not directly store data in its memory space. It stores the address of the memory space where the actual data is stored.

4. Class objects are instances of that `class`.

5. Using the operator `new` to create a `class` object is called an instantiation of that `class`.

6. To use a predefined method in a program, you must know the name of the `class` containing the method, know the name of the `package` containing the `class`, and import the `package` into the program. In addition, you need to know the name of the method, the number of parameters the method takes, and the type of each parameter. You must also be aware of what the method is going to do.

7. In Java, the dot (.) is called the member access operator. The dot separates the `class` name from the member, or method, name. Dot notation is also used when a reference variable of a `class` type accesses a certain member of that `class`.

8. The `class` `String` is used to manipulate strings.

9. The assignment operator is defined for the `class` `String` and it works the same way as does the operator `new`.

10. The method `substring` of the `class` `String` returns a substring from another string.

11. The `class` `String` contains many other useful methods such as—`charAt`, `indexOf`, `compareTo`, `concat`, `equals`, `length`, `replace`, `toLowerCase`, and `toUpperCase`.

12. The method `showInputDialog` of the `class` `JOptionPane` is used to create an input dialog box.

13. The method `showMessageDialog` of the **class JOptionPane** is used to create an output message dialog box.

14. The **class JOptionPane** is contained in the **package javax.swing**.

15. If a program uses input and output dialog boxes, it must also use the statement `System.exit(0)`.

16. The **class StringTokenizer**, contained in the package `java.util`, is used to tokenize a string, that is, divide it up into smaller meaningful units called tokens.

17. The method `nextToken` of the **class StringTokenizer** is used to return the next token in the string.

18. The tokens of a string are usually delimited by whitespace characters.

19. Whitespace characters include the space and certain nonprintable characters such as the tab and the newline character.

20. The **class DecimalFormat** is used to format decimal numbers to a certain number of decimal places.

21. To input data from a file, you use the **class FileReader**, and to send output to a file, you use the **classes FileWriter** and **PrintWriter**.

22. File I/O is a four-step process: (i) import the necessary classes from the **package java.io** in the program; (ii) Declare and associate appropriate variables to the input/output sources; (iii) use the appropriate methods associated with the class variables created in Step ii to input/output data; and (iv) close the output file.

EXERCISES

1. Mark the following statements as true or false.

    a. A variable declared using a **class** is called an object.

    b. In the statement `x = keyboard.readLine();`, `x` must be a variable.

    c. You generate the newline character by pressing the Enter (return) on the keyboard.

    d. The **class DecimalFormat** is used to format a decimal number to a specific number of decimal places.

2. How does a variable of a primitive type differ from a reference variable?

3. What is an object?

4. What does the operator **new** do?

5. Suppose that `str` is a **String** variable. Write a Java statement that uses the operator **new** to instantiate the object `str` and assign the string `"Java Programming"` to `str`.

6. Consider the following statements:

```
String str = "Going to the amusement park.";
char ch;
int len;
int position;
```

a. What value is stored in `ch` by the following statement?

`ch = str.charAt(0);`

b. What value is stored in `ch` by the following statement?

`ch = str.charAt(10);`

c. What value is stored in `len` by the following statement?

`len = str.length();`

d. What value is stored in `position` by the following statement?

`position = str.indexOf('t');`

e. What value is stored in `position` by the following statement?

`position = str.indexOf("park");`

7. Assume the declaration in Exercise 6. What is the output of the following statements?

a. `System.out.println(str.substring(0,5));`

b. `System.out.println(str.substring(13,22));`

c. `System.out.println(str.toUpperCase());`

d. `System.out.println(str.toLowerCase());`

e. `System.out.println(str.replace('t', '*'));`

8. a. What method is used to create an input dialog box?

b. What method is used to create an output dialog box?

c. What is the name of the `class` that contains the methods to create input and output dialog boxes?

d. What is the name of the `package` that contains the `class` described in c?

9. What does the following statement do? (Assume that `scoreStr` is a `String` variable.)

`scoreStr = JOptionPane.showInputDialog("Enter the score:");`

10. Write a Java statement that creates the output dialog box in Figure 3-20.

Figure 3-20   Figure for Exercise 10, Chapter 3

11. Write a Java statement that creates the output dialog box in Figure 3-21.

Figure 3-21   Figure for Exercise 11, Chapter 3

12. Consider the following statements:

```
double x = 75.3987;
double y = 982.89764;
DecimalFormat twoDigits = new DecimalFormat("0.00");
DecimalFormat threeDigits = new DecimalFormat("0.000");
```

What is the output of the following statements?

a. `System.out.println(twoDigits.format(x));`

b. `System.out.println(twoDigits.format(y));`

c. `System.out.println(threeDigits.format(x));`

d. `System.out.println(threeDigits.format(y));`

13. Consider the statements

```
int x, y;
char ch;
```

and the input
46 A 49

Write the Java statements that would store 46 into x, A into ch, and 49 into y. (You must include appropriate statements to tokenize the input line.)

14. The following program is supposed to read two numbers from a file named Ex14Input.txt, and write the sum of the numbers to a file named Ex14Output.dat. However, it fails to do so. Rewrite the program so that it performs correctly. (You may assume that both numbers are on the same line. Also the input and output files on the floppy disk A.)

```
import java.io.*;
public class Ch3Ex14
{
```

```
public static void main(String[] args)
{
    BufferedReader inFile = new
        BufferedReader(new FileReader("a:\\Ex14Input.txt"));

    StringTokenizer tokenizer;

    int num1, num2;

    num1 = Integer.parseInt(tokenizer.nextToken());
    num2 = Integer.parseInt(tokenizer.nextToken());
    outFile.println("Sum = " + (num1 + num2));

    outFile.close();
}
}
```

15. A program reads data from a file called `inputFile.dat` and, after doing some calculations, writes the results to a file called `outFile.dat`. Answer the following questions:

a. After the program executes, what are the contents of the file `inputFile.dat`?

b. After the program executes, what are the contents of the file `outFile.dat` if this
file was empty before the program executed?

c. After the program executes, what are the contents of the file `outFile.dat` if this
file contained 100 numbers before the program executed?

d. What would happen if the file `outFile.dat` did not exist before the program
executed?

PROGRAMMING EXERCISES

1. Consider the following incomplete Java program:

```
public class Ch3_PrExercise1
{
    public static void main(String[] args)
    {
        ...
    }
}
```

a. Write a statement that imports the classes `BufferedReader`, `FileReader`,
`PrintWriter`, and `FileWriter` from the package `java.io`. Also write the statement that imports the class `StringTokenizer` from the package `java.util`.

b. Write statements that declare `inFile` to be a reference variable of the type
`BufferedReader` and `outFile` to be a reference variable of the type
`PrintWriter`.

c. The program will read data from the file `inData.txt` and write output to the file `outData.dat`. Write statements to open both these files, associate `inFile` with `inData.txt`, and associate `outFile` with `outData.dat`.

d. Suppose that the file `inData.txt` contains the following data:

```
56 38
A
7 8
```

Write statements so that after the program executes, the contents of the file `outData.dat` are as shown below. If necessary, declare additional variables. Your statements should be general enough so that if the content of the input file changes and the program is run again (without editing and recompiling), it outputs the appropriate results.

```
The sum of 56 and 38 = 94.
The character that comes after A in the Unicode set is B.
The product of 7 and 8 = 56.
```

e. Write the statement that closes the output file.

f. Write a Java program that tests the statements in parts a-e.

2. Write a program that prompts the user to enter a decimal number and then outputs this number rounded to two decimal places.

3. The manager of a football stadium wants you to write a program that calculates the total ticket sales after each game. There are four types of tickets—box, sideline, premium, and general admission. After each game, data is stored in a file in the following form:

```
ticketPrice     numberOfTicketsSold
...
```

Sample data are shown below:

```
250 5750
100 28000
50 35750
25 18750
```

The first line indicates that the box ticket price is $250 and that 5750 tickets were sold at that price. Output the number of tickets sold and the total sale amount. Format your output with two decimal places.

4. Write a program to calculate the property tax. Property tax is calculated on 92% of the assessed value of the property. For example, if the assessed value is $100000, the property tax is on $92000. Assume that the property tax rate is $1.05 for each $100 of the assessed value. Your program should prompt the user to enter the assessed value of the property. Store the output in a file in the following sample format.

```
Assessed Value:          $100000.00
Taxable Amount:          $92000.00
```

```
Tax Rate for each $100.00:   $1.05
Property Tax:                $966.00
```

Format your output to have two decimal places.

5. Write a program that converts a temperature from degrees Fahrenheit to degrees centi-grade. The formula for converting the temperature from degrees Fahrenheit to degrees centigrade is:

```
C = (5/9) (F - 32)
```

Your program should prompt the user to enter a temperature given in degrees Fahrenheit. The program should output the temperature both in degrees Fahrenheit and in degrees centigrade. Format your output to have two decimal places.

6. Write a program that calculates and prints the monthly paycheck for an employee. The net pay is calculated after taking the following deductions:

```
Federal Income Tax:       15%
State Tax:                3.5%
Social Security Tax:      5.75%
Medicare/Medicaid Tax:    2.75%
Pension Plan:             5%
Health Insurance:         $75.00
```

Your program should prompt the user to input the gross amount and the employee name. The output will be stored in a file. Format your output to have two decimal places. A sample output follows:

```
Allison Nields
Gross Amount:             $3575.00
Federal Tax:              $536.25
State Tax:                $125.12
Social Security Tax:      $205.56
Medicare/Medicaid Tax:    $98.31
Pension Plan:             $178.75
Health Insurance:         $75.00
Net Pay:                  $2356.00
```

4

CONTROL STRUCTURES I

Selection

In this chapter, you will:

♦ Learn about control structures

♦ Examine relational and logical operators

♦ Explore how to form and evaluate logical (Boolean) expressions

♦ Learn how to use the selection control structures `if`, `if...else`, and `switch` in a program

---

Chapter 2 defined a program as a sequence of statements whose objective is to accomplish some task. The programs you have examined so far have been simple and straightforward. In executing programs, the computer starts at the first executable statement and executes the statements in order until it comes to the end. In this chapter and in Chapter 5, you will learn how to tell a computer that it does not have to follow a simple sequential order of statements; it can also make decisions and repeat certain statements over and over until certain conditions are met.

CONTROL STRUCTURES

A computer can process a program in one of three ways: in **sequence**; by making a selection or a choice, which is also called a **branch**; or by repetition, executing a statement over and over using a structure called a **loop**. These three kinds of program flow are shown in Figure 4-1. The programming examples in Chapters 2 and 3 included simple sequential programs. With such a program, the computer starts at the beginning and follows the statements in order. No choices are made; there is no repetition. Control structures provide alternatives to sequential program execution and are used to alter the flow of execution. The two most common control structures are selection and repetition. In **selection**, the program executes particular statements depending on some condition(s). In **repetition**, the program repeats particular statements a certain number of times depending on some condition(s). This chapter introduces selection (branching), and Chapter 5 introduces repetition (looping).

Branch: Altering the flow of program execution by making a selection or choice.

Loop: Altering the flow of program execution by repetition of statement(s).

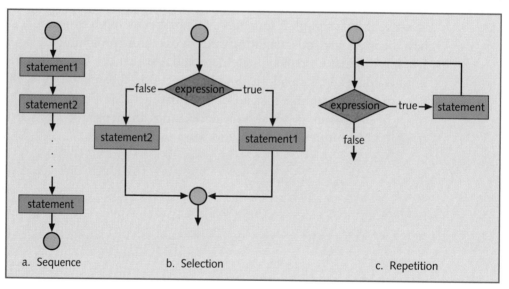

Figure 4-1 Flow of execution

Before you can learn about selection and repetition, you must understand the nature of conditional statements and how to use them. Consider the following three statements (notice that these are not Java statements):

```
1. if(score is greater than or equal to 90)
      grade is A
```

2. if(hours worked are less than or equal to 40)
    wages = rate * hours
  otherwise
    wages = (rate * 40) + 1.5 * (rate * (hours - 40))

3. if(temperature is greater than 70 degrees and it is not
    raining)
      recommended activity is golfing

These statements are examples of conditional statements. You can see that these statements are to be executed only if certain conditions are met. A condition is met if it evaluates to true. For example, in statement 1,

score is greater than or equal to 90

is true if the value of score is greater than or equal to 90; it is false otherwise. For example, if the value of score is 95, the statement evaluates to true. Similarly, if the value of score is 86, the statement evaluates to false.

It would be useful if the computer could recognize these types of statements to be true for appropriate values. Furthermore, in certain situations, the truth or falsity of a statement could depend on more than one condition. For example, in statement 3, both temperature is greater than 70 degrees and it is not raining must be true for the recommended activity to be golfing.

As you can see from these examples, to make decisions, the computer must be able to react to conditions that exist when the program executes. The next few sections discuss how to represent and evaluate conditional statements in Java.

RELATIONAL OPERATORS

To make decisions, you must be able to express conditions and make comparisons. For example, the interest rate and service charges on a checking account might depend on the balance at the end of the month. If the balance is less than some minimum balance, not only is the interest rate lower, but there is also usually a service charge. Therefore, to determine the interest rate, you must be able to state the minimum balance (a condition) and compare the account balance with the minimum balance. The premium on an insurance policy is also determined by stating conditions and making comparisons. For example, to determine an insurance premium, you must be able to check the smoking status of the policyholder. Nonsmokers (the condition) receive lower premiums than smokers. Both of these examples involve comparing items. Certain items are compared for equality against a particular condition; others are compared for inequality—greater than or less than—against a particular condition.

An expression that has a value of either true or false is called a **logical (Boolean) expression**. The values true and false are called **logical (Boolean) values**. In Java, a condition is represented by a logical (Boolean) expression.

Logical (Boolean) expression: An expression that has a value of either `true` or `false`.

Suppose `i` and `j` are integers. Consider the expression:

```
i > j
```

If this expression is a logical expression, it will have the value `true` if the value of `i` is greater than the value of `j`; otherwise, it will have the value `false`. You can think of the symbol > as an operator that (in this case) takes integer operands and yields a logical value. Here, the symbol > is similar to the operators + and − that yield integer or real results. In fact, the symbol > is called a **relational operator** because the value of `i > j` is `true` only when the relationship "greater than" holds between `i` and `j`.

Relational operator: An operator that allows you to make comparisons in a program.

Java includes six relational operators that allow you to state conditions and make comparisons. Table 4-1 lists the relational operators.

Table 4-1 Relational Operators in Java

Operator	Description
==	equal to
!=	not equal to
<	less than
<=	less than or equal to
>	greater than
>=	greater than or equal to

 In Java, the symbol ==, which consists of two equal signs, is called the **equality operator**. Recall that the symbol = is called the assignment operator. Remember that the equality operator, ==, determines whether two expressions are equal, whereas the assignment operator, =, assigns the value of an expression to a variable.

Each of the relational operators is a binary operator; that is, it requires two operands. Because the result of a comparison is `true` or `false`, expressions using these operators evaluate to `true` or `false`.

RELATIONAL OPERATORS AND PRIMITIVE DATA TYPES

You can use the relational operators with integral and floating-point primitive data types. For example, the following expressions use both integers and real numbers:

Expression	Meaning	Value
8 < 15	8 is less than 15	true
6 != 6	6 is not equal to 6	false
2.5 > 5.8	2.5 is greater than 5.8	false
5.9 <= 7.5	5.9 is less than or equal to 7.5	true

 It is important to remember that the comparison of real numbers for equality may not behave as you would expect; see Example 4-1.

Example 4-1

Consider the following program:

```
public class FloatingPointNumbers
{
    public static void main(String[] args)
    {
        System.out.println("3.0 / 7.0 = " + (3.0 / 7.0));
        System.out.println("2.0 / 7.0 = " + (2.0 / 7.0));
        System.out.println("3.0 / 7.0 + 2.0 / 7.0 + 2.0 / 7.0 = "
                   + (3.0 / 7.0 + 2.0 / 7.0 + 2.0 / 7.0));
    }
}
```

Output

```
3.0 / 7.0 = 0.42857142857142855
2.0 / 7.0 = 0.2857142857142857
3.0 / 7.0 + 2.0 / 7.0 + 2.0 / 7.0 = 0.9999999999999999
```

From the output, it follows that the following equality evaluates to `false`:

```
1.0 == 3.0 / 7.0 + 2.0 / 7.0 + 2.0 / 7.0
```

The preceding program and its output show that you should be careful when comparing floating-point numbers for equality.

For `char` values, whether an expression using relational operators evaluates to `true` or `false` depends on the collating sequence of the Unicode character set. Table 4-2 shows how expressions using the Unicode character set are evaluated.

Table 4-2 Evaluating Expressions Using Relational Operators and the Unicode (ASCII) Collating Sequence

Expression	Value of the Expression	Explanation
`' ' < 'a'`	`true`	The Unicode value of `' '` is 32, and the Unicode value of `'a'` is 97. Because 32 < 97 is `true`, it follows that `' ' < 'a'` is `true`.
`'R' > 'T'`	`false`	The Unicode value of `'R'` is 82, and the Unicode value of `'T'` is 84. Because 82 > 84 is `false`, it follows that `'R' > 'T'` is `false`.
`'+' < '*'`	`false`	The Unicode value of `'+'` is 43, and the Unicode value of `'*'` is 42. Because 43 < 42 is `false`, it follows that `'+' < '*'` is `false`.
`'6' <= '>'`	`true`	The Unicode value of `'6'` is 54, and the Unicode value of `'>'` is 62. Because 54 <= 62 is `true`, it follows that `'6' <= '>'` is `true`.

 Consider the following expression:

`8 < '5'`

You might think that 8 is being compared with 5. This is not the case. Here the integer 8 is being compared with the character 5. That is, 8 is being compared with the collating sequence of `'5'`, which is 53. The Java system uses implicit type conversion, changes `'5'` to 53, and compares 8 with 53. Therefore, the expression `8 < '5'` always evaluates to `true`. However, the expression `8 < 5` always evaluates to `false`.

Expressions such as `4 < 6` and `'R' > 'T'` are examples of logical (Boolean) expressions. When Java evaluates a logical expression, it returns the `boolean` value `true` if the logical expression evaluates to `true`; it returns the `boolean` value `false` otherwise.

COMPARING STRINGS

In Java, strings are compared character by character, starting with the first character and using the collating sequence. The character-by-character comparison continues until either a mismatch is found or the last characters have been compared and are equal.

For example, the string `"Air"` is smaller than the string `"Big"` because the first character `'A'` of `"Air"` is smaller than the first character `'B'` of `"Big"`. The string `"Air"` is smaller than the string `"An"` because the first characters of `"Air"` and `"An"` are the same, but the second character `'i'` of `"Air"` is smaller than the second character `'n'` of `"An"`. Moreover, the string `"Hello"` is smaller than the string `"hello"` because the first character `'H'` of `"Hello"` is smaller than the first character `'h'` of `"hello"`.

If two strings of different lengths are compared and the character-by-character comparison is equal until it reaches the last character of the shorter string, the shorter string is evaluated as less than the larger string. For example, the string `"Bill"` is smaller than the string `"Billy"` and the string `"Sun"` is smaller than the string `"Sunny"`.

The **class** `String` provides the method `compareTo`, to compare objects of the **class** `String`. The syntax to use the method `compareTo` is

```
str1.compareTo(str2)
```

4

where `str1` and `str2` are `String` variables. Moreover, `str2` can also be a `String` constant. This expression returns an integer value as follows:

$$str1.compareTo(str2) = \begin{cases} \text{an integer value less than 0 if string } str1 \text{ is less than string } str2 \\ 0 \text{ if string } str1 \text{ is equal to string } str2 \\ \text{an integer value greater than 0 if string } str1 \text{ is greater than string } str2 \end{cases}$$

Consider the following statement:

```
String str1 = "Hello";
String str2 = "Hi";
String str3 = "Air";
String str4 = "Bill";
String str5 = "Bigger";
```

Using these variable declarations, Table 4–3 shows how the method `compareTo` works.

Table 4-3 Comparing Strings with the Method `compareTo`

Expression	Value
`str1.compareTo(str2)`	< 0
`str1.compareTo("Hen")`	< 0
`str4.compareTo(str3)`	> 0
`str1.compareTo("hello")`	< 0
`str2.compareTo("Hi")`	0
`str4.compareTo("Billy")`	< 0
`str5.compareTo("Big")`	> 0

The program in Example 4–2 evaluates the expressions in Table 4–3.

Example 4-2

```java
//The String method compareTo

public class StringComparison
{
    public static void main(String[] args)
    {
        String str1 = "Hello";                          //Line 1
        String str2 = "Hi";                             //Line 2
        String str3 = "Air";                            //Line 3
        String str4 = "Bill";                           //Line 4
        String str5 = "Bigger";                         //Line 5

        System.out.println("Line 6: " +
                        "str1.compareTo(str2) evaluates to "
                    +  str1.compareTo(str2));            //Line 6

        System.out.println("Line 7: " +
                        "str1.compareTo(\"Hen\") evaluates to "
                    +  str1.compareTo("Hen"));           //Line 7

        System.out.println("Line 8: " +
                        "str4.compareTo(str3) evaluates to "
                    +  str4.compareTo(str3));            //Line 8

        System.out.println("Line 9: " +
                        "str1.compareTo(\"hello\") evaluates to "
                    +  str1.compareTo("hello"));         //Line 9

        System.out.println("Line 10: " +
                        "str2.compareTo(\"Hi\") evaluates to "
                    +  str2.compareTo("Hi"));            //Line 10

        System.out.println("Line 11: " +
                        "str4.compareTo(\"Billy\") evaluates to "
                    +  str4.compareTo("Billy"));         //Line 11

        System.out.println("Line 12: " +
                        "str5.compareTo(\"Big\") evaluates to "
                    +  str5.compareTo("Big"));           //Line 12
    }
}
```

Output

```
Line 6: str1.compareTo(str2) evaluates to -4
Line 7: str1.compareTo("Hen") evaluates to -2
Line 8: str4.compareTo(str3) evaluates to 1
Line 9: str1.compareTo("hello") evaluates to -32
```

```
Line 10: str2.compareTo("Hi") evaluates to 0
Line 11: str4.compareTo("Billy") evaluates to -1
Line 12: str5.compareTo("Big") evaluates to 3
```

Notice that the values, such as −4, −2, 1, and so on, printed in Lines 6 through 12 are the differences of the collating sequences of the first unmatched characters of the strings. The only thing we need to know is whether the value is positive, negative, or zero. The output is self-explanatory.

In addition to the method **compareTo**, you can also use the method **equals** of the **class String** to determine if two **String** objects contain the same value. However, the method **equals** returns the value **true** or **false**. For example, the expression

```
str1.equals("Hello")
```

evaluates to **true**, while the expression

```
str1.equals(str2)
```

evaluates to **false**, where **str1** and **str2** are as defined in Example 4-2.

 You can apply the relational operators == and != to variables of **String** type, such as the variables **str1** and **str2**. However, when these operators are applied to these variables they compare the values of these variables, not the values of the **String** objects they point to. For example, the expression (**str1** == **str2**) determines if the values of **str1** and **str2** are the same, that is, if **str1** and **str2** point to the same **String** object. Similarly, the expression (**str1** != **str2**) determines if the values of **str1** and **str2** are *not* the same, that is, if **str1** and **str2** do not point to the same **String** object.

Consider the statement:

```
String str = "Sunny";
```

As explained in Chapter 3, when this statement executes, memory is allocated to store the string **"Sunny"** and the address of the allocated memory is stored in the variable **str**. In reality, the computer checks if there already is a **String** object with the value **"Sunny"**, then the address of that object is stored in **str**. The following further explains it. Consider the following statements:

```
String str1 = "Hello";
String str2 = "Hello";
```

When the first statement executes, a **String** object with the value **"Hello"** is created and its address is assigned to **str1**. When the second statement executes, because there already exists a **String** object with the value **"Hello"**, the address of this **String** object is stored in **str2**. Therefore, if you evaluate the expression (**str1** == **str2**) after these statements, then this expression evaluates to **true**. Moreover, here the expression **str1.equals(str2)** also evaluates to **true**.

If you later assigned a different string, say the string `"Cloudy"`, to `str2`, then if no `String` object exists with the value `"Cloudy"`, a `String` object with this value is created and its address is stored in `str2`. However, `str1` would still point to the string `"Hello"`. In other words, changing the value of the string `str2` does not change the value of the string `str1`.

LOGICAL (BOOLEAN) OPERATORS AND LOGICAL EXPRESSIONS

This section describes how to form and evaluate logical expressions that are combinations of other logical expressions. **Logical (Boolean) operators** enable you to combine logical expressions. Java has three logical (Boolean) operators, as shown in Table 4–4.

Table 4-4   Logical (Boolean) Operators in Java

Operator	Description
`!`	not
`&&`	and
`||`	or

Logical operators take only logical values as operands and yield only logical values as results. The operator `!` is unary, so it has only one operand. The operators `&&` and `||` are binary.

Table 4–5 shows that when you use the `!` operator, `!true` is `false` and `!false` is `true`. Putting `!` in front of a logical expression reverses the value of that logical expression. Example 4-3 gives examples of the `!` operator.

Table 4-5   The `!` (not) Operator

Expression	!(Expression)
`true`	`false`
`false`	`true`

Example 4-3

Expression	**Value**	**Explanation**
`!('A' > 'B')`	`true`	Because `'A' > 'B'` is `false`, `!('A' > 'B')` is `true`.
`!(6 <= 7)`	`false`	Because `6 <= 7` is `true`, `!(6 <= 7)` is `false`.

Table 4-6 defines the operator `&&` (and). From this table, it follows that `Expression1&&Expression2` is `true` if and only if both `Expression1` and `Expression2` are `true`; otherwise `Expression1&&Expression2` evaluates to `false`. Example 4-4 gives examples of the `&&` operator.

Table 4-6 The `&&` (and) Operator

Expression1	Expression2	Expression1 && Expression2
true	true	true
true	false	false
false	true	false
false	false	false

Example 4-4

Expression	Value	Explanation
`(14 >= 5) && ('A' < 'B')`	true	Because `(14 >= 5)` is `true`, `('A' < 'B')` is `true`, and `true && true` is `true`, the expression evaluates to `true`.
`(24 >= 35) && ('A' < 'B')`	false	Because `(24 >= 35)` is `false`, `('A' < 'B')` is `true`, and `false && true` is `false`, the expression evaluates to `false`.

Table 4-7 defines the operator `||` (or). From this table, it follows that `Expression1||Expression2` is `true` if and only if at least one of the expressions, `Expression1` or `Expression2`, is `true`; otherwise, `Expression1||Expression2` evaluates to `false`. Example 4-5 gives examples of the `||` operator.

Table 4-7 The `||` (or) Operator

Expression1	Expression2	Expression1 || Expression2
true	true	true
true	false	true
false	true	true
false	false	false

Example 4-5

Expression	Value	Explanation
`(14 >= 5) || ('A' > 'B')`	`true`	Because `(14 >= 5)` is `true`, `('A' > 'B')` is `false`, and `true || false` is `true`, the expression evaluates to `true`.
`(24 >= 35) || ('A' > 'B')`	`false`	Because `(24 >= 35)` is `false`, `('A' > 'B')` is `false`, and `false || false` is `false`, the expression evaluates to `false`.
`('A' <= 'a') || (7 != 7)`	`true`	Because `('A' <= 'a')` is `true`, `(7 != 7)` is `false`, and `true || false` is `true`, the expression evaluates to `true`.

ORDER OF PRECEDENCE

Complex logical expressions can be difficult to evaluate. Consider the following logical expression:

`11 > 5 || 6 < 15 && 7 >= 8`

This logical expression yields different results depending on whether `||` or `&&` is evaluated first. If `||` is evaluated first, it evaluates to `false`. If `&&` is evaluated first, it evaluates to `true`.

To work with complex logical expressions, there must be some priority scheme for determining which operators to evaluate first. Because an expression might contain arithmetic, relational, and logical operators, as in the expression `5 + 3 <= 9 && 2 > 3`, an order of precedence for all Java operators must be established. Table 4-8 shows the order of precedence of some Java operators, including the arithmetic, relational, and logical operators. (See Appendix B for the precedence of all Java operators.)

Table 4-8 Precedence of Operators

Operators	Precedence
`!, +, -` (unary operators)	first
`*, /, %`	second
`+, -`	third
`<, <=, >=, >`	fourth
`==, !=`	fifth
`&&`	sixth
`||`	seventh
`=` (assignment operator)	last

Using the precedence rules given in Table 4-8, in an expression, relational and logical operators are evaluated from left to right. Because relational and logical operators are evaluated from left to right, the **associativity** of these operators is said to be from left to right.

Example 4-6 illustrates how logical expressions consisting of variables are evaluated.

Example 4-6

Suppose you have the following declarations:

```
boolean found = true;
boolean flag = false;
int num = 1;
double x = 5.2;
double y = 3.4;
int a = 5, b = 8;
int n = 20;
char ch = 'B';
```

Consider the following expressions:

Expression	Value	Explanation
!found	false	Because found is true, !found is false.
x > 4.0	true	Because x is 5.2 and 5.2 > 4.0 is true, the expression x > 4.0 evaluates to true.
!found && (x >= 0)	false	In this expression, !found is false. Also, because x is 5.2 and 5.2 >= 0 is true, x >= 0 is true. Therefore, the value of the expression !found && (x >= 0) is false && true, which evaluates to false.
!(found && (x >= 0))	false	In this expression, found && (x >= 0) is true && true, which evaluates to true. Therefore, the value of the expression !(found && (x >= 0)) is !true, which evaluates to false.
x + y <= 20.5	true	Because x + y = 5.2 + 3.4 = 8.6 and 8.6 <= 20.5, it follows that x + y <= 20.5 evaluates to true.
(n >= 0) && (n <= 100)	true	Here n is 20. Because 20 >= 0 is true, n >= 0 is true. Also, because 20 <= 100 is true, n <= 100 is true. Therefore, the value of the expression (n >= 0) && (n <= 100) is true && true, which evaluates to true.

4

('A' <= ch && ch <= 'Z') true		In this expression, the value of ch is 'B'. Because 'A' <= 'B' is true, 'A' <= ch evaluates to true. Also, because 'B' <= 'Z' is true, ch <= 'Z' evaluates to true. Therefore, the value of the expression ('A' <= ch && ch <= 'Z') is true && true, which evaluates to true.
(a + 2 <= b) && !flag true		Now a + 2 = 5 + 2 = 7 and b is 8. Because 7 < 8 is true, the expression a + 2 < b evaluates to true. Also, because flag is false, !flag is true. Therefore, the value of the expression (a + 2 <= b) && !flag is true && true, which evaluates to true.

You can also write a Java program to evaluate the logical expressions given in Example 4-6, as shown in Example 4-7.

Example 4-7

The following program evaluates and outputs the values of the logical expressions given in Example 4-6.

```java
//Chapter 4: Logical operators

public class LogicalOperators
{
    public static void main(String[] args)
    {
        boolean found = true;
        boolean flag = false;
        int num = 1;
        double x = 5.2;
        double y = 3.4;
        int a = 5, b = 8;
        int n = 20;
        char ch = 'B';

        System.out.println("Line 1: !found evaluates to "
                         + !found);                              //Line 1
        System.out.println("Line 2: x > 4.0 evaluates to "
                         + (x > 4.0));                           //Line 2
        System.out.println("Line 3: !found && (x >= 0) "
                         + "evaluates to "
                         + (!found && (x >= 0)));                //Line 3
        System.out.println("Line 4: !(found && (x >= 0)) "
                         + "evaluates to "
                         + !(found && (x >= 0)));                //Line 4
```

```
            System.out.println("Line 5: x + y <= 20.5 evaluates to "
                            + (x + y <= 20.5));              //Line 5
            System.out.println("Line 6: (n >= 0) && (n <= 100) "
                            + "evaluates to "
                            + ((n >= 0) && (n <= 100)));     //Line 6
            System.out.println("Line 7: ('A' <= ch && ch <= 'Z') "
                            + "evaluates to "
                            + ('A' <= ch && ch <= 'Z'));     //Line 7
            System.out.println("Line 8: (a + 2 <= b) && !flag "
                            + "evaluates to "
                            + ((a + 2 <= b) && !flag));      //Line 8
    }
}
```

Output

```
Line 1: !found evaluates to false
Line 2: x > 4.0 evaluates to true
Line 3: !found && (x >= 0) evaluates to false
Line 4: !(found && (x >= 0)) evaluates to false
Line 5: x + y <= 20.5 evaluates to true
Line 6: (n >= 0) && (n <= 100) evaluates to true
Line 7: ('A' <= ch && ch <= 'Z') evaluates to true
Line 8: (a + 2 <= b) && !flag evaluates to true
```

You can insert parentheses into an expression to clarify its meaning. You can also use parentheses to override the precedence of operators. Using the standard order of precedence, the expression

```
11 > 5 || 6 < 15 && 7 >= 8
```

is equivalent to

```
11 > 5 || (6 < 15 && 7 >= 8)
```

In this expression,

```
11 > 5 is true,
6 < 15 is true,
```

and

```
7 >= 8 is false.
```

Substitute these values in the expression

```
11 > 5 || (6 < 15 && 7 >= 8)
```

to get

```
true || (true && false) = true || false = true.
```

Therefore, the expression 11 > 5 || (6 < 15 && 7 >= 8) evaluates to **true**.

Example 4-8

Evaluate the following expression:

```
(17 < 4 * 3 + 5) || (8 * 2 == 4 * 4) && !(3 + 3 == 6)
```

Now,

```
  (17 < 4 * 3 + 5) || (8 * 2 == 4 * 4) && !(3 + 3 == 6)
= (17 < 12 + 5) || (16 == 16) && !(6 == 6)
= (17 < 17) || true && !(true)
= false || true && false
= false || false (Because true && false is false)
= false
```

Therefore, the value of the original logical expression is `false`.

Short-Circuit Evaluation

Logical expressions in Java are evaluated using a highly efficient algorithm. This algorithm is illustrated with the help of the following statements:

```
(x > y) || (x == 5)
(a == b) && (x >= 7)
```

In the first statement, the two operands of the operator `||` are the expressions `(x > y)` and `(x == 5)`. This expression evaluates to `true` if either the operand `(x > y)` is `true` or the operand `(x == 5)` is `true`. With **short-circuit evaluation**, the computer evaluates the logical expression from left to right. As soon as the value of the entire logical expression is known, the evaluation stops. For example, in the first statement, if the operand `(x > y)` evaluates to `true`, then the entire expression evaluates to `true` because `true || true` is `true` and `true || false` is `true`. Therefore, the value of the operand `(x == 5)` has no bearing on the final outcome.

Similarly, in the second statement, the two operands of the operator `&&` are `(a == b)` and `(x >= 7)`. Now, if the operand `(a == b)` evaluates to `false`, then the entire expression evaluates to `false` because `false && true` is `false` and `false && false` is `false`.

Short-circuit evaluation (of a logical expression): A process in which the computer evaluates a logical expression from left to right and stops as soon as the value of the expression is known.

Example 4-9

Consider the following expressions:

```
(age >= 21) || ( x == 5)        //Line 1
(grade == 'A') && (x >= 7)       //Line 2
```

For the expression in Line 1, suppose that the value of `age` is 25. Because `(25 >= 21)` is `true` and the logical operator used in the expression is `||`, the expression evaluates to `true`. Due to short-circuit evaluation, the computer does not evaluate the expression `(x == 5)`. Similarly, for the expression in Line 2, suppose that the value of `grade` is `'B'`. Because `('A' == 'B')` is `false` and the logical operator used in the expression is `&&`, the expression evaluates to `false`. The computer does not evaluate `(x >= 7)`.

 In Java, `&` and `|` are also operators. You can use the operator `&` in place of the operator `&&` in a logical expression. Similarly, you can use the operator `|` in place of the operator `||` in a logical expression. However, there is no short-circuit evaluation of the logical expressions if `&` is used in place of `&&` or `|` is used in place of `||`.

The `boolean` Data Type and Logical (Boolean) Expressions

Recall that Java contains the built-in data type `boolean`, which has the logical (Boolean) values `true` and `false`. Therefore, you can manipulate logical (Boolean) expressions using the `boolean` data type. Also, recall that in Java, `boolean`, `true`, and `false` are reserved words.

Suppose that you have the following statement:

```
boolean legalAge;
int age;
```

The statement

```
legalAge = true;
```

sets the value of the variable `legalAge` to `true`. The statement

```
legalAge = (age >= 21);
```

assigns the value `true` to `legalAge` if the value of `age` is greater than or equal to 21. This statement assigns the value `false` to `legalAge` if the value of `age` is less than 21. For example, if the value of `age` is 25, the value assigned to `legalAge` is `true`. Similarly, if the value of `age` is 16, the value assigned to `legalAge` is `false`.

 Be careful when forming logical expressions. Some beginners make the following common mistake: Suppose that num is an `int` variable. Further suppose that you want to write a logical expression that evaluates to `true` if the value of num is between 0 and 10, including 0 and 10, and that evaluates to `false` otherwise. The following expression appears to represent a comparison of 0, num, and 10 that will yield the desired result:

```
0 <= num <= 10
```

This statement is not legal in Java and you will get a syntax error. This is because the associativity of the operator `<=` is from left to right. Therefore, the preceding expression is equivalent to:

```
(0 <= num) <= 10
```

The value of the expression (0 <= num) is either `true` or `false`. Since you cannot compare the `boolean` values `true` and `false` with other data types, the expression would result in a syntax error. One of the correct ways to write this expression in Java is:

```
0 <= num && num <= 10
```

When creating a complex logical expression, take care to use the proper logical operators.

SELECTION: `if` AND `if...else`

Although there are only two logical values, `true` and `false`, they are extremely useful because they permit programs to incorporate decision making that alters the processing flow. The remainder of this chapter discusses ways to incorporate decisions into a program. In Java, there are two selection or branch control structures: `if` statements and the `switch` structure. This section discusses how `if` and `if...else` statements can be used to create one-way selection, two-way selection, and multiple selections. The `switch` structure is discussed later in this chapter.

One-Way Selection

A bank wants to send a notice to a customer if her or his checking account balance falls below the required minimum balance. That is, if the checking account balance is below the required minimum balance, the bank should send a notice to the customer; otherwise, it should do nothing. Similarly, if the policyholder of an insurance policy is a nonsmoker, the company wants to apply a 10% discount to the policy premium. Both of these examples involve one-way selection. In Java, one-way selections are incorporated using the `if` statement. The syntax of one-way selection is:

```
if(expression)
    statement
```

Note the elements of this syntax. It begins with the reserved word `if`, followed by an `expression` contained within parentheses, followed by a `statement`. The `expression` is sometimes called a **decision maker** because it decides whether to execute the `statement` that follows it. The `expression` is a logical expression. If the value of the `expression` is `true`, the `statement` executes. If the value is `false`, the `statement` does not execute and the computer goes on to the next statement in the program. The `statement` following the `expression` is sometimes called the **action statement**. Figure 4-2 shows the flow of execution of the `if` statement (one-way selection).

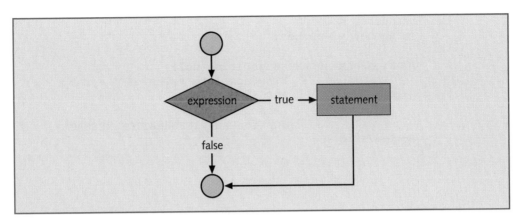

Figure 4-2 One-way selection

Example 4-10

```
if(score >= 90)

    grade = 'A';
```

In this code, if the expression (`score >= 90`) evaluates to `true`, the assignment statement, `grade = 'A';`, executes. If the expression evaluates to `false`, the statements (if any) following the `if` structure execute. For example, if the value of `score` is 95, the value assigned to the variable `grade` is A.

Example 4-11

The following Java program finds the absolute value of an integer.

```
//Determine the absolute value of an integer

import javax.swing.JOptionPane;

public class AbsoluteValue
{
    public static void main(String[] args)
    {
        int number;
        int temp;
        String numString;

        numString =
            JOptionPane.showInputDialog("Enter an integer:"); //Line 1

        number = Integer.parseInt(numString);                 //Line 2
        temp = number;                                        //Line 3
```

```
        if(number < 0)                                      //Line 4
            number = -number;                               //Line 5

        JOptionPane.showMessageDialog(null,
                        "The absolute value of " + temp
                        + " is " + number,
                        "Absolute Value",
                        JOptionPane.INFORMATION_MESSAGE);    //Line 6
        System.exit(0);
    }
}
```

Sample Run: Figure 4-3 shows the sample run.

Figure 4-3 Sample run for Example 4-11

The statement in Line 1 displays the input dialog box and prompts the user to enter an integer. The entered number is stored as a string in **numString**. The statement in Line 2 uses the method **parseInt** of the **class Integer**, converts the **numString** into the number, and stores the number in the variable **number**. The statement in Line 3 copies the value of **number** into **temp**. The statement in Line 4 checks whether **number** is negative. If **number** is negative, the statement in Line 5 changes **number** to a positive number. The statement in Line 6 displays the message dialog box and shows the original number, stored in **temp**, and the absolute value of the number stored in **number**.

Example 4-12

Consider the following statement:

```
if score >= 90
    grade = 'A';
```

This statement illustrates an incorrect version of an `if` statement. The parentheses around the logical expression are missing, which is a syntax error.

Putting a semicolon after the parentheses following the expression in an `if` statement (that is, before the statement) is a semantic error. If the semicolon immediately follows the closing parenthesis, the `if` statement will operate on the empty statement.

Example 4-13

Consider the following Java statements:

```
if(score >= 90);          //Line 1
    grade = 'A';          //Line 2
```

This statement represents a one-way selection. Because there is a semicolon at the end of the expression in Line 1, the `if` statement terminates at Line 1, the action of the `if` statement is null, and the statement in Line 2 is not part of the `if` statement. Because of the first semicolon, the statement in Line 2 executes regardless of how the `if` statement evaluates.

Two-Way Selection

In the previous section, you learned how to implement one-way selections in a program. There are many situations in which you must choose between two alternatives. For example, if a part-time employee works overtime, the paycheck is calculated using the overtime payment formula; otherwise, the paycheck is calculated using the regular formula. This is an example of two-way selection. To choose between two alternatives—that is, to implement two-way selections—Java provides the `if...else` statement. Two-way selection uses the following syntax:

```
if(expression)
    statement1
else
    statement2
```

Take a moment to examine this syntax. It begins with the reserved word `if`, followed by a logical expression contained within parentheses, followed by a statement, followed by the reserved word `else`, followed by a second statement. Statements 1 and 2 can be any valid Java statements. In a two-way selection, if the value of the **expression** is **true**, **statement1** executes. If the value of the **expression** is **false**, **statement2** executes. Figure 4-4 shows the flow of execution of the **if...else** statement (two-way selection).

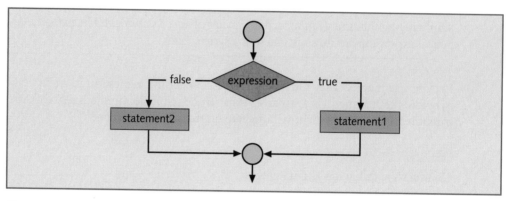

Figure 4-4   Two-way selection

Example 4-14

Consider the following statements:

```
if(hours > 40.0)                                    //Line 1
    wages = 40.0 * rate +
            1.5 * rate * (hours - 40.0);            //Line 2
else                                                //Line 3
    wages = hours * rate;                           //Line 4
```

If the value of the variable **hours** is greater than **40.0**, then the **wages** include overtime payment. Suppose that **hours** is **50**. The expression in the **if** statement in Line 1 evaluates to **true**, so the statement in Line 2 executes. On the other hand, if **hours** is **30**, or any number less than or equal to **40**, the expression in the **if** statement in Line 1 evaluates to **false**. In this case, the program skips the statement in Line 2 and executes the statement in Line 4—that is, the statement following the reserved word **else** executes.

In a two-way selection statement, putting a semicolon after the right parenthesis and before **statement1** creates a syntax error. If the **if** statement ends with a semicolon, **statement1** is no longer part of the **if** statement, and the **else** part of the **if...else** statement stands by itself. There is no stand-alone **else** statement in Java. That is, the **else** statement cannot be separated from the **if** statement.

Example 4-15

The following statements show an example of a syntax error:

```
if(hours > 40.0);                              //Line 1
    wages = 40.0 * rate +
            1.5 * rate * (hours - 40.0);       //Line 2
                                               //Line 3
else                                           //Line 4
    wages = hours * rate;
```

Because a semicolon follows the closing parenthesis of the `if` statement (Line 1), the `else` statement stands alone. The semicolon at the end of the `if` statement (see Line 1) ends the `if` statement, so the statement at Line 2 separates the `else` clause from the `if` statement. That is, `else` is by itself. Since there is no separate `else` statement in Java, this code generates a syntax error.

Example 4-16

The following program determines an employee's weekly wages. If the `hours` worked exceed **40**, `wages` include overtime payment.

```
//Chapter 4: Weekly Wages

import java.io.*;
import java.text.DecimalFormat;

public class WeeklyWages
{
    public static void main(String[] args) throws IOException
    {
        double wages, rate, hours;                              //Line 1
        DecimalFormat twoDigits = new DecimalFormat("0.00");    //Line 2

        System.out.print("Line 3: Enter working hours: ");      //Line 3
        hours = Double.parseDouble((keyboard.readLine());       //Line 4
        System.out.println();                                   //Line 5

        System.out.print("Line 6: Enter pay rate: ");           //Line 6
        rate = Double.parseDouble((keyboard.readLine());        //Line 7
        System.out.println();                                   //Line 8

        if(hours > 40.0)                                        //Line 9
            wages = 40.0 * rate +
                    1.5 * rate * (hours - 40.0);                //Line 10
        else                                                   //Line 11
            wages = hours * rate;                               //Line 12
```

```
        System.out.println("Line 13: The wages are $"
                        + twoDigits.format(wages));        //Line 13
    }
}
```

Sample Run: In this sample run, the user input is shaded:
Line 3: Enter working hours: 75.50

Line 6: Enter pay rate: 12.50

Line 13: The wages are $1165.62

The statement in Line 1 declares the appropriate variables. The statement in Line 2 declares twoDigits to be a reference variable of the **DecimalFormat** type and instantiates the object twoDigits to output decimal numbers to two decimal places. The statement in Line 3 prompts the user to input the number of hours worked. The statement in Line 4 inputs and stores the working hours in the variable hours. The statement in Line 6 prompts the user to input the pay rate. The statement in Line 7 inputs and stores the pay rate into the variable rate. The statement in Line 9 checks whether the value of the variable hours is greater than 40.0. If hours is greater than 40.0, then the wages are calculated by the statement in Line 5, which includes overtime payment. Otherwise, the wages are calculated by the statement in Line 12. The statement in Line 13 outputs the wages.

Now let's consider more examples of if statements and examine some of the common errors made by beginning programmers.

Example 4-17

Consider the following statements:

```
if(score >= 90)                                          //Line 1
    grade = 'A';                                         //Line 2
    System.out.println("The grade is " + grade);         //Line 3
```

Here you might think that just because the statements in Lines 2 and 3 are aligned, both these statements are the action statements of the if statement. However, this is not the case. The if statement acts on only one statement, which is grade = 'A';. The output statement executes regardless of whether (score >= 90) is true or false.

Example 4-18 illustrates another common mistake.

Example 4-18

Consider the following statements:

```
if(score >= 60)
    System.out.println("Passing");
    System.out.println("Failing");
```

If the expression (score >= 60) evaluates to false, the output would be Failing. That is, this set of statements performs the same action as an else statement. It will execute the second output statement rather than the first. For example, if the value of score is 50, these statements will output the following line:

```
Failing
```

However, if the expression score >= 60 evaluates to true, the program will write both statements, giving an unsatisfactory result. For example, if the value of score is 70, these statements will output the following lines:

```
Passing
Failing
```

The correct code to print Passing or Failing, depending on the value of score, is:

```
if(score >= 60)
    System.out.println("Passing");
else
    System.out.println("Failing");
```

Compound (Block of) Statements

The if and if...else structures control only one statement at a time. Suppose, however, that you want to execute more than one statement if the expression in an if or if...else statement evaluates to true. To permit more complex statements, Java provides a structure called a **compound statement** or a **block** of statements. A compound statement takes the following form:

```
{
    statement1
    statement2
       .
       .
       .
    statementn
}
```

That is, a compound statement or block consists of a sequence of statements enclosed in curly braces, { and }. In an if or if...else structure, a compound statement functions as if it were a single statement. Thus, instead of having a simple two-way selection similar to the following code,

```
if(age > 18)
    System.out.println("Eligible to vote.");
else
    System.out.println("Not eligible to vote.");
```

you could include compound statements, similar to the following code:

```
if(age > 18)
{
    System.out.println("Eligible to vote.");
    System.out.println("No longer a minor.");
}
else
{
    System.out.println("Not eligible to vote.");
    System.out.println("Still a minor.");
}
```

The compound statement is very useful and will be used in most of the ensuing structured statements in this chapter.

Multiple Selections: Nested `if`

In the previous sections, you learned how to implement one-way and two-way selections in a program. However, some problems require the implementation of more than two alternatives. For example, suppose that if the checking account balance is more than $50000, the interest rate is 7%; if the balance is between $25000 and $49999.99, the interest rate is 5%; if the balance is between $1000 and $24999.99, the interest rate is 3%; otherwise, the interest rate is 0%. This particular problem has four alternatives—that is, multiple selection paths. You can include multiple selection paths in a program by using an `if...else` structure, if the action statement itself is an `if` or `if...else` statement. When one control statement is located within another, it is said to be **nested**.

Example 4-19

Suppose that `balance` and `interestRate` are variables of the type `double`. The following statements determine the `interestRate` depending on the value of the `balance`:

```
if(balance > 50000.00)                          //Line 1
    interestRate = 0.07;                        //Line 2
else                                            //Line 3
    if(balance >= 25000.00)                     //Line 4
        interestRate = 0.05;                    //Line 5
    else                                        //Line 6
        if(balance >= 1000.00)                  //Line 7
            interestRate = 0.03;                //Line 8
        else                                    //Line 9
            interestRate = 0.00;                //Line 10
```

The statements in Example 4-19 illustrate how to incorporate multiple selections using a nested `if...else` structure.

A nested if...else structure demands the answer to an important question: How do you know which else is paired with which if? Recall that in Java there is no stand-alone else statement. Every else must be paired with an if. The rule to pair an else with an if is as follows:

Pairing an else with an if: In a nested if statement, Java associates an else with the most recent incomplete if—that is, the most recent if that has not been paired with an else.

Using this rule, in Example 4-19, the else at Line 3 is paired with the if at Line 1. The else at Line 6 is paired with the if at Line 4, and the else at Line 9 is paired with the if at Line 7.

To avoid excessive indentation, the code in Example 4-19 can be rewritten as follows:

```
if(balance > 50000.00)                      //Line 1
    interestRate = 0.07;                    //Line 2
else if(balance >= 25000.00)                //Line 3
        interestRate = 0.05;                //Line 4
else if(balance >= 1000.00)                 //Line 5
        interestRate = 0.03;                //Line 6
else                                        //Line 7
        interestRate = 0.00;                //Line 8
```

Example 4-20

Assume that **score** is a variable of the type int. Based on the value of **score**, the following code determines the grade:

```
if(score >= 90)
    System.out.println("The grade is A");
else if(score >= 80)
        System.out.println("The grade is B");
else if(score >= 70)
        System.out.println("The grade is C");
else if(score >= 60)
        System.out.println("The grade is D");
else
    System.out.println("The grade is F");
```

The following examples will further help you see the various ways in which you can use nested if structures to implement multiple selection.

Example 4-21

Assume that all variables are properly declared, and consider the following statements:

```
if(temperature >= 50)                       //Line 1
    if(temperature >= 80)                   //Line 2
```

```
        System.out.println("Good day for swimming.");    //Line 3
    else                                                 //Line 4
        System.out.println("Good day for golfing.");     //Line 5
  else                                                   //Line 6
      System.out.println("Good day to play tennis.");    //Line 7
```

In this Java code, the else in Line 4 is paired with the if in Line 2, and the else in Line 6 is paired with the if in Line 1. Note that the else in Line 4 cannot be paired with the if in Line 1. If you pair the else in Line 4 with the if in Line 1, the if in Line 2 becomes the action statement part of the if in Line 1, leaving the else in Line 6 dangling. Also, the statements in Lines 2 though 5 form the statement part of the if in Line 1.

Example 4-22

Assume that all variables are properly declared, and consider the following statements:

```
if(temperature >= 70)                                    //Line 1
    if(temperature >= 80)                                //Line 2
        System.out.println("Good day for swimming.");    //Line 3
    else                                                 //Line 4
        System.out.println("Good day for golfing.");     //Line 5
```

In this code, the else in Line 4 is paired with the if in Line 2. Note that for the else in Line 4, the most recent incomplete if is the if in Line 2. In this code, the if in Line 1 has no else and is a one-way selection.

Example 4-23

Assume that all variables are properly declared, and consider the following statements:

```
if(GPA >= 2.0)                                           //Line 1
    if(GPA >= 3.9)                                       //Line 2
        System.out.println("Dean\'s Honor List.");       //Line 3
else                                                     //Line 4
    System.out.println("Current GPA below graduation "
                    + "requirement. "   +
                    "\nSee your academic advisor.");      //Line 5
```

This code won't work the way we want it to work. Let us explore why. Following the rule of pairing an else with an if, the else in Line 4 is paired with the if in Line 2. However, this pairing produces an unsatisfactory result. Suppose that the GPA is 3.8. The expression in the if at Line 1 evaluates to true, and the statement part of the if, which is an if...else structure, executes. Because GPA is 3.8, the expression in the if at Line 2 evaluates to false, and the else associated with this if executes, producing the following output:

```
Current GPA below graduation requirement.
See your academic advisor.
```

However, a student with a GPA of 3.8 would graduate with some type of honor. In fact, the code intended to print the message

```
Current GPA below graduation requirement.
See your academic advisor.
```

only if the GPA is less than 2.0, and the message

```
Dean's Honor List.
```

if the GPA is greater than or equal to 3.9. To achieve that result, the else in Line 4 must be paired with the if in Line 1. To pair the else in Line 4 with the if in Line 1, you must use a compound statement, as follows:

```
if(GPA >= 2.0)                                              //Line 1
{
    if(GPA >= 3.9)                                          //Line 2
        System.out.println("Dean\'s Honor List.");         //Line 3
}
else                                                       //Line 4
    System.out.println("Current GPA below graduation "
                  + "requirement. "   +
                  "\nSee your academic advisor.");          //Line 5
```

In cases such as this one, the general rule is that you cannot look inside a block (that is, inside the braces) to pair an else with an if. The else in Line 4 cannot be paired with the if in Line 2 because the if statement in Line 2 is enclosed within braces, and the else in Line 4 cannot look inside those braces. Therefore, the else in Line 4 is paired with the if in Line 1.

Comparing if...else Statements with a Series of if Statements

Consider the following Java program segments, both of which accomplish the same task.

(a)

```
if(month == 1)                                   //Line 1
    System.out.println("January");               //Line 2
else if(month == 2)                              //Line 3
        System.out.println("February");          //Line 4
else if(month == 3)                              //Line 5
        System.out.println("March");             //Line 6
else if(month == 4)                              //Line 7
        System.out.println("April");             //Line 8
else if(month == 5)                              //Line 9
        System.out.println("May");               //Line 10
else if(month == 6)                              //Line 11
        System.out.println("June");              //Line 12
```

(b)

```
if(month == 1)
    System.out.println("January");
```

```
if(month == 2)
    System.out.println("February");
if(month == 3)
    System.out.println("March");
if(month == 4)
    System.out.println("April");
if(month == 5)
    System.out.println("May");
if(month == 6)
    System.out.println("June");
```

Program segment (a) is written as a sequence of **if...else** statements; program segment (b) is written as a series of **if** statements. Both program segments accomplish the same thing. If **month** is 3, then both program segments output **March**. If **month** is 1, then in program segment (a), the expression in the **if** statement at Line 1 evaluates to **true**. The statement (at Line 2) associated with this **if** then executes; the rest of the structure, which is the **else** of this **if** statement, is skipped; and the remaining **if** statements are not evaluated. In program segment (b), the computer has to evaluate the expression in each **if** statement because there is no **else** statement. As a consequence, program segment (b) executes more slowly than does program segment (a).

The Conditional Operator (? :)

The reader can skip this section without any discontinuation.

Certain **if...else** statements can be written more concisely by using Java's conditional operator. The **conditional operator**, written as **?:**, is a **ternary operator**, which means that it takes three arguments. The syntax for using the conditional operator is:

```
expression1 ? expression2 : expression3
```

This type of statement is called a **conditional expression**. The conditional expression is evaluated as follows: If **expression1** evaluates to **true**, the result of the conditional expression is **expression2**. Otherwise, the result of the conditional expression is **expression3**.

Consider the following statements:

```
if(a >= b)
    max = a;
else
    max = b;
```

You can use the conditional operator to simplify the writing of this `if...else` statement as follows:

```
max = (a >= b) ? a : b;
```

switch STRUCTURES

Recall that there are two selection, or branch, structures in Java. The first selection structure, which is implemented with `if` and `if...else` statements, usually requires the evaluation of a (logical) expression. The second selection structure, which does not require the evaluation of a logical expression, is called the `switch` structure. Java's `switch` structure gives the computer the power to choose from many alternatives.

The general syntax of the `switch` statement is:

```
switch(expression)
{
case value1: statements1
             break;
case value2: statements2
             break;
   ...
case valuen: statementsn
             break;
default: statements
}
```

In Java, `switch`, `case`, `break`, and `default` are reserved words. In a `switch` structure, the **expression** is evaluated first. The value of the **expression** is then used to perform the actions specified in the statements that follow the reserved word `case`. (Recall that, in a syntax template, shading indicates an optional part of the definition.)

Although it need not be, the **expression** is usually an identifier. Whether it is an identifier or an expression, the value of the identifier or the expression can be only *integral*. The **expression** is sometimes called the **selector**. Its value determines which statement is selected for execution. A particular `case` value must appear only once. One or more statements may follow a `case` label, so you do not need to use braces to turn multiple statements into a single compound statement. The `break` statement may or may not appear after each statement. Figure 4-5 shows the flow of execution of the `switch` statement.

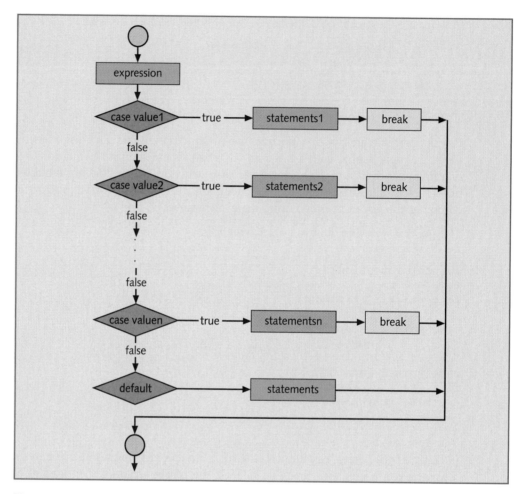

Figure 4-5 `switch` statement

The `switch` statement executes according to the following rules:

1. When the value of the **expression** is matched against a **case** value (also called a label), the statements execute until either a **break** statement is found or the end of the **switch** structure is reached.

2. If the value of the **expression** does not match any of the **case** values, the statements following the **default** label execute. If the **switch** structure has no **default** label, and if the value of the **expression** does not match any of the **case** values, the entire **switch** statement is skipped.

3. A **break** statement causes an immediate exit from the **switch** structure.

Example 4-24

Consider the following statements (assume that `grade` is a `char` variable):

```
switch(grade)
{
case 'A': System.out.println("The grade is A.");
          break;
case 'B': System.out.println("The grade is B.");
          break;
case 'C': System.out.println("The grade is C.");
          break;
case 'D': System.out.println("The grade is D.");
          break;
case 'F': System.out.println("The grade is F.");
          break;
default:  System.out.println("The grade is invalid.");
}
```

In this example, the expression in the `switch` statement is a variable identifier. The variable `grade` is of the type `char`, which is an integral type. The valid values of `grade` are `'A'`, `'B'`, `'C'`, `'D'`, and `'F'`. Each `case` label specifies a different action to take, depending on the value of `grade`. If the value of `grade` is `'A'`, the output is:

```
The grade is A.
```

Example 4-25

The following program illustrates the effect of the **break** statement. It asks the user to input a number between 0 and 10.

```
//Effect of break statements in a switch structure

import java.io.*;

public class BreakStatementsInSwitch
{
    static BufferedReader keyboard = new
            BufferedReader(new InputStreamReader(System.in));

    public static void main (String[] args) throws IOException
    {

        int num;

        System.out.print("Enter an integer between "
                    + "0 and 10: ");                        //Line 1
        System.out.flush();                                 //Line 2
```

```
        num = Integer.parseInt(keyboard.readLine());        //Line 3

        System.out.println("\nThe number you entered is "
                            + num);                          //Line 4

        switch(num)                                          //Line 5
        {
        case 0:                                              //Line 6
        case 1: System.out.print("Hello ");                 //Line 7
        case 2: System.out.print("there. ");                //Line 8
        case 3: System.out.print("I am ");                  //Line 9
        case 4: System.out.println("Mickey.");              //Line 10
                break;                                       //Line 11
        case 5: System.out.print("How ");                   //Line 12
        case 6:                                              //Line 13
        case 7:                                              //Line 14
        case 8: System.out.println("are you?");             //Line 15
                break;                                       //Line 16
        case 9: break;                                       //Line 17
        case 10: System.out.println("Have a nice day.");    //Line 18
                 break;                                      //Line 19
        default: System.out.println("Sorry the number is out "
                            + "of range.");                  //Line 20
        }

        System.out.println("Out of switch structure.");     //Line 21
    }
}
```

Sample Runs

These outputs were obtained by executing the preceding program several times. In each of these outputs, the user input is shaded.

Sample Run 1:

```
Enter an integer between 0 and 10: 0

The number you entered is 0
Hello there. I am Mickey.
Out of switch structure.
```

Sample Run 2:

```
Enter an integer between 0 and 10: 1

The number you entered is 1
Hello there. I am Mickey.
Out of switch structure.
```

Sample Run 3:

Enter an integer between 0 and 10: 3

The number you entered is 3
I am Mickey.
Out of switch structure.

Sample Run 4:

Enter an integer between 0 and 10: 4

The number you entered is 4
Mickey.
Out of switch structure.

Sample Run 5:

Enter an integer between 0 and 10: 5

The number you entered is 5
How are you?
Out of switch structure.

Sample Run 6:

Enter an integer between 0 and 10: 7

The number you entered is 7
are you?
Out of switch structure.

Sample Run 7:

Enter an integer between 0 and 10: 9

The number you entered is 9
Out of switch structure.

Sample Run 8:

Enter an integer between 0 and 10: 10

The number you entered is 10
Have a nice day.
Out of switch structure.

Sample Run 9:

Enter an integer between 0 and 10: 11

The number you entered is 11
Sorry number is out of range.
Out of switch structure.

A walk-through of this program, using certain values of the **switch** expression, num, can help you understand how the **break** statement functions. If the value of num is 0, the value of the **switch** expression matches the **case** value 0. All statements following **case   0:** execute until a **break** statement appears.

The first **break** statement appears at Line 11, just before the **case** value of 5. Even though the value of the **switch** expression does not match any of the **case** values (1, 2, 3, or 4), the statements following these values execute.

When the value of the **switch** expression matches a **case** value, *all* statements execute until a **break** is encountered, and the program skips all **case** labels in between. Similarly, if the value of num is 3, it matches the **case** value of 3 and the statements following this label execute until the **break** statement is encountered at Line 11. If the value of num is 9, it matches the **case** value of 9. In this situation, the action is empty, because only the **break** statement, at Line 17, follows the **case** value of 9.

Example 4-26

Although a **switch** structure's **case** values (labels) are limited, the **switch** statement **expression** can be as complex as necessary. Consider the following **switch** statement:

```
switch(score / 10)
{
case 0: case 1: case 2:
case 3: case 4: case 5:  grade = 'F';
                         break;
case 6: grade = 'D';
        break;
case 7: grade = 'C';
        break;
case 8: grade = 'B';
        break;
case 9: case 10: grade = 'A';
                 break;
default: System.out.println("Invalid test score.");
}
```

Assume that **score** is an **int** variable with values between 0 and 100. If **score** is 75, then **score** / 10 = 75 / 10 = 7 and the grade assigned is **'C'**. If the value of **score** is between 0 and 59, then the grade is **'F'**. If **score** is between 0 and 59, **score** / 10 is 0, 1, 2, 3, 4, or 5; each of these values corresponds to the grade **'F'**.

Therefore, in this **switch** structure, the action statements of **case 0, case 1, case 2, case 3, case 4,** and **case 5** are all the same. Rather than write the statement **grade = 'F';** followed by the **break** statement for each of the **case** values of 0, 1, 2, 3, 4, and 5, you can simplify the programming code by first specifying all of the case values (as shown in the preceding code) and then specifying the desired action statement. The **case** values of 9 and 10 follow similar conventions.

As you can see from the preceding examples, the `switch` statement is an elegant way to implement multiple selections. You will see a `switch` statement used in the programming example at the end of this chapter. No fixed rules exist that can be applied to decide whether to use an `if...else` structure or a `switch` structure to implement multiple selections, but you should remember the following considerations. If multiple selections involve a range of values, you should use either an `if...else` structure or a `switch` structure, wherein you convert each range to a finite set of values.

For instance, in Example 4-26, the value of **grade** depends on the value of **score**. If **score** is between 0 and 59, **grade** is `'F'`. Because **score** is an `int` variable, 60 values correspond to the grade of `'F'`. If you list all 60 values as the **case** values, the `switch` statement could be very long. However, dividing by 10 reduces these 60 values to only 6 values: 0, 1, 2, 3, 4, and 5.

If the range of values is infinite and you cannot reduce them to a set containing a finite number of values, you must use the `if...else` structure. For example, if **score** is a `double` variable, the number of values between 0 and 60 is infinite. However, you can use the expression `(int)(score) / 10` and reduce this infinite number of values to just six values.

PROGRAMMING EXAMPLE: CABLE COMPANY BILLING

This programming example demonstrates a program that calculates a customer's bill for a local cable company. There are two types of customers: residential and business. There are two rates for calculating a cable bill: one for residential customers and one for business customers.

For residential customers, the following rates apply:

- Bill-processing fee: `$4.50`
- Basic service fee: `$20.50`
- Premium channel: `$7.50` per channel

For business customers, the following rates apply:

- Bill-processing fee: `$15.00`
- Basic service fee: `$75.00` for first 10 connections; `$5.00` for each additional connection
- Premium channel: `$50.00` per channel for any number of connections

The program should ask the user for an account number (an integer) and a customer code. Assume that R or **r** stands for a residential customer, and B or **b** stands for a business customer.

Input   Input to the program is the customer's account number, customer code, number of premium channels to which the customer subscribes, and, in the case of business customers, number of basic service connections.

Output   Customer's account number and the billing amount.

Problem Analysis and Algorithm Design

The purpose of this program is to calculate and print the billing amount. To calculate the billing amount, you need to know the customer for whom the billing amount is calculated (whether the customer is residential or business) and the number of premium channels to which the customer subscribes. In the case of a business customer, you need to know the number of basic service connections and the number of premium channels. Other data needed to calculate the bill, such as bill-processing fees and the cost of a premium channel, are known quantities. The program should print the billing amount to two decimal places, which is standard for monetary amounts. This problem analysis translates into the following algorithm:

1. Declare and initialize an appropriate **DecimalFormat** variable, to output decimal numbers to two decimal places.
2. Prompt the user for the account number and customer type.
3. Determine the number of premium channels and basic service connections, compute the bill, and print the bill based on the customer type:
   a. If the customer type is **R** or **r**,
      (i)   Prompt the user for the number of premium channels.
      (ii) Compute the bill.
      (iii) Print the bill.
   b. If the customer type is **B** or **b**,
      (i)   Prompt the user for the number of basic service connections and number of premium channels.
      (ii) Compute the bill.
      (iii) Print the bill.

Variables

Because the program will ask the user to input the customer account number, customer code, number of premium channels, and number of basic service connections, you need variables to store all of this information. Also, because the program will calculate the billing amount, you need a variable to store the billing amount. Thus, the program needs at least the following variables to compute and print the bill:

```
int    accountNumber;    //variable to store customer's
                         //account number
char   customerType;     //variable to store customer code
int    numberOfPremiumChannels;  //variable to store number
                         //of premium channels to which the
                         //customer subscribes
```

```
int   numberOfBasicServiceConnections;  //variable to store
                     //number of basic service connections
                     //to which the customer subscribes
double amountDue;   //variable to store the billing amount
```

Named Constants

As you can see, the bill-processing fees, the cost of a basic service connection, and the cost of a premium channel are fixed; these values are needed to compute the bill. Although these values are constants in the program, they can change with little warning. To simplify the process of modifying the program later, instead of using these values directly in the program, you should declare them as named constants. Based on the problem analysis, you need to declare the following named constants:

```
        //Named constants - residential customers
static final double R_BILL_PROC_FEE = 4.50;
static final double R_BASIC_SERV_COST = 20.50;
static final double R_COST_PREM_CHANNEL = 7.50;

        //Named constants - business customers
static final double B_BILL_PROC_FEE = 15.00;
static final double B_BASIC_SERV_COST = 75.00;
static final double B_BASIC_CONN_COST = 5.00;
static final double B_COST_PREM_CHANNEL = 50.00;
```

Formulas

The program uses a number of formulas to compute the billing amount. To compute the residential bill, you need to know only the number of premium channels to which the user subscribes. The following statement calculates the billing amount for a residential customer:

```
amountDue = R_BILL_PROC_FEE + R_BASIC_SERV_COST +
            numberOfPremiumChannels * R_COST_PREM_CHANNEL;
```

To compute the business bill, you need to know the number of basic service connections and the number of premium channels to which the user subscribes. If the number of basic service connections is less than or equal to 10, the cost of basic service connections is fixed. If the number of basic service connections exceeds 10, you must add the cost for each connection over 10. The following statement calculates the business billing amount:

```
if(noOfBasicServiceConnections <= 10)
   amountDue =   B_BILL_PROC_FEE + B_BASIC_SERV_COST +
                 numberOfPremiumChannels * B_COST_PREM_CHANNEL;
else
   amountDue =   B_BILL_PROC_FEE + B_BASIC_SERV_COST +
                 (noOfBasicServiceConnections - 10) *
                 B_BASIC_CONN_COST +
                 numberOfPremiumChannels * B_COST_PREM_CHANNEL;
```

Main Algorithm

Based on the preceding discussion, you can now write the main algorithm.

1. To output floating-point numbers with two decimal places, create an appropriate `DecimalFormat` object.
2. Prompt the user to enter the account number.
3. Get the customer account number.
4. Prompt the user to enter the customer code.
5. Get the customer code.
6. If the customer code is `r` or `R`:
   a. Prompt the user to enter the number of premium channels.
   b. Get the number of premium channels.
   c. Calculate the billing amount.
   d. Print the account number.
   e. Print the billing amount.
7. If the customer code is `b` or `B`:
   a. Prompt the user to enter the number of basic service connections.
   b. Get the number of basic service connections.
   c. Prompt the user to enter the number of premium channels.
   d. Get the number of premium channels.
   e. Calculate the billing amount.
   f. Print the account number.
   g. Print the billing amount.
8. If the customer code is something other than `r`, `R`, `b`, or `B`, output an error message.

For Steps 6 and 7, the program uses a `switch` statement to calculate the bill for the desired customer.

Complete Program Listing

```java
//Chapter 4: Cable Company Billing

import java.io.*;
import java.text.DecimalFormat;

public class CableCompanyBilling
{
    static BufferedReader keyboard = new
            BufferedReader(new InputStreamReader(System.in));

        //Named constants - residential customers
    static final double R_BILL_PROC_FEE = 4.50;
```

```
static final double R_BASIC_SERV_COST = 20.50;
static final double R_COST_PREM_CHANNEL = 7.50;

    //Named constants - business customers
static final double B_BILL_PROC_FEE = 15.00;
static final double B_BASIC_SERV_COST = 75.00;
static final double B_BASIC_CONN_COST = 5.00;
static final double B_COST_PREM_CHANNEL = 50.00;

public static void main(String[] args) throws IOException
{
    //Variable declaration
    int    accountNumber;
    char   customerType;
    int    numberOfPremiumChannels;
    int    noOfBasicServiceConnections;
    double amountDue;

    DecimalFormat twoDigits =
                new DecimalFormat("0.00");                    //Step 1

    System.out.println("This program computes a cable bill.");

    System.out.print("Enter account number: ");              //Step 2
    accountNumber =
        Integer.parseInt(keyboard.readLine());               //Step 3
    System.out.println();

    System.out.print("Enter customer type: R or r (Residential), "
                + "B or b (Business): ");                     //Step 4
    customerType = (keyboard.readLine()).charAt(0);          //Step 5
    System.out.println();

    switch(customerType)
    {
    case 'r':                                                //Step 6
    case 'R': System.out.print("Enter the number "
                    +"of premium channels: ");//Step 6a
            numberOfPremiumChannels =
                Integer.parseInt(keyboard.readLine());
                                                             //Step 6b
            System.out.println();

            amountDue = R_BILL_PROC_FEE +                    //Step 6c
                    R_BASIC_SERV_COST +
                    numberOfPremiumChannels *
                    R_COST_PREM_CHANNEL;
```

```
                    System.out.println("Account number = "
                                   + accountNumber);          //Step 6d
                    System.out.println("Amount due = $"
                                + twoDigits.format(amountDue));//Step 6e
                    break;
        case 'b':                                             //Step 7
        case 'B': System.out.print("Enter the number of basic "
                                + "service connections: ");
                                                              //Step 7a
                    noOfBasicServiceConnections =
                         Integer.parseInt(keyboard.readLine());
                                                              //Step 7b
                    System.out.println();
                    System.out.print("Enter the number "
                             + "of premium channels: ");      //Step 7c
                    numberOfPremiumChannels =
                         Integer.parseInt(keyboard.readLine());
                                                              //Step 7d
                    System.out.println();

                    if(noOfBasicServiceConnections <= 10)     //Step 7e
                       amountDue =  B_BILL_PROC_FEE +
                                    B_BASIC_SERV_COST +
                                    numberOfPremiumChannels *
                                    B_COST_PREM_CHANNEL;
                    else
                       amountDue =  B_BILL_PROC_FEE +
                                    B_BASIC_SERV_COST +
                                    (noOfBasicServiceConnections - 10)
                                    * B_BASIC_CONN_COST +
                                    numberOfPremiumChannels *
                                    B_COST_PREM_CHANNEL;

                    System.out.println("Account number = "
                                   + accountNumber);          //Step 7f
                    System.out.println("Amount due = $"
                            + twoDigits.format(amountDue));    //Step 7g
                    break;
        default: System.out.println("Invalid customer type.");//Step 8
        }//end switch
    }
}
```

Sample Run: In this sample run, the user input is shaded.

```
This program computes a cable bill.
Enter account number: 12345

Enter customer type: R or r (Residential), B or b (Business): b

Enter the number of basic service connections: 16

Enter the number of premium channels: 8

Account number = 12345
Amount due = $520.00
```

QUICK REVIEW

1. Control structures alter the normal flow of control.

2. The two most common control structures are selection and repetition.

3. Selection structures incorporate decisions in a program.

4. The Java relational operators are == (equality), < (less than), <= (less than or equal to), > (greater than), >= (greater than or equal to), and != (not equal to).

5. Including a space between the relational operators ==, <=, >=, and != creates a syntax error.

6. Characters are compared using the collating sequence of the Unicode character set.

7. To compare strings, you use the method `compareTo` of the `class String`.

8. To use the method `compareTo`, you use the expression

   `str1.compareTo(str2)`

   where `str1` and `str2` are `String` variables. Moreover, `str2` can also be a `String` constant. The expression `str1.compareTo(str2)` evaluates as follows:

   $$str1.compareTo(str2) = \begin{cases} \text{an integer value less than 0 if string } str1 \text{ is less than string } str2 \\ \text{0 if string } str1 \text{ is equal to string } str2 \\ \text{an integer value greater than 0 if string } str1 \text{ is greater than string } str2 \end{cases}$$

9. Logical (Boolean) expressions evaluate to **true** or **false**.

10. In Java, **boolean** variables are used to store the value of a logical expression.

11. In Java, the logical operators are ! (**not**), && (**and**), and || (**or**).

12. In Java, there are two selection structures.

13. One-way selection takes the following form:

```
if(expression)
    statement
```

If `expression` is `true`, the `statement` executes; otherwise, the computer executes the statement following the `if` statement.

14. Two-way selection takes the following form:

```
if(expression)
    statement1
else
    statement2
```

If `expression` is `true`, then `statement1` executes; otherwise, `statement2` executes.

15. The expression in an `if` or `if...else` structure is a logical expression.

16. Including a semicolon before the `statement` in a one-way selection creates a semantic error. In this case, the action of the `if` statement is empty.

17. Including a semicolon before `statement1` in a two-way selection creates a syntax error.

18. There is no stand-alone `else` statement in Java. Every `else` has a related `if`.

19. An `else` is paired with the most recent `if` that has not been paired with any other `else`.

20. A sequence of statements enclosed between braces, { and }, is called a compound statement or block of statements. A compound statement is treated as a single statement.

21. The `switch` structure is used to handle multiple selections.

22. The execution of a `break` statement in a `switch` statement immediately exits the `switch` structure.

EXERCISES

1. Mark the following statements as true or false.

   a. The result of a logical expression cannot be assigned to an `int` variable.

   b. In a one-way selection, if a semicolon is placed after the expression in an `if` statement, the expression in the `if` statement is always `true`.

   c. Every `if` statement must have a corresponding `else`.

   d. The expression

   ```
   (ch >= 'A' && ch <= 'Z')
   ```

   evaluates to `false` if either ch < 'A' or ch >= 'Z'.

e. Suppose input is **5**. (Assume that all variables are properly declared.) The output of the code

```
num = Integer.parseInt(keyboard.readLine());
if(num > 5)
    System.out.println(num);
    num = 0;
else
    System.out.println("Num is zero");
```

is:

```
Num is zero.
```

4

f. The expression in a **switch** statement should evaluate to a value of a primitive data type.

g. The expression !(x > 0) is true only if x is a negative number.

h. In Java, both ! and != are logical operators.

i. The order in which statements execute in a program is called the flow of control.

2. Circle the best answer.

a.

```
if(6 < 2 * 5)
        System.out.print("Hello");
        System.out.print(" There");
```

outputs the following:

(i) `Hello There`   (ii) `Hello`   (iii) `Hello`   (iv) `There`
                                        `There`

b.

```
if('a' > 'b' || 66 > (int)('A'))
    System.out.println("#*#");
```

outputs the following:

(i) `#*#`   (ii) `#`   (iii) `*`   (iv) none of these
              `*`
              `#`

c.

```
if(7 <= 7)
        System.out.println(6 - 9 * 2 / 6);
```

outputs the following:

(i) `-1`   (ii) `3`   (iii) `3.0`   (iv) none of these

d.

```java
if(7 < 8)
{
    System.out.println("2 4 6 8");
    System.out.println("1 3 5 7");
}
```

outputs the following:

(i) 2 4 6 8   (ii) 1 3 5 7   (iii) none of these
    1 3 5 7

e.

```java
if(5 < 3)
    System.out.println("*");
else
    if(7 == 8)
        System.out.println("&");
    else
        System.out.println("$");
```

outputs the following:

(i) *   (ii) &   (iii) $ (iv) none of these

3. What is the output of the following Java code?

```java
x = 100;
y = 200;

if(x > 100 && y <= 200)
    System.out.println(x + " " + y + " " + (x + y));
else
    System.out.println(x + " " + y + " " + (2 * x - y));
```

4. Write Java statements that output Male if the gender is 'M', Female if the gender is 'F', and invalid gender otherwise.

5. Correct the following code so that it prints the correct message.

```java
if(score >= 60)
    System.out.println("You pass.");
else;
    System.out.println("You fail.");
```

6. Suppose that you have the following declaration:

```java
int j = 0;
```

The output of the statement

```java
if((8 > 4) || (j++ == 7))
    System.out.println("j = " + j);
```

is:

```
j = 0
```

while the output of the statement

```
if((8 > 4) | (j++ == 7))
    System.out.println("j = " + j);
```

is:

```
j = 1
```

Explain why.

7. State whether the following are valid **switch** statements. If not, explain why. Assume that n and **digit** are **int** variables.

a.

```
switch(n <= 2)
{
case 0: System.out.println("Draw.");
        break;
case 1: System.out.println("Win.");
        break;
case 2: System.out.println("Lose.");
        break;

}
```

b.

```
switch (digit / 4)
{
case 0: case 1: System.out.println("low.");
                break;
case 1: case 2: System.out.println("middle.");
                break;
case 3: System.out.println("high.");
}
```

c.
```
switch(n % 6)
 {
  case 1: case 2: case 3: case 4: case 5: System.out.println(n);
                                          break;
  case 0: System.out.println();
          break;
 }
```

d.

```
switch (n % 10)
 {
  case 0: case 2: case 4: case 6:
  case 8: System.out.println("Even");
          break;
  case 1: case 3: case 5: case 7: System.out.println("Odd");
                                  break;
 }
```

8. Suppose the input is 5. What is the value of `alpha` after the following Java code executes? (Assume that `alpha` is an `int` variable and `keyboard` is a `BufferedReader` object initialized to the keyboard.)

```
alpha = Integer.parseInt(keyboard.readLine());

switch(alpha)
{
case 1:
case 2: alpha = alpha + 2;
        break;
case 4: alpha++;
case 5: alpha = 2 * alpha;
case 6: alpha = alpha + 5;
        break;
default: alpha--;
}
```

9. Suppose the input is 3. What is the value of `beta` after the following Java code executes? (Assume that all variables are properly declared.)

```
beta = Integer.parseInt(keyboard.readLine());

switch(beta)
{
case 3: beta = beta + 3;
case 1: beta++;   break;
case 5: beta = beta + 5;
case 4: beta = beta + 4;
}
```

10. Suppose the input is 6. What is the value of `a` after the following Java code executes? (Assume that all variables are properly declared.)

```
a = Integer.parseInt(keyboard.readLine());

if(a > 0)
   switch(a)
   {
   case 1: a = a + 3;
   case 3: a++;
           break;
   case 6: a = a + 6;
   case 8: a = a * 8;
           break;
   default: a--;
   }
else
      a = a + 2;
```

11. In the following code, correct any errors that would prevent the program from compiling or running.

```
public class Errors
{
```

```
public static void main(String[] args)
{
        int a,b;
        boolean found;

        System.out.print("Enter the first integers: ");
        a = Integer.parseInt(keyboard.readLine());
        System.out.println();

        System.out.print("Enter the second integers: ");
        b = Integer.parseInt(keyboard.readLine());

        if  a > a*b  &&  10 < b
             found = 2* a > b;
        else
        {
           found = 2 * a < b;
           if found
               a = 3;
               c = 15;
           if b
           {
               b = 0;
               a = 1;
           }
        }
   }
}
```

12. The following program contains errors. Correct them so that the program will run and output w = 21.

```
public class Mystery
{
   static final int ONE = 5;

   public static void main(String[] args)
   {
        int  x, y, w, z;
        z = 9;

        if z > 10
           x = 12;   y = 5,    w = x + y + one;
        else
           x = 12;   y = 4,    w = x + y + one;

        System.out.println("w = " + w);
   }
}
```

PROGRAMMING EXERCISES

1. Write a program that prompts the user to input a number. The program should then output the number and a message saying whether the number is positive, negative, or zero.

2. Write a program that prompts the user to input three numbers. The program should then output the numbers in ascending order.

3. Write a program that prompts the user to input a number between 0 and 35. If the number is less than or equal to 9, the program should output the number; otherwise, it should output A for 10, B for 11, C for 12, ..., and Z for 35. (*Hint:* Use the cast operator, (char), for numbers >= 10.)

4. The cost of an international call from New York to New Delhi is calculated as follows: connection fee, $1.99; $2.00 for the first three minutes; and $0.45 for each additional minute. Write a program that prompts the user to enter the number of minutes the call lasted and outputs the amount due. Format your output with two decimal places.

5. In a right triangle, the square of the length of one side is equal to the sum of the squares of the lengths of the other two sides. Write a program that prompts the user to enter the lengths of three sides of a triangle and then outputs a message indicating whether the triangle is a right triangle.

6. The roots of the quadratic equation $ax^2 + bx + c = 0$, where a, b, and c are real numbers, and $a \neq 0$, are given by the following formula:

$$\frac{-b \pm \sqrt{b^2 - 4ac}}{2a}$$

   In this formula, the term $b^2 - 4ac$ is called the discriminant. If $b^2 - 4ac = 0$, then the equation has a single (repeated) root. If $b^2 - 4ac > 0$, the equation has two real roots. If $b^2 - 4ac < 0$, the equation has two complex roots. Write a program that prompts the user to input the value of a (the coefficient of x^2), b (the coefficients of x), and c (the constant term), and outputs the type of roots of the equation. Furthermore, if $b^2 - 4ac > 0$, the program should output the roots of the quadratic equation. (*Hint:* Use the function sqrt from the class Math to calculate the square root. Math.sqrt(x) is the square root of x, where $x \geq 0$.)

7. Write a program that prompts the user to input the x-y coordinate of a point in a Cartesian plane. The program should then output a message indicating whether the point is the origin, is located on the x (or y) axis, or appears in a particular quadrant.

   For example:

   ```
   (0,0) is the origin
   (4,0) is on the x-axis
   (0,-3) is on the y-axis
   (-2,3) is in the second quadrant
   ```

8. Write a program that mimics a calculator. The program should take as input two integers and the operation to be performed. It should then output the numbers, the operator, and the result. (For division, if the denominator is zero, output an appropriate message.) Some sample output follows:

```
3 + 4 = 7
13 * 5 = 65
```

9. Redo Exercise 8 to handle floating-point numbers. (Format your output to two decimal places.)

10. A bank in your town updates its customers' accounts at the end of each month. The bank offers two types of accounts: savings and checking. Every customer must maintain a minimum balance. If a customer's balance falls below the minimum, there is a service charge of $10.00 for savings accounts and $25.00 for checking accounts. If the balance at the end of the month is at least the minimum balance, the account receives interest as follows:

   ■ Savings accounts receive 4% interest.

   ■ Checking accounts with balances of up to $5000 more than the minimum balance receive 3% interest; otherwise, the interest is 5%.

   Write a program that reads a customer's account number (**int** type), account type (**char**; s for savings, c for checking), minimum balance that the account should maintain, and current balance. The program should then output the account number, account type, current balance, and an appropriate message. Test your program by running it five times, using the following data:

```
46728 S 1000 2700
87324 C 1500 7689
79873 S 1000 800
89832 C 2000 3000
98322 C 1000 750
```

11. Write a program that implements the algorithm given in Example 1-2 (Chapter 1), which determines the monthly wages of a salesperson.

12. Write a program that calculates and prints the bill for a cellular telephone company. The company offers two types of service: regular and premium. Its rates vary depending on the type of service. The rates are computed as follows:

   Regular service: $10.00 plus first 50 minutes are free. Charges for over 50 minutes are $0.20 per minute.

   Premium service: $25.00 plus:

   a. For calls made from 6:00 A.M. to 6:00 P.M., the first 75 minutes are free; charges for over 75 minutes are $0.10 per minute.

   b. For calls made from 6:00 P.M. to 6:00 A.M., the first 100 minutes are free; charges for over 100 minutes are $0.05 per minute.

Your program should prompt the user to enter an account number, a service code (type **char**), and the number of minutes the service was used. A service code of **r** or **R** means regular service; a service code of **p** or **P** means premium service. Treat any other character as an error. Your program should output account number, type of service, number of minutes the telephone service was used, and amount due from the user.

For the premium service, the customer may be using the service during the day and at night. Therefore, to calculate the bill, you must ask the user to input the number of minutes the service was used during the day and the number of minutes the service was used at night.

5

CONTROL STRUCTURES II

Repetition

In this chapter, you will:

♦ Learn about repetition (looping) control structures

♦ Explore how to construct and use count-controlled, sentinel-controlled, flag-controlled, and EOF-controlled repetition structures

♦ Examine `break` and `continue` statements

♦ Discover how to form and use nested control structures

In Chapter 4, you learned how decisions are incorporated in programs. In this chapter, you learn how repetitions are incorporated in programs.

WHY IS REPETITION NEEDED?

Suppose you want to add five integers to find their average. From what you have learned so far, you know that you could proceed as follows. (Assume that all variables are properly declared.)

```
num1 = Integer.parseInt(keyboard.readLine());     //read num1
num2 = Integer.parseInt(keyboard.readLine());     //read num2
num3 = Integer.parseInt(keyboard.readLine());     //read num3
num4 = Integer.parseInt(keyboard.readLine());     //read num4
num5 = Integer.parseInt(keyboard.readLine());     //read num5
sum = num1 + num2 + num3 + num4 + num5;           //add the numbers
average = sum/5;                                  //find the average
```

But suppose you want to add and average 1000 or more numbers. You would have to declare that many variables, and list them again in input statements, and perhaps again in the output statements. This would take an exorbitant amount of typing as well as time. Also, if you wanted to run this program again with different values, or with a different number of values, you would have to rewrite the program.

Suppose you want to add the following numbers:

5
3
7
9
4

Consider the following statements, in which **sum** and **num** are variables of type int:

```
sum = 0;                                          //Line 1
num = Integer.parseInt(keyboard.readLine());      //Line 2
sum = sum + num;                                  //Line 3
```

The statement in Line 1 initializes **sum** to 0. Let's execute the statements in Lines 2 and 3. The statement in Line 2 stores 5 in num; the statement in Line 3 updates the value of **sum** by adding num to it. After Line 3, the value of **sum** is 5.

Let's repeat the statements in Lines 2 and 3. After Line 2 (after the programming code reads the next number),

num = 3

After Line 3,

sum = sum + num = 5 + 3 = 8

At this point, **sum** contains the sum of the first two numbers. Let's repeat the statements in Lines 2 and 3 a third time. After Line 2 executes (after the programming code reads the next number),

num = 7

After Line 3 executes,

```
sum = sum + num = 8 + 7 = 15
```

Now **sum** contains the sum of the first three numbers. If you repeat the statements in Lines 2 and 3 two more times, **sum** will contain the sum of all five numbers.

If you want to add 10 integers, you can repeat the statements in Lines 2 and 3 ten times. And if you want to add 100 numbers, you can repeat the statements one hundred times. In either case, you do not have to declare any additional variables as you did in the first code in the chapter. The preceding Java code, Line 1 to Line 3, with variables of type int can be used to add any set of integers, whereas the earlier code requires that you drastically change the code.

There are many situations in which it is necessary to repeat a set of statements. For example, for each student in a class, the formula to determine the course grade is the same. Java has three repetition, or looping, structures that let you repeat statements over and over until certain conditions are met: **while**, **for**, and **do...while**. These three looping (repetition) structures are discussed in the following sections.

5

THE while LOOPING (REPETITION) STRUCTURE

In the previous section, you saw that sometimes it is necessary to repeat a set of statements several times. One way to repeat a set of statements is to type the set of statements in the program over and over. For example, if you want to repeat a set of statements 100 times, you type the set of statements 100 times in the program. However, this way of repeating a set of statements is impractical, if not impossible. Fortunately, there is a better way to repeat a set of statements. As noted earlier, Java has three repetition, or looping, structures that allow you to repeat a set of statements until certain conditions are met. This section discusses the first looping structure, a **while** loop.

The general form of the **while** statement is:

```
while(expression)
      statement
```

In Java, **while** is a reserved word. The **statement** can be either a simple or compound statement. The **expression**, called a **loop condition**, acts as a *decision-maker* and is a logical expression. The **statement** is called the body of the loop. Note that the parentheses around the **expression** are part of the syntax. Figure 5-1 shows the flow of execution of a **while** loop.

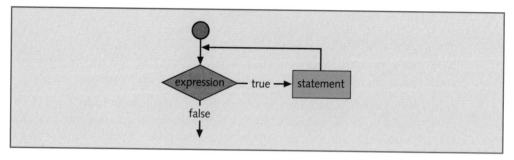

Figure 5-1 `while` loop

The `expression` provides an entry condition. If it initially evaluates to `true`, the `statement` executes. The loop condition—the `expression`—is then reevaluated. If it again evaluates to `true`, the `statement` executes again. The `statement` (body of the loop) continues to execute until the `expression` is no longer `true`. A loop that continues to execute endlessly is called an **infinite loop**. To avoid an infinite loop, make sure that the loop's body contains one or more statements that ensure that the loop condition—the `expression` in the `while` statement—will eventually be `false`.

Example 5-1

Consider the following Java program segment:

```
i = 0;                                //Line 1

while(i <= 20)                        //Line 2
{
        System.out.print(i + " ");    //Line 3
        i = i + 5;                    //Line 4
}

System.out.println();                 //Line 5
```

Output:

```
0 5 10 15 20
```

At Line 1, the variable i is set to 0. The **expression** in the `while` statement (in Line 2), i <= 20, is evaluated. Since the expression i <= 20 evaluates to `true`, the body of the `while` loop executes next. The body of the `while` loop consists of the statements in Lines 3 and 4. The statement in Line 3 outputs the value of i, which is 0. The statement in Line 4 changes the value of i to 5. After executing the statements in Lines 3 and 4, the **expression** in the `while` loop (at Line 2) is evaluated again. Since i is 5, the expression i <= 20 evaluates to `true` and the body of the `while` loop executes again. This process of evaluating the **expression** and executing the body of the `while` loop continues until the **expression** i <= 20 (at Line 2) no longer evaluates to `true`.

The variable i (Line 2) in the expression is called the **loop control variable**.

Note the following from the preceding example:

1. Within the loop i becomes 25, but is not printed because the entry condition is `false`.

2. If you omit the statement

    ```
    i = i + 5;
    ```

    from the body of the loop, you will have an infinite loop, continually printing rows of zeros.

3. You must initialize the loop control variable i before you execute the loop. If the statement

    ```
    i = 0;
    ```

    (at Line 1) is omitted, either the loop might not execute at all or the compiler will generate an error. (Recall that not all variables in Java are automatically initialized.)

4. In the above program segment, if the two statements in the body of the loop are interchanged, the result may be drastically altered. For example, consider the following statements:

    ```
    i = 0;

    while(i <= 20)
    {
          i = i + 5;
          System.out.print(i + " ");
    }

    System.out.println();
    ```

Here the output is:

```
5 10 15 20 25
```

Typically this would be a semantic error because you rarely want a condition to be `true` for i <= 20, and yet produce results for i > 20.

Example 5-2

Consider the following Java program segment:

```
i = 20;                                  //Line 1
while(i < 20)                            //Line 2
{
      System.out.print(i + " ");         //Line 3
      i  =  i + 5;                        //Line 4
}
```

```
System.out.println();                              //Line 5
```

It is easy to overlook the difference between this example and Example 5-1. At Line 1, `i` is set to 20. Since `i` is 20, the expression `i < 20` in the **while** statement (Line 2) evaluates to **false**. Initially the loop entry condition, `i < 20`, is **false**, so the body of the **while** loop never executes. Hence, no values are output and the value of `i` remains 20.

When a program needs to be tested again and again on certain data, or if the program will operate on a large amount of data, using the keyboard to enter data is not practical. In such situations, you can store data on an external device such as a disk and instruct the program to read the data from the device. For simplicity, assume that the data is stored on a disk (floppy or hard) and is free of errors or otherwise not defective. This situation has four possibilities, as described in the next four sections.

Counter-Controlled `while` Loops

Suppose you know exactly how many pieces of data (or entries) need to be read. In this case, the **while** loop assumes the form of a **counter-controlled `while` loop**. Suppose the file has N data items. You can set up a `counter` (initialized to 0 before the **while** statement) to track how many items have been read. Before executing the body of the **while** statement, the `counter` is compared with N. If `counter < N`, the body of the **while** statement executes. The body of the loop continues to execute until the value of `counter >= N`. Thus, inside the body of the **while** statement, the value of the `counter` increments after it reads a new item. In this case, the **while** loop might look like the following:

```
counter = 0;
while(counter < N)
{
       .
       .
       .
    counter++;
       .
       .
       .
}
```

The value of N (the number of items in the file) can be determined in any of several ways. The program can prompt you to specify the number of items in the file, and an input statement can read the value. Alternatively, you can specify the first item in the file as the number of items in the file, so that you need not remember the number of input values (items). This is useful if someone other than the programmer enters the data. Consider Example 5-3.

Example 5-3

Suppose the input is:

12 8 9 2 3 90 38 56 8 23 89 7 2 8 3 8

The first number, 12, specifies the number of values in the data set. Suppose you want to add these numbers and find their average. Note that only 12 values are read; the others are discarded. The complete program is as follows:

```java
//Counter-controlled while loop
import java.io.*;
import java.util.*;

public class CounterControlledWhileLoop
{
    static BufferedReader keyboard =
            new BufferedReader(new InputStreamReader(System.in));

    public static void main(String[] args) throws IOException
    {
        int limit;      //store the number of items
                        //in the list
        int number;     //variable to store the number
        int sum;        //variable to store the sum
        int counter;    //loop control variable

        StringTokenizer tokenizer;   //variable to tokenize
                                     //the input line

        System.out.println("Line 1: Enter data for "
                    + "processing");                        //Line 1

        tokenizer =
                new StringTokenizer(keyboard.readLine()); //Line 2
        limit = Integer.parseInt(tokenizer.nextToken());  //Line 3

                                                            //Line 4
        sum = 0;                                            //Line 5
        counter = 0;

        while(counter < limit)                              //Line 6
        {
            number =
                Integer.parseInt(tokenizer.nextToken()); //Line 7
            sum = sum + number;                             //Line 8
            counter++;                                      //Line 9
        }

        System.out.println("Line 10: The sum of "
                    + limit + " numbers = "
                    + sum);                                 //Line 10
```

5

```
    if(counter != 0)                                        //Line 11
        System.out.println("Line 12: The average = "
                        + (sum / counter));                 //Line 12
    else                                                    //Line 13
        System.out.println("Line 14: No input.");           //Line 14
    }
}
```

Sample Run: In this sample run, the user input is shaded.

```
Line 1: Enter data for processing
12 8 9 2 3 90 38 56 8 23 89 7 2 8 3 8
Line 10: The sum of 12 numbers = 335
Line 12: The average = 27
```

The preceding program works as follows. The statement in Line 1 prompts the user to input data for processing. The statement in Line 2 reads the next input line and stores it in the object `tokenizer`. The statement in Line 3 retrieves the next token from `tokenizer`, converts it into an `int` value, and stores it in the variable `limit`. The value of `limit` indicates the number of items in the list. The statements in Lines 4 and 5 initialize the variables `sum` and `counter` to 0. The `while` statement in Line 6 checks the value of `counter` to determine how many items have been read. If `counter` is less than `limit`, the `while` loop proceeds for the next iteration. The statement in Line 7 stores the next number in the variable `number`. The statement in Line 8 updates the value of `sum` by adding the value of `number` to the previous value. The statement in Line 9 increments the value of `counter` by 1. The statement in Line 10 outputs the sum of the numbers. The statements in Lines 11–14 output either the average or the text `Line 14: No input.`

Note that in the preceding program, in Line 4, `sum` is initialized to 0. At Line 8, after storing the next number in `number` in Line 7, the program adds the next number to the sum of all the numbers scanned before the current number. The first number read is added to zero (since `sum` is initialized to 0), giving the correct sum of the first number. To find the average, divide `sum` by `counter`. If `counter` is 0, then dividing by 0 terminates the program and you get an error message. Therefore, before dividing `sum` by `counter`, you must check whether or not `counter` is 0.

The program in Example 5-3 assumes that all numbers are entered in the same line. If all numbers are entered in more than one line, replace the `while` loop between Lines 6-9 with the following `while` loop and renumber the remaining lines. (If you enter numbers in more than one line, then enter at least one number per line.)

```
while(counter < limit)                                      //Line 6
{
    if(!tokenizer.hasMoreTokens())                          //Line 7
        tokenizer = new
                StringTokenizer(keyboard.readLine()); //Line 8
    number =
```

```
        Integer.parseInt(tokenizer.nextToken());    //Line 9
        sum = sum + number;                          //Line 10
        counter++;                                   //Line 11
    }
```

Sentinel-Controlled while Loops

You might not know how many pieces of data (or entries) need to be read, but you do know that the last entry is a special value, called a **sentinel**. In this case, you read the first item before entering the while statement. If this item does not equal the sentinel, the body of the while statement executes. The while loop continues to execute as long as the program has not read the sentinel. Such a while loop is called a **sentinel-controlled** while **loop**. In this case, a while loop might look like the following:

```
input the first data item into variable
while(variable != sentinel)
{
    .
    .
    .
    input a data item into variable
}
```

Example 5-4

Suppose you want to read some positive integers and average them, but you do not have a preset number of data items in mind. Suppose the number –999 marks the end of the data. You can proceed as follows:

```
//Sentinel-controlled while loop

import java.io.*;
import java.util.*;

public class SentinelControlledWhileLoop
{
    static BufferedReader keyboard =
            new BufferedReader(new InputStreamReader(System.in));

    static final int SENTINEL = -999;

    public static void main (String[] args) throws IOException
    {
        int number;        //variable to store the number
        int sum = 0;       //variable to store the sum
        int count = 0;     //variable to store the total
                           //numbers read
```

5

```
        StringTokenizer tokenizer;   //variable to tokenize the
                                     //input line


        System.out.println("Line 1: Enter numbers ending with "
                       + SENTINEL);                      //Line 1

        tokenizer =
              new StringTokenizer(keyboard.readLine());   //Line 2
        number = Integer.parseInt(tokenizer.nextToken()); //Line 3

        while(number != SENTINEL)                        //Line 4
        {
            sum = sum + number;                          //Line 5
            count++;                                     //Line 6
            number =
                  Integer.parseInt(tokenizer.nextToken()); //Line 7
        }

        System.out.println("Line 8: The sum of "
                       + count + " numbers = "
                       + sum);                           //Line 8

        if(count != 0)                                   //Line 9
            System.out.println("Line 10: The average = "
                       + (sum / count));                 //Line 10
        else                                             //Line 11
            System.out.println("Line 12: No input.");    //Line 12
    }
}
```

Sample Run: In this sample run, the user input is shaded.

```
Line 1: Enter numbers ending with -999
34 23 9 45 78 0 77  8 3 5 -999
Line 8: The sum of 10 numbers = 282
Line 10: The average = 28
```

This program works as follows. The statement in Line 1 prompts the user to enter numbers ending with -999. The statement in Line 2 reads the next input line and stores it in the object tokenizer. The statement in Line 3 retrieves the next token from tokenizer, converts it into an int value, and stores it in the variable number. The while statement in Line 4 checks whether number is not equal to SENTINEL. If number is not equal to SENTINEL, the body of the while loop executes. The statement in Line 5 updates the value of sum by adding number to it. The statement in Line 6 increments the value of count by 1. The statement in Line 7 stores the next number in the variable number. The statements in Lines 5–7 repeat until the program reads -999. The statement in Line 8 outputs the sum of the numbers, and the statements in Lines 9–12 output the average of the numbers.

The program in Example 5-4 assumes that all numbers are entered in the same line. If all numbers are entered in more than one line, replace the `while` loop between Lines 4–7 with the following `while` loop and renumber the remaining lines. (If you enter numbers in more than one line, then enter at least one number per line.)

```
while(number != SENTINEL)                                   //Line 4
{
    sum = sum + number;                                     //Line 5
    count++;                                                //Line 6
    if(!tokenizer.hasMoreTokens())                          //Line 7
        tokenizer = new
            StringTokenizer(keyboard.readLine());  //Line 8
    number =
        Integer.parseInt(tokenizer.nextToken());     //Line 9
}
```

Next consider another example of a sentinel-controlled `while` loop. In this example, the user is prompted to enter the value to be processed. If the user wants to stop the program, he or she can enter the sentinel.

Example 5-5 Telephone Digits

The following program reads the letter codes `'A'` to `'Z'` and prints the corresponding telephone digit. This program uses a sentinel-controlled `while` loop. To stop the program, the user is prompted for the sentinel, which is either `'Q'` or `'Z'`. This is also an example of a nested control structure, where `if... else`, `switch`, and the `while` loop are nested.

```
//***************************************************
// Program:  Telephone Digits
// This is an example of a sentinel-controlled loop. This
// program converts uppercase letters to their
// corresponding telephone digits.
//***************************************************

import javax.swing.JOptionPane;

public class TelephoneDigitProgram
{
    public static void main(String[] args)
    {
        char letter;                                    //Line 1
        String inputMessage;                            //Line 2
        String inputString;                             //Line 3
        String outputMessage;                           //Line 4
        int phoneDigit = 0;                             //Line 5


        inputMessage = "This program converts uppercase "
                    + "letters to their corresponding "
```

```
                    + "telephone digits.\n"
                    + "To stop the program enter Q or Z.\n"
                    + "Enter a letter:";                    //Line 6
        inputString =
              JOptionPane.showInputDialog(inputMessage);    //Line 7
        letter = inputString.charAt(0);                      //Line 8

        while(letter != 'Q' && letter != 'Z')                //Line 9
        {
           outputMessage = "The letter you entered is: "
                           + letter + "\n"
                           + "The corresponding telephone "
                           + "digit is: ";                   //Line 10
           if(letter >= 'A' && letter <= 'Z')                //Line 11
           {
              switch(letter)                                 //Line 12
              {
              case 'A': case 'B': case 'C': phoneDigit = 2;  //Line 13
                                   break;                    //Line 14
              case 'D': case 'E': case 'F': phoneDigit = 3;  //Line 15
                                   break;                    //Line 16
              case 'G': case 'H': case 'I': phoneDigit = 4;  //Line 17
                                   break;                    //Line 18
              case 'J': case 'K': case 'L': phoneDigit = 5;  //Line 19
                                   break;                    //Line 20
              case 'M': case 'N': case 'O': phoneDigit = 6;  //Line 21
                                   break;                    //Line 22
              case 'P': case 'R': case 'S': phoneDigit = 7;  //Line 23
                                   break;                    //Line 24
              case 'T': case 'U': case 'V': phoneDigit = 8;  //Line 25
                                   break;                    //Line 26
              case 'W': case 'X': case 'Y': phoneDigit = 9;  //Line 27
              }

              outputMessage = outputMessage + phoneDigit;    //Line 28
           }
           else                                              //Line 29
              outputMessage = outputMessage
                              + "Invalid input";             //Line 30

           JOptionPane.showMessageDialog(null, outputMessage,
                           "Telephone Digit",
                           JOptionPane.PLAIN_MESSAGE); //Line 31
           inputMessage = "Enter another uppercase letter "
                          + "to be converted to the corresponding "
                          + "telephone digit.\n"
                          + "To stop the program enter Q or Z.\n"
                          + "Enter a letter:";               //Line 32
```

```
        inputString =
              JOptionPane.showInputDialog(inputMessage); //Line 33
        letter = inputString.charAt(0);                  //Line 34
    }//end while

        System.exit(0);                                  //Line 35
    }
}
```

Sample Run: Figure 5-2 shows the sample run.

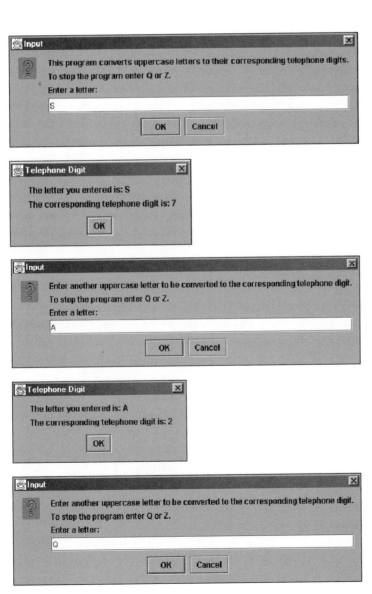

Figure 5-2   Sample run for telephone digit program

The program in Example 5-5 works as follows. The statements in Lines 1-5 declare appropriate variables. The statement in Line 6 creates the appropriate string to be included in the input dialog box. The statement in Line 7 displays the input dialog box informing the user what to do. This statement also retrieves the string entered by the user and assigns the string to the object `inputString`. (Notice that even though the user enters a single letter, it is still considered a string.) The statement in Line 8 retrieves the letter from `inputString` and stores it in `letter`. The `while` loop at Line 9 checks that the letter is neither Q nor Z. If the letter entered by the user is neither Q nor Z, the body of the `while` loop executes. The statement in Line 10 creates the appropriate string to be displayed in the output dialog box.

The `if` statement in Line 11 checks whether the letter entered by the user is uppercase. If the letter entered by the user is uppercase, the `expression` in the `if` statement (at Line 11) evaluates to `true` and the `switch` statement executes, which determines the appropriate telephone digit (see the statements in Lines 13–27). The telephone digit is appended to `outputMessage` at Line 28. If the letter entered by the user is not uppercase, the `else` (Line 29) executes and the statement in Line 30 appends the string `"Invalid input"` to `outputMessage`. The statement in Line 31 displays the output dialog box showing the result of the input.

Once the current letter is processed, the statement in Line 32 creates the message string, and the statement in Line 33 displays the input dialog box informing the user what to do next. The statement in Line 34 copies the letter entered by the user in `letter`. (Note that the statement in Line 32 is similar to the statement in Line 6, and that the statements in Lines 33 and 34 are the same as the statements in Lines 7 and 8.) After the statement in Line 34 (at the end of the `while` loop) executes, the control goes back to the top of the `while` loop and the same process begins again. When the user enters either Q or Z, the program terminates.

 In the program in Example 5-5, you can write the statements between Lines 11 and 30 using just a `switch` structure, that is, without the `if` in Line 11 and the `else` in Line 29. (See Programming Exercise 4 at the end of this chapter.)

Flag-Controlled while Loops

A **flag-controlled** while **loop** uses a boolean variable to control the loop. Suppose found is a boolean variable. The flag-controlled while loop takes the following form:

```
found = false;

while(!found)
{
    .
    .
    .

    if(expression)
        found = true;
    .
    .
    .
}
```

The variable found, which is used to control the execution of the while loop, is called a **flag variable**.

EOF-Controlled while Loops

If the data file is frequently altered (for example, if data is frequently added or deleted), it's best not to read the data with a sentinel value. Someone might accidentally erase the sentinel value or add data past the sentinel, especially if the programmer and data entry person are different people. Also, the programmer sometimes does not know what the sentinel is. In such situations, you can use an **EOF (End Of File)-controlled** while **loop**.

The general form of the EOF-controlled while loop is:

```
input the first data item
while(not_end_of_input_file)
{
        .
        .
        .
        input a data item
}
```

Recall that the method **read** is used to read a stream of characters one character at a time. However, rather than return the character, the method **read** returns the integer value (collating sequence) of the character. For example, if you enter the character **A**, it returns **65**. Of course, you can use the data type **char** as the cast operator and convert **65** into **A**. The method **read** returns −1 when the end of the input file is reached. We can therefore use the value returned by the method **read** to determine whether the end of the input file is reached.

Suppose that **inFile** is a **BufferedReader** object initialized to the input file. In this case, the EOF-controlled **while** loop takes the following form. (Assume that **ch** is a variable of the type **char** and **nextValue** is a variable of the type **int**.)

```
nextValue = inFile.read();

while(nextValue != -1)
{
        ch = (char) nextValue;
        ...
        nextValue = inFile.read();
}
```

Chapter 3 discussed how to use the **class StringTokenizer** to break an input line into meaningful tokens. To get the next line from the input stream we use the method **readLine**. The method **readLine** returns the value **null** when trying to read past the end of the input file.

Suppose that **inFile** is a **BufferedReader** object initialized to the input file, and you have the following declaration:

```
String inputLine;
StringTokenizer tokenizer;
```

You can use the value returned by the method **readLine** to determine whether the end of file is reached. In this case, the EOF-controlled **while** loop takes the following form:

```
inputLine = inFile.readLine();

while(inputLine != null)
{
        tokenizer = new StringTokenizer(inputLine);
        .
        .
        .
        inputLine = inFile.readLine();
}
```

The following programming example illustrates how to use an EOF-controlled **while** loop in a program.

In the Windows console environment, the end-of-file marker is entered using **Ctrl+z** (hold the **Ctrl** key and press z). In the UNIX environment, the end-of-file marker is entered using **Ctrl+d** (hold the **Ctrl** key and press d).

PROGRAMMING EXAMPLE: CHECKING ACCOUNT BALANCE

A local bank in your town is looking for someone to write a program that calculates a customer's checking account balance at the end of each month. The data is stored in a file in the following form:

```
467343 23750.40
W 250.00
D 1200
W 75.00
I 120.74
.
.
.
```

The first line of data shows the account number followed by the account balance at the beginning of the month. Thereafter, each line has two entries: the transaction code and the transaction amount. The transaction code W or w means withdrawal, D or d means deposit, and I or i means interest paid by the bank. The program updates the balance after each transaction. If at any time during the month the balance goes below $1000.00, a $25.00 service fee is charged. The program prints the following information: account number, balance at the beginning of the month, balance at the end of the month, interest paid by the bank, total amount of deposit, number of deposits, total amount of withdrawal, number of withdrawals, and service charge if any.

Input   A file consisting of data in the above format

Output   The output is of the following form:

```
Account Number: 467343
Beginning Balance: $23750.40
Ending Balance: $24611.49

Interest Paid: $366.24

Amount Deposited: $2230.50
Number of Deposits: 3

Amount Withdrawn: $1735.65
Number of Withdrawals: 6
```

Problem Analysis and Algorithm Design

The first entries in the input file are the account number and the beginning balance. Therefore, the program first reads the account number and the beginning balance. Thereafter, each entry in the file is of the following form:

```
transactionCode transactionAmount
```

To determine the account balance at the end of the month, you need to process each entry that contains the transaction code and transaction amount. Begin with the starting balance and then update the account balance after processing each entry. If the transaction code is D, d, I, or i, the transaction amount is added to the account balance. If the transaction code is W or w, the transaction amount is subtracted from the balance. Since the program also outputs the number of withdrawals and deposits, you need to keep separate counts of withdrawals and deposits. This discussion translates into the following algorithm:

1. Declare the necessary variables and objects.
2. Initialize the variables.
3. Get the account number and beginning balance.
4. Get the transaction code and transaction amount.
5. Analyze the transaction code and update the appropriate variables.
6. Repeat Steps 4 and 5 until there is no more data.
7. Print the result.

Variables and Objects

The program outputs the account number, beginning balance, balance at the end of the month, interest paid, amount deposited, number of deposits, amount withdrawn, number of withdrawals, and service charge if any. So far you need the following variables to store all this information:

```
acctNumber              //variable to store the account number
beginningBalance        //variable to store the beginning balance
accountBalance          //variable to store the account balance at the
                        //end of the month
amountDeposited         //variable to store the total amount deposited
numberOfDeposits        //variable to store the number of deposits
amountWithdrawn         //variable to store the total amount withdrawn
numberOfWithdrawals     //variable to store the number of withdrawals
interestPaid            //variable to store the interest amount paid
```

Since the program reads the data from a file and the output is stored in a file, the program needs both input and output stream objects. After the first line, the data in each line is the transaction code and the transaction amount; the program needs a variable to store this information.

Whenever the account balance goes below the minimum balance, a service charge for that month is applied. After each withdrawal, you need to check the account balance. If the balance goes below the minimum after a withdrawal, a service charge is applied. You can potentially have several withdrawals in a month; once the account balance goes below the minimum, a subsequent deposit might bring the balance above the minimum, and another withdrawal might again reduce it below the minimum. However, the service charge is applied only once.

To implement this idea, the program uses a `boolean` variable, `isServiceCharged`, which is initialized to `false` and set to `true` whenever the account balance goes below the minimum. Before applying a service charge, the program checks the value of the variable `isServiceCharged`. If the account balance is less than the minimum and `isServiceCharged` is `false`, a service charge is applied. The program needs the following variables:

```
int       acctNumber;
double    beginningBalance;
double    accountBalance;

double    amountDeposited;
int       numberOfDeposits;

double    amountWithdrawn;
int       numberOfWithdrawals;

double    interestPaid;
char      transactionCode;
double    transactionAmount;

boolean   isServiceCharged;
```

Suppose input data is in the file `money.txt` on a floppy disk in drive `A:`. Also suppose that the output will be stored in the file `money.out` on a floppy disk in drive `A:`. The following statements create the appropriate input and output stream objects:

```
BufferedReader inFile =
        new BufferedReader(new FileReader("a:\\money.txt"));
PrintWriter outfile =
        new PrintWriter(new FileWriter("a:\\money.out"));
```

Since there is more than one token in each line, we use the `class StringTokenizer` to tokenize each input line. We therefore need to declare the reference variable `tokenizer`, of the type `StringTokenizer`, to tokenize each input line. Also, we will use the method `nextToken` of the `class StringTokenizer` to retrieve the next token. The method `readLine` returns the value `null` when trying to read past the end of the input file. We first assign the next input line returned by the method `readLine` to the `String` variable `inputLine`. When the method `readLine` reads past the end of the input file, the value `null` is stored in `inputLine`, indicating the end of the input file. The value of `inputLine` is assigned to the `StringTokenizer` object `tokenizer` to tokenize the input line. Therefore, we also need the following variables:

```
String inputLine;
StringTokenizer tokenizer;
```

Named Constants

The minimum account balance and the service charge amount are fixed, so the program uses two named constants to store them:

```
static final double MINIMUM_BALANCE = 1000.00;
static final double SERVICE_CHARGE = 25.00;
```

Because this program is more complex than previous ones, before writing the main algorithm, the preceding seven steps are described more fully here:

1. **Declare variables and objects:** Declare variables and objects as discussed above.

2. **Initialization:** After each deposit, the total amount deposited is updated and the number of deposits is incremented by one. Before the first deposit, the total amount deposited is 0 and the number of withdrawals is 0. Therefore, the variables `amountDeposited` and `numberOfDeposits` must be initialized to 0. Similarly, the variables `amountWithdrawn`, `numberOfWithdrawals`, and `interestPaid` must be initialized to 0. Also, as discussed earlier, the variable `isServicedCharged` is initialized to `false`. Of course, you can initialize these variables when you declare them.

   Before the first deposit, withdrawal, or interest paid, the account balance is the same as the beginning balance. Therefore, after reading the beginning balance in the variable `beginningBalance` from the file, you need to initialize the variable `accountBalance` to the value of the variable `beginningBalance`.

3. **Get account number and starting balance:** This is accomplished by the following statements:

```
inputLine = inFile.readLine();
tokenizer = new StringTokenizer(inputLine);
acctNumber = Integer.parseInt(tokenizer.nextToken());
beginningBalance =
        Double.parseDouble(tokenizer.nextToken());
```

4. **Get the transaction code and transaction amount:** This is accomplished by the following input statement:

```
inputLine = inFile.readLine();
tokenizer = new StringTokenizer(inputLine);
transactionCode = tokenizer.nextToken().charAt(0);
transactionAmount =
        Double.parseDouble(tokenizer.nextToken());
```

5. **Analyze transaction code and update appropriate variables:** If `transactionCode` is `'D'` or `'d'`, update `accountBalance` by adding `transactionAmount`, update `amountDeposited` by adding `transactionAmount`, and increment `numberOfDeposits`. If `transactionCode` is `'I'` or `'i'`, update `accountBalance` by adding `transactionAmount` and update `interestPaid` by adding

transactionAmount. If transactionCode is 'W' or 'w', update accountBalance by subtracting transactionAmount, update amountWithdrawn by adding transactionAmount, increment numberOfWithdrawals, and if the account balance is below the minimum and service charges have not been applied, subtract the service charge from the account balance and mark the service charge as having been applied. The following switch statement does this:

```java
switch(transactionCode)
{
case 'D':
case 'd': accountBalance = accountBalance
                          + transactionAmount;
          amountDeposited = amountDeposited
                          + transactionAmount;
          numberOfDeposits++;
          break;
case 'I':
case 'i': accountBalance = accountBalance
                          + transactionAmount;
          interestPaid = interestPaid
                          + transactionAmount;
          break;
case 'W':
case 'w': accountBalance = accountBalance
                          - transactionAmount;
          amountWithdrawn = amountWithdrawn
                          + transactionAmount;
          numberOfWithdrawals++;

          if((accountBalance < MINIMUM_BALANCE)
             && (!isServiceCharged))
          {
            accountBalance = accountBalance
                          - SERVICE_CHARGE;
            isServiceCharged = true;
          }
          break;

default: System.out.println("Invalid transaction code");
} //end switch
```

6. **Repeat Steps 4 and 5 until there is no more data:** Because the number of entries in the input file is not known, the program needs an EOF-controlled while loop.

7. **Print result:** This is accomplished by using output statements.

This proceding process translates into the following algorithm:

Main Algorithm

1. Declare and initialize the variables and input and output stream objects.
2. To output floating-point numbers in a fixed decimal format, create a `DecimalFormat` object and initialize it to format the output of decimal numbers to two decimal places.
3. Read the next input line and tokenize it.
4. Get `accountNumber` and `beginningBalance`.
5. Set `accountBalance` to `beginningBalance`.
6. Read the next input line.
7. While (not end of input file):
   a. Tokenize the input line.
   b. Get `transactionCode`.
   c. Get `transactionAmount`.
   d. If `transactionCode is 'D'`:
      i.   Add `transactionAmount` to `accountBalance`.
      ii. Add `transactionAmount` to `amountDeposited`.
      iii. Increment `numberOfDeposits`.
   e. If `transactionCode is 'I'`:
      i. Add `transactionAmount` to `accountBalance`.
      ii. Add `transactionAmount` to `interestPaid`.
   f. If `transactionCode is 'W'`:
      i.   Subtract `transactionAmount` from `accountBalance`.
      ii. Add `transactionAmount` to `amountWithdrawn`.
      iii. Increment `numberOfWithDrawals`.
      iv. If `(accountBalance < MINIMUM_BALANCE`
          `&& !isServicedCharged)`:
         1. Subtract `SERVICE_CHARGE` from `accountBalance`.
         2. Set `isServiceCharged` to `true`.
   g. If `transactionCode` is other than `'D'`, `'d'`, `'I'`, `'i'`, `'W'`, or `'w'`, output an error message.
   h. Read the next input line.
8. Output the results.

```java
//*****************************************************
// Program -- Checking Account Balance.
// This program calculates a customer's checking account
// balance at the end of the month.
//*****************************************************
import java.io.*;
import java.text.DecimalFormat;
import java.util.*;

public class CheckingAccountBalance
{
  static final double MINIMUM_BALANCE = 1000.00;
  static final double SERVICE_CHARGE = 25.00;

  public static void main(String[] args) throws
                          FileNotFoundException, IOException
  {
            //Declare and initialize variables      //Step 1
      int acctNumber;
      double beginningBalance;
      double accountBalance;

      double amountDeposited = 0.0;
      int numberOfDeposits = 0;

      double amountWithdrawn = 0.0;
      int numberOfWithdrawals = 0;

      double interestPaid = 0.0;

      char transactionCode;
      double transactionAmount;

      boolean isServiceCharged = false;

      String inputLine;
      StringTokenizer tokenizer;

      BufferedReader inFile =
            new BufferedReader(new FileReader("a:\\money.txt"));
      PrintWriter outfile =
            new PrintWriter(new FileWriter("a:\\money.out"));

      DecimalFormat twoDecimal =
            new DecimalFormat("0.00");                //Step 2

      inputLine = inFile.readLine();                  //Step 3
```

```
tokenizer = new StringTokenizer(inputLine);       //Step 3
acctNumber =
      Integer.parseInt(tokenizer.nextToken());    //Step 4
beginningBalance =
      Double.parseDouble(tokenizer.nextToken());  //Step 4

accountBalance = beginningBalance;                 //Step 5

inputLine = inFile.readLine();                      //Step 6

while(inputLine != null)                            //Step 7
{
    tokenizer = new StringTokenizer(inputLine);    //Step 7a
    transactionCode =
            tokenizer.nextToken().charAt(0);       //Step 7b
    transactionAmount =
        Double.parseDouble(tokenizer.nextToken()); //Step 7c

    switch(transactionCode)
    {
    case 'D':                                       //Step 7d
    case 'd': accountBalance = accountBalance
                             + transactionAmount;
              amountDeposited = amountDeposited
                             + transactionAmount;
              numberOfDeposits++;
              break;
    case 'I':                                       //Step 7e
    case 'i': accountBalance = accountBalance
                             + transactionAmount;
              interestPaid = interestPaid
                             + transactionAmount;
              break;
    case 'W':                                       //Step 7f
    case 'w': accountBalance = accountBalance
                             - transactionAmount;
              amountWithdrawn = amountWithdrawn
                             + transactionAmount;
              numberOfWithdrawals++;

              if((accountBalance < MINIMUM_BALANCE)
                 && (!isServiceCharged))
              {
                  accountBalance = accountBalance
                             - SERVICE_CHARGE;
                  isServiceCharged = true;
              }
              break;
```

```
            default: System.out.println("Invalid transaction "
                                  + "code");                //Step 7g
        } //end switch

        inputLine = inFile.readLine();                      //Step 7h
    }//end while

            //Output Results                                //Step 8
    outfile.println("Account Number: " + acctNumber);
    outfile.println("Beginning Balance: $"
                + twoDecimal.format(beginningBalance));
    outfile.println("Ending Balance: $"
                + twoDecimal.format(accountBalance));
    outfile.println();
    outfile.println("Interest Paid: $"
                + twoDecimal.format(interestPaid));
    outfile.println();
    outfile.println("Amount Deposited: $"
                + twoDecimal.format(amountDeposited));
    outfile.println("Number of Deposits: "
                + numberOfDeposits);
    outfile.println();
    outfile.println("Amount Withdrawn: $"
                + twoDecimal.format(amountWithdrawn));
    outfile.println("Number of Withdrawals: "
                + numberOfWithdrawals);
    outfile.println();

    if(isServiceCharged)
        outfile.println("Service Charge: $"
                    + twoDecimal.format(SERVICE_CHARGE));
    outfile.close();
    }
}
```

Sample Run: Contents of the output file **money.out**:

```
Account Number: 467343
Beginning Balance: $23750.40
Ending Balance: $24611.49

Interest Paid: $366.24

Amount Deposited: $2230.50
Number of Deposits: 3

Amount Withdrawn: $1735.65

Number of Withdrawals: 6
```

Input File: `money.txt`

```
467343 23750.40
W 250.00
D 1200.00
W 75.00
I 120.74
W 375.00
D 580.00
I 245.50
W 400.00
W 600.00
D 450.50
W 35.65
```

PROGRAMMING EXAMPLE: FIBONACCI NUMBER

So far, you have seen several examples of loops. A `while` loop is used mainly to read data, although it has other uses. In Java, `while` loops are used when a certain statement(s) must be executed repeatedly until certain conditions are met. The following program uses a `while` loop to find a **Fibonacci number**.

Consider the following sequence of numbers:

```
1, 1, 2, 3, 5, 8, 13, 21, 34, ....
```

Given the first two numbers of the sequence (say a_1 and a_2), the nth number a_n, n >= 3, of this sequence is given by the formula:

$$a_n = a_{n-1} + a_{n-2}$$

Thus

$$
\begin{aligned}
a_3 &= a_2 + a_1 \\
&= 1 + 1 \\
&= 2, \\
a_4 &= a_3 + a_2 \\
&= 1 + 2 \\
&= 3,
\end{aligned}
$$

and so on.

Such a sequence is called a **Fibonacci sequence**. In the preceding sequence, $a_2 = 1$ and $a_1 = 1$. However, given any first two numbers, using this process you can determine the nth number, a_n, n >= 3, of the sequence. The number determined this way is called the **nth Fibonacci number**. Suppose $a_2 = 6$ and $a_1 = 3$. Then

$$a_3 = a_2 + a_1 = 6 + 3 = 9; \quad a_4 = a_3 + a_2 = 9 + 6 = 15.$$

Next, we write a program that determines the nth Fibonacci number, given the first two numbers.

Input   The first two Fibonacci numbers and the desired Fibonacci number

Output   The nth Fibonacci number

Problem Analysis and Algorithm Design

To find a_{10}, the tenth Fibonacci number of a sequence, you must first find a_9 and a_8, which requires you to find a_7 and a_6 and so on. Therefore, to find a_{10}, you must first find $a_3, a_4, a_5, \ldots, a_9$. This discussion translates into the following algorithm:

1. Get the first two Fibonacci numbers.
2. Get the desired Fibonacci number. That is, get the position, n, of the Fibonacci number in the sequence.
3. Calculate the next Fibonacci number by adding the previous two elements of the Fibonacci sequence.
4. Repeat Step 2 until the nth Fibonacci number is found.
5. Output the nth Fibonacci number.

Variables

Because you must know the last two numbers to find the current Fibonacci number, you need the following variables: two variables—say, `previous1` and `previous2`—to hold the previous two numbers of the Fibonacci sequence; and one variable—say, `current`—to hold the current Fibonacci number. The number of times that Step 2 of the algorithm repeats depends on the position of the Fibonacci number you are calculating. For example, if you want to calculate the 10th Fibonacci number, you must execute Step 3 eight times. (Remember—the user gives the first two numbers of the Fibonacci sequence.) Therefore, you need a variable to store the number of times that Step 3 should execute. You also need a variable—the loop control variable—to track the number of times that Step 3 has executed. Therefore, you need five variables for the data manipulation:

```
int previous1;    //Variable to store the first
                  //Fibonacci number
int previous2,    //Variable to store the second
                  //Fibonacci number
int current;      //Variable to store the current
                  //Fibonacci number
int counter;      //Loop control variable
int nthFibonacci; //Variable to store the desired
                  //Fibonacci number
```

To calculate the third Fibonacci number, add the value of `previous1` and `previous2` and store the result in `current`. To calculate the fourth Fibonacci number, add the value of the second Fibonacci number (that is, `previous2`) and the value of the third Fibonacci number (that is, `current`). Thus, when the fourth Fibonacci number is calculated, you no longer need the first Fibonacci number. Instead of declaring additional variables, which could be several, after calculating a Fibonacci number to determine the next Fibonacci number, `current` becomes `previous2` and `previous2` becomes `previous1`. Therefore, you can again use the variable `current` to store the next Fibonacci number. This process is repeated until the desired Fibonacci number is calculated. Initially, `previous1` and `previous2` are the first two elements of the sequence, supplied by the user. From the preceding discussion, it follows that you need five variables.

Main Algorithm

1. Display the input dialog box to prompt the user for the first Fibonacci number—that is, `previous1`. Store the string representing `previous1` into `inputString`.
2. Retrieve the string from `inputString` and store the first Fibonacci number into `previous1`.
3. Display the input dialog box to prompt the user for the second Fibonacci number—that is, `previous2`. Store the string representing `previous2` into `inputString`.
4. Retrieve the string from `inputString`, and store the second Fibonacci number into `previous2`.
5. Create the `outputString` and append `previous1` and `previous2`.
6. Display the input dialog box to prompt the user for the desired Fibonacci number—that is, `nthFibonacci`. Store the string representing `nthFibonacci` into `inputString`.
7. Retrieve the string from `inputString`, and store the desired *n*th Fibonacci number into `nthFibonacci`.
8. a. `if(nthFibonacci == 1)`

   the desired Fibonacci number is the first Fibonacci number. Copy the value of `previous1` into `current`.

   b. `else if(nthFibonacci == 2)`

   the desired Fibonacci number is the second Fibonacci number. Copy the value of `previous2` into `current`.

   c. `else` calculate the desired Fibonacci number as follows:

   Since you already know the first two Fibonacci numbers of the sequence, start by determining the third Fibonacci number.

   c.1. Initialize `counter` to 3, to keep track of the calculated Fibonacci numbers.

   c.2. Calculate the next Fibonacci number, as follows:

   ```
   current = previous2 + previous1;
   ```

   c.3. Assign the value of `previous2` to `previous1`.

   c.4. Assign the value of `current` to `previous2`.

   c.5. Increment `counter`.

Repeat Steps 8c.2–8c.5 until the Fibonacci number you want is calculated. The following `while` loop executes Steps 8c.2–c.5 and determines the *n*th Fibonacci number:

```
while(counter <= nthFibonacci)
{
       current = previous2 + previous1;
       previous1 = previous2;
       previous2 = current;
       counter++;
}
```

9. Append the nth Fibonacci number to `outputString`. Notice that the nth Fibonacci number is stored in `current`.

10. Display the output dialog box showing the first two and the nth Fibonacci numbers.

Complete Program Listing

```java
// Program: nth Fibonacci number

import javax.swing.JOptionPane;

public class FibonacciNumber
{
   public static void main (String[] args)
   {
                  //Declare variables
      String inputString;
      String outputString;
      int previous1;
      int previous2;
      int current = 0;
      int counter;
      int nthFibonacci;

      inputString =
         JOptionPane.showInputDialog("Enter the first "
                              + "Fibonacci number");//Step 1
      previous1 =  Integer.parseInt(inputString);      //Step 2

      inputString =
         JOptionPane.showInputDialog("Enter the second "
                              + "Fibonacci number");//Step 3
      previous2 = Integer.parseInt(inputString);       //Step 4

      outputString = "The first two Fibonacci numbers are "
                  + previous1 + " and " + previous2;//Step 5
```

```
        inputString =
            JOptionPane.showInputDialog("Enter the desired "
                            + "Fibonacci number to "
                            + "be determined: ");        //Step 6
        nthFibonacci = Integer.parseInt(inputString);    //Step 7

        if(nthFibonacci == 1)                            //Step 8.a
            current = previous1;
        else if(nthFibonacci == 2)                       //Step 8.b
                current = previous2;
        else                                             //Step 8.c
        {
            counter = 3;                                 //Step 8.c.1

                //Steps 8.c.2-8.c.5
            while(counter <= nthFibonacci)
            {
                current = previous2 + previous1;         //Step 8.c.2
                previous1 = previous2;                   //Step 8.c.3
                previous2 = current;                     //Step 8.c.4
                counter++;                               //Step 8.c.5
            }
        }

        outputString = outputString + "\nThe " + nthFibonacci
                    + "th Fibonacci number is: "
                    + current;                           //Step 9
        JOptionPane.showMessageDialog(null,outputString,
                    "Fibonacci Number",
                    JOptionPane.INFORMATION_MESSAGE);    //Step 10
        System.exit(0);
    }
}
```

Sample Run: Figure 5-3 shows the sample run.

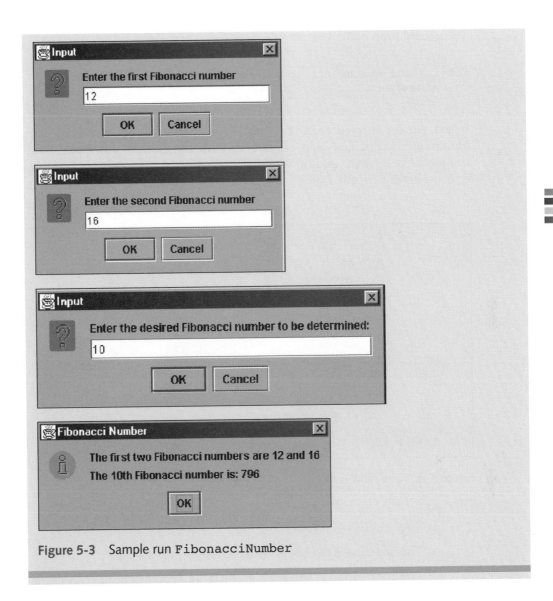

Figure 5-3   Sample run `FibonacciNumber`

THE for LOOPING (REPETITION) STRUCTURE

The **while** loop discussed in the previous section is general enough to implement all forms of repetitions. The Java **for** looping structure is a specialized form of the **while** loop. Its primary purpose is to simplify the writing of count-controlled loops. For this reason, the **for** loop is typically called a **counted** or **indexed for** loop.

The general form of the for statement is:

```
for(initial statement; loop condition; update statement)
    statement
```

In Java, for is a reserved word. The initial statement, loop condition, and update statement (called for loop **control statements**) are enclosed within parentheses and control the body (statement) of the for statement. A for loop can have either a simple or compound statement. Figure 5-4 shows the flow of execution of a for loop.

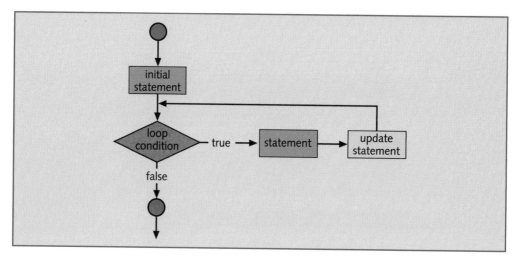

Figure 5-4 for loop

The for loop executes as follows:

1. The initial statement executes.

2. The loop condition is evaluated. If the loop condition evaluates to true:

a. Execute the for loop statement.

b. Execute the update statement (the third expression in the parentheses).

3. Repeat Step 2 until the loop condition evaluates to false.

The initial statement usually initializes a variable (called the for loop control, or indexed, variable).

 As the name implies, the initial statement in the for loop is the first statement to execute; it executes only once.

Example 5-6

The following `for` loop prints the first 10 positive integers:

```
for(i = 1; i <= 10; i++)
    System.out.print(i + " ");

System.out.println();
```

The `initial statement`, i = 1;, initializes the `int` variable i to 1. Next, the loop condition, i <= 10, is evaluated. Since 1 <= 10 is `true`, the print statement executes and outputs 1. The `update statement` i++ then executes, which sets the value of i to 2. Once again, the `loop condition` is evaluated, which is still `true`, and so on. When i becomes 11, the `loop condition` evaluates to `false`, the `for` loop terminates, and the statement following the `for` loop executes.

The following examples further illustrate how a `for` loop executes.

Example 5-7

1. The following `for` loop outputs the word `Hello` and a star (on separate lines) five times:

```
for(i = 1; i <= 5; i++)
{
    System.out.println("Hello");
    System.out.println("*");
}
```

2. Now consider the following `for` loop:

```
for(i = 1; i <= 5; i++)
    System.out.println("Hello");
    System.out.println("*");
```

This loop outputs the word `Hello` five times and the star only once. In this case, the `for` loop controls only the first output statement because the two output statements are not made into a compound statement using curly braces. Therefore, the first output statement executes five times because the `for` loop executes five times. After the `for` loop executes, the second output statement executes only once.

Example 5-8

The following `for` loop executes five empty statements:

```
for(i = 1; i <= 5; i++);          //Line 1
    System.out.println("*");      //Line 2
```

The semicolon at the end of the `for` statement (before the output statement in Line 1) terminates the `for` loop. The action of this `for` loop is empty.

The preceding examples show that care is required to get a **for** loop to perform the desired action.

Some additional comments on **for** loops follow:

- If the loop condition is initially **false**, the loop body does not execute.

- The update expression, when executed, changes the value of the loop control variable (initialized by the initial expression), which eventually sets the value of the loop condition to **false**. The **for** loop executes indefinitely if the loop condition is always **true**.

- If you put a semicolon at the end of the **for** statement (just before the body of the loop), the action of the **for** loop is empty.

- In the **for** statement, if the **loop condition** is omitted, it is assumed to be **true**.

- In a **for** statement, you can omit all three statements—**initial statement**, **loop condition**, and **update statement**. The following is a legal **for** loop:

```
for(;;)
    System.out.println("Hello");
```

This is an infinite **for** loop, continuously printing the world **Hello**.

More examples of **for** loops follow.

Example 5-9

1. You can count backward using a **for** loop if the **for** loop control expressions are set correctly. For example, consider the following **for** loop:

```
for(i = 10; i >= 1; i--)
    System.out.print(" " + i);

System.out.println();
```

The output is:

```
10 9 8 7 6 5 4 3 2 1
```

In this **for** loop, the variable i is initialized to 10. After each iteration of the loop, i is decremented by 1. The loop continues to execute as long as i >= 1.

2. You can increment (or decrement) the loop control variable by any fixed number. In the following **for** loop, the variable is initialized to 1; at the end of the **for** loop, i is incremented by 2. This **for** loop outputs the first 10 positive odd integers:

```
for(i = 1; i <= 20; i = i + 2)
    System.out.print(" " + i);

System.out.println();
```

Example 5-10

Consider the following examples, where i is an int variable.

1.

```
for(i = 10; i <= 9; i++)
    System.out.print(i + " ");

System.out.println();
```

In this for loop, the initial statement sets i to 10. Since initially the loop condition (i <= 9) is false, nothing happens.

2.

```
for(i = 9; i >= 10; i--)
    System.out.print(i + " ");

System.out.println();
```

In this for loop, the initial statement sets i to 9. Since initially the loop condition (i >= 10) is false, nothing happens.

3.

```
for(i = 10; i <= 10; i++)
    System.out.print(i + " ");

System.out.println();
```

In this for loop, the output statement executes once.

4.

```
for(i = 1; i <= 10; i++);
    System.out.print(i + " ");

System.out.println();
```

This for loop has no effect on the output statement. The semicolon at the end of the for statement terminates the for loop; the action of the for loop is thus empty. The output statement is all by itself and executes only once.

5.

```
for(i = 1; ; i++)
    System.out.print(i + " ");

System.out.println();
```

In this for loop, since the loop condition is omitted from the for statement, the loop condition is always true. This is an infinite loop.

In this example, a `for` loop reads five integers and finds their sum and average. Consider the following program code, in which i, `newNum`, `sum`, and `average` are `int` variables, `inputLine` is a `String` variable, and `tokenizer` is a reference variable of the type `StringTokenizer`. For simplicity, assume that all five numbers are entered in the same line.

```
sum = 0;
inputLine = keyboard.readLine();
tokenizer = new StringTokenizer(inputLine);

for(i = 1; i <= 5; i++)
{
    newNum = Integer.parseInt(tokenizer.nextToken());
    sum = sum + newNum;
}

average = sum / 5;
System.out.println("The sum is " + sum);
System.out.println("The average is " + average);
```

In the preceding `for` loop, after getting a `newNum`, this value is added to the previously calculated (partial) `sum` of all the numbers read before the current number. The variable `sum` is initialized to 0 before the `for` loop. Thus, after the program gets the first number and adds it to the value of `sum`, the variable `sum` holds the correct `sum` of the first number.

The following Java program finds the sum of the first n positive integers.

```
//Program: sum first n numbers
//This program finds the sum of the first n positive integers.

import java.io.*;

public class SumFirstNNumbers
{
    static BufferedReader keyboard =
            new BufferedReader(new InputStreamReader(System.in));

    public static void main(String[] args) throws IOException
    {
        int counter;        //loop control variable
        int sum;            //variable to store the sum of the numbers
        int N;              //variable to store the number of
                            //first positive integers to be added
```

```
System.out.print("Line 1: Enter the number of positive "
              + "integers to be added: ");          //Line 1
System.out.flush();                                 //Line 2
N = Integer.parseInt(keyboard.readLine());          //Line 3
System.out.println();                               //Line 4
sum = 0;                                            //Line 5

for(counter = 1; counter <= N; counter++)           //Line 6
    sum = sum + counter;                            //Line 7

System.out.println("Line 8: The sum of the first "
              + N + " positive integers is "
              + sum);                               //Line 8
    }
}
```

Sample Run: In this sample run, the user input is shaded.

Line 1: Enter the number of positive integers to be added: 100

Line 8: The sum of the first 100 positive integers is 5050

The statement in Line 1 prompts the user to enter the number of first positive integers to be added. The statement in Line 3 stores the number entered by the user in N and the statement in Line 5 initializes sum to 0. The for loop in Line 6 executes N times. (In the sample run, N is 100.) In the for loop, counter is initialized to 1 and is incremented by 1 after each iteration of the loop. Therefore, counter ranges from 1 to N. Each time through the loop, the value of counter is added to sum. Because sum was initialized to 0, counter ranges from 1 to N, and the current value of counter is added to the value of sum. After the for loop executes, sum contains the sum of the first N values, which in the sample run is 100 positive integers.

Recall that putting one control structure statement inside another is called **nesting**. The following programming example demonstrates a simple instance of nesting, and also nicely demonstrates counting.

PROGRAMMING EXAMPLE: CLASSIFY NUMBERS

This program reads a given set of integers and then prints the number of odd and even integers. It also outputs the number of zeros.

The program reads 20 integers, but you can easily modify it to read any set of numbers. In fact, you can modify the program so that it first prompts the user to specify how many integers are to be read.

Input 20 integers—positive, negative, or zeros

Output The number of zeros, even numbers, and odd numbers

Problem Analysis and Algorithm Design

After reading a number, you need to check whether it is even or odd. Suppose the value is stored in **number**. Divide **number** by 2 and check the remainder. If the remainder is zero, **number** is even. Increment the even count and then check whether **number** is zero. If it is, increment the zero count. If the remainder is not zero, increment the odd count.

The program uses a **switch** statement to decide whether **number** is odd or even. Suppose that **number** is odd. Dividing by 2 gives the remainder 1 if **number** is positive and the remainder –1 if negative. If **number** is even, dividing by 2 gives the remainder 0 whether **number** is positive or negative. You can use the mod operator, **%**, to find the remainder. For example:

```
6 % 2 = 0,  -4 % 2 = 0,  -7 % 2 = -1,  15 % 2 = 1
```

Repeat the preceding process of analyzing a number for each number in the list.

This discussion translates into the following algorithm:

1. For each number in the list:
   a. Get the number.
   b. Analyze the number.
   c. Increment the appropriate count.
2. Print the results.

Variables

Because you want to count the number of zeros, even numbers, and odd numbers, you need three variables of type **int**—say **zeros**, **evens**, and **odds**, to track the counts. You also need a variable—say, **number**—to read and store the number to be analyzed, and another variable—say, **counter**—to count the numbers analyzed. Your program needs the following variables:

```
int counter;    //loop control variable
int number;     //variable to store the number read
int zeros;      //variable to store the zero count
int evens;      //variable to store the even count
int odds;       //variable to store the odd count
```

Clearly, you must initialize the variables **zeros**, **evens**, and **odds** to zero. You can initialize these variables when you declare them.

Main Algorithm

1. Initialize the variables.
2. Prompt the user to enter 20 numbers.

3. Read the next input line and tokenize it.

4. For each number in the list:

   a. Get the next number from the tokenizer.

   b. Output the number (echo input).

   c. If the number is even:

   {

   i. Increment the even count.

   ii. If the number is zero, increment the zero count.

   }

   otherwise

       Increment the odd count.

   d. If there are no more numbers left in the tokenizer, get the next input line and tokenize it.

5. Print the results.

Before writing the Java program, let's describe Steps 1–5 in more detail. It will be much easier for you to then write the instructions in Java.

1. Initialize the variables. You can initialize the variables **zeros**, **evens**, and **odds** when you declare them.

2. Use an output statement to prompt the user to enter 20 numbers.

3. Read the next input line and tokenize it.

4. For Step 4, you can use a **for** loop to process and analyze the 20 numbers. In pseudocode, this step is written as follows:

```
for(counter = 1; counter <= 20; counter++)
{
    a.  get the number;
    b.  output number;
    c.  switch(number % 2)      // check the remainder
        {
        case 0:  increment even count;
                 if(number == 0)
                     increment zero count;
                 break;
        case 1: case -1: increment odd count;
        }//end switch
    d.  If no more numbers are left in the tokenizer, read and tokenize the next
        input line.
}//end for
```

5. Print the result. Output the value of the variables **zeros, evens,** and **odds.**

Complete Program Listing

```java
//**********************************************************
// Program: ClassifyNumbers
// This program counts the number of odd and even numbers.
// The program also counts the number of zeros.
//**********************************************************

import java.io.*;

public class ClassifyNumbers
{
    static BufferedReader keyboard = new
            BufferedReader(new InputStreamReader(System.in));

    static final int N = 20;

    public static void main(String[] args) throws IOException
    {
            //Declare variables
        int counter;        //loop control variable
        int number;         //variable to store the new number
        StringTokenizer tokenizer;  //variable to tokenize the
                                    //input line

        int zeros = 0;                                      //Step 1
        int odds = 0;                                       //Step 1
        int evens = 0;                                      //Step 1

        System.out.println("Please enter " + N + " integers, "
                    + "positive, negative, or zeros.");     //Step 2

        tokenizer =
            new StringTokenizer(keyboard.readLine());       //Step 3

        for(counter = 1; counter <= N; counter++)           //Step 4
        {
            number =
                Integer.parseInt(tokenizer.nextToken());    //Step 4a
            System.out.print(number + " ");                 //Step 4b

                                                            //Step 4c
```

```
            switch(number % 2)
            {
            case 0: evens++;
                    if(number == 0)
                        zeros++;
                    break;
            case 1:
            case -1: odds++;
            } //end switch

            if(!tokenizer.hasMoreTokens())              //Step 4d
                tokenizer = new StringTokenizer(keyboard.readLine());
        } //end for loop

        System.out.println();

                                                        //Step 5
        System.out.println("There are " + evens + " evens, "
                        + "which also includes "
                        + zeros + " zeros");
        System.out.println("Total number of odds is: " + odds);
    }
}
```

Sample Run: In this sample run, the user input is shaded.

```
Please enter 20 integers, positive, negative, or zeros.
0 0 -2 -3 -5 6 7 8 0 3 0 -23 -8 0 2 9 0 12 67 54
0 0 -2 -3 -5 6 7 8 0 3 0 -23 -8 0 2 9 0 12 67 54

There are 13 evens, which also includes 6 zeros
Total number of odds is: 7
```

We recommend that you do a walk-through of this program using the above sample input. When you execute this program, after entering the 20 numbers in a line(s), press the Enter key twice.

THE do...while LOOPING (REPETITION) STRUCTURE

This section describes the third type of looping or repetition structure—a do...while loop. The general form of a do...while statement is:

```
do
   statement
while(expression);
```

In Java, **do** is a reserved word. As with the other repetition structures, the **do...while statement** can be either a simple or a compound statement. If it is a compound statement, enclose it between curly braces. The **expression** is called the **loop condition**. Figure 5-5 shows the flow of execution of a **do...while** loop.

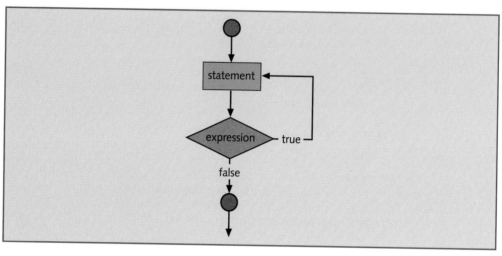

Figure 5-5 **do...while** loop

The **statement** executes first, and then the **expression** is evaluated. If the **expression** evaluates to **true**, the **statement** executes again. As long as the **expression** in a **do...while** statement is **true**, the **statement** executes. To avoid an infinite loop, you must, once again, make sure that the loop body contains a statement that ultimately makes the **expression false** and assures that it exits properly.

Example 5-13

```
i = 0;
do
{
    System.out.print(i + " ");
    i = i + 5;
}
while(i <= 20);
```

The output of this code is:

```
0 5 10 15 20
```

After the value **20** is output, the statement

```
i = i + 5;
```

changes the value of **i** to **25**, so **i <= 20** becomes **false**, which halts the loop.

Because the `while` and `for` loops both have entry conditions, these loops might never activate. The `do...while` loop, on the other hand, has an exit condition and therefore always goes through at least once.

In a `while` and `for` loop, the loop condition is evaluated before executing the body of the loop. Therefore, `while` and `for` loops are called **pre-test loops**. On the other hand, the loop condition in a `do...while` loop is evaluated after executing the body of the loop. Therefore, `do...while` loops are called **post-test loops**.

Example 5-14

Consider the following two loops:

(a)

```
i = 11;
while(i <= 10)
{
        System.out.print(i + " ");
        i = i + 5;
}

System.out.println();
```

(b)

```
i = 11;
do
{
    System.out.print(i + " ");
    i = i + 5;
}
while(i <= 10);

System.out.println();
```

In (a), the `while` loop produces nothing. In (b), the `do...while` loop outputs the number 11 and also changes the value of `i` to 16.

The `do...while` loop is useful when it does not make sense to check a condition until after the action occurs. For example, it is suitable when the action is to read data that is then checked against the exit condition, such as in monitoring devices used in hospitals. The following program illustrates this idea.

Example 5-15

```
//***********************************************************
//  Program: Warning Message
//  This program reads a value and prints a warning
//  message when a value falls outside a given range.
//***********************************************************

import java.io.*;
public class WarningMessage
{
    static BufferedReader keyboard =
            new BufferedReader(new InputStreamReader(System.in));

    static final int LOW = 60;
    static final int HIGH = 100;

    public static void main(String[] args) throws IOException
    {
        int pressure;
        StringTokenizer tokenizer;

        tokenizer = new StringTokenizer(keyboard.readLine());

        do
        {
          if(tokenizer.hasMoreTokens())
             pressure = Integer.parseInt(tokenizer.nextToken());
          else
             tokenizer = new StringTokenizer(keyboard.readLine());
        }
        while((pressure > LOW) && (pressure < HIGH));

        System.out.println("Help");
    }
}
```

All three loops have their place in Java. You can usually replace one with another, but it's often awkward. For example, you can rewrite the `while` loop in the program `SentinelControlledWhileLoop` (see Example 5-4) as a `do...while` loop. To do so, however, takes the awkward form:

```
if(number != -999)
   do
   {
        .
        .
        .
   }
   while(number != -999);
```

That is,

```
if(expression)
   do
        action
   while(expression);
```

replaces the simpler

```
while(expression)
      action
```

break AND continue STATEMENTS

The **break** and **continue** statements alter the flow of control in a program. As you have seen, the **break** statement, when executed in a **switch** structure, provides an immediate exit from the **switch** structure. Similarly, you can use the **break** statement in **while, for,** and **do...while** loops to immediately exit from these structures. The **break** statement is typically used for two purposes:

- To exit early from a loop

- To skip the remainder of the **switch** structure

After the **break** statement executes, the program continues to execute with the first statement after the structure.

Suppose that you have the following declaration:

```
static BufferedReader keyboard =
        new BufferedReader(new InputStreamReader(System.in));
StringTokenizer tokenizer;

int sum;
int num;
boolean isNegative;
```

The use of a **break** statement in a loop can eliminate the use of certain **boolean** variables. The following Java code segment helps illustrate this idea:

```
sum = 0;
isNegative = false;
tokenizer = new StringTokenizer(keyboard.readLine());
```

```
while(tokenizer.hasMoreTokens() && !isNegative)
{
    num = Integer.parseInt(tokenizer.nextToken());
    if(num < 0)    //if number is negative, terminate the
                   //loop after the next iteration
    {
        System.out.println("Negative number found in the data");
        isNegative = true;
    }
    else
    {
        sum = sum + num;
        if(!tokenizer.hasMoreTokens())
            tokenizer = new StringTokenizer(keyboard.readLine());
    }
}
```

This while loop is supposed to find the sum of a set of positive numbers. If the data set contains a negative number, the loop terminates with an appropriate error message. This while loop uses the flag variable isNegative to accomplish the desired result. The variable isNegative is initialized to false before the while loop. Before adding num to sum, check whether num is negative. If num is negative, an error message appears on the screen and isNegative is set to true. In the next iteration, when the expression in the while statement is evaluated, it evaluates to false since !isNegative is false. (Note that because isNegative is true, !isNegative is false).

The following while loop is written without using the variable isNegative:

```
sum = 0;
tokenizer = new StringTokenizer(keyboard.readLine());

while(tokenizer.hasMoreTokens())
{
    num = Integer.parseInt(tokenizer.nextToken());
    if(num < 0)    //if number is negative, terminate the loop
    {
        System.out.println("Negative number found in the data");
        break;
    }

    sum = sum + num;
    if(!tokenizer.hasMoreTokens())
        tokenizer = new StringTokenizer(keyboard.readLine());
}
```

In this form of the while loop, when a negative number is found, the expression in the if statement evaluates to true; after printing an appropriate message, the break statement terminates the loop. (After executing the break statement in a loop, the remaining statements in the loop are skipped.)

The `continue` statement is used in `while`, `for`, and `do...while` structures. When the `continue` statement is executed in a loop, it skips the remaining statements in the loop and proceeds with the next iteration of the loop. In a `while` and `do...while` structure, the `expression` (that is, the loop-continue test) is evaluated immediately after the `continue` statement. In a `for` structure, the `update statement` is executed after the `continue` statement, and then the `loop condition` (that is, the loop-continue test) executes.

If the previous program segment encounters a negative number, the `while` loop terminates. If you want to ignore the negative number and read the next number rather than terminate the loop, replace the `break` statement with the `continue` statement, as shown in the following example:

```
sum = 0;
tokenizer = new StringTokenizer(keyboard.readLine());

while(tokenizer.hasMoreTokens())
{
    num = Integer.parseInt(tokenizer.nextToken());
    if(num < 0)    //if number is negative, terminate the loop
    {
        System.out.println("Negative number found in the data");

        if(!tokenizer.hasMoreTokens())
            tokenizer = new StringTokenizer(keyboard.readLine());

        continue;
    }

    sum = sum + num;

    if(!tokenizer.hasMoreTokens())
        tokenizer = new StringTokenizer(keyboard.readLine());
}
```

 As stated earlier, all three loops have their place in Java and one loop can often replace another. The execution of a `continue` statement, however, is where a `while` structure differs from a `for` structure. In a `while` loop, when the `continue` statement is executed, if the `update statement` appears after the `continue` statement, the `update statement` is not executed. In a `for` loop, the `update statement` always executes.

NESTED CONTROL STRUCTURES

This section briefly reviews the control structures discussed so far in this chapter and in Chapter 4. You have seen that by placing one control structure within another, you can achieve dramatic and fruitful results; nesting of control structures provides new power, subtlety, and complexity. Consider the following program:

```java
import java.io.*;

public class NestedControlStructure
{
    static BufferedReader keyboard =
            new BufferedReader(new InputStreamReader(System.in))
    public static void main(String[] args) throws IOException
    {
        String studentId;
        int    testScore;
        int    count = 0;

        System.out.print("Enter student Id "
                        + "(Enter ZZZ to end): ");
        System.out.flush();
        studentId = keyboard.readLine();
        System.out.println();

        while(!studentId.equals("ZZZ"))
        {
            count++;

            System.out.print("Enter test score: ");
            System.out.flush();
            testScore =
                    Integer.parseInt(keyboard.readLine());;
            System.out.println();

            System.out.print("Student Id = " + studentId
                            + ", test score = "
                            + testScore + ", and grade = ");
            if(testScore >= 90)
                System.out.println("A.");
            else if(testScore >= 80)
                    System.out.println("B.");
            else if(testScore >= 70)
                    System.out.println("C.");
            else if(testScore >= 60)
                    System.out.println("D.");
            else
                System.out.println("F.");

            System.out.print("Enter student Id "
                            + "(Enter ZZZ to end): ");
            System.out.flush();
            studentId = keyboard.readLine();
            System.out.println();
        }// end while

        System.out.println("\nStudents in class = " + count);
    }
}
```

How would this program work if you wrote it as a sequence of `if...` statements (with no `else` or as a `switch` structure) within the `while` loop?

Consider another example of nesting. Suppose you want to create the following pattern:

```
*
**
***
****
*****
```

Clearly, you want to print five lines of stars. In the first line you want to print one star, in the second line two stars, and so on. To print five lines, start with the following `for` statement:

```
for(i = 1; i <= 5 ; i++)
```

The value of `i` in the first iteration is 1, in the second iteration it is 2, and so on. You can use the value of `i` as the limiting condition in another `for` loop nested within this loop to control the number of stars in a line. A little more thought produces the following code:

```
for(i = 1; i <= 5 ; i++)
{
    for(j = 1; j <= i; j++)
       System.out.print("*");

    System.out.println();
}
```

A walk-through of this code shows that the `for` loop starts with `i = 1`. When `i` is 1, the inner `for` loop outputs one star and the insertion point moves to the next line. Then `i` becomes 2, the inner `for` loop outputs two stars, the insertion point moves to the next line, and so on. This process continues until `i` becomes 6 and the loop stops.

What pattern does this code produce if you replace the first `for` statement with the following?

```
for(i = 5; i >= 1; i--)
```

To learn more about the nesting of `for` loops, see Exercise 30 at the end of this chapter.

QUICK REVIEW

1. Java has three looping (repetition) structures: `while`, `for`, and `do...while`.
2. The syntax of the `while` statement is:

```
while(expression)
statement
```

3. In Java, `while` is a reserved word.
4. In the `while` statement, the parentheses around the **expression**, the decision maker, are important; they mark the beginning and end of the expression.

5. The **statement** is called the body of the loop.

6. The body of the **while** loop must contain a statement that eventually sets the expression to **false** to terminate the loop.

7. A counter-controlled **while** loop uses a counter to control the loop.

8. In a counter-controlled **while** loop, you must initialize the counter before the loop, and the body of the loop must contain a statement that changes the value of the counter variable.

9. A sentinel is a special value that marks the end of input data. The sentinel must be similar, yet differ, from all the data items.

10. A sentinel-controlled **while** loop uses a sentinel to control the **while** loop. The **while** loop continues to execute until the sentinel is read.

11. An EOF-controlled **while** loop continues to execute until the program detects the end-of-file marker.

12. The method **read** returns −1 when trying to read past the end of the input file.

13. The method **readLine** returns the value **null** when trying to read past the end of the input file.

14. In the Windows console environment, the end-of-file marker is entered using **Ctrl+z** (hold the **Ctrl** key and press **z**). In the UNIX environment, the end-of-file marker is entered using **Ctrl+d** (hold the **Ctrl** key and press **d**).

15. In Java, **for** is a reserved word.

16. A **for** loop simplifies the writing of a count-controlled **while** loop.

17. The syntax of the **for** loop is:

```
for(initialize statement; loop condition; update statement)
    statement
```

The **statement** is called the body of the **for** loop.

18. If you put a semicolon at the end of the **for** loop (before the body of the **for** loop), the action of the **for** loop is empty.

19. The syntax of the **do...while** statement is:

```
do
    statement
while(expression);
```

20. The **statement** is called the body of the **do...while** loop.

21. The **while** and **for** loops might not execute at all, but the **do...while** loop always executes at least once.

22. Executing a **break** statement in the body of a loop immediately terminates the loop.

23. Executing a `continue` statement in the body of a loop skips the loop's remaining statements and proceeds with the next iteration.

24. When a `continue` statement executes in a `while` or `do...while` loop, the expression update statement in the body of the loop might not execute.

25. After a `continue` statement executes in a `for` loop, the update statement is the next statement executed.

26. In a `while` and `for` loop, the loop condition is evaluated before executing the body of the loop. Therefore, `while` and `for` loops are called pre-test loops.

27. In a `do...while` loop, the loop condition is evaluated after executing the body of the loop. Therefore, `do...while` loops are called post-test loops.

5

EXERCISES

1. Mark the following statements as true or false.

   a. In a counter-controlled `while` loop, it is not necessary to initialize the loop control variable.

   b. It is possible that the body of a `while` loop might not execute at all.

   c. In an infinite `while` loop, the loop condition is initially false, but after the first iteration it is always true.

   d. The `while` loop

   ```
   j = 0;
   while(j <= 10)
           j++;
   terminates when j > 10.
   ```

   e. A sentinel-controlled `while` loop is an event-controlled `while` loop whose termination depends on a special value.

   f. A loop is a control structure that causes certain statements to execute over and over.

   g. To read data from a file of unspecified length, an EOF-controlled loop is a good choice.

   h. When a `while` loop terminates, the control first goes back to the statement just before the `while` statement, and then the control goes to the statement immediately following the `while` loop.

2. What is the output of the following Java code?

   ```
   count = 1;
   y = 100;
   while(count < 100)
   {
      y = y - 1;
      count++;
   }
   System.out.println(" y = " + y + " and count = " + count);
   ```

3. What is the output of the following Java code?

```java
num = 5;
while(num > 5)
   num = num + 2;
System.out.println(num);
```

4. What is the output of the following Java code?

```java
num = 1;
while(num < 10)
{
    System.out.print(num + " ");
    num = num + 2;
}
System.out.println();
```

5. When does the following `while` loop terminate?

```java
ch = 'D';
while('A' <= ch && ch <= 'Z')
      ch = (char)((int)(ch) + 1));
```

6. Suppose that the input is:

```
38
45
71
4
-1
```

What is the output of the following code? Assume all variables are properly declared.

```java
sum = Integer.parseInt(keyboard.readLine());
num = Integer.parseInt(keyboard.readLine());
for(j = 1; j <= 3; j++)
{
   num = Integer.parseInt(keyboard.readLine());
   sum = sum + num;
}
System.out.println("Sum = " + sum);
```

7. Suppose that the input is:

```
38
45
71
4
-1
```

What is the output of the following code? Assume all variables are properly declared.

```java
sum = Integer.parseInt(keyboard.readLine());
num = Integer.parseInt(keyboard.readLine());
while(num != -1)
```

```
{
    sum = sum + num;
    num = Integer.parseInt(keyboard.readLine());
}
System.out.println("Sum = " + sum);
```

8. Suppose that the input is:

```
38
45
71
4
-1
```

What is the output of the following code? Assume all variables are properly declared.

```
num = Integer.parseInt(keyboard.readLine());
sum = num;
while(num != -1)
{
    num = Integer.parseInt(keyboard.readLine());
    sum = sum + num;
}
System.out.println("Sum = " + sum);
```

9. Suppose that the input is:

```
38
45
71
4
-1
```

What is the output of the following code? Assume all variables are properly declared.

```
sum = 0;
num = Integer.parseInt(keyboard.readLine());
while(num != -1)
{
    sum = sum + num;
    num = Integer.parseInt(keyboard.readLine());
}
System.out.println("Sum = " + sum);
```

10. Correct the following code so that it finds the sum of 10 numbers.

```
sum = 0;
while(count < 10)
    num = Integer.parseInt(keyboard.readLine());
    sum = sum + num;
    count++;
```

11. What is the output of the following program?

```java
public class WhatIsTheOutput
{
    public static void main(String[] args)
    {
        int  x, y, z;

        x = 4;
        y = 5;
        z = y + 6;

        while(((z-x) % 4) != 0)
        {
            System.out.print(z + " ");
            z = z + 7;
        }
        System.out.println();
    }
}
```

12. Suppose that the input is:

58   23   46   75   98   150   12   176   145 -999

What is the output of the following program?

```java
import java.io.*;
import java.util.*;

public class FindTheOutput
{
    static BufferedReader inputStream =
            new BufferedReader(new InputStreamReader(System.in));

    public static void main(String[] args) throws IOException
    {
        int num;
        StringTokenizer tokenizer;

        tokenizer = new StringTokenizer(inputStream.readLine());
        num = Integer.parseInt(tokenizer.nextToken());

        while(num != -999)
        {
            System.out.print(num % 25 + "  ");
            num = Integer.parseInt(tokenizer.nextToken());
        }

        System.out.println();
    }
}
```

13. Given the following code:

```
for(i = 12; i <= 25; i++)
    System.out.println(i);
System.out.println();
```

Answer the following questions:

a. The seventh integer printed is _____.

b. The statement produces _____ lines of output.

c. If i++ were changed to i--, a compilation error would result. True or false?

14. Given that the following code is correctly inserted into a program, state its entire output as to content and form.

```
num = 0;
for(i = 1; i <= 4; i++)
{
    num = num + 10 * (i - 1);
    System.out.print(num + " ");
}
System.out.println();
```

15. Given that the following code is correctly inserted into a program, state its entire output as to content and form.

```
j = 2;
for(i = 0; i <= 5; i++)
{
    System.out.print(j + " ");
    j = 2 * j + 3;
}
System.out.println();
```

16. Assume that the following code is correctly inserted into a program:

```
s = 0;
for(i = 0; i < 5; i++)
{
    s = 2 * s + i;
    System.out.print(s + " ");
}

System.out.println();
```

a. What is the final value of s?

    (i) 11   (ii) 4   (iii) 26   (iv) none of these

b. If a semicolon is inserted after the right parentheses in the for loop control expressions, what is the final value of s?

    (i) 0   (ii) 1   (iii) 2   (iv) 5   (v) none of these

c. If the 5 is replaced with a 0 in the for loop control expression, what is the final value of s?

    (i) 0   (ii) 1   (iii) 2   (iv) none of these

17. State what output, if any, results in each of the following statements:

a.
```
for(i = 1; i <= 1; i++)
    System.out.print("*");
System.out.println();
```

b.
```
for(i = 2; i >= 1; i++)
    System.out.print("*");
System.out.println();
```

c.
```
for(i = 1; i <= 1; i--)
    System.out.print("*");
System.out.println();
```

d.
```
for(i = 12; i >= 9; i--)
    System.out.print("*");
System.out.println();
```

e.
```
for(i = 0; i <= 5; i++)
    System.out.print("*");
System.out.println();
```

f.
```
for(i = 1; i <= 5; i++)
{
    System.out.print("*");
    i = i + 1;
}
System.out.println();
```

18. Write a **for** statement to add all multiples of 3 between 1 and 100.

19. What is the exact output of the following program?

```
public class Mystery
{
    public static void main (String[] args)
    {
        int counter;

        for(counter = 7; counter <= 16; counter++)
            switch (counter % 10)
            {
            case 0: System.out.print(", ");
                    break;
            case 1: System.out.print("OFTEN ");
                    break;
            case 2: case 8: System.out.print("IS ");
                            break;
            case 3: System.out.print("NOT ");
                    break;
            case 4: case 9: System.out.print("DONE ");
                            break;
```

```
            case 5: System.out.print("WELL");
                    break;
            case 6: System.out.print(".");
                    break;
            case 7: System.out.print("WHAT ");
                    break;
            default: System.out.print("Bad number. ");
            }

        System.out.println();
        }
    }
```

20. Suppose that the input is:

```
5
3
8
```

What is the output of the following code? Assume all variables are properly declared.

```
a = Integer.parseInt(keyboard.readLine());
b = Integer.parseInt(keyboard.readLine());
c = Integer.parseInt(keyboard.readLine());
for(j = 1; j < a; j++)
{
    d = b + c;
    b = c;
    c = d;
    System.out.print(c + "   ");
}
System.out.println();
```

21. What is the output of the following Java program segment? Assume all variables are properly declared.

```
for(j = 0; j < 8; j++)
{
    System.out.print(j * 25 + " - ");
    if(j != 7)
        System.out.println((j + 1) * 25 - 1);
    else
        System.out.println((j + 1) * 25);
}
```

22. The following program has more than five mistakes that prevent it from compiling and/or running. Correct all such mistakes.

```
public class Exercise22
{
    final int N = 2,137;

    public static main(String[] args)
```

```
{
    int a, b, c, d:

    a := 3;
    b = 5;
    c = c + d;
    N = a + n;
    for(i = 3; i <= N; i++)
    {
        System.out.print(" " + i);
        i = i + 1;
    }

    System.out.println();
}
}
```

23. Which of the following apply to the `while` loop only? To the `do...while` loop only? To both?

    a. It is considered a conditional loop.

    b. The body of the loop executes at least once.

    c. The logical expression controlling the loop is evaluated before the loop is entered.

    d. The body of the loop might not execute at all.

24. How many times will each of the following loops execute? What is the output in each case?

    a.
    ```
    x = 5;   y = 50;
    do
        x = x + 10;
    while(x < y);

    System.out.println(x + " " + y);
    ```
    b.
    ```
    x = 5;   y = 80;
    do
        x = x * 2;
    while(x < y);

    System.out.println(x + " " + y);
    ```
    c.
    ```
    x = 5;   y = 20;
    do
        x = x + 2;
    while(x >= y);

    System.out.println(x + " " + y);
    ```

d.

```
x = 5;   y = 35;
while(x < y)
      x = x + 10;

System.out.println(x + " " + y);
```

e.

```
x = 5;   y = 30;
while(x <= y)
      x = x * 2;

System.out.println(x + " " + y);
```

f.

```
x = 5;   y = 30;
while(x > y)
      x = x + 2;

System.out.println(x + " " + y);
```

25. The **do...while** loop in the following program is supposed to read some numbers until it reaches a sentinel (in this case, **-1**). It is supposed to add all of the numbers except for the sentinel. If the data looks like

```
12
5
30
48
-1
```

the program fails to do what it is purported to do. Make any necessary corrections.

```
import java.io.*;
public  class Strange
{
    static BufferedReader keyboard = new
            BufferedReader(new InputStreamReader(System.in));
    public static void main(String[] args)
    {
        int total = 0,
            number;
        do
        {
            number = Integer.parseInt(keyboard.readLine());
            total = total + number;
        }
        while(number != -1);
```

```
System.out.println("The sum of the numbers entered is "
                   + total);
        }
}
```

26. Using the data from Exercise 25, the following two loops also fail. Correct them.

    a.
    ```
    number = Integer.parseInt(keyboard.readLine());
    while(number != -1)
            total =  total + number;
            number = Integer.parseInt(keyboard.readLine());
    ```

    b.
    ```
    number = Integer.parseInt(keyboard.readLine());
    while(number != -1)
    {
        number = Integer.parseInt(keyboard.readLine());
        total = total + number;
    }
    ```

27. Given the following program segment

    ```
    for(number = 1; number <= 10; number++)
        System.out.print(number + " ");
    System.out.println();
    ```

    write a **while** and a **do...while** loop that have the same output.

28. Given the following program segment

    ```
    j = 2;
    for(i = 1; i <= 5; i++);
    {
        System.out.print(j + " ");
        j = j + 5;
    }
    System.out.println();
    ```

    write a **while** and a **do...while** loop that have the same output.

29. What is the output of the following program?

    ```
    public class Mystery
    {
      public static void main(String[] args)
        {
            int  x, y, z;

            x = 4;
            y = 5;
    ```

```
        z = y + 6;
        do
        {
            System.out.print(z + " ");
            z = z + 7;
        }
        while(((z - x) % 4) != 0);

        System.out.println();
    }
}
```

30. To further learn how nested **for** loops work, do a walk-through of the following program segments and, in each case, determine the exact output.

a.
```
int i,j;
for(i = 1; i <= 5; i++)
{
    for(j = 1; j <= 5; j++)
        System.out.print(i * j + "\t");
    System.out.println();
}
```

b.
```
int i,j;
for(i = 1; i <= 5; i++)
{
    for(j = 1; j <= 5; j++)
        System.out.print(i + "\t");
    System.out.println();
}
```

c.
```
int i,j;
for(i = 1; i <= 5; i++)
{
    for(j = (i + 1); j <= 5; j++)
        System.out.print(j + "\t");
    System.out.println();
}
```

d.
```
int i,j;
for(i = 1; i <= 5; i++)
{
    for(j = 1; j <= i; j++)
        System.out.print(j + "\t");
    System.out.println();
}
```

e.
```
final int m = 10;
final int n = 10;
int i,j;
```

5

```
for(i = 1; i <= m; i++)
{
    for(j = 1; j <= n; j++)
        System.out.print((m * (i - 1) + j) + "\t");
    System.out.println();
}
```

f. int i,j;

```
for(i = 1; i <= 9; i++)
{
    for(j = 1; j <= (9 - i); j++)
        System.out.print(" ");
    for(j = 1; j <= i; j++)
        System.out.print(j);
    for(j = (i - 1); j >= 1; j--)
        System.out.print(j);
    System.out.println();
}
```

PROGRAMMING EXERCISES

1. An integer is divisible by 9 if the sum of its digits is divisible by 9. Write a program that prompts the user to input an integer. The program should then output the number and a message stating whether the number is divisible by 9. It does so by first adding the digits and then checking whether the sum of the digits is divisible by 9.

2. Write a program that prompts the user to input an integer and then outputs both the individual digits of the number and the sum of the digits. For example, the program should: output the individual digits of 3456 as 3 4 5 6; output the individual digits of 8030 as 8 0 3 0; and output the individual digits of 2345526 as 2 3 4 5 5 2 6; output the individual digits of 4000 as 4 0 0 0; output the individual digits of -2345 as 2 3 4 5.

3. Write a program that prompts the user to input an integer and then outputs the number with the digits reversed. For example, if the input is 12345, the output should be 54321. Your program must also output 5000 as 0005 and 980 as 089.

4. Rewrite the program of Example 5-5, Telephone Digits. Replace the statements from Line 10 to Line 28 so that the program uses only a **switch** structure to find the digit that corresponds to an uppercase letter.

5. The program Telephone Digits outputs only telephone digits that correspond to uppercase letters. Rewrite the program so that it processes uppercase and lowercase letters and outputs the corresponding telephone digit. If the input is other than an uppercase or lowercase letter, the program must output an appropriate error message.

6. Write a program that reads a set of integers, and then finds and prints the sum of the even and odd integers.

7. Write a program that prompts the user to input a positive integer. It should then output a message indicating whether the number is a prime number. (*Note:* An even number is prime if it is 2. An odd integer is prime if it is not divisible by any odd integer less than or equal to the square root of the number.)

8. Write a program that uses a `while` loop to perform the following steps:

   a. Prompt the user to input two integers: `firstNum` and `secondNum` (`firstNum` must be less than `secondNum`).

   b. Output all odd numbers between `firstNum` and `secondNum`.

   c. Output the sum of all even numbers between `firstNum` and `secondNum`.

   d. Output the numbers and their square between 1 and 10.

   e. Output the sum of the square of odd numbers between `firstNum` and `secondNum`.

   f. Output all uppercase letters.

9. Redo Exercise 8 using a `for` loop.

10. Redo Exercise 8 using a `do...while` loop.

11. For research purposes and to assist students, the admissions office of your local university wants to know how well female and male students perform in certain courses. You receive a file that contains female and male student GPAs for certain courses. Due to confidentiality, the letter code `f` is used for female students; `m` is used for male students. Every file entry consists of a letter code followed by a GPA. Each line has one entry. The number of entries in the file is unknown. Write a program that computes and outputs the average GPA for both female and male students. Format your results to two decimal places.

12. If interest is compounded annually, it grows as follows. Suppose `P0` is the initial amount and `INT` is the interest rate per year. If `P1`, `P2`, and `P3` represent the balance at the end of the first, second, and third year, respectively, then:

```
P1 = P0 + P0 * INT = P0 * (1 + INT)
P2 = P1 + P1 * INT = P1 * (1 + INT) = P0 * (1 + INT) * (1 + INT)
   = P0 * (1 + INT)²
P3 = P2 + P2 * INT = P2 * (1 + INT)
   = P0 * (1 + INT) * (1 + INT) * (1 + INT)
   = P0 * (1 + INT)³
```

and so on . . .

When money is deposited in an IRA account it is usually sheltered from taxes until the money is withdrawn after the age of 59. Suppose that someone dear to you opened such an account for you on your 16th birthday at 10% interest, and then he or she forgot about it (so no money was added or withdrawn). On your 60th birthday, some fortune hunters notify you about this account. The money has been compounded annually at the 10% rate. Write a program that reads an initial amount and computes the total in the account on your 60th birthday.

You decide to leave the money in for another year. Starting from your 61ˢᵗ birthday, you decide to withdraw each year's interest income. In other words, you withdraw the interest and leave the rest of the money untouched. How much income would you have per month for the rest of your life?

Design your program to accept any integer input. Test it with initial investments of $1700, $3600, and $8500. (*Note:* Use a loop to compute the amount at your 60ᵗʰ birthday. Do *not* use the predefined method **pow**.) The program should do all the computing needed, and output all the relevant data as follows:

```
The initial investment was $_____. The total amount
accumulated after  _____  years, if $_____  is
allowed to compound with an interest rate of 10.00%, comes to
$_____ .

The total amount accumulated after  _____  (years + 1)
years, if $ _____  is allowed to compound with an
interest rate of 10%, comes to $_____ .

The interest earned during this year is $_____. If
interest is withdrawn each year thereafter, my income is
$_____  per month.
```

6

GRAPHICAL USER INTERFACE (GUI) AND OBJECT-ORIENTED DESIGN (OOD)

In this chapter, you will:

♦ Learn about basic GUI components

♦ Explore how the GUI components `JFrame`, `JLabel`, `JTextField`, and `JButton` work

♦ Become familiar with the concept of event-driven programming

♦ Discover events and event handlers

♦ Explore object-oriented design

♦ Learn how to identify objects, classes, and members of a class

Java is equipped with many powerful, yet easy-to-use graphical user interface (GUI) components, such as the input and output dialog boxes you learned about in Chapter 3. You can use these to make your programs attractive and user friendly. The first half of this chapter introduces you to some basic Java GUI components.

In Chapter 1, you were introduced to the object-oriented design (OOD) problem-solving methodology. The second half of this chapter outlines a general approach to solving problems using OOD, and provides several examples to clarify this problem-solving methodology.

GRAPHICAL USER INTERFACE (GUI) COMPONENTS

In Chapter 3, you learned how to use input and output dialog boxes to input data into a program and show the output of a program. Before introducing the various GUI components, we will use input and output dialog boxes to write a program to determine the area and perimeter of a rectangle. We will then discuss how to use different GUI components to create a different graphical user interface to determine the area and perimeter of a rectangle.

The program in Example 6-1 prompts the user to input the length and width of a rectangle and then display its area and perimeter. We will use the method `showInputDialog` to create an input dialog box and the method `showMessageDialog` to create an output dialog box. Recall that these methods are contained in the **class JOptionPane** and this class is contained in the package `javax.swing`.

Example 6-1: (Area and Perimeter of a Rectangle)

```java
// This Java Program determines the area and
// perimeter of a rectangle.

import javax.swing.JOptionPane;

public class Rectangle
{
    public static void main(String[] args)
    {
        double width, length, area, perimeter;             //Line 1

        String lengthStr, widthStr, outputStr;             //Line 2

        lengthStr =
           JOptionPane.showInputDialog("Enter the length: "); //Line 3
        length = Double.parseDouble(lengthStr);            //Line 4

        widthStr =
           JOptionPane.showInputDialog("Enter the width: ");  //Line 5
        width = Double.parseDouble(widthStr);              //Line 6

        area = length * width;                             //Line 7
        perimeter = 2 * (length + width);                  //Line 8

        outputStr = "Length: " + length + "\n" +
                    "Width: " + width + "\n" +
                    "Area: " + area + " square units\n" +
                    "Perimeter: " + perimeter + " units\n"; //Line 9

        JOptionPane.showMessageDialog(null, outputStr,
                             "Rectangle",
                       JOptionPane.INFORMATION_MESSAGE);   //Line 10
```

```
        System.exit(0);                                    //Line 11
    }
}
```

Sample Run: Figure 6-1 shows the sample run.

Figure 6-1   Sample run for area and perimeter of a rectangle

The program in Example 6-1 works as follows: The statements in Lines 1 and 2 declare various variables to manipulate data. The statement in Line 3 displays the first dialog box of the sample run and prompts the user to enter the length of the rectangle. The entered length is assigned as a string to `lengthStr`. The statement in Line 4 retrieves the length and stores it in the variable `length`.

The statement in Line 5 displays the second dialog box of the sample run and prompts the user to enter the width of the rectangle. The entered width is assigned as a string to `widthStr`. The statement in Line 6 retrieves the width and stores it in the variable `width`.

The statement in Line 7 determines the area, and the statement in Line 8 determines the perimeter of the rectangle. The statement in Line 9 creates the string containing the desired output and assigns this string to `outputStr`. The statement in Line 10 uses the output dialog box to display the desired output, which is shown in the third dialog box of the sample run. Finally, the statement in Line 11 terminates the program.

The program in Example 6-1 uses input and output dialog boxes to accomplish its job. When you run this program, you see only one dialog box at a time.

However, suppose that you want the program to display all input and output in one dialog box, as shown in Figure 6-2.

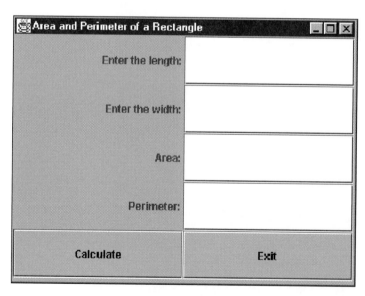

Figure 6-2   GUI to find the area and perimeter of a rectangle

In Java terminology, such a dialog box is called a GUI, or simply a user interface. In this GUI, the user enters the length and width in the top two white boxes. When the user clicks the `Calculate` button, the program displays the area and the perimeter in their respective locations. When the user clicks the `Exit` button, the program terminates.

In this interface, the user can:

- See the entire input and output simultaneously

- Input values for length and width, in any order the user prefers

- Input values that can be corrected after entering them and before clicking the `Calculate` button

- Enter another set of input values and click the `Calculate` button to obtain the area and perimeter of another rectangle

The interface shown in Figure 6-2 contains various Java GUI components that are labeled in Figure 6-3.

Figure 6-3 Java GUI components

As you can see in Figure 6-3, the white areas used to get input and show results are called `JTextFields`. The labels for these text fields, such as `Enter the length:` are called `JLabels`, the buttons `Calculate` and `Exit` are each called a `JButton`. All these components are placed in a window, called `JFrame`.

Creating this type of user interface is not difficult. Java has done all the work; you only need to learn how to use the tools provided by Java to create such an interface. For example, to create an interface like the one shown in Figures 6-2 and 6-3 that contains labels, text areas, buttons, and windows, you need to learn the statements that create these components. In the following sections you will learn how to create the following GUI components:

- Windows
- Labels
- Text areas
- Buttons

The GUI components, such as labels, are placed in an area called the **content pane** of the window. You can think of a content pane as the inner area of the window, below the title bar and inside the border. You will also learn how to place these GUI components in the content pane of a window.

In Figure 6-2, when you click on the `Calculate` button, the program displays the area and the perimeter of the rectangle you have specified. This means that clicking the `Calculate` button causes the program to execute the code to calculate the area and the perimeter and then display the results. When the `Calculate` button is clicked, we say that an **event** has occurred. The Java system is very prompt in listening for the events generated by a program and then reacting to those events. Therefore, in this chapter you will briefly learn how to write the code that needs to be executed when a particular event occurs, such as when a button is clicked. So, in addition to creating windows, labels, text areas, and buttons, in the next few sections, you will learn:

- How to access the content pane
- How to create event listeners
- How to process or handle events

We begin by describing how to create a window.

Creating a Window

GUI components such as windows and labels, are, in fact, objects. Recall that an object is an instance of a particular class. Therefore, these components (objects) are instances of a particular class type. `JFrame` is a `class` and the GUI component `window` can be created by using a `JFrame` object. There are various attributes associated with a window. For example:

- Every window has a title.
- Every window has width and height.

JFrame

The class JFrame provides various methods to control the attributes of a window. For example, it has methods to set the window title and methods to specify the height and width of the window. Table 6-1 describes some of the methods provided by the class JFrame.

Table 6-1 Some Methods Provided by the class JFrame

Method / Description / Example

```public JFrame()```
 //This is used when an object of the type JFrame is
 //instantiated and the window is created without any title.
 //Example: JFrame myWindow = new JFrame();
 //   myWindow is a window with no title

```public JFrame(String s)```
 //This is used when an object of the type JFrame is
 //instantiated and the title of the window is also specified.
 //Example: JFrame myWindow = new JFrame("Rectangle");
 //   myWindow is a window with title Rectangle

```public void setSize(int w, int h)```
 //Method to set the size of the window
 //Example: myWindow.setSize(400,300);
 //   sets the width of the window to 400 pixels and
 //   the height to 300 pixels.

```public void setTitle(String s)```
 //Method to set the title of the window
 //Example: myWindow.setTitle("Rectangle");
 //   sets the title of the window to Rectangle

```public void setVisible(boolean b)```
 //Method to display window in the program. If the value of b is true
 //the window will be displayed on the screen.
 //Example: myWindow.setVisible(true);
 // After the execution of this statement the window will be shown
 // during program execution.

```public void setDefaultCloseOperation(int operation)```
 //Method to determine the action to be taken when the user clicks on
 //the window closing button, ×, to close the window.
 //Choices for the parameter operation are the named constants –
 //EXIT_ON_CLOSE, HIDE_ON_CLOSE, DISPOSE_ON_CLOSE, and
 //DO_NOTHING_ON_CLOSE. The named constant EXIT_ON_CLOSE is defined in
 //the class JFrame. The last three named constants are defined in
 //javax.swing.WindowConstants.
 //Example: The statement
 //   setDefaultCloseOperation(EXIT_ON_CLOSE);
 //sets the default close option of the window closing to close the
 //window and terminate the program when the user clicks the
 //window closing button, ×.

```public void addWindowListener(WindowEvent e)```   //Method to register a window listener object to a JFrame

The **class JFrame** also contains methods to set the color of a window. Chapter 13 describes these methods.

There are two ways to make an application program create a window. The first way is to declare an object of the type **JFrame**, instantiate the object, and then use various methods to manipulate the window. In this case, the object created can use the various applicable methods of the class.

The second way is to create the class containing the application program by *extending* the definition of the **class JFrame**, that is, the class containing the application program is built "on top of" the **class JFrame**. In Java, this way of creating a class utilizes the mechanism of **inheritance**. Inheritance means that a new class can be derived from or based on an already existing class. The new class "inherits" features such as methods from the existing class; this saves a lot of time for programmers. For example, we could define a new **class RectangleProgram** that would extend the definition of **JFrame**. The class **RectangleProgram** would be able to use variables and methods from **JFrame**, but also add some functionality of its own (such as the ability to calculate the area and perimeter of a rectangle).

When you use inheritance, the class containing your application program will have more than one method. In addition to the method **main**, you will have at least one other method that will be used to create a window object containing the required GUI components (such as labels and text fields). This additional method is a special type of method called a **constructor**. A constructor is a method of a class that is automatically executed when an object of the class is created. Typically, a constructor is used to initialize an object. The name of the constructor is always the same as the name of the class. For example, the constructor for the **class RectangleProgram** would be named **RectangleProgram**.

Chapter 11 discusses the principles of inheritance in detail. Constructors are covered in detail in Chapter 8.

Because inheritance is an important concept in programming languages such as Java, we will use the second way of creating a window. We will extend the definition of the **class JFrame** by using the modifier **extends**. For example, the definition of the **class RectangleProgram**, containing the application program to calculate the area and perimeter of a rectangle, is as follows:

```
public class RectangleProgram extends JFrame
{
    public RectangleProgram()        //constructor
    {
        //Necessary code
    }
```

```
    public static void main(String[] args)
    {
        //Code for the method main
    }
}
```

In Java, **extends** is a reserved word. The remainder of this section describes the necessary code to create a window.

An important property of inheritance is that the class—called a **subclass**—that extends the definition of an existing class—called a **superclass**—inherits all the properties of the superclass. For example, all `public` methods of the superclass can be *directly* accessed in the subclass. In our example, the `class RectangleProgram` is a subclass of the `class JFrame`, so it can access the `public` methods of the `class JFrame`. Therefore, to set the title of the window to `Area and Perimeter of a Rectangle`, you use the method `setTitle` of the `class JFrame` as follows:

```
setTitle("Area and Perimeter of a Rectangle");        //Line 1
```

Similarly, the statement

```
setSize(400,300);                                     //Line 2
```

sets the window's width to 400 pixels and its height to 300 pixels. (A **pixel** is the smallest unit of space on your screen that you can write. The term pixel stands for *picture element*.) Note that since the pixel size depends on the current monitor setting, it is impossible to predict the exact width and height of a window in centimeters or inches.

Next, to display the window, you must invoke the method `setVisible`. The following statement accomplishes this:

```
setVisible(true);                                     //Line 3
```

To terminate the application program when the user closes the window, use the following statement (as described in Table 6-1):

```
setDefaultCloseOperation(EXIT_ON_CLOSE);              //Line 4
```

The statements in Lines 1, 2, 3, and 4 will be placed in the constructor (that is, in the method whose heading is `public RectangleProgram()`). Thus, you can write the constructor as follows:

```
public RectangleProgram()
{
    setTitle("Area and Perimeter of a Rectangle");
    setSize(400,300);
    setVisible(true);
    setDefaultCloseOperation(EXIT_ON_CLOSE);
}
```

You could create a `window` by using an object of the type `JFrame`. However, for our program, if we do so, then the window created will not have a title or the required size unless we specify the necessary statements similar to the ones in the preceding code. Because

`RectangleProgram` is also a **`class`**, we can create objects of the type `RectangleProgram`. Because the **`class`** `RectangleProgram` **`extends`** the definition of the **`class`** `JFrame`, it inherits the properties of the **`class`** `JFrame`. If we create an object of the type `RectangleProgram`, not only do we create a `window`, but the created `window` also will have a title and a specific size, and the `window` will be displayed when the program executes.

Consider the following statement:

```
RectangleProgram rectObject = new RectangleProgram();   //Line 5
```

This statement creates the object `rectObject` of the type `RectangleProgram`.

The statement in Line 5 causes the window shown in Figure 6-4 to appear on the screen.

Figure 6-4 Window with the title `Area and Perimeter of a Rectangle`

You can close the window in Figure 6-4 by clicking the "close" button, the button containing ✕, in the upper-right corner. The window in Figure 6-4 is empty because we have not yet created labels, text fields, and so on.

The program to create the window shown in Figure 6-4 uses the **`class`** `JFrame` and this class is contained in the package `javax.swing`. Therefore, the program must include either of the following two statements in the program:

```
import javax.swing.*;
```

or

```
import javax.swing.JFrame;
```

After making minor changes in the statements described in this section, the program to create the window shown in Figure 6-4 is as follows:

```java
//Java program to create a window

import javax.swing.*;

public class RectangleProgram extends JFrame
{
    private static final int WIDTH = 400;
    private static final int HEIGHT = 300;

    public RectangleProgram()
    {
        setTitle("Area and Perimeter of a Rectangle");
        setSize(WIDTH,HEIGHT);
        setVisible(true);
        setDefaultCloseOperation(EXIT_ON_CLOSE);
    }

    public static void main(String[] args)
    {
        RectangleProgram rectProg = new RectangleProgram();

    }

}
```

Let's review the important points introduced in this section:

- The preceding application program has exactly one class: `RectangleProgram`.

- The `class RectangleProgram` contains the constructor `RectangleProgram` and the `main` method.

- You created the new `class RectangleProgram` by extending the existing class, `JFrame`. Therefore, `JFrame` is the superclass of `RectangleProgram`, and `RectangleProgram` is a subclass of `JFrame`.

- Whenever there is a superclass-subclass relationship, the subclass inherits all data members and methods of the superclass. The methods `setTitle`, `setSize`, `setVisible`, and `setDefaultCloseOperation` are methods of the `class` `JFrame`, and these methods can be inherited by its subclasses.

The next few sections describe how to create GUI labels, text fields, and buttons, which can all be placed in the content pane of a window. Before you can place GUI components in the content pane, you must learn how to access the content pane.

Getting Access to the Content Pane

If you can visualize **JFrame** as a window, think of the content pane as the inner area of the window (below the title bar and inside the border). The **class JFrame** has the method **getContentPane** that you can use to access the content pane of the window. However, the **class JFrame** does not have the necessary tools to manage the components of the content pane. The components of the content pane are managed by declaring a reference variable of the **Container** type and then using the method **getContentPane** as shown next.

Consider the following statements:

```
Container pane;                          //Line 1
pane = getContentPane();                 //Line 2
```

The statement in Line 1 declares **pane** to be a reference variable of the **Container** type. The statement in Line 2 gets the content pane of the window as a container, that is, the reference variable **pane** now points to the content pane. You can now access the content pane to add GUI components to it by using the reference variable **pane**.

The statements in Lines 1 and 2 can be combined into one statement:

```
Container pane = getContentPane();       //Line 3
```

If you look back at Figure 6-2, you will see that the labels, text areas, and the buttons are laid out, that is, arranged, in 5 rows and 2 columns. To control the layout—where in the content pane to place the GUI components—you set the layout of the content pane. The layout used in Figure 6-2 is called the grid layout. The **class Container** provides the method **setLayout**, as described in Table 6-2, to set the layout of the content pane. To add components such as labels and text fields to the content pane, you use the method **add** of the **class Container**, which is also described in Table 6-2.

Table 6-2   Some Methods of the **class Container**

Method / Description
`public void add(Object obj)` `//Method to add an object to the pane`
`public void setLayout(Object obj)` `//Method to set the layout of the pane`

The **class Container** is contained in the package **java.awt**. To use this **class** in your program, you need to include either the statement

```
import java.awt.*;
```

or

```
import java.awt.Container;
```

As noted earlier, the method `setLayout` is used to set the layout of the content pane, `pane`. To set the layout of the container to a grid, you use the `class GridLayout`. Consider the following statement:

```
pane.setLayout(new GridLayout(5,2));
```

This statement creates an object belonging to the `class GridLayout` and assigns that object as the layout of the content pane, `pane`, by invoking the `setLayout` method. Moreover, this statement sets the layout of the content pane, `pane`, to 5 rows and 2 columns. This will allow you to add 10 components arranged in 5 rows and 2 columns.

If you do not specify a layout, Java will use a default layout. If you specify a layout, you must set the layout before adding any components. Once the layout is set, you can use the method `add` to add components in the pane; this process is described in the next section.

JLabel

Now you will learn how to create labels and add them to the pane. We assume the following statements:

```
Container pane = getContentPane();

pane.setLayout(new GridLayout(4,1));
```

Labels are objects of a particular `class` type. The Java `class` that you use to create labels is `JLabel`. Therefore, to create labels, you instantiate objects of the type `JLabel`. The `class JLabel` is contained in the package `javax.swing`.

Just like a window, there are various attributes associated with a label. For example, every label has a title, width, and a height. The `class JLabel` contains various methods to control the display of labels. Table 6-3 describes some of the methods provided by the `class JLabel`.

Table 6-3 Some Methods Provided by the `class JLabel`

Method / Description/ Example

`public JLabel(String str)`
`//Constructor to create a label with left-aligned text specified`
`//by str`
`//Example: JLabel lengthL;`
`//          lengthL = new JLabel("Enter the length:")`
`//     Creates the label lengthL with the title Enter the length:`

`public JLabel(String str, int align)`
`//Constructor to create label with text specified by str.`
`//     The value of align can be any one of the following:`
`//     SwingConstants.LEFT, SwingConstants.RIGHT,`
`//     SwingConstants.CENTER`
`//Example:`
`//   JLabel lengthL;`
`//   lengthL = new JLabel("Enter the length:",`
`//                   SwingConstants.RIGHT);`
`//   The label lengthL is right aligned.`

6

Table 6-3 Some Methods Provided by the `class JLabel` (continued)

Method / Description/ Example

`public JLabel(String t, Icon icon, int align)`
`//Constructs a JLabel with both text and an icon.`
`//The icon is to the left of text.`

`public JLabel(Icon icon)` `//Constructs a JLabel with an icon.`

 In Table 6-3, `SwingConstants.LEFT`, `SwingConstants.RIGHT`, and `SwingConstants.CENTER` are constants defined in the `class SwingConstants`. They specify whether to set the string describing the label as left-justified, right-justified, or centered.

Consider the statements:

```
JLabel lengthL;
lengthL = new JLabel("Enter the length:",SwingConstants.RIGHT);
```

After the execution of these statements, the label shown in Figure 6-5 is created.

Enter the length:

Figure 6-5 `JLabel` with the text `Enter the length:`

Now consider the following statements:

```
private JLabel lengthL, widthL, areaL, perimeterL;              //Line 1

lengthL =
    new JLabel("Enter the length: ",SwingConstants.RIGHT); //Line 2
widthL =
    new JLabel("Enter the width: ",SwingConstants.RIGHT);  //Line 3
areaL = new JLabel("Area: ",SwingConstants.RIGHT);         //Line 4
perimeterL =
    new JLabel("Perimeter: ",SwingConstants.RIGHT);        //Line 5
```

The statement in Line 1 declares four reference variables, `lengthL`, `widthL`, `areaL`, and `perimeterL`, of the `JLabel` type. The statement in Line 2 instantiates the object `lengthL`, assigns it the title Enter the length:, and sets the title alignment to right-justified. The statements in Lines 3-5 instantiate the objects widthL, areaL, and perimeterL with appropriate titles and text alignment.

Next we add these labels to the pane declared at the beginning of this section. The following statements accomplish this. (Recall from the preceding section that we use the method add to add components to a pane.)

```
pane.add(lengthL);
pane.add(widthL);
pane.add(areaL);
pane.add(perimeterL);
```

Since we have specified a grid layout for the pane with four rows and one column, the label lengthL is added to the first row, the label widthL is added to the second row, and so on.

Now that you know how to add the components to the pane, you can put together the program to create these labels. RectangleProgramTwo builds on the RectangleProgram of the preceding section and, like RectangleProgram, is a subclass of JFrame.

```
//Java program to create a window and place four labels

import javax.swing.*;
import java.awt.*;

public class RectangleProgramTwo extends JFrame
{
    private static final int WIDTH = 400;
    private static final int HEIGHT = 300;

    private JLabel lengthL, widthL, areaL, perimeterL;

    public RectangleProgramTwo()
    {
        setTitle("Area and Perimeter of a Rectangle");

        lengthL =
            new JLabel("Enter the length: ",SwingConstants.RIGHT);
        widthL =
            new JLabel("Enter the width: ",SwingConstants.RIGHT);
        areaL = new JLabel("Area: ",SwingConstants.RIGHT);
        perimeterL =
            new JLabel("Perimeter: ",SwingConstants.RIGHT);

        Container pane  = getContentPane();
        pane.setLayout(new GridLayout(4,1));
```

6

```
        pane.add(lengthL);
        pane.add(widthL);
        pane.add(areaL);
        pane.add(perimeterL);

        setSize(WIDTH, HEIGHT);
        setVisible(true);
        setDefaultCloseOperation(EXIT_ON_CLOSE);
    }

    public static void main( String[] args)
    {
        RectangleProgramTwo rectObject = new RectangleProgramTwo();
    }
}
```

Sample Run: Figure 6-6 shows the sample run.

Figure 6-6   Sample run for `RectangleProgramTwo`

Now you are ready to create and place the text fields and buttons. The good news is that the techniques for creating and placing components such as **JTextField** and **JButton** in a container are similar to the ones used for **JLabel**, and are described in the next two sections.

JTextField

As you may recall, text fields are objects belonging to the `class JTextField`. Therefore, you can create a text field by declaring a reference variable of the type `JTextField` followed by an instantiation of the object.

Table 6-4 describes some of the methods of the `class JTextField`.

Table 6-4 Some Methods of the `class JTextField`

Method / Description
`public JTextField(int columns)` `//Constructor to set the size of the text field`

`public JTextField(String str)`
`//Constructor to initialize the object with the text specified`
`//by str`

`public JTextField(String str, int columns)`
`//Constructor to initialize the object with the text specified`
`//by str`
`//and to set the size of the text field`

`public void setText(String str)`
`//Method to set the text of the text field to string specified`
`//by str`

`public String getText()` `//Method to  return the text contained in text field`

`public void setEditable(Boolean b)`
`//If the value of the Boolean variable b is false, user cannot`
`//type in the text field.`
`//In this case, the text field is used as a tool to display`
`//the result.`

`public void addActionListener(ActionListener obj)` `//Method to register a listener object to a JTextField`

Consider the following statements:

```
private JTextField lengthTF, widthTF, areaTF,
                   perimeterTF;                    //Line 1
lengthTF = new JTextField(10);                     //Line 2
widthTF = new JTextField(10);                      //Line 3
areaTF = new JTextField(10);                       //Line 4
perimeterTF = new JTextField(10);                  //Line 5
```

The statement in Line 1 declares four reference variables, `lengthTF`, `widthTF`, `areaTF`, and `perimeterTF`, of the type `JTextField`. The statement in Line 2 instantiates the object `lengthTF` and sets the width of this text field to 10 characters. That is, this text field can display no more than 10 characters. The meaning of the other statements is similar.

Placing these objects involves using the **add** method of the **class Container** as described in the previous section. The following statements add these components to the container:

```
pane.add(lengthTF);
pane.add(widthTF);
pane.add(areaTF);
pane.add(perimeterTF);
```

The container **pane** now would contain 8 objects—four labels and four text fields. We want to place the object **lengthTF** adjacent to the label **lengthL** in the same row, and use similar placements for the other objects. So we need to expand the grid layout to 4 rows and 2 columns. The following statements create the required grid layout and the necessary objects:

```
pane.setLayout(new GridLayout(4,2));
pane.add(lengthL);
pane.add(lengthTF);
pane.add(widthL);
pane.add(widthTF);
pane.add(areaL);
pane.add(areaTF);
pane.add(perimeterL);
pane.add(perimeterTF);
```

The following program, **RectangleProgramThree**, summarizes our discussion so far:

```java
//Java program to create a window
//and place four labels and four text fields

import javax.swing.*;
import java.awt.*;

public class RectangleProgramThree extends JFrame
{
    private static final int WIDTH = 400;
    private static final int HEIGHT = 300;

    private JLabel lengthL, widthL, areaL, perimeterL;
    private JTextField lengthTF, widthTF, areaTF,
                        perimeterTF;

    public RectangleProgramThree()
    {
        setTitle("Area and Perimeter of a Rectangle");
```

```
    lengthL =
        new JLabel("Enter the length: ",SwingConstants.RIGHT);
    widthL =
        new JLabel("Enter the width: ",SwingConstants.RIGHT);
    areaL =
        new JLabel("Area: ",SwingConstants.RIGHT);
    perimeterL =
        new JLabel("Perimeter: ",SwingConstants.RIGHT);

    lengthTF = new JTextField(10);
    widthTF = new JTextField(10);
    areaTF = new JTextField(10);
    perimeterTF = new JTextField(10);

    Container pane  = getContentPane();
    pane.setLayout(new GridLayout(4,2));

    pane.add(lengthL);
    pane.add(lengthTF);
    pane.add(widthL);
            pane.add(widthTF);
    pane.add(areaL);
    pane.add(areaTF);
    pane.add(perimeterL);
    pane.add(perimeterTF);

    setSize(WIDTH,HEIGHT);
    setVisible(true);
    setDefaultCloseOperation(EXIT_ON_CLOSE);
}

public static void main(String[] args)
{
    RectangleProgramThree rectObject =
                        new RectangleProgramThree();
}
}
```

Sample Run: Figure 6-7 shows the sample run.

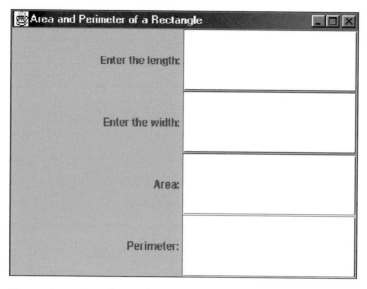

Figure 6-7   Sample run for `RectangleProgramThree`

To complete the design of the user interface, you now learn how to create buttons.

JButton

To create a button, Java provides the **class JButton**. Thus, to create objects belonging to the **class JButton**, we use a technique similar to the one we used to create instances of `JLabel` and `JTextField`. Table 6-5 shows some methods of the **class JButton**.

Table 6-5 Commonly Used Methods of the **class JButton**

Method / Description

`public JButton(Icon ic)`
`//Constructor to initialize the button object with the icon`
`//specified by ic`

`public JButton(String str)`
`//Constructor to initialize the button object to the text specified`
`//by str`

`public JButton(String str, Icon ic)`
`//Constructor to initialize the button object to the text specified`
`//by str and icon specified by ic`

`public void setText(String str)` `//Method to set the text of button to the string specified by str`
`public String getText()` `//Method to return the text contained in button`

Table 6-5 Commonly Used Methods of the `class` `JButton` (continued)

Method / Description

`public void setEditable(boolean b)`
`//If the Boolean value b is false, user cannot type in. In this case,`
`//the text field is used only to display the result.`

`public void addActionListener(ActionListener obj)` `//Method to register a listener object to the button object`

The following three lines will create two buttons, `Calculate` and `Exit`, shown earlier in Figure 6-2.

```
JButton calculateB, exitB;              //Line 1
calculateB = new JButton("Calculate");  //Line 2
exitB = new JButton("Exit");            //Line 3
```

The statement in Line 1 declares `calculateB` and `exitB` to be reference variables of the type `JButton`. The statement in Line 2 instantiates the button object `calculateB` and sets the text for the button to the string `Calculate`. Similarly, the statement in Line 3 instantiates the button object `exitB` and sets the text for `exitB` to the string `Exit`.

The buttons `calculateB` and `exitB` can be placed into the container `pane` by using the method `add`. The following statements add these buttons to the `pane`:

```
pane.add(calculateB);
pane.add(exitB);
```

Now you have two more objects in the container, so you need to modify the `GridLayout` to accommodate 5 rows and 2 columns, and then add all the components. The following statements create the required grid layout and add the labels, text fields, and the buttons to the container `pane`.

```
pane.setLayout(new GridLayout(5,2));//specify the layout
pane.add(lengthL);                   //add the label lengthL
pane.add(lengthTF);                  //add the text field lengthTF
pane.add(widthL);                    //add the label widthL
pane.add(widthTF);                   //add the text field lengthTF
pane.add(areaL);                     //add the label areaL
pane.add(areaTF);                    //add the text field areaTF
pane.add(perimeterL);                //add the label perimeterL
pane.add(perimeterTF);               //add the text field perimeterTF
pane.add(calculateB);                //add the button calculateB
pane.add(exitB);                     //add the button exitB
```

Notice that the preceding `add` statements place components from left to right and from top to bottom.

Handling an Event

You have now learned how to create a window, how to create a container, and how to create labels, text fields, and buttons.

Now that you can create a button, such as `calculateB`, you need to specify how such a button should behave when you click on it. For example, when you click on the button `calculateB`, you want the program to calculate the area and perimeter of the rectangle and display these values in their respective text fields. Similarly, when you click on the button `exitB`, the program should terminate.

When you click on a `JButton` an event is created, known as an **action event**, which sends a message to another object, known as an **action listener**. When the listener receives the message, it performs some action. Sending a message or an event to a listener object simply means that some method in the listener object is invoked with the event as the argument. This invocation happens automatically; you will not see the code corresponding to the method invocation. However, you must specify two things:

- For each `JButton`, you must specify the corresponding listener object. In Java, this is known as **registering** the listener.

- You must define the methods that will be invoked when the event is sent to the listener. Normally, you will write these methods and you will never write the code for invocation.

Java provides various classes to handle different kinds of events. The action event is handled by the `class ActionListener`, which contains only the method `actionPerformed`. In the method `actionPerformed`, you include the code that you want the system to execute when an action event is generated.

The `class ActionListener` that handles the action event is a special type of class called an `interface`. In Java, `interface` is a reserved word. Roughly speaking, an `interface` is a class that contains only the methods headings and each methods heading is terminated with a semicolon. For example, the definition of the `interface ActionListener` containing the method `actionPerformed` is:

```
public interface ActionListener
{
    public void actionPerformed(ActionEvent e);
}
```

Because the method `actionPerformed` does not contain a body, Java does not allow you to instantiate an object of the type `ActionListener`. So how do you register an action listener with the object `calculateB`?

One way this can be done is the following (there are other ways not discussed here): Because you cannot instantiate an object of the type `ActionListener`, first we need to create a class on top of `ActionListener` so that the required object can be instantiated. The class created must provide the necessary code for the method `actionPerformed`.

You will create the **class CalculateButtonHandler** to handle the event generated by clicking the button **calculateB**.

The **class CalculateButtonHandler** is created on top of the **interface ActionListener**. The definition of the **class CalculateButtonHandler** is:

```
private class CalculateButtonHandler implements
                                    ActionListener   //Line 1
{
   public void actionPerformed(ActionEvent e)         //Line 2
   {
      //The code for calculating the area and the perimeter
      //and displaying these quantities goes here
   }
}
```

Notice the following:

- The **class CalculateButtonHandler** starts with the modifier **private**. This is because you want this class to be used only within your **RectangleProgram**.

- This class uses another modifier, **implements**. This is how you build classes on top of classes that are interfaces. Notice that you have not yet provided the code for the method **actionPerformed**. You will do that shortly.

In Java, **implements** is a reserved word.

Next we illustrate how to create a listener object of the type **CalculateButtonHandler**. Consider the following statements:

```
CalculateButtonHandler cbHandler;
cbHandler = new CalculateButtonHandler();   //instantiate the object
```

As described, these statements create the listener object. Having created a listener, you next must associate (or in Java terminology, register) this handler with the corresponding **JButton**. The following line of code registers **cbHandler** as the listener object of **calculateB**:

```
calculateB.addActionListener(cbHandler);
```

The complete definition of the **class CalculateButtonHandler** including the code for the method **actionPerformed** is:

```
private class CalculateButtonHandler implements
                                    ActionListener     //Line 1
{
   public void actionPerformed(ActionEvent e)          //Line 2
   {
      double width, length, area, perimeter;           //Line 3

      length
          = Double.parseDouble(lengthTF.getText());  //Line 4
```

6

```
    width
        = Double.parseDouble(widthTF.getText());    //Line 5
    area = length * width;                           //Line 6
    perimeter = 2 * (length + width);                //Line 7

    areaTF.setText("" + area);                       //Line 8
    perimeterTF.setText("" + perimeter);             //Line 9
    }
}
```

In the preceding program segment, Line 1 declares the **class CalculateButtonHandler** and makes it an action listener by including the phrase **implements ActionListener**. Note that all of this code is just a new class definition. This class has one method and Line 2 is the first statement of that method. Let us look at the statement in Line 4:

```
length = Double.parseDouble(lengthTF.getText());
```

The length of the rectangle is stored in the text field **lengthTF**. We use the method **getText** to retrieve the string from this text field, specifying the length. Now the value of the expression **lengthTF.getText()** is the length, but it is in a string form. So we need to use the method **parseDouble** to convert the length string into an equivalent decimal number. The length is then stored in the variable **length**. The statement in Line 5 works similarly for the width.

The statements in Lines 6 and 7 compute the area and the perimeter, respectively. The statement in Line 8 uses the method **setText** of the **class JTextField** to display the area. Since **setText** requires that the argument be a string, you need to convert the value of the variable **area** into a string. The easiest way to do this is to concatenate the value of **area** to an empty string. Similar conventions apply for the statement in Line 9.

It follows that the method **actionPerformed** displays area and perimeter in corresponding **JTextField**s.

Before creating an action listener for the **JButton exitB**, let us summarize what we've done so far to create and register an action event listener:

1. Created a class that implements the **interface ActionListener**. For example, for the **JButton calculateB** we created the **class CalculateButtonHandler**.

2. Provided the definition of the method **actionPerformed** within the class that you created in Step 1. The method **actionPerformed** contains the code that the program executes when the specific event is generated. For example, when you click on the **JButton calculateB**, the program should calculate and display the area and the perimeter of the rectangle.

3. Created and instantiated an object of the class type created in Step 1. For example, for the **JButton calculateB** we created the object **cbHandler**.

4. Registered the event handler created in Step 3 with the object that generates an action event using the method **addActionListener**. For example, for JButton **calculateB** the following statement registers the object **cbHandler** to listen and register the action event:

```
calculateB.addActionListener(cbHandler);
```

We can now repeat these four steps to create and register the action listener with the JButton **exitB**.

```
private class ExitButtonHandler implements ActionListener
{
    public void actionPerformed(ActionEvent e)
    {
        System.exit(0);
    }
}
```

The following statements create the action listener object for the button **exitB**:

```
ExitButtonHandler ebHandler;
ebHandler = new ExitButtonHandler();
exitB.addActionListener(ebHandler);
```

The **interface ActionListener** is contained in the package **java.awt.event**. Therefore, to use this interface to handle events, your program must include the statement

```
import java.awt.event.*;
```

or

```
import java.awt.event.ActionListener;
```

The complete program to calculate the perimeter and area of a rectangle is:

```
//Given the length and width of a rectangle, this Java
//program determines its area and perimeter.

import javax.swing.*;
import java.awt.*;
import java.awt.event.*;

public class RectangleProgram extends JFrame
{
    private JLabel lengthL, widthL, areaL, perimeterL;

    private JTextField lengthTF, widthTF, areaTF, perimeterTF;

    private JButton calculateB, exitB;

    private CalculateButtonHandler cbHandler;
    private ExitButtonHandler ebHandler;
```

6

```
private static final int WIDTH = 400;
private static final int HEIGHT = 300;

public RectangleProgram()
{
        //Create four labels
    lengthL = new JLabel("Enter the length: ",
                            SwingConstants.RIGHT);
    widthL = new JLabel("Enter the width: ",
                        SwingConstants.RIGHT);
    areaL = new JLabel("Area: ",SwingConstants.RIGHT);
    perimeterL = new JLabel("Perimeter: ",
                            SwingConstants.RIGHT);

        //Create four text fields
    lengthTF = new JTextField(10);
    widthTF = new JTextField(10);
    areaTF = new JTextField(10);
    perimeterTF = new JTextField(10);

        //Create Calculate Button
    calculateB = new JButton("Calculate");
    cbHandler = new CalculateButtonHandler();
    calculateB.addActionListener(cbHandler);

        //Create Exit Button
    exitB = new JButton("Exit");
    ebHandler = new ExitButtonHandler();
    exitB.addActionListener(ebHandler);

        //Set the title of the window
    setTitle("Area and Perimeter of a Rectangle");

        //Get the container
    Container pane = getContentPane();

        //Set the layout
    pane.setLayout(new GridLayout(5,2));

        //Place the components in the pane
    pane.add(lengthL);
    pane.add(lengthTF);
    pane.add(widthL);
    pane.add(widthTF);
    pane.add(areaL);
    pane.add(areaTF);
    pane.add(perimeterL);
    pane.add(perimeterTF);
```

```
        pane.add(calculateB);
        pane.add(exitB);

              //set the size of the window and display it
        setSize(WIDTH,HEIGHT);
        setVisible(true);
        setDefaultCloseOperation(EXIT_ON_CLOSE);
    }

    private class CalculateButtonHandler implements ActionListener
    {
        public void actionPerformed(ActionEvent e)
        {
            double width, length, area, perimeter;

            length = Double.parseDouble(lengthTF.getText());
            width = Double.parseDouble(widthTF.getText());
            area = length * width;
            perimeter = 2 * (length + width);

            areaTF.setText(""+ area);
            perimeterTF.setText(""+ perimeter);
        }
    }

    private class ExitButtonHandler implements ActionListener
    {
        public void actionPerformed(ActionEvent e)
        {
            System.exit(0);
        }
    }

    public static void main(String[] args)
    {
        RectangleProgram rectObject = new RectangleProgram();
    }
}
```

6

Sample Run: Figure 6-8 shows the sample run.

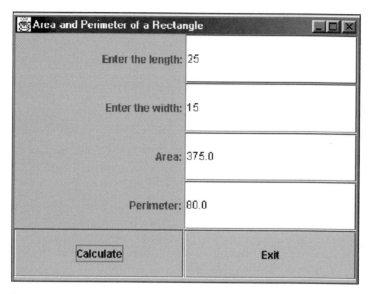

Figure 6-8   Sample run for the final `RectangleProgram`

PROGRAMMING EXAMPLE: TEMPERATURE CONVERSION

Write a program that creates the GUI shown in Figure 6-9, to convert temperature from Fahrenheit to Centigrade and from Centigrade to Fahrenheit.

Figure 6-9   GUI for the temperature conversion program

When the user enters the temperature in the text field adjacent to the label **Temp in Centigrade** and presses the **Enter** key, the program displays the equivalent temperature in the text field adjacent to the label **Temp in Fahrenheit**. Similarly, when the user enters the temperature in Fahrenheit and presses the **Enter** key, the program displays the equivalent temperature in Centigrade.

Input   Temperature in Fahrenheit or Centigrade

Output   Temperature in Centigrade if the input is Fahrenheit; and Temperature in Fahrenheit if the input is Centigrade

Problem Analysis, GUI Design, and Algorithm Design

Suppose that the variable `centigrade` represents the temperature in Centigrade and the variable `fahrenheit` represents the temperature in Fahrenheit. If the user enters the temperature in Fahrenheit, the formula for calculating the equivalent temperature in Centigrade is:

```
centigrade = (5.0 / 9.0) * (fahrenheit - 32)
```

For example, if `fahrenheit` is `98.6`, then:

```
centigrade = 5.0 / 9.0 * (98.6 - 32) = 37.00
```

Similarly, if the user enters the temperature in Centigrade, then the formula for calculating the equivalent temperature in Fahrenheit is:

```
fahrenheit = 9.0 / 5.0 * centigrade + 32
```

For example, if `centigrade` is `20`, then:

```
fahrenheit = 9.0 / 5.0 * 20 + 32 = 68.0
```

The GUI in Figure 6-9 contains a window, a container, two labels, and two text fields. The labels and text fields are placed in the container of the window. As we did in the rectangle program in this chapter, we can create the window by making the application extend the `class JFrame`. To get access to the container, we will use a reference variable of the `Container` type. To create labels, we use objects of the type `JLabel`; to create text fields, we use objects of the type `JTextField`. Suppose that we have the following declarations:

```
JLabel centigradeLabel;        //label Centigrade
JLabel fahrenheitLabel;        //label Fahrenheit

JTextField centigradeTF;       //text field Centigrade
JTextField fahrenheitTF;       //text field Fahrenheit
```

When the user enters the temperature in the text field `centigradeTF` and presses the `Enter` key, we want the program to show the equivalent temperature in the text field `fahrenheitTF` and vice versa.

Recall that when you click on a `JButton`, it generates an action event. Moreover, the action event is handled by the method `actionPerformed` of the `interface ActionListener`. Similarly, when you press the `Enter` key in a text field, it generates an action event. Therefore, we can register an action event listener with the text fields `centigradeTF` and `fahrenheitTF` to take appropriate action.

Based on this analysis and the GUI shown in Figure 6-9, you can design an event-driven algorithm as follows:

  1. Have a listener in each text field.
  2. Register an event handler with each text field.

3. Let the event handler registered with a text field do the following:
   a. Get the data from the text field once the user presses the ENTER key.
   b. Apply the corresponding formula to perform the conversion.
   c. Set the value of the other text field.

The process of adding an event listener and then registering the event listener to a text field is similar to the process we used to register an event listener to a JButton earlier in the chapter. (This process will be described later in this programming example.)

Variables, Objects, and Named Constants

The input to the program is either the temperature in Centigrade or the temperature in Fahrenheit. If the input is a value for Centigrade, then the program calculates the equivalent temperature in Fahrenheit. Similarly, if the input is a value for Fahrenheit, then the program calculates the equivalent temperature in Centigrade. Therefore, the program needs the following variables:

```
double centigrade;            //variable to hold Centigrade
double fahrenheit;            //variable to hold Fahrenheit
```

Notice that these variables are needed in each event handler.

The formulas to convert temperature from Fahrenheit to Centigrade and vice versa use the special values 32, 9.0/5.0, and 5.0/9.0, which we will declare as named constants as follows:

```
private static final double FTOC = 5.0/9.0;
private static final double CTOF = 9.0/5.0;
private static final int OFFSET = 32;
```

As in the GUI, you need two labels—one to label the text field corresponding to the Centigrade value and another to label the text field corresponding to the Fahrenheit value. Therefore, the following statements are needed:

```
JLabel centigradeLabel;              //label Centigrade
JLabel fahrenheitLabel;              //label Fahrenheit

centigradeLabel = new JLabel("Temp in Centigrade: ",
                SwingConstants.RIGHT);//object instantiation
fahrenheitLabel = new JLabel("Temp in Fahrenheit: ",
                SwingConstants.RIGHT);//object instantiation
```

You also need two JTextField objects. The necessary Java code is:

```
JTextField centigradeTF;                //text field Centigrade
JTextField  fahrenheitTF;               //text field Fahrenheit

centigradeTF = new JTextField(7);       //object instantiation
fahrenheitTF = new JTextField(7);       //object instantiation
```

Now you need a window to display the labels and the text fields. Since a window is an object of the type **JFrame**, the class containing the application program that we create will extend the definition of the **class JFrame**. We will set the width of the window to 500 pixels and the height to 50 pixels. We'll call the class containing the application program **TempConversion**. The application will look like this:

```java
//Java program to convert temperature from Centigrade to
//Fahrenheit and vice versa.

import javax.swing.*;

public class TempConversion extends JFrame
{
    private static final int WIDTH = 500;
    private static final int HEIGHT = 50;

    private static final double FTOC = 5.0/9.0;
    private static final double CTOF = 9.0/5.0;
    private static final int OFFSET = 32;

    public TempConversion()
    {
        setTitle("Temperature Conversion");
        setSize(WIDTH,HEIGHT);
        setVisible(true);
        setDefaultCloseOperation(EXIT_ON_CLOSE);
    }

    public static void main( String[] args)
    {
        TempConversion tempConv = new TempConversion();
    }
}
```

Now you need to access the container content pane to place the GUI components and set the required layout of the pane. Therefore, as before, you need the following statements:

```java
Container c = getContentPane();    //get the Container
c.setLayout(new GridLayout(1,4));  //create a new layout

c.add(centigradeLabel);        //add the label centigradeLabel
                               //to the container
c.add(centigradeTF);           //add the text field centigradeTF
                               //to the container
c.add(fahrenheitLabel);        //add the label fahrenheitLabel
                               //to the container
c.add(fahrenheitTF);           //add the text field fahrenheitTF
                               //to the container
```

You want your program to respond to the events generated by `JTextFields`. Just as when you click on a `JButton` an action event is generated, when you press the `Enter` key in a `JTextField`, it generates an action event. Therefore, to register event listeners with `JTextFields`, we use the four steps outlined in the section Handling an Event earlier in this chapter: (1) create a class that implements the `interface ActionListener`; (2) provide the definition of the method `actionPerformed` within the class that you created in Step 1; (3) create and instantiate an object of the class created in Step 1; and (4) register the event handler created in Step 3 with the object that generates an action event using the method `addActionListener`.

Next we create and register an action listener with the `JTextField centigradeTF`.

First we create the `class CentHandler`, implementing the `interface ActionListener`. Then we provide the definition of the method `actionPerformed` of the `class CentHandler`. When the user enters the temperature in the `JTextField centigradeTF` and presses the `Enter` key, the program needs to calculate and display the equivalent temperature in the `JTextField fahrenheitTF`. The necessary code is placed within the body of the method `actionPerformed`.

We now describe the steps of the method `actionPerformed`. The temperature in Centigrade is contained in the `JTextField centigradeTF`. We use the method `getText` of the `class JTextField` to retrieve the temperature in `centigradeTF`. However, the value returned by the method `getText` is in string form, so we use the method `parseDouble` of the `class Double` to convert the numeric string into a decimal value. It follows that we need a variable of the type `double`, say `centigrade`, to store the temperature in Centigrade. We accomplish this with the following statement:

```
centigrade = Double.parseDouble(centigradeTF.getText());
```

We also need a variable of the type `double`, say `fahrenheit`, to store the equivalent temperature in Fahrenheit. Since we want to display the temperature to two decimal places, we need to create an appropriate object of the type `DecimalFormat`.

We can now write the definition of the `class CentHandler` as follows:

```
private class CentHandler implements ActionListener
{
    public void actionPerformed(ActionEvent e)
    {

        double centigrade, fahrenheit;
        DecimalFormat twoDigits = new DecimalFormat("0.00");

        centigrade =
            Double.parseDouble(centigradeTF.getText());
        fahrenheit =  centigrade * CTOF + OFFSET;
        fahrenheitTF.setText(""+twoDigits.format(fahrenheit));
    }
}
```

We can now create an object of the type `CentHandler` as follows:

```
CentHandler centigradeHandler;
centigradeHandler = new CentHandler();
```

Having created a listener, you have to associate this handler with the corresponding `JTextField centigradeTF`; this is accomplished by the following code:

```
centigradeTF.addActionListener(centigradeHandler);
```

Similarly, we can create and register an action listener with the text field `fahrenheitTF`. The necessary code is as follows:

```
private class FahrHandler implements ActionListener
{
    public void actionPerformed(ActionEvent e)
    {
        double centigrade, fahrenheit;
        DecimalFormat twoDigits = new DecimalFormat("0.00");

        fahrenheit =
                 Double.parseDouble(fahrenheitTF.getText());
        centigrade = (fahrenheit – OFFSET)/CTOF;
        centigradeTF.setText(""+twoDigits.format(centigrade));
    }
}

FahrHandler fahrenheitHandler;
fahrenheitHandler = new FahrHandler(); //instantiate the object

fahrenheitTF.addActionListener(fahrenheitHandler);
                                   //add action listener
```

Now that we have created the necessary GUI components and the programming code, in the next section we put everything together to create the complete program.

Putting It Together

You can start with the window creation program and then add all the components, handlers, and classes developed. You also need the necessary **import** statements. In this case they are:

```
import java.awt.*;             //due to the class Container
import java.awt.event.*;       //due to events
import javax.swing.*;          //due to JLabel and JTextField
import java.text.DecimalFormat; //to format decimal number
```

Thus, you have the following Java program:

```
//Java program to convert temperature between Centigrade and
//Fahrenheit.
```

```java
import java.awt.*;
import java.awt.event.*;
import javax.swing.*;
import java.text.DecimalFormat;

public class TempConversion extends JFrame
{
    private JLabel centigradeLabel;
    private JLabel  fahrenheitLabel;
    private JTextField centigradeTF;
    private JTextField  fahrenheitTF;
    private CentHandler centigradeHandler;
    private FahrHandler fahrenheitHandler;

    private static final int WIDTH = 500;
    private static final int HEIGHT = 50;
    private static final double FTOC = 5.0/9.0;
    private static final double CTOF = 9.0/5.0;
    private static final int OFFSET = 32;

    public TempConversion()
    {
        setTitle("Temperature Conversion");
        Container c = getContentPane();
        c.setLayout(new GridLayout(1,4));

        centigradeLabel = new JLabel("Temp in Centigrade: ",
                                    SwingConstants.RIGHT);
        fahrenheitLabel = new JLabel("Temp in Fahrenheit: ",
                                    SwingConstants.RIGHT);

        centigradeTF = new JTextField(7);
        fahrenheitTF = new JTextField(7);

        c.add(centigradeLabel);
        c.add(centigradeTF);
        c.add(fahrenheitLabel);
        c.add(fahrenheitTF);

        centigradeHandler = new CentHandler();
        fahrenheitHandler = new FahrHandler();

        centigradeTF.addActionListener(centigradeHandler);
        fahrenheitTF.addActionListener(fahrenheitHandler);

        setSize(WIDTH,HEIGHT);
        setVisible(true);
```

```java
        setDefaultCloseOperation(EXIT_ON_CLOSE);
    }

    private class CentHandler implements ActionListener
    {
        public void actionPerformed(ActionEvent e)
        {
            double centigrade, fahrenheit;
            DecimalFormat twoDigits = new DecimalFormat("0.00");

            centigrade =
                    Double.parseDouble(centigradeTF.getText());

            fahrenheit =  centigrade * CTOF + OFFSET;
            fahrenheitTF.setText(""+ twoDigits.format(fahrenheit));
        }
    }

    private class FahrHandler implements ActionListener
    {
      public void actionPerformed(ActionEvent e)
      {
        double centigrade, fahrenheit;
        DecimalFormat twoDigits = new DecimalFormat("0.00");

        fahrenheit =
                Double.parseDouble(fahrenheitTF.getText());

        centigrade = (fahrenheit - OFFSET) * FTOC;
        centigradeTF.setText(""+ twoDigits.format(centigrade));
      }
    }

    public static void main( String[] args)
    {
        TempConversion tempConv = new TempConversion();
    }
}
```

Sample Run: Figure 6-10 shows the display after the user typed **98.6** and pressed the **Enter** key in the text field labeled **Temp in Fahrenheit**.

Figure 6-10   Sample run for **TempConversion**

OBJECT-ORIENTED DESIGN

In the preceding sections you came across various GUI components such as labels, buttons, text fields, and windows. To use these GUI components, you learned about classes such as `JFrame`, `JLabel`, `JTextField`, and `JButton`. Recall that one of the buttons we created was `Calculate`. To create this button, we declared and instantiated an object of the type `JButton`. We have stressed several times that objects are instances of a particular class.

In this section, we delve a little deeper into the general concept of objects and how they are used in object-oriented design (OOD). OOD is a major field of study in its own right; most likely there are courses in your university on the topic. This section by no means presents an in-depth treatise on OOD. Rather, we review its general concepts and give a simplified methodology for using the OOD approach to problem solving.

Since the beginning of this chapter you have been using objects belonging to various classes such as `JFrame`, `JLabel`, `JTextField`, `JButton`, and `String`. In fact, in your daily life you use objects such as a VCR, CD player, and so on without even realizing how they might be conceptualized as objects or classes. For example, regarding a VCR, the following facts are obvious:

- In order to use a VCR, you do not need to know how the VCR is made. In other words, you do not need to know the internal parts of a VCR or how they work. These are hidden from you.

- In order to use a VCR, you need to know the functions of various buttons and how to use them.

- Once you know how to use a VCR, you can use it either as a stand-alone device or you can combine it with other devices to create an entertainment system.

- You cannot modify the functions of a VCR. The Record button will always function as a Record button.

Now think about any Java objects, such as labels, buttons, and strings, that you have encountered. They also possess the properties mentioned above: You can use the objects and their methods, but you don't need to know how they work.

The aim of OOD is to build software from components called classes so that if someone wants to use a class, all they need to know is the various methods provided by that class.

Recall that in OOD, an object combines data and operations on that data in a single unit, a feature called **encapsulation**. In OOD, we first identify the object, then identify the relevant data, and then identify operations needed to manipulate the object.

For example, the relevant data for a `String` object is the actual string and the length of the string, that is, the number of characters in the string. Every `String` object must have memory space to store the relevant data, that is, the string and its length. Next we must identify the type of operations performed on a string. Some of the operations on a string might be to replace a particular character of a string, extract part of a string, change a string from upper-case to lowercase, and so on. The **class String** provides the necessary operations to be performed on a string.

As another example of how an object contains both data and operations on that data, con-sider objects of the type **JButton**. Since every button has a label, which is a string, every button must have memory space to store its label. Some of the operations on a button that you have encountered are to set the label of the button and add a listener object to a button. Other operations that can be performed on a button are to set its size and location. These operations are the methods of a class. Thus the **class JButton** provides methods to set a button's size and location.

A Simplified OOD Methodology

Now that you have an overview of objects and the essential components of OOD, you may be eager to learn how to solve a particular problem using OOD methodology. The best way to learn is by practice. A simplified OOD methodology can be expressed in the following steps:

1. Write down a detailed description of the problem.

2. Identify all (relevant) nouns and verbs.

3. From the list of nouns, select objects. Identify data components of each object.

4. From the list of verbs, select the operations.

In Step 3, after identifying objects or classes, usually you will realize that several objects func-tion in the same way. That is, they have the same data components and same operations. In other words, they will lead to the construction of the same class.

Remember that objects are nothing but instances of a particular class. Therefore, in order to create objects you will have to learn how to create classes. In other words, in order to create objects you first need to create classes; to know what type of classes to create, you need to know what an object stores and what operations are needed to manipulate an object's data. You can see that objects and classes are closely related. Because an object consists of data and operations on data in a single unit, in Java we use the mechanism of classes to combine data and its operations in a single unit. In OOD methodology, we therefore identify classes, data members of classes, and operations. In Java, data members are also known as **fields**.

In the remainder of this chapter, we give various examples to illustrate how objects, data components of objects, and operations of data are identified. In these examples, nouns (objects) are in bold type, and verbs (operations) are in italics.

Example 6-2

Consider the problem presented in Example 6-1. In simple terms, the problem can be stated as follows:

"Write a program to *input* the **length** and **width** of a **rectangle** and *calculate* and *print* the **perimeter** and **area** of the **rectangle**."

Step 1: Identify all nouns.

Length

Width

Rectangle

Perimeter

Area

Step 2: Identify class(es).

Considering all five nouns, it is clear that:

- Perimeter is the perimeter of a rectangle.

- Area is the area of a rectangle.

- Length is the length of a rectangle.

- Width is the width of a rectangle.

Notice that four of the five nouns are related to the fifth one, namely, `rectangle`. Therefore, choose `Rectangle` as a class. From the `class Rectangle`, you can instantiate rectangles of various dimensions. The `class Rectangle` can be graphically represented as in Figure 6-11.

Figure 6-11 `class Rectangle`

Step 3: Identify data members for each of the classes.

In this step, you evaluate the remaining nouns and determine the information essential to fully describe each class. Therefore, consider each noun—perimeter, area, length, and width—and ask: "Is each of these nouns essential for describing the rectangle?"

- Perimeter is not needed, as it can be computed from length and width. Perimeter is not a data member.

- Area is not needed, as it can be computed from length and width. Area is not a data member.

■ Length is required. Length is a data member.

■ Width is required. Width is a data member.

Having made these choices, the **class Rectangle** can be represented with data members, as shown in Figure 6-12.

Figure 6-12   **class Rectangle** with data members

Step 4: Identify operations for each of the classes.

Many operations for a class or an object can be determined by looking at the list of verbs. Let us consider the verbs *input, calculate,* and *print.* The possible operations on a rectangle object are *input* length and width, *calculate* perimeter and area, and *print* the perimeter and area. In this step, we focus on the functionalities of the class(es) involved. By carefully reading the problem statement, you may conclude that you need at least the following operations:

■ **setLength:** Set the length of the rectangle.

■ **setWidth:** Set the width of the rectangle.

■ **computePerimeter:** Calculate the perimeter of the rectangle.

■ **computeArea:** Calculate the area of the rectangle.

■ **print:** Print the area and perimeter of the rectangle.

It is customary to include operations to retrieve the values of the data members of an object. Therefore, you also need the following operations:

■ **getLength:** Retrieve the length of the rectangle.

■ **getWidth:** Retrieve the width of the rectangle.

Figure 6-13 shows the **class Rectangle** with data members and operations.

Figure 6-13 class Rectangle with data members and operations

With these steps completed, you can design an algorithm for each operation of an object (class) and implement each algorithm in Java.

Example 6-3

Consider the following problem:

A **place** to buy **candy** is from a **candy machine**. A new candy machine is bought for the **gym**, but it is not working properly. The candy machine has four **dispensers** to hold and release **items** sold by the candy machine and a **cash register**. The machine sells four products—**candies, chips, gum**, and **cookies**—each stored in a separate dispenser. You have been asked to write a program for this candy machine so that it can be put into operation.

The program should do the following:

- *Show* the **customer** the different **products** sold by the **candy machine**.
- Let the **customer** *make* the selection.
- *Show* the **customer** the **cost of the item** selected.
- *Accept* **money** from the **customer**.
- *Return* **change**.
- *Release* the **item**, that is, *make* the sale.

The OOD solution of this problem proceeds as follows:

Step 1: Identify all nouns.

- place
- candy
- candy machine

- dispenser

- items

- cash register

- gym

- chips

- gum

- cookies

- customer

- products

- cost of the item

- money

- change

In this description of the problem, products stand for items such as candy, chips, gum, and cookies. In fact, the actual product in the machine is not that important. What *is* important is to note that there are four dispensers, each capable of dispensing one product. Further, there is one cash register. Thus, the candy machine consists of four dispensers and one cash register. Graphically, this can be represented as in Figure 6-14.

Figure 6-14   CandyMachine and its components

In Figure 6-14, the number 4 on top of the box `Dispenser` indicates that there are 4 dispensers in the candy machine. Similarly, the number 1 on top of the box `CashRegister` indicates that the candy machine has 1 cash register.

Step 2: Identify class(es).

You can see that the program you are about to write is supposed to deal with dispensers and cash registers. That is, the main objects are four dispensers and a cash register. Because all dispensers are of the same type, you need to create a class, say `Dispenser`, to create dispensers. Similarly, you need to create a class, say `CashRegister`, to create a cash register. We will create the `class CandyMachine` containing the four dispensers, a cash register, and the application program.

Step 3: Identify data members for each of the class(es).

Dispenser To make the sale, there has to be at least one item on hand and the customer must know the cost of the product. Therefore, the data members of a dispenser are:

- Product cost

- Number of items in the dispenser

Cash Register The cash register accepts money and returns change. Therefore, the cash register has only one data member, which we call `cashOnHand`.

Candy Machine The `class CandyMachine` has four dispensers and a cash register. You can name the four dispensers by the items they store. Therefore, the candy machine has five data members—four dispensers and a cash register.

Step 4: Identify operations for each of the objects (classes).

The relevant verbs are *show* (selections), *make* (selections), *show* (cost), *accept* (money), *return* (change), and *make* (sale).

The verbs *show* (selections) and *make* (selections) relate to the candy machine. The verbs *show* (cost) and *make* (sale) relate to the dispenser. Similarly, the verbs *accept* (money) and *return* (change) relate to the cash register.

Dispenser The verb *show* (cost) applies to either printing or retrieving the value of the data member `cost`. The verb *make* (sale) applies to reduce the number of items in the dispenser by 1. Of course, the dispenser has to be nonempty. You must also provide an operation to set the cost and the number of items in the dispenser. Thus, the operations for a dispenser object are:

- `getCost`: Retrieve the cost of the item.

- `makeSale`: Reduce the number of items in the dispenser by 1.

- `setCost`: Set the cost of the product.

- `setNumberOfProducts`: Set the number of items in the dispenser.

Cash Register The verb *accept* (money) applies to updating the money in the cash register by adding the money deposited by the customer. Similarly, the verb *return* (change) applies to reducing the money in the cash register by reducing the amount to be returned to the customer. You also need to (initially) set the money in the cash register and also retrieve the money from the cash register. Thus, the possible operations on a cash register are:

- `acceptAmount`: Update the amount in the cash register.

- `returnChange`: Return change.

- `getCashOnHand`: Retrieve the amount in the cash register.

- `setCashOnHand`: Set the amount in the cash register.

Candy Machine   The verbs *show* (selection) and *make* (selection) apply to the candy machine. Thus, the two possible operations are:

- `showSelection`: Show the number of products sold by the candy machine.

- `makeSelection`: Allow the customer to select the product.

The result of the OOD for this problem is shown in Figure 6-15.

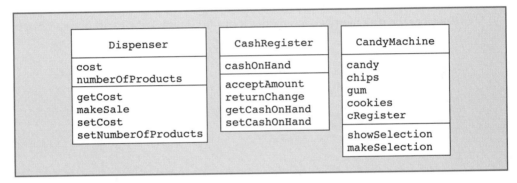

Figure 6-15   Classes `Dispenser`, `CashRegister`, `CandyMachine`, and their members

IMPLEMENTING CLASSES AND OPERATIONS

From the preceding examples, it is clear that once the relevant classes, data members of each class, and relevant operations for each class are identified, the next step is to implement these things in Java. Since objects are nothing but instances of classes, we need to learn how to implement classes in Java. Implementing data members, that is, fields, of classes, is simple, as you need variables to store data.

What about operations? In Java, to implement operations we write algorithms. Since there is usually more than one operation on an object, each algorithm is implemented with the help of Java's methods. In Chapter 3 we briefly introduced methods and described some predefined methods. However, Java does not provide all the methods that you will ever need. Therefore, to learn how to design and implement classes, you first must learn how to construct and implement your own methods. Since methods are an essential part of Java (or any programming language), Chapter 7 is devoted to teaching you how to create methods.

The class IntClass

Chapter 3 showed you how to use certain mathematical functions and how to pass numbers as parameters. In this chapter, we also passed objects as parameters to methods such as adding a button and labels to a container and registering a listener to a button and a text field. You can also pass `String` objects and `Integer` objects as parameters. Java provides the classes `Integer`, `Double`, `Character`, `Long`, and `Float` so that values of primitive data types can be treated as objects. These classes are called **wrappers**. They wrap primitive type values. However, these classes have limitations. You can create objects of the type, say `Integer`, to store `int` values, but (as stated in Chapter 3) you cannot change the value stored in the objects. Parameter passing, as you will see, is a fundamental concept in any programming language. Therefore, we have created the classes `IntClass` and `DoubleClass`, which are similar to the classes `Integer` and `Double`, respectively. You can create objects of the type `IntClass` and/or `DoubleClass`, store, and/or change values of the objects. Table 6-6 describes the data member and methods of the `class IntClass` (see also Appendix D).

Table 6-6 The class IntClass

data member: int x; //variable to store the number

public IntClass()
//constructor
//When the object is instantiated, the value of x is initialized
//to 0.

public IntClass(int num)
//constructor
//When the object is instantiated, the value of x is initialized
//to num.

public void setNum(int num)
//Method to set the data member x
//The value of num is copied into x

public int getNum()
//Method to retrieve the value of x
//The value of x is returned

public void addToNum(int num)
//Method to update the value of x by adding the value of num
//x = x + num;

public void multiplyToNum(int num)
//Method to update the value of x by multiplying by the value
//of num
//x = x * num;

public int compareTo(int num)
//Method to compare the value of x with the value of num
//Returns a value < 0 if x < num
//Returns 0 if x == num
//Returns a value > 0 if x > num

Table 6-6 The class IntClass (continued)

```
public boolean equals(int num)
//Method to compare x with num for equality
//Returns true if x == num; otherwise it returns false
```

```
public String toString()
//Method to return the value of x as a string
```

Consider the following statements:

```
IntClass firstNum = new IntClass();        //Line 1
IntClass secondNum = new IntClass(5);      //Line 2
int num;                                   //Line 3
```

The statement in Line 1 creates the object firstNum and initializes it to 0. The statement in Line 2 creates the object secondNum and initializes it to 5. The statement in Line 3 declares num to be an int variable. Now consider the following statements:

```
firstNum.setNum(24);                       //Line 4
secondNum.addToNum(6);                     //Line 5
num = firstNum.getNum();                   //Line 6
```

The statement in Line 4 sets the value of firstNum (in fact, the value of the data member x of firstNum) to 24. The statement in Line 5 updated the value of secondNum to 11 (the previous value 5 is update by adding 6 to it). The statement in Line 6 retrieves the value of the object firstNum (the value of the data member x), and assigns it to num. After this statement executes, the value of num is 24.

The following statements output the values of firstNum and secondNum (in fact, the values of their data members):

```
System.out.println("firstNum = " + firstNum);
System.out.println("secondNum = " + secondNum);
```

 The class DoubleClass is similar to the class IntClass. In other words, the class DoubleClass has one data member of the type double and similar methods with the same name. (See Appendix D.)

QUICK REVIEW

1. GUI stands for graphical user interface.

2. Every GUI program requires a window.

3. Various components are added to the content pane of the window and not to the window itself.

4. You must create a layout before you add a component to the content pane.

5. Pixel stands for picture element. Windows are measured in pixels of height and width.

6. `JFrame` is a class and the GUI component `window` can be created as an instance of `JFrame`.

7. `JLabel` is used to label other GUI components as well as to display information to the user.

8. A `JTextField` can be used both for input and for output.

9. A `JButton` generates an event.

10. An event handler is a Java method that determines the action to be performed as the event happens.

11. When you click on a button, an action event is created and sent to another object known as an action listener.

12. An action listener must have a method called `actionPerformed`.

13. A `class` is a collection of data members and methods associated with those data members.

14. OOD starts with a problem statement and attempts to identify the classes required by identifying nouns appearing in the problem statement.

15. Methods of a class are identified with the help of verbs appearing in the problem specification.

EXERCISES

1. Mark the following statements as true or false.

   a. Every window has width and height.

   b. In Java, `JFrame` is a class.

   c. To display the window you need not invoke a method such as `setVisible.`

   d. In Java, the reserved word `extends` allows you to create a new class from an existing one.

   e. The window you see displayed on your screen is a class.

   f. Labels are used to display the output of a program.

   g. Every GUI component you need has to be created and added to a container.

   h. In Java, `implements` is a keyword.

   i. Clicking a button is an example of an action event.

   j. In a problem statement, every verb is a possible class.

   k. In a problem statement, every noun is a possible method.

   l. In order to use an object, you must know how it is implemented.

2. Name some commonly used GUI components and their uses.

3. Name a GUI component that can be used both for input and for output.

4. Name two input GUI components.

5. Why do you need labels in a GUI program?

6. Why would you prefer a GUI program over a non-GUI version?

7. What are the advantages of problem analysis, GUI design, and algorithm design over directly writing a program?

8. Modify the temperature conversion program to convert centimeters to inches, and vice versa.

9. Modify the program to compute the area and perimeter of a rectangle so that your new program will compute the sum and product of two numbers.

10. Fill in the blanks in each of the following:

a. A(n) _____ places GUI components in a container.

b. Clicking a button is a(n) _____.

c. The method _____ is invoked when a button is pressed and a(n) _____ is registered to handle the event.

d. _____ operator is needed to instantiate an object.

e. A class has two types of members: _____ and _____.

f. To create a window, you extend the _____ class.

g. Every GUI program is a(n) _____ program.

h. The method _____ gets the string in the `JTextField` and the method _____ changes the string displayed in a `JTextField`.

i. If `Student` is a class and you create a new class `GradStudent` by extending `Student`, then `Student` is a(n) _____ and `GradStudent` is a(n) _____.

j. Event and event listener classes are contained in the package _____.

k. The unit of measure of length in a window is _____.

11. Write necessary statements to create the following GUI components:

a. A `JLabel` with text the string `"Enter number of courses"`

b. A `JButton` with text the string `"Run"`

c. A `JTextField` that can display 15 characters

d. A window with the title `"Welcome Home!"`

e. A window with a width of 200 pixels and a height of 400 pixels

f. A `JTextField` that displays the string `"Apple tree"`

12. Correct the syntax errors in the following program and add additional statements necessary to make the program work:

```java
import javax.jswing.*;

public class ROne extends JFrame
{
        static private final int WIDTH = 400;
        static private final int HEIGHT = 300;

        public RectangleProgramOne()
        {
                setTitle("Welcome");
                setSize(WIDTH,HEIGHT);
                SetVisible(true);
                setDefaultCloseOperation(EXIT_ON_CLOSE);
        }

        public static void main( String args[] )
        {
                ROne r1 = r1();
        }
}
```

13. Correct the syntax errors in the following program:

```java
public class RTwo extends JFrame
{
        public RTwoProgram()
        {
           private JLabel length, width, area;

           setTitle("Good day Area");

           length =   JLabel("Enter the length);
           width = JLabel("Enter the width);
           area = JLabel("Area: ");
           containerPane  = ContentPane();
           pane.setLayout(GridLayout(4,1));
           setSize(WIDTH,HEIGHT);
           setVisible();
           setDefaultCloseOperation(EXIT_ON_CLOSE);
        }

        public static void main( String args[] )
        {
                RTwoProgram R2 = new RTwoProgram ();
        }
}
```

14. Consider a common VCR. What are the methods of a VCR?

15. What are the methods of an ATM?

16. Do an OOD analysis of the following problem: Write a program to input the dimensions of a cylinder, and calculate and print the surface area and volume.

17. Lead County Credit Union (LCCU) has recently upgraded its software systems to an OOD design. List at least five classes that you think should be included in this design. For each class, identify some of the data members and methods.

18. Your local public library wants to design new software to keep track of patrons, books, and lending activity. List at least three classes you think should be in the design. For each class, identify some data members and methods.

19. The Custom Consulting Company (CCC) places temporary computer professionals in companies that request such employees. CCC's business can be explained as follows:

CCC keeps a list of professionals willing to work or currently working on a temporary assignment. A professional may have up to three qualifications, including programmer, senior programmer, analyst, tester, designer, and so on. A company always requests a professional with a single specific qualification. CCC keeps a list of all its clients (that is, a list of other companies) and their current needs. If CCC can find a match, a professional with the required qualification is assigned to a specific opening at one of CCC's clients.

Identify at least five classes and, for each class, list possible data members and methods.

6

PROGRAMMING EXERCISES

1. Design a GUI program to find the weighted average of four test scores. The four test scores and their respective weights are given in the following format:

```
testscore1 weight1
...
```

For example, the sample data is as follows:

```
75 0.20
95 0.35
85 0.15
65 0.30
```

The user is supposed to enter the data and press a Calculate button. The program must display the weighted average.

2. Write a GUI program that converts seconds to years, weeks, days, hours, and minutes. For this problem, assume 1 year is 365 days.

3. Design and implement a GUI program to compare two strings and display the larger one.

4. Write a GUI program to convert a character to a corresponding integer, and vice versa.

5. Write a GUI program to convert all letters in a string to uppercase letters. For example, `Alb34ert` will be converted to `ALB34ERT`.

6. Write a GUI program to convert all lowercase letters in a string to uppercase letters, and vice versa. For example, `Alb34eRt` will be converted to `aLB34ErT`.

7. Write a GUI program to compute the amount of a certificate of deposit on maturity. The sample data are as follows:

```
Amount deposited: 80000.00
Years: 15
Interest rate: 7.75
```

Hint: To solve this problem, compute `80000.00 (1 + 7.75 / 100)`^{15}.

8. Write a GUI program that will accept three (integer) input values, say `x`, `y`, and `z`, and then verify whether or not `x * x + y * y = z * z`.

9. Design and implement a GUI program to convert a positive number given in one base to another base. For this problem, assume that both bases are less than or equal to 10. Consider the sample data:

```
number = 2010, base = 3 and new base = 4.
```

In this case, first convert `2010` in base `3` into the equivalent number in base `10` as follows:

$$2 * 3^3 + 0 * 3^2 + 1 * 3 + 0 \doteq 54 + 0 + 3 + 0 \ = 57$$

To convert `57` to base `4`, you need to find the remainders obtained by dividing by `4`, as shown in the following:

```
57 % 4 = 1, quotient = 14
14 % 4 = 2, quotient = 3
3 % 4 = 3, quotient = 0.
```

Therefore, `57` in base `4` is `321`.

7

USER-DEFINED METHODS

In Chapter 2, you learned that a Java application program is a collection of classes; and that a class is a collection of methods and data members. One such method is `main`. The programs in Chapters 2 through 5 use only the method `main`; all programming instructions are packed into one method. This technique, however, is good only for short programs. For large programs, it is not practical (although it is possible) to put the entire programming instructions into one method, as you will soon discover. You must learn to break the problem into manageable pieces. This chapter first discusses previously defined methods and then discusses user–defined methods.

Let's imagine an automobile factory. When an automobile is manufactured, it is not made from basic raw materials; it is put together from previously manufactured parts. Some parts are made by the company itself, others are manufactured by different companies.

Methods in Java are like the automobile parts; they are building blocks. Methods are used to divide complicated programs into manageable pieces. There are **predefined methods**, methods that are already written and provided by Java; and there are **user-defined methods**, methods that you create.

Using methods has several advantages:

- While working on one method, you can focus on just that part of the program and construct it, debug it, and perfect it.

- Different people can work on different methods simultaneously.

- If a method is needed in more than one place in a program, or in different programs, you can write it once and use it many times.

- Using methods greatly enhances the program's readability because it reduces the complexity of the method `main`.

Methods are often called *modules*. They are like miniature programs; you can put them together to form a larger program. When user-defined methods are discussed, you will see that this is the case. This ability is less apparent with predefined methods because their programming code is not available to us. However, since predefined methods are already written for us, you will learn these first so that you can use them when needed. To use a predefined method in your programs, you need to know only how to use it.

PREDEFINED METHODS

Before formally discussing Java's predefined methods, let's review a concept from a college algebra course. In algebra, a function can be considered a rule or correspondence between values, called the function's arguments, and the unique value of the function associated with the arguments. Thus, if $f(x) = 2x + 5$, then $f(1) = 7$, $f(2) = 9$, and $f(3) = 11$, where 1, 2, and 3 are arguments of f, and 7, 9, and 11 are the corresponding values of the function f.

In Java, the concept of a method, predefined or user-defined, is similar to that of a function in an algebra course. For example, every method has a name and depending on the values specified by the user it does some computation. This section discusses various predefined methods.

Some of the predefined mathematical methods are `pow(x, y)` and `sqrt(x)`.

The *power* method, `pow(x, y)`, calculates x^y; that is, the value of `pow(x, y)` = x^y. For example, `pow(2, 3)` = `8.0` and `pow(2.5,3)` = `15.625`. Since the value of `pow(x, y)` is of the type `double`, we say that the method `pow` is of the type `double` or that the method `pow` returns a value of the type `double`. Moreover, `x` and `y` are called the **parameters** (or **arguments**) of the method `pow`. The method `pow` has two parameters.

The *square root* method, `sqrt(x)`, calculates the non-negative square root of `x` for `x >= 0.0`. For example, `sqrt(2.25)` is `1.5`. The method `sqrt` is of the type `double` and has only one parameter.

In Java, predefined methods are organized as a collection of classes, called **class libraries**. For example, the `class Math` contains mathematical methods. Table 7-1 lists some of Java's predefined mathematical methods. The table gives the name of the method, number of parameters, the data type of the parameters, and the method type. The **method type** is the data type of the value returned by the method. The name of the method is shown in bold. The table also shows how a method works and how to use it. The `class Math` is contained in the package `java.lang`. (For a list of additional classes and their associated methods, see Appendix E.)

Table 7-1 Some Predefined Mathematical Methods

class **Math** (**Package:** java.lang)

Expression	Description
`Math.abs(x)`	Returns the absolute value of `x`. If `x` is of the type `int`, it returns a value of the type `int`; if `x` is of the type `long`, it returns a value of the type `long`; if `x` is of the type `float`, it returns a value of the type `float`; if `x` is of the type `double`, it returns a value of the type `double`. **Example:** `Math.abs(-67)` returns the value 67. `Math.abs(35)` returns the value 35. `Math.abs(-75.38)` returns the value 75.38.
`Math.ceil(x)`	`x` is of the type `double`. Returns a value of the type `double`, which is the smallest integer value that is not less than `x`. **Example:** `Math.ceil(56.34)` returns the value 57.0.
`Math.exp(x)`	`x` is of the type `double`. Returns e^x, value of the type `double`, where e is approximately 2.7182818284590455. **Example:** `Math.exp(3)` returns the value 20.085536923187668.
`Math.floor(x)`	`x` is of the type `double`. Returns a value of the type `double`, which is the largest integer value less than `x`. **Example:** `Math.floor(65.78)` returns the value 65.0.
`Math.log(x)`	`x` is of the type `double`. Returns a value of the type `double`, which is the natural logarithm of `x`. **Example:** `Math.log(2)` returns the value 0.6931471805599453.
`Math.max(x, y)`	Returns the larger of `x` and `y`. If `x` and `y` are of the type `int`, it returns a value of the type `int`; if `x` and `y` are of the type `long`, it returns a value of the type `long`; if `x` and `y` are of the type `float`, it returns a value of the type `float`; if `x` and `y` are of the type `double`, it returns a value of the type `double`. **Example:** `Math.max(15, 25)` returns the value 25. `Math.max(23.67, 14.28)` returns the value 23.67. `Math.max(45, 23.78)` returns the value 45.00.

Table 7-1 Some Predefined Mathematical Methods (continued)

Expression	Description
Math.min(x, y)	Returns the smaller of x and y. If x and y are of the type int, it returns a value of the type int; if x and y are of the type long, it returns a value of the type long; if x and y are of the type float, it returns a value of the type float; if x and y are of the type double, it returns a value of the type double. **Example:** Math.min(15, 25) returns the value 15. Math.min(23.67, 14.28) returns the value 14.28. Math.min(12, 34.78) returns the value 12.00.
Math.pow(x, y)	x and y are of the type double. Returns a value of the type double, which is x^y. **Example:** Math.pow(2.0, 3.0) returns the value 8.0. Math.pow(4, 0.5) returns the value 2.0.
Math.round(x)	Returns a value which is the integer closest to x. If x is of the type float, it returns a value of the type int; if x is of the type long, it returns a value of the type double. **Example:** Math.round(24.56) returns the value 25. Math.round(18.35) returns the value 18.
Math.sqrt(x)	x is of the type double. Returns a value of the type double, which is the square root of x. **Example:** Math.sqrt(4.0) returns the value 2.0. Math.sqrt(2.25) returns the value 1.5.
Math.cos(x)	x is of the type double. Returns the cosine of x measured in radians. **Example:** Math.cos(0) returns the value 1.0.
Math.sin(x)	x is of the type double. Returns the sine of x measured in radians. **Example:** Math.sin(0) returns the value 0.0.
Math.tan(x)	x is of the type double. Returns the tangent of x measured in radians. **Example:** Math.tan(0) returns the value 0.0.

Java also provides methods, contained in the **class Character**, to manipulate characters. Table 7-2 describes some of the methods of the **class Character** contained in the package **java.lang**. As in Table 7-1, Table 7-2 shows the name of the method in bold, and examples of how to use the methods are given.

Table 7-2 Some Predefined Methods for Character Manipulation

class **Character** (Package: `java.lang`)	
Expression	**Description**
`Character.isDigit(ch)`	ch is of the type `char`. Returns `true` if ch is a digit; `false` otherwise. **Example:** `Character.isDigit('8')` returns the value `true`. `Character.isDigit('*')` returns the value `false`.
`Character.isLetter(ch)`	ch is of the type `char`. Returns `true` if ch is a letter; `false` otherwise. **Example:** `Character.isLetter('a')` returns the value `true`. `Character.isLetter('*')` returns the value `false`.
`Character.isLowerCase(ch)`	ch is of the type `char`. Returns `true` if ch is a lowercase letter; `false` otherwise. **Example:** `Character.isLowerCase('a')` returns the value `true`. `Character.isLowerCase('A')` returns the value `false`.
`Character.isUpperCase(ch)`	ch is of the type `char`. Returns `true` if ch is an upper-case letter; `false` otherwise. **Example:** `Character.isUpperCase('B')` returns the value `true`. `Character.isUpperCase('k')` returns the value `false`.
`Character.isSpaceChar(ch)`	ch is of the type `char`. Returns `true` if ch is the space character; `false` otherwise. **Example:** `Character.isSpaceChar(' ')` returns the value `true`. `Character.isSpaceChar('*')` returns the value `false`.
`Character.isWhitespace(ch)`	ch is of the type `char`. Returns `true` if ch is a white-space character; `false` otherwise. **Example:** `Character.isWhitespace('\n')` returns the value `true`. `Character.isWhitespace('\t')` returns the value `true`. `Character.isWhitespace('\r')` returns the value `true`. `Character.isWhitespace(' ')` returns the value `true`. `Character.isWhitespace('*')` returns the value `false`.

7

Table 7-2 Some Predefined Methods for Character Manipulation (continued)

Expression	Description
`Character.toLowerCase(ch)`	ch is of the type `char`. Returns the character that is the lowercase equivalent of ch. If ch does not have a corresponding lowercase letter, it returns ch. **Example:** `Character.toLowerCase('D')` returns the value d. `Character.toLowerCase('*')` returns the value *.
`Character.toUpperCase(ch)`	ch is of the type `char`. Returns the character that is the uppercase equivalent of ch. If ch does not have a corresponding uppercase letter, it returns ch. **Example:** `Character.toUpperCase('j')` returns the value J. `Character.toUpperCase('8')` returns the value 8.

In general, to use predefined methods of a class in a program, you must `import` the `class` from the package containing the class. For example, to use the method `readLine` of the `class BufferedReader` contained in the `package java.io`, we import this `class` from the `package java.io`. Similarly, to use the method `nextToken` of the `class StringTokenizer`, contained in the `package java.util`, we import this `class` from the `package java.util`. However, as stated in Chapter 2, if a `class` is contained in the `package java.lang` and you want to use a method of this `class`, then Java does not require you to explicitly include any `import` statement to import that `class`. For example, to use any method of the `class String`, contained in the `package java.lang`, in a program we do not need any `import` `statement`. By default Java automatically imports classes from the package `java.lang`. Therefore, if you use a method from the `class Math` or `Character` you do not need to explicitly import these classes in your program.

Example 7-1

This example shows you how to use some of the predefined methods:

```
//How to use predefined methods

import java.text.DecimalFormat;

public class PredefinedMethods
{
    public static void main(String[] args)
    {
        int    x;
        double  u,v;
        DecimalFormat twoDigits = new DecimalFormat("0.00");
```

```
System.out.println("Line 1: Uppercase a is "
           + Character.toUpperCase('a'));      //Line 1
u = 4.2;                                        //Line 2
v = 3.0;                                        //Line 3
System.out.println("Line 4: " + u
           + " to the power of "
           + v + " = "
           + twoDigits.format(Math.pow(u,v))); //Line 4

System.out.println("Line 5: 5 to the power of 4 = "
           + twoDigits.format(Math.pow(5,4))); //Line 5

u = u + Math.pow(3,3);                          //Line 6
System.out.println("Line 7: u = "
           + twoDigits.format(u));             //Line 7

x = -15;                                        //Line 8
System.out.println("Line 9: Absolute value of " +
           + x + " = " + Math.abs(x));         //Line 9
    }
}
```

Output

```
Line 1: Uppercase a is A
Line 4: 4.2 to the power of 3.0 = 74.09
Line 5: 5 to the power of 4 = 625.00
Line 7: u = 31.20
Line 9: Absolute value of -15 = 15
```

This program works as follows. The statement at Line 1 outputs the uppercase letter that corresponds to 'a', which is 'A'. In the statement at Line 4, the method **pow** (of the **class Math**) is used to output u^v. In Java terminology, it is said that the method **pow** is called with the parameters u and v. In this case, the values of u and v are passed to the method **pow**. The statement in Line 5 uses the method **pow** to output 5^4. The statement in Line 6 uses the method **pow** to determine 3^3, adds this value to the value of u, and then stores the new value into u. The statement in Line 7 outputs the value of u. The statement in Line 8 stores -15 into x, and the statement in Line 9 outputs the absolute value of x.

USER-DEFINED METHODS

Since Java does not provide every method that you will ever need, and designers cannot possibly know a user's specific needs, you must learn to write your own methods.

User-defined methods in Java are classified into two categories:

- Methods that have a type, called **value-returning methods**
- Methods that do not have a type, called **void methods**

The next section discusses value-returning methods. Many concepts regarding value-returning methods also apply to void methods. Void methods are discussed later in this chapter.

Value-Returning Methods

The section Predefined Methods introduced some predefined Java methods such as **pow**, **sqrt**, **isLowerCase**, and **toUpperCase**. These are examples of value-returning methods; that is, methods that calculate and return a value. To use these methods in your programs, you must know:

1. The name of the method

2. The number of **parameters**, if any

3. The data type of each parameter

4. The data type of the value computed (that is, the value returned) by the method, called the type of the method

Since the value returned by a value-returning method is unique, it is natural for you to use the value in one of three ways:

- Save the value for further calculation.
- Use the value in some calculation.
- Print the value.

This suggests that a value-returning method is used in either an assignment statement or an output statement. That is, a value-returning method is used in an expression.

In addition to the four properties just described, one more thing is associated with methods (both value-returning and void):

5. The code required to accomplish the task

Before we look at the syntax of a user-defined value-returning method, let's review the things associated with such methods. The first four properties become part of what is called the **heading** of the method; the fifth property is called the **body** of the method. Together, these five properties form what is called the **definition** of the method.

 For predefined methods, you need to be concerned only with the first four properties. Software companies do not give out the actual source code, which is the body of the method.

For example, for the method **abs** (*absolute*), the heading might look like:

```
public static int abs(int number)
```

Similarly, the method **abs** might have the following definition:

```
public static int abs(int number)
{
      if(number < 0)
         number = -number;

      return number;
}
```

The variable declared in the heading, within the parentheses, of the method **abs** is called the **formal parameter** of the method **abs**. Thus, the formal parameter of **abs** is **number**.

The program in Example 7-1 contains several statements that use the method **pow**. In Java terminology, we say that the method **pow** was *called* several times. Later in this chapter, we discuss what happens when a method is called.

Suppose that the heading of the method **pow** is:

```
public static double pow(double base, double exponent)
```

In this heading, you can see that the formal parameters of **pow** are **base** and **exponent**. Consider the following statements:

```
double u = 2.5;
double v = 3.0;
double x, y, w;

x = Math.pow(u, v);          //Line 1
y = Math.pow(2.0, 3.2);      //Line 2
w = Math.pow(u, 7);          //Line 3
```

In Line 1, the method **pow** is called with the parameters u and v. In this case, the values of u and v are passed to the method **pow**. In fact, the value of u is copied into **base** and the value of v is copied into **exponent**. The variables u and v that appear in the call to the method **pow** in Line 1 are called **actual parameters** of that call. In Line 2, the method **pow** is called with the parameters **2.0** and **3.2**. In this call, the value **2.0** is copied into **base** and **3.2** is copied into **exponent**. In this call of the method **pow**, the actual parameters are **2.0** and **3.2**, respectively. Similarly, in Line 3, the actual parameters of the method **pow** are u and 7. The value of u is copied into **base**, and **7.0** is copied into **exponent**.

We can now formally present the following two definitions:

Formal parameter: A variable declared in the method heading.

Actual parameter: A variable or expression listed in a call to a method.

Syntax: Value-Returning Method

The syntax of a value-returning method is:

```
modifier(s) returnType methodName(formal parameter list)
{
        statements
}
```

In this syntax:

- **modifier(s)** indicates the visibility of the method, that is, where in a program the method can be used (called). Some of the modifiers are `public`, `private`, `protected`, `static`, `abstract`, and `final`. If you include more than one modifier, they must be separated with spaces. You can select one modifier among `public`, `protected`, and `private`. The modifier `public` specifies that the method can be called outside the class, and the modifier `private` specifies that the method cannot be used outside the class. Similarly, you can choose one of the modifiers `static` or `abstract`. More information about these modifiers is provided when we discuss classes in general. Meanwhile, we use the modifiers `public` and/or `static`, as used in the method `main`.

- **returnType** is the type of value that the method calculates and returns. This type is also called the type of the value-returning method.

- **methodName** is a Java identifier, giving a name to the method.

- Statements enclosed between curly braces form the body of the method.

In Java, `public`, `protected`, `private`, `static`, and `abstract` are reserved words.

Syntax: Formal Parameter List

The syntax of the formal parameter list is:

```
dataType identifier, dataType identifier,...
```

Method Call

The syntax to call a value-returning method is:

```
methodName(actual parameter list)
```

Syntax: Actual Parameter List

The syntax of the actual parameter list is:

```
expression or variable, expression or variable, ...
```

Thus, to call a value-returning method, you use its name, with the actual parameters (if any) in parentheses.

A method's formal parameter list can be empty, but the parentheses are still needed. If the formal parameter list is empty, the method heading of the value-returning method takes the following form:

```
modifiers(s) returnType methodName()
```

If the formal parameter list is empty in a method call, the actual parameter list is also empty. In the case of an empty formal parameter list, in a method call the empty parentheses are still needed. Thus, a call to a value-returning method with an empty formal parameter list is:

```
methodName()
```

In a method call, the number of actual parameters, together with their data types, must match the formal parameters in the order given. That is, actual and formal parameters have a one-to-one correspondence.

As stated previously, a value-returning method is called in an expression. The expression can be part of an assignment statement, or an output statement, or a parameter in a method call. A method call in a program causes the body of the called method to execute.

Next we describe how a value-returning method returns its value.

The `return` Statement

Once a value-returning method computes the value, the method returns this value via the `return` statement; in other words, it passes this value outside the method via the `return` statement.

Syntax: `return` Statement

The `return` statement has the following syntax:

```
return expr;
```

where `expr` is a variable, constant value, or expression. The `expr` is evaluated and its value is returned. The data type of the value that `expr` computes must match the method type.

In Java, `return` is a reserved word.

When a `return` statement executes in a method, the method immediately terminates and the control goes back to the caller.

To put the ideas of this section to work, we'll write a method that determines the larger of two numbers. Because the method compares two numbers, it follows that this method has two parameters and that both parameters are numbers. Assume that the data type of these numbers is floating-point (decimal)—say `double`. Since the larger number is of the type `double`, the method's data type is also `double`. Let's name this method `larger`. The only thing you need to complete this method is the body of the method. Thus, following the syntax of a method, you can write this method as follows:

```java
public static double larger(double x, double y)
{
    double max;

    if(x >= y)
        max = x;
    else
        max = y;

    return max;
}
```

You can also write this method as follows:

```java
public static double larger(double x, double y)
{
    if(x >= y)
        return x;
    else
        return y;
}
```

The first form of the method `larger` requires that you use an additional variable `max` (called a **local declaration**, where `max` is a variable local to the method `larger`); the second form does not.

 1. In the method definition, x and y are formal parameters.
2. The `return` statement can appear anywhere in the method. Recall that once a `return` statement executes, all subsequent statements are skipped. Thus, it's a good idea to return the value as soon as it is computed.

Example 7-2

Suppose that you have the following declaration:

```
static BufferedReader keyboard = new
            BufferedReader(new InputStreamReader(System.in));
```

The following Java code illustrates how to use the method `larger` in the method `main`:

```
public static void main(String[] args) throws IOException
{
        double one, two, maxNum;                              //Line 1

        System.out.println("Larger of 5 and 6 is "
                        + larger(5,6));                       //Line 2

        System.out.print("Enter the first number: ");   //Line 3
        System.out.flush();                              //Line 4
        one = Double.parseDouble(keyboard.readLine());   //Line 5
        System.out.println();                            //Line 6

        System.out.print("Enter the second number: ");  //Line 7
        System.out.flush();                              //Line 8
        two = Double.parseDouble(keyboard.readLine());   //Line 9
        System.out.println();                            //Line 10

        System.out.println("Larger of " + one + " and "
                        + two + " is " +
                        larger(one,two));                //Line 11
        System.out.println("Larger of " + one
                        + " and 29 is "
                        + larger(one,29));               //Line 12
        maxNum = larger(38.45, 56.78);                   //Line 13
        System.out.println("maxNum = " + maxNum);        //Line 14
}
```

1. In Example 7-2, the expression `larger(5,6)` in Line 2 is a method call, and 5 and 6 are actual parameters.
2. In Example 7-2, the expression `larger(one, two)` in Line 11 is a method call. Here, one and two are actual parameters.
3. In Example 7-2, the expression `larger(one, 29)` in Line 12 is also a method call. Here, one and 29 are actual parameters.
4. In Example 7-2, the expression `larger(38.45, 56.78);` in Line 13 is a method call. In this call, the actual parameters are 38.45 and 56.78. In this statement, the value returned by the method `larger` is assigned to the variable `maxNum`.

In a method call, you specify only the actual parameter, not its data type. For example, notice that in Example 7-2 the statements in Lines 2, 11, 12, and 13 show how to call the method `larger` with actual parameters. However, the following statements contain incorrect calls to the method `larger` and would result in syntax errors. (Assume that all variables are properly declared.)

```
x = larger(int one, 29); //illegal
y = larger(int one, int 29); //illegal
System.out.println(larger(int one, int two)); //illegal
```

Once a method is written, you can use it anywhere it is "visible" in the program (the rules for visibility within a class, called scope, are discussed later in this chapter). The method `larger` compares two numbers and returns the larger of the two. Let's now write another method that uses this method to determine the largest of three numbers. We call this method `compareThree`.

```
public static double compareThree(double x, double y, double z)
{
    return larger(x,larger(y,z));
}
```

In the definition of the method `compareThree`, first the larger of `y` and `z` is determined, which is then compared with `x`. Finally, the `return` statement returns the largest number. In the method heading, x, y, and z are formal parameters.

Final Program

You now know enough to write the entire program, compile it, and run it. The following program uses the functions `larger`, `compareThree`, and `main` to determine the larger/largest of two or three numbers.

```
//Program: Largest of three numbers

import java.io.*;

public class LargerNumber
{

    static BufferedReader keyboard = new
            BufferedReader(new InputStreamReader(System.in));

    public static void main(String[] args) throws IOException
    {
        double num1, num2;                                      //Line 1

        System.out.println("Line 2: Larger of 5.6 and 10.8 is "
                        + larger(5.6,10.8));                    //Line 2
        System.out.print("Line 3: Enter the first number: ");//Line 3
```

```
        System.out.flush();                                    //Line 4
        num1 = Double.parseDouble(keyboard.readLine());        //Line 5

        System.out.print("Line 6: Enter the second number: ");//Line 6
        System.out.flush();                                    //Line 7
        num2 = Double.parseDouble(keyboard.readLine());        //Line 8

        System.out.println("Line 9: Larger of "
                      + num1 + " and " + num2 + " is "
                      + larger(num1,num2));                     //Line 9
        System.out.println("Line 10: Largest of 23.5, 34.6, "
                      + "and 12 is "
                      + compareThree(23.5,34.6,12));            //Line 10
    }

    public static double larger(double x, double y)
    {
        if(x >= y)
            return x;
        else
            return y;
    }

    public static double compareThree(double x, double y, double z)
    {
        return larger(x, larger(y, z));
    }
}
```

Sample Run: In this sample run, the user input is shaded.

```
Line 2: Larger of 5.6 and 10.8 is 10.8
Line 3: Enter the first number: 34
Line 6: Enter the second number: 43
Line 9: Larger of 34.0 and 43.0 is 43.0
Line 10: Largest of 23.5, 34.6, and 12 is 34.6
```

> **NOTE** You can put methods within a class in any order.

Following is an example of a method that returns a Boolean value.

PROGRAMMING EXAMPLE: PALINDROME NUMBER

In this example, we write a program that determines whether an integer is a palindrome. An integer is a **palindrome** if it reads forward and backward in the same way. For example, the integers 5, 44, 434, −1881, and 789656987 are all palindromes.

Input An integer (positive or negative)

Output A message indicating whether the integer is a palindrome

Problem Analysis and Algorithm Design

The first thing the program does is read the integer. Since input to the program is a string, the string containing the integer is converted into the integer. If the integer is negative, the program changes it to positive. The next step is to convert the integer back to a string and then determine whether the string is a palindrome.

1. Read the string containing the integer.
2. Convert the string into the integer.
3. If the integer is negative, change it to positive.
4. Convert the integer into a string.
5. Determine whether the string is a palindrome.

Next we design the method `isPalindrome` that returns `true` if a string is a palindrome and `false` otherwise.

The Method `isPalindrome` The method `isPalindrome` takes a string as a parameter and returns `true` if the string is a palindrome, `false` otherwise. Suppose that the `String` variable `str` refers to the string. To be specific, suppose that `str` refers to the string `"845548"`. The length of this string is 6. Recall that the position of the first character of a string is 0, the position of the second character is 1, and so on.

To determine whether the string `str`, `"845548"` is a palindrome, first we compare the character at position 0 with the character at position 5. If these two characters are the same, then we compare the character at position 1 with the character at position 4; if these two characters are the same, then we compare the characters at position 2 and 3. When we find mismatched characters, the string `str` is not a palindrome, and the method returns `false`. It follows that we need two variables, `i` and `j`; `i` is initialized to 0 and `j` is initialized to the last character of the string. We then compare the characters at positions `i` and `j`. If the characters at position `i` and `j` are the same, we then increment `i` and decrement `j`, and continue this process. If the characters at position `i` and `j` are not the same, then return `false`. Note that we only need to compare the characters in the first half of the string with characters in the second half of the string in the order described above. This discussion translates into the following algorithm:

1. Find the length of the string. Since `str` is a `String` variable, we can use the method `length` of the `class String` to find the length of the string. Suppose `len = str.length();`.

2. Set `j = len − 1`. (Recall that in a string, the position of the first character is 0, the position of the second character is 1, and so on. Therefore, the position of the last character in the string `str` is `len − 1`.)

3. Use a `for` loop to compare the characters in the first half of the string with those in the second half as follows:

```
for(i = 0; i < (len - 1)/2; i++)
{
  a. if(str.charAt(i) is not equal to str.charAt(j))
        return false;
  b. j--;
}
```

4. Return `true`.

The following method implements this algorithm:

```
public static boolean isPalindrome(String str)
{
    int len = str.length();                        //Step 1
    int i, j;

    j = len - 1;                                   //Step 2

    for(i = 0; i < (len - 1)/2; i++)               //Step 3
    {
        if(str.charAt(i) !=  str.charAt(j))        //Step 3.a
            return false;
        j--;                                       //Step 3.b
    }

    return true;                                   //Step 4
}
```

Complete Program Listing

```
//Program Palindrome

import javax.swing.JOptionPane;

public class Palindrome
```

```
{
    public static void main(String[] args)
    {
        long num, temp;
        String inputStr, outputStr;

        inputStr =
            JOptionPane.showInputDialog("Enter an integer, "
                                      + "positive or negative");

        num = Long.parseLong(inputStr);
        temp = num;

        if(num <= 0)
        {
            num = -num;
            inputStr = inputStr.valueOf(num);
        }

        if(isPalindrome(inputStr))
            outputStr = temp + " is a palindrome";
        else
            outputStr = temp + " is not a palindrome";

        JOptionPane.showMessageDialog(null, outputStr,
                        "Palindrome Program",
                        JOptionPane.INFORMATION_MESSAGE);

        System.exit(0);
    }

    public static boolean isPalindrome(String str)
    {
        int len = str.length();                          //Step 1
        int i, j;

        j = len - 1;                                     //Step 2

        for(i = 0; i < (len - 1)/2; i++)                 //Step 3
        {
            if(str.charAt(i) !=  str.charAt(j))          //Step 3.a
                return false;
            j--;                                         //Step 3.b
        }

        return true;                                     //Step 4
    }
}
```

Sample Run 1: Figure 7-1 shows Sample Run 1.

Figure 7-1   Sample Run 1 of the Palindrome program

Sample Run 2: Figure 7-2 shows Sample Run 2.

Figure 7-2   Sample Run 2 of the Palindrome program

FLOW OF EXECUTION

As you know, a Java application program is a collection of classes, and a class is a collection of methods and data members. In a Java program, methods can appear in any order. However, when the program executes, the first statement in the method `main` always executes first, regardless of where in the program the method `main` is placed. Other methods execute only when they are called.

A method call statement transfers control to the first statement in the body of the method. In general, after the last statement of the called method executes, control is passed back to the point immediately following the method call. A value-returning method returns a value. Therefore, for value-returning methods, after executing the method when the control goes back to the caller, the value that the method returns replaces the method call statement. The execution continues at the point immediately following the method call.

PROGRAMMING EXAMPLE: LARGEST NUMBER

In this programming example, the method `larger` is used to determine the largest number from a set of numbers, in this case the largest number from a set of 10 numbers. You can easily modify this program to accommodate any set of numbers.

Input   A set of 10 numbers

Output   The largest of 10 numbers

Problem Analysis and Algorithm Design

Suppose that the input data is:

```
15 20 7 8 28 21 43 12 35 3
```

Get the first number of the data set. Since this is the only number read to this point, you can assume that it is the largest number and call it `max`. Read the second number and call it `num`. Now compare `max` and `num`, and store the larger number into `max`. Now `max` contains the larger of the first two numbers. Read the third number. Compare it with `max` and store the larger number into `max`. At this point, `max` contains the largest of the first three numbers. Read the next number, compare it with `max`, and store the larger into `max`. Repeat this process for each remaining number in the data set. Eventually, `max` will contain the largest number in the data set. This discussion translates into the following algorithm:

1. Get the first number. Since this is the only number that you have read so far, it is the largest number so far. Save it in a variable called `max`.

2. For each remaining number in the list:

  a. Get the next number. Store it in a variable called num.

  b. Compare num and max. If max < num, then num is the new largest number; update the value of max by copying num into max. If max >= num, discard num; that is, do nothing.

3. Because max now contains the largest number, print it.

To find the larger of two numbers, the program uses the method larger.

Complete Program Listing

```java
//Program: Largest number

import java.io.*;
import java.util.*;

public class LargestNumber
{
    static BufferedReader keyboard = new
            BufferedReader(new InputStreamReader(System.in));

    public static void main(String[] args) throws IOException
    {
        double num; //variable to hold the current number
        double max; //variable to hold the larger number
        int count;  //loop control variable

        StringTokenizer tokenizer;

        System.out.println("Enter 10 numbers in the same line.");

        tokenizer =
            new StringTokenizer(keyboard.readLine());   //Step 1
        max = Double.parseDouble(tokenizer.nextToken()); //Step 1

        for(count = 1; count < 10; count++)             //Step 2
        {
            num =
                Double.parseDouble(tokenizer.nextToken()); //Step 2a
            max = larger(max, num);                     //Step 2b
        }

        System.out.println("The largest number is "
                            + max);                     //Step 3
    }
```

```
public static double larger(double x, double y)
{
    if(x >= y)
        return x;
    else
        return y;
}
}
```

Sample Run: In this sample run, the user input is shaded. (When you execute this program, enter all numbers in the same line.)

```
Enter 10 numbers in the same line.
10.5 56.34 73.3 42 22 67 88.55 26 62 11
The largest number is 88.55
```

VOID METHODS

Void methods (methods that do not have a type) and value-returning methods have similar structures. Both have a heading part and a statement part. You can place user-defined void methods either before or after the method `main`. However, program execution always begins with the first statement in the method `main`. Because a void method does not have a data type, `methodType` in the heading part and the `return` statement in the body of the void method are meaningless. However, in a void method, you can use the `return` statement without any value; it is typically used to exit the method early. Like value-returning methods, void methods may or may not have formal parameters.

Because void methods do not have a data type, they are not used (that is, called) in an expression. A call to a void method is a stand-alone statement. Thus, to call a void method, you use the method name together with the actual parameters (if any) in a stand-alone statement.

Void Methods without Parameters

This section discusses void methods that do not have formal parameters.

Method Definition

The general form (syntax) of a void method without parameters is as follows:

```
modifier(s) void methodName()
{
    statements
}
```

where `modifier(s)` are as previously described. (Until we discuss classes in general, we will use the modifiers `public` and/or `static`.)

Method Call (Within the Class)

The method call has the following syntax:

```
methodName();
```

Because these methods do not have parameters, within a class such methods are usually good for displaying information about the program or for printing statements. Consider the program in Example 7-3.

Example 7-3

Suppose you want to print the following banner to announce the annual spring sale. (See a similar program in Chapter 2, Programming Exercise 3.)

```
******************************
******************************
********** Annual   **********
******************************
******************************
******* Spring Sale **********
******************************
******************************
```

The banner starts with two lines of stars. After printing the line containing the text `Annual`, you need to print another two lines of stars. After printing the line containing the text `Spring Sale`, you need to print two more lines of stars. You can write a method that prints two lines of stars and call it whenever you need it. The complete program looks like this:

```java
public class Banner
{
    public static void main (String[] args)
    {
        printStars();                                    //Line 1
        System.out.println("********** Annual   **********");//Line 2
        printStars();                                    //Line 3
        System.out.println("******* Spring Sale **********");//Line 4
        printStars();                                    //Line 5

    }
```

```
public static void printStars()
{
    System.out.println("*******************************");
    System.out.println("*******************************");
}
}
```

Output:

```
*******************************
*******************************
********** Annual   **********
*******************************
*******************************
****** Spring Sale **********
*******************************
*******************************
```

In Line 1, the method **printStars** is called and it outputs the first two lines of the output. The statement in Line 2 outputs the line of stars containing the text **Annual**, which is the third line of the output. In Line 3, the method **printStars** is called again and it outputs the next two lines of the output. The statement in Line 4 then outputs the line of stars containing the text **Spring Sale**, which is the sixth line of the output. At Line 5, the method **printStars** is called again and it outputs the last two lines of the output.

 The statement **printStars();** in the method **main** is a method call.

In the previous program, you can replace the method **printStars** with the following method:

```
public static void printStars()
{
    int stars, lines;

    for(lines = 1; lines <= 2; lines++)        //Line 1
    {
        for(stars = 1; stars <= 30; stars++)   //Line 2
            System.out.print("*");             //Line 3

        System.out.println();                  //Line 4
    }
}
```

In this method definition, the outer **for** loop (Line 1) executes twice. For each iteration of the outer **for** loop (Line 1), the inner **for** loop (Line 2) executes 30 times, each time printing 30 stars in a line. The statement at Line 3 prints each star. The output statement at Line 4 positions the insertion point at the beginning of the next line on the standard output device.

Because the outer `for` loop executes twice, this method outputs two lines of stars with 30 stars in each line.

You would agree that the definition of the method `printStars` using `for` loops to output 2 lines of stars with 30 stars in each line is much easier to modify than the definition of `printStars` given in Example 7-3. If you need to output 5 lines of stars instead of 2 lines, for instance, you can replace the number 2 (in the first `for` loop, Line 1) with the number 5. Similarly, if you need to output 40 stars instead of 30 stars in each line, you can replace the number 30 (in the second `for` loop, Line 2) with the number 40. As you will soon discover, the definition of the method `printStars` using `for` loops is much easier to modify in order to establish the communication links with the calling method (such as the method `main`) and to do different things each time the method `printStars` is called.

Void Methods with Parameters

In the previous program, the method `printStars` always prints two lines of stars, with 30 stars in each line. Suppose that you want to print the following pattern (a triangle of stars):

You could write a method similar to the method `printStars`. However, if you need to extend this pattern to 20 lines, the method `printStars` will have 20 lines. Every time you call the method `printStars`, it prints the same number of lines; the method `printStars` is inflexible. However, if you can somehow tell the method `printStars` how many lines to print, you can considerably enhance its flexibility. A communication link must exist between the calling method and the called method. Parameters provide this link between the calling method (such as `main`) and the called method. They enable methods to manipulate different data each time they are called.

Method Definition

The definition of a void method with parameters has the following syntax:

```
modifier(s) void methodName(formal parameter list)
{
    statements
}
```

Formal Parameter List

The formal parameter list has the following syntax:

```
dataType variable, dataType variable, ...
```

Method Call

The method call has the following syntax:

```
methodName(actual parameter list);
```

Actual Parameter List

The actual parameter list has the following syntax:

```
expression or variable, expression or variable, ...
```

As with value-returning methods, in a method call the number of actual parameters, together with their data types, must match the formal parameters in the order given. Actual and formal parameters have a one-to-one correspondence. A method call results in the execution of the body of the called method. Two examples of void methods with parameters follow:

Example 7-4

Consider the following method heading:

```
public static void funexp(int a, double b, char c, String name)
```

The method `funexp)` has four formal parameters: (1) `a`, a parameter of the type `int;`, (2) `b`, a parameter of the type `double;`, (3) `c`, a parameter of the type `char`, and (4) `name`, a parameter of the type `String`.

Example 7-5

Consider the following method heading:

```
public static void expfun(int one, DoubleClass two, char three,
                          String four)
```

The method `expfun` has four formal parameters: (1) `one`, a parameter of the type `int;`, (2) `two`, a parameter of the `DoubleClass;` type, (3) `three`, a parameter of the type `char`, and (4) `four`, a parameter of the type `String`.

Let's now write the Java program to print the pattern (triangle of stars) given at the beginning of this section.

Example 7-6

The following Java program prints a triangle of stars:

```java
//Program: Print a triangle of stars

import java.io.*;

public class TriangleOfStars
{
    static BufferedReader keyboard =
              new BufferedReader(new InputStreamReader(System.in));

    public static void main (String[] args) throws IOException
    {
        int numberOfLines;
        int counter;
        int numberOfBlanks;

        System.out.print("Enter the number of star lines (1 to 20)"
                         + " to be printed--> ");             //Line 1
        System.out.flush();                                  //Line 2
        numberOfLines =
                Integer.parseInt(keyboard.readLine());       //Line 3

        while(numberOfLines < 0 || numberOfLines > 20)       //Line 4
        {
                System.out.println("Number of star lines should be "
                              + "between 1 and 20");          //Line 5
                System.out.print("Enter the number of star lines (1 "
                          + "to 20 to be printed--> ");       //Line 6
                System.out.flush();                           //Line 7
                numberOfLines =
                     Integer.parseInt(keyboard.readLine());   //Line 8
        }

        numberOfBlanks = 30;                                  //Line 9

        for(counter = 1; counter <= numberOfLines; counter++)//Line 10
        {
            printStars(numberOfBlanks, counter);              //Line 11
            numberOfBlanks--;                                 //Line 12
        }
    }
}
```

```
public static void printStars(int blanks, int starsInLine)
{
    int count;

    for(count = 1; count <= blanks; count++)                //Line 13
        System.out.print(" ");                              //Line 14
    for(count = 1; count <= starsInLine; count++)           //Line 15
        System.out.print(" *");                             //Line 16
    System.out.println();                                   //Line 17
}
}
```

Sample Run: In this sample run, the user input is shaded.

Enter the number of star lines (1 to 20) to be printed--> 15

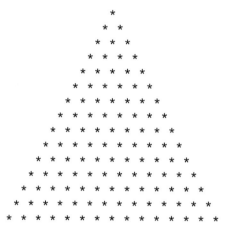

In this program, the statement (see Line 11)

```
printStars(numberOfBlanks, counter);
```

in the method **main** is a method call. The variables **numberOfBlanks** and **counter** are actual parameters.

The method **printStars** works as follows. The method **printStars** has two parameters. Whenever the method **printStars** executes, it outputs a line of stars with a certain number of blanks before the stars. The number of blanks and the number of stars in a line are passed as parameters to the method **printStars**. The first parameter, **blanks**, tells how many blanks to print; the second parameter, **starsInLine**, tells how many stars to print in a line. If the value of the parameter **blanks** is 30, for instance, then the first **for** loop (Line 13) in the method **printStars** executes 30 times and prints 30 blanks. Also, because you want to print spaces between the stars, every iteration of the second **for** loop (Line 15) in the method **printStars** prints the string " *" (Line 16)—that is, a blank followed by a star.

The statement in Line 17 ensures that when the program terminates, the buffer containing the output is emptied.

In the method `main`, the user is first asked to specify how many lines of stars to print (Line 1). (In this program, the user is restricted to 20 lines because a triangular grid of up to 20 lines fits nicely on the screen.) Because the program is restricted to only 20 lines, the `while` loop in Lines 4–8 ensures that the program prints the triangular grid of stars only if the number of lines is between 1 and 20.

The `for` loop (Line 10) in the method `main` calls the method `printStars` (Line 11). Every iteration of this `for` loop specifies the number of blanks followed by the number of stars to print in a line, using the variables `numberOfBlanks` and `counter`. Every call of the method `printStars` receives one fewer blank and one more star than the previous call. For example, the first iteration of the `for` loop in the method `main` specifies 30 blanks and 1 star (which are passed as the parameters, `numberOfBlanks` and `counter`, to the method `printStars`). The `for` loop then:

1. Decrements the number of blanks by 1. This is done by executing the following statement in Line 12:

   ```
   numberOfBlanks--;
   ```

2. At the end of the `for` loop, the number of stars is incremented by 1 for the next iteration. This is done by executing the update statement, `counter++` (Line 10), in the `for` statement, which increments the value of the variable `counter` by 1.

In other words, the second call of the method `printStars` receives 29 blanks and 2 stars as parameters.

PRIMITIVE DATA TYPE VARIABLES AS PARAMETERS

In Chapter 3 you learned that there are two categories of variables in Java—variables of a primitive type and reference variables. Before considering examples of void methods with parameters, let's make the following observation about variables of primitive types and reference variables. When a method is called, the value of the actual parameter is copied into the corresponding formal parameter. If a formal parameter is a variable of a primitive data type, then after copying the value of the actual parameter, there is no connection between the formal parameter and the actual parameter. That is, the formal parameter has its own copy of the data. Therefore, during program execution, the formal parameter manipulates the data stored in its own memory space. The program in Example 7-7 further illustrates how a primitive data type formal parameter works.

Example 7-7

The following program shows how a formal parameter of a primitive data type works:

```
//Example 7-7
//Program illustrating how a formal parameter of
//primitive data type works.

public class PrimitiveTypeParameters
{
    public static void main(String[] args)
    {
        int number = 6;                                    //Line 1

        System.out.println("Line 2: Before calling the "
                        + " method funcPrimFormalParam, "
                        + "number = " + number);           //Line 2

        funcPrimFormalParam(number);                       //Line 3

        System.out.println("Line 4: After calling the "
                        + "method funcPrimFormalParam, "
                        + "number = " + number);           //Line 4
    }

    public static void funcPrimFormalParam(int num)
    {
        System.out.println("Line 5: In the method "
                        + "funcPrimFormalParam, before "
                        + "changing, num = " + num);       //Line 5

        num = 15;                                          //Line 6

        System.out.println("Line 7: In the method "
                        + "funcPrimFormalParam, after "
                        + "changing, num = " + num);       //Line 7
    }

}
```

Output:

```
Line 2: Before calling the method funcPrimFormalParam, number = 6
Line 5: In the method funcPrimFormalParam, before changing, num = 6
Line 7: In the method funcPrimFormalParam, after changing, num = 15
Line 4: After calling the method funcPrimFormalParam, number = 6
```

The preceding program works as follows. The execution begins at the method main. The statement in Line 1 declares and initializes the int variable number. The statement in

Line 2 outputs the value of `number` before calling the method `funcPrimFormalParam`. The statement in Line 3 calls the method `funcPrimFormalParam`. The value of the variable `number` is passed to the formal parameter `num`. The control now transfers to the method `funcPrimFormalParam`. The statement in Line 5 outputs the value of `num` before changing its value. The statement in Line 6 changes the value of `num` to `15`, and the statement in Line 7 outputs the value of `num`. After this statement executes, the method `funcPrimFormalParam` exits and the control goes back to the method `main` at Line 4. The statement in Line 4 outputs the value of `number` after calling the method `funcPrimFormalParam`. As you can see from the output, the value of `number`, as shown by the output of statements in Lines 2 and 4, remains the same even though the value of its corresponding formal parameter `num` was changed witihin the method `funcPrimFormalParam`.

After copying data, a formal parameter of the primitive type has no connection with the actual parameter, so a formal parameter of the primitive type cannot pass any result back to the calling method. When the method executes, any changes made to the formal parameters do not in any way affect the actual parameters. The actual parameter has no knowledge of what is happening to the formal parameter. Thus, formal parameters of the primitive data types cannot pass information outside the method. Formal parameters of the primitive data types provide only a one-way link between actual parameters and formal parameters. Hence, methods with formal parameters only of the primitive data types have limitations.

REFERENCE VARIABLES AS PARAMETERS

The program in Example 7-7 illustrates how a formal parameter of a primitive data type works. Now suppose that a formal parameter is a reference variable. Here, also, the value of the actual parameter is copied into a formal parameter, but there is a slight difference. Recall that a reference variable does not store data directly in its own memory space. We use the operator `new` to allocate memory for an object belonging to a specific class, and a reference variable of that class type contains the address of the allocated memory space. Therefore, when we pass the value of the actual parameter to the corresponding formal parameter, after copying the value of the actual parameter, both the actual and the formal parameters refer to the same memory space, that is, the same object. Therefore, if the formal parameter changes the value of the object, it also changes the value of the object of the actual parameter.

Because a reference variable contains the address (that is, memory location) of the actual data, both the formal and the value parameters refer to the same object. Therefore, reference variables can pass one or more values from a method and can change the value of the actual parameter.

Reference variables as parameters are useful in three situations:

- When you want to return more than one value from a method

- When the value of the actual object needs to be changed
- When passing the address would save memory space and time, relative to copying a large amount of data

As illustrated by the program in Example 7-7, if a formal parameter is of the primitive data type and the corresponding actual parameter is a variable, then the formal parameter cannot change the value of the actual parameter. In other words, changing the value of a formal parameter of the primitive data type has no effect on the actual parameter. So, how do we pass the values of primitive data types outside the method? As described in the preceding paragraph, only reference variables can pass values outside the method. Corresponding to each primitive data type, Java provides a class so that values of primitive data types can be considered objects. For example, you can use the class `Integer` to treat `int` values as objects, the class `Double` to treat `double` values as objects, and so on. These wrapper classes were described in Chapter 6. As discussed in Chapter 3, even though you can uses the class `Integer` to treat `int` values as objects, the class `Integer` does not provide any method to change the value of an existing `Integer` object. The same is true of other wrapper classes. Chapter 6 introduced the class `IntClass` so that values of `int` type could be wrapped in an object. The class `IntClass` also provides methods to change the value of an `IntClass` object. You can review these classes in Chapter 6 and Appendix D. Appendix D also shows how to use these classes in a program.

Example 7-8: Calculate Grade

Consider the following program. Given a course score (a value between 0 and 100), it determines a student's course grade. This program to determine the course grade based on the course score has three methods: **main**, **getScore**, and **printGrade**. These three methods are described as follows:

1. **main**

    a. Get the course score.

    b. Print the course grade.

2. **getScore**

    a. Prompt the user for the input.

    b. Get the input.

    c. Print the course score.

3. **printGrade**

    a. Calculate the course grade.

    b. Print the course grade.

The complete program is as follows:

```
//Program: Compute grade.
//This program reads a course score and prints the
//associated course grade.

import java.io.*;

public class Example7_8
{
    static BufferedReader keyboard =
            new BufferedReader(new InputStreamReader(System.in));

    public static void main (String[] args) throws IOException
    {
        DoubleClass courseScore = new DoubleClass();

        System.out.println("Line 1: Based on the course score, "
                        + "this program computes the "
                        + "course grade.");              //Line 1

        getScore(courseScore);                           //Line 2
        printGrade(courseScore.getNum());                //Line 3
    }

    public static void getScore(DoubleClass score)   throws
                                                   IOException
    {
        double s;                                        //Line 4
        System.out.print("Line 5: Enter course score: "); //Line 5
        System.out.flush();                              //Line 6
        s = Double.parseDouble(keyboard.readLine());     //Line 7
        score.setNum(s);                                 //Line 8
        System.out.println("\nLine 9: Course score is "
                        + s);                            //Line 9
    }

    public static void printGrade(double testScore)
    {
        System.out.print("Line 10: Your grade for "
                        + "the course is ");             //Line 10

        if(testScore >= 90)                              //Line 11
            System.out.println("A");
        else if(testScore >= 80)
                System.out.println("B");
        else if(testScore >= 70)
                System.out.println("C");
        else if(testScore >= 60)
```

7

```
                        System.out.println("D");
            else
                System.out.println("F");
    }
}
```

Sample Run: In this sample run, the user input is shaded.

```
Line 1: Based on the course score, this program computes the course grade.
Line 5: Enter course score: 90.50

Line 9: Course score is 90.5
Line 10: Your grade for the course is A
```

This program works as follows. The program starts to execute at Line 1, which prints the first line of the output (see the Sample Run). The statement in Line 2 calls the method `getScore` with the actual parameter `courseScore` (a reference variable of the `DoubleClass` type declared in `main`). The formal parameter `score`, of the method `getScore`, is a reference variable of the `DoubleClass` type, which receives the value of `courseScore`. Thus, both `score` and `courseScore` point to the same object. Any changes that `score` makes to the object immediately change the value of the object to which `courseScore` points.

Control is then transferred to the method `getScore`. The statement in Line 4 declares the variable `s` of the type `double`. The statement in Line 5 prints the second line of output (see the Sample Run). This statement prompts the user to enter the course `score`. The statement in Line 7 reads and stores the value entered by the user (`90.50` in the Sample Run) in `s`. The statement in Line 8 copies the value of `s` into the object to which `score` points. Thus, at this point, the value of the object that `score` and `courseScore` point to is `90.50`. Next the statement in Line 9 outputs the value of `s` as shown by the third line of the sample output. After the statement in Line 9 executes, control goes back to the method `main`.

The statement in Line 3 executes next. It is a method call to the method `printGrade` with the actual parameter `courseScore.getNum()`. In the expression `courseScore.getNum()`, the method `getNum` of the `class DoubleClass` returns the value of the object pointed to by `courseScore`, which is the course score. Now that the formal parameter `testScore` of the method `printScore` is of a primitive data type, the parameter `testScore` receives the course score. Thus, the value of `testScore` is `90.50`. Now the program executes the statement in Line 10, which outputs the fourth line (see the statement marked Line 10 in the Sample Run). The `if...else` statement in Line 11 determines and outputs the grade for the course. Notice that the output of the `if...else` statement is part of the fourth line of the output (see the Sample Run). After the `if...else` statement executes, control goes back to the method `main`. Because there are no more statements in method `main`, the program terminates.

In this program, the method `main` first calls the method `getScore` to get the course score from the user. The method `main` then calls the method `printGrade` to calculate and print the grade based on the course score. The course score is returned by the method `getScore`; later this course score is used by the method `printGrade`. Because the value retrieved by the `getScore` method is used later in the program, the method `getScore` must pass this value outside. Thus, the formal parameter that holds this value must be an object.

Parameters and Memory Allocation

When a method is called, memory for its formal parameters and variables declared in the body of the method, called **local variables**, is allocated in the method data area. The value of the actual parameter is copied into the memory cell of its corresponding formal parameter. If the parameter is an object (of a class type), both the actual parameter and formal parameter refer to the same memory space.

Reference Variables of the `String` Type as Parameters: A Precaution

Recall that reference variables do not directly contain the data. Reference variables contain the address of the memory space where the data is stored. Moreover, we use the operator `new` to allocate memory space of a specific type. However, in the case of reference variables of the type `String`, we can use the assignment operator to allocate memory space to store a string and assign the string to a `String` variable. Consider the following statement:

```
String str;                        //Line 1
```

The statement

```
str = "Hello";                     //Line 2
```

is equivalent to the statement

```
str = new String("Hello");         //Line 3
```

Figure 7-3 illustrates this concept.

Figure 7-3   Variable `str` and the string object

We assume that the address of the memory space where the string `"Hello"` is stored is 1500. Now suppose that you execute either the statement:

```
str = "Hello There";
```

or the statement

```
str = str + " There";
```

The effect of either of these statements is illustrated by Figure 7-4.

Figure 7-4   `str` after the statement `str = "Hello There";` or
`str = str + " There";` executes

Note that the string `"Hello There"` is stored at a different location. It is now clear that any time you use the assignment operator (or the operator **new**) to assign a string to a **String** variable, the computer allocates different memory space large enough to store the string. In other words, when a string is created and assigned to a **String** variable, the *string cannot be changed.* Moreover, the **class** String does not contain any method that allows you to change an existing string.

If you pass a **String** variable, that is, a reference variable of the **String** type, as a parameter to a method, and within the method you use the assignment operator to change the string, you might think that you have changed the string assigned to the actual parameter. But this does not happen. The string of the actual parameter remains unchanged; a new string is assigned to the formal parameter. This is further illustrated by the following example.

Example 7-9: **String objects as parameters**

Consider the following program:

```
//Program: String Objects as Parameters

public class StringObjectsAsParameters
{
    public static void main(String[] args)
    {
        String str = "Hello";                              //Line 1

        System.out.println("Line 2: str before calling "
                    + "the method stringParameter: "
                    + str);                                //Line 2
        stringParameter(str);                              //Line 3
        System.out.println("Line 4: str after calling "
                    + "the method stringParameter: "
                    + str);                                //Line 4
    }
```

```
    public static void stringParameter(String pStr)
    {
        System.out.println("Line 5: In the method "
                        + "stringParameter");            //Line 5
        System.out.println("Line 6: pStr before changing "
                        + "its value: " + pStr);         //Line 6
        pStr = "Sunny Day";                              //Line 7
        System.out.println("Line 8: pStr after changing "
                        + "its value: " + pStr);         //Line 8

    }
}
```

Output:

```
Line 2: str before calling the method stringParameter: Hello
Line 5: In the method stringParameter
Line 6: pStr before changing its value: Hello
Line 8: pStr after changing its value: Sunny Day
Line 4: str after calling the method stringParameter: Hello
```

The preceding program works as follows. The statement in Line 1 declares `str` to be a `String` variable and assigns the string `"Hello"` to it. The statement in Line 2 outputs the first line of output. The statement in Line 3 calls the method `stringParameter`. The actual parameter is `str` and the formal parameter is `pStr`, so the value of `str` is copied into `pStr`. Since both these parameters are reference variables, `str` and `pStr` point to the same string, which is `"Hello"`.

The control is transferred to the method `stringParameter`. The next statement executed is in Line 5, which outputs the second line of the output. The statement in Line 6 outputs the third line of the output. Notice that this statement also outputs the string referenced by `pStr` and the printed value is the string `"Hello"`. The next statement executed is in Line 7. This statement uses the assignment operator and assigns the string `"Sunny Day"` to `pStr`. After the execution of the statement in Line 7, `str` no longer refers to the same string as does `pStr`. The statement in Line 7, in fact, uses the operator `new` to allocate memory space, stores the string in it, and assigns this string to `pStr`.

The statement in Line 8 outputs the fourth line. Notice that the printed value is the string `"Sunny Day"`. After the execution of this statement control, goes back to the method `main` at Line 4. Therefore, the next statement executed is in Line 4, which outputs the last line of the output. Notice that `str` still refers to the same string, which is `"Hello"`.

 The preceding example shows that you should be careful when passing `String` variables as parameters.

The class StringBuffer

If you want to pass strings as parameters to a method and want to change the actual parameter, you can use the class StringBuffer. The class StringBuffer is similar to the class String. However, strings assigned to StringBuffer variables can be altered.

The class StringBuffer contains the method append, which allows you to append a string to an existing string, and the method delete, which allows you to delete all characters of the string. It also contains other methods to manipulate a string. (See Appendix E for various methods associated with the class StringBuffer.)

 The assignment operator *cannot* be used with StringBuffer variables. You must use the operator new to (*initially*) allocate memory space for a string.

The following example illustrates how objects of the type StringBuffer are passed as parameters.

Example 7-10

```
//Program: StringBuffer Objects as Parameters

public class StringBufferObjectsAsParameters
{
    public static void main (String[] args)
    {
        StringBuffer str = new StringBuffer("Hello");      //Line 1

        System.out.println("Line 2: str before calling "
                        + "the method stringParameter: "
                        + str);                            //Line 2
        stringParameter(str);                              //Line 3
        System.out.println("Line 4: str after calling "
                        + "the method stringParameter: "
                        + str);                            //Line 4
    }

    public static void stringParameter(StringBuffer pStr)
    {
        System.out.println("Line 5: In the method "
                        + "stringParameter");              //Line 5
        System.out.println("Line 6: pStr before changing "
                        + "its value: " + pStr);           //Line 6
        pStr.append(" There");                             //Line 7
        System.out.println("Line 8: pStr after changing "
                        + "its value: " + pStr);           //Line 8
    }
}
```

Output:

```
Line 2: str before calling the method stringParameter: Hello
Line 5: In the method stringParameter
Line 6: pStr before changing its value: Hello
Line 8: pStr after changing its value: Hello There
Line 4: str after calling the method stringParameter: Hello There
```

The preceding program works as follows. The statement in Line 1 declares `str` to be a reference variable of the `StringBuffer` type and assigns the string `"Hello"` to it. The statement in Line 2 outputs the first line of output. The statement in Line 3 calls the method `stringParameter`. The actual parameter is `str` and the formal parameter `pStr`. The value of `str` is copied into `pStr`. Since both of these parameters are reference variables, `str` and `pStr` point to the same string, which is `"Hello"`.

The control is transferred to the method `stringParameter`. The next statement executed is in Line 5, which outputs the second line of the output. The statement in Line 6 outputs the third line of the output. Notice that this statement also outputs the string to which `pStr` points, and the printed value is that string. The next statement executed is in Line 7. This statement uses the method `append` to append the string `" There"` to the string referenced by `pStr`. After the execution of this statement, `pStr` refers to the string `"Hello There"`. However, this also changes the string that was assigned to the variable `str`. After the execution of the statement in Line 7, `str` points to the same string as does `pStr`.

The statement in Line 8 outputs the fourth line of output. Notice that the printed value is the string `"Hello There"`, which is the string referenced by `pStr`. After the execution of this statement control goes back to the method `main` at Line 4. Therefore, the next statement executed is in Line 4, which outputs the last line of the output. Notice that `str` refers to the string `"Hello There"`.

Because parameter passing is fundamental to any programming language, Example 7-11 further illustrates this concept.

Example 7-11

```java
//Example 7-11


public class Example7_11
{
    public static void main(String[] args)
    {
        int num1;                              //Line 1
        IntClass num2 = new IntClass();        //Line 2
        char ch;                               //Line 3
        StringBuffer str;                      //Line 4
```

7

```
        num1 = 10;                                //Line 5
        num2.setNum(15);                          //Line 6
        ch = 'A';                                 //Line 7
        str = new StringBuffer("Sunny");          //Line 8

        System.out.println("Line 9: Inside main: "
                          + "num1 = " + num1
                          + ", num2 = " + num2.getNum()
                          + ", ch = " + ch
                          + ", and str = "
                          + str);                 //Line 9


        funcOne(num1, num2, ch, str);             //Line 10

        System.out.println("Line 11: After funcOne: "
                          + "num1 = " + num1
                          + ", num2 = " + num2.getNum()
                          + ", ch = " + ch
                          + ", and str = "
                          + str);                 //Line 11
    }

    public static void funcOne(int a, IntClass b,
                         char v, StringBuffer pStr)
    {
        int num;                                  //Line 12
        int len;                                  //Line 13

        num = b.getNum();                         //Line 14
        a++;                                      //Line 15
        b.addtoNum(12);                           //Line 16
        v = 'B';                                  //Line 17
        len = pStr.length();                      //Line 18
        pStr.delete(0, len);                      //Line 19
        pStr.append("Warm");                      //Line 20

        System.out.println("Line 21: Inside funcOne: \n"
                          + "            a = " + a
                          + ", b = " + b.getNum()
                          + ", v = " + v
                          + ", pStr = " + pStr
                          + ", len = " + len
                          + ", and num = " + num); //Line 21
    }
}
```

Output:

```
Line 9: Inside main: num1 = 10, num2 = 15, ch = A, and str = Sunny
Line 21: Inside funOne:
         a = 11, b = 27, v = B, pStr = Warm, len = 5, and num = 15
Line 11: After funcOne: num1 = 10, num2 = 27, ch = A, and str = Warm
```

Let's walk through this program. The lines are numbered for easy reference, and the values of the variables are shown before and/or after each statement executes.

Just before the statement in Line 5 executes, memory is allocated only for the variables and objects of the method **main**. Moreover, **num1**, **ch**, and **str** are not initialized. The variable **num2** at Line 2 is declared, and the memory for the data is also allocated and initialized to **0**. This is because **num2** is a reference variable of **IntClass** type and the **class IntClass** automatically initializes the allocated memory space of the object to **0**. Just before the statement in Line 5 executes, the variables and objects are as shown in Figure 7-5.

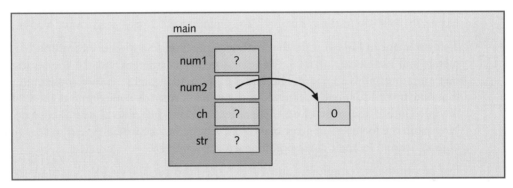

Figure 7-5   Variables and objects just before the statement in Line 5 executes

The statement in Line 5 stores **10** into **num1;**, the statement in Line 6 stores **15** in the object pointed to by **num2;**, the statement in Line 7 stores the character **'A'** into **ch;**, and the statement in Line 8 allocates memory space to store the string **"Sunny"** into it and assigns this string to **str**. After the statement in Line 8 executes, the variables and objects of the method **main** are as shown in Figure 7-6.

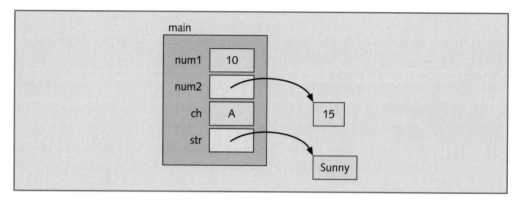

Figure 7-6   Variables and objects after the statement in Line 8 executes

Line 9 produces the following output:

```
Line 9: Inside main: num1 = 10, num2 = 15, ch = A, and str = Sunny
```

The statement in Line 10 calls the method funcOne. The method funcOne has four parameters and two local variables. Memory for the parameters and the local variable of the method funcOne is allocated. The values of the actual parameters are copied into the corresponding formal parameters. Therefore, the value of num1 is copied into a, the value of num2 is copied into b, the value of ch is copied into v, and the value of str is copied into pStr. Now both the formal parameter b and pStr are reference variables, and so they point to the objects referred by their corresponding actual parameters.

Just before the statement in Line 14 executes, the variables and objects are as shown in Figure 7-7.

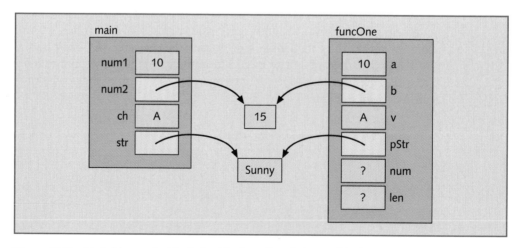

Figure 7-7   Variables and objects just before the statement in Line 14 executes

The statement in Line 14 retrieves the value of b and stores it into num. After the statement in Line 14 executes, the variables and objects are as shown in Figure 7-8.

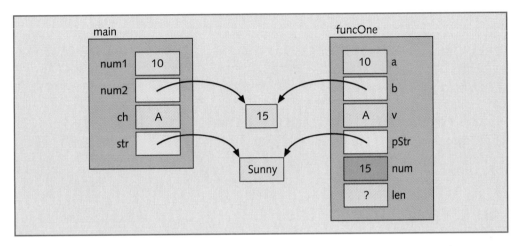

Figure 7-8   Variables and objects after the statement, num = b.getNum();, in Line 14 executes

The statement in Line 15 increments the value of a by 1. After the statement in Line 15 executes, the variables and objects are as shown in Figure 7-9.

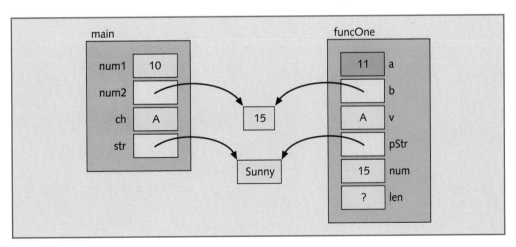

Figure 7-9   Variables and objects after the statement, a++;, in Line 15 executes

The statement in Line 16 adds **12** to the previous value of the object referred by **b**. After the statement in Line 16 executes, the variables and objects are as shown in Figure 7-10.

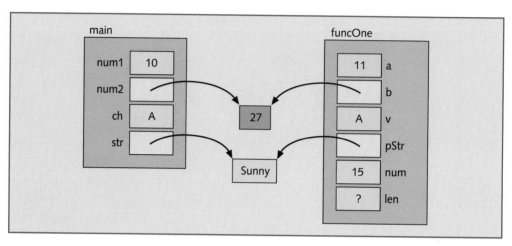

Figure 7-10   Variables and objects after the statement, `b.addtoNum(12);`, in Line 16 executes

The statement in Line 17 stores the character **'B'** into **v**. After the statement in Line 17 executes, the variables and objects are as shown in Figure 7-11.

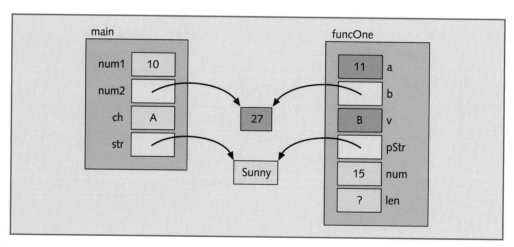

Figure 7-11   Variables and objects after the statement, `v = 'B';`, in Line 17 executes

The statement in Line 18 stores the length of the string referred by **pStr** into **len**. After the statement in Line 18 executes, the variables and objects are as shown in Figure 7-12. (Notice that the length of the string **"Sunny"** is 5.)

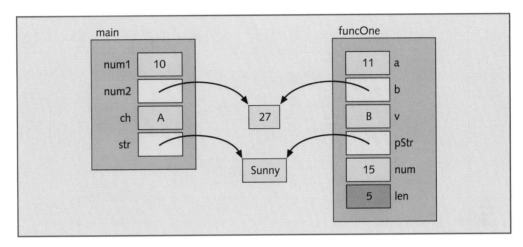

Figure 7-12   Variables and objects after the statement, `len = pStr.length();`, in Line 17 executes

The statement in Line 19 uses the method **delete** of the **class StringBuffer** and deletes the string **"Sunny"**. After the statement in Line 19 executes, the variables and objects are as shown in Figure 7-13.

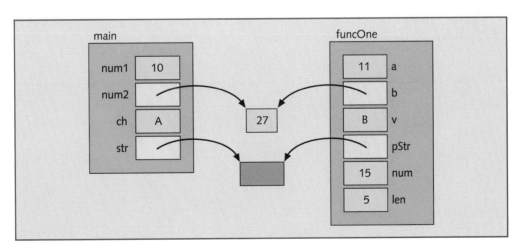

Figure 7-13   Variables and objects after the statement, `pStr.delete(0,len);`, in Line 19 executes

The statement in Line 20 uses the method **append** of the **class StringBuffer** and appends the string **"Warm"** to the string referred by **pStr**. After the statement in Line 20 executes, the variables and objects are as shown in Figure 7-14.

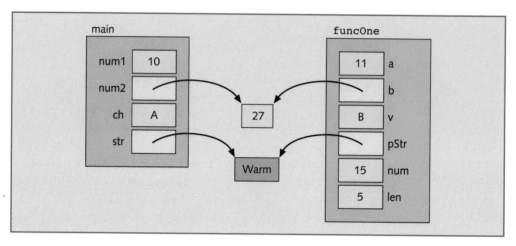

Figure 7-14   Variables and objects after the statement, **pStr.append("Warm");**, in Line 20 executes

The statement in Line 21 produces the following output:

```
Line 21: Inside funcOne:
         a = 11, b = 27, v = B, pStr = Warm, len = 5, and num = 15
```

After the statement in Line 21 executes, control goes to Line 11. The memory allocated for the variables of method **funcOne** is deallocated. The values of the variables of the method **main** are as shown in Figure 7-15.

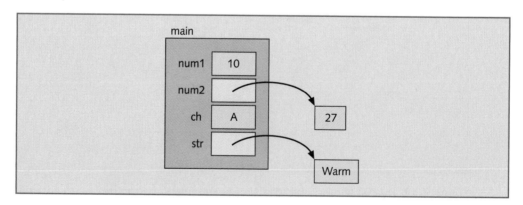

Figure 7-15   Variables and objects of **main** when the control goes back to **main**

Line 11 produces the following output:

```
Line 11: After funcOne: num1 = 10, num2 = 27, ch = A, and str = Warm
```

After the statement in Line 11 executes, the program terminates.

SCOPE OF AN IDENTIFIER WITHIN A CLASS

The previous sections presented several examples of programs with user-defined methods. In these examples, and in Java in general, identifiers are declared in a method heading, within a block, or outside a block. (Recall that an identifier is the name of something in Java such as a variable or method.) A question naturally arises: Are you allowed to access any identifier anywhere in the program? The answer is no. Certain rules exist that you must follow to access an identifier. The **scope** of an identifier refers to what other parts of the program can "see" an identifier, that is, where it is accessible (visible). For example, a **local identifier** is an identifier declared within a method or block that can be accessed only by code within that same method or block.

This section examines the scope of an identifier. Let's first define the following widely used term.

Local identifier: Identifier declared within a method or block and that is visible only within that method or block.

Java does not allow the nesting of methods. That is, you cannot include the definition of one method in the body of another method.

Within a class, an identifier is accessible throughout the class, with the exception that a `static` method cannot access nonstatic identifiers. The scope rules for identifiers declared within a block follow. The identifier declared within a block is accessible:

- Only within the block from the point at which it is declared until the end of the block

- By those blocks that are nested within that block if the nested block does not have an identifier with the same name as that of the outside block (the block that encloses the nested block)

Within a method, an identifier used to name a variable in the outer block of the method cannot be used to name any other variable in an inner block of the method.

Within a `class`, any method can call any other method, with the exception that a `static` method cannot call a nonstatic method.

Before you consider an example which explains these scope rules, first note the scope of the identifier declared in the `for` statement. Java allows the programmer to declare a variable in the initialization statement of the `for` statement. For example, the following `for` statement

```
for(int count = 1; count < 10; count++)
    System.out.println(count);
```

declares the variable count and initializes it to 1. The scope of the variable count is limited only to the body of the for loop.

Example 7-12 illustrates the scope rules.

Example 7-12

Consider the following Java program.

```java
public class ScopeRules
{
    static final double rate = 10.50;
    static int z;
    static double t;

    public static void main(String[] args)
    {
        int num;
        double x, z;
        char ch;

        //...
    }

    public static void one(int x, char y)
    {
        //...
    }

    public static int w;

    public static void two(int one, int z)
    {
        char ch;
        int a;


            //block three
        {
            int x = 12;

            //...
        }//end block three
        //...
    }
}
```

Table 7-3 summarizes the scope (visibility) of the identifiers in Example 7-12.

Table 7-3 Scope (Visibility) of the Identifiers

Identifier	Visibility in one	Visibility in two	Visibility in block three	Visibility in main
rate (before main)	Y	Y	Y	Y
z (before main)	Y	Y	N	N
t (before main)	Y	Y	Y	Y
main	Y	Y	Y	Y
local variables of main	N	N	N	Y
one (method name)	Y	Y	Y	Y
x (one's formal parameter)	Y	N	N	N
y (one's formal parameter)	Y	N	N	N
w (before method two)	Y	Y	Y	Y
two (method name)	Y	Y	Y	Y
one (two's formal parameter)	N	Y	Y	N
z (two's formal parameter)	N	Y	Y	N
local variables of two	N	Y	Y	N
x (block three's local variable)	N	N	Y	N

Before we look at some programming examples, we will explore the concept of method overloading.

METHOD OVERLOADING: AN INTRODUCTION

In Java, within a `class` several methods can have the same name. This is called **method overloading**. If several methods within a `class` have the same name, every method must have:

- A different number of formal parameters, or
- If the number of formal parameters is the same, then the data type of the formal parameter, in the order you list, must differ in at least one position.

The types of parameters determine which method to execute.

Method overloading: Creating several methods, within a `class`, with the same name.

Suppose you need to write a method that determines the larger of two items. Both items can be integers, floating-point numbers, characters, or strings. You could write several methods as follows. (We only give the method heading.)

```
int largerInt(int x, int y)
char largerChar(char first, char second)
```

```
double largerDouble(double u, double v)
String largerString(String first, String second)
```

The method `largerInt` determines the larger of two integers, the method `largerChar` determines the larger of two characters, and so on. All of these methods perform similar operations. Instead of giving different names to these methods, you can use the same name—say, `larger`—for each method; that is, you can overload the method `larger` as follows:

```
int larger(int x, int y)
char larger(char first, char second)
double larger(double u, double v)
String larger(String first, String second)
```

If the call is `larger(5,3)`, for example, the first method executes because the actual parameters match the formal parameters of the first method. If the call is `larger('A', '9')`, the second method executes, and so on.

Method overloading is used when you have the same action for different sets of data. Of course, for method overloading to work, you must give the definition of each method.

PROGRAMMING EXAMPLE: DATA COMPARISON

This programming example illustrates:

1. How to read data from more than one file in the same program
2. How to send output to a file
3. How to generate bar graphs
4. With the help of methods and parameter passing, how to use the same program segment on different (but similar) sets of data
5. How to use structured design to solve a problem and how to perform parameter passing

This program is broken into two parts. First, you learn how to read data from more than one file. Second, you learn how to generate bar graphs.

Two groups of students at a local university are enrolled in certain special courses during the summer semester. The courses are offered for the first time and are taught by different teachers. At the end of the semester, both groups are given the same tests for the same courses and their scores are recorded in separate files. The data in each file is in the following form:

```
courseNo  score1, score2, ..., scoreN -999
courseNo  score1, score2, ..., scoreM -999
   .
   .
   .
```

Let's write a program that finds the average course score for each course for each group. The output is of the following form:

```
Course No   Group No    Course Average
   CSC          1           83.71
                2           80.82

   ENG          1           82.00
                2           78.20
    .
    .
    .
Avg for group 1: 82.04
Avg for group 2: 82.01
```

Input Because data for the two groups are recorded in separate files, input data appear in two separate files

Output As shown above

Problem Analysis and Algorithm Design

Reading input data from both files is straightforward. Suppose the data are stored in the file **group1.txt** for group 1 and in the file **group2.txt** for group 2; these files are on floppy disk **A**. After processing the data for one group, we can process data for the second group for the same course, and continue until we run out of data. Processing data for each course is similar and uses the following process:

    a. Sum the scores for the course.

    b. Count the number of students in the course.

    c. Divide the total score by the number of students to find the course average.

    d. Output the results.

We are comparing only the averages of the corresponding courses in each group. The data in each file is ordered according to course ID. To ensure that only the averages of the corresponding courses are compared, we compare the course IDs for each group. If the corresponding course IDs are not the same, we output an error message and terminate the program.

This discussion suggests that we should write a method, **calculateAverage**, to find the course average. We should also write another method, **printResult**, to output the data in the form given. By passing the appropriate parameters, we can use the same methods, **calculateAverage** and **printResult**, to process each course's data for both groups. (In the second part of the program, we modify the method **printResult**.)

The preceding discussion translates into the following algorithm:

    1. Initialize the variables.

    2. Get the course IDs for group 1 and group 2.

3. If the course IDs are different, print an error message and exit the program.
4. Calculate the course average for group 1 and group 2.
5. Print the results in the form given earlier.
6. Repeat Steps 2–6 for each course.
7. Print the final results.

Variables (Method `main`)

The preceding discussion suggests that the program needs the following variables for data manipulation in the method `main`:

```
String courseId1;                          //course ID for group 1
String courseId2;                          //course ID for group 2
int numberOfCourses;
DoubleClass avg1 = new DoubleClass(); //average for a course
                                           //in group 1
DoubleClass avg2 = new DoubleClass(); //average for a course
                                           //in group 2
double avgGroup1;                          //average group 1
double avgGroup2;                          //average group 2

String inputGroup1;                        //retrieve group1 data
String inputGroup2;                        //retrieve group2 data
StringTokenizer tokenizer1;                //tokenizer for group1 data
StringTokenizer tokenizer2;                //tokenizer for group2 data

BufferedReader group1 =
        new BufferedReader(new FileReader("a:\\group1.txt"));
BufferedReader group2 =
        new BufferedReader(new FileReader("a:\\group2.txt"));
PrintWriter outfile =
        new PrintWriter(new FileWriter("a:\\student.out"));

DecimalFormat twoDecimal = new DecimalFormat("0.00");
```

Next, we discuss the methods `calculateAverage` and `printResult`. Then we will put the method `main` together.

Method `calculateAverage`

This method calculates the average for a course. Because the input is stored in a file and the input file is opened in the method `main`, we must pass the variable associated with the input file to this method. Also, because the input line was read in the method `main`, the tokenizer might have some test scores in it. Therefore, we need to pass the tokenizer to this method. Furthermore, after calculating the course average, this method must pass the course average to the method `main`. Therefore, this method has three parameters.

To find the course average, we must first find the sum of all scores for the course and the number of students who took the course; we then divide the sum by the number of students. Thus, we need a variable to find the sum of the scores, a variable to find the number of students, and a variable to read and store a score. Of course, we must initialize the variables to find the sum and the number of students to zero.

Local Variables (Method `calculateAverage`)

In the previous discussion of data manipulation, we identified three variables for the method `calculateAverage`:

```
double totalScore;     //to store the sum of scores
int numberOfStudents;//to store the number of students
int score;             //to read and store a course score
```

The above discussion translates into the following algorithm for the method `calculateAverage`:

    a. Declare variables.

    b. Initialize `totalScore` to `0.0`.

    c. Initialize `numberOfStudents` to `0`.

    d. Get the (next) course score.

    e. `while (score != -999)`:

        i. Update `totalScore` by adding the course score read in step d.

        ii. Increment `numberOfStudents` by 1.

        iii. Get the next course score.

    f. `courseAvg.setNum(totalScore / numberOfStudents);`

A `while` loop is used to repeat steps d, e, and f.

We are now ready to write the definition of the method `calculateAverage`.

```
public static void calculateAverage(BufferedReader inp,
                                    StringTokenizer tok,
                                    DoubleClass courseAvg)
                                       throws IOException
{
    double totalScore = 0.0;          //Steps a and b
    int numberOfStudents = 0;         //Steps a and c
    int score = 0;                    //Steps a

    if(!tok.hasMoreTokens())
        tok = new StringTokenizer(inp.readLine());  //Step d
    score = Integer.parseInt(tok.nextToken());       //Step d

    while(score != -999)                              //Step e
    {
        totalScore = totalScore + score;             //Step e.i
        numberOfStudents++;                          //Step e.ii
        if(!tok.hasMoreTokens())
```

```
                     tok = new StringTokenizer(inp.readLine());
                                                    //Step e.iii
              score = Integer.parseInt(tok.nextToken());  //Step e.iii
       }//end while

       courseAvg.setNum(totalScore / numberOfStudents);//Step f
}//end calculate Average
```

Method `printResult`

The method `printResult` prints the group's course ID, group number, and course average. The output is stored in a file. We must pass four parameters to this method: the variable associated with the output file, the group number, the course ID, and the course average for the group. Also, from the output, it is clear that we print the course ID only before group 1. In pseudocode, the algorithm is:

```
if(group number == 1)
   print course ID
else
   print a blank

print group number and course average
```

The definition of the method `printResult` follows:

```
public static void printResult(PrintWriter outp, String courseId,
                               int groupNo, DoubleClass avg)
{
     DecimalFormat twoDecimal =
                 new DecimalFormat("0.00");

     if(groupNo == 1)
        outp.print("  " + courseId + "   ");
     else
        outp.print("           ");

     outp.println("\t" + groupNo + "\t    "
                 + twoDecimal.format(avg.getNum()));
}
```

Now that we have designed and defined the methods `calculateAverage` and `printResults`, we can describe the algorithm for the method `main`. Before outlining the algorithm, however, note the following: It is quite possible that in both input files the data are ordered according to the course IDs, but one file might have fewer courses than the other. We discover this error only after we have processed both files and discover that one file has unprocessed data. Make sure to check for this error before printing the final answer—that is, the average for group 1 and group 2.

Main Algorithm: Method `main`

1. Declare the variables (local declaration).
2. Create and initialize variables to open input and output files.
3. To output floating-point numbers in a fixed decimal format with two decimal places, declare a `DecimalFormat` variable and initialize this variable to the appropriate string.
4. Initialize the course average for group 1 to `0.0`.
5. Initialize the course average for group 2 to `0.0`.
6. Initialize the number of courses to `0`.
7. Print the heading.
8. Get the next input line for group 1.
9. Get the next input line for group 2.
10. For each course in group 1 and group 2:
    a. Retrieve `courseId1`, for group 1.
    b. Retrieve, `courseId2`, for group 2.
    c. `if(courseId1 != courseId2)`
       ```
       {
           System.out.println("Data error: Course IDs do not match");
           return;
       }
       ```
    d. `else`
       ```
       {
       ```
       i.   Calculate the course average for group 1 (call the method `calculateAverage` and pass the appropriate parameters).
       ii. Calculate the course average for group 2 (call the method `calculateAverage` and pass the appropriate parameters).
       iii. Print the results for group 1 (call the method `printResult` and pass the appropriate parameters).
       iv. Print the results for group 2 (call the method `printResult` and pass the appropriate parameters).
       v.   Update the average for group 1.
       vi. Update the average for group 2.
       vii. Increment the number of courses.
       ```
       }
       ```
    e. Get the next input line for group 1.
    f. Get the next input line for group 2.
11. a. if not_end_of_file on group 1 and end_of_file on group 2
       print "Ran out of data for group 2 before group 1"

b. else

    if end_of_file on group 1 and not_end_of_file on group 2

    print "Ran out of data for group 1 before group 2"

c. else

    print the average of group 1 and group 2.

12. Close the output file.

Complete Program Listing

```java
//Program: Comparison of Class Averages.

import java.io.*;
import java.util.*;
import java.text.DecimalFormat;

public class DataComparison
{
    public static void main (String[] args) throws
                                FileNotFoundException,
                                IOException

    {
                                            //Step 1
        String courseId1;                   //course ID for group 1
        String courseId2;                   //course ID for group 2
        int numberOfCourses;
        DoubleClass avg1 = new DoubleClass();//average for a course
                                            //in group 1
        DoubleClass avg2 = new DoubleClass();//average for a course
                                            //in group 2
        double avgGroup1;                   //average group 1
        double avgGroup2;                   //average group 2

        String inputGroup1;
        String inputGroup2;
        StringTokenizer tokenizer1 = null;
        StringTokenizer tokenizer2 = null;


                    //Step 2 Open input and output files
        BufferedReader group1 =
            new BufferedReader(new FileReader("a:\\group1.txt"));
        BufferedReader group2 =
```

```java
        new BufferedReader(new FileReader("a:\\group2.txt"));
PrintWriter outfile =
        new PrintWriter(new FileWriter("a:\\student.out"));

DecimalFormat twoDecimal =
            new DecimalFormat("0.00");          //Step 3

avgGroup1 = 0.0;                                //Step 4
avgGroup2 = 0.0;                                //Step 5

numberOfCourses = 0;                            //Step 6

                //print heading: Step 7
outfile.println("Course No    Group No    Course Average");

inputGroup1 = group1.readLine();               //Step 8
inputGroup2 = group2.readLine();               //Step 9

while((inputGroup1 != null) &&
      (inputGroup2 != null))                   //Step 10
{
    tokenizer1 = new StringTokenizer(inputGroup1);
    courseId1 = tokenizer1.nextToken();        //Step 10a
    tokenizer2 = new StringTokenizer(inputGroup2);
    courseId2 = tokenizer2.nextToken();        //Step 10b

    if(!courseId1.equals(courseId2))           //Step 10c
    {
        System.out.println("Data error: Course IDs "
                        + "do not match.");
        System.out.println("Program terminates.");
        outfile.println("Data error: Course IDs "
                        + "do not match.");
        outfile.println("Program terminates.");
        outfile.close();
        return;
    }
    else                                       //Step 10d
    {
        calculateAverage(group1, tokenizer1, avg1);//Step 10d.i
        calculateAverage(group2, tokenizer2, avg2);//Step 10d.ii
        printResult(outfile,courseId1,1,avg1);   //Step 10d.iii
        printResult(outfile,courseId2,2,avg2);   //Step 10d.iv
        avgGroup1 = avgGroup1 + avg1.getNum();   //Step 10d.v
        avgGroup2 = avgGroup2 + avg2.getNum();   //Step 10d.vi
        outfile.println();
            numberOfCourses++;                   //Step 10d.vii
    }
```

```
            inputGroup1 = group1.readLine();           //Step 10e
            inputGroup2 = group2.readLine();           //Step 10f
        }//end while

    if((inputGroup1 != null) && (inputGroup2 == null))
                                                       //Step 11a
        System.out.println("Ran out of data for group 2 "
                        + "before group 1.");
    else                                               //Step 11b
        if((inputGroup1 == null) && (inputGroup1 != null))
            System.out.println("Ran out of data for "
                            + "group 1 before group 2.");
        else                                           //Step 11c
        {
            outfile.println("Avg for group 1: " +
                twoDecimal.format(avgGroup1 / numberOfCourses));
            outfile.println("Avg for group 2: " +
                twoDecimal.format(avgGroup2 / numberOfCourses));
        }

    outfile.close();                                   //Step 12
}

public static void calculateAverage(BufferedReader inp,
                                    StringTokenizer tok,
                                    DoubleClass courseAvg)
                                       throws IOException
{
    double totalScore = 0.0;                           //Steps a and b
    int numberOfStudents = 0;                          //Steps a and c
    int score = 0;                                     //Steps a

    if(!tok.hasMoreTokens())
        tok = new StringTokenizer(inp.readLine());
                                                       //Step d
    score = Integer.parseInt(tok.nextToken()); //Step d

    while(score != -999)                               //Step e
    {
        totalScore = totalScore + score;               //Step e.i
        numberOfStudents++;                            //Step e.ii
        if(!tok.hasMoreTokens())
            tok = new StringTokenizer(inp.readLine());
                                                       //Step e.iii
```

```
        score = Integer.parseInt(tok.nextToken()); //Step e.iii
    }//end while

    courseAvg.setNum(totalScore / numberOfStudents);//Step f
}//end calculate Average

public static void printResult(PrintWriter outp,
                               String courseId,
                               int groupNo, DoubleClass avg)
{

    DecimalFormat twoDecimal =
            new DecimalFormat("0.00");

    if(groupNo == 1)
        outp.print("  " + courseId + "   ");
    else
        outp.print("        ");

    outp.println("\t" + groupNo + "\t    "
            + twoDecimal.format(avg.getNum()));
    }
}
```

Sample Output

```
Course No   Group No     Course Average
  CSC          1            83.71
               2            80.82

  ENG          1            82.00
               2            78.20

  HIS          1            77.69
               2            84.15

  MTH          1            83.57
               2            84.29

  PHY          1            83.22
               2            82.60
```

```
Avg for group 1: 82.04
Avg for group 2: 82.01
```

Input Data Group 1

```
CSC 80 100 70 80 72 90 89 100 83 70 90 73 85 90 -999
ENG 80 90 80 94 90 74 78 63 83 80 90 -999
HIS 90 70 80 70 90 50 89 83 90 68 90 60 80  -999
MTH 74 80 75 89 90 73 90 82 74 90 84 100 90 79 -999
PHY 100 83 93 80 63 78 88 89 75 -999
```

Input Data Group 2

```
CSC 90 75 90 75 80 89 100 60 80 70 80 -999
ENG 80 80 70 68 70 78 80 90 90 76 -999
HIS 100 80 80 70 90 76 88 90 90 75 90 85 80 -999
MTH 80 85 85 92 90 90 74 90 83 65 72 90 84 100 -999
PHY 90 93 73 85 68 75 67 100 87 88 -999
```

Bar Graphs

In the business world, company executives often like to see results in a visual form, such as bar graphs. Many currently available software packages can analyze data in several forms and then display the results in such visual forms as bar graphs or pie charts. The second part of this program will display the earlier results in the form of bar graphs, as shown below:

```
Course        Course Average
   ID    0   10   20   30   40   50   60   70   80   90   100
         |....|....|....|....|....|....|....|....|....|....|
   CSC   ******************************************
         ########################################

   ENG   ******************************************
         ########################################


Group 1 -- ****
Group 1 -- ####

Avg for group 1: 64.48
Avg for group 2: 65.22
```

Each symbol (* or #) in the bar graph represents 2 points. If a course average is less than 2, no symbol is printed.

Because the output is in the form of a bar graph, we need to modify the method `printResult`.

Method printResult

The method `printResult` prints the course ID and the bar graph representing the average for a course. The output is stored in a file. So we must pass four parameters to this method: the variable associated with the output file, the group number (to print * or #), the course ID, and the course average for the department.

To print the bar graph, we can use a loop to print a symbol for each two points. If the average is `78.45`, for example, we must print `39` symbols to represent this average. To find the number of symbols to print, we can use integer division as follows:

```
numberOfSymbols = (int)(average)/2;
```

For example, `(int)(78.45)/2 = 78/2 = 39`.

Following this outline, the definition of the method `printResult` is:

```
public static void printResult(PrintWriter outp, String courseId,
                               int groupNo, DoubleClass avg)
{
        int noOfSymbols;
        int count;

        if(groupNo == 1)
           outp.print(" " + courseId + "     ");
        else
           outp.print("          ");

        noOfSymbols = (int)(avg.getNum())/2;

        if(groupNo == 1)
           for(count = 1; count <= noOfSymbols; count++)
              outp.print("*");
        else
           for(count = 1; count <= noOfSymbols; count++)
              outp.print("#");

        outp.println();
}//end printResults
```

We also include a method, `printHeading`, to print the first two lines of the output. The definition of this method is:

```
public static void printHeading(PrintWriter outp)
{
    outp.println("Course          Course Average");
    outp.println("  ID      0   10   20   30   40   50   60   70"
             + "   80   90   100");
    outp.println("          |....|....|....|....|....|....|....|"
             + "....|....|....|");
}//end printHeading
```

If you replace the method `printResult` in the preceding program, include the method `printHeading`, include the statements to output—Group 1 -- **** and Group 2 -- ####—and rerun the program, then the output for the previous data is as follows:

Sample Output:

```
Course          Course Average
    ID      0   10   20   30   40   50   60   70   80   90   100
            |....|....|....|....|....|....|....|....|....|....|....|
   CSC      ********************************************
            ######################################

   ENG      *******************************************
            ######################################

   HIS      *****************************************
            ########################################

   MTH      ******************************************
            ########################################

   PHY      ******************************************
            ######################################

Group 1 -- ****
Group 2 -- ####
Avg for group 1: 82.04
Avg for group 2: 82.01
```

Compare both outputs. Which one do you think is better?

QUICK REVIEW

1. Methods are like miniature programs and are called modules.

2. Methods enable you to divide a program into manageable tasks.

3. The Java system provides standard (predefined) methods.

4. In general, to use a predefined method, you must:

   a. Know the name of the name of the class containing the method, and the name of the package containing the class that contains the method.

   b. Import the class in the program.

   c. Know the name and type of the method, and number and types of the parameters (arguments).

5. To use a method of a class contained in the package `java.lang` in a program, you do not need to explicitly import these classes in your program.

6. There are two types of user-defined methods: value-returning methods and void methods.

7. Variables defined in a method heading are called formal parameters.

8. Expressions, variables, or constant values used in a method call are called actual parameters.

9. In a method call, the number of actual parameters and their types must match the formal parameters in the order given.

10. To call a method, use its name together with the actual parameter list.

11. A value-returning method returns a value. Therefore, a value-returning method is usually used (called) in either an expression or an output statement, or as a parameter in a method call.

12. The general syntax of a user-defined method is:

```
modifier(s) methodType  methodName(formal parameter list)
{
    statements
}
```

13. The line

```
modifier(s) methodType methodName(formal parameter list)
```

is called the method heading (or method header). Statements enclosed between curly braces, { and }, are called the body of the method.

14. The method heading and the body of the method are called the definition of the method.

15. If a method has no parameters, you still need the empty parentheses in both the method heading and the method call.

16. A value-returning method returns its value via the `return` statement.

17. A method can have more than one `return` statement. However, whenever a `return` statement executes in a method, the remaining statements are skipped and the method exits.

18. When the program executes, the execution always begins with the first statement in the method `main`.

19. User-defined methods execute only when they are called.

20. A call to a method transfers control from the caller to the called method.

21. In a method call statement, you specify only the actual parameters, not their data type or the method type.

22. When a method exits, the control goes back to the caller.

23. A method that does not have a type is called a **void** method.

24. A return statement without any value can be used in a **void** method.

25. If a return statement is used in a **void** method, it is typically used to exit the method early.

26. The heading of a **void** method starts with the word **void**.

27. In Java, **void** is a reserved word.

28. A **void** method may or may not have parameters.

29. To call a **void** method, you use the method name together with the actual parameters in a stand-alone statement.

30. The formal parameter receives a copy of its corresponding actual parameter.

31. If a formal parameter is of the primitive data type, it directly stores the value of the actual parameter.

32. If a formal parameter is a reference variable, it copies the value of its corresponding actual parameter, which is the address of the object where the actual data is stored. Therefore, if a formal parameter is a reference variable, both the formal and actual parameters refer to the same object.

33. If a formal parameter needs to change the value of an actual parameter, in the method heading you must declare this formal parameter as an appropriate reference variable.

34. The scope of an identifier refers to those parts of the program where it is accessible.

35. Variables declared within a method (or block) are called local variables.

36. Within a **class**, any method can call any other method with the exception that a **static** method cannot call a nonstatic method.

37. Specific scope rules are defined in the section, Scope of an Identifier.

38. In Java, a method can be overloaded (more than one method can have the same name).

39. If a method is overloaded, all methods with the same name must have a different number of formal parameters, or if the number of formal parameters is the same, then the data type of the formal parameter, in the order you list, must differ in at least one position.

EXERCISES

1. Mark the following statements as true or false.

   a. To use a predefined method of a **class** contained in the package **java.lang** in a program, you need to know only what the name of the method is and how to use it.

   b. A value-returning method returns only one value.

   c. Parameters allow you to use different values each time the method is called.

   d. When a **return** statement executes in a user-defined method, the method immediately exits.

   e. A value-returning method returns only integer values.

f. If a Java method does not use parameters, parentheses around the empty parameter list are still needed.

g. In Java, the names of the corresponding formal and actual parameters must be the same.

h. In Java, method definitions can be nested; that is, the definition of one method can be enclosed in the body of another method.

2. What is the output of the following Java program?

```java
public class Exercise2
{
    public static void main(String[] args)
    {
        int counter;

        for(counter = 1; counter <= 100; counter++)
            if(Math.pow(Math.floor(Math.sqrt(counter)),2) == counter)
                System.out.print(counter + " ");
        System.out.println();
    }
}
```

3. Which of the following method headings are valid? If they are invalid, explain why.

```java
public static one(int a, int b)
public static int thisone(char x)
public static char another(int a, b)
public static double yetanother
```

4. Consider the following statements:

```java
double num1, num2, num3;
int int1, int2, int3;
int value;

num1 = 5.0; num2 = 6.0; num3 = 3.0;
int1 = 4;  int2 = 7; int3 = 8;
```

and the method heading:

```java
public static double cube(double a, double b, double c)
```

Which of the following statements are valid? If they are invalid, explain why.

a. `value = cube (num1, 15.0, num3);`

b. `System.out.println(cube(num1, num3, num2));`

c. `System.out.println(cube(6.0, 8.0, 10.5));`

d. `System.out.println(num1 + " " + num3);`

e. `System.out.println(cube(num1, num3));`

f. `value = cube(num1, int2, num3);`

g. `value = cube(7, 8, 9);`

5. Consider the following methods:

```
public static int secret(int x)
{
    int i, j;

    i = 2 * x;

    if(i > 10)
        j = x / 2;
    else
        j = x / 3;

    return j - 1;
}
```

```
public static int another(int a, int b)
{
    int i , j;

    j = 0;

    for(i = a; i <= b; i++)
        j = j + i;

    return j;
}
```

What is the output of each of the following program segments?

a. `x = 10;`
   `System.out.println(secret(x));`

b. `x = 5; y = 8;`
   `System.out.println(another(x, y));`

c. `x = 10; k = secret(x);`
   `System.out.println(x + " " + k + " "`
   `                    + another(x, k));`

d. `x = 5; y = 8;`
   `System.out.println(another(y, x));`

6. Consider the following method headings:

```
public static int test (int x, char ch, double d, int y)
public static double two(double d1, double d2)
public static char three(int x, int y, char ch, double d)
```

Answer the following questions.

a. How many parameters does the method `test` have? What is the type of the method `test`?

b. How many parameters does method `two` have? What is the type of method `two`?

c. How many parameters does method `three` have? What is the type of method `three`?

d. How many actual parameters are needed to call the method `test`? What is the type of each parameter, and in what order should you use these parameters in a call to the method `test`?

e. Write a Java statement that prints the value returned by the method `test` with the actual parameters `5, 5, 7.3,` and `'z'`.

f. Write a Java statement that prints the value returned by method `two` with the actual parameters `17.5` and `18.3`, respectively.

g. Write a Java statement that prints the next character returned by method `three`. (Use your own actual parameters.)

7. Consider the following method:

```
public static int mystery(int x, double y, char ch)
{
    int u;

    if('A' <= ch && ch <= 'R')
        return(2 * x + (int)(y));
    else
        return((int)(2 * y) - x);
}
```

What is the output of the following Java statements?

a. `System.out.println(mystery(5,4.3,'B'));`

b. `System.out.println(mystery(4,9.7,'v'));`

c. `System.out.println(2 * mystery(6,3.9,'D'));`

7

8. Consider the following method:

```java
public static int secret(int one)
{
int i;
int prod = 1;

for(i = 1; i <= 3; i++)
     prod = prod * one;
return prod;
}
```

a. What is the output of the following Java statements?

  i. `System.out.println(secret(5));`

  ii. `System.out.println(2 * secret(6));`

b. What does the method `secret` do?

9. Show the output of the following program.

```java
public class MysteryClass
{
    public static void main(String[] args)
    {
        int n;

        for(n = 1; n <= 5; n++)
            System.out.println(mystery(n));
    }

    public static int mystery(int k)
    {
        int x, y;

        y = k;

        for(x = 1; x <= (k - 1); x++)
            y = y * (k - x);

        return y;
    }
}
```

10. Show the output of the following program.

```java
public class StrangeClass
{
    public static void main(String[] args)
    {
        int num = 0;
```

```
            while(num <= 29)
            {
                    if(strange(num))
                        System.out.println("True");
                    else
                        System.out.println("False");

                    num = num + 4;
            }
    }

    public static boolean strange(int n)
    {
            if(n % 2 == 0 && n % 3 == 0)
                return true;
            else
                return false;
    }
}
```

11. In the program fragment shown below, identify the following items: method heading, method body method definition, formal parameters, actual parameters, method call, and local variables.

```
public class Exercise11                             //Line 1
{                                                   //Line 2
    public static void main(String[] args)          //Line 3
    {                                               //Line 4
        int x;                                      //Line 5
        double y;                                   //Line 6
        char z;                                     //Line 7
        //...                                       //Line 8
        hello(x,y,z);                               //Line 9
        //...                                       //Line 10
        hello(x + 2, y - 3.5, 'S');                 //Line 11
        //...                                       //Line 12
    }                                               //Line 13

    public static void hello(int first, double second, //Line 14
                          char ch)                  //Line 15
    {                                               //Line 16
        int num;                                    //Line 17
        double y;                                   //Line 18
        //...                                       //Line 19
    }                                               //Line 20
}
```

12. For the program in Exercise 11, fill in the blanks below with variable names to show the matching that occurs between the actual and the formal parameter list in each of the two calls.

First Call to `hello`			Second Call to `hello`	
Formal	Actual		Formal	Actual
1. ———	———	1.	———	———
2. ———	———	2.	———	———
3. ———	———	3.	———	———

13. What is the output of the following program?

```
public class Exercise13
{
    public static void main(String[] args)
    {
        int num1;
        IntClass num2 ;

        num1 = 5;
        num2 = new IntClass(10);
        test(24, num2);
        test(num1, num2);
        test(num1 * num1, num2);
        test(num1 + num1, num2);
    }

    public static void test(int first, IntClass second)
    {
        int third;

        third = first + second.getNum() * second.getNum() + 2;
        first = second.getNum() - first;
        second.setNum(2 * second.getNum());
        System.out.println(first + " "+ second + " "
                           + third);
    }
}
```

14. Assume the following input values:

```
7 3 6 4
2 6 3 5
```

Show the output of the following program:

```java
import java.io.*;
import java.util.*;

public class Exercise14
{
    static BufferedReader inputStream =
            new BufferedReader(new InputStreamReader(System.in));

    public static void main(String[] args) throws IOException
    {
        int first, third;
        IntClass second, fourth;

        first = 3;
        second = new IntClass(4);
        third = 6;
        fourth = new IntClass(7);
        System.out.println(first + "   " + second.getNum()
                            + "   " + third + "   "
                            + fourth.getNum());
        goofy(first, second, third, fourth);
        System.out.println(first + "   " + second.getNum()
                            + "   " + third + "   "
                            + fourth.getNum());
        fourth.setNum(first * second.getNum() + third +
                        fourth.getNum());
        goofy(third, fourth, first, second);
        System.out.println(first + "   " + second.getNum()
                            + "   " + third + "   "
                            + fourth.getNum());
    }

    public static void goofy(int a, IntClass b, int c,
                            IntClass d) throws IOException
    {
        StringTokenizer tokenizer;

        tokenizer = new
        StringTokenizer(inputStream.readLine());

        a = Integer.parseInt(tokenizer.nextToken());
        b.setNum(Integer.parseInt(tokenizer.nextToken()));
        c = Integer.parseInt(tokenizer.nextToken());
        d.setNum(Integer.parseInt(tokenizer.nextToken()));

        b.setNum(a * b.getNum() - c);
```

7

```
                    d.setNum(b.getNum() + d.getNum());
        }
    }
```

15. In the following program, number the marked statements to show the order in which they will execute (the logical order of execution).

```
import java.io.*;

public class Exercise15
{
static BufferedReader keyboard = new
    BufferedReader(new InputStreamReader(System.in));

public static void main(String[] args) throws IOException
{
        int num1, num2;
_____  System.out.println("Please enter two integers "
                            + "on separate lines");
_____  num1 = Integer.parseInt(keyboard.readLine());
_____  num2 = Integer.parseInt(keyboard.readLine());
_____  func (num1, num2);
_____  System.out.println("The two integers are " + num1
                            + ", " + num2);
}

public static void func (int val1, int val2)
{
        int val3, val4;
_____  val3 = val1 + val2;
_____  val4 = val1 * val2;
_____  System.out.println("The sum and product are " + val3
                            + " and " + val4);
}
```

16. Consider the following program. What is its exact output? Show the values of the variables after each line executes, as in Example 7-11.

```
public class Exercise16
{
    public static void main(String[] args)
    {
      int num1;
      IntClass num2;

      num1 = 10;                            //Line 1
      num2 = new IntClass(20);              //Line 2
```

```
            System.out.println("Line 3: In main: num1 = "
                            + num1 + ", num2 = "
                            + num2.getNum());                    //Line 3
        funOne(num1, num2);                                      //Line 4
        System.out.println("Line 5: In main after funOne: "
                            + "num1 = " + num1 +   ", num2 = "
                            + num2.getNum());                    //Line 5
    }

    public static void funOne(int a, IntClass b)
    {
        int x;
        int z;

        x = b.getNum() ;                                         //Line 6
        z = a + x;                                               //Line 7

        System.out.println("Line 8: In funOne: a = " + a
                            + ", b = " + b.getNum()
                            + ", x = " + x
                            + ", and z = " + z);                 //Line 8

        x = x + 5;                                               //Line 9

        System.out.println("Line 10: In funOne: a = " + a
                            + ", b = " + b.getNum()
                            + ", x = " + x
                            + ", and z = " + z);                 //Line 10

        a = a + 8;                                               //Line 11
        b.setNum(a + x + z);                                     //Line 12

        System.out.println("Line 13: In funOne: a = " + a
                            + ", b = " + b.getNum()
                            + ", x = " + x
                            + ", and z = " + z);                 //Line 13
    }
}
```

7

PROGRAMMING EXERCISES

1. Write a value-returning method, isVowel, that returns the value **true** if a given character is a vowel, and otherwise returns **false**.

2. Write a program that prompts the user to input a sequence of characters and outputs the number of vowels. (Use the method isVowel written in Programming Exercise 1.)

3. Consider the following program segment:

```java
public class Ch7Ex3
{
    public static void main(String[] args)
    {
        int num;
        double dec;
        .
        .
        .

    }

    public static int one(int x, int y)
    {
        .
        .
        .

    }

    public static double two(int x, double a)
    {
        int first;
        double z;
        .
        .
        .

    }
}
```

a. Write the definition of method **one** so that it returns the sum of x and y if x is greater than y; otherwise, it should return x minus 2 times y.

b. Write the definition of method **two** as follows:

   i. Read a number and store it in z.

   ii. Update the value of z by adding the value of a to its previous value.

   iii. Assign the variable **first** the value returned by method **one** with the parameters 6 and 8.

   iv. Update the value of **first** by adding the value of x to its previous value.

   v. If the value of z is more than twice the value of **first**, return z; otherwise, return 2 times **first** minus z.

c. Write a Java program that tests parts a and b. (Declare additional variables in the method **main**, if necessary.)

4. Write a method, **reverseDigit**, that takes an integer as a parameter and returns the number with its digits reversed. For example, the value of **reverseDigit(12345)** is 54321. Also write a program to test your method.

5. The following formula gives the distance between two points (x_1, y_1) and (x_2, y_2) in the Cartesian plane:

$$\sqrt{(x_2-x_1)^2+(y_2-y_1)^2}$$

Given the center and a point on a circle, you can use this formula to find the radius of the circle. Write a program that prompts the user to enter the center and a point on the circle. The program should then output the circle's radius, diameter, circumference, and area. Your program must have at least the following methods:

a. `distance`: This method takes as its parameters four numbers that represent two points in the plane and returns the distance between them.

b. `radius`: This method takes as its parameters four numbers that represent the center and a point on the circle, calls the method `distance` to find the radius of the circle, and returns the circle's radius.

c. `circumference`: This method takes as its parameter a number that represents the radius of the circle and returns the circle's circumference. (If r is the radius, the circumference is $2\pi r$.)

d. `area`: This method takes as its parameter a number that represents the radius of the circle and returns the circle's area. (If r is the radius, the area is πr^2.)

e. Assume that $\pi = 3.1416$.

6. If P is the population on the first day of the year, B is the birth rate, and D is the death rate, the estimated population at the end of the year is given by the formula:

$$P + \frac{B*P}{100} - \frac{D*P}{100}$$

The population growth rate is given by the formula:

$$B - D$$

Write a program that prompts the user to enter the starting population, birth and death rates, and n, the number of years. The program should then calculate and print the estimated population after n years. Your program must consist of the following methods:

a. `growthRate`: This method takes as its parameters the birth and death rates, and it returns the population growth rate.

b. `estimatedPopulation`: This method takes as its parameters the current population, population growth rate, and n, the number of years. It returns the estimated population after n years.

Your program should not accept a negative birth rate, negative death rate, or a population less than 2.

7. Rewrite the Programming Example Cable Company Billing (from Chapter 4) so that it uses the following methods to calculate the billing amount:

a. `residentialCustomer`: This method calculates and returns the billing amount for the residential customer.

b. `businessCustomer`: This method calculates and returns the billing amount for the service business customer.

7

8. Rewrite the program in Programming Exercise 12 from Chapter 4 (cell phone company) so that it uses the following methods to calculate the billing amount. (In this programming exercise, do not output the number of minutes during which the service is used.)

a. `regularBill`: This method calculates and returns the billing amount for regular service.

b. `premiumBill`: This method calculates and returns the billing amount for premium service.

9. Consider the following program segment (with the method `main`):

```
public class Ch7Ex9
{
    public static void main(String[] arg)
    {
        IntClass x, y;
        CharClass   z;
        double rate, hours;
        double amount;

        .
        .
        .

    }
}
```

Write the following definitions:

a. Write the definition of the method `initialize` that initializes `x` and `y` to 0 and `z` to the blank character.

b. Write the definition of the method `getHoursRate` that prompts the user to input the hours worked and rate per hour to initialize the variables `hours` and `rate` of the method `main`.

c. Write the definition of the value-returning method `payCheck` that calculates and returns the amount to be paid to an employee, based on the hours worked and rate per hour. The hours worked and rate per hour are stored in the variables `hours` and `rate`, respectively, of the method `main`. The formula for calculating the amount to be paid is as follows: for the first 40 hours, the rate is the given rate; for hours over 40, the rate is 1.5 times the given rate.

d. Write the definition of the method `printCheck` that prints the hours worked, rate per hour, and the amount due.

e. Write the definition of the method `funOne` that prompts the user to input a number. The method then changes the value of `x` to 2 times the old value of `x` plus the value of `y` minus the value entered by the user.

f. Write the definition of the method `nextChar` that sets the value of `z` to the next character stored in `z`.

g. Write the definition of a method `main` that tests each of these methods. Also write a complete program to test the methods of (a)–(e).

10. The method **printGrade** of this chapter's Example 7-8, is written as a **void** method to compute and output the course grade. The course score is passed as a parameter to the method **printGrade**. Rewrite the method **printGrade** as a value-returning method so that it computes and returns the course grade. (The course grade must be output in the method **main**.) Also, change the name of the method to **calculateGrade**.

11. In this exercise, you are to rewrite the Programming Example Classify Numbers (from Chapter 5). As written, the program inputs data from the standard input device (keyboard) and outputs results on the standard output device (screen). The program can process only 20 numbers. Re-write the program to incorporate the following requirements:

   a. Data to the program is input from a file of unspecified length; that is, the program does not know in advance how many numbers are in the file.

   b. Save the output of the program in a file.

   c. Write the method **getNumber** so that it reads a number from the input file (opened in the method **main**), outputs the number to the output file (opened in the method **main**), and sends the number read to the method **main**. Print only 10 numbers per line.

   d. Have the program find the sum and average of the numbers.

   e. Write the method **printResult** so that it outputs the final results to the output file (opened in the method **main**). Other than outputting the appropriate counts, the definition of the method **printResult** should also output the sum and average of the numbers.

12. Rewrite the program developed in Programming Exercise 11 in Chapter 5, so that the method **main** is merely a collection of method calls. Your program should use the following methods:

   a. Method **initialize**: This method initializes variables such as **countFemale**, **countMale**, **sumFemaleGPA**, and **sumMaleGPA**.

   b. Method **sumGrades**: This method finds the sum of female and male students' GPAs.

   c. Method **averageGrade**: This method finds the average GPA for female and male students.

   d. Method **printResults**: This method outputs the relevant results.

   Use appropriate parameters to pass information in and out of methods.

13. Write a program that prints the day number of the year, given the date is in the form month-day-year. For example, if the input is 1-1-03, the day number is 1; if the input is 12-25-03, the day number is 359. The program should check for a leap year. A year is a leap year if it is divisible by 4 but not divisible by 100. For example, 1992 and 2008 are divisible by 4, but not by 100. A year that is divisible by 100 is a leap year if it is also divisible by 400. For example, 1600 and 2000 are divisible by 400. However, 1800 is not a leap year because 1800 is not divisible by 400.

14. Write a program that reads a student's name together with his or her test scores. The program should then compute the average test score for each student and assign the appropriate grade. The grade scale is as follows: 90–100, A; 80–89, B; 70–79, C; 60–69, D; 0–59, F.

Your program must use the following methods:

a. A void method, `calculateAverage`, to determine the average of five test scores for each student. Use a loop to read and sum the five test scores. (This method does not output the average test score. That task must be done in the method `main`.)

b. A value-returning method, `calculateGrade`, to determine and return each student's grade. (This method does not output the grade. That task must be done in the method `main`.)

Test your program on the following data. Read the data from a file and send the output to a file. Do not use any global variables. Use the appropriate parameters to pass values in and out of methods.

```
Balto 85 83 77 91 76
Mickey 80 90 95 93 48
Minnie 78 81 11 90 73
Doc 92 83 30 69 87
Goofy 23 45 96 38 59
Duckey 60 85 45 39 67
Grumpy 27 31 52 74 83
Sunny 93 94 89 77 97
Piggy 79 85 28 93 82
Pluto 85 72 49 75 63
```

Sample Output: The output should be of the following form: Fill the last two columns and the last line showing the class average.

Student	Test1	Test2	Test3	Test4	Test5	Average	Grade
Balto	85	83	77	91	76		
Mickey	80	90	95	93	48		
Minnie	78	81	11	90	73		
Doc	92	83	30	69	87		
Goofy	23	45	96	38	59		
Duckey	60	85	45	39	67		
Grumpy	27	31	52	74	83		
Sunny	93	94	89	77	97		
Piggy	79	85	28	93	82		
Pluto	85	72	49	75	63		

```
Class Average =
```

15. Write a program to process text files. The program should read a text file and output the data in the file as is. The program should also output the number of words, number of lines, and number of paragraphs.

You must write and use the following methods:

a. `initialize`: This method initializes all variables of the method `main`.

b. `processBlank`: This method reads and writes blanks. Whenever it hits a nonblank (except whitespace characters), it increments the number of words in a line (this number is set back to zero in the method `updateCount`). The method exits after processing blanks.

c. `copyText`: This method reads and writes nonblank characters. Whenever it hits a blank, it exits.

d. `updateCount`: This method takes place at the end of each line. It increments the number of lines and sets the number of words on a line back to zero. If there are no words in a line, it increments the number of paragraphs. One blank line (between paragraphs) is used to distinguish paragraphs and should not be counted with the number of lines. This method also updates the total word count.

e. `printTotal`: This method outputs the number of words, number of lines, and number of paragraphs.

Your program should read data from a file and send output to a file. Use appropriate parameters to pass values in and out of methods. Test your program using the method `main` that looks like:

```
public static void main(String[] args)
{
    variables declaration
    open files

    read a character
    while (not end of file)
    {
        while(not end of line)
        {
            processBlank(parameters);
            copyText(parameters);
        }
        updateCount(parameters);
        read a character;
        ...

    }
    printTotal(parameters);
        close files;
}
```

8

USER-DEFINED CLASSES AND ADTs

In this chapter, you will:

♦ Learn about classes

♦ Learn about `private`, `protected`, `public`, and `static` members of a class

♦ Explore how classes are implemented

♦ Learn about the various operations on classes

♦ Examine constructors and finalizers

♦ Examine the method `toString`

♦ Learn about the abstract data type (ADT)

In the preceding chapters, you learned how to use various classes and their methods to manipulate data. Java does not provide all the classes that you will ever need. Therefore, you must learn to create your classes. In this chapter, we discuss how to create classes and objects.

CLASSES

As you learned in earlier chapters, the first step in problem-solving with object-oriented design (OOD) is to identify components called objects. An object combines data and the operations on that data in a single unit; the mechanism in Java that allows you to combine data and the operations on that data in a single unit is called a class. Now that you know how to store and manipulate data in computer memory and how to construct your own methods, you are ready to learn how objects are constructed.

A **class** is a collection of a fixed number of components. The components of a `class` are called the **members** of the `class`.

The general syntax for defining a `class` is

```
modifier(s) class ClassIdentifier modifier(s)
{
     classMembers
}
```

where `modifier(s)` are used to alter the behavior of the class, and, usually, `classMembers` consist of named constants, variable declarations and/or methods. That is, usually a member of a `class` can be either a variable (to store data) or a method. Some of the modifiers that we have encountered are `public`, `private`, and `static`.

- If a member of a class is a named constant, you declare it just like any other named constant.

- If a member of a class is a variable, you declare it just like any other variable.

- If a member of a class is a method, you define it just like any other method.

- If a member of a class is a method, it can (directly) access any member of the class—data members and method members. That is, when you write the definition of the member method, you can directly access any data member of the class without passing it as a parameter.

In Java, `class` is a reserved word, and it defines only a data type; no memory is allocated. It announces the declaration of a class. In Java, the data members of a `class` are also called **fields**.

The members of a `class` are usually classified into three categories: `private`, `public`, and `protected`. This chapter discusses the first two categories: `private` and `public`. Chapter 11 discusses `protected` members.

Following are some facts about `public` and `private` members of a class:

- If a member of a class is `private`, you *cannot* access it outside the class.

- If a member of a class is `public`, you *can* access it outside the class.

Recall that a package is collection of related classes. Later in this chapter, you will learn how to create your own packages. If a class member is declared/defined without any modifier, then that class member can be accessed from anywhere in the package.

In Java, `private`, `protected`, and `public` are reserved words.

Suppose that we want to define the **class Clock** to implement the time of day in a program. Further suppose that the time is represented as a set of three integers: one to represent the hours, one to represent the minutes, and one to represent the seconds. We also want to perform the following operations on the time:

1. Set the time.

2. Return hours.

3. Return minutes.

4. Return seconds.

5. Print the time.

6. Increment the time by one second.

7. Increment the time by one minute.

8. Increment the time by one hour.

9. Compare two times for equality.

10. Copy the time.

11. Return a copy of the time.

To implement these 11 operations, we write algorithms, which we implement as methods—11 methods to implement these 11 operations. So far, the **class Clock** has 14 members: 3 data members and 11 method members. Suppose that the 3 data members are `hr`, `min`, and `sec`, each of the type `int`.

Some members of the **class Clock** will be `private`; others will be `public`. Deciding which members to make `public` and which to make `private` depends on the nature of each member. The general rule is that any member that needs to be accessed from outside the class is declared `public`; any member that should not be accessed directly by the user should be declared `private`. For example, the user should be able to set the time and print the time. Therefore, the methods that set the time and print the time should be declared `public`.

Similarly, the method to increment the time and compare the time for equality should be declared `public`. On the other hand, users should not control the *direct* manipulation of the data members `hr`, `min`, and `sec`, so we will declare them `private`. Note that if the user has direct access to the data members, methods such as `setTime` are not needed.

The data members for the **class Clock** are:

```
private int hr;   //store hours
```

8

```
private int min; //store minutes
private int sec; //store seconds
```

The (non `static`) data members of a `class` are called **instance variables**. Therefore, the variables `hr`, `min`, and `sec` are the instance variables of the `class Clock`.

Suppose the 11 methods to implement the 11 operations are as follows. (We also specify the headings of the methods.)

1. `setTime` sets the time to the time specified by the user. The method heading is:

   ```
   public void setTime(int hours, int minutes, int seconds)
   ```

2. `getHours` returns hours. The method heading is:

   ```
   public int getHours()
   ```

3. `getMinutes` returns minutes. The method heading is:

   ```
   public int getMinutes()
   ```

4. `getSeconds` returns seconds. The method heading is:

   ```
   public int getSeconds()
   ```

5. `printTime` prints the time in the form `hh:mm:ss`. The method heading is:

   ```
   public void printTime()
   ```

6. `incrementSeconds` increments the time by one second. The method heading is:

   ```
   public void incrementSeconds()
   ```

7. `incrementMinutes` increments the time by one minute. The method heading is:

   ```
   public void incrementMinutes()
   ```

8. `incrementHours` increments the time by one hour. The method heading is:

   ```
   public void incrementHours()
   ```

9. `equals` compares the two times to determine whether they are equal. The method heading is:

   ```
   public boolean equals(Clock otherClock)
   ```

10. `makeCopy` copies the time of one object into another object. The method heading is:

    ```
    public void makeCopy(Clock otherClock)
    ```

11. `getCopy` returns a copy of the time. A copy of the object's time is created and a reference of the copy is returned. The method heading is:

    ```
    public Clock getCopy()
    ```

The member methods of a class are called the **instance methods** of the class.

In the definition of the **class** **Clock**, all data members are **private** and all method members are **public**. However, a method member can also be **private**. For example, if a method member is used only to implement other method members of the class, and the user does not need to access this method, you make it **private**. Similarly, a data member of a **class** can also be **public**.

Notice that we have not yet written the definitions of the methods of the **class** **Clock**. (You will learn how to write them in the section Definitions of the Constructors and Methods of the **class** **Clock**.) Also notice that the method **equals** has only one parameter, although you need two things to make a comparison. Similarly, the method **makeCopy** has only one parameter. An example later in this chapter will help explain this concept.

Before giving the definition of the **class** **Clock**, we first introduce another important concept related to classes—constructors.

Constructors

In addition to the methods necessary to implement operations, every class has a *special* type of method called constructors. A **constructor** has the same name as the class, and it executes automatically when an object of that class is created. Constructors are used to guarantee that the instance variables of the class initialize to specific values.

There are two types of constructors: with parameters and without parameters. The constructor without parameters is called the **default constructor**.

Constructors have the following properties:

- The name of a constructor is the same as the name of the class.

- A constructor, even though it is a method, has no type. That is, it is neither a value-returning method nor a **void** method.

- A class can have more than one constructor. However, all constructors of a class have the same name.

- If a class has more than one constructor, either they have a different number of formal parameters or If the number of formal parameters is the same, then the data types of the formal parameters, in the order you list, must differ in at least one position.

- Constructors are automatically executed when a class object is instantiated. Because they have no types, they cannot be called like other methods.

- If there are multiple constructors, which constructor executes depends on the type of values passed to the class object when the class object is instantiated.

For the **class** **Clock**, we will include two constructors: the default constructor and a constructor with parameters. The default constructor initializes the instance variables to store hours, minutes, and seconds, each to 0. Similarly, the constructor with parameters initializes the instance variables to the values specified by the user. We will illustrate shortly how constructors are invoked.

The heading of the default constructor is:

```
public Clock()
```

The heading of the constructor with parameters is:

```
public Clock(int hours, int minutes, int seconds)
```

It now follows that the definition of the `class Clock` has 16 members: 11 methods to implement the 11 operations, 2 constructors, and 3 instance variables to store hours, minutes, and seconds.

 If you do not include any constructor in a class, then Java *automatically* provides the default constructor. Therefore, when you create an object, the instance variables are initialized to their default values. For example, `int` variables are initialized to 0. If you provide at least one constructor and do not include the default constructor, then Java *will not automatically* provide the default constructor. Generally, if a class includes constructors, you also include the default constructor.

Unified Modeling Language Diagrams

A class and its members can be described graphically using **Unified Modeling Language (UML)** notation. For example, the UML diagram of the `class Clock` is shown in Figure 8-1.

```
                          Clock
        ┌─────────────────────────────────────┐
        │ -hr: int                            │
        │ -min: int                           │
        │ -sec: int                           │
        ├─────────────────────────────────────┤
        │ +Clock()                            │
        │ +Clock(int, int, int)               │
        │ +setTime(int, int, int): void       │
        │ +getHours(): int                    │
        │ +getMinutes(): int                  │
        │ +getSeconds(): int                  │
        │ +printTime(): void                  │
        │ +incrementSeconds(): int            │
        │ +incrementMinutes(): int            │
        │ +incrementHours(): int              │
        │ +equalTime(Clock): boolean          │
        │ +makeCopy(Clock): void              │
        │ +getCopy(): Clock                   │
        └─────────────────────────────────────┘
```

Figure 8-1 UML diagram of the `class Clock`

The top box in the UML diagram contains the name of the class. The middle box contains the data members and their data types. The last box contains the member method names, parameter list, and return types. The + (plus) sign in front of a member indicates that it is a public member; the − (minus) sign indicates that it is a private member. The # symbol before a member name indicates that it is a protected member.

Variable Declaration and Object Instantiation

Once a class is defined, you can declare reference variables of that class type. For example, the following statement declares myClock to be a reference variable of the type Clock:

```
Clock   myClock;
```

The preceding statement *does not* allocate memory space to store hours, minutes, and seconds. Next we explain how to allocate memory space to store hours, minutes, and seconds and how to access that memory space using the variable myClock.

The class Clock has three instance variables. To store hours, minutes, and seconds, we need to create a Clock object, which is accomplished by using the operator new. Every Clock object then has three data members.

The general syntax for using the operator new is:

```
new className()                                          //Line 1
```

or

```
new className(argument1, argument2, ..., argumentN)   //Line 2
```

The expression in Line 1 instantiates the object and initializes the instance variables of the object using the default constructor. The expression in Line 2 instantiates the object and initializes the instance variables using a constructor with parameters.

For the expression in Line 2:

- The number of arguments and their type should match the formal parameters (in the order given) of one of the constructors.

- If the type of the arguments does not match the formal parameters of any constructor (in the order given), Java uses type conversion and looks for the best match. For example, an integer value might be converted to a floating-point value with a zero decimal part. Any ambiguity will result in a compile-time error.

Consider the following statements:

```
myClock = new Clock();                                   //Line 3
yourClock = new Clock(9,35,15);                          //Line 4
```

The statement in Line 3 allocates memory space for a **Clock** object, initializes each instance variable of the object to **0**, and stores the address of the object into **myClock**. The statement in Line 4 allocates memory space for a **Clock** object, initializes the instance variables **hr**, **min**, and **sec** of the object to **9, 35**, and **15**, respectively; and stores the address of the object into **yourClock**. See Figure 8-2.

Figure 8-2   Variables **myClock** and **yourClock** and **Clock** objects

To be specific, we call the object to which **myClock** points the object **myClock** and the object to which **yourClock** points the object **yourClock**. See Figure 8-3.

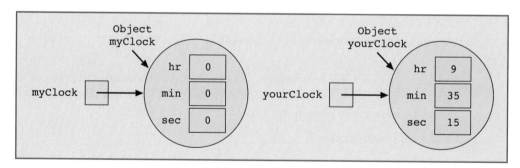

Figure 8-3   Objects **myClock** and **yourClock**

Of course, you can combine the statements to declare the variable and instantiate the object into one statement, as follows:

```
Clock myClock = new Clock();    //declare and instantiate
                                //myClock
```

This statement declares `myClock` to be a reference variable of the type `Clock`, and instantiates the object `myClock` to store hours, minutes, and seconds. Each instance variable of the object `myClock` is initialized to 0 by the default constructor.

Similarly, the statement

```
Clock yourClock = new Clock(9,35,15);   //declare and
                                        //instantiate yourClock
```

declares `yourClock` to be a reference variable of the type `Clock`, and instantiates the object `yourClock` to store hours, minutes, and seconds. The instance variables `hr`, `min`, and `sec` of the object `yourClock` are initialized to 9, 35, and 15, respectively, by the constructor with parameters.

 When we use phrases such as "create an object of a `class` type," we mean (i) declare a reference variable of the `class` type; (ii) instantiate the `class` object; and (iii) store the address of the object into the reference variable declared. For example, the following statements create the object `tempClock` of the `Clock` type:

```
Clock tempClock = new Clock();
```

The object `tempClock` is accessed via the reference variable `tempClock`.

8

Recall from Chapter 3 that a `class` object is called an **instance** of that `class`.

Accessing Class Members

Once an object is created, you can access the **public** members of the `class`. The general syntax to access a data member of a `class` object or a `class` method is:

`referenceVariableName.memberName`

Recall that in Java, the dot **.** (period) is called the **member access operator**.

Example 8-1 illustrates how to access the members of a class.

Example 8-1

Suppose that the objects `myClock` and `yourClock` have been created as before. Consider the following statements:

```
myClock.setTime(5,2,30);
myClock.printTime();
yourClock.setTime(x,y,z);   //Assume x, y, and z are
                            //variables of the type int
                            //and they have been initialized

if(myClock.equals(yourClock))
.
.
.
```

These statements are legal; that is, they are syntactically correct. Note the following:

- In the first statement, `myClock.setTime(5,2,30);`, the method `setTime` is executed. The values 5, 2, and 30 are passed as parameters to the method `setTime`, and the method uses these values to set the values of `hr`, `min`, and `sec` of the object `myClock` to 5, 2, and 30, respectively.

- Similarly, the second statement executes the method `printTime` and outputs the values of `hr`, `min`, and `sec` of the object `myClock`.

- In the third statement, the values of the variables `x`, `y`, and `z` are used to set the values of `hr`, `min`, and `sec` of the object `yourClock`.

- In the fourth statement, the method `equals` executes and compares the instance variables of the object `myClock` with the corresponding instance variables of the object `yourClock`. Because in this statement the method `equals` is invoked by the variable `myClock`, it has direct access to the instance variables of the object `myClock`. So it needs one more object, which in this case, is the object `yourClock`, to compare. This explains why the method `equals` has only one parameter.

You can access only `public` members of the class. The following statements are illegal because `hr` and `min` are `private` members of the `class Clock` and, therefore, cannot be accessed by `myClock` and `yourClock`:

```
myClock.hr = 10;                //illegal
myClock.min = yourClock.min;    //illegal
```

Built-in Operations on Classes

Most of Java's built-in operations do not apply to classes. You cannot perform arithmetic operations on `class` objects. For example, you cannot use the operator + to add the values of two `Clock` objects. Also, you cannot use relational operators to compare two class objects.

The built-in operation that is valid for classes is the dot operator, (`.`). A reference variable uses the dot operator to access a `public` member; classes can use the dot operator to access `static public` members.

The Assignment Operator and Classes: A Precaution

This section discusses how the assignment operator works with reference variables and objects.

Suppose that the objects `myClock` and `yourClock` are as shown in Figure 8-4.

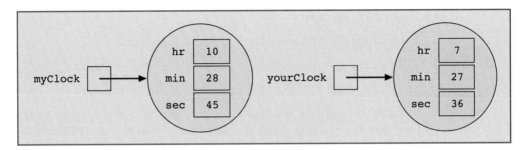

Figure 8-4   `myClock` and `yourClock` example

The statement

`myClock = yourClock;`

copies the value of the reference variable `yourClock` into the reference variable `myClock`. After this statement executes, both `yourClock` and `myClock` refer to the same object. Figure 8-5 illustrates this situation.

8

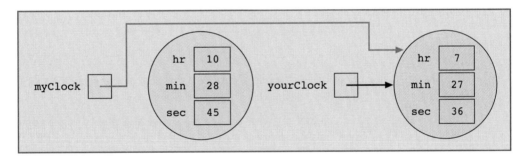

Figure 8-5   `myClock` and `yourClock` after the statement `myClock = yourClock;` executes

This is called shallow copying of data. In **shallow copying**, two or more reference variables of the same type point to the same object.

To copy the instance variables of the object `yourClock` into the corresponding instance variables of the object `myClock`, you need to use the method `makeCopy`. This is accomplished by the following statement:

`myClock.makeCopy(yourClock);`

After this statement executes:

1. The value of `yourClock.hr` is copied into `myClock.hr`.

2. The value of `yourClock.min` is copied into `myClock.min`.

3. The value of `yourClock.sec` is copied into `myClock.sec`.

In other words, the values of the three instance variables of the object `yourClock` are copied into the corresponding instance variables of the object `myClock`, as shown in Figure 8-6.

Figure 8-6 Objects `myClock` and `yourClock` after the statement `myClock.makeCopy(yourClock);` executes

This is called deep copying of data. In **deep copying**, each reference variable refers to its *own* object, as in Figure 8-6, *not* the same object, as in Figure 8-5.

Another way to avoid shallow copying of data is to have the object being copied create a copy of itself, and then return a reference to the copy. This is accomplished by the method `getCopy`. Consider the following statement:

```
myClock = yourClock.getCopy();
```

In this statement, the expression `yourClock.getCopy()` makes a copy of the object `yourClock` and returns the address, that is, the reference of the copy. The assignment statement stores this address into `myClock`.

 The methods `makeCopy` and `getCopy` are both used to avoid shallow copying of data. The main difference between these two methods is: To use the method `makeCopy`, both the objects—the object whose data is being copied and the object that is copying the data—must be instantiated before invoking this method. To use the method `getCopy`, the object whose data is being copied must be instantiated before invoking this method, while the object of the reference variable receiving a copy of the data need not be instantiated. Moreover, note that `makeCopy` and `getCopy` are user-defined methods.

Class Scope

A reference variable has the same scope as other variables. A member of a class is local to the class. You access a `public class` member outside the `class` through the reference variable name or the `class` name (for `static` members) and the member access operator (`.`).

Methods and Classes

Reference variables can be passed as parameters to methods and returned as method values. Recall from Chapter 7 that when a reference variable is passed as a parameter to a method, both the formal and actual parameters point to the same object.

Definitions of the Constructors and Methods of the `class` `Clock`

We now give the definition of the methods of the `class` `Clock`, and then we will write the complete definition of this class. First note the following:

1. The `class` `Clock` has 11 methods: `setTime`, `getHours`, `getMinutes`, `getSeconds`, `printTime`, `incrementSeconds`, `incrementMinutes`, `incrementHours`, `equals`, `makeCopy`, and `getCopy`. It has two constructors and three instance variables: `hr`, `min`, and `sec`.

2. The three instance variables—`hr`, `min`, and `sec`—are `private` to the `class` and cannot be accessed outside the class.

3. The 11 methods—`setTime`, `getHours`, `getMinutes`, `getSeconds`, `printTime`, `incrementSeconds`, `incrementMinutes`, `incrementHours`, `equals`, `makeCopy`, and `getCopy`—can directly access the instance variables (`hr`, `min`, and `sec`). In other words, we do not pass instance variables or data members as parameters to member methods. Similarly, constructors directly access the instance variables.

Let's first write the definition of the method `setTime`. The method `setTime` has three parameters of the type `int`. This method sets the instance variables to the values specified by the user, which are passed as parameters to this function. The definition of the method `setTime` follows:

```
public void setTime(int hours, int minutes, int seconds)
{
    if(0 <= hours && hours < 24)
        hr = hours;
    else
        hr = 0;

    if(0 <= minutes && minutes < 60)
        min = minutes;
    else
        min = 0;
```

8

```
        if(0 <= seconds && seconds < 60)
            sec = seconds;
        else
            sec = 0;
    }
```

Note that the definition of the method **setTime** checks for valid values of **hours, minutes,** and **seconds.** If these values are out of range, the instance variables **hr, min,** and **sec** are initialized to 0. Now let's look at how the method **setTime** works.

The method **setTime** is a **void** method and has three parameters. Therefore:

- A call to this method is a stand-alone statement.

- We must use three parameters in a call to this method.

Furthermore, recall that because **setTime** is a member of the **class Clock,** it can directly access the instance variables **hr, min,** and **sec,** as shown in the definition of **setTime.**

Suppose that the object **myClock** is as shown in Figure 8-7.

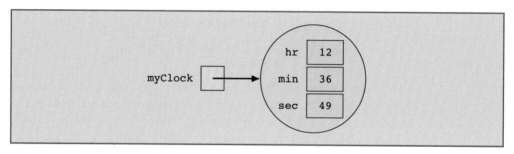

Figure 8-7 Object **myClock**

Consider the following statement:

```
myClock.setTime(3,48,52);
```

The variable **myClock** accesses the member **setTime.** In the statement **myClock.setTime(3,48,52);,** **setTime** is accessed by the variable **myClock.** Therefore, the three variables—**hr, min,** and **sec**—referred to in the body of the method **setTime** are the three instance variables of the object **myClock.** Thus, the values **3, 48,** and **52,** which are passed as parameters in the preceding statement, are assigned to the three instance variables of the object **myClock** by the method **setTime** (see the body of the method **setTime**). After the previous statement executes, **myClock** is as shown in Figure 8-8.

Figure 8-8   `myClock` after statement `myClock.setTime(3, 48, 52);` executes

Next let's give the definitions of the other methods of the `class Clock`. These definitions are simple and easy to follow.

```java
public int getHours()
{
    return hr;          //return the value of hr
}

public int getMinutes()
{
    return min;         //return the value of min
}

public int getSeconds()
{
    return sec;         //return the value of sec
}

public void printTime()
{
    if(hr < 10)
        System.out.print("0");
    System.out.print(hr + ":");

    if(min < 10)
        System.out.print("0");
    System.out.print(min + ":");

    if(sec < 10)
        System.out.print("0");
    System.out.print(sec);
}
```

```
public void incrementHours()
{
    hr++;              //increment the value of hr by 1
    if(hr > 23)        //if hr is greater than 23,
        hr = 0;        //set hr to 0
}
public void incrementMinutes()
{
    min++;                 //increment the value of min by 1
    if(min > 59)           //if min is greater than 59
    {
        min = 0;                //set min to 0
        incrementHours();   //increment hours
    }
}
public void incrementSeconds()
{
    sec++;                 //increment the value of sec by 1
    if(sec > 59)           //if sec is greater than 59
    {
        sec = 0;                //set sec to 0
        incrementMinutes(); //increment minutes
    }
}
```

From the definitions of the methods `incrementMinutes` and `incrementSeconds`, you can see that a method of a `class` can call other methods of the `class`.

The method `equals` has the following definition:

```
public boolean equals(Clock otherClock)
{
        return(hr == otherClock.hr
            && min == otherClock.min
            && sec == otherClock.sec);
}
```

Let's see how the member method `equals` works.

Suppose that `myClock` and `yourClock` are as shown in Figure 8-9.

Figure 8-9 Objects `myClock` and `yourClock`

Consider the following statement:

```
if(myClock.equals(yourClock))
```
.
.
.

In the expression

```
myClock.equals(yourClock)
```

myClock accesses the method **equals**. The value of the parameter **yourClock** is passed to the formal parameter **otherClock**, as shown in Figure 8-10.

Figure 8-10   Object **myClock** and parameter **otherClock**

Note that **otherClock** and **yourClock** refer to the same object. The instance variables **hr, min,** and **sec** of the object **otherClock** have the values 12, 27, and 15, respectively. In other words, when the body of the method **equals** executes, the value of **otherClock.hr** is 12, the value of **otherClock.min** is 27, and the value of **otherClock.sec** is 15. The method **equals** is a member of **myClock**. When the method **equals** executes, the variables **hr, min,** and **sec** in the body of the method **equals** are the instance variables of the object **myClock**. Therefore, the instance variable **hr** of the object **myClock** is compared with **otherClock.hr**, the instance variable **min** of the object **myClock** is compared with **otherClock.min**, and the instance variable **sec** of the object **myClock** is compared with **otherClock.sec**.

Once again, in the expression

```
myClock.equals(yourClock)
```

the method **equals** is invoked by **myClock** and compares the object **myClock** with the object **yourClock**. It follows that the method **equals** needs only one parameter.

The method `makeCopy` copies the instance variables of its parameter, `otherClock`, into the corresponding instance variables of the object referenced by the variable using this method. Its definition is:

```
public void makeCopy(Clock otherClock)
{
    hr = otherClock.hr;
    min = otherClock.min;
    sec = otherClock.sec;
}
```

Consider the following statement:

```
myClock.makeCopy(yourClock);
```

In this statement, the method `makeCopy` is invoked by `myClock`. The three instance variables `hr`, `min`, and `sec` in the body of the method `makeCopy` are the instance variables of the object `myClock`. The variable `yourClock` is passed as a parameter to `makeCopy`. Therefore, `yourClock` and `otherClock` refer to the same object, which is the object `yourClock`. Thus, after the preceding statement executes, the instance variables of the object `yourClock` are copied into the corresponding instance variables of the object `myClock`.

The method `getCopy` creates a copy of an object's `hr`, `min`, and `sec` and returns the address of the copy of the object. That is, the method `getCopy` creates a new `Clock` object, initializes the instance variables of the object, and returns the address of the object created. The definition of the method `getCopy` is:

```
public Clock getCopy()
{
    Clock temp = new Clock();        //Line 1

    temp.hr = hr;                    //Line 2
    temp.min = min;                  //Line 3
    temp.sec = sec;                  //Line 4

    return temp;                     //Line 5
}
```

The following illustrates how the method `getCopy` works. Suppose that `yourClock` is as shown in Figure 8-11.

Figure 8-11   Object `yourClock`

Consider the following statement:

```
myClock = yourClock.getCopy();          //Line A
```

In this statement, because the method `getCopy` is invoked by `yourClock`, the three variables `hr`, `min`, and `sec` in the body of the method `getCopy` are the instance variables of the object `yourClock`. The body of the method `getCopy` executes as follows. The statement in Line 1 creates the `Clock` object `temp`. The statement in Lines 2 through 4 copies the instance variables of the object `yourClock` into the corresponding instance variables of `temp`. In other words, the object referenced by `temp` is a copy of the object `yourClock` (see Figure 8-12).

Figure 8-12   Objects `temp` and `yourClock`

The statement in Line 5 returns the value of `temp`, which is the address of the object holding a copy of the data. The value returned by the method `getCopy` is copied into `myClock`. Therefore, after the statement in Line A executes, `myClock` and `yourClock` are as shown in Figure 8-13.

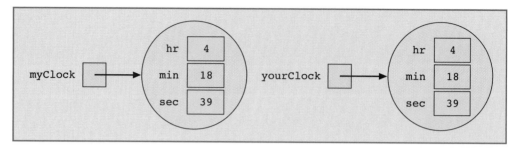

Figure 8-13 Objects `myClock` and `yourClock`

Next we give the definitions of the constructors. The default constructor initializes each instance variable to 0. Its definition is:

```
public Clock()
{
    hr = 0;
    min = 0;
    sec = 0;
}
```

You can also write the definition of the default constructor using the method `setTime` as follows:

```
public Clock()
{
    setTime(0,0,0);
}
```

The definition of the constructor with parameters is the same as the definition of the method `setTime`. It initializes the instance variables to the values specified by the user. Its definition is:

```
public Clock(int hours, int minutes, int seconds)
{
    if(0 <= hours && hours < 24)
        hr = hours;
    else
        hr = 0;

    if(0 <= minutes && minutes < 60)
        min = minutes;
    else
        min = 0;

    if(0 <= seconds && seconds < 60)
        sec = seconds;
    else
        sec = 0;
}
```

As in the case of the default constructor, you can write the definition of the constructor with parameters using the method `setTime` as follows:

```
public Clock(int hours, int minutes, int seconds)
{
     setTime(hours, minutes, seconds);
}
```

This definition of the constructor with parameters makes debugging easier as only code for the method `setTime` needs to be checked.

Definition of the `class` Clock

Now that you have defined the methods of the **class** Clock, we can give the complete definition of the **class** Clock. Before the definition of a method we include comments specifying preconditions and/or postconditions.

Precondition: A statement specifying the condition(s) that must be true before the function is called.

Postcondition: A statement specifying what is true after the function call is completed:

The definition of the **class** Clock is:

```
public class Clock
{
     private int hr;  //store hours
     private int min; //store minutes
     private int sec; //store seconds

         //Constructor with parameters, to set the time
         //The time is set according to the parameters
         //Postcondition: hr = hours; min = minutes; sec = seconds
     public Clock(int hours, int minutes, int seconds)
     {
         setTime(hours, minutes, seconds);
     }
         //Default constructor
         //Postcondition: hr = 0; min = 0; sec = 0
     public Clock()
     {
         setTime(0, 0, 0);
     }
```

8

```java
        //Method to set the time
        //The time is set according to the parameters
        //Postcondition: hr = hours; min = minutes; sec = seconds
public void setTime(int hours, int minutes, int seconds)
{
    if(0 <= hours && hours < 24)
       hr = hours;
    else
       hr = 0;

    if(0 <= minutes && minutes < 60)
       min = minutes;
    else
       min = 0;

    if(0 <= seconds && seconds < 60)
       sec = seconds;
    else
       sec = 0;
}

    //Method to return the hours
    //Postcondition: the value of hr is returned
public int getHours()
{
    return hr;
}

    //Method to return the minutes
    //Postcondition: the value of min is returned
public int getMinutes()
{
    return min;
}

    //Method to return the seconds
    //Postcondition: the value of sec is returned
public int getSeconds()
{
    return sec;
}
```

```
      //Method to print the time
      //Postcondition: Time is printed in the form hh:mm:ss
public void printTime()
{
    if(hr < 10)
       System.out.print("0");
    System.out.print(hr + ":");

    if(min < 10)
       System.out.print("0");
    System.out.print(min + ":");

    if(sec < 10)
       System.out.print("0");
    System.out.print(sec);
}

      //Method to increment the time by one second
      //Postcondition: The time is incremented by one second
      //If the before-increment time is 23:59:59, the time
      //is reset to 00:00:00
public void incrementSeconds()
{
    sec++;
    if(sec > 59)
    {
       sec = 0;
       incrementMinutes(); //increment minutes
    }
}

      //Method to increment the time by one minute
      //Postcondition: The time is incremented by one minute
      //If the before-increment time is 23:59:53, the time
      //is reset to 00:00:53
public void incrementMinutes()
{
    min++;
    if(min > 59)
    {
       min = 0;
       incrementHours(); //increment hours
    }
}
```

8

```
    //Method to increment the time by one hour
    //Postcondition: The time is incremented by one hour
    //If the before-increment time is 23:45:53, the time
    //is reset to 00:45:53
public void incrementHours()
{
    hr++;
    if(hr > 23)
        hr = 0;
}

    //Method to compare the two times
    //Postcondition: Returns true if this time is equal to
    //               otherTime; otherwise returns false
public boolean equals(Clock otherClock)
{
    return(hr == otherClock.hr
           && min == otherClock.min
           && sec == otherClock.sec);
}
    //Method to copy time
    //Postcondition: The instance variables of otherTime are
    //               copied into the corresponding data
    //               members of this time.
    //               hr = otherTime.hr; min = otherTime.min;
    //               sec = otherTime.sec;
public void makeCopy(Clock otherClock)
{
    hr = otherClock.hr;
    min = otherClock.min;
    sec = otherClock.sec;
}

    //Method to return a copy of time
    //Postcondition: A copy of the object is created
    //               and a reference of the copy is returned
public Clock getCopy()
{
    Clock temp = new Clock();

    temp.hr = hr;
    temp.min = min;
    temp.sec = sec;

    return temp;
}
}
```

In a class definition, it is a common practice to list all the instance variables, named constants, other data members, or variable declarations first, then constructors, and then the methods.

Example 8-2

```
//Program to test the various operations of the class Clock

import java.io.*;

public class TestProgClock
{
    static BufferedReader keyboard =
            new BufferedReader(new InputStreamReader(System.in));
    public static void main(String[] args) throws IOException
    {
        Clock myClock = new Clock(5,4,30);              //Line 1
        Clock yourClock = new Clock();                  //Line 2

        int hours;                                      //Line 3
        int minutes;                                    //Line 4
        int seconds;                                    //Line 5

        System.out.print("Line 6: myClock: ");          //Line 6
        myClock.printTime();                            //Line 7
        System.out.println();                           //Line 8

        System.out.print("Line 9: yourClock: ");        //Line 9
        yourClock.printTime();                          //Line 10
        System.out.println();                           //Line 11

        yourClock.setTime(5,45,16);                     //Line 12

        System.out.print("Line 13: After setting - "
                        + "yourClock: ");               //Line 13
        yourClock.printTime();                          //Line 14
        System.out.println();                           //Line 15

        if(myClock.equals(yourClock))                   //Line 16
           System.out.println("Line 17: Both times "
                            + "are equal.");            //Line 17
        else                                            //Line 18
           System.out.println("Line 19: The two times "
                            + "are not equal");         //Line 19

        System.out.print("Line 20: Enter hours: ");     //Line 20
        System.out.flush();                             //Line 21
        hours = Integer.parseInt(keyboard.readLine());  //Line 22
        System.out.println();                           //Line 23

        System.out.print("Line 24: Enter minutes: ");   //Line 24
        System.out.flush();                             //Line 25
        minutes = Integer.parseInt(keyboard.readLine()); //Line 26
        System.out.println();                           //Line 27

        System.out.print("Line 28: Enter seconds: ");   //Line 28
        System.out.flush();                             //Line 29
        seconds = Integer.parseInt(keyboard.readLine()); //Line 30
        System.out.println();                           //Line 31
```

8

```
        myClock.setTime(hours,minutes,seconds);          //Line 32

        System.out.print("Line 33: New myClock: ");      //Line 33
        myClock.printTime();                             //Line 34
        System.out.println();                            //Line 35

        myClock.incrementSeconds();                      //Line 36

        System.out.print("Line 37: After incrementing "
                    + "the clock by one second, "
                    + "myClock: ");                       //Line 37
        myClock.printTime();                             //Line 38
        System.out.println();                            //Line 39

        yourClock.makeCopy(myClock);                     //Line 40
        System.out.print("Line 41: After copying "
                    + "myClock: into yourClock; "
                    + "yourClock: ");                     //Line 41
        yourClock.printTime();                           //Line 42
        System.out.println();                            //Line 43
    }//end main
}
```

Sample Run: In this sample run, the user input is shaded.

```
Line 6: myClock: 05:04:30
Line 9: yourClock: 00:00:00
Line 13: After setting - yourClock: 05:45:16
Line 19: The two times are not equal
Line 20: Enter hours: 11

Line 24: Enter minutes: 22

Line 28: Enter seconds: 59

Line 33: New myClock: 11:22:59
Line 37: After incrementing the clock by one second, myClock:
11:23:00
Line 41: After copying myClock: into yourClock; yourClock: 11:23:00
```

A walkthrough of the preceding program is left as an exercise for you.

THE COPY CONSTRUCTOR

Suppose that you have the following statement.

```
Clock myClock = new Clock(8, 45, 22);          //Line 1
```

You can use the object myClock to declare and instantiate another Clock object. Consider the following statement:

```
Clock aClock = new Clock(myClock);          //Line 2
```

This statement declares **aClock** to be a reference variable of the type **Clock**, instantiates the object **aClock**, and initializes the instance variables of the object **aClock** using the values of the corresponding instance variables of the object **myClock**. However, to successfully execute the statement in Line 2, you need to include a special constructor, called a **copy constructor**, in the **class Clock**. The copy constructor executes when an object is instantiated and initialized using an existing object.

The syntax of the heading of the copy constructor is:

```
public ClassName(ClassName otherObject) //copy constructor heading
```

For example, the heading of the copy constructor for the **class Clock** is:

```
public Clock(Clock otherClock)
```

The definition of the copy constructor for the **class Clock** is

```
public Clock(Clock otherClock)
{
    hr = otherClock.hr;
    min = otherClock.min;
    sec = otherClock.sec;
}
```

If you include this definition of the copy constructor in the **class Clock**, then the statement in Line 2 declares **aClock** to be a reference variable of the type **Clock**, instantiates the object **aClock**, and initializes the instance variables of the object **aClock** using the values of the instance variables of the object **myClock**.

The copy constructor is very useful and will be included in most of the classes.

CLASSES AND THE METHOD toString

Suppose that **x** is an **int** variable and the value of **x** is **25**. The statement

```
System.out.println(x);
```

outputs

```
25
```

However, the output of the statement

```
System.out.println(myClock);
```

is

```
Clock@f617d64b
```

which looks strange. This is because whenever you create a **class**, the Java system provides the method **toString** to the **class**. The method **toString** is used to convert an object to a `String` object. The methods `print` and `println` output the string created by the method `toString`.

The default definition of the method `toString` creates a string that is the name of the object's `class`, followed by the hash code of the object. For example, in the preceding statement, `Clock` is the name of the object `myClock`'s `class` and the hash code for the object referenced by `myClock` is `@f617d64b`.

The method `toString` is a `public` value-returning method. It does not take any parameters and returns the address of a `String` object. The heading of the method `toString` is:

```
public String toString()
```

You can *override* the default definition of the method `toString` to convert an object to a desired string. Suppose that for the objects of the `class Clock` you want the method `toString` to create the string hh:mm:ss—the string consists of the object's hour, minutes, seconds, and the colons as shown. The string created by the method `toString` is the same as the string output by the method `print` of the `class Clock`. This is easily accomplished by providing the following definition of the method `toString`:

```
public String toString()
{
      String str = "";

    if(hr < 10)
        str = "0";
    str = str + hr + ":";

    if(min < 10)
        str = str + "0" ;
    str = str + min + ":";

    if(sec < 10)
        str = str + "0";
    str = str + sec;

    return str;
}
```

In the preceding code, `str` is a `String` variable used to create the required string.

The preceding definition of the method `toString` must be included in the `class Clock`. In fact, after including the method `toString` in the `class Clock`, we can remove the method `print`. If the values of the instance variables `hr`, `min`, and `sec` of `myClock` are 8, 25, and 56, respectively, then the output of the statement

```
System.out.println(myClock)
```

is

```
08:25:56
```

You can see that the method `toString` is quite useful for outputting the values of the instance variables.

STATIC MEMBERS OF A CLASS

In Chapter 7, we described the `classes Math` and `Character`. In Example 7-1 (of Chapter 7), we used several methods of the `classes Math` and `Character`, however, we did not need to create any object to use these methods. We simply used the name of the class, the dot operator, and the method's name. For example, to use the method **pow** of the **class Math**, we used expressions such as:

```
Math.pow(5,3)
```

Can we do the same with the **class Clock**? The answer is no. Although the methods of the **classes Math** and **Character** are **public**, they also are defined using the modifier **static**. For example, the heading of the method **pow** of the **class Math** is:

```
public static double pow(double base, double exponent)
```

The modifier **static** in the heading specifies that the method can be invoked by using the name of the **class**. Similarly, if a data member of a **class** is declared using the modifier **static**, it can be accessed by using the name of the **class**.

The following example clarifies the effect of the modifier **static**.

8

Example 8-3

Consider the following definition of the **class Illustrate**:

```
public class Illustrate
{
    private int x;
    private static int y;
    public static int count;

    public Illustrate()
    {
        x = 0;
    }

    public Illustrate(int a)
    {
        x = a;
    }

    public void print()
    {
        System.out.println("x = " + x
                        + ", y = " + y
                        + ", count = " + count);
    }
```

```
    public static void incrementCount()
    {
        count++;
    }
}
```

Further, suppose that you have the following declaration:

```
Illustrate illusObject = new Illustrate();
```

The reference variable `illusObject` can access any `public` member of the `class` `Illustrate`. Now, because the method `incrementCount` is `static` and `public`, the following statement is legal:

```
Illustrate.incrementCount();
```

Similarly, because the data member `count` is `static` and `public`, the following statement is legal:

```
Illustrate.count++;
```

`static` Variables (Data Members) of a Class

Suppose that you have a `class`, say `MyClass`, with data members (`static` and non-`static`). When you instantiate objects of the type `MyClass`, only non-`static` data members of the `class` `MyClass` become the data members of each object. What about the memory for the `static` data members of `MyClass`? For each `static` member of the `class`, Java allocates only one memory space. All `MyClass` objects refer to the same memory space. In fact, `static` data members of a `class` *exist* even when no object of the `class` type is instantiated. Moreover, `static` variables are initialized to their default values. You can access the `public` `static` data members outside the `class`, as explained in the previous section.

The following example further clarifies how memory space is allocated for `static` and non-`static` data members of a class.

Suppose that you have the `class` `Illustrate`, as given in Example 8-3. Then memory space exists for the `static` data members `y` and `count`.

Consider the following statement:

```
Illustrate illusObject1 = new Illustrate(3);    //Line 1
Illustrate illusObject2 = new Illustrate(5);    //Line 2
```

The statements in Line 1 and Line 2 declare `illusObject1` and `illusObject2` to be reference variables of `Illustrate` type and instantiate these objects (see Figure 8-14).

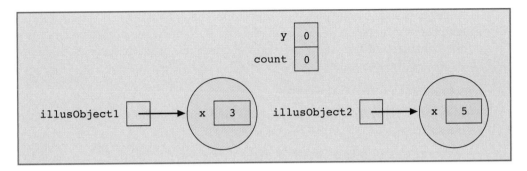

Figure 8-14   `illusObject1` and `illusObject2`

Now consider the following statements:

```
Illustrate.incrementCount();
Illustrate.y++;
```

The output of the statement

```
illusObject1.print();          //Line 3
```

is

```
x = 3, y = 1, count = 1
```

Similarly, the output of the statement

```
illusObject2.print();          //Line 4
```

is

```
x = 5, y = 1, count = 1
```

FINALIZERS

Like constructors, **finalizers** are also special types of methods. However a finalizer is a `void` method. Moreover, a `class` can have only one finalizer, and the finalizer can have no parameters. The name of the finalizer is `finalize`. The method `finalize` automatically executes when the class object goes out of scope.

CREATING YOUR OWN PACKAGES

Recall that a package is a collection of related classes. As you develop classes, you can create packages and categorize your classes. You can import your classes in the same way that you import classes from the packages provided by Java.

Every Java SDK usually contains a directory where the compiled versions of the classes are stored. For example, if you are using the Sun JDK, the name of this directory is *classes*. Both the compiler and the interpreter know the location of the directory. On some versions of JDK 1.4, the location of this directory is:

```
c:\j2sdk1.4.0-rc\jre\lib
```

You can check your SDK's documentation to find the directory where compiled codes of classes are stored.

To create a package and add a class to the package so that the class can be used in a program, you do the following:

1. Define the class to be **public**. If the class is not **public**, it can be used only within the package.

2. Choose a name for the package. To organize your packages, you can create subdirectories within the directory that contains the compiled code of classes. For example, you could create a directory for classes you create in this book. Since the title of this book is *Java Programming: From Problem Analysis to Program Design*, you could create a directory named **jpfpatpd**. You could make subdirectories for the classes used in each chapter, such as the subdirectory **ch08** within the directory **jpfpatpd**.

Suppose that you want to create a **package** to group classes related to time. You could call this **package clockPackage**. To add the **class Clock** to this package and to place the package **clockPackage** within the subdirectory **ch08** of the directory **jpfpatpd**, you include the following package statement with the file containing the **class Clock**:

```
package jpfpatpd.ch08.clockPackage;
```

This statement is put before the definition of the **class**, like this:

```
package jpfpatpd.ch08.clockPackage;

public class Clock
{
    //put instance variables and methods, as before, here
}
```

The name of the file containing the **package** statement and the definition of the **class Clock** is **Clock.java**. The next step is to compile the file **Clock.java** using the compile command in the SDK you are using.

For example, if you are using **jdk1.4**, which contains a command-line compiler, you include the option **–d** to only compile the file **Clock.java** as follows:

```
javac –d c:\j2sdk1.4.0-rc\jre\lib Clock.java
```

If the directories **jpfpatpd**, **ch08**, and **clockPackage** do not exist, then the compiler automatically creates these directories. To be absolutely certain about the correct directory path, check your system's documentation.

Once the `package` is created, you can use the appropriate `import` command in your program to make use of the `class`. For example, to use the `class Clock`, as created in the preceding code, you use the following `import` statement in your program:

```
import jpfpatpd.ch08.clockPackage.Clock;
```

In Java, `package` is a reserved word.

Multiple File Programs

In the preceding section, you learned how to create a `package`. Creating a `package` to group related `class`(es) is very useful if the classes are to be used again and again. On the other hand, if a `class` is to be used in only one program, or if you have divided your program so that it uses more than one `class`, rather than create a `package`, you can directly add the file(s) containing the `class`(es) to the program.

The Java SDKs, Forte for Java, J++ Builder, and CodeWarrior put the editor, compiler, and linker all into one program. With one command, a program is compiled and linked with the other necessary files. These SDKs also manage multiple-file programs in the form of a project. A **project** consists of several files, called the project files. These SDKs include a command that will allow you to add several files to a project. Also, these SDKs usually have commands like **build**, **rebuild**, or **make** (check your software's documentation) to automatically compile and link all files required to create the executable code. When one or more files in the project change, you can use these commands to recompile and relink the files.

Example 8-4 further illustrates how classes are designed and implemented. The `class Person` that we create in this example is very useful; we will use this `class` in subsequent chapters.

Example 8-4

Two common attributes of a person are the person's first name and last name. The typical operations on a person's name are to set the name and print the name. The following statements define a `class` with these properties. (See Figure 8-15.)

```java
public class Person
{
    private String firstName; //store the first name
    private String lastName;  //store the last name

        //Constructor with parameters
        //Set firstName and lastName according to the parameters
        //Postcondition: firstName = first; lastName = last;
    public Person (String first, String last)
    {
        firstName = first;
        lastName = last;
    }
```

```java
    //Default constructor;
    //Initialize firstName and lastName to empty string
    //Postcondition: firstName = ""; lastName = "";
public Person()
{
    firstName = "";
    lastName = "";

}


    //Method to output the first name and last name
    //in the form firstName lastName
public String toString()
{
    return (firstName + " " + lastName);
}


    //Method to set firstName and lastName according to
    //the parameters
    //Postcondition: firstName = first; lastName = last;
public void setName(String first, String last)
{
    firstName = first;
    lastName = last;
}


    //Method to return the firstName
    //Postcondition: the value of firstName is returned
public String getFirstName()
{
    return firstName;
}


    //Method to return the lastName
    //Postcondition: the value of lastName is returned
public String getLastName()
{
    return lastName;
}
}
```

Figure 8-15   UML diagram of the class Person

The following program tests the class Person:

```java
import java.io.*;

public class TestProgPerson
{
    public static void main(String[] args)
    {
        Person name = new Person();                            //Line 1

        Person emp = new Person("Donald", "Doc");              //Line 2

        System.out.println("Line 3: name: " + name);           //Line 3

        name.setName("Sleeping", "Beauty");                    //Line 4
        System.out.println("Line 5: name: " + name);           //Line 5

        System.out.println("Line 6: emp: " + emp);             //Line 6

        emp.setName("Sandy", "Smith");                         //Line 7
        System.out.println("Line 8: emp: " + emp);             //Line 8
    }//end main
}
```

Output:

```
Line 3: name:
Line 5: name: Sleeping Beauty
Line 6: emp: Donald Doc
Line 8: emp: Sandy Smith
```

THE REFERENCE this

In this chapter, we defined the **class** Clock. Suppose that myClock is a reference variable of the type Clock. Moreover, assume that the object myClock has been created. Consider the following statements:

```
myClock.setTime(5,6,59);          //Line 1
myClock.incrementSeconds();        //Line 2
```

The statement in Line 1 uses the method setTime to set the instance variables hr, min, and sec of the object myClock to 5, 6, and 59, respectively. The statement in Line 2 uses the method incrementSeconds to increment the time of the object myClock by one second. The statement in Line 2 calls the method incrementMinutes because after incrementing the value of sec by 1, the value of sec becomes 60, which then is reset to 0, and the method incrementMinutes is invoked.

How do you think Java makes sure that the statement in Line 1 sets the instance variables of the object myClock and not of another Clock object? How does Java make sure that when the method incrementSeconds calls the method incrementMinutes, the method incrementMinutes increments the value of the instance variable min of the object myClock and not of another Clock object?

The answer is that every object has access to a reference to itself. The name of this reference is this. In Java, this is a reserved word.

Java implicitly uses the reference this to refer to both the instance variables and the methods of a class. Recall that the definition of the method setTime is:

```
public void setTime(int hours, int minutes, int seconds)
{
    if(0 <= hours && hours < 24)
        hr = hours;
    else
        hr = 0;

    if(0 <= minutes && minutes < 60)
        min = minutes;
    else
        min = 0;

    if(0 <= seconds && seconds < 60)
        sec = seconds;
    else
        sec = 0;
}
```

In the method setTime, the statement

```
hr = hours;
```

is in fact, equivalent to the statement

```
this.hr = hours;
```

In this statement, the reference this is explicitly used. You can explicitly use the reference this and write the equivalent definition of the method setTime as follows:

```
public void setTime(int hr, int min, int sec)
{
    if(0 <= hr && hr < 24)
        this.hr = hr;
    else
        this.hr = 0;

    if(0 <= min && min < 60)
        this.min = min;
    else
        this.min = 0;

    if(0 <= sec && sec < 60)
        this.sec = sec;
    else
        this.sec = 0;
}
```

Notice that in the preceding definition of the method setTime, the name of the formal parameters and the name of the instance variables are the same. In this definition of the method setTime, the expression this.hr means the instance variable hr, not the formal parameter hr, and so on. Because the code explicitly uses the reference this, the compiler can distinguish between the instance variables and the formal parameters. Of course you could have kept the name of the formal parameters as before and still used the reference this as shown in the code.

Similarly, explicitly using the reference this, you can write the definition of the method incrementSeconds as follows:

```
public void incrementSeconds()
{
    this.sec++;
    if(this.sec > 59)
    {
        this.sec = 0;
        this.incrementMinutes(); //increment minutes
    }
}
```

Cascaded Method Calls

 This section may be omitted without any discontinuation.

In addition to explicitly referring to the instance variables and methods of an object, the reference this has another use. It can be used to implement cascaded method calls. We explain this with the help of an example.

Example 8-4 shows a class we designed to implement a person's name in a program. Here, we extend the definition of the class Person to individually set a person's first name and last name, and then return a reference of the object. The following code is the extended definition of the class Person. (The methods setFirstName and setLastName are added to this definition of the class Person.)

```
public class Person
{
    private String firstName; //store the first name
    private String lastName;  //store the last name

        //Constructor with parameters
        //Set firstName and lastName according to the parameters
        //Postcondition: firstName = first; lastName = last;
    public Person(String first, String last)
    {
        firstName = first;
        lastName = last;
    }

        //Default constructor;
        //Initialize firstName and lastName to empty string
        //Postcondition: firstName = ""; lastName = "";
    public Person()
    {
        firstName = "";
        lastName = "";
    }


        //Method to return the first name and last name
        //in the form firstName lastName
    public String toString()
    {
        return (firstName + " " + lastName);
    }


        //Method to set firstName and lastName according to
        //the parameters
        //Postcondition: firstName = first; lastName = last;
    public void setName(String first, String last)
    {
        firstName = first;
        lastName = last;
    }


        //Method to set the last name
        //Postcondition: lastName = last;
```

```
        //        After setting the last name, a reference
        //        of the object is returned
    public Person setLastName(String last)
    {
        lastName = last;

        return this;
    }

        //Method to set the first name
        //Postcondition: firstName = first;
        //        After setting the first name, a reference
        //        of the object is returned
    public Person setFirstName(String first)
    {
        firstName = first;

        return this;
    }

        //Method to return the firstName
        //Postcondition: the value of firstName is returned
    public String getFirstName()
    {
        return firstName;
    }

        //Function to return the lastName
        //Postcondition: the value of lastName is returned
    public String getLastName()
    {
        return lastName;
    }
}
```

Consider the following function main. (Assume that the definition of the class Person, as created in this section, is in the package jpfpatpd.ch08.PersonNew.)

```
import jpfpatpd.ch08.PersonNew.*;

public class CascadedMethodCalls
{
    public static void main(String[] args)
    {
        Person student1 =
                    new Person("Angela", "Clodfelter");     //Line 1

        Person student2 = new Person();                     //Line 2

        Person student3 = new Person();                     //Line 3
```

```
        System.out.println("Line 4 -- Student 1: "
                    + student1);                        //Line 4

        student2.setFirstName("Shelly").setLastName("Malik");//Line 5

        System.out.println("Line 6 -- Student 2: "
                    + student2);                        //Line 6

        student3.setFirstName("Chelsea");               //Line 7

        System.out.println("Line 8 -- Student 3: "
                    + student3);                        //Line 8

        student3.setLastName("Tomek");                  //Line 9

        System.out.println("Line 10 -- Student 3: "
                    + student3);                        //Line 10

    }
}
```

Output

```
Line 4 -- Student 1: Angela Clodfelter
Line 6 -- Student 2: Shelly Malik
Line 8 -- Student 3: Chelsea
Line 10 -- Student 3: Chelsea Tomek
```

The statements in Lines 1, 2, and 3 declare the variables `student1`, `student2`, and `student3` and also instantiate the objects. The instance variables of the objects `student2` and `student3` are initialized to empty strings. The statement in Line 4 outputs the value of `student1`. The statement in Line 5 works as follows. In the statement

```
student2.setFirstName("Shelly").setLastName("Malik");
```

first the expression

```
student2.setFirstName("Shelly")
```

is executed because the associativity of the dot operator is from left to right. This expression sets the first name to `"Shelly"` and returns a reference of the object, which is object `student2`. Thus, the next expression executed is

```
student2.setLastName("Malik")
```

which sets the last name of the object `student2` to `"Malik"`. The statement in Line 6 outputs the value of `student2`. The statement in Line 7 sets the first name of `student3` to `"Chelsea"`, and the statement in Line 8 outputs `student3`. Notice the output in Line 8. The output shows only the first name, not the last name, because we have not yet set the last name of the object `student3`. The last name of the object `student3` is still empty, which was set by the statement in Line 3 when `student3` was declared. Next, the statement in Line 9 sets the last name of the object `student3`, and the statement in Line 10 outputs the `student3`.

INNER CLASSES

The classes defined thus far in this chapter are said to have file scope, that is, they are contained within a file, but not within another class. In Chapter 6, while designing the `class RectangleProgram`, we defined the `class CalculateButtonHandler` to handle an action event. The definition of the `class CalculateButtonHandler` is contained within the `class RectangleProgram`. Classes that are defined within other classes are called **inner classes**.

An inner class can be either a complete class definition, such as the `class CalculateButtonHandler`, or an anonymous inner class definition. Anonymous classes are classes with no name.

One of the main uses of inner classes is to handle events—as we did in Chapter 6.

ABSTRACT DATA TYPES

To help you understand an abstract data type (ADT), and how it might be used, we'll provide an analogy. The following items seem unrelated:

- A deck of playing cards
- A set of index cards containing contact information
- Telephone numbers stored in your cellular phone

All three of these items share the following structural properties:

- Each one is a collection of elements.
- There is a first element.
- There is a second element, third element, and so on.
- There is a last element.
- Given an element other than the last element, there is a "next" element.
- Given an element other than the first element, there is a "previous" element.
- An element can be removed from the collection.
- An element may be added to the collection.
- A specified element can be located in the collection by systematically going through the collection.

In your programs, you may want to keep a collection of various elements such us addresses, students, employees, departments, and projects. Thus, this structure commonly appears in various applications, and it is worth studying in its own right. We call this organization a *list* and list is an example of an ADT.

There is a data type called `Vector` (discussed in Chapter 10) with basic operations such as:

- Insert an item

- Delete an item

- Find an item

You could use it to create an address book. You would not need to write a program to insert an address, delete an address, or find an item in your address book. Java also allows you to create your own abstract data types through classes.

An ADT is an abstraction of a commonly appearing data structure, along with a set of defined operations on the data structure.

Abstract data type (ADT): A data type that specifies the logical properties without the implementation details.

Historically, the concept of ADT in computer programming developed as a way of abstracting the common data structure and the associated operations. Along the way, ADT provided **information hiding**. That is, ADT *hides* the implementation details of the operations and the data from the users of the ADT. Users can use the operations of an ADT without knowing how the operation is implemented.

PROGRAMMING EXAMPLE: CANDY MACHINE

A new candy machine is bought for the gym, but it is not working properly. The machine sells candies, chips, gum, and cookies. In this programming example, we write a program to create a Java application program for this candy machine so that it can be put into operation.

We divide this program in two parts. In the first part we design a non-GUI application program. In the second part we design an application program that will create a GUI as described in the second part.

The non-GUI application program should do the following:

1. Show the customer the different products sold by the candy machine.
2. Let the customer make the selection.
3. Show the customer the cost of the item selected.
4. Accept money from the customer.
5. Release the item.

Input The item selection and the cost of the item

Output The selected item

In the next section, we design the candy machine's basic components, which are required by either type of application program—GUI or non-GUI. The difference between the two types is evident when we write the main program to put the candy machine into operation.

Problem Analysis and Algorithm Design

A candy machine has three main components: a built-in cash register, several dispensers to hold and release the products, and the candy machine itself. Therefore, we need to define a class to implement the cash register, a class to implement the dispenser, and a class to implement the candy machine. First we describe the classes to implement cash register and dispenser, and then we use these classes to describe the candy machine.

Cash Register   Let's first discuss the properties of a cash register. The register has some cash on hand, it accepts the amount from the customer, and if the amount entered is more than the cost of the item, then—if possible—it returns the change. For simplicity, we assume that the user enters the exact amount for the product. The cash register should also be able to show the candy machine's owner the amount of money in the register at any given time. Let's call the class implementing the cash register `CashRegister`.

The members of the `class CashRegister` are listed below and shown in Figure 8-16.

Instance Variables

```java
private int cashOnHand;
```

Methods

```java
public CashRegister(int cashIn)
   //Constructor with parameters
   //Postcondition: cashOnHand = cashIn;

public CashRegister()
   //Default constructor with parameters
   //To set the cash in the register 500 cents
   //Postcondition: cashOnHand = 500;

public int currentBalance()
   //Method to show the current amount in the cash register
   //Postcondition: The value of the instance variable
   //               cashOnHand is returned

public void acceptAmount(int amountIn)
   //Method to receive the amount deposited by
   //the customer and updates the amount in the register.
   //Postcondition: cashOnHand = cashOnHand + amountIn
```

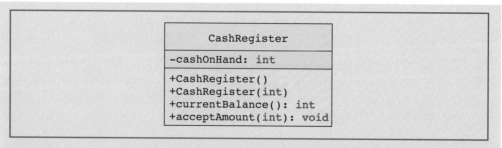

Figure 8-16 UML diagram of the class `CashRegister`

Next we give the definition of the methods to implement the operations of the **class** **CashRegister**. The definition of these methods is simple and easy to follow.

The method **currentBalance** shows the current amount in the cash register. The amount stored in the cash register is in cents. Its definition is:

```
public int currentBalance()
{
    return cashOnHand;
}
```

The method **acceptAmount** accepts the amount entered by the customer. It updates the cash in the register by adding the amount entered by the customer to the previous amount in the cash register. The definition of this method is:

```
public void acceptAmount(int amountIn)
{
    cashOnHand = cashOnHand + amountIn;
}
```

The constructor with the parameter sets the value of the instance variable to the value specified by the user. The value is passed as a parameter to the constructor. The definition of the constructor with the parameter is:

```
public CashRegister(int cashIn)
{
    if(cashIn >= 0)
       cashOnHand = cashIn;
    else
       cashOnHand = 500;
}
```

Note that the definition of the constructor checks for valid values of the parameter **cashIn**. If the value of **cashIn** is less than 0, the value assigned to the instance variable **cashOnHand** is 500.

The default constructor sets the value of the instance variable `cashOnHand` to 500 cents. Its definition is:

```
public CashRegister()
{
    cashOnHand = 500;
}
```

Now that we have the definitions of all the methods necessary to implement operations of the `class CashRegister`, we can give the definitions of `CashRegister`. (This `class` is placed in the `package candyMachine`.) Its definition is:

```
//class CashRegister

package jpfpatpd.ch08.candyMachine;

public class CashRegister
{
    private int cashOnHand;    //variable to store the cash
                               //in the register

        //Constructor with parameters
        //To set the cash in the register to a specific amount
        //Postcondition: cashOnHand = cashIn;
    public CashRegister(int cashIn)
    {
        if(cashIn >= 0)
            cashOnHand = cashIn;
        else
            cashOnHand = 500;
    }


        //Default constructor with parameters
        //To set the cash in the register to 500 cents
        //Postcondition: cashOnHand = 500;
    public CashRegister()
    {
        cashOnHand = 500;
    }


        //Method to show the current amount in the cash register
        //Postcondition: The value of the instance variable
        //               cashOnHand is returned
    public int currentBalance()
    {
        return cashOnHand;
    }
```

```
         //Method to receive the amount deposited by
         //the customer and update the amount in the register.
         //Postcondition: cashOnHand = cashOnHand + amountIn
      public void acceptAmount(int amountIn)
      {
            cashOnHand = cashOnHand + amountIn;
      }
}
```

Dispenser   The dispenser releases the selected item if it is not empty. It should show the number of items in the dispenser and the cost of the item. Let's call the class implementing a dispenser `Dispenser`. The members necessary to implement the `class Dispenser` are listed below and shown in Figure 8-17.

Instance Variables

```
private int numberOfItems; //variable to store the number of
                           //items in the dispenser
private int cost;          //variable to store the cost of an item
```

Methods

```
public int getCount()
   //Method to show the number of items in the machine
   //Postcondition: The value of the instance variable
   //               numberOfItems is returned

public int getProductCost()
   //Method to show the cost of the item
   //Postcondition: The value of the instance
   //               variable cost is returned

public void makeSale()
   //Method to reduce the number of items by 1
   //Postcondition: numberOfItems = numberOfItems - 1;

public Dispenser(int setNoOfItems, int setCost)
   //Constructor with parameters to set the cost and number
   //of items in the dispenser specified by the user
   //Postcondition: numberOfItems = setNoOfItems;
   //               cost = setCost;

public Dispenser()
   //Default constructor to set the cost and number of
   //items to the default values
   //Postcondition: numberOfItems = 50; cost = 50;
```

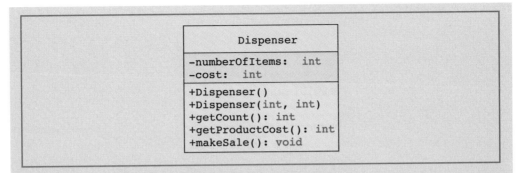

Figure 8-17   UML diagram of the `class` `Dispenser`

Because the candy machine sells four types of items, we will create four objects of the type `Dispenser`. The statement

`Dispenser chips = new Dispenser(100,65);`

creates the object `chips`, sets the number of chip bags in this dispenser to `100`, and sets the cost of each chip bag to `65` cents. (See Figure 8–18.)

Figure 8-18   The object `chips`

Next we discuss the definitions of the methods to implement the operations of the `class` `Dispenser`.

The method `getCount` returns the number of items of a particular product. Because the number of items currently in the dispenser is stored in the instance variable numberOfItems, the method getCount returns the value of the instance variable numberOfItems. The definition of this method is:

```
public int getCount()
{
    return numberOfItems;
}
```

The method getProductCost returns the cost of a product. Because the cost of a product is stored in the instance variable cost, it returns the value of the instance variable cost. The definition of this method is:

```
public int getProductCost()
{
    return cost;
}
```

When a product is sold, the number of items in that dispenser is reduced by 1. Therefore, the method makeSale reduces the number of items in the dispenser by 1. That is, it decrements the value of the instance variable numberOfItems by 1. The definition of this method is:

```
public void makeSale()
{
    numberOfItems--;
}
```

The definition of the constructor checks for valid values of the parameters. If these values are less than 0, the default values are assigned to the instance variables. The definition of the constructor is:

```
    //constructor with parameters
public Dispenser(int setNoOfItems, int setCost)
{
    if(setNoOfItems >= 0)
        numberOfItems = setNoOfItems;
    else
        numberOfItems = 50;

    if(setCost >= 0)
        cost = setCost;
    else
        cost = 50;
}
```

The default constructor assigns the default values to the instance variables:

```java
public Dispenser()
{
    numberOfItems = 50;
    cost = 50;
}
```

The definition of the **class Dispenser** is (we put this **class** in the **package candyMachine**):

```java
//class Dispenser

package jpfpatpd.ch08.candyMachine;

public class Dispenser
{
    private int numberOfItems;   //variable to store the number of
                                 //items in the dispenser
    private int cost;     //variable to store the cost of an item

        //Constructor with parameters to set the cost and number
        //of items in the dispenser specified by the user
        //Postconditions: numberOfItems = setNoOfItems;
        //                cost = setCost;
    public Dispenser(int setNoOfItems, int setCost)
    {
        if(setNoOfItems >= 0)
            numberOfItems = setNoOfItems;
        else
            numberOfItems = 50;

        if(setCost >= 0)
            cost = setCost;
        else
            cost = 50;
    }

        //Default constructor to set the cost and number of
        //items to the default values
        //Postconditions: numberOfItems = 50;
        //                cost = 50;
    public Dispenser()
    {
        numberOfItems = 50;
        cost = 50;
    }

        //Method to show the number of items in the machine
        //Postconditions: The value of the instance variable
        //                numberOfItems is returned
```

```
    public int getCount()
    {
        return numberOfItems;
    }


    //Method to show the cost of the item
    //Postconditions: The value of the instance variable
    //                cost is returned
    public int getProductCost()
    {
        return cost;
    }


    //Method to reduce the number of items by 1
    //Postconditions: numberOfItems = numberOfItems - 1;
    public void makeSale()
    {
        numberOfItems--;
    }
}
```

 We will create the `package jpfpatpd.ch08.candyMachine` and place the classes `CashRegister` and `Dispenser` in this package. The main program can import these classes from this package.

Main Program

When the program executes, it must do the following:

1. Show the different products sold by the candy machine.
2. Show how to select a particular product.
3. Show how to terminate the program.

Furthermore, these instructions must be displayed after processing each selection (except exiting the program), so that the user need not remember what to do if he or she wants to buy additional items. Once the user makes the appropriate selection, the candy machine must act accordingly. If the user opts to buy an available product, the candy machine should show the cost of the product and ask the user to deposit the money. If the money deposited is at least the cost of the item, the candy machine should sell the item and display an appropriate message.

This discussion translates into the following algorithm:

1. Show the selection to the customer.
2. Get the selection.
3. If the selection is valid and the dispenser corresponding to the selection is not empty, sell the product.

We divide this program into three functions—showSelection, sellProduct, and main.

Method showSelection   This method displays the necessary information to help the user select and buy a product. Essentially, it contains the following output statements. (We assume that the candy machine sells four types of products.)

```
*** Welcome to One Stop Candy Shop ***"
To select an item, enter
1 for Candy
2 for Chips
3 for Gum
4 for Cookies
9 to exit
```

The definition of the function showSelection is:

```
public static void showSelection()
{
   System.out.println("*** Welcome to One Stop Candy Shop ***");
   System.out.println("To select an item, enter ");
   System.out.println("1 for Candy");
   System.out.println("2 for Chips");
   System.out.println("3 for Gum");
   System.out.println("4 for Cookies");
   System.out.println("9 to exit");
}//end showSelection
```

Next we describe the method sellProduct.

Method sellProduct   This method attempts to sell a particular product selected by the customer. The candy machine contains four dispensers, which correspond to the four products. The first thing this method does is check whether the dispenser holding the product is empty. If the dispenser is empty, the method informs the customer that this product is sold out. If the dispenser is nonempty, it tells the user to deposit the necessary amount to buy the product. For simplicity, we assume that this program does not return the extra money deposited by the customer. Therefore, the cash register is updated by adding the money entered by the user.

From this discussion, it follows that the method sellProduct must have access to the dispenser holding the product (to decrement the number of items in the dispenser by 1 and to show the cost of the item) as well as access to the cash register (to update the cash). Therefore, this method has two parameters: one corresponding to the dispenser, and the other corresponding to the cash register.

In pseudocode, the algorithm for this method is:

1. If the dispenser is nonempty
   a. Get the product cost.
   b. Set the variable `coinsRequired` to the price of the product.
   c. Set the variable `coinsInserted` to 0.
   d. While `coinsRequired` is greater than 0
      i.   Show and prompt the customer to enter the additional amount.
      ii. Calculate the total amount entered by the customer.
      iii. Determine the amount needed.
   e. Update the amount in the cash register.
   f. Sell the product—that is, decrement the number of items in the dispenser by 1.
   g. Display an appropriate message.
2. If the dispenser is empty, tell the user that this product is sold out.

This definition of the method `sellProduct` is:

```
public static void sellProduct(Dispenser product,
                               CashRegister cRegister)
                                        throws IOException
{
    int price;        //variable to hold the product price
    int coinsInserted; //variable to hold the amount entered
    int coinsRequired; //variable to show the extra amount needed

    if(product.getCount() > 0)                          //Step 1
    {
        price = product.getProductCost();               //Step 1a
        coinsRequired = price;                          //Step 1b
        coinsInserted = 0;                              //Step 1c

        while(coinsRequired > 0)                         //Step 1d
        {
            System.out.println("Please deposit "
                    + coinsRequired + " cents");       //Step 1d.i

                                                        //Step 1d.ii
            coinsInserted = coinsInserted
                        + Integer.parseInt(keyboard.readLine());

            coinsRequired = price - coinsInserted; //Step 1d.iii
        }

        cRegister.acceptAmount(coinsInserted);         //Step 1e
        product.makeSale();                            //Step 1f
```

```
            System.out.println("Collect your item at the "
                        + "bottom and enjoy.");      //Step 1g
    }
    else
        System.out.println("Sorry this item is sold out.");
}//end sellProduct
```

Method main   The algorithm for the method main follows:

1. Create the cash register—that is, create and initialize a CashRegister object.
2. Create four dispensers—that is, create and initialize four objects of the type Dispenser. For example, the statement

```
Dispenser candy = new Dispenser(100, 50);
```

   creates a dispenser object, candy, to hold the candies. The number of items in the dispenser is 100, and the cost of an item is 50 cents.

3. Declare additional variables as necessary.
4. Show the selection; call the method showSelection.
5. Get the selection.
6. While not done (a selection of 9 exits the program):
   a. Sell the product; call the method sellProduct.
   b. Show the selection; call the method showSelection.
   c. Get the selection.

The definition of the method main follows:

```
public static void main(String[] args) throws IOException
{
    CashRegister cashRegister = new CashRegister (); //Step 1
    Dispenser candy = new Dispenser (100,50);        //Step 2
    Dispenser chips = new Dispenser (100,65);        //Step 2
    Dispenser gum = new Dispenser (75,45);           //Step 2
    Dispenser cookies = new Dispenser (100,85);      //Step 2

    int choice;  //variable to hold the selection    //Step 3

    showSelection();                                 //Step 4
    choice = Integer.parseInt(keyboard.readLine());  //Step 5

    while(choice != 9)                               //Step 6
    {
        switch(choice)                               //Step 6a
        {
        case 1: sellProduct(candy, cashRegister);
                break;
        case 2: sellProduct(chips, cashRegister);
                break;
```

```
            case 3: sellProduct(gum, cashRegister);
                    break;
            case 4: sellProduct(cookies, cashRegister);
                    break;
            default: System.out.println("Invalid Selection");
            }//end switch

            showSelection();                                    //Step 6b
            choice =
                    Integer.parseInt(keyboard.readLine());  //Step 6c
        }//end while
}//end main
```

Main Program Listing

```
// Program candy machine

import java.io.*;
import jpfpatpd.ch08.candyMachine.*;

public class CandyMachine
{
    static BufferedReader keyboard =
            new BufferedReader(new InputStreamReader(System.in));

    //Place the definition of the method main as given above here

    //Place the definition of the method showSelection as
    //given above here

    //Place the definition of the method sellProduct as
    //given above here
}
```

Sample Run: In this sample run, the user input is shaded.

```
*** Welcome to One Stop Candy Shop ***
To select an item, enter
1 for Candy
2 for Chips
3 for Gum
4 for Cookies
9 to exit
1
Please deposit 50 cents
50
```

```
Collect your item at the bottom and enjoy
*** Welcome to One Stop Candy Shop ***
To select an item, enter
1 for Candy
2 for Chips
3 for Gum
4 for Cookies
9 to exit
3
Please deposit 45 cents
45
Collect your item at the bottom and enjoy
*** Welcome to One Stop Candy Shop ***
To select an item, enter
1 for Candy
2 for Chips
3 for Gum
4 for Cookies
9 to exit
9
```

Candy Machine: Creating a GUI

 If you skipped the GUI part of Chapter 6, you can skip this section.

We will now design an application program that will create the GUI shown in Figure 8-19.

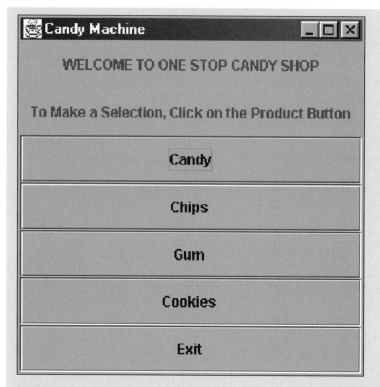

Figure 8-19   GUI for the candy machine

The program should do the following:
1. Show the customer the above GUI.
2. Let the customer make the selection.
3. When the user clicks on a product, show the customer its cost, and prompt the customer to enter the money for the product using an input dialog box shown in Figure 8-20.

Figure 8-20   Input dialog box to enter money for the candy machine

4. Accept money from the customer.
5. Make the sale and display a dialog box as shown in Figure 8-21.

Figure 8-21   Output dialog box to show the output of the candy machine

In the first part of this programming example, we designed and implemented the classes **CashRegister** and **Dispenser**. Our final step is to revise the main program of the first part to create a GUI.

Main Program

We now describe how to create the candy machine using the classes **CashRegister** and **Dispenser** and the GUI components. When the program executes, it must display the GUI shown earlier in Figure 8-19.

The GUI contains a window, two labels and five buttons. The labels and buttons are placed into the content pane of the window. As you learned in Chapter 6, to create the window, the application program will be created by extending the definition of the class JFrame. Thus, we need the following GUI components:

```
private JLabel headingMainL;    //label for the first line
private JLabel selectionL;      //label for the second line

private JButton exitB, candyB, chipsB, gumB, cookiesB;
```

The following statements create and instantiate these labels and button objects:

```
headingMainL = new JLabel("WELCOME TO ONE STOP CANDY SHOP",
                          SwingConstants.CENTER);
selectionL = new JLabel("To Make a Selection, "
                  + "Click on the Product Button",
                    SwingConstants.CENTER);

candyB = new JButton("Candy");

chipsB = new JButton("Chips");

gumB = new JButton("Gum");

cookiesB = new JButton("Cookies");

exitB = new JButton("Exit");
```

Now these components are to be placed in the content pane of the window. The seven components—labels and buttons—are arranged in seven rows. Therefore, the content pane layout will be a grid of 7 rows and 1 column. The following statements get the content pane and add these components to the content pane:

```
Container pane  = getContentPane();
setSize(300, 300);

pane.setLayout(new GridLayout(7,1));

pane.add(headingMainL);
pane.add(selectionL);
pane.add(candyB);
pane.add(chipsB);
pane.add(gumB);
pane.add(cookiesB);
pane.add(exitB);
```

Event Handling

When the user clicks on a product button, it generates an action event. There are five buttons, each generating an action event. To handle these action events, we use the same process as that used in Chapter 6. That is:

1. Create a class implementing the interface ActionListener.

2. Provide the definition of the method `actionPerformed`.
3. Create and instantiate an object, action listener, of the class type created in Step 1.
4. Register the listener of Step 3 to each button.

In Chapter 6, we created a separate class for each of the buttons and then created separate listener for each button. In this new program, rather than create a separate class for each button, we create only one class. Recall that the heading of the method `actionPerformed` is:

```
public void actionPerformed(ActionEvent e)
```

In Chapter 6, while providing the definition of this method, we ignored the formal parameter `e`. The formal parameter `e` is a reference variable of the `ActionEvent` type. The `class ActionEvent` contains `getActionCommand` (a method without parameters), which can be used to identify which button generated the event. For example, the expression

```
e.getActionCommand()
```

returns the string containing the label of the component generating the event. We can now use the appropriate `String` method to determine the button generating the event.

If the user clicks on one of the product buttons, then the candy machine attempts to sell the product. Therefore, the action of clicking on a product button is to sell. For this we write the method `sellProduct` (discussed later in this programming example). If the user clicks on the `Exit` button, the program should terminate. Let's call the class to handle the events `ButtonHandler`. Its definition is:

```
private class ButtonHandler implements ActionListener
{
    public void actionPerformed (ActionEvent e)
    {
        if(e.getActionCommand().equals("Exit"))
            System.exit(0);
        else if(e.getActionCommand().equals("Candy"))
                sellProduct(candy, "Candy");
        else if(e.getActionCommand().equals("Chips"))
                sellProduct(chips, "Chips");
        else if(e.getActionCommand().equals("Gum"))
                sellProduct(gum, "Gum");
        else if(e.getActionCommand().equals("Cookies"))
                sellProduct(cookies, "Cookies");
    }
}
```

You can now declare, instantiate, and register the listener as follows:

```
private ButtonHandler pbHandler;   //declare the listener
```

```
pbHandler = new ButtonHandler();   //instantiate the object

    //register the listener with each button
candyB.addActionListener(pbHandler);
chipsB.addActionListener(pbHandler);
gumB.addActionListener(pbHandler);
cookiesB.addActionListener(pbHandler);
exitB.addActionListener(pbHandler);
```

Next we describe the method `sellProduct`.

Method `sellProduct`   The definition of this method is similar to the one we designed for the non GUI program. (We give its definition for the sake of completeness.) This method attempts to sell a particular product selected by the customer. The candy machine contains four dispensers which correspond to the four products. These dispensers will be declared as instance variables. Moreover, we will write separate methods for each dispenser to sell the product. Therefore, the dispenser of the product to be sold and the name of the product are passed as parameters to this method. Since cash register will be declared as an instance variable, this method can directly access the cash register.

This definition of the method `sellProduct` is:

```
private void sellProduct(Dispenser product, String productName)
{
   int coinsInserted = 0;
   int price, coinsRequired;
   String str;

   if(product.getCount() > 0)
   {
      price = product.getProductCost();
      coinsRequired = price - coinsInserted;

      while(coinsRequired > 0)
      {
         str = JOptionPane.showInputDialog("To buy "
                            + productName
                            + " please insert "
                            + coinsRequired + " cents");
         coinsInserted = coinsInserted
                      + Integer.parseInt(str);
         coinsRequired = price - coinsInserted;
      }

      cashRegister.acceptAmount(coinsInserted);
      product.makeSale();

      JOptionPane.showMessageDialog(null,"Please pick up your "
```

```
                            + productName + " and enjoy",
                            "Thank you, Come again!",
                            JOptionPane.PLAIN_MESSAGE);
    }
    else                //dispenser is empty
        JOptionPane.showMessageDialog(null,"Sorry "
                            + productName
                            + " is sold out\n" +
                            "Make another selection",
                            "Thank you, Come again!",
                            JOptionPane.PLAIN_MESSAGE);
}//end sellProduct
```

We have described the method `sellProduct` and other necessary components, so next we write the Java application program for the candy machine.

The algorithm is as follows:

1. Create the cash register—that is, declare a reference variable of the type `CashRegister` and instantiate the object.

2. Create four dispensers—that is, declare four reference variables of the type `Dispenser` and instantiate appropriate `Dispenser` objects. For example, the statement

   ```
   Dispenser candy = new Dispenser(100, 50);
   ```

   declares `candy` to be a reference variable of the `Dispenser` type and instantiates the object `candy` to hold the candies. The number of items in the object `candy` is 100, and the cost of a candy is 50 cents.

3. Create other objects, such as labels and buttons, as previously described.

4. Display the GUI showing the candy machine as described at the beginning of this programming example.

5. Get and process the selection.

The complete list of the class containing the application program is:

```
//Candy Machine Program

import javax.swing.*;
import java.awt.*;
import java.awt.event.*;
import jpfpatpd.ch08.candyMachine.*;

public class CandyMachine extends JFrame
{
    private static final int WIDTH = 300;
    private static final int HEIGHT = 300;
```

```java
      //Instance variables
private CashRegister cashRegister = new CashRegister();
private Dispenser candy = new Dispenser(100,50);
private Dispenser chips = new Dispenser(100,65);
private Dispenser gum = new Dispenser(75,45);
private Dispenser cookies = new Dispenser(100,85);

private JLabel headingMainL;
private JLabel selectionL;

private JButton exitB, candyB, chipsB, gumB, cookiesB;
private ButtonHandler pbHandler;

public CandyMachine()
{
   setTitle("Candy Machine");      //set window title
   setSize(WIDTH, HEIGHT);         //set window size

   Container pane  = getContentPane();  //get the container
   pane.setLayout(new GridLayout(7,1)); //set pane layout

   pbHandler = new ButtonHandler();  //instantiate listener
                                     //object

   headingMainL = new JLabel("WELCOME TO ONE STOP CANDY SHOP",
                    SwingConstants.CENTER); //instantiate
                                            //the first label
   selectionL = new JLabel("To Make a Selection, "
                     + "Click on the Product Button",
                    SwingConstants.CENTER);  //instantiate
                                             //the second label

   pane.add(headingMainL);   //add the first label to the pane
   pane.add(selectionL);     //add the second label to the pane

   candyB = new JButton("Candy");  //instantiate the candy
                                   //button
   candyB.addActionListener(pbHandler);   //register the
                                          //listener to the
                                          //candy button
   chipsB = new JButton("Chips");  //instantiate the chips
                                   //button
   chipsB.addActionListener(pbHandler);   //register the
                                          //listener to the
                                          //chips button
```

```
      gumB = new JButton("Gum");         //instantiate the gum button
      gumB.addActionListener(pbHandler); //register the listener
                                         //to the gum button


      cookiesB = new JButton("Cookies");    //instantiate the
                                            //cookies button
      cookiesB.addActionListener(pbHandler); //register the
                                //listener to the cookies button


      exitB = new JButton("Exit");      //instantiate the exit button
      exitB.addActionListener(pbHandler); //register the listener
                                          //to the exit button


      pane.add(candyB);       //add the candy button to the pane
      pane.add(chipsB);       //add the chips button to the pane
      pane.add(gumB);         //add the gum button to the pane
      pane.add(cookiesB);     //add the cookies button to the pane
      pane.add(exitB);        //add the exit button to the pane


      setVisible(true);       //show window and its contents
      setDefaultCloseOperation(EXIT_ON_CLOSE);

   } //end constructor

         //class to handle button events
   private class ButtonHandler implements ActionListener
   {
      public void actionPerformed (ActionEvent e)
      {
           if(e.getActionCommand().equals("Exit"))
              System.exit(0);
           else if(e.getActionCommand().equals("Candy"))
                  sellProduct(candy, "Candy");
           else if(e.getActionCommand().equals("Chips"))
                  sellProduct(chips, "Chips");
           else if(e.getActionCommand().equals("Gum"))
                  sellProduct(gum, "Gum");
           else if(e.getActionCommand().equals("Cookies"))
                  sellProduct(cookies, "Cookies");

      }
   }
```

```
      //Method to sell a product
   private void sellProduct(Dispenser product, String productName)
   {
     int coinsInserted = 0;
     int price, coinsRequired;
     String str;

     if(product.getCount() > 0)
     {
        price = product.getProductCost();
        coinsRequired = price - coinsInserted;

        while(coinsRequired > 0)
        {
           str = JOptionPane.showInputDialog("To buy "
                             + productName
                             + " please insert "
                             + coinsRequired + " cents");
           coinsInserted = coinsInserted
                             + Integer.parseInt(str);
           coinsRequired = price - coinsInserted;
        }

        cashRegister.acceptAmount(coinsInserted);
        product.makeSale();

        JOptionPane.showMessageDialog(null,"Please pick up your "
                             + productName + " and enjoy",
                              "Thank you, Come again!",
                              JOptionPane.PLAIN_MESSAGE);
     }
     else            //dispenser is empty
        JOptionPane.showMessageDialog(null,"Sorry "
                             + productName
                             + " is sold out\n" +
                             "Make another selection",
                             "Thank you, Come again!",
                             JOptionPane.PLAIN_MESSAGE);
   }//end sellProduct


   public static void main(String[] args)
   {
       CandyMachine candyShop = new CandyMachine();
   }
}
```

Sample Run: Figure 8-22 shows the sample run.

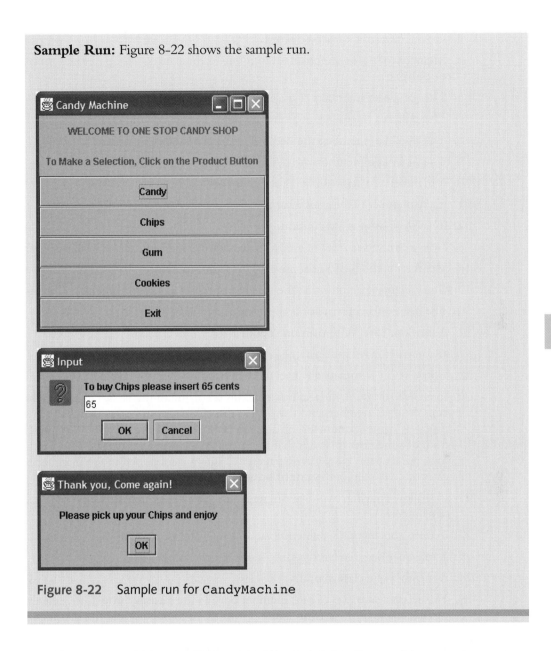

Figure 8-22   Sample run for `CandyMachine`

QUICK REVIEW

1. A `class` is a collection of a fixed number of components.
2. Components of a `class` are called the members of the class.
3. Members of a `class` are accessed by name.

4. In Java, **class** is a reserved word.

5. Members of a class are classified into one of three categories: **private**, **protected**, or **public**.

6. The **private** members of a class are not accessible outside the class.

7. The **public** members of a class are accessible outside the class.

8. The **public** members are declared using the modifier **public**.

9. The **private** members are declared using the modifier **private**.

10. A member of a class can be a method or a variable.

11. If any member of a class is a variable, it is declared like any other variable.

12. In Java, a **class** is a definition.

13. Non-**static** variables of a **class** are called instance variables of that **class**.

14. Member methods of a class are called instance methods.

15. Constructors guarantee that the data members are initialized when an object is declared.

16. The name of a constructor is the same as the name of the class.

17. A class can have more than one constructor.

18. A constructor without parameters is called the default constructor.

19. Constructors automatically execute when a class object is created.

20. In a UML diagram, the top box contains the name of the class. The middle box contains the data members and their data types. The bottom box contains the member methods' names, parameter list, and the return type of the method. A + (plus) sign in front of a member indicates that the member is a **public** member; a − (minus) sign indicates that this is a **private** member. The **#** symbol before the member name indicates that the member is a **protected** member.

21. In shallow copying, two or more reference variables of the same type refer to the same object.

22. In deep copying, each reference variable refers to its own object.

23. A reference variable has the same scope as other variables.

24. A member of a class is local to the class.

25. You access a **public class** member outside the **class** through the reference variable name or the **class** name (for **static** members) and the member access operator (**.**).

26. The copy constructor executes when an object is instantiated and initialized using an existing object.

27. The method **toString** is a **public** value-returning method. It does not take any parameters and returns the address of a **String** object.

28. The methods **print** and **println** output the string created by the method **toString**.

29. The default definition of the method **toString** creates a **String** that is the name of the object's **class** name followed by the hash code of the object.

30. The modifier **static** in the heading of the method of a class specifies that the method can be invoked by using the name of the class.

31. If a data member of a class is declared using the modifier **static**, that data member can be invoked by using the name of the class.

32. **static** data members of a **class** *exist* even when no object of the **class** type is instantiated. Moreover, **static** variables are initialized to their default values.

33. Finalizers automatically execute when a class object goes out of scope.

34. A **class** can have only one finalizer, and the finalizer has no parameters.

35. The name of the finalizer is **finalize**.

36. You can create your own packages using the **package** statement.

37. Java implicitly uses the reference **this** to refer to both the instance variables and the methods of a class.

38. Classes that are defined within another class are called inner classes.

39. A data type that specifies the logical properties without the implementation details is called an abstract data type (ADT).

8

EXERCISES

1. Mark the following statements as true or false:

   a. The instance variables of a class must be of the same type.

   b. The methods of a class must be **public**.

   c. A class can have more than one constructor.

   d. A class can have more than one finalizer.

   e. Constructors and finalizers can both have parameters.

2. Find the syntax errors in the definitions of the following classes:

   a.

```
public class AA
{
    private int x;
    private int y;

    public void print()
    {
        System.out.println(x + " " + y);
    }
```

```java
        public int sum()
        {
            return x + y ;
        }

        public AA()
        {
            x = 0 ;
            y = 0 ;
        }

        public int AA(int a, int b)
        {
            x = a ;
            y = b ;
        }
    }
```

b.

```java
    public class BB
    {
        private int one ;
        private int two;

        public boolean equal()
        {
            return (one == two);
        }

        public print()
        {
            System.out.println(one + " " + two);
        }

        public BB(int a, int b)
        {
            one = a;
            two = b;
        }
    }
```

3. Consider the definition of the following class:

```java
    class CC
    {
        private int u;
        private int v;
        private double w;

        public CC()                                    //Line 1
        {
        }
```

```
    public CC(int a)                         //Line 2
    {
    }
    public CC(int a, int b)                  //Line 3
    {
    }
    public CC(int a, int b, double d)        //Line 4
    {
    }
}
```

a. Give the line number containing the constructor that is executed in each of the following declarations:

(i) CC one = new CC();

(ii) CC two = new CC(5, 6);

(iii) CC three = new CC(2, 8, 3.5);

b. Write the definition of the constructor at Line 1 so that the instance variables are initialized to 0.

c. Write the definition of the constructor at Line 2 so that the instance variable u is initialized according to the value of the parameter, and the instance variables v and w are initialized to 0.

d. Write the definition of the constructor at Line 3 so that the instance variables u and v are initialized according to the values of the parameters a and b, respectively, and the instance variable w is initialized to 0.0.

e. Write the definition of the constructors at Line 4 so that the instance variables u, v, and w are initialized according to the values of the parameters a, b, and d, respectively.

4. Write a Java statement that creates the object mysteryClock of the Clock type, and initialize the instance variables hr, min, and sec of mysteryClock to 7, 18, and 39, respectively.

5. Given the statements

```
Clock firstClock = new Clock(2,6,35);
Clock secondClock = new Clock(6,23,17);

firstClock = secondClock;
```

what is the output of the following statements?

```
firstClock.print();
System.out.println();
secondClock.print();
System.out.println();
```

6. Consider the following declarations:

```
public class XClass
{
    private int u;
    private double w;

    public XClass()
    {
    }

    public XClass(int a, double b)
    {
    }

    public void func()
    {

    }

    public void print()
    {
    }
}

XClass x = new XClass(10, 20.75);
```

   a. How many members does **class XClass** have?

   b. How many **private** members does **class XClass** have?

   c. How many constructors does **class XClass** have?

   d. Write the definition of the member **func** so that u is set to **10** and w is set to **15.3**.

   e. Write the definition of the member **print** that prints the contents of u and w.

   f. Write the definition of the default constructor of the **class XClass** so that the instance variables are initialized to 0.

   g. Write the definition of the constructor with parameters of the **class XClass** so that the instance variable u is initialized to the value of **a** and the instance variable **v** is initialized to the value of **b**.

   h. Write a Java statement that prints the values of the instance variables of **x**.

   i. Write a Java statement that creates the **XClass** object **t** and initializes the instance variables of **t** to **20** and **35.0**, respectively.

7. Explain shallow copying.

8. Explain deep copying.

9. Suppose that two reference variables, say **aa** and **bb**, of the same type point to two different objects. What happens when you use the assignment operator to copy the value of **aa** into **bb**?

10. Assume that the method **toString** is defined for the **class Clock** as given in this chapter. What is the output of the following statements?

```
Clock firstClock;
Clock secondClock = new Clock(6,23,17);

firstClock = secondClock.getCopy();

System.out.println(firstClock);
```

11. What is the purpose of the copy constructor?

12. How does Java use the reference **this**?

13. Suppose that you have created the **class Mystery**. Write the Java statement that would put this class into the **package strangeClasses** in the subdirectory **ch08** of the directory **jpfpatpd**.

14. Can you use the relational operator **==** to determine if two different objects of the same **class** type contain the same data?

15. Consider the definition of the following **class**:

```
class TestClass
{

    private int x;
    private int y;

        //default constructor
        //initialize the instance variables to 0
    public TestClass()
    {
    }

        //constructors with parameters
        //initialize the instance variables to the values
        //specified by the parameters
        //Postcondition: x = a; y = b;
    TestClass(int a, int b)
    {
    }

        //return the sum of the instance variables
    public int sum()
    {
    }
```

8

```
        //print the values of the instance variables
    public void print()
    {
    }
}
```

a. Write the definitions of the methods as described in the definition of the `class` `TestClass`.

b. Write a test program to test the various operations of the `class` `TestClass`.

PROGRAMMING EXERCISES

1. Write a program that converts a number entered in Roman numerals to decimal. Your program should consist of a `class`, say `Roman`. An object of the type `Roman` should do the following:

   a. Store the number as a Roman numeral.

   b. Convert and store the number into decimal.

   c. Print the number as a Roman numeral or decimal number as requested by the user.

   The decimal values of the Roman numerals are:

M	1000
D	500
C	100
L	50
X	10
V	5
I	1

   d. Test your program using the following Roman numerals: `MCXIV`, `CCCLIX`, and `MDCLXVI`.

2. Design and implement the `class Day` that implements the day of the week in a program. The `class Day` should store the day, such as `Sun` for Sunday. The program should be able to perform the following operations on an object of the type `Day`:

   a. Set the day.

   b. Print the day.

   c. Return the day.

   d. Return the next day.

   e. Return the previous day.

   f. Calculate and return the day by adding certain days to the current day. For example, if the current day is Monday and we add 4 days, the day to be returned is Friday. Similarly, if today is Tuesday and we add 13 days, the day to be returned is Monday.

   g. Add the appropriate constructors.

h. Write the definitions of the methods to implement the operations for the **class Day** as defined in a–g.

i. Write a program to test various operations on the **class Day**.

3. a. Example 8-4 defined the **class Person** to store the name of a person. The member methods that we included merely print the name and set the name of a person. Redefine the **class Person** so that, in addition to what the existing **class** does, you can:

   i.   Set the last name only.

   ii. Set the first name only.

   iii. Store and set the middle name.

   iv. Check whether a given last name is the same as the last name of this person.

   v.   Check whether a given first name is the same as the first name of this person.

   b. Add the method **equals** that returns true if two objects contains the same first and last name.

   c. Add the method **makeCopy** that copies the instance variables of a **Person** object into another **Person** object.

   d. Add the method **getCopy** that creates and returns the address of the object, which is a copy of another **Person** object.

   e. Add the copy constructor.

   f. Write the definition of the methods of the **class Person** to implement the operations for this **class**.

   g. Write a program that tests various operations of the **class Person**.

4. a. Some of the characteristics of a book are the title, author(s), publisher, ISBN, price, and year of publication. Design the **class Book** that defines the book as an ADT.

   Each object of the **class Book** can hold the following information about a book: title, up to four authors, publisher, ISBN, price, and number of copies in stock. To keep track of the number of authors, add another instance variable.

   Include the member methods to perform the various operations on the objects of **Book**. For example, the usual operations that can be performed on the title are to show the title, set the title, and check whether a title is the actual title of the book. Similarly, the typical operations that can be performed on the number of copies in stock are to show the number of copies in stock, set the number of copies in stock, update the number of copies in stock, and return the number of copies in stock. Add similar operations for the publisher, ISBN, book price, and authors. Add the appropriate constructors and a finalizer (if one is needed).

   b. Write the definition of the member methods of the **class Book**.

   c. Write a program that uses the **class Book** and tests various operations on the objects of **class Book**. Declare an array of 100 components of type **Book**. Some of the operations that you should perform are to search for a book by its title, search by ISBN, and update the number of copies of a book.

8

5. In this exercise, you will design the **class Member**.

   a. Each object of **Member** can hold the name of a person, member ID, number of books bought, and amount spent.

   b. Include the member methods to perform the various operations on the objects of **Member**—for example, modify, set, and show a person's name. Similarly, update, modify, and show the number of books bought and the amount spent.

   c. Add the appropriate constructors and a finalizer (if one is needed).

   d. Write the definitions of the methods of the **class Member**.

6. Using the classes designed in programming Exercises 4 and 5, write a program to simulate a bookstore. The bookstore has two types of customers: those who are members of the bookstore and those who buy books from the bookstore only occasionally. Each member has to pay a $10 yearly membership fee and receives a 5% discount on each book bought.

   For each member, the bookstore keeps track of the number of books bought and the total amount spent. For every eleventh book that a member buys, the bookstore takes the average of the total amount of the last 10 books bought, applies this amount as a discount, and then resets the total amount spent to 0.

   Write a program that can process up to 1000 book titles and 500 members. Your program should contain a menu that gives the user different choices to effectively run the program; in other words, your program should be menu-driven.

7. Rational fractions are of the form a / b, where a and b are integers and $b \neq 0$. In this exercise, by "fractions" we mean rational fractions. Suppose a / b and c / d are fractions. Arithmetic operations on fractions are defined by the following rules:

   $a / b + c / d = (ad + bc) / bd$

   $a / b - c / d = (ad - bc) / bd$

   $a / b \times c / d = ac / bd$

   $(a / b) / (c / d) = ad / bc$, where $c / d \neq 0$

   Fractions are compared as follows: a / b *op* c / d if ad *op* bc, where *op* is any of the relational operations. For example, $a / b < c / d$ if $ad < bc$.

   Design the **class Fraction** that can be used to manipulate fractions in a program. Among others, the **class Fraction** must include methods to add, subtract, multiply, and divide fractions. When you add, subtract, multiply, or divide fractions, your answer need not be in the lowest terms. Also override the method **toString** so that the fraction can be output using the output statement.

   Write a Java program that, using the **class Fraction**, performs operations on fractions.

ARRAYS

In this chapter, you will:

♦ Learn about arrays

♦ Explore how to declare and manipulate data into arrays

♦ Understand the meaning of "array index out of bounds"

♦ Become familiar with the restrictions on array processing

♦ Discover how to pass an array as a parameter to a method

♦ Discover how to manipulate data in a two-dimensional array

♦ Learn about multidimensional arrays

In previous chapters, you worked with primitive data types and learned how to construct your own classes. Recall that a variable of a primitive data type can store only one value at a time; on the other hand, a `class` object can store more than one value at a time. This chapter introduces a special data structure called arrays, which allow the user to group data items of the same type and process them in a convenient way.

WHY DO WE NEED ARRAYS?

Before we formally define an array, let's consider the following problem. We want to write a Java program that reads five numbers, finds their sum, and prints the numbers in reverse order.

In Chapter 5, you learned how to read numbers, print them, and find their sum. What's different here is that we want to print the numbers in reverse order. We cannot print the first four numbers until we have printed the fifth, and so on. This means that we need to store all the numbers before we can print them in reverse order. From what we have learned so far, the following program accomplishes this task:

```java
//Program to read five numbers, find their sum, and print the
//numbers in reverse order.

import java.io.*;

public class ReversePrintI
{
    static BufferedReader keyboard =
      new BufferedReader(new InputStreamReader(System.in));

    public static void main(String[] args) throws IOException
    {
        int  item0, item1, item2, item3, item4;
        int sum;

        System.out.println("Enter five integers one "
                     +  "number per line");
        item0 = Integer.parseInt(keyboard.readLine());
        item1 = Integer.parseInt(keyboard.readLine());
        item2 = Integer.parseInt(keyboard.readLine());
        item3 = Integer.parseInt(keyboard.readLine());
        item4 = Integer.parseInt(keyboard.readLine());

        sum = item0 + item1 + item2 + item3 + item4;

        System.out.println("The sum of the numbers = " + sum);
        System.out.print("The numbers in reverse order are: ");
        System.out.println(item4 + " " + item3 + " " + item2 + " "
                     + item1 + " " + item0);
    }
}
```

This program works fine. However, to read 100 (or more) numbers and print them in reverse order, you would have to declare 100 or more variables and write many input and output statements. Thus, for large amounts of data, this type of program is not desirable.

Note the following in the preceding program:

1. Five variables must be declared because the numbers are to be printed in reverse order.

2. All variables are of the type `int`—that is, of the same data type.

3. The way in which these variables are declared indicates that the variables to store these numbers have the same name except for the last character, which is a number.

Statement 1 tells you that you have to declare five variables. Statement 3 tells you that it would be convenient if you could somehow put the last character, which is a number, into a counter variable and use one `for` loop to count from 0 to 4 for reading, and use another `for` loop to count from 4 to 0 for printing. Finally, because all variables are of the same type, you should be able to specify how many variables must be declared—and their data type—with a simpler statement than the one used earlier.

The data structure that lets you do all of these things in Java is called an array.

ARRAYS

An **array** is a collection of a fixed number of components, wherein all the components are of the same data type. A **one-dimensional array** is an array in which the components are arranged in a list form. The remainder of this section discusses one-dimensional arrays. Arrays of two or more dimensions are discussed later in this chapter.

The general form of declaring a one-dimensional array is

```
dataType[] arrayName;     //Line 1
```

where `dataType` is the component type.

In Java, an array is an object, just like the objects discussed in Chapter 8. Because an array is an object, `arrayName` is a reference variable. Therefore, the preceding statement only declares a reference variable. To store data we must instantiate the array object.

The general syntax to instantiate an array object is

```
arrayName = new dataType[intExp];     //Line 2
```

where `intExp` is any expression that evaluates to a positive integer. Also, the value of `intExp` specifies the number of components in the array.

You can combine the statements in Lines 1 and 2 in one statement as follows:

```
dataType[] arrayName = new dataType[intExp];     //Line 3
```

We will usually use statements similar to the statement in Line 3 to create arrays to manipulate data.

 When an array is instantiated, Java automatically initializes its components to their default values. For example, numeric arrays are initialized to 0.

Example 9-1

The statement

```
int[] num = new int[5];
```

declares and creates the array `num` of 5 components. Each component is of the type `int`. The components are num[0], num[1], num[2], num[3], and num[4]. Figure 9-1 illustrates the array `num`.

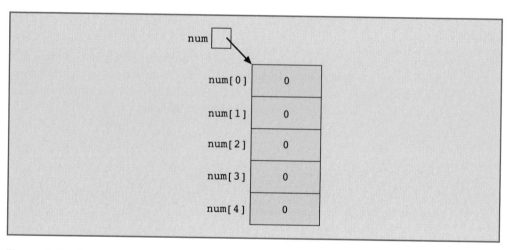

Figure 9-1 Array num

Alternate Ways to Declare an Array

Java allows you to declare arrays as follows:

```
int list[];              //Line 1
```

Here the operator [ ] appears after the identifier list, not after the data type int.

You should be careful when declaring arrays as in Line 1. Consider the following statements:

```
int  alpha[], beta;   //Line 2
int[] gamma, delta;   //Line 3
```

The statement in Line 2 declares the variables alpha and beta. Similarly, the statement in Line 3 declares the variables gamma and delta. However, the statement in Line 2 declares only alpha to be an array reference variable, while the variable beta is an int variable. On the other hand, the statement in Line 3 declares both gamma and delta to be array reference variables.

Traditionally, Java programmers declare arrays as shown in Line 3. We recommend that you also declare arrays as in Line 3.

Accessing Array Components

The general form (syntax) used for accessing an array component is

9

```
arrayName[indexExp]
```

where indexExp, called **index**, is an expression whose value is a non-negative integer less than the size of the array. The index value specifies the position of the component in the array. In Java, the array index starts at 0.

In Java, [ ] is an operator, called the **array subscripting operator**.

Consider the following statement:

```
int[] list = new int[10];
```

This statement declares an array list of 10 components. The components are list[0], list[1], ..., list[9]. In other words, we have declared 10 variables of the type int. See Figure 9-2.

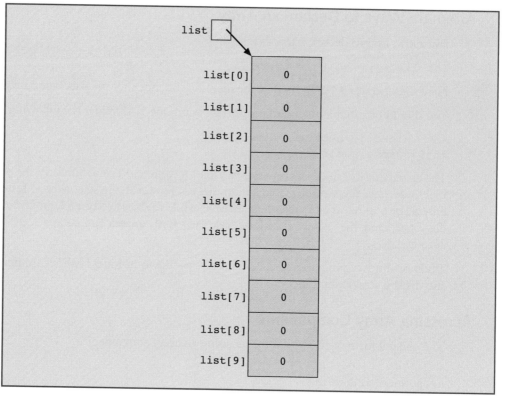

Figure 9-2   Array `list`

The assignment statement

`list[5] = 34;`

stores 34 in `list[5]`, which is the sixth component of the array `list`. See Figure 9-3.

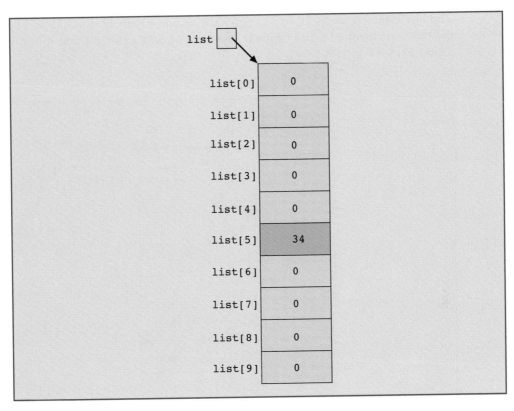

Figure 9-3 Array `list` after execution of the statement `list[5]= 34;`

Suppose `i` is an `int` variable. Then the assignment statement

```
list[3] = 63;
```

is equivalent to the assignment statements

```
i = 3;
list[i] = 63;
```

If `i` is 4, then the assignment statement

```
list[2 * i - 3] = 58;
```

stores 58 in `list[5]`, because `2 * i - 3` evaluates to 5. The index expression is evaluated first, giving the position of the component in the array.

Next consider the following statements:

```
list[3] = 10;
list[6] = 35;
list[5] = list[3] + list[6];
```

The first statement stores 10 in list[3], the second statement stores 35 in list[6], and the third statement adds the contents of list[3] and list[6] and stores the result in list[5]. See Figure 9-4.

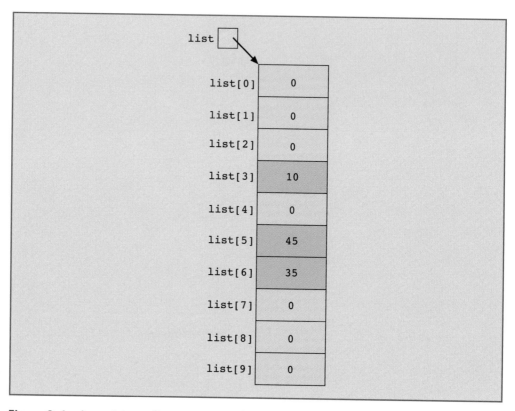

Figure 9-4   Array list after execution of the statements list[3]= 10;, list[6]= 35;, and list[5] = list[3] + list[6];

Example 9-2

You can also declare arrays as follows:

```
final int ARRAY_SIZE = 10;
int[] list = new int[ARRAY_SIZE];
```

That is, you can first declare a named constant of an integral type such as int and then use the value of the named constant to specify the size of the array.

Specifying Array Size During Program Execution

When you include a statement in a program to instantiate an array object, it is not necessary to know the size of the array at compile time. During program execution you can first prompt the user to specify the size of the array and then instantiate the object. The following statements illustrate this concept:

```
int arraySize;                                         //Line 1

System.out.print("Enter the size of the array: ");     //Line 2
arraySize  = Integer.parseInt(keyboard.readLine());    //Line 3
System.out.println();                                  //Line 4

int[] list = new int[arraySize];                       //Line 5
```

The statement in Line 2 asks the user to enter the size of the array when the program executes. The statement in Line 3 inputs the size of the array into `arraySize`. During program execution, the system uses the value of the variable `arraySize` to instantiate the object `list`. For example, if the value of `arraySize` is 15, `list` is an array of size 15. Arrays that are created, that is, instantiated, during program execution are called **dynamic arrays**.

Arrays and the Instance Variable `length`

Recall that an array is an object; therefore, to store data, the array object must be instantiated. Associated with each array that has been instantiated (that is, memory has been allocated to store data), there is a **public** instance variable `length`. The variable `length` contains the size of the array. Since `length` is a **public** member, it can be directly accessed in a program using the array name and the dot operator.

Consider the following declaration:

```
int[] list = {10, 20, 30, 40, 50, 60};
```

This statement creates the array `list` of six components and initializes the components using the values given. Here `list.length` is 6.

Consider the following statements:

```
int[] numList = new int[10];
```

This statement creates the array `numList` of 10 components and initializes each component to 0. Because the number of components of `numList` is 10, the value of `numList.length` is 10. Now consider the following statements:

```
numList[0]  = 5;
numList[1]  = 10;
numList[2]  = 15;
numList[3]  = 20;
```

These statements store 5, 10, 15, and 20, respectively, in the first four components of `numList`. Even though we put the data into the first four components, the value of `numList.length` is 10, the total number of array components.

Processing One-Dimensional Arrays

Some of the basic operations performed on a one-dimensional array are to initialize the array, input data, output data stored in an array, and find the largest and/or smallest element in an array. If the data type of the array component is numeric, a common operation is to find the sum and average of the elements of the array. Each of these operations requires the ability to step through the elements of the array. Stepping through the elements of an array is easily accomplished by a loop. Suppose that we have the following statements:

```
int[] list = new int[100];       //list is an array of size 100
int i;
```

The following **for** loop steps through each element of the array **list** starting at the first element of **list**:

```
for(i = 0; i < 100; i++)                                  //Line 1
    //process list[i], the (i + 1)th element of list      //Line 2
```

If processing **list** requires inputting data into **list**, the statement in Line 2 takes the form of an input statement, such as in the following code. The following statements read 100 numbers from the keyboard and store the numbers in **list**:

```
for(i = 0; i < 100; i++)                                  //Line 1
    list[i] = Integer.parseInt(keyboard.readLine());      //Line 2
```

Similarly, if processing **list** requires outputting data, then the statement in Line 2 takes the form of an output statement. Example 9-3 further illustrates how to process one-dimensional arrays.

Example 9-3

This example shows how loops are used to process arrays. The following declaration is used throughout this example:

```
double[] sale = new double[10];
int index;
double largestSale, sum, average;
```

The first statement creates the array **sale** of 10 components with each component the type **double**. The meaning of the other statements is clear. Also, notice that the value of **sale.length** is 10.

Loops can be used to process arrays in several ways:

1. **Initializing an array to a specific value:** To initialize every component of the array **sale** to a specific value, say **10.00**, you can use the following loop.

   ```
   for(index = 0; index < sale.length; index++)
       sale[index] = 10.00;
   ```

2. **Reading data into an array:** The following loop inputs data in the array
   `sale`. For simplicity, we assume that the data is entered at the keyboard one
   number per line.

   ```
   for(index = 0; index < sale.length; index++)
       sale[index] = Integer.parseInt(keyboard.readLine());
   ```

3. **Printing an array:** The following loop outputs the array `sale`. For simplicity,
   we assume that the output goes to the screen.

   ```
   for(index = 0; index < sale.length; index++)
       System.out.print(sale[index] + " ");
   ```

4. **Finding the sum and average of an array:** Because the array `sale`, as its
   name implies, represents certain sales data, it is natural to find the total sale and
   average sale amounts. The following Java code finds the sum of the elements of the
   array `sale` (total sales) and the average sale amount.

   ```
   sum = 0;
   for(index = 0; index < sale.length; index++)
       sum = sum + sale[index];

   if(sale.length != 0)
       average = sum / sale.length;
   else
       average = 0.0;
   ```

5. **Determining the Largest element in the array:** We now discuss the algorithm to find the largest element in an array—that is, the array component with
   the largest value. However, the user is usually more interested in determining the
   location of the largest element in the array. Of course, if you know the location
   (the index of the largest element in the array), you can easily determine the value
   of the largest element in the array. So let's describe the algorithm to determine the
   index of the largest element in an array—in particular, the index of the largest sale
   amount in the array `sale`.

   We assume that `maxIndex` will contain the index of the largest element in the
   array `sale`. The general algorithm is as follows. Initially, we assume that the first
   element in the list is the largest element, so `maxIndex` is initialized to 0. We then
   compare the element to which `maxIndex` points with every element in the list.
   Whenever we find an element in the array larger than the element to which
   `maxIndex` points, we update `maxIndex` so that it points to the new larger element. The code to implement this algorithm is as follows:

   ```
   maxIndex = 0;
   for(index = 1; index < sale.length; index++)
       if(sale[maxIndex] < sale[index])
           maxIndex = index;

   largestSale = sale[maxIndex];
   ```

9

The way this code works can be demonstrated with an example. Suppose the array `sale` is as given in Figure 9-5, and we want to determine the largest element in the array.

	[0]	[1]	[2]	[3]	[4]	[5]	[6]	[7]	[8]	[9]
sale	12.50	8.35	19.60	25.00	14.00	39.43	35.90	98.23	66.65	35.64

Figure 9-5   Array `sale`

Before the `for` loop begins, `maxIndex` is initialized to 0 and the `for` loop initializes `index` to 1. In Table 9-1, we show the values of `maxIndex`, `index`, and certain array elements during each iteration of the `for` loop:

Table 9-1   Values of `sale` Array Elements During `for` Loop Iterations

index	maxIndex	sale[maxIndex]	sale[index]	sale[maxIndex]< sale[index]
1	0	12.50	8.35	12.50 < 8.35 is false
2	0	12.50	19.60	12.50 < 19.60 is true; maxIndex = 2
3	2	19.60	25.00	19.60 < 25.00 is true; maxIndex = 3
4	3	25.00	14.00	25.00 < 14.00 is false
5	3	25.00	39.43	25.00 < 39.43 is true; maxIndex = 5
6	5	39.43	35.90	39.43 < 35.90 is false
7	5	39.43	98.23	39.43 < 98.23 is true; maxIndex = 7
8	7	98.23	66.65	98.23 < 66.65 is false
9	7	98.23	35.64	98.23 < 35.64 is false

After the `for` loop executes, `maxIndex = 7`, giving the index of the largest element in the array `sale`. Thus, `largestSale = sale[maxIndex] = 98.23`.

The algorithm to find the smallest element in the array is similar to the algorithm for finding the largest element in an array. (See Programming Exercise 2 at the end of this chapter.)

Now that we know how to declare and process arrays, let's rewrite the program that we discussed in the beginning of this chapter. Recall that this program reads five numbers, finds the sum, and prints the numbers in reverse order.

Example 9-4

```java
//Program to read five numbers, find their sum, and
//print the numbers in reverse order.

import java.io.*;

public class ReversePrintII
{
    static BufferedReader keyboard =
            new BufferedReader(new InputStreamReader(System.in));

    public static void main (String[] args) throws IOException
    {
        int[] item = new int[5]; //declare an array item of five
                                 //components
        int sum;
        int counter;

        System.out.println("Enter five integers, one "
                        + "integer per line");

        sum = 0;

        for(counter = 0; counter < 5; counter++)
        {
            item[counter] = Integer.parseInt(keyboard.readLine());
            sum = sum + item[counter];
        }

        System.out.println("The sum of the numbers = " + sum);
        System.out.print("The numbers in the reverse order are: ");

            //print the numbers in reverse order
        for(counter = 4; counter >= 0; counter-)
            System.out.print(item[counter] + " ");

        System.out.println();

    }
}
```

Sample Run: In this sample run, the user input is shaded.

```
Enter five integers, one integer per line.
12
76
34
52
89
The sum of the numbers is: 263
The numbers in the reverse order are: 89  52  34  76  12
```

Array Initialization During Declaration

Like any other primitive data type variable, an array can also be initialized to specific values when it is declared. For example, the following Java statement declares an array, `list`, of five components and initializes those components to specific values:

```
double[]  sales = {12.25, 32.50, 16.90, 23, 45.68};
```

The values, called **initial values**, are placed between braces and separated by commas. Here `sales[0] = 12.25`, `sales[1] = 32.50`, `sales[2] = 16.90`, `sales[3] = 23.00`, and `sales[4]= 45.68`. Notice that the value of `sales.length` is 5.

Note the following about initializing and declaring arrays:

- When declaring and initializing arrays, the size of the array is determined by the number of initial values within the braces.

- If an array is declared and initialized at the same time, we *do not* use the operator `new` to instantiate the array object.

Array Index Out of Bounds Exception

Consider the following declaration:

```
double[] num = double[10];
int  i;
```

The component `num[i]` is valid, that is, `i` is a valid index if `i` = 0, 1, 2, 3, 4, 5, 6, 7, 8, or 9.

The index—say, `index`—of an array is **in bounds** if `index >= 0` and `index <= arraySize - 1`. If either `index < 0` or `index > arraySize - 1`, then we say that the index is **out of bounds**.

In Java, if an array index goes out of bounds during program execution, it throws an `ArrayIndexOutOfBoundsException` exception. If the program does not handle this exception, the program terminates with an appropriate error message.

A loop such as the following can set the index out of bounds:

```
for(i = 0; i <= 10; i++)
    list[i] = 0;
```

Here we assume that `list` is an array of 10 components. When `i` becomes 10, the loop test condition `i <= 10` evaluates to `true`, and the body of the loop executes, and the program tries to access `list[10]`, which does not exist.

The Assignment Operator, the Relational Operators, and Arrays: A Precaution

Consider the following statements:

```
int[] listA = {5, 10, 15, 20, 25, 30, 35};   //Line 1
int[] listB = new int[listA.length];          //Line 2
```

The statement in Line 1 creates the array `listA` of size 7 and also initializes the array. Note that the value of `listA.length` is 7. The statement in Line 2 uses the value of `listA.length` to create the array `listB` of size 7. See Figure 9-6.

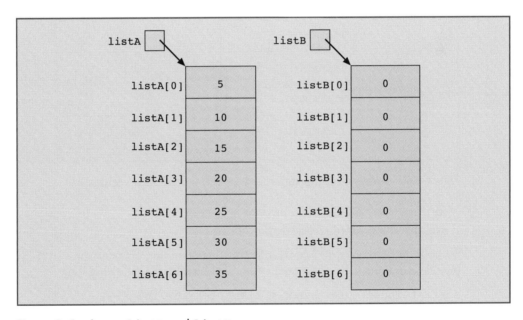

Figure 9-6   Arrays `listA` and `listB`

You can use the assignment operator to assign `listA` to `listB` and you can use relational operators to compare `listA` with `listB`. However, the results obtained might not be what you expect.

For example, consider the following statement:

```
listB = listA;
```

Here you might expect that elements of `listA` are copied into the corresponding elements of `listB`. However, this is not the case. Because `listA` is a reference variable, its value is a reference, that is, a memory address. Therefore, the preceding statement copies the value of `listA` into `listB`, and so after the execution of this statement both `listA` and `listB` refer to the same array. See Figure 9-7.

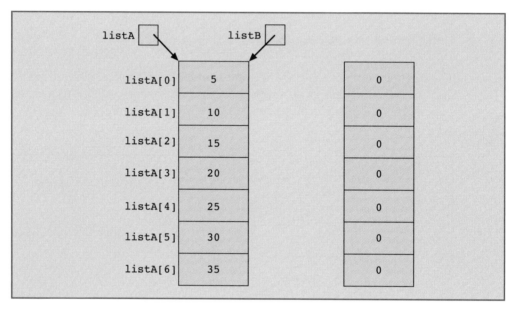

Figure 9-7 Arrays after the statement `listB = listA;` executes

Recall that this is called *shallow copying* of data.

To copy the elements of `listA` into the corresponding elements of `listB`, you need to provide component-by-component copy as shown by the following loop:

```
for(int index = 0; index < listA.length; index++)
    listB[index] = listA[index];
```

After the execution of this statement, `listA` and `listB` still refer to their own arrays and the elements of `listA` are copied into the corresponding elements of `listB`. See Figure 9-8.

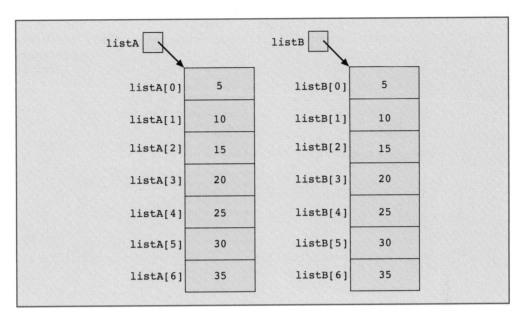

Figure 9-8 Arrays after the `for` loop executes

Recall that this is called *deep copying* of data.

In addition to the assignment operator, you can use the relational operators `==` and `!=` to compare arrays. However, you must be aware of what you are comparing. For example, in the statement

```
if(listA == listB)
...
```

the expression `listA == listB` determines if the values of `listA` and `listB` are the same and thus determines whether `listA` and `listB` refer to the same array. That is, this statement does *not* determine whether `listA` and `listB` contain the same elements.

To determine whether `listA` and `listB` contain the same elements, you need to compare them component by component. You can in fact write a method that returns `true` if two `int` arrays contain the same elements. For example, consider the following method:

```
boolean isEqualArray(int[] firstArray, int[] secondArray)
{
    boolean flag = true;

    if(firstArray.length != secondArray.length)
        return false;
```

```
        for(int index = 0; index < firstArray.length; index++)
            if(firstArray[index] != secondArray[index]) //corresponding
                                                         //elements are
                                                         //different
        {
            flag = false;      //set flag to false
            break;             //terminate the loop
        }

    return flag;
}
```

Now consider the following statement:

```
if(isEqualArray(listA, listB))
...
```

The expression `isEqualArray(listA, listB)` evaluates to `true` if the arrays `listA` and `listB` contain the same elements; `false` otherwise.

Arrays as Parameters to Methods

Just like other objects, arrays can be passed as parameters to methods. The following method takes as an argument any `int` array and outputs data stored in each component:

```
public static void printArray(int[] list)
{
    int index;
    for(index = 0; index < list.length; index++)
        System.out.print(list[index] + " ");
}
```

Methods such as the preceding one process data of an entire array. Sometimes the number of elements in the array might be less than the length of the array. For example, the number of elements in an array storing student data might increase or decrease as students drop or add courses. In situations like this, we want to process only the components of the array that hold actual data. To write methods to process such arrays, in addition to declaring an array as a formal parameter, we declare another formal parameter specifying the number of elements in the array, as in the following method:

```
public static void printArray(int[] list, int noOfElements)
{
    int index;
    for(index = 0; index < noOfElements; index++)
        System.out.print(list[index] + " ");
}
```

The first parameter of the method `printArray` is an `int` array of any size. When the method `printArray` is called, the number of elements in the actual array is passed as the second parameter of the method `printArray`.

Example 9-5

This example shows how to write methods for array processing and declare an array as a formal parameter. (Here we write general-purpose methods and so we also pass the number of elements as a parameter to the methods.) In the preceding code, we assume that the variable `keyboard` is as declared in Example 9-6.

```
//Method to input data and store in an array
public static void fillArray(int[] list, int noOfElements)
                                              throws IOException
{
    int index;
    StringTokenizer tokenizer;

    tokenizer = new StringTokenizer(keyboard.readLine());

    for(index = 0; index < noOfElements; index++)
    {
        list[index] = Integer.parseInt(tokenizer.nextToken());
        if(!tokenizer.hasMoreTokens())
            tokenizer = new StringTokenizer(keyboard.readLine());
    }
}

//Method to print the array
public static void printArray(int[] list, int noOfElements)
{
    int index;

    for(index = 0; index < noOfElements; index++)
        System.out.print(list[index] + " ");
}

//Method to find and return the sum of an array
public static int sumArray(int[] list, int noOfElements)
{
    int index;
    int sum = 0;

    for(index = 0; index < noOfElements; index++)
        sum = sum + list[index];

    return sum;
}
```

```
        //Method to find and return the index of the
        //largest element of an array
public static int indexLargestElement(int[] list, int noOfElements)
{
     int index;
     int maxIndex = 0; //Assume first element is the largest

     for(index = 1; index < noOfElements; index++)
          if(list[maxIndex] < list[index])
               maxIndex = index;

     return maxIndex;
}

        //Method to copy one array into another array
public static void copyArray(int[] list1, int[] list2,
                              int noOfElements)
{
     int index;

     for(index = 0; index < noOfElements; index++)
          list2[index] = list1[index];
}
```

Note that for the method **copyArray** to work correctly, the array **list2** must be at least as large as the number of elements in the array **list1**.

Base Address of an Array

The **base address** of an array is the address (memory location) of the first array component. For example, if **list** is a one-dimensional array, then the base address of **list** is the address of the component **list[0]**. The value of the variable **list** is the base address of the array—the address of **list[0]**. It follows that when you pass an array as a parameter, the base address of the actual array is passed to the formal parameter.

Example 9-6

The following program illustrates how arrays are passed as actual parameters in a method call.

```
//Arrays as parameters to methods

import java.io.*;
import java.util.*;
```

```java
public class ArraysAsParameters
{
    static final int ARRAY_SIZE = 10;
    static BufferedReader keyboard =
            new BufferedReader(new InputStreamReader(System.in));

    public static void main(String[] args) throws IOException
    {
        int[] listA = new int[ARRAY_SIZE];                    //Line 1
        int[] listB = new int[ARRAY_SIZE];                    //Line 2

        System.out.print("Line 3: listA elements: ");         //Line 3
        printArray(listA, listA.length);                      //Line 4
        System.out.println();                                 //Line 5

        System.out.print("Line 6: Enter " + listA.length
                        + " integers: ");                     //Line 6
        fillArray(listA, listA.length);                       //Line 7
        System.out.println();                                 //Line 8

        System.out.println("Line 9: After filling "
                        + "listA, the elements are:"
                        + "\n");                               //Line 9
        printArray(listA, listA.length);                      //Line 10
        System.out.println("\n");                             //Line 11

        System.out.println("Line 12: Sum of the "
                        + "elements of listA is: "
                        + sumArray(listA, listA.length)
                        + "\n");                               //Line 12

        System.out.println("Line 13: Location of "
                    + "the largest element in "
                    + "listA is: "
                    + (indexLargestElement(listA, listA.length) + 1)
                    + "\n");                                   //Line 13
        System.out.println("Line 14: Largest element in "
                    + "listA is: "
                    + listA[indexLargestElement(listA, listA.length)]
                    + "\n");                                   //Line 14

        copyArray(listA, listB, listA.length);                //Line 15
        System.out.print("Line 16: After copying the "
                    + "elements of listA into listB\n"
                    + "          listB elements are: ");       //Line 16
        printArray(listB, listB.length);                      //Line 17
        System.out.println();                                 //Line 18
    }
```

```
//Place the definition of the methods fillArray and so on
//here. Example 9-5 gives the definitions of these methods.

}
```

Sample Run: In this sample run, the user input is shaded.

```
Line 3: listA elements: 0 0 0 0 0 0 0 0 0 0
Line 6: Enter 10 integers: 33 77 25 63 56 48 98 39 5 12

Line 9: After filling listA, the elements are:
33 77 25 63 56 48 98 39 5 12

Line 12: Sum of the elements of listA is: 456

Line 13: Location of the largest element in listA is: 7
Line 14: Largest element in listA is: 98

Line 16: After copying the elements of listA into listB
         listB elements are: 33 77 25 63 56 48 98 39 5 12
```

The output of this program is straightforward. The statement in Line 1 creates the array listA of 10 components and initializes each component of listA to 0. The statement in Line 2 creates the array listB of 10 components. The statement at Line 4 calls the method printArray and outputs the values stored in listA. The statement in Line 7 calls the method fillArray to input data into array listA. The statement in Line 12 calls the method sumArray and outputs the sum of all elements of listA. Similarly, the statement in Line 14 outputs the value of the largest element in listA.

 When you execute the preceding program, enter all numbers in the same line and, after entering the numbers, press the Enter key twice.

PARALLEL ARRAYS

Two (or more) arrays are called **parallel** if their corresponding components hold related information.

Suppose you need to keep track of students' course grades, together with their ID numbers, so that grades can be posted at the end of the semester. Further suppose that there are 50 students in a class and their IDs are 5 digits long. Because there are 50 students, you need 50 variables to store the students' IDs and 50 variables to store their grades. You can declare two arrays: studentId of the type int and courseGrade of the type char. Each array has 50 components. Furthermore, studentId[0] and courseGrade[0] will store the ID and course grade of the first student, studentId[1] and courseGrade[1] will store the ID and course grade of the second student, and so on.

The statements

```
int[] studentId = new int[50];
char[] courseGrade = new char[50];
```

declare and instantiate these two arrays.

ARRAYS OF OBJECTS

In the previous sections, you learned how to use an array to store and manipulate values of primitive data types such as `int` and `double`. You can also use arrays to manipulate objects.

Suppose that you have 100 employees who are paid on an hourly basis and you need to keep track of their arrival and departure time. In Chapter 8, we designed and implemented the `class Clock` to implement time in a program. You can declare two arrays—`arrivalTimeEmp` and `departureTimeEmp`—of 100 components each, wherein each component is a reference variable of the `Clock` type. Consider the following statement:

```
Clock[] arrivalTimeEmp = new Clock[100];          //Line 1
```

The statement in Line 1 creates the array shown in Figure 9-9.

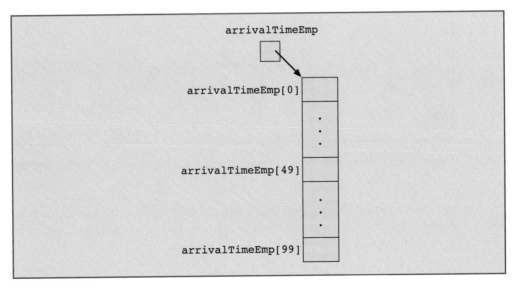

Figure 9-9   Array `arrivalTimeEmp`

The statement in Line 1 creates only the array, not the objects `arrivalTimeEmp[0]`, `arrivalTimeEmp[1]`, ..., `arrivalTimeEmp[99]`. We still need to instantiate `Clock` objects for each array component. Consider the following statements:

```
for(int j = 0; j < arrivalTimeEmp.length; j++)        //Line 2
    arrivalTimeEmp[j] = new Clock();                   //Line 3
```

The statement in Lines 2 and 3 instantiates the objects `arrivalTimeEmp[0]`, `arrivalTimeEmp[1]`, ..., `arrivalTimeEmp[99]`, shown in Figure 9-10.

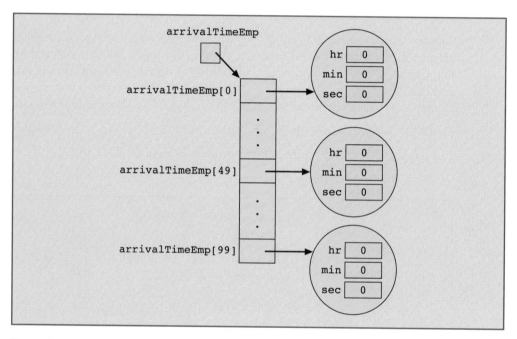

Figure 9-10 Array `arrivalTime` after instantiating objects for each component

You can now use the methods of the **class Clock** to manipulate time for each employee. For example, the following statement sets arrival time, that is, `hr`, `min`, and `sec` of employee **49** to **8, 5, 10**, respectively. See Figure 9-11.

```
arrivalTimeEmp[49].setTime(8,5,10);                   //Line 4
```

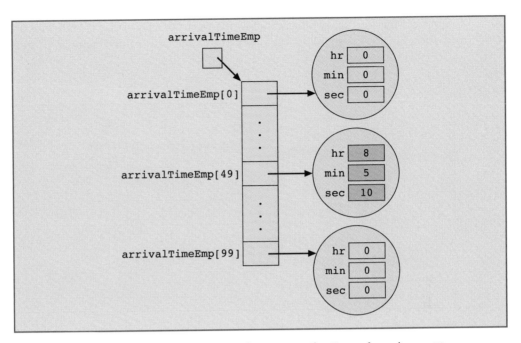

Figure 9-11   Array `arrivalTimeEmp` after setting the time of employee `49`

To output the arrival time of each employee you can use a loop such as the following:

```
for(int j = 0; j < arrivalTimeEmp.length; j++)        //Line 5
    System.out.println("Employee " +  (j + 1)
                    + " arrival time: "
                    + arrivalTimeEmp[j]);              //Line 6
```

The statement in Line 6 assumes that the method `toString` is defined for the `class Clock`, as described in Chapter 8, to return the time in the form `hr:min:sec`.

To keep track of the departure time of each employee you can use the array `departureTimeEmp`.

In a similar manner, you can use arrays to manage a list of names or other objects.

TWO-DIMENSIONAL ARRAYS

In the previous section, you learned how to use one-dimensional arrays to manipulate data. If the data is provided in a list form, you can use one-dimensional arrays. However, sometimes data is provided in a table form.

Suppose you want to keep track of how many cars of a particular color a local dealership has in stock. The dealership sells 6 types of cars in 5 different colors. Figure 9-12 shows a sample data table.

inStock	[Red]	[Brown]	[Black]	[White]	[Gray]
[GM]	10	7	12	10	4
[Ford]	18	11	15	17	10
[Toyota]	12	10	9	5	12
[BMW]	16	6	13	8	3
[Nissan]	10	7	12	6	4
[Volvo]	9	4	7	12	11

Figure 9-12   Table inStock

You can see that the data is in a table format. The table has 30 entries, and every entry is an integer. Because all table entries are of the same type, you can declare a one-dimensional array of 30 components of the type int. The first 5 components of the one-dimensional array can store the data of the first row of the table, the next 5 components of the one-dimensional array can store the data of the second row of the table, and so on. In other words, you can simulate the data given in a table format in a one-dimensional array.

If you do so, the algorithms to manipulate the data in the one-dimensional array will be somewhat complicated because you must carefully note where one row ends and another begins. You must also correctly compute the index of particular elements. Java simplifies manipulating data given in a table form by using **two-dimensional arrays**. This section first discusses how to declare two-dimensional arrays and then looks at ways to manipulate data in a two-dimensional array.

Two-dimensional array: A collection of a fixed number of components arranged in rows and columns (that is, in two dimensions), wherein all components are of the same type.

The syntax for declaring a two-dimensional array is

```
dataType[][]  arrayName;
```

where **dataType** is the data type of the array components.

Because an array is an object, we must instantiate the object to allocate memory space to store data. The general syntax to instantiate a two-dimensional array object is

```
arrayName = new dataType[intExp1][intExp2];
```

where `intExp1` and `intExp2` are expressions yielding positive integer values. The two expressions, `intExp1` and `intExp2`, specify the number of rows and the number of columns, respectively, in the array.

The preceding two statements can be combined into one statement as follows:

```
dataType[][] arrayName = new dataType[intExp1][intExp2];
```

For example, the statement

```
double[][] sales = new double[10][5];
```

declares a two-dimensional array `sales` of 10 rows and 5 columns, where every component is of the type `double`. As in a one-dimensional array, the rows are numbered 0...9 and the columns are numbered 0...4. See Figure 9-13.

sales	[0]	[1]	[2]	[3]	[4]
[0]	0.0	0.0	0.0	0.0	0.0
[1]	0.0	0.0	0.0	0.0	0.0
[2]	0.0	0.0	0.0	0.0	0.0
[3]	0.0	0.0	0.0	0.0	0.0
[3]	0.0	0.0	0.0	0.0	0.0
[4]	0.0	0.0	0.0	0.0	0.0
[5]	0.0	0.0	0.0	0.0	0.0
[6]	0.0	0.0	0.0	0.0	0.0
[7]	0.0	0.0	0.0	0.0	0.0
[8]	0.0	0.0	0.0	0.0	0.0
[9]	0.0	0.0	0.0	0.0	0.0

Figure 9-13   Two-dimensional array `sales`

From now on in this book, whenever we instantiate a two-dimensional array and draw its diagram, we will not show all the default values as we have in Figure 9-13.

Accessing Array Components

To access the components of a two-dimensional array, you need a pair of indices: one for the row position and one for the column position.

The syntax to access a component of a two-dimensional array is

```
arrayName[indexExp1][indexExp2]
```

where `indexExp1` and `indexExp2` are expressions yielding non-negative integer values. `indexExp1` specifies the row position; `indexExp2` specifies the column position. Moreover, the value of `indexExp1` must be less than the number of rows, and the value of `indexExp2` must be less than the number of columns in the array.

The statement

```
sales[5][3] = 25.75;
```

stores `25.75` into row number `5` and column number `3` (the `6th` row and the `4th` column) of the array `sales`. See Figure 9-14.

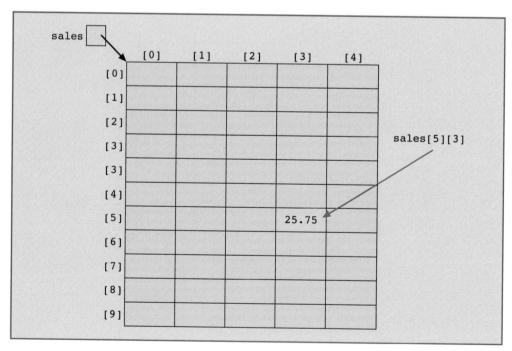

Figure 9-14   `sales[5][3]`

Suppose that:

```
int i = 5;
int j = 3;
```

Then the previous statement

```
sales[5][3] = 25.75;
```

is equivalent to

```
sales[i][j] = 25.75;
```

So the indices can also be variables.

Two-Dimensional Arrays and the Instance Variable `length`

Just as in one-dimensional arrays, you can use the instance variable `length` to determine the number of rows as well as number of columns (in each row). Consider the following statement:

```
int[][] matrix = new int[20][15];
```

This statement declares and instantiates a two-dimensional array `matrix` of 20 rows and 15 columns. The value of the expression

```
matrix.length
```

is 20, the number of rows.

Each row of `matrix` is a one-dimensional array and `matrix[0]`, in fact, refers to the first row. Therefore, the value of the expression

```
matrix[0].length
```

is 15, the number of columns in the first row. Similarly, `matrix[1].length` gives the number of columns in the second row, which in this case is 15, and so on.

Two-Dimensional Arrays: Special Cases

The two-dimensional arrays created in the preceding sections are quite straightforward; each row has same number of columns. However, Java allows you to specify a different number of columns for each row. In this case, each row must be instantiated separately. Consider the following statement:

```
int[][] board;
```

Suppose that you want to create the array `board`, as shown in Figure 9-15.

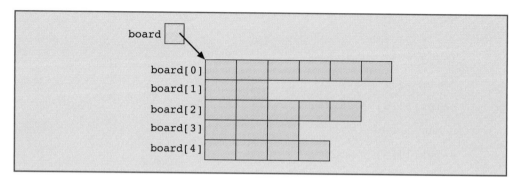

Figure 9-15   Two-dimensional array `board`

It follows from Figure 9-15 that the number of rows in `board` is 5; the number of columns in the first row is 6; the number of columns in the second row is 2; the number of columns in the third row is 5; the number of columns in the fourth row is 3; and the number of columns in the fifth row is 4. To create this two-dimensional array, first we create the one-dimensional array `board` of 5 rows. Then we instantiate each row, specifying the required number of columns as follows:

```
board = new int[5];       //Create the number of rows
board[0] = new int[6];    //Create the columns for the first row
board[1] = new int[2];    //Create the columns for the second row
board[2] = new int[5];    //Create the columns for the third row
board[3] = new int[3];    //Create the columns for the fourth row
board[4] = new int[4];    //Create the columns for the fifth row
```

Because the number of columns of each row is not the same, such arrays are called **ragged arrays**. To process these types of two-dimensional arrays, you must know the exact number of columns for each row.

Notice that here `board.length` is 5, the number of rows in the array `board`. Similarly, `board[0].length` is 6, the number of columns in the first row; `board[1].length` is 2, the number of columns in the second row; `board[2].length` is 5, the number of columns in the third row; `board[3].length` is 3, the number of columns in the fourth row; and `board[4].length` is 4, the number of columns in the fifth row.

Two-Dimensional Array Initialization During Declaration

Like one-dimensional arrays, two-dimensional arrays can be initialized when they are declared. The example in the following statement helps illustrate this concept:

```
int[][] board = {{2, 3, 1},
                 {15, 25, 13},
                 {20, 4, 7},
                 {11, 18, 14}};       //Line 1
```

This statement declares **board** to be a two-dimensional array of 4 rows and 3 columns. The components of the first row are 2, 3, and 1; the components of the second row are 15, 25, and 13; the components of the third row are 20, 4, and 7; and the components of the fourth row are 11, 18, and 14, respectively. Figure 9-16 shows the array **board**.

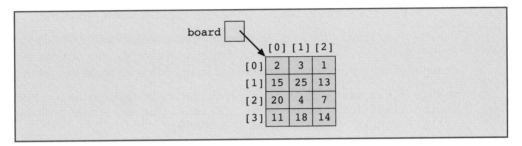

Figure 9-16   Two-dimensional array **board**

To initialize a two-dimensional array when it is declared:

- The elements of each row are enclosed within braces and separated by commas.

- All rows are enclosed within braces.

Now consider the following statement:

```
int[][] table = {{2, 1, 3, 5},
                 {15, 25},
                 {4, 23, 45}};
```

Here you see that the number of values specified for the first row of the array **table** is 4; the number of values specified for the second row is 2; and the number of values specified for the third row is 3. Since the number of values specified for the first row is 4, only four columns are assigned to the first row. Similarly, the number of columns assigned to the second and third row is 2 and 3, respectively. See Figure 9-17.

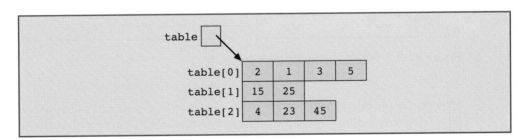

Figure 9-17   Two-dimensional array **table**

Processing Two-Dimensional Arrays

A two-dimensional array can be processed in three ways:

1. Process the entire array.

2. Process a particular row of the array, called **row processing**.

3. Process a particular column of the array, called **column processing**.

Initializing and printing the array are examples of processing the entire two–dimensional array. Finding the largest element in a row or column, or finding the sum of a row or column are examples of row (column) processing. We will use the following declaration for our discussion:

```
static final int ROWS = 7;      //this can be set to any number
static final int COLUMNS = 6; //this can be set to any number
int[][] matrix = new int[ROWS][COLUMNS];
int row;
int col;
int sum;
int largest;
int temp;
```

Figure 9-18 shows the array `matrix`.

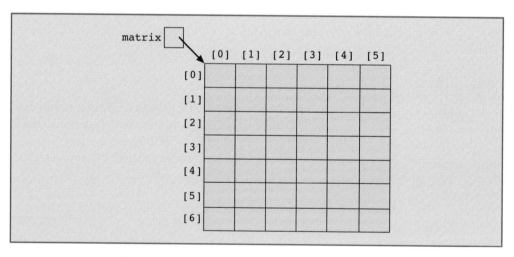

Figure 9-18   Two-dimensional array `matrix`

 For the two-dimensional array `matrix`, the value of `matrix.length` is 7, which is same as the value of the named constant ROWS. Also, the values of `matrix[0].length, matrix[1].length, . . ., matrix[6].length` gives the number of columns in row 0, row 1, . . ., row 6, respectively. And notice that the number of columns in each row is 6.

Because all the components of a two-dimensional array are of the same type, the components of any row or column are of the same type. This means that in a two-dimensional array, each row and each column is a one-dimensional array. Therefore, when processing a particular row or column of a two-dimensional array, we use algorithms similar to those that process one-dimensional arrays. We further explain this concept with the help of the two-dimensional array `matrix`, as declared previously.

Suppose that we want to process row number **5** of `matrix` (the `sixth` row of `matrix`). The components of row number **5** of `matrix` are:

```
matrix[5][0], matrix[5][1], matrix[5][2], matrix[5][3],
matrix[5][4], matrix[5][5]
```

In these components, the first index (the row position) is fixed at **5**. The second index (the column position) ranges from **0** to **5**. Therefore, we can use the following **for** loop to process row number **5**:

```
for(col = 0; col < matrix[5].length; col++)
    //process matrix[5][col]
```

This **for** loop is equivalent to the following **for** loop:

```
row = 5;
for(col = 0; col < matrix[row].length; col++)
    //process matrix[row][col]
```

Similarly, suppose that we want to process column number **2** of `matrix`—the third column of `matrix`. The components of this column are:

```
matrix[0][2], matrix[1][2], matrix[2][2], matrix[3][2],
matrix[4][2], matrix[5][2], matrix[6][2]
```

Here the second index (the column position) is fixed at **2**. The first index (the row position) ranges from **0** to **6**. In this case, we use the following **for** loop to process column **2** of `matrix`:

```
for(row = 0; row < matrix.length; row++)
    //process matrix[row][2]
```

This **for** loop is equivalent to the following **for** loop:

```
col = 2;
for(row = 0; row < matrix.length; row++)
    //process matrix[row][col]
```

Next we discuss specific algorithms for processing two-dimensional arrays.

Initialization

Suppose that you want to initialize row number **4** to **10**, that is, the 5th row to **10**. As explained earlier, the following **for** loop initializes row number **4** to **10**:

```
row = 4;
for(col = 0; col < matrix[row].length; col++)
    matrix[row][col] = 10;
```

If you want to initialize the entire `matrix` to 10, you can also put the first index (the row position) in a loop. By using the following nested `for` loops, you can initialize each component of `matrix` to 10:

```
for(row = 0; row < matrix.length; row++)
    for(col = 0; col < matrix[row].length; col++)
        matrix[row][col] = 10;
```

Print

By using a nested `for` loop, you can output the components of `matrix`. The following nested `for` loops print the components of `matrix`, one row per line:

```
for(row = 0; row < matrix.length; row++)
{
    for(col = 0; col < matrix[row].length; col++)
        System.out.print(matrix[row][col] + "\t");

    System.out.println();
}
```

Input

The following `for` loop inputs data into row number 4, that is, the 5th row of `matrix`:

```
row = 4;
for(col = 0; col < matrix[row].length; col++)
    matrix[row][col] = Integer.parseInt(keyboard.readLine());
```

As before, by putting the row number in a loop, you can input data into each component of `matrix`. The following `for` loop inputs data into each component of `matrix`:

```
for(row = 0; row < matrix.length; row++)
    for(col = 0; col < matrix[row].length; col++)
        matrix[row][col] = Integer.parseInt(keyboard.readLine());
```

Sum by Row

The following `for` loop finds the sum of row number 4 of `matrix`; that is, it adds the components of row number 4:

```
sum = 0;
row = 4;
for(col = 0; col < matrix[row].length; col++)
    sum = sum + matrix[row][col];
```

Once again, by putting the row number in a loop, you can find the sum of each row separately. The Java code to find the sum of each individual row follows:

```
//Sum of each individual row
for(row = 0; row < matrix.length; row++)
{
    sum = 0;
    for(col = 0; col < matrix[row].length; col++)
        sum = sum + matrix[row][col];

    System.out.println("Sum of row " + (row+1) + " = "+ sum);
}
```

Sum by Column

As in the case of sum by row, the following nested **for** loop finds the sum of each individual column. (Notice that **matrix[0].length** gives the number of columns in each row.)

```
//Sum of each individual column
for(col = 0; col < matrix[0].length; col++)
{
    sum = 0;
    for(row = 0; row < matrix.length; row++)
        sum = sum + matrix[row][col];

    System.out.println("Sum of column " + (col+1) + " = " + sum);
}
```

Largest Element in Each Row and Each Column

As stated earlier, another possible operation on a two-dimensional array is finding the largest element in each row and each column. Next we give the Java code to perform this operation.

The following **for** loop determines the largest element in row number 4:

```
row = 4;
largest = matrix[row][0]; //assume that the first element of the
                          //row is the largest
for(col = 1; col < matrix[row].length; col++)
    if(largest < matrix[row][col])
        largest = matrix[row][col];
```

The following Java code determines the largest element in each row and each column:

```
//Largest element in each row
for(row = 0; row < matrix.length; row++)
{
    largest = matrix[row][0]; //assume that the first element
                              //of the row is the largest
    for(col = 1; col < matrix[row].length; col++)
        if(largest < matrix[row][col])
            largest = matrix[row][col];
```

```
    System.out.println("Largest element of row " + (row+1)
                    + " = " + largest);
}

//Largest element in each column
for(col = 0; col < matrix[0].length; col++)
{
    largest = matrix[0][col]; //assume that the first element of
                              //the column is the largest
    for(row = 1; row < matrix.length; row++)
        if(largest < matrix[row][col])
            largest = matrix[row][col];

    System.out.println("Largest element of col " + (col+1)
                    + " = " + largest);
}
```

Reversing Diagonals

Suppose that `matrix` is a square array, that is, it has the same number of rows and columns. Then `matrix` has a main diagonal and an opposite diagonal. To be specific, suppose that we have the following:

```
final int ROWS = 4;
final int COLUMNS = 4;
```

The components of the main diagonal of `matrix` are `matrix[0][0]`, `matrix[1][1]`, `matrix[2][2]`, and `matrix[3][3]`. The components of the opposite diagonal are `matrix[0][3]`, `matrix[1][2]`, `matrix[2][1]`, and `matrix[3][0]`.

We want to write Java code to reverse both the diagonals of `matrix`. Assume that the array `matrix` is as shown in Figure 9-19.

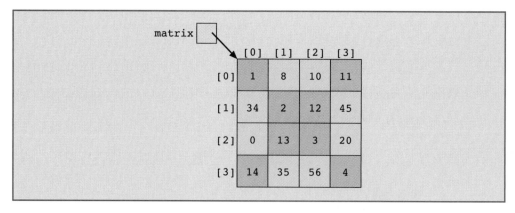

Figure 9-19 Two-dimensional array `matrix` before reversing diagonals

After reversing both the diagonals, the array `matrix` is as shown in Figure 9-20.

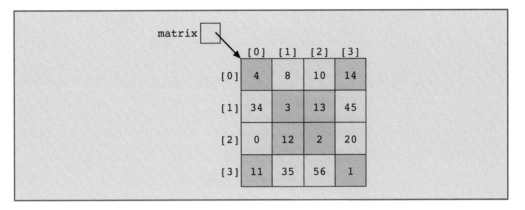

Figure 9-20   Two-dimensional array `matrix` after reversing diagonals

To reverse the main diagonal, we do the following:

Swap `matrix[0][0]` with `matrix[3][3]`.
Swap `matrix[1][1]` with `matrix[2][2]`.

To reverse the opposite diagonal, we do the following:

Swap `matrix[0][3]` with `matrix[3][0]`.
Swap `matrix[1][2]` with `matrix[2][1]`.

The following **for** loops reverse the diagonals:

```
        //Reverse the main diagonal
for(row = 0; row < matrix.length / 2; row++)
{
        temp = matrix[row][row];
        matrix[row][row] =
                matrix[matrix.length-1-row][matrix.length-1-row];
        matrix[matrix.length-1-row][matrix.length-1-row] = temp;
}

        //Reverse the opposite diagonal
for(row = 0; row < matrix.length / 2; row++)
{
        temp = matrix[row][matrix.length-1-row];
        matrix[row][matrix.length-1-row] =
                                matrix[matrix.length-1-row][row];
        matrix[matrix.length-1-row][row] = temp;
}
```

N
O   This Java code to reverse the diagonals works for any square two-dimensional array.
T
E

Passing Two-Dimensional Arrays as Parameters to Methods

Just like one-dimensional arrays, two-dimensional arrays can be passed as parameters to a method.

In the section, Processing Two-Dimensional Arrays, we described various algorithms to process the elements of a two-dimensional array. Using those algorithms, we can write methods that can be used in a variety of applications. In this section we write some of these methods. In these methods, for simplicity, we assume that we are processing the entire two-dimensional array.

The following method outputs the elements of a two-dimensional array, one row per line:

```
public static void printMatrix(int[][] matrix)
{
        int row, col;

        for(row = 0; row < matrix.length; row++)
        {
            for(col = 0; col < matrix[row].length; col++)
                System.out.print(matrix[row][col] + "\t");
            System.out.println();
        }
}
```

In a similar way, the following method outputs the sum of the elements of each row of a two-dimensional array whose elements are of the type `int`:

```
public static void sumRows(int[][] matrix)
{
        int row, col;
        int sum;

          //sum of each individual row
        for(row = 0; row < matrix.length; row++)
        {
            sum = 0;

            for(col = 0; col < matrix[row].length; col++)
                sum = sum + matrix[row][col];

            System.out.println("Sum of row " + (row+1) + " = " + sum);
        }
}
```

The following method determines the largest element in each row:

```
public static void largestinRows(int[][] matrix)
{
        int row, col;
        int largest;
```

```
        //Largest element in each row
    for(row = 0; row < matrix.length; row++)
    {
        largest = matrix[row][0]; //assume that the first element
                                  //of the row is largest
        for(col = 1; col < matrix[row].length; col++)
            if(largest < matrix[row][col])
                largest = matrix[row][col];

        System.out.println("Largest element of row " + (row+1)
                            + " = " + largest);
    }
}
```

In a similar fashion, you can write methods to find the sum of the elements of each column, read data into a two-dimensional array, find the largest and/or smallest element in each row or each column, and so on.

Example 9-7 shows how the preceding methods are used in a program.

Example 9-7

The following program illustrates how two-dimensional arrays are passed as parameters to methods:

```
public class TwoDimArraysAsParam
{
    public static void main(String[] args)
    {
        int[][] board ={{23,5,6,15,18},
                        {4,16,24,67,10},
                        {12,54,23,76,11},
                        {1,12,34,22,8},
                        {81,54,32,67,33},
                        {12,34,76,78,9}};        //Line 1
        printMatrix(board);                      //Line 2
        System.out.println();                    //Line 3
        sumRows(board);                          //Line 4
        System.out.println();                    //Line 5
        largestinRows(board);                    //Line 6
    }

    //Place the definitions of the methods printMatrix,
    //sumRows, and largestinRows as described above here
}
```

9

Sample Run:

```
23        5         6         15        18
4         16        24        67        10
12        54        23        76        11
1         12        34        22        8
81        54        32        67        33
12        34        76        78        9
```

```
Sum of row 1 = 67
Sum of row 2 = 121
Sum of row 3 = 176
Sum of row 4 = 77
Sum of row 5 = 267
Sum of row 6 = 209
```

```
Largest element of row 1 = 23
Largest element of row 2 = 67
Largest element of row 3 = 76
Largest element of row 4 = 34
Largest element of row 5 = 81
Largest element of row 6 = 78
```

In the preceding program, the statement in Line 1 declares and initializes **board** to be a two-dimensional array of 6 rows and 5 columns. The statement in Line 2 uses the method **printMatrix** to output the elements of **board** (see the first six lines of the Sample Run). The statement in Line 4 uses the method **sumRows** to calculate and print the sum of each row. The statement in Line 6 uses the method **largestinRows** to find and print the largest element in each row.

When storing a two-dimensional array in the computer's memory, Java uses the **row order form**. That is, the first row is stored first, followed by the second row, followed by the third row, and so on.

MULTIDIMENSIONAL ARRAYS

Earlier in this chapter, we defined an array as a collection of a fixed number of elements (called components) of the same type. A one-dimensional array is an array in which the elements are arranged in a list form; in a two-dimensional array, the elements are arranged in a table form. We can also define three-dimensional or larger arrays. In Java, there is no limit on the dimensions of arrays. Following is the general definition of an array:

Array: A collection of a fixed number of elements (called components) arranged in n dimensions (n >= 1), called an **n-dimensional array**.

The general syntax for declaring and instantiating an n-dimensional array is

```
dataType[][]...[] arrayName
              = new dataType[intExp1][intExp2] ... [intExpn];
```

where `intExp1`, `intExp2`, ..., and `intExpn` are constant expressions yielding positive integer values.

The syntax to access a component of an n-dimensional array is

```
arrayName[indexExp1][indexExp2] ... [indexExpn]
```

where `indexExp1`, `indexExp2`, ..., and `indexExpn` are expressions yielding non-negative integer values. Moreover, for each `i` the value of `indexExpi` must be less than the size of the `i`th dimension. `indexExpi` gives the position of the array component in the `i`th dimension.

For example, the statement

```
double[][][] carDealers = new double [10][5][7];
```

declares `carDealers` to be a three-dimensional array. The size of the first dimension is `10`, the size of the second dimension is `5`, and the size of the third dimension is `7`. The first dimension ranges from `0` to `9`, the second dimension ranges from `0` to `4`, and the third dimension ranges from `0` to `6`. The base address of the array `carDealers` is the address of the first array component—the address of `carDealers[0][0][0]`. The total number of components in the array `carDealers` is `10*5*7 = 350`.

The statement

```
carDealers[5][3][2] = 15564.75;
```

sets the value of the component `carDealers[5][3][2]` to `15564.75`.

You can use loops to process multidimensional arrays. For example, the nested `for` loops

```
for(i = 0; i < 10; i++)
    for(j = 0; j < 5; j++)
        for(k = 0; k < 7; k++)
            carDealers[i][j][k] = 10.00;
```

initialize each component of the array to `10.00`.

During program execution, if an array index goes out of bounds, the program throws an **ArrayIndexOutOfBoundsException**. Exception handling is discussed in detail in Chapter 12.

PROGRAMMING EXAMPLE: TEXT PROCESSING

Let's now write a program that reads a given text, outputs the text as is, and prints the number of lines and the number of times each letter appears in the text. An uppercase letter and a lowercase letter are treated as being the same; that is, they are tallied together.

Because there are 26 letters, we use an array of **26** components to perform the letter count. We also need a variable to store the line count.

The text is stored in a file, which we will call **text.txt**; it is on a floppy disk, which we will assume is **a**. The output will be stored in a file, which we will call **textCh.out**.

Input A file containing the text to be processed.

Output A file containing the text, number of lines, and the number of times a letter appears in the text.

Problem Analysis and Algorithm Design

Based on the desired output, it is clear that we must output the text as is. That is, if the text contains any whitespace characters, they must be output as well.

Let's first describe the variables that are necessary to develop the program. This will simplify the discussion that follows.

Variables We need to store the letter count and the line count. Therefore, we need a variable to store the line count and 26 variables to perform the letter count. We will use an array of 26 components to perform the letter count. We also need a variable to read and store each character in turn, because the input file will be read character by character. Because data will be read from an input file and output will be saved in a file, we need an input stream object to open the input file and an output stream object to open the output file. These statements indicate that the method **main** needs (at least) the following variables:

```
int lineCount = 0;      //variable to store the line count
int[] letterCount = new int[26]; //array to store the letter count

IntClass next = new IntClass();      //variable to read a character

FileReader inputStream = new FileReader("a:\\text.txt");
PrintWriter outfile =
          new PrintWriter(new FileWriter("a:\\textCh.out"));
```

We assume that the input file is **text.txt**, output will be stored in the file **textCh.out**, and both these files are on floppy disk A.

In this declaration, **letterCount[0]** stores the **A** count, **letterCount[1]** stores the **B** count, and so on. Clearly, the variable **lineCount** and the array **letterCount** must be initialized to **0**.

The algorithm for the program is:

1. Declare and initialize the variables.
2. Create objects to open the input and output files.
3. While there is more data in the input file:
    a. For each character in a line:
        i.   Read and write the character.
        ii. Increment the appropriate letter count.
    b. Increment the line count.
4. Output the line count and letter counts.
5. Close the files.

To simplify the method `main`, we divide it into three methods:

- Method `copyText`
- Method `characterCount`
- Method `writeTotal`

The following sections describe each method in detail. Then, with the help of these methods, we describe the algorithm for the method `main`.

`copyText`   This method reads a line and outputs the line. Whenever a nonblank character is found, it calls the method `characterCount` to update the letter count. Clearly, this method has four parameters: an input stream object, an output stream object, a variable to read the character, and the array to update the letter count.

Note that the method `copyText` does not perform the letter count, but we still pass the array `letterCount` to it. We do this because this method calls the method `characterCount`, which needs the array `letterCount` to update the appropriate letter count. Therefore, we must pass the array `letterCount` to the `copyText` method so that it can pass the array to the method `characterCount`.

```
static void copyText(FileReader infile, PrintWriter outfile,
              IntClass next, int[] letterC) throws IOException
{
   while(next.getNum() != (int)'\n') //Process the entire line
   {
      outfile.print((char)(next.getNum())); //Output the character
      chCount((char)(next.getNum()), letterC); //Call the
                                       //method chCount

      next.setNum(infile.read());        //Read the next character
   }
   outfile.println();                    //Output the newline character
}
```

`characterCount` This method increments the letter count. To increment the appropriate letter count, the method must know what the letter is. Therefore, the `characterCount` method has two parameters: a **char** variable and the array to update the letter count. In pseudocode, this method is:

   a. Convert the letter to uppercase.

   b. Find the index of the array corresponding to this letter.

   c. If the index is valid, increment the appropriate count. At this step, we must ensure that the character is a letter. We are counting only letters, so other characters—such as commas, hyphens, and periods—are ignored.

Following this algorithm, the definition of this method is:

```
static void chCount(char ch, int[] letterC)
{
    int index;
    int i;

    ch = Character.toUpperCase(ch);        //Step a
    index = (int) ch - 65;                 //Step b
    if(index >= 0 && index < 26)           //Step c
        letterC[index]++;
}
```

`writeTotal` This method outputs the line count and the letter count. It has three parameters: the output stream object, the line count, and the array to output the letter count. The definition of this method is:

```
static void writeTotal(PrintWriter outfile, int lines,
                       int[] letters)
{
   int i;

   outfile.println("The number of lines =  " + lines);

   for(i = 0; i < 26; i++)
       outfile.println((char)(i+65) + " count = " + letters[i]);
}
```

We now describe the algorithm for the method `main`.

Main Algorithm

   1. Declare and initialize the variables.

   2. Open the input and output files.

   3. If the input file does not exist, exit the program.

   4. Open the output file.

   5. Read the first character.

6. while (not end of input file):
   a. Process the next line; call the method `copyText`.
   b. Increment the line count. (Increment the variable `lineCount`.)
   c. Read the next character.
7. Output the line count and letter counts. Call the method `writeTotal`.
8. Close the files.

Complete Program Listing

```java
//Program: Line and letter count

import java.io.*;

public class CharacterCount
{
    public static void main (String[] args)
                    throws FileNotFoundException, IOException
    {
        int lineCount = 0;
        int[] letterCount = new int[26];

        IntClass next = new IntClass();

        FileReader inputStream = new FileReader("a:\\text.txt");
        PrintWriter outfile =
                new PrintWriter(new FileWriter("a:\\textCh.out"));

        next.setNum(inputStream.read());
        while(next.getNum() != -1)
        {
            copyText(inputStream, outfile, next, letterCount);
            lineCount++;
            next.setNum(inputStream.read());
        }   // end while loop
         writeTotal(outfile,lineCount,letterCount);

        outfile.close();
    }
```

```
static void copyText(FileReader infile, PrintWriter outfile,
            IntClass next, int[] letterC) throws IOException
{
    while(next.getNum() != (int)'\n')
    {
        outfile.print((char)(next.getNum()));
        chCount((char)(next.getNum()), letterC);
        next.setNum(infile.read());
    }
    outfile.println();
}

static void chCount(char ch, int[] letterC)
{
    int index;
    int i;

    ch = Character.toUpperCase(ch);             //Step a
    index = (int) ch - 65;                      //Step b
    if(index >= 0 && index < 26)                //Step c
        letterC[index]++;
}

static void writeTotal(PrintWriter outfile, int lines,
                    int[] letters)
{
  int i;

  outfile.println("The number of lines =  " + lines);

  for(i = 0; i < 26; i++)
      outfile.println((char)(i+65) + " count = " + letters[i]);
}
}
```

QUICK REVIEW

1. An array is a structured data type with a fixed number of components. Every component is of the same type, and components are accessed using their relative positions in the array.

2. Elements of a one-dimensional array are arranged in the form of a list.

3. An array index can be any expression that evaluates to a non-negative integer. The value of the index must always be less than the size of the array.

4. In Java, an array index starts with 0.

5. In Java, [ ] is an operator, called the array subscripting operator.

6. When an array object is instantiated, its components are initialized to their default values.

7. Arrays that are created, that is, instantiated, during program execution are called dynamic arrays.

8. Arrays can be initialized when they are created.

9. Associated with each array that has been instantiated, (that is, memory has been allocated to store data), there is a `public` instance variable `length`. The variable `length` contains the size of the array.

10. If array index goes out of bounds, the program throws an `ArrayIndexOutOfBoundsException`.

11. The base address of an array is the address (that is, memory location) of the first array component.

12. Arrays can be passed as parameters to methods.

13. In a method call statement, when passing an array as an actual parameter, you use only its name.

14. Individual array components can be passed as parameters to methods.

15. You can create an array of objects.

16. Parallel arrays are used to hold related information.

17. A two-dimensional array is an array in which the elements are arranged in a table form.

18. To access an element of a two-dimensional array, you need a pair of indices: one for the row position and one for the column position.

19. In row processing, a two-dimensional array is processed one row at a time.

20. In column processing, a two-dimensional array is processed one column at a time.

21. Java stores two-dimensional arrays in a row order form in computer memory.

9

EXERCISES

1. Mark the following statements as true or false.

   a. A `double` type is an example of a primitive data type.

   b. A one-dimensional array is an example of a structured data type.

   c. Arrays can be passed as parameters to a method.

   d. A method can return a value of the type `array`.

   e. The size of an array is determined at compile time.

f. Given the declaration

```
int[] list = new int[10];
```

the statement

```
list[5] = list[3] + list[2];
```

updates the content of the fifth component of the array `list`.

g. If an array index goes out of bounds, the program terminates in an error.

2. Write Java statements to do the following:

a. Declare an array `alpha` of 15 components of the type `int`.

b. Output the value of the tenth component of the array `alpha`.

c. Set the value of the fifth component of the array `alpha` to 35.

d. Set the value of the ninth component of the array `alpha` to the sum of the sixth and thirteenth components of the array `alpha`.

e. Set the value of the fourth component of the array `alpha` to three times the value of the eighth component, minus 57.

f. Output `alpha` so that five components per line are printed.

3. Consider the method headings

```
void funcOne(int[] alpha, int size)
int funcSum(int x, int y)
void funcTwo(int[] alpha, int[] beta)
```

and the declarations

```
int[] list = new int[50];
int[] Alist = new int[60];
int num;
```

Write Java statements that do the following:

a. Call the method `funcOne` with the actual parameters, `list` and 50, respectively.

b. Print the value returned by the method `funcSum` with the actual parameters, 50 and the fourth component of `list`, respectively.

c. Print the value returned by the method `funcSum` with actual parameters, the thirtieth and tenth components of the `list`, respectively.

d. Call the method `funcTwo` with the actual parameters, `list` and `Alist`, respectively.

4. Suppose `list` is an array of five components of the type `int`. What is stored in `list` after the following Java code executes?

```
for(i = 0; i < 5; i++)
{
    list[i] = 2 * i + 5;
    if(i % 2 == 0)
        list[i] = list[i] - 3;
}
```

5. Suppose `list` is an array of six components of the type `int`. What is stored in `list` after the following Java code executes?

```java
list[0] = 5;
for(int i = 1; i < 6; i++)
{
    list[i] = i * i + 5;

    if(i > 2)
        list[i] = 2 * list[i] - list[i - 1];
}
```

6. What is the output of the following program?

```java
public class Exercise6
{
    public static void main(String[] args)
    {
        int count;
        int[] alpha = new int[5];

        alpha[0] = 5;
        for(count = 1; count < 5; count++)
        {
            alpha[count] = 5 * count + 10;
            alpha[count - 1] = alpha[count] - 4;
        }

        System.out.print("List elements: ");

        for(count = 0; count < 5; count++)
            System.out.print(alpha[count] + " ");
        System.out.println();
    }
}
```

7. What is the output of the following program?

```java
public class Exercise7
{
    public static void main(String[] args)
    {
        int j;
        int[] one = new int[5];
        int[] two = new int[10];

        for(j = 0; j < 5; j++)
            one[j] = 5 * j + 3;

        System.out.print("One contains: ");
```

9

```
        for(j = 0; j < 5; j++)
            System.out.print(one[j] + " ");

    System.out.println();

        for(j = 0; j < 5; j++)
        {
            two[j] = 2 * one[j] - 1;
            two[j + 5] = one[4 - j] + two [j];
        }

        System.out.print("Two contains: ");
        for(j = 0; j < 10; j++)
            System.out.print(two[j] + " ");

        System.out.println();
    }
}
```

8. Consider the following declarations:

```
const int carTypes = 5;
const int colorTypes = 6;

double[][] sales = new double [carTypes][colorTypes];
```

   a. How many components does the array **sales** have?

   b. What is the number of rows in the array **sales**?

   c. What is the number of columns in the array **sales**?

   d. To sum the sales by **carTypes**, what kind of processing is required?

   e. To sum the sales by **colorTypes**, what kind of processing is required?

9. Write Java statements that do the following:

   a. Declare an array **alpha** of 10 rows and 20 columns of the type **int**.

   b. Initialize the array **alpha** to 0.

   c. Store 1 in the first row and 2 in the remaining rows.

   d. Store 5 in the first column, and make sure that the value in each remaining column is twice the value in the previous column.

   e. Print the array **alpha** one row per line.

   f. Print the array **alpha** one column per line.

10. Consider the following declaration:

```
int[][] beta = new int[3][3];
```

What is stored in **beta** after the each of the following statements executes?

a.
```
for(i = 0; i < 3; i++)
    for(j = 0; j < 3; j++)
        beta[i][j] = 0;
```

b.
```
for(i = 0; i < 3; i++)
    for(j = 0; j < 3; j++)
        beta[i][j] = i + j;
```

c.
```
for(i = 0; i < 3; i++)
    for(j = 0; j < 3; j++)
        beta[i][j] = i * j;
```

d.
```
for(i = 0; i < 3; i++)
    for(j = 0; j < 3; j++)
        beta[i][j] =  2 * (i + j) % 4;
```

PROGRAMMING EXERCISES

1. Write a Java program that declares an array **alpha** of 50 components of the type **double**. Initialize the array so that the first 25 components are equal to the square of the index variable, and the last 25 components are equal to three times the index variable. Output the array so that 10 elements per line are printed.

2. Write a Java method, **smallestIndex**, that takes as its parameters an **int** array and its size, and returns the index of the smallest element in the array. Also write a program to test your method.

3. Write a program that reads a file consisting of students' test scores in the range 0–200. It should then determine the number of students having scores in each of the following ranges: 0–24, 25–49, 50–74, 75–99, 100–124, 125–149, 150–174, and 175–200. Output the score ranges and the number of students. Run your program with the following input data: 76, 89, 150, 135, 200, 76, 12, 100, 150, 28, 178, 189, 167, 200, 175, 150, 87, 99, 129, 149, 176, 200, 87, 35, 157, 189.

4. In a gymnastics or diving competition, each contestant's score is calculated by dropping the lowest and highest scores and then adding the remaining scores. Write a program that allows the user to enter eight judges' scores and outputs the points received by the contestant. Format your output with two decimal places. A judge awards points between 1 and 10, with 1 being the lowest and 10 being the highest. For example, if the scores are 9.2, 9.3, 9.0, 9.9, 9.5, 9.5, 9.6, and 9.8, the contestant receives a total of 56.90 points.

5. Write a program that prompts the user to input a string and outputs the string in uppercase letters. (Use a character array to store the string.)

9

6. The history teacher at your school needs help grading a True/False test. The students' IDs and test answers are stored in a file. The first entry in the file contains answers to the test in the form

   TFFTFFTTTTFFTFTFTFT

   Every other entry in the file is the student ID, followed by a blank, followed by the student's response. For example, the entry

   ABC54301 TFTFTFTT TFTFTFFTTFT

   indicates that the student ID is ABC54301 and the answer to question 1 is True, the answer to question 2 is False, and so on. This student did not answer question 9. The exam has 20 questions, and the class has more than 150 students. Each correct answer is awarded two points, each wrong answer gets -1 point, and no answer gets 0 points. Write a program that processes the test data. The output should be the student's ID, followed by the answers, followed by the test score, followed by the test grade. Assume the following grade scale: 90%–100%, A; 80%–89.99%, B; 70%–79.99%, C; 60%–69.99%, D; and 0%–59.99%, F.

7. Write a program that allows the user to enter the last names of five candidates in a local election and the votes received by each candidate. The program should then output each candidate's name, votes received by that candidate, and the percentage of the total votes received by the candidate. Your program should also output the winner of the election. A sample output is:

   ```
   Candidate     Votes Received      % of Total Votes
   Johnson           5000                 25.91
   Miller            4000                 20.72
   Duffy             6000                 31.09
   Robinson          2500                 12.95
   Ashtony           1800                  9.33
   Total            19300
   The Winner of the Election is Duffy.
   ```

8. Write a program that allows the user to enter the students' names followed by their test score and outputs the following information. (Assume that the maximum number of students in the class is 50.)

   a. Class average

   b. Names of all students whose test scores are below the class average, with an appropriate message

   c. Highest test score and the names of all students having the highest score

9. Consider the following method `main`:

```
public static void main(String[] args)
{
    int[][] inStock = new int[10][4];
    int[] alpha = new int[20];
    int[] beta = new int[20];
    int[] gamma = {11, 13, 15, 17};
    int[] delta = {3, 5, 2, 6, 10, 9, 7, 11, 1, 8};

         .
         .
         .
}
```

a. Write the definition of the method `inputArray` that prompts the user to input 20 numbers and stores the numbers in `alpha`.

b. Write the definition of the method `doubleArray` that initializes the elements of `beta` to two times the corresponding elements in `alpha`. Make sure that you prevent the method from modifying the elements of `alpha`.

c. Write the definition of the method `copyGamma` that sets the elements of the first row of `inStock` to `gamma` and the remaining rows of `inStock` to three times the previous row of `inStock`. Make sure that you prevent the method from modifying the elements of `gamma`.

d. Write the definition of the method `copyAlphaBeta` that stores `alpha` into the first five rows of `inStock` and `beta` into the last five rows of `inStock`. Make sure that you prevent the method from modifying the elements of `alpha` and `beta`.

e. Write the definition of the method `printArray` that prints any one-dimensional array of the type `int`. Print 15 elements per line.

f. Write the definition of the method `setInStock` that prompts the user to input the elements for the first column of `inStock`. The method should then set the elements in the remaining columns to two times the corresponding element in the previous column, minus the corresponding element in `delta`.

g. Write Java statements that call each of the methods in parts a through f.

h. Write a Java program that tests the method `main` and the methods discussed in parts a through f.

10. Write a program that uses a two-dimensional array to store the highest and lowest temperatures for each month of the year. The program should output the average high, average low, and highest and lowest temperatures of the year. Your program must consist of the following methods:

a. Method `getData`: This method reads and stores data in the two-dimensional array.

b. Method `averageHigh`: This method calculates and returns the average high temperature of the year.

c. Method `averageLow`: This method calculates and returns the average low temperature of the year.

    d. Method `indexHighTemp`: This method returns the index of the highest tempera-
ture in the array.

    e. Method `indexLowTemp`: This method returns the index of the lowest temperature
in the array.

(These methods must all have the appropriate parameters.)

11. Write a program that reads in a set of positive integers and outputs how many times a
particular number appears in the list. You may assume that the data set has at most 100
numbers and `-999` marks the end of the input data. The numbers must be output in
increasing order. For example, for the data

```
15 40 28 62 95 15 28 13 62 65 48 95 65 62 65 95 95 -999
```

the output is:

```
Number      Count
13          1
15          2
28          2
40          1
48          1
62          3
65          3
95          4
```

12. **Airplane Seating Assignment:** Write a program that can be used to assign seats for a
commercial airplane. The airplane has 13 rows, with 6 seats in each row. Rows 1 and 2
are first class; the remaining rows are economy class. Rows 1 through 7 are nonsmoking. Your program must prompt the user to enter the following information:

Ticket type (first class or economy class)

For economy class, the smoking or nonsmoking section

Desired seat

Output the seating plan in the following form:

```
        A B C   D E F
Row 1   * * X   * X X
Row 2   * X *   X * X
Row 3   * * X   X * X
Row 4   X * X   * X X
Row 5   * X *   X * *
Row 6   * X *   * * X
Row 7   X * *   * X X
Row 8   * X *   X X *
Row 9   X * X   X * X
Row 10  * X *   X X X
Row 11  * * X   * X *
Row 12  * * X   X * X
Row 13  * * *   * X *
```

Here, * indicates that the seat is available; X indicates that the seat has been assigned. Make this a menu-driven program; show the user's choices and allow the user to make the appropriate choices.

13. Magic Square:

a. Write a method `createArithmeticSeq` that prompts the user to input two numbers, `first` and `diff`. The method then creates a one-dimensional array of 16 elements ordered in an arithmetic sequence. It also outputs the arithmetic sequence. For example, if `first` = 21 and `diff` = 5, the arithmetic sequence is 21 26 31 36 41 46 51 56 61 66 71 76 81 86 91 96.

b. Write a method `matricize` that takes a one-dimensional array of 16 elements and a two-dimensional array of 4 rows and 4 columns as parameters. (Other values, such as the sizes of the arrays, must also be passed as parameters.) This method puts the elements of the one-dimensional array into the two-dimensional array. For example, if A is the one-dimensional array created in part a and B is a two-dimensional array, then after putting the elements of A into B, the array B is:

```
21 26 31 36
41 46 51 56
61 66 71 76
81 86 91 96
```

c. Write a method `reverseDiagonal` that reverses both diagonals of a two-dimensional array. For example, if the two-dimensional array is as in part b, after reversing the diagonals, the two-dimensional array is:

```
96 26 31 81
41 71 66 56
61 51 46 76
36 86 91 21
```

d. Write a method `magicCheck` that takes a one-dimensional array of size 16, a two-dimensional array of 4 rows and 4 columns, and the sizes of the arrays as parameters. By adding all of the elements of the one-dimensional array and dividing by 4, this method determines the `magicNumber`. The method then adds each row, each column, and each diagonal of the two-dimensional array and compares each sum with the magic number. If the sum of each row, each column, and each diagonal is equal to the `magicNumber`, the method outputs "It is a magic square"; otherwise, it outputs "It is not a magic number". Do not print the sum of each row, each column, and the diagonals.

e. Write a method `printMatrix` that outputs the elements of a two-dimensional array, one row per line. This output should be as close to a square form as possible.

f. The methods written in parts a through e should be general enough to apply to an array of any size. (The work should be done by using loops.) The method `magicCheck` works better if it calls two separate methods: one to add rows and columns and one to add the diagonals. (In this case, the program compares the magic number with each sum (row, column, and diagonal) in the respective method.)

Test the methods you wrote in parts a through f using the following method `class` and the method `main`:

```
public class MagicSquare
{
    static final int rows = 4;
    static final int columns = 4;

    static final int listSize = 16;
    ...
    public static void main(String[] args)
    {

        int[] list = new int[listSize];
        int[][] matrix = new int[rows][columns];

        createArithmeticSeq(list);
        matricize(list,matrix);
        printMatrix(matrix);
        reverseDiagonal(matrix);
        printMatrix(matrix);
        magicCheck(list, matrix);
    }
}
```

CHAPTER 10

APPLICATIONS OF ARRAYS AND STRINGS

In this chapter, you will:

♦ Learn how to implement the sequential search algorithm

♦ Explore how to sort an array using the selection sort algorithm

♦ Learn how to implement the binary search algorithm

♦ Become aware of the `class Vector`

♦ Learn more about manipulating strings using the `class String`

Chapter 9 introduced arrays, a structured data type. Arrays are a convenient way to store and process data values of the same type. You learned how to effectively use loops with arrays for input/output, initialization, and other operations. You also learned how to pass the entire set of values as a parameter with a single statement. This chapter continues the discussion of arrays and shows you how to use them effectively for processing lists. This chapter also discusses how to use the `class Vector` to overcome some limitations of arrays, and revisits the `class String` to show you additional methods for manipulating strings.

LIST PROCESSING

A **list** is a set of values of the same type. Since all values are of the same type, it is convenient to store a list in an array, particularly a one-dimensional array. The size of a list is the number of elements in the list. Because a list's size can increase and decrease, the array you use to store the list should be declared to be the maximum size of the list.

Some basic operations performed on a list are:

- Search the list for a given item.
- Sort the list.
- Insert an item in the list.
- Delete an item from the list.

The following sections discuss algorithms to perform some of these operations.

Searching

Searching a list for a given item is one of the most common operations performed on a list. To search the list, you need the following:

1. The list, that is, the array containing the list.
2. The length of the list.
3. The item for which you are searching.

After the search is completed:

4. If the item is found, then report "success" and the location where the item was found.
5. If the item is not found, then report "failure."

To accommodate (4) and (5), we will write a value-returning method as follows: If the search item is found in the list, the method returns the location in the list where the search item is found; otherwise it returns -1, indicating an unsuccessful search. From this, it is clear that the value-returning method we will write has three parameters:

a. The array, `list`, containing the list
b. The length of the list, `listLength` (Note that `listLength <=` the size of the array.)
c. The item, `searchItem`, for which you are searching

The search algorithm described here is called the **sequential search** or **linear search**. As the name implies, you sequentially search the array starting from the first array component. You compare the `item` with the elements in the array (the list) and continue the search until either you find the item or no more data is left in the `list` to compare with the `item`.

Consider the list of seven elements shown in Figure 10-1.

Figure 10-1 List of seven elements

Suppose that you want to determine whether 27 is in the list. Sequential search works as follows: First you compare 27 with list[0], that is, compare 27 with 35. Since list[0] ≠ 27, you then compare 27 with list[1] (that is, with 12, the second item in the list). Since list[1] ≠ 27, compare 27 with the next element in the list, that is, compare 27 with list[2]. Since list[2] = 27, the search stops. This search is successful.

Let's now search for 10. As before, the search starts at the first element in the list, that is, at list[0]. Proceeding as before, we see that this time the search item, which is 10, is compared with every item in the list. Eventually, no more data is left in the list to compare with the search item. This is an unsuccessful search.

It now follows that, as soon as you find an element in the list that is equal to the search item, you must stop the search and report "success." (In this case, you usually also tell the location in the list where the search item was found.) Otherwise, after the search item is unsuccessfully compared with every element in the list, you must stop the search and report failure.

Suppose that the name of the array containing the list elements is list. The previous discussion translates into the following algorithm for the sequential search:

```
found is set to false;

for(loc = 0; loc < length; loc++)
    if(list[loc] is equal to searchItem)
    {
        found is set to true
        exit loop
    }

if(found)
    return loc;
else
    return -1;
```

The following method performs a sequential search on a list. To be specific, and for illustration purposes, we assume that the list elements are of the type int.

```
int seqSearch(int[] list, int listLength, int searchItem)
{
    int loc;
    bool found = false;
```

10

```
    for(loc = 0; loc < listLength; loc++)
        if(list[loc] == searchItem)
        {
            found = true;
            break;
        }

    if(found)
        return loc;
    else
        return -1;
}
```

If the method `seqSearch` returns a value greater than or equal to `0`, it is a successful search; otherwise it is an unsuccessful search.

As you can see from this algorithm, you start the search by comparing the `searchItem` with the first element in the `list`. If the `searchItem` is equal to the first element in the `list`, you exit the loop; otherwise `loc` is incremented by 1 to point to the next element in the `list`. You then compare the `searchItem` with the next element in the `list`, and so on. Suppose that you have a list with 1000 elements. See Figure 10-2.

Figure 10-2 List of 1000 elements

If the search item is the second item in the list, the sequential search makes two **key comparisons** (also called **item comparisons**) to determine whether the search item is in the list. Similarly, if the search item is the 900th item in the list, the sequential search makes 900 key comparisons to determine whether the search item is in the list. If the search item is not in the list, the sequential search makes 1000 key comparisons.

If the `searchItem` for which we are searching is always at the bottom of the `list`, it will take many comparisons to find the `searchItem`. Also, if the `searchItem` for which we are searching is not in the `list`, then we will compare the `searchItem` with every element in the `list`. A sequential search is therefore not efficient for large lists. In fact, it can be proved that, on average, the number of comparisons (that is, key comparisons) made by a sequential search is equal to half the size of the list. So, for a list size of 1000, on average, the sequential search makes about 500 comparisons.

This search algorithm does not assume that the `list` is sorted. If the `list` is sorted, then you can somewhat improve the search algorithm. Next we discuss how to sort a `list`.

Sorting a List: Selection Sort

Many sorting algorithms are available in the literature. The sorting algorithm discussed here is called the **selection sort**.

In a selection sort, a list is sorted by selecting an element in the list and moving it to its proper position. This algorithm finds the location of the smallest element in the unsorted portion of the list and moves it to the top of the unsorted portion of the list. The first time we locate the smallest item in the entire list, the second time we locate the smallest item in the list starting from the second element in the list, and so on. For example, suppose you have the list shown in Figure 10-3.

	[0]	[1]	[2]	[3]	[4]	[5]	[6]	[7]	[8]	[9]
list	16	30	24	7	25	62	45	5	65	50

Figure 10-3   List of 10 elements

Initially, the entire list is unsorted. So we find the smallest item in the list. The smallest item is at position 7, as shown in Figure 10-4.

Figure 10-4   Smallest element of unsorted list

Because this is the smallest item, it must be moved to position 0. So swap 16 (that is, `list[0]`) with 5 (that is, `list[7]`), as shown in Figure 10-5.

Figure 10-5 Swap elements `list[0]` and `list[7]`

After swapping these elements, the resulting list is as shown in Figure 10-6.

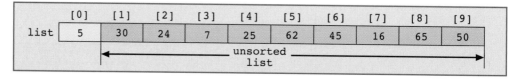

Figure 10-6 List after swapping `list[0]` and `list[7]`

Now the unsorted list is `list[1]...list[9]`. So find the smallest element in the unsorted list. The smallest element is at position 3, as shown in Figure 10-7.

Figure 10-7 Smallest element in unsorted portion of `list`

Since the smallest element in the unsorted list is at position 3, it must be moved to position 1. Swap 7 (that is, `list[3]`) with 30 (that is, `list[1]`), as shown in Figure 10-8.

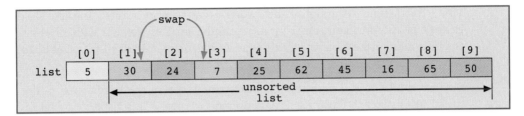

Figure 10-8   Swap `list[1]` with `list[3]`

After swapping `list[1]` with `list[3]`, the resulting list is as shown in Figure 10-9.

	[0]	[1]	[2]	[3]	[4]	[5]	[6]	[7]	[8]	[9]
list	5	7	24	30	25	62	45	16	65	50

Figure 10-9   `list` after swapping `list[1]` with `list[3]`

Now the unsorted list is `list[2]...list[9]`. So we repeat the preceding process of finding the (position of the) smallest element in the unsorted portion of the list and moving it to the beginning of the unsorted portion of the list. The selection sort thus involves the following steps.

In the unsorted portion of the list:

  a. Find the location of the smallest element.

  b. Move the smallest element to the beginning of the unsorted list.

Initially, the entire list, that is, `list[0]...list[length - 1]`, is the unsorted list. After executing steps a and b, the unsorted list is `list[1]...list[length - 1]`. After executing steps a and b the second time, the unsorted list is `list[2]...list[length - 1]`, and so on. We can keep track of the unsorted portion of the list and repeat steps a and b with the help of the following **for** loop:

```
for(index = 0; index < length - 1; index++)
{
        a. find the location, smallestIndex, of the smallest element
           in list[index]...list[length].
        b. Swap the smallest element with list[index]. That is, swap
           list[smallestIndex] with list[index].
}
```

The first time through the loop we locate the smallest element in list[0]...list[length - 1] and swap the smallest element with list[0]. The second time through the loop we locate the smallest element in list[1]...list[length - 1] and swap the smallest element with list[1], and so on.

Step a is similar to the algorithm of finding the index of the largest item in the list, as discussed in Chapter 9. (Also see Programming Exercise 2 in Chapter 9.) Here we find the index of the smallest item in the list. The general form of step a is:

```
smallestIndex = index; //assume first element is the smallest

for(minIndex = index + 1; minIndex < length; minIndex++)
    if(list[minIndex] < list[smallestIndex])
        smallestIndex = minIndex; //current element in the list is
                                  //smaller then the smallest so
                                  //far, so update smallestIndex
```

Step b swaps the contents of list[smallestIndex] with list[index]. The following statements accomplish this task:

```
temp = list[smallestIndex];
list[smallestIndex] = list[index];
list[index] = temp;
```

Before writing the selection sort method, let's apply the preceding algorithm to sort the list shown in Figure 10-10.

	[0]	[1]	[2]	[3]	[4]	[5]
list	14	6	23	2	9	20

Figure 10-10 Unsorted list

Let's call this array containing the list elements list. The length of list is 6, that is, length = 6.

Iteration 1: Sort list[0]...list[5].

Step a: Find the index of the smallest element in list[0]...list[5]. See Figure 10-11.

Figure 10-11 Smallest element in unsorted list is at position 3

Step b: Swap `list[smallestIndex]` with `list[index]`. That is, swap `list[3]` with `list[0]`. Figure 10-12 shows the resulting array.

Figure 10-12 `list` after swapping `list[3]` with `list[0]`

Iteration 2: Sort `list[1]...list[5]`. Here `index` = 1.

Step a: Find the index of the smallest element in `list[1]...list[5]`. See Figure 10-13.

Figure 10-13 Smallest element in the unsorted list is at position 1

Step b: Swap `list[smallestIndex]` with `list[index]`. That is, swap `list[1]` with `list[1]`. Figure 10-14 shows the resulting array.

Figure 10-14   list after swapping list[1] with list[1]

Iteration 3: Sort list[2]...list[5].

Step a: Find the index of the smallest element in list[2]...list[5]. See Figure 10-15.

Figure 10-15   Smallest element in unsorted list is at position 4

Step b: Swap list[smallestIndex] with list[index]. That is, swap list[4] with list[2]. Figure 10-16 shows the resulting array.

Figure 10-16   list after swapping list[4] with list[2]

Iteration 4: Sort list[3]...list[5].

Step a: Find the index of the smallest element in list[3]...list[5]. See Figure 10-17.

Figure 10-17 Smallest element in the unsorted list is at position 3

Step b: Swap `list[smallestIndex]` with `list[index]`. That is, swap `list[3]` with `list[3]`. Figure 10-18 shows the resulting array.

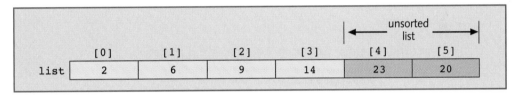

Figure 10-18 `list` after swapping `list[3]` with `list[3]`

10

Iteration 5: Sort `list[4]...list[5]`.

Step a: Find the index of the smallest element in `list[4]...list[5]`. See Figure 10-19.

Figure 10-19 Smallest element in the unsorted list is at position 5

Step b: Swap `list [smallestIndex]` with `list[index]`. That is, swap `list[5]` with `list[4]`. Figure 10-20 shows the resulting array.

	[0]	[1]	[2]	[3]	[4]	[5]
list	2	6	9	14	20	23

Figure 10-20   list after swapping list[4] with list[5]

After 5 iterations of Steps a and b, the list is in order, that is, sorted. Note that the length of the list is 6, but we needed to repeat Steps a and b only 5 times, that is, length − 1 times.

We can now write the method to sort a list. Let's call this method selectionSort. The definition of the method selectionSort is:

```
void selectionSort(int[] list, int length)
{
    int index;
    int smallestIndex;
    int minIndex;
    int temp;

    for(index = 0; index < length - 1; index++)
    {
            //Step a
        smallestIndex = index;

        for(minIndex = index + 1; minIndex < length; minIndex++)
            if(list[minIndex] < list[smallestIndex])
                smallestIndex = minIndex;

            //Step b
        temp = list[smallestIndex];
        list[smallestIndex] = list[index];
        list[index] = temp;
    }
}
```

Sequential Search on an Ordered List

Now that you know how to sort a list, let's rewrite the sequential search and take advantage of a sorted list. Consider the sorted list of seven elements shown in Figure 10-21.

	[0]	[1]	[2]	[3]	[4]	[5]	[6]	[7]	
list	4	12	27	38	45	53	58		. . .

Figure 10-21   Sorted list of seven elements

Suppose that you want to determine whether 38 is in the list. You start the search at the first element of the list. Of course, the search stops at `list[3]`. Now suppose that you want to determine whether 40 is in the list. From the description of the list, it follows that you should not search the list past `list[4]` because `list[4] >= 40`.

From these two cases, it follows that you search the `list` until either you arrive at an item in the list that is greater than or equal to the `searchItem` you are searching for, or until the `list` has no elements left to compare with the `searchItem`. The general form of the sequential search on a sorted list is:

```
found is set to false;

for(loc = 0; loc < listLength; loc++)
    if(list[loc] is greater than or equal to searchItem)
    {
        found is set to true
        exit loop
    }
```

Note that the loop stops (that is, `found` is set to `true`) if you find an element in the `list` that is either greater than or equal to the item for which you are searching. But `found` should be `true` only if the item is equal to some element in the `list`. So you must correctly set the value of `found` outside the loop. The following statement accomplishes this:

```
if(found)
    if(list[loc] == searchItem)
        return loc;
    else
        return -1;
else
        return -1;
```

Now we can complete the definition of the method `seqOrderedSearch` to perform a search on a sorted list.

```
int seqOrderedSearch(int[] list, int listLength, int searchItem)
{
    int loc;                                    //Line 1
    boolean found = false;                      //Line 2

    for(loc = 0; loc < listLength; loc++)       //Line 3
        if(list[loc] >= searchItem)             //Line 4
        {
            found = true;                       //Line 5
            break;                              //Line 6
        }

    if(found)                                   //Line 7
        if(list[loc] == searchItem)             //Line 8
            return loc;                         //Line 9
```

10

```
        else                              //Line 10
            return -1;                     //Line 11
      else                                //Line 12
          return -1;                       //Line 13
}
```

Let's trace this algorithm on the list shown in Figure 10-22.

	[0]	[1]	[2]	[3]	[4]	[5]	[6]	[7]
list	4	18	29	35	44	59	65	98

Figure 10-22 Sorted list of eight elements

The length of the list is 8. So `length = 8`.

Suppose that the item for which you are searching is 35. Therefore, `searchItem = 35`. Before the `for` loop executes, `loc = 0`, and `found = false`. In the following, we trace the execution of the `for` loop, showing the values of `loc`, `found`, and certain list elements during each iteration:

Iteration	loc	found	list[loc]	list[loc] >= searchItem
1	0	false	4	4 >= 35 is false; loc = 1
2	1	false	18	18 >= 35 is false; loc = 2
3	2	false	29	29 >= 35 is false; loc = 3
4	3	false	35	35 >= 35 is true; found = true

During the fourth iteration of the `for` loop, `found` becomes `true` and the `break` statement exits the loop. After the `for` loop, the following statement executes:

```
if(found)                            //Line 7
   if(list[loc] == searchItem)       //Line 8
      return loc;                    //Line 9
   else                              //Line 10
      return -1;                     //Line 11
else                                 //Line 12
   return -1;                        //Line 13
```

Since `found` is `true`, the `if` statement at Line 8 executes. Because `list[loc] = 35` and `searchItem = 35`, the expression

`list[loc] == searchItem`

evaluates to `true` and the `return` statement at Line 9 returns the value of `loc`, which is 3. This was a successful search.

Let us now search for 40. So searchItem = 40. Before the for loop executes, loc = 0, and found = false. In the following, we trace the execution of the for loop, showing the values of loc, found, and certain list elements during each iteration:

Iteration	loc	found	list[loc]	list[loc] >= searchItem
1	0	false	4	4 >= 40 is false; loc = 1
2	1	false	18	18 >= 40 is false; loc = 2
3	2	false	29	29 >= 40 is false; loc = 3
4	3	false	35	35 >= 40 is false; found = 4
5	4	false	44	44 >= 40 is true; found = true

During the fifth iteration of the for loop, found becomes true and the break statement exits the loop. After the for loop, we execute the statements between Lines 7 and 13, that is, the statements:

```
if(found)                             //Line 7
    if(list[loc] == searchItem)       //Line 8
        return loc;                   //Line 9
    else                              //Line 10
        return -1;                    //Line 11
else                                  //Line 12
    return -1;                        //Line 13
```

Because found is true, the if statement at Line 8 executes. Since list[loc] = 44 and searchItem = 40, the expression

```
list[loc] == searchItem
```

evaluates to false, the statement at Line 9 is skipped, and the return statement at Line 11 executes, which returns -1. This was an unsuccessful search.

It can be proven that to determine whether an item is in a list, a sequential search on an ordered list, on average, searches half the list. That is, for a list of 1000 elements (in a successful case) a sequential search, on average, makes 500 comparisons.

Binary Search

A sequential search performs a bit better on a sorted list, but is still not efficient for large lists. It typically still searches about half the list. However, if the list is sorted, you can use another search algorithm, called a **binary search**. A binary search is much faster than a sequential search, but a binary search can only be performed on a sorted list. Binary search uses the divide and conquer technique to search the list. First the search item is compared with the middle element of the list. If the search item is less than the middle element of the list, the search is restricted to the first half of the list; otherwise the second half of the list is searched.

Consider the following sorted list of length = 12, shown in Figure 10-23.

10

Figure 10-23 List of length = 12

Suppose that we want to determine whether 75 is in the list. Initially, the entire list is the search list. See Figure 10-24.

Figure 10-24 Search list `list[0]...list[11]`

First we compare 75 with the middle element, `list[5]` (which is 39), in the list. Since 75 ≠ `list[5]` and 75 > `list[5]`, next we restrict our search in the list `list[6]...list[11]`, as shown in Figure 10-25.

Figure 10-25 Search list `list[6]...list[11]`

The above process is now repeated on the list `list[6]...list[11]`, which is a list of length = 6.

Since we frequently need to determine the middle element of the list, binary search algorithm is usually implemented for array-based lists. To determine the middle element of the list, we add the starting index, `first`, and the ending index, `last`, of the search list and divide by 2 to calculate its index. That is, $mid = \dfrac{first+last}{2}$.

Initially, `first = 0` and (since array index in Java starts at `0` and `length` denotes the number of elements in the list) `last = length - 1`.

The following Java method implements the binary search algorithm. If the search item is found in the list, its location is returned. If the search item is not in the list, `-1` is returned.

```java
int binarySearch(int[] list, int listLength, int searchItem)

{
        int first = 0;
        int last = listLength - 1;
        int mid;

        boolean found = false;

        while(first <= last && !found)
        {
                mid = (first + last) / 2;

                if(list[mid] == searchItem)
                    found = true;
                else
                    if(list[mid] > searchItem)
                        last = mid - 1;
                    else
                        first = mid + 1;
        }

        if(found)
            return mid;
        else
            return -1;
}//end binarySearch
```

Note that in the binary search algorithm, each time through the loop two key (item) comparisons are made, except in the successful case the last time through the loop, when only one item key comparison is made.

Next, we walk through the binary search algorithm on the list shown in Figure 10-26.

	[0]	[1]	[2]	[3]	[4]	[5]	[6]	[7]	[8]	[9]	[10]	[11]
list	4	8	19	25	34	39	45	48	66	75	89	95

Figure 10-26   Sorted list for binary search

The size of the list in Figure 10-26 is 12, that is, length = 12. Suppose that the item for which we are searching is 89, that is, searchItem = 89. Before the while loop executes, first = 0, last = 11, and found = false. In the following, we trace the execution of the while loop, showing the values of first, last, and mid, and number of key comparisons during each iteration:

Iteration	first	last	mid	list[mid]	No. of key comparisons
1	0	11	5	39	2
2	6	11	8	66	2
3	9	11	10	89	1 (found is true)

The item is found at location 10 and the total number of key comparisons is 5.

Next let's search the list for 34, that is, searchItem = 34. Before the while loop executes, first = 0, last = 11, and found = false. In the following, as before, we trace the execution of the while loop, showing the values of first, last, and mid, and number of key comparisons during each iteration:

Iteration	first	last	mid	list[mid]	No. of key comparisons
1	0	11	5	39	2
2	0	4	2	19	2
3	3	4	3	25	2
4	4	4	4	34	1 (found is true)

The item is found at location 4 and the total number of key comparisons is 7.

Let's now search for 22, that is, searchItem = 22. Before the while loop executes, first = 0, last = 11, and found = false. In the following, as before, we trace the execution of the while loop, showing the values of first, last, and mid, and number of key comparisons during each iteration:

Iteration	first	last	mid	list[mid]	No. of key comparisons
1	0	11	5	39	2
2	0	4	2	19	2
3	3	4	3	25	2
4	3	2	The loop stops (since first > last) unsuccessful search		

This is an unsuccessful search. The total number of key comparisons is 6.

From these tracings of the binary search algorithm, you can see that every time you go through the loop, you cut the size of the sublist by half. That is, the size of the sublist you search the next time through the loop is half the size of the previous sublist.

Performance of Binary Search

Suppose that L is a sorted list of 1000 elements, and suppose that you want to determine whether x is in L. Because L is sorted, you can apply the binary search algorithm to search for x. Suppose L is as shown in Figure 10-27.

[0] [1]   [249]   [499]   [999]

Figure 10-27   List L

The first iteration of the while loop searches for x in L[0]...L[999], which is a list of 1000 items. This iteration of the while loop compares x with L[499]. See Figure 10-28.

Figure 10-28   Search list

Suppose that x ≠ L[499]. If x < L[499], the next iteration of the while loop looks for x in L[0]...L[498]; otherwise, the while loop looks for x in L[500]...L[999]. Suppose that x < L[499]. Then the next iteration of the while loop looks for x in L[0]...L[498], which is a list of 499 items, as shown in Figure 10-29.

Figure 10-29   Search list after first iteration

This iteration of the while loop compares x with L[249]. Once again, suppose that x ≠ L[249]. Further suppose that x > L[249]. The next iteration of the while loop searches for x in L[250]...L[498], which is a list of 249 items, as shown in Figure 10-30.

Figure 10-30   Search list after second iteration

From these observations, it follows that every iteration of the `while` loop cuts the size of the search list by half. Since $1000 \approx 1024 = 2^{10}$, the `while` loop will have, at most, 11 iterations to determine whether `x` is in `L`. Because every iteration of the `while` loop makes two item (key) comparisons, that is, `x` is compared twice with the elements of `L`, the binary search will make, at most, 22 comparisons to determine whether `x` is in `L`. On the other hand, recall that a sequential search on average will make 500 comparisons to determine whether `x` is in `L`.

To better understand how fast binary search is compared to sequential search, suppose that `L` is of size `1000000`. Since $1000000 \approx 1048576 = 2^{20}$, it follows that the `while` loop in binary search will have at most `21` iterations to determine whether an element is in `L`. Every iteration of the `while` loop makes two key (that is, item) comparisons. Therefore, to determine whether an element is in `L`, binary search makes at most `42` item comparisons. On the other hand, on average, a sequential search will make `500000` key (item) comparisons to determine whether an element is in `L`.

In general, if `L` is a sorted list of size `n`, to determine whether an element is in `L`, the binary search makes at most `2 * `$\log_2 n$` + 2` key (item) comparisons.

Now that you've learned how arrays can be used to manipulate data, in the next section we describe how to use the `class Vector` to manipulate data and overcome some of the limitations of the arrays with which we've worked so far.

THE `class Vector`

Chapter 9 and the preceding sections of this chapter described how arrays can be used to implement and process lists. One of the limitations of arrays discussed so far is that once you create an array, its size remains fixed. This means that only a fixed number of elements can be stored in an array. Also, inserting an element in the array at a specific position might require that the elements of the array be shifted. Similarly, removing an element from the array also could require shifting the elements of the array, as we typically do not leave empty positions between array positions holding data. Usually, empty positions are at the end of an array.

In addition to arrays, Java provides the `class Vector` to implement a list. Unlike an array, the size of a `Vector` object can grow and shrink during program execution. Therefore, you do not need to worry about the number of data elements. Before describing how a Vector object is used to manage a list, Table 10-1 describes some of the members of the class Vector.

Table 10-1   Various Members of the class Vector

```
protected int elementCount;
protected Object[] elementData;  //Array of references
```

Constructors

```
public Vector()
  //Creates an empty vector of default length 10
```

```
public Vector(int size)
  //Creates an empty vector of the length specified by size
```

Methods

```
public void addElement(Object insertObj)
  //Add the object insertObj at the end.
```

```
public void insertElementAt(Object insertObj, int index)
  //Insert the object insertObj at the position specified by index.
  //If index is out of range, this method throws
  //ArrayIndexOutOfBoundsException.
```

```
public Object clone()
  //Returns a copy of the vector
```

```
public boolean contains(Object obj)
  //Returns true if the Vector object contains the element specified
  //by obj; otherwise it returns false.
```

```
public void copyInto(Object[] dest)
  //Copy the elements of this vector into the array dest.
```

```
public Object elementAt(int index)
  //Returns the element of the vector at location specified by index
```

```
public Object firstElement()
  //Returns the first element of the vector
  //If the vector is empty, the method throws NoSuchElementException.
```

```
public Object lastElement()
  //Returns the last element of the vector
  //If the vector is empty, the method throws NoSuchElementException.
```

```
public int indexOf(Object obj)
  //Returns the position of the first occurrence of the element
  //specified by obj in the vector
  //If obj is not in the vector, the method returns -1.
```

10

Table 10-1 Various Members of the `class` `Vector` (continued)

Methods

```
public int indexOf(Object obj, int index)
    //Starting at index, the method returns the position of the
    //first occurrence of the element specified by obj in the vector.
    //If item is not in the vector, the method returns -1.
```

```
public boolean isEmpty()
    //Returns true if the vector is empty; otherwise it returns false.
```

```
public int lastIndexOf(Object obj)
    //Starting at the last element, using a backward search, this
    //method returns the position of the first occurrence of the
    //element specified by obj in the vector.
    //If obj is not in the vector, the method returns -1.
```

```
public int lastIndexOf(Object item, int index)
    //Starting at the position specified by index and using a backward
    //search, this method returns the position of the first occurrence
    //of the element specified by obj in the vector.
    //If item is not in the vector, the method returns -1.
```

```
public void removeAllElements()
    //Removes all elements of the vector.
```

```
public boolean removeElement(Object obj)
    //If an element specified by obj exists in the list, the element
    //is removed and the value true is returned; otherwise the value
    //false is returned.
```

```
public void removeElementAt(int index)
    //If an element at position specified by index exists, it is
    //removed from the vector.
    //If index is out of range, this method throws
    //ArrayIndexOutOfBoundsException.
```

```
public void setElementAt(Object obj, int index)
    //The element specified by obj is stored at position specified by
    //index.
    //If index is out of range, this method throws
    //ArrayIndexOutOfBoundsException.
```

```
public int size()
    //Returns the number of elements in the vector
```

```
public String toString()
    //Returns a string representation of this vector
```

From Table 10-1, it follows that every element of a **Vector** object is a reference variable of the type **Object**. In Java, **Object** is a predefined class, and a reference variable of **Object** type can store the address of any object. Because every component of a **Vector** object is a reference, to add an element into a **Vector** object, you must first create the appropriate object and store the data into that object. You can then store the address of the object holding the data into a **Vector** object element. Because every string in Java is considered a **String** object, we will illustrate some of the operations on a **Vector** object using string data.

Consider the following statement:

```
Vector stringList = new Vector();        //Line 1
```

This statement declares **stringList** to be a reference variable of the **Vector** type, instantiates an empty **Vector** object, and stores the address of the object into **stringList**. Next consider the following statements:

```
stringList.addElement("Spring");
stringList.addElement("Summer");
stringList.addElement("Fall");
stringList.addElement("Winter");
```

After these statements execute, **stringList** is as shown in Figure 10-31.

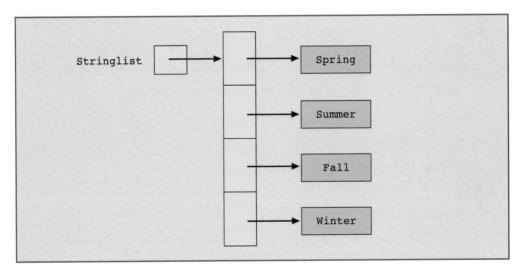

Figure 10-31   **stringList** after adding four strings

The statement

```
System.out.println(stringList);
```

outputs the elements of **stringList** in the following form:

```
[Spring, Summer, Fall, Winter]
```

Now consider the following statement:

```
stringList.addElement("Cool",1);
```

This statement adds the string **"Cool"** at position 1, as shown in Figure 10-32.

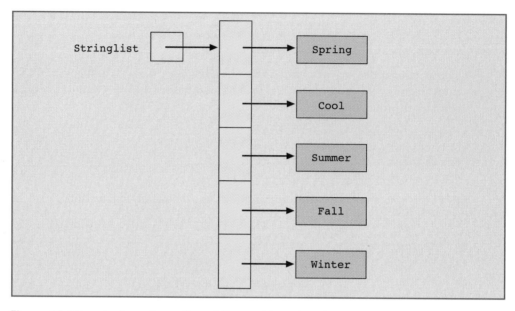

Figure 10-32 **stringList** after adding a string at position 1

Now the output of the statement

```
System.out.println(stringList);
```

is:

```
[Spring, Cool, Summer, Fall, Winter]
```

The **class Vector** is contained in the package **java.util**. Therefore, to use the **class Vector**, your program must include either the statement

```
import java.util.*;
```

or the statement

```
import java.util.Vector;
```

The program in Example 10-1 further illustrates how a **Vector** object works.

Example 10-1

```
//StringVectorExample

import java.io.*;
import java.util.Vector;
```

```java
public class StringVectorExample
{
    public static void main(String[] args)
    {
        Vector stringList = new Vector();                       //Line 1

        System.out.println("Line 2: Empty stringList?: "
                        + stringList.isEmpty());                //Line 2
        System.out.println("Line 3: Size stringList?: "
                        + stringList.size());                   //Line 3
        System.out.println();                                   //Line 4

        stringList.addElement("Spring");                        //Line 5
        stringList.addElement("Summer");                        //Line 6
        stringList.addElement("Fall");                          //Line 7
        stringList.addElement("Winter");                        //Line 8
        stringList.addElement("Sunny");                         //Line 9

        System.out.println("Line 10: **** After adding "
                        + "elements to stringList ****");       //Line 10
        System.out.println("Line 11: Empty stringList?: "
                        + stringList.isEmpty());                //Line 11
        System.out.println("Line 12: Size stringList?: "
                        + stringList.size());                   //Line 12
        System.out.println("Line 13: stringList: "
                        + stringList);                          //Line 13

        System.out.println("Line 14: stringList contains Fall?: "
                        + stringList.contains("Fall"));         //Line 14
        System.out.println();                                   //Line 15

        stringList.insertElementAt("Cool", 1);                  //Line 16
        System.out.println("Line 17: **** After adding an "
                        + "element at position 1 ****");        //Line 17
        System.out.println("Line 18: stringList: "
                        + stringList);                          //Line 18

        System.out.println();                                   //Line 19

        stringList.removeElement("Fall");                       //Line 20
        stringList.removeElementAt(2);                          //Line 21
        System.out.println("Line 22: **** After the remove "
                        + "operations ****");                   //Line 22
        System.out.println("Line 23: stringList: "
                        + stringList);                          //Line 23
        System.out.println("Line 24: Size stringList?: "
                        + stringList.size());                   //Line 24
```

10

```
        System.out.println("Line 25: indexOf(\"Sunny\"): "
                        + stringList.indexOf("Sunny"));   //Line 25
    }
}
```

Sample Run:

```
Line 2: Empty stringList?: true
Line 3: Size stringList?: 0

Line 10: **** After adding elements to stringList ****
Line 11: Empty stringList?: false
Line 12: Size stringList?: 5
Line 13: stringList: [Spring, Summer, Fall, Winter, Sunny]
Line 14: stringList contains Fall?: true

Line 17: **** After adding an element at position 1 ****
Line 18: stringList: [Spring, Cool, Summer, Fall, Winter, Sunny]

Line 22: **** After the remove operations ****
Line 23: stringList: [Spring, Cool, Winter, Sunny]
Line 24: Size stringList?: 4
Line 25: indexOf("Sunny"): 3
```

 In this example we restricted a Vector object to manage elements of the same type. In the program in Example 10-1, the object stringList manages strings. As stated earlier, every element of a Vector object is a reference that can point to any object, and the same Vector object can be used to manage various types of objects. For example, see Exercise 7 at the end of this chapter.

Primitive Data Types and the class Vector

As described in the preceding section, every component of a Vector object is a reference. Therefore, values of primitive data types cannot be directly assigned to a Vector element. You must first wrap the primitive data type element into an appropriate wrapper class, such as the class Integer for int values.

Suppose that you have the declaration:

```
Vector list = new Vector();
```

The following statements create Integer objects with int values 13 and 25, and the Integer objects are assigned to list:

```
list.addElement(new Integer(13));
list.addElement(new Integer(25));
```

PROGRAMMING EXAMPLE: ELECTION RESULTS

The election for president of the student council of your local university is about to be held. To ensure confidentiality, the election committee chair wants to computerize the voting. The chair is looking for someone to write a program to analyze the data and report the winner. Let's write a program to help the election committee.

The university has four major divisions, and each division has several departments. For election purposes, the four divisions are labeled Region 1, Region 2, Region 3, and Region 4. Each department in each division holds its own voting and directly reports the votes received by each candidate to the election committee. The voting is reported in the form:

```
candidate_name region# number_of_votes_for_this_candidate
```

The election committee wants the output in the following tabular form:

```
---------------Election Results--------------

Candidate                 Votes
Name        Region1 Region2 Region3 Region4 Total
----        ------- ------- ------- ------- ------
Balto          0       0       0      272    272
Doc           25      71      156      97    349
Donald       110     158       0        0    268
.
.
.


Winner: ???,  Votes Received: ???
Total votes polled: ???
```

The names of the candidates in the output must be in alphabetical order.

For this program, we assume that six candidates are running for student council president. This program can be enhanced to any number of candidates.

The data is provided in two files. One file, `candData.txt`, consists of the names of candidates. The names of the candidates in the file are in no particular order. In the second file, `voteData.txt`, each line consists of voting results in the following form:

```
candidateName regionNumber numberOfVotesForTheCandidate
```

That is, each line in the file `voteData.txt` consists of the candidate name, region number, and the votes received by the candidate in this region. There is one entry per line. For example, the input file containing voting data looks like:

```
Donald 1 23
Pluto 2 56
```

```
Doc 1 25
Pluto 4 23
   .
   .
   .
```

The first line indicates that Donald received 23 votes from region 1.

Input Two files, one containing the candidates' names and the other containing the voting data as described previously.

Output Election results in a tabular form as described previously, and the winner.

Problem Analysis and Algorithm Design

From the output, it is clear that the program must organize the voting data by regions. The program must also calculate the total votes received by each candidate, and the total votes polled for the election. Furthermore, the names of the candidates must appear in alphabetical order.

Since the data type of a candidate's name (which is a string) and the data type of the number of votes (which is an integer) are different, we need separate arrays—one to hold the candidates' names and the other to hold the voting data. The array to hold the names of the candidates is a one-dimensional array, and each component of this array is a string. Instead of using one two-dimensional array to hold the voting data, we will use a two-dimensional array to hold the next four columns of the output, that is, the votes by region data, and we will use a one-dimensional array to hold the total votes received by each candidate. These three arrays are parallel arrays. See Figure 10-33.

Figure 10-33   Parallel arrays: candidatesName, votesByRegion, and totalVotes

The data in the first row of these three arrays correspond to the candidate whose name is stored in the first row of the array candidatesName, and so on. In the voting by region array, column 1 corresponds to Region 1, column 2 corresponds to Region 2, and so on. Recall that, in Java, an array index starts at 0. Therefore, if the name of this array in the program is, say, `votesByRegion`, `votesByRegion[ ][ 0 ]` refers to the first column and so Region 1, and so on.

For easy reference, for the rest of the discussion, assume that in the program we are writing, the name of the candidates' name array is `candidatesName`, the name of the voting by region array is `votesByRegion`, and the name of the array total votes is `totalVotes`.

The first thing we must do in this program is read the candidates' names from the input file `candData.txt` into the array `candidatesName`. Once the candidates' names are stored in the array `candidatesName`, we must sort this array.

Next we process the voting data. Every entry in the file `voteData.txt` contains `candidatesName`, `regionNumber`, and `numberOfVotesForTheCandidate`. To process this entry, we find the appropriate entry in the array `votesByRegion` and update this entry by adding `numberOfVotesForTheCandidate` to this entry. Therefore, it follows that array `votesByRegion` must be initialized to zero. Processing voting data is described in detail later in this section.

After processing the voting data, the next step is to calculate the total votes received by each candidate. This is accomplished by adding the votes received in each region. Therefore, we must initialize the array `totalVotes` to zero. Finally, we output the results as shown earlier.

This discussion translates into the following algorithm:

1. Read the candidates' names into the array `candidatesName`.
2. Sort the array `candidatesName`.
3. Process the voting data.
4. Calculate the total votes received by each candidate.
5. Output the results as shown earlier.

Notice that the arrays `votesByRegion` and `totalVotes` are automatically initialized when they are created. Since input data is provided in two separate files, in this program we must open two files. We open both input files in the method `main`.

To implement the preceding five steps, the program consists of several methods, which are described next.

Method `getCandidatesName` This method reads data from the input file `candData.txt` and fills the array `candidatesName`. The input file is opened in the method `main`. Note that this method has two parameters: a parameter corresponding to the input file and a parameter corresponding to the array `candidatesName`. Essentially, this method is:

```
public static void getCandidatesName(BufferedReader inp,
                                String[] cNames) throws IOException
{
    int i;

    for(i = 0; i < cNames.length; i++)
        cNames[i] = inp.readLine();
}
```

After a call to this method, the arrays to hold the data are as shown in Figure 10-34.

candidatesName		votesByRegion					totalVotes	
			[0]	[1]	[2]	[3]		
[0]	Goofy	[0]	0	0	0	0	[0]	0
[1]	Mickey	[1]	0	0	0	0	[1]	0
[2]	Donald	[2]	0	0	0	0	[2]	0
[3]	Pluto	[3]	0	0	0	0	[3]	0
[4]	Doc	[4]	0	0	0	0	[4]	0
[5]	Balto	[5]	0	0	0	0	[5]	0

Figure 10-34   Arrays `candidatesName`, `votesByRegion`, and `totalVotes` after reading candidates' names

Method `sortCandidatesName`   This method uses a selection sort algorithm (as discussed in this chapter) to sort the array `candidatesName`. This method has only one parameter: the parameter corresponding to the array `candidatesName`. Essentially, this method is:

```
public static void sortCandidatesName(String[] cNames)
{
    int i, j;
    int min;
    String temp;

    //selection sort
    for(i = 0; i < cNames.length - 1; i++)
    {
        min = i;

        for(j = i + 1; j < cNames.length; j++)
            if(cNames[j].compareTo(cNames[min]) < 0)
                min = j;

        temp = cNames[i];
        cNames[i] = cNames[min];
        cNames[min] = temp;
    }
```

```
        System.gc();
}
```
After a call to this method, the arrays are as shown in Figure 10-35.

candidatesName		votesByRegion					totalVotes	
			[0]	[1]	[2]	[3]		
[0]	Balto	[0]	0	0	0	0	[0]	0
[1]	Doc	[1]	0	0	0	0	[1]	0
[2]	Donald	[2]	0	0	0	0	[2]	0
[3]	Goofy	[3]	0	0	0	0	[3]	0
[4]	Mickey	[4]	0	0	0	0	[4]	0
[5]	Pluto	[5]	0	0	0	0	[5]	0

Figure 10-35   Arrays `candidatesName`, `votesByRegion`, and `totalVotes` after sorting names

Process Voting Data   Processing voting data is quite straightforward. Each entry in the file `voteData.txt` is in the following form:

`candidatesName regionNumber numberOfVotesForTheCandidate`

The general algorithm to process the voting data follows.

For each entry in the file `voteData.txt`:
   a. Tokenize the input line and get `candidatesName, regionNumber`, and `numberOfVotesForTheCandidate`.
   b. Find the row number in the array `candidatesName` corresponding to this candidate. This will give the corresponding row number in the array `votesByRegion` for this candidate.
   c. Find the column in the array `votesByRegion` corresponding to this `regionNumber`.
   d. Update the appropriate entry in the array `votesByRegion` by adding `numberOfVotesForTheCandidate`.

Step b requires us to search the array `candidatesName` to find the location, that is, row number, of a particular candidate. Since the array `candidatesName` is sorted, we can use the binary search algorithm to find the row number corresponding to a particular candidate. Therefore, the program also includes the method `binSearch` to implement the binary search algorithm on the array `candidatesName`. We will write the definition of the method `binSearch` shortly. First we discuss how to update the array `votesByRegion`.

Suppose that the three arrays are as shown in Figure 10-36.

Figure 10-36 Arrays `candidatesName`, `votesByRegion`, and `totalVotes`

Further suppose that the next entry read from the input file is:

`Donald 2 35`

Next we locate the row in the preceding grid that corresponds to this candidate. To find the row, we search the array `candidatesName` to find the row that corresponds to this name. Now `Donald` corresponds to row number 2 in the array `candidatesName`, as shown in Figure 10-37.

Figure 10-37 Position of `Donald` and `region = 2`

To process this entry, we access row number 2 of the array `votesByRegion`. Since `Donald` received 35 votes from Region 2, we access row 2 and column number 1, that is, `votesByRegion[2][1]`, and update this entry by adding 35 to its previous value. The following statement accomplishes this:

`votesByRegion[2][1] = votesByRegion[2][1] + 35;`

After processing this entry, the three arrays are as shown in Figure 10-38.

Figure 10-38   Arrays `candidatesName`, `votesByRegion`, and `totalVotes` after processing the entry `Donald 2 35`

We now describe the method `binSearch` and the method `processVotes` to process the voting data.

Method `binSearch`   This method implements the binary search algorithm on the array `candidatesName`. It is similar to the method `binarySearch`. Its definition is:

```
public static int binSearch(String[] cNames, String name)
{
    int first, last, mid = 0;
    boolean found;

    first = 0;
    last = cNames.length - 1;
    found = false;

    while(!found && first <= last)
    {
        mid = (first + last) / 2;

        if(cNames[mid].equals(name))
            found = true;
        else
            if(cNames[mid].compareTo(name) > 0)
                last = mid - 1;
            else
                first = mid + 1;
    }

    if(found)
        return mid;
```

```
        else
           return -1;
    }
```

Method processVotes This method processes the voting data. Clearly, this method must have access to the arrays `candidatesName` and `votesByRegion`, and to the input file, `voteData.txt`. Thus, this method has three parameters: a parameter to access the input file `voteData.txt`, a parameter corresponding to the array `candidatesName`, and a parameter corresponding to the array `votesByRegion`. The definition of this method is:

```
public static void processVotes(BufferedReader inp,
                            String[] cNames, int[][] vbRegion)
                                    throws IOException
{
    String candName;
    int region;
    int noOfVotes;
    int loc;
    String inputLine;
    StringTokenizer tokenizer;

    inputLine = inp.readLine();                              //Step a

    while(inputLine != null)
    {
        tokenizer = new StringTokenizer(inputLine);
        candName = tokenizer.nextToken();                    //Step a
        region =
            Integer.parseInt(tokenizer.nextToken()); //Step a
        noOfVotes =
            Integer.parseInt(tokenizer.nextToken()); //Step a

        loc =  binSearch(cNames,candName);                   //Step b

        if(loc != -1)
           vbRegion[loc][region - 1] = vbRegion[loc][region - 1]
                               + noOfVotes; //Steps c and d
        inputLine = inp.readLine();                          //Step a
    }
}
```

Calculate Total Votes (Method addRegionsVote) After processing the voting data, the next step is to calculate the total votes for each candidate. Suppose that after processing the voting data, the arrays are as shown in Figure 10-39.

candidatesName	votesByRegion				totalVotes
	[0]	[1]	[2]	[3]	
[0] Balto	[0] 0	0	0	272	[0] 0
[1] Doc	[1] 25	71	156	97	[1] 0
[2] Donald	[2] 110	158	0	0	[2] 0
[3] Goofy	[3] 0	34	0	0	[3] 0
[4] Mickey	[4] 112	141	156	89	[4] 0
[5] Pluto	[5] 285	56	0	46	[5] 0

Figure 10-39   Arrays `candidatesName`, `votesByRegion`, and `totalVotes` after processing the voting data

After calculating the total votes received by each candidate, the three arrays are as shown in Figure 10-40.

candidatesName	votesByRegion				totalVotes
	[0]	[1]	[2]	[3]	
[0] Balto	[0] 0	0	0	272	[0] 272
[1] Doc	[1] 25	71	156	97	[1] 349
[2] Donald	[2] 110	158	0	0	[2] 268
[3] Goofy	[3] 0	34	0	0	[3] 34
[4] Mickey	[4] 112	141	156	89	[4] 498
[5] Pluto	[5] 285	56	0	46	[5] 387

Figure 10-40   Arrays `candidatesName`, `votesByRegion`, and `totalVotes` after calculating the total votes received by each candidate

To calculate the total votes received by each candidate, we add the contents of each row in the `votesByRegion` array and store the sum in the corresponding row in the `totalVotes` array. This is accomplished by the method `addRegionsVote`, which is described next.

The method `addRegionsVote` calculates the total votes received by each candidate. This method must access the arrays `votesByRegion` and `totalVotes`. This method has two parameters: a parameter corresponding to the array `votesByRegion`, and a parameter corresponding to the array `totalVotes`. The definition of this method is:

```
public static void addRegionsVote(int[][] vbRegion, int[] tVotes)
{
    int i,j;
    for(i = 0; i < tVotes.length; i++)
        for(j = 0; j < vbRegion[0].length; j++)
            tVotes[i] = tVotes[i] + vbRegion[i][j];
}
```

The remaining methods to get the desired output are described next.

Method `printHeading` The method `printHeading` outputs the first four lines of input, so it contains certain output statements. The definition of this method is:

```
public static void printHeading()
{
    System.out.println("  ---------------Election Results"
                    + "--------------\n");
    System.out.println("Candidate\t\t   Votes");
    System.out.println("Name\t   Region1 Region2 Region3 "
                    + "Region4 Total");
    System.out.println("----\t   ------- ------- ------- "
                    + "------- ------");
}
```

Method `printResults` The method `printResults` outputs the remaining lines of the output. Clearly this method must have access to each of the three arrays. (Note that each array has the same number of rows.) Thus, this method has three parameters. Suppose that the parameter `cName` corresponds to `candidatesName`, the parameter `vbRegion` corresponds to `votesByRegion`, and the parameter `tVotes` corresponds to `totalVotes`.

Further suppose that the variable `sumVotes` holds the total votes polled for the election, the variable `largestVotes` holds the largest number of votes received by a candidate, and the variable `winLoc` holds the index of the winning candidate in the array `candidatesName`. The algorithm for this method is:

1. Initialize `sumVotes`, `largestVotes`, and `winLoc` to 0.
2. For each row in each array:
   a. `if(largestVotes < tVotes[i])`
      ```
      {
          largestVotes = tVotes[i];
          winLoc = i;
      }
      ```
   b. `sumVotes = sumVotes + tVotes[i];`
   c. Output data from corresponding rows of each array.
3. Output the final lines of output.

The definition of this method is:

```
public static void printResults(String[] cNames,
                                int[][] vbRegion, int[] tVotes)
{
    int i, j;
    int largestVotes = 0;                          //Step i
    int winLoc = 0;                                //Step i
    int sumVotes = 0;                              //Step i

    for(i = 0; i < tVotes.length; i++)             //Step ii
    {
        if(largestVotes < tVotes[i])               //Step ii.a
        {
            largestVotes = tVotes[i];
            winLoc = i;
        }

        sumVotes = sumVotes + tVotes[i];           //Step ii.b

                                                   //Step ii.c
        System.out.print(cNames[i] + " \t    ");

        for(j = 0; j < vbRegion[0].length; j++)
            System.out.print(vbRegion[i][j] + "\t    ");
        System.out.println(tVotes[i]);
    }
                                                   //Step iii
    System.out.println("\n\n\nWinner: " + cNames[winLoc]
                   + ",  Votes Received: " + tVotes[winLoc]);
    System.out.println("Total votes polled: " + sumVotes);
}
```

Main Algorithm: method main   Suppose that the variables in the method **main** are:

```
String[] candidatesName = new String[noOfCandidates]; //array
                                     //to store candidates' names
int[][] votesByRegion =
            new int [noOfCandidates][noOfRegions]; //array to
                                    //hold voting data by region
int[] totalVotes = new int [noOfCandidates];  //array to hold
                                      //total votes received by
                                      //each candidate

BufferedReader infile;   //input file variable
```

Further suppose that candidate names are in the file **candData.txt**, and the voting data is in the file **voteData.txt**.

The algorithm for **main** is:

1. Declare and initialize the variables and the objects.
2. Open the input file **candData.txt**.
3. Read the data from the file **candData.txt** into the array **candidatesName**.
4. Sort the array **candidatesName**.
5. Open the input file **voteData.txt**.
6. Process the voting data and store the results in the array **votesByRegion**.
7. Calculate the total votes received by each candidate and store the results in the array **totalVotes**.
8. Print the heading.
9. Print the results.

Complete Program Listing

```
//ElectionResults


import java.io.*;
import java.util.*;

public class ElectionResults
{
    final static int noOfCandidates = 6;
    final static int noOfRegions = 4;

    public static void main (String[] args) throws
                             FileNotFoundException,
                             IOException
    {
                                                         //Step 1
        String[] candidatesName = new String[noOfCandidates];
        int[][] votesByRegion = new int[noOfCandidates][noOfRegions];
        int[] totalVotes = new int[noOfCandidates];

        BufferedReader infile = new
            BufferedReader(new FileReader("a:\\candData.txt"));
                                                         //Step 2

        getCandidatesName(infile, candidatesName);       //Step 3
        sortCandidatesName(candidatesName);              //Step 4

        infile = null;
        infile = new
            BufferedReader(new FileReader("a:\\voteData.txt"));
                                                         //Step 5
```

```
    processVotes(infile, candidatesName, votesByRegion);//Step 6
    addRegionsVote(votesByRegion, totalVotes);            //Step 7

    printHeading();                                       //Step 8
    printResults(candidatesName,votesByRegion,
                 totalVotes);                             //Step 9
}

public static void getCandidatesName(BufferedReader inp,
                        String[] cNames) throws IOException
{
    int i;

    for(i = 0; i < cNames.length; i++)
        cNames[i] = inp.readLine();
}

public static void sortCandidatesName(String[] cNames)
{
    int i, j;
    int min;
    String temp;

        //selection sort
    for(i = 0; i < cNames.length - 1; i++)
    {
        min = i;

        for(j = i + 1; j < cNames.length; j++)
            if(cNames[j].compareTo(cNames[min]) < 0)
                min = j;

        temp = cNames[i];
        cNames[i] = cNames[min];
        cNames[min] = temp;
    }

    System.gc();
}

public static int binSearch(String[] cNames, String name)
{
    int first, last, mid = 0;
    boolean found;

    first = 0;
    last = cNames.length - 1;
    found = false;
```

```
        while(!found && first <= last)
        {
            mid = (first + last) / 2;

            if(cNames[mid].equals(name))
                found = true;
            else
                if(cNames[mid].compareTo(name) > 0)
                    last = mid - 1;
                else
                    first = mid + 1;
        }

        if(found)
            return mid;
        else
            return -1;
    }

    public static void processVotes(BufferedReader inp,
                        String[] cNames, int[][] vbRegion)
                                        throws IOException
    {
        String candName;
        int region;
        int noOfVotes;
        int loc;
        String inputLine;
        StringTokenizer tokenizer;

        inputLine = inp.readLine();

        while(inputLine != null)
        {
            tokenizer = new StringTokenizer(inputLine);
            candName = tokenizer.nextToken();
            region =
                Integer.parseInt(tokenizer.nextToken());
            noOfVotes =
                Integer.parseInt(tokenizer.nextToken());

            loc = binSearch(cNames,candName);

            if(loc != -1)
                vbRegion[loc][region - 1] = vbRegion[loc][region - 1]
                                        + noOfVotes;
            inputLine = inp.readLine();
```

```java
    }
}

public static void addRegionsVote(int[][] vbRegion,
                                  int[] tVotes)
{
    int i,j;

    for(i = 0; i < tVotes.length; i++)
        for(j = 0; j < vbRegion[0].length; j++)
            tVotes[i] = tVotes[i] + vbRegion[i][j];
}

public static void printHeading()
{
    System.out.println("  --------------Election Results"
                + "--------------\n");
    System.out.println("Candidate\t\t   Votes");
    System.out.println("Name\t   Region1 Region2 Region3 "
                + "Region4 Total");
    System.out.println("----\t   ------- ------- ------- "
                + "------- ------");
}

public static void printResults(String[] cNames,
                                int[][] vbRegion, int[] tVotes)
{
    int i, j;
    int largestVotes = 0;
    int winLoc = 0;
    int sumVotes = 0;

    for(i = 0; i < tVotes.length; i++)
    {
        if(largestVotes < tVotes[i])
        {
            largestVotes = tVotes[i];
            winLoc = i;
        }

        sumVotes = sumVotes + tVotes[i];

        System.out.print(cNames[i] + " \t    ");
        for(j = 0; j < vbRegion[0].length; j++)
            System.out.print(vbRegion[i][j] + "\t    ");
        System.out.println(tVotes[i]);
    }
```

```
            System.out.println("\n\n\nWinner: " + cNames[winLoc]
                        + ",   Votes Received: " + tVotes[winLoc]);
            System.out.println("Total votes polled: " + sumVotes);
    }
}
```

Sample Run:

```
---------------Election Results---------------

Candidate                  Votes
Name        Region1 Region2 Region3 Region4 Total
----        ------- ------- ------- ------- ------
Balto         0       0       0      272     272
Doc          25      71      156     97      349
Donald      110      158      0       0      268
Goofy         0      34       0       0       34
Mickey      112      141     156     89      498
Pluto       285      56       0       46     387


Winner: Mickey,  Votes Received: 498
Total votes polled: 1808
```

Input Files:

candData.txt   **voteData.txt**

```
Goofy        Goofy 2 34
Mickey       Mickey 1 56
Donald       Donald 2 56
Pluto        Pluto 1 78
Doc          Doc 4 29
Balto        Balto 4 78
             Mickey 2 63
             Donald 1 23
             Pluto 2 56
             Doc 1 25
             Pluto 4 23
             Doc 4 12
             Balto 4 82
             Mickey 3 67
             Donald 2 67
             Doc 3 67
             Balto 4 23
             Mickey 1 56
             Donald 2 35
             Pluto 1 27
             Doc 2 34
```

```
                    Pluto 4 23
                    Mickey 4 89
                    Pluto 1 23
                    Doc 3 89
                    Mickey 3 89
                    Pluto 1 67
                    Doc 2 37
                    Balto 4 89
                    Mickey 2 78
                    Donald 1 87
                    Pluto 1 90
                    Doc 4 56
```

THE class String (REVISITED)

Chapter 3 introduced the **class String** and discussed how to manipulate strings using various string methods. You learned about the **String** method **substring** in detail and also how the **String** methods **length**, **charAt**, and **indexOf** work in a program. As you now know, the **class String** is a very important class in Java. This section introduces some other **String** methods.

Table 3-1 (in Chapter 3) described various **String** methods. This section further illustrates how the methods described in Table 3-1 work. Table 10-2 expands on Table 3-1, and shows additional **String** methods.

Table 10-2 Additional String Methods

```
String(String str)
    //Constructor: Creates a string object and initializes the string
    //object with characters specified by str.
char charAt(int index)
    //Returns the character at the position specified by index.
int indexOf(char ch)
    //Returns the index of the first occurrence of the character
    //specified by ch; if the character specified by ch does not
    //appear in the string, it returns -1.
int indexOf(char ch, int pos)
    //Returns the index of the first occurrence of the character
    //specified by ch; the parameter pos specifies from where to begin
    //the search; if the character specified by ch does not
    //appear in the string, it returns -1.
```

Table 10-2 Additional `String` Methods (continued)

```
int indexOf(String str)
  //Returns the index of the first occurrence of the string
  //specified by str; if the string specified by str does not
  //appear in the string, it returns -1.
```

```
int indexOf(String str, int pos)
  //Returns the index of the first occurrence of the String
  //specified by str; the parameter pos specifies where to begin
  //the search; if the string specified by str does not appear
  //in the string, it returns -1.
```

```
int compareTo(String str)
  //Compares two strings character by character.
  //Returns a negative value if this string is less than str.
  //Returns 0 if this string is the same as str.
  //Returns a positive value if this string is greater than str.
```

```
String concat(String str)
  //Returns the strings that is this string concatenated with str
```

```
boolean equals(String str)
  //Returns true if this string is the same as str.
```

```
int length()
  //Returns the length of this string.
```

```
String replace(char charToBeReplaced, char charReplacedWith)
  //Returns the string in which every occurrence of
  //charToBeReplaced is replaced with charReplaced.
```

```
String substring(int startIndex, int endIndex)
  //Returns the string which is a substring of this string
  //starting at startIndex until endIndex - 1.
```

```
String toLowerCase()
  //Returns the string that is the same as this string except that
  //all uppercase letters of this string are replaced with
  //their equivalent lowercase letters.
```

```
String toUpperCase()
  //Returns the string that is the same as this string except
  //that all lowercase letters of this string are replaced with
  //their equivalent uppercase letters.
```

```
boolean startsWith(String str)
  //Returns true if the string begins with the string specified by
  //str; otherwise, this methods returns false.
```

```
boolean endsWith(String str)
  //Returns true if the string ends with the string specified by str;
  //otherwise, this methods returns false.
```

```
boolean regionMatches(int ind, String str, int strIndex, int len)
  //Returns true if the substring of str starting at strIndex and
  //length specified by len is the same as the substring of this
  //String object starting at ind and having the same length.
```

Table 10-2 Additional String Methods (continued)

```
boolean regionMatches(boolean ignoreCase, int ind,
                    String str, int strIndex, int len)
   //Returns true if the substring of str starting at strIndex and
   //length specified by len is the same as the substring of this
   //String object starting at ind and having the same length. If
   //ignoreCase is true, then during character comparison case is
   //ignored.
```

The method substring was discussed in Chapter 3. Also, the program in Example 3-4 shows how to use the methods charAt, length, concat, replace, and toUpperCase. The methods compareTo and equals were discussed in Chapter 4.

The next example shows how the String methods startsWith, endsWith, toLowerCase, and regionMatches work.

Example 10-2

Consider the following statements:

```
String sentence;
String str1;
String str2;
String str3;
String str4;

sentence = "It is sunny and warm.";
str1 = "warm.";
str2 = "Programming with Java";
str3 = "sunny";
str4 = "Learning Java Programming is exciting";
```

The effect of these statements is shown in Table 10-3:

Table 10-3 Effect of some String methods

Expression	Effect
sentence.startsWith("It")	Returns true
sentence.startsWith(str1)	Returns false
sentence.endsWith("hot")	Returns false
sentence.endsWith(str1)	Returns true
str2.toLowerCase()	Returns the reference of the string "programming with java"
sentence.regionMatches(6,str3,0,5)	Returns true

Table 10-3 Effect of some `String` methods (continued)

Expression	Effect
`sentence.regionMatches(true,6,"Sunny",0,5)`	Returns `true`
`str4.regionMatches(9,str2,17,4)`	Returns `true`

For the most part, the statements are straightforward. Let's look at the last three statements, which use the method `regionMatches`.

`sentence.regionMatches(6,str3,0,5)`

In this statement, we want to determine whether `str3` appears as a substring in the string `sentence` starting at position 6. Notice that the last three arguments, `str3`, 0, and 5, specify that in `str3` the starting index is 0 and the length of the substring is 5. The substring in `sentence` starting at position 6 and of length 5 matches `str3`. So this expression returns `true`.

The expression

`sentence.regionMatches(true,6,"Sunny",0,5)`

is similar to the previous expression, except that when the substrings are compared, case is ignored, that is, uppercase and lowercase letters are considered the same. Next let's look at the expression:

`str4.regionMatches(9,str2,17,4)`

In this expression, we want to determine if the substring in `str2` starting at position 17 and of length 4 is the same as the substring in `str4` starting at position 9 and of length 4. This expression returns `true` because these substrings are the same.

The following program evaluates the preceding expressions:

```
//String methods - startsWith, endsWith, toLowerCase,
//                  and regionMatches

public class StringMethods
{
  public static void main (String[] args)
  {
    String sentence = "It is cloudy and warm.";          //Line 1
    String str1 = "warm.";                               //Line 2
    String str2 = "Programming with Java";               //Line 3
    String str3 = "cloudy";                              //Line 4
    String str4 = "Learning Java Programming is exciting"; //Line 5
```

```
        System.out.println("Line 6: sentence = \""
                        + sentence + "\"");                    //Line 6
        System.out.println("Line 7: str1 = \""
                        + str1 + "\"");                        //Line 7

        System.out.println("Line 8: sentence starts with It?: "
                        + sentence.startsWith("It"));          //Line 8
        System.out.println("Line 9: sentence starts with str1?: "
                        + sentence.startsWith(str1));          //Line 9

        System.out.println("Line 10: sentence in lower case = \""
                        + sentence.toLowerCase() + "\"");      //Line 10

        System.out.println("Line 11: sentence ends with hot: "
                        + sentence.endsWith("hot"));           //Line 11
        System.out.println("Line 12: sentence ends with str1: "
                        + sentence.endsWith(str1));            //Line 12

        System.out.println("Line 13: str2 = \""
                        + str2 + "\"");                        //Line 13
        System.out.println("Line 14: str2 in lowercase: "
                        + str2.toLowerCase());                 //Line 14
        System.out.println("Line 15: str3 = \""
                        + str3 + "\"");                        //Line 15

        System.out.println("Line 16: "
                + "sentence.regionMatches(6,str3,0,6): "
                + sentence.regionMatches(6,str3,0,6));         //Line 16
        System.out.println("Line 17: "
            + "sentence.regionMatches(true,6,\"Cloudy\",0,6): "
          + sentence.regionMatches(true,6,"Cloudy",0,6));      //Line 17

        System.out.println("Line 18: str4 = \""
                        + str4 + "\"");                        //Line 18
        System.out.println("Line 19: "
                + "str4.regionMatches(9,str2,17,4): "
                + str4.regionMatches(9,str2,17,4));            //Line 19
    }
}
```

10

Output:

```
Line 6: sentence = "It is cloudy and warm."
Line 7: str1 = "warm."
Line 8: sentence starts with It?: true
Line 9: sentence starts with str1?: false
Line 10: sentence in lower case = "it is cloudy and warm."
Line 11: sentence ends with hot: false
Line 12: sentence ends with str1: true
Line 13: str2 = "Programming with Java"
```

```
Line 14: str2 in lowercase: programming with java
Line 15: str3 = "cloudy"
Line 16: sentence.regionMatches(6,str3,0,6): true
Line 17: sentence.regionMatches(true,6,"Cloudy",0,6): true
Line 18: str4 = "Learning Java Programming is exciting"
Line 19: str4.regionMatches(9,str2,17,4): true
```

The **class String** also contains the following overloaded **static** methods:

```
public static String valueOf(boolean b)
public static String valueOf(char ch)
public static String valueOf(int num)
public static String valueOf(long num)
public static String valueOf(double decNum)
public static String valueOf(float decNum)
```

The method **valueOf** returns a string representation of its parameter. Because this is a **static** method, it can be called by using the class name, the dot operator, and the method name. For example:

`String.valueOf(true)`	returns	`"true"`
`String.valueOf('A')`	returns	`"A"`
`String.valueOf(4567)`	returns	`"4567"`
`String.valueOf(16.78)`	returns	`"16.78"`

PROGRAMMING EXAMPLE: PIG LATIN STRINGS

In this programming example, we write a program that prompts the user to input a string and then outputs the string in pig Latin form. The rules for converting a string into pig Latin form follow:

1. If the string begins with a vowel, add the string **"-way"** at the end of the string. For example, the pig Latin form of the string **"eye"** is **"eye-way"**.

2. If the string does not begin with a vowel, first add **"-"** at the end of the string. Then rotate the string one character at a time; that is, move the first character of the string to the end of the string until the first character of the string becomes a vowel. Then add the string **"ay"** at the end. For example, the pig Latin form of the string **"There"** is **"ere-Thay"**.

3. Strings such as **"by"** contain no vowels. In such cases, the letter **y** is considered a vowel. So, for this program the vowels are **a, e, i, o, u, y, A, E, I, O, U,** and **Y.** Therefore, the pig Latin form of **"by"** is **"y-bay"**.

4. Strings such as "1234" contain no vowels. The pig Latin form of the string "1234" is "1234-way". That is, the pig Latin form of a string that has no vowels is the string followed by the string "-way".

Input   Input to the program is a string.

Output   Output of the program is the string in pig Latin form.

Problem Analysis and Algorithm Design

Suppose that str denotes a string. To convert str into pig Latin form, check the first character, str[0], of str. If str[0] is a vowel, add "-way" at the end of str—that is, str = str + "-way".

Suppose that the first character of str, str[0], is not a vowel. First add "-" at the end of the string. Then remove the first character of str and put it at the end of str. Now the second character of str is the first character of str. Checking the first character of str and moving it to the end of str if the first character of str is not a vowel is repeated until either the first character of str is a vowel or all characters of str are processed, in which case str does not contain any vowels.

In this program, we write the method isVowel, to determine whether a character is a vowel; the method rotate, to move the first character of str to the end of str; and the method pigLatinString, to find the pig Latin form of str. The previous discussion translates into the following algorithm:

1. Get str.
2. Find the pig Latin form of str by using the method pigLatinString.
3. Output the pig Latin form of str.

Before writing the main algorithm, each of these methods is described in detail.

Method isVowel   The method isVowel takes a character as a parameter and returns true if the character is a vowel, and false otherwise. The definition of the method isVowel is:

```java
public static boolean isVowel(char ch)
{
    switch(ch)
    {
    case 'A': case 'E':
    case 'I': case 'O':
    case 'U': case 'Y':
    case 'a': case 'e':
    case 'i': case 'o':
    case 'u': case 'y': return true;
    default: return false;
    }
}
```

Method rotate   The method **rotate** takes a string as a parameter, removes the first character of the string, and places it at the end of the string. This is done by extracting the substring starting at position 1 (which is the second character) until the end of the string, and then adding the first character of the string. The new string is returned as the value of this method. Essentially, the definition of the method **rotate** is:

```
public static String rotate(String pStr)
{
    int len = pStr.length();

    String rStr;

    rStr = pStr.substring(1,len) + pStr.charAt(0);

    return rStr;
}
```

Method pigLatinString   The method **pigLatinString** takes a string, **pStr**, as a parameter and returns the pig Latin form of **pStr**. There are three possible cases: **pStr.charAt(0)** is a vowel; **pStr** contains a vowel and the first character of **pStr** is not a vowel; and **pStr** contains no vowels. Suppose that **pStr.charAt(0)** is not a vowel. Move the first character of **pStr** to the end of **pStr**. This process is repeated until either the first character of **pStr** has become a vowel or all characters of **pStr** are checked, in which case **pStr** does not contain any vowels. This discussion translates into the following algorithm:

1. If **pStr.charAt(0)** is a vowel, add **"-way"** at the end of **pStr**.
2. Suppose **pStr.charAt(0)** is not a vowel.
3. Move the first character of **pStr** to the end of **pStr**. The second character of **pStr** becomes the first character of **pStr**. Now **pStr** may or may not contain a vowel. We use a Boolean variable, **foundVowel**, which is set to **true** if **pStr** contains a vowel, and **false** otherwise.
   a. Suppose that **len** denotes the length of **pStr**.
   b. Initialize **foundVowel** to **false**.
   c. If **pStr.charAt(0)** is not a vowel, move **pStr.charAt(0)** to the end of **pStr** by calling the method **rotate**.
   d. Repeat Step b until either the first character of **pStr** becomes a vowel or all characters of **pStr** have been checked.
4. Convert **pStr** into pig Latin form.
5. Return **pStr**.

The definition of the method `pigLatinString` is:

```
public static String pigLatinString(String pStr)
{
    int len;

    boolean foundVowel;

    int counter;

    if(isVowel(pStr.charAt(0)))                     //Step 1
        pStr = pStr + "-way";
    else                                            //Step 2
    {
        pStr = pStr + "-";
        pStr = rotate(pStr);                        //Step 3

        len = pStr.length();                        //Step 3.a
        foundVowel = false;                         //Step 3.b

        for(counter = 1; counter < len - 1; counter++) //Step 3.d
            if(isVowel(pStr.charAt(0)))
            {
                foundVowel = true;
                break;
            }
            else                                    //Step 3.c
                pStr = rotate(pStr);

        if(!foundVowel)                             //Step 4
            pStr = pStr.substring(1,len) + "-way";
        else
            pStr = pStr + "ay";
    }

    return pStr;                                    //Step 5
}
```

Main Algorithm

1. Get the string.
2. Call the method `pigLatinString` to find the pig Latin form of the string.
3. Output the pig Latin form of the string.

```java
//Program PigLatin Strings

import java.io.*;

public class PigLatin
{
    static BufferedReader keyboard =
            new BufferedReader(new InputStreamReader(System.in));

    public static void main(String[] args) throws IOException
    {
        String str;

        System.out.print("Enter a string: ");
        System.out.flush();
        str = keyboard.readLine();
        System.out.println();

        System.out.println("The pig Latin form of " + str
                        + " is: " + pigLatinString(str));
    }

    public static boolean isVowel(char ch)
    {
        switch(ch)
        {
        case 'A': case 'E':
        case 'I': case 'O':
        case 'U': case 'Y':
        case 'a': case 'e':
        case 'i': case 'o':
        case 'u': case 'y': return true;
        default: return false;
        }
    }

    public static String rotate(String pStr)
    {
        int len = pStr.length();

        String rStr;

        rStr = pStr.substring(1,len) + pStr.charAt(0);

        return rStr;
    }
```

```
    public static String pigLatinString(String pStr)
    {
        int len;

        boolean foundVowel;

        int counter;

        if(isVowel(pStr.charAt(0)))              //Step 1
            pStr = pStr + "-way";
        else                                     //Step 2
        {
            pStr = pStr + "-";
            pStr = rotate(pStr);                 //Step 3

            len = pStr.length();                 //Step 3.a
            foundVowel = false;                  //Step 3.b

            for(counter = 1; counter < len - 1; counter++)
                                                 //Step 3.d
                if(isVowel(pStr.charAt(0)))
                {
                    foundVowel = true;
                    break;
                }
                else                             //Step 3.c
                    pStr = rotate(pStr);

            if(!foundVowel)                      //Step 4
                pStr = pStr.substring(1,len) + "-way";
            else
                pStr = pStr + "ay";
        }

        return pStr;                             //Step 5
    }
}
```

Sample Run 1: In this and the following sample runs, the user input is shaded.

Enter a string: Hello

The pig Latin form of Hello is: ello-Hay

Sample Run 2:

Enter a string: Eye

The pig Latin form of Eye is: Eye-way

Sample Run 3:

Enter a string: `123456`

The pig Latin form of 123456 is: 123456-way

QUICK REVIEW

1. A list is a set of elements of the same type.
2. The length of a list is the number of elements in the list.
3. A one-dimensional array is a convenient place to store and process lists.
4. A sequential search algorithm searches the list for a given item starting with the first element in the list. It continues comparing the item with elements in the list until either the item is found, or the list has no more elements left to compare with the search item.
5. On average, a sequential search searches half the list.
6. A sequential search is good only for very short lists.
7. A binary search is much faster than a sequential search.
8. A binary search requires the list elements to be in order, that is, sorted.
9. For a list of length `1024`, to determine whether an item is in the list, a binary search algorithm requires no more than **22** key comparisons.
10. Selection sort sorts the list by finding the smallest (or equivalently largest) element in the list and moving it to the beginning (or end) of the list.
11. In addition to arrays, Java provides the **class Vector** to implement a list.
12. Unlike an array, the size of a **Vector** object can grow and shrink during program execution.
13. The **class String** contains various methods to manipulate a string.

EXERCISES

1. Mark the following statements as true or false.

   a. A sequential search of a list assumes that the list is in ascending order.

   b. A binary search of a list assumes that the list is in sorted order.

   c. A binary search is faster on ordered lists and slower on unordered lists.

   d. A binary search is faster on large lists, but a sequential search is faster on small lists.

    e. Elements of a **Vector** object are sorted.

    f. The **String** method **regionMatches** can be used to determine if two strings have the same substring.

2. Consider the following list:

```
63 45 32 98 46 57 28 100
```

Using a sequential search, how many comparisons are required to determine whether the following items are in the list or not? (Recall that comparisons mean item comparisons, not index comparisons.)

    a. 90

    b. 57

    c. 63

    d. 120

3. Consider the following list:

```
5 12 17 35 46 65 78 85 93 110 115
```

Using a sequential search on ordered lists, how many comparisons are required to determine whether the following items are in the list or not? (Recall that comparisons mean item comparisons, not index comparisons.)

    a. 35

    b. 60

    c. 78

    d. 120

4. Consider the following list:

```
2 10 17 45 49 55 68 85 92 98 110
```

Using the binary search, how many comparisons are required to determine whether the following items are in the list or not? Show the values of **first**, **last**, and **middle** and the number of comparisons after each iteration of the loop.

    a. 15

    b. 49

    c. 98

    d. 99

5. What is the effect of the following statement?

```
Vector list = new Vector();
```

6. Suppose that you have the following **Vector** object **list**:

```
list = ["One", "Two", "Three", "Four"];
```

10

What are the elements of `list` after the following statements execute?

```
list.addElement("Five");
list.insertElementAt("Six", 1);
```

7. Suppose that you have the following `Vector` object `names`:

names = ["Goofy", "Duckey", "Mickey", "Pluto", "Balto"];

What are the elements of `list` after the following statements execute?

```
list.removeElementAt(1);
list.removeElement("Pluto");
```

8. What is the output of the following program?

```
import java.util.Vector;

public class Exercise_8
{
    public static void main(String[] args)
    {
        Vector list = new Vector();

        list.addElement("Hello");
        list.addElement(new Integer(10));
        list.addElement("Happy");
        list.addElement(new Integer(20));
        list.addElement("Sunny");
        list.addElement(new Integer(30));

        System.out.println(list);

        list.insertElementAt("Joy", 2);

        list.removeElement(new Integer(20));
        System.out.println(list);
    }
}
```

9. Suppose that you have the following statements:

```
String str;
String str1 = "programming";
String str2;
String str3;
```

str = "Java programming: from problem analysis to program design";

What is the value of the following expressions?

a. `str.indexOf("analysis")`

b. `str.substring(5, 16)`

c. `str.startsWith("Java")`

d. `str.startsWith("J")`

e. `str.endsWith(".")`

f. `str.regionMatches(6, str1, 0, str1.length())`

g. `str.regionMatches(true, 31, "Analysis", 0, 8)`

PROGRAMMING EXERCISES

1. Write a method, **remove**, that takes three parameters: an array of integers, the length of the array, and an integer, say, **removeItem**. The method should find and delete the first occurrence of **removeItem** in the array. If the value does not exist or the array is empty, output an appropriate message. (Note that after deleting the element, the array size is reduced by 1.) You may assume that the array is unsorted.

2. Write a method, **removeAt**, that takes three parameters: an array of integers, the length of the array, and an integer, say, **index**. The method deletes the array element indicated by **index**. If **index** is out of range or the array is empty, output an appropriate message. (Note that after deleting the element, the array size is reduced by 1.) You may assume that the array is unsorted.

3. Write a method, **removeAll**, that takes three parameters: an array of integers, the length of the array, and an integer, say, **removeItem**. The method should find and delete all occurrences of **removeItem** in the array. If the value does not exist or the array is empty, output an appropriate message. (Note that after deleting the element, the array size will be reduced.) You may assume that the array is unsorted.

4. Redo Programming Exercises 1, 2, and 3 for a sorted array.

5. Write a method, **insertAt**, that takes four parameters: an array of integers; the length of the array; an integer, say, **insertItem**; and an integer, say **index**. The method inserts **insertItem** in the array at the position specified by the **index**. If the **index** is out of range, output an appropriate message. (Note that **index** must be between 0 and **maxSize**, that is, 0 ≤ **index** < **maxSize**.) You may assume that the array is unsorted.

6. Write a version of a sequential search that can be used to search a string **Vector** object. Also write a program to test your algorithm.

7. Write a version of a selection sort that can be used to sort a string **Vector** object. Also write a program to test your algorithm.

8. Write a version of a binary search that can be used to search a string **Vector** object. Also write a program to test your algorithm. (Use the selection sort algorithm you developed in Programming Exercise 7 to sort the Vector.)

9. Redo the Programming Example: Election Results so that the names of the candidates and the total votes are stored in **Vector** objects.

10

10. The Programming Example: Pig Latin Strings converts a string into pig Latin form, but it processes only one word. Rewrite the program so that it can be used to process a text of unspecified length. If a word ends with a punctuation mark, in pig Latin form put the punctuation at the end of the string. For example, the pig Latin form of `Hello:` is `ello-Hay:`. Assume that the text contains the following punctuation marks: `,` (comma), `.` (period), `?` (question mark), `;` (semicolon), and `:` (colon).

INHERITANCE AND COMPOSITION

Classes were introduced in Chapter 8. Using classes, you can combine data and operations in a single unit, a process called encapsulation. Through encapsulation, an object becomes a self-contained entity. Operations can directly access the data, but the internal state of an object cannot be manipulated directly.

In addition to implementing encapsulation, classes have other capabilities. For instance, you can create new classes from existing classes. This important feature encourages code reuse and saves programmers an enormous amount of time. In Java, you can relate two or more classes in more than one way. This chapter examines two common ways to relate classes:

- **Inheritance** ("is-a" relationship)

- **Composition** ("has-a" relationship)

INHERITANCE

Suppose that you want to design a `class`, `PartTimeEmployee`, to implement and process the characteristics of a part-time employee. The main features associated with a part-time employee are the name, pay rate, and number of hours worked. In Example 8-4 (in Chapter 8), we designed the `class Person` to implement a person's name. Every part-time employee is a person. Therefore, rather than design the `class PartTimeEmployee` from scratch, we want to be able to extend the definition of the `class Person` from Example 8-4 by adding additional members (data and/or methods).

Of course, we do not want to make the necessary changes directly to the `class Person`— that is, edit the `class Person`, and add and/or delete members. We want to create the `class PartTimeEmployee` without making any physical changes to the `class Person`, by adding only the members that are necessary. For example, because the `class Person` already has data members to store the first name and last name, we will not include any such members in the `class PartTimeEmployee`. In fact, these data members will be *inherited* from the `class Person`. (We will design `class PartTimeEmployee` in Example 11-3.)

In Chapter 8, we extensively studied and designed the `class Clock` to implement the time of day in a program. The `class Clock` has three data members (instance variables) to store the hours, minutes, and seconds. Certain applications, in addition to hours, minutes, and seconds, might also require that we store the time zone. In this case, we want to *extend* the definition of the `class Clock` and create a `class`, `ExtClock`, to accommodate this new information. That is, we want to derive the `class ExtClock` by adding a data member— `timeZone`—and the necessary method members to manipulate the time. In Java, the mechanism that allows us to accomplish this task is the principle of **inheritance**. Inheritance implies an "is-a" relationship; for instance, "every employee is a person."

Inheritance lets you create new classes from existing classes. Any new class that you create from an existing class is called a **subclass** or **derived class**; existing classes are called **superclasses** or **base classes**. The subclass inherits the properties of the superclass. Rather than create completely new classes from scratch, you can take advantage of inheritance and reduce software complexity.

Inheritance can be viewed as a tree-like, or hierarchical, structure wherein a superclass is shown with its subclasses. Consider the diagram in Figure 11-1, which shows the relationship between various shapes.

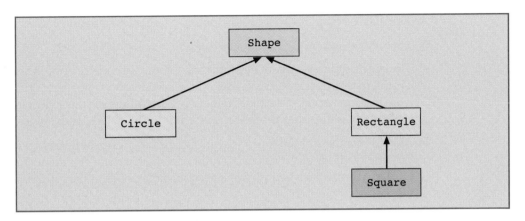

Figure 11-1 Inheritance hierarchy

In this diagram, **Shape** is the superclass. **Circle** and **Rectangle** are derived from **Shape**, and the **class Square** is derived from **Rectangle**. Every **Circle** and every **Rectangle** is a **Shape**. Every **Square** is a **Rectangle**.

The general syntax of deriving a class from an existing class is:

```
modifier(s) class ClassName extends ExistingClassName modifier(s)
{
    memberList
}
```

In Java, **extends** is a reserved word.

Example 11-1

Suppose that we have defined a **class** called **Shape**. The following statements specify that the **class Circle** is derived from **Shape**:

```
public class Circle extends Shape
{
    .
    .
    .
}
```

The following facts about superclasses and subclasses should be kept in mind:

1. The **private** members of the superclass are **private** to the superclass; hence, the members of the subclass cannot directly access them. In other words, when you write the definitions of the methods of the subclass, you cannot directly access the **private** members of the superclass.

2. The subclass can directly access the `public` members of the superclass.

3. The subclass can include additional data and/or method members.

4. The subclass can override, that is, redefine the `public` methods of the superclass. That is, in the subclass, you can have a method with the same name, number, and types of parameters as a method in the superclass. However, this redefinition applies only to the objects of the subclass, not to the objects of the superclass.

5. All data members of the superclass are also data members of the subclass. Similarly, the methods of the superclass (unless overridden) are also the methods of the subclass. (Remember Rule 1 when accessing a member of the superclass in the subclass.)

Each subclass, in turn, becomes a superclass for a future subclass. Inheritance can be either single or multiple. In **single inheritance**, the subclass is derived from a single superclass; in **multiple inheritance**, the subclass is derived from more than one superclass. Java only supports single inheritance; that is, in Java a class can *extend* the definition of only one class.

The next sections describe two important issues related to inheritance. The first issue is using the methods of the superclass in the subclass. While discussing this issue, we will also address how to access the `private` (data) members of the superclass in the subclass. The second key inheritance issue is related to the constructor. The constructor of a subclass *cannot directly access* the `private` data members of the superclass. Thus, you must ensure that `private` data members that are inherited from the superclass are initialized when a constructor of the subclass executes.

Using Methods of the Superclass in a Subclass

Suppose that a `class SubClass` is derived from a `class SuperClass`. Further assume that both `SubClass` and `SuperClass` have some data members. It then follows that the data members of the `class SubClass` are its own data members, together with the data members of `SuperClass`. Similarly, in addition to its own methods, the subclass also inherits the methods of the superclass. The subclass can give some of its methods the same name as given by the superclass. For example, suppose that `SuperClass` contains a method, `print`, that prints the values of the data members of `SuperClass`. `SubClass` contains data members in addition to the data members inherited from `SuperClass`. Suppose that you want to include a method in `SubClass` that prints the data members of `SubClass`. You can give any name to this method. However, in the `class SubClass`, you can also name this method `print` (the same name used by `SuperClass`). This is called **overriding**, or **redefining**, the method of the superclass.

To override a `public` method of the superclass in the subclass, the corresponding method in the subclass must have the same name, the same type, and the same formal parameter list. In other words, the method being overridden in the subclass must have the same name, the same type, and the same set of formal parameters. If the corresponding method in the superclass and the subclass has the same name but different parameters, then this is method **overloading** in the subclass, which is also allowed.

Whether you override a method of the superclass or overload a method of the superclass in the subclass, you must know how to specify a call to the method of the superclass that has the same name as used by a method of the subclass. We illustrate these concepts with the help of the following example.

Consider the definition of the following class (see Figure 11-2):

```
public class Rectangle
{
    private double length;
    private double width;

    public Rectangle()
    {
        length = 0;
        width = 0;
    }

    public Rectangle(double l, double w)
    {
        setDimension(l, w);
    }

    public void setDimension(double l, double w)
    {
        if(l >= 0)
            length = l;
        else
            length = 0;

        if(w >= 0)
            width = w;
        else
            width = 0;
    }

    public double getLength()
    {
        return length;
    }

    public double getWidth()
    {
        return width;
    }
```

11

```
    public double area()
    {
        return length * width;
    }

    public double perimeter()
    {
        return 2 * (length + width);
    }

    public void print()
    {
        System.out.print("Length = "  + length
                        + "; Width = " + width);
    }
}
```

Figure 11-2   UML diagram of the `class Rectangle`

The `class Rectangle` has 10 members.

Now consider the following definition of the `class Box`, derived from the `class Rectangle` (see Figure 11-3):

```
public class Box extends Rectangle
{
    private double height;

    public Box()
    {
        //The definition is as given below
    }
```

```
    public Box(double l, double w, double h)
    {
        //The definition is as given below
    }

    public void setDimension(double l, double w, double h)
    {
        //Sets the length, width, and height of the box
        //The definition is as given below
    }

    public double getHeight()
    {
        return height;
    }

    public double area()
    {
        //Returns the surface area
        //The definition is as given below
    }

    public double volume()
    {
        //Returns the volume
        //The definition is as given below
    }

    public void print()
    {
        //Outputs length, width, and height of the box
        //The definition is as given below
    }
}
```

11

Figure 11-3   UML diagram of the `class` Box and the inheritance hierarchy

From the definition of the **class Box**, it is clear that the **class Box** is derived from the **class Rectangle**. Therefore, all **public** members of **Rectangle** are **public** members of **Box**. The **class Box** overrides the methods **print** and **area**, and overloads the method **setDimension**.

In general, when writing the definition of the methods of a subclass to specify a call to a **public** method of a superclass, you do the following:

- If the subclass overrides a **public** method of a superclass, then you specify a call to that **public** method of the superclass by using the reserved word **super** followed by the dot operator followed by the method name with an appropriate parameter list.

- If the subclass does not override a **public** method of the superclass, you can specify a call to that **public** method by using the name of the method and an appropriate parameter list.

Next let's write the definition of the method **print** of the **class Box**.

The **class Box** has three data members: **length**, **width**, and **height**. The method **print** of the **class Box** prints the values of these three data members. To write the definition of the method **print** of the **class Box**, remember the following:

- The instance variables **length** and **width** are **private** members of the **class Rectangle** and so cannot be directly accessed in the **class Box**. Therefore, when writing the definition of the method **print** of the **class Box**, you cannot directly reference **length** and **width**.

- The instance variables **length** and **width** of the **class Rectangle** are accessible in the **class Box** through the **public** methods of the **class Rectangle**. Therefore, when writing the definition of the method **print** of the **class Box**, you first call the method **print** of the **class Rectangle** to print the values of **length** and **width**. After printing the values of **length** and **width**, you output the values of **height**.

As remarked above, to call the method **print** of **Rectangle** in the definition of the method **print** of **Box**, you must use the following statement:

```
super.print();
```

This statement ensures that you call the method **print** of the superclass **Rectangle**, not of the **class Box**.

The definition of the method **print** of the **class Box** is:

```
public void print()
{
    super.print();
    System.out.print("; Height = " + height);
}
```

Let's write the definition of the remaining methods of the `class Box`.

```
public void setDimension(double 1, double w, double h)
{
    super.setDimension(1, w);

    if(h >= 0)
        height = h;
    else
        height = 0;
}
```

 Notice that the `class Box` overloads the method `setDimension` of the `class Rectangle`. Therefore, in the preceding definition of the method `setDimension` of the `class Box`, you can also specify a call to the method `setDimension` of the `class Rectangle` without the reserved word `super` and the dot operator.

The definition of the method `getHeight` is:

```
public double getHeight()
{
    return height;
}
```

The method **area** of the `class Box` determines the surface area of the box. To do so, we need to access the length and width of the box which are declared as `private` members of the `class Rectangle`. Therefore, we use the methods `getLength` and `getWidth` of the `class Rectangle` to retrieve the length and width, respectively. Because the `class Box` does not override the methods `getLength` and `getWidth`, we call these methods of the `class Rectangle` without using the reserved word `super`.

```
public double area()
{
    return  2 * (getLength() * getWidth()
              + getLength() * height
              + getWidth() * height);
}
```

The method **volume** of the `class Box` determines the volume of the box. To determine the box's volume, you multiply the length, width, and height of the box or multiply the area of the base of the box by its height. Let's write the definition of the method **volume** by using the second alternative. To do so, you can use the method **area** of the `class Rectangle` to determine the area of the base. Because the `class Box` overrides the method **area**, to specify a call to the method **area** of the `class Rectangle`, we use the reserved word **super**, as shown in the following definition.

```
public double volume()
{
    return super.area() * height;
}
```

In the next section, we discuss how to specify a call to the constructor of the superclass when writing the definition of a constructor of the subclass.

Constructors of the Superclass and Subclass

A subclass can have its own `private` data members, so a subclass also can have its own constructors. A constructor typically serves to initialize instance variables. When we instantiate a subclass object, this object inherits the instance variables of the superclass, but the subclass object cannot directly access the `private` instance variables of the superclass. The same is true for the methods of a subclass. That is, the methods of the subclass cannot directly access the `private` members of the superclass.

As a consequence, the constructors of the subclass can (directly) initialize only the instance variables of the subclass. Thus, when a subclass object is instantiated, to initialize the (`private`) instance variables it must also automatically execute one of the constructors of the superclass. A call to a constructor of the superclass is specified in the definition of a subclass constructor by using the reserved word `super`.

In the preceding section we defined the `class Rectangle` and derived the `class Box` from it. Moreover, we illustrated how to override a method of the `class Rectangle`. We now discuss how to write the definition of the constructors of the `class Box`.

The `class Rectangle` has two constructors and two instance variables. The `class Box` has three instance variables: `length`, `width`, and `height`. The instance variables `length` and `width` are inherited from the `class Rectangle`.

To write the definitions of the constructors of the `class Box`, we first write the definition of the default constructor of the `class Box`. Recall that if a class contains the default constructor and no values are specified during object instantiation, the default constructor executes and initializes the object. Because the `class Rectangle` contains the default constructor, when we write the definition of the default constructor of the `class Box`, we use the reserved word `super` with no parameters, as shown in the following code. Moreover, a call to the (default) constructor of the superclass *must* be the first statement.

```
public Box()
{
    super();
    height = 0;
}
```

Next we discuss how to write the definitions of constructors with parameters.

To specify a call to a constructor with parameters of the superclass, we use the reserved word `super` with appropriate parameters. A call to the constructor of the superclass must be the first statement.

Consider the following definition of the constructor with parameters of the `class Box`:

```
public Box(double l, double w, double h)
{
    super(l, w);
    height = h;
}
```

This definition specifies the constructor of `Rectangle` with two parameters. When this constructor of `Box` executes, it triggers the execution of the constructor with two parameters of the type `double` of `class Rectangle`.

As an exercise, try writing the complete definition of the `class Box`.

Consider the following statements:

```
Rectangle myRectangle = new Rectangle(5, 3);          //Line 1
Box myBox = new Box(6, 5, 4);                         //Line 2
```

The statement in Line 1 creates the `Rectangle` object `myRectangle`. Thus, the object `myRectangle` has two instance variables: `length` and `width`. The statement in Line 2 creates the `Box` object `myBox`. Thus, the object `myBox` has three instance variables: `length`, `width`, and `height`. See Figure 11-4.

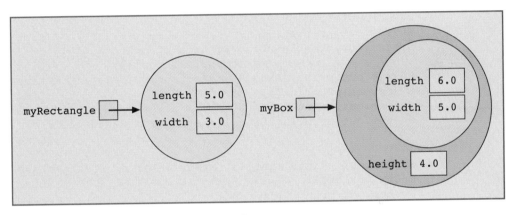

Figure 11-4 Objects `myRectangle` and `myBox`

Consider the following statements:

```
myRectangle.print();                                  //Line 3
System.out.println();                                 //Line 4
myBox.print();                                        //Line 5
System.out.println();                                 //Line 6
```

In the statement in Line 3, the method `print` of the `class Rectangle` is executed; in the statement in Line 5, the method `print` associated with the `class Box` is executed. Recall that if a subclass overrides a method of the superclass, the redefinition applies only to the objects of the subclass. Thus, the output of the statement in Line 3 is:

```
Length = 5.0; Width = 3.0
```

The output of the statement in Line 5 is:

```
Length = 6.0; Width = 5.0; Height = 4.0
```

The program in Example 11-2 shows how the objects of a superclass and a base class behave.

Example 11-2

Consider the following Java application program.

```
public class SubClassSuperClassMethods
{
    public static void main(String[] args)
    {
        Rectangle myRectangle1 = new Rectangle();          //Line 1
        Rectangle myRectangle2 = new Rectangle(8, 6);      //Line 2

        Box myBox1 = new Box();                            //Line 3
        Box myBox2 = new Box(10, 7, 3);                    //Line 4

        System.out.print("Line 5: myRectangle1: ");        //Line 5
        myRectangle1.print();                              //Line 6
        System.out.println();                              //Line 7
        System.out.println("Line 8: Area of myRectangle1: "
                        + myRectangle1.area());            //Line 8
        System.out.print("Line 9: myRectangle2: ");        //Line 9
        myRectangle2.print();                              //Line 10
        System.out.println();                              //Line 11
        System.out.println("Line 12: Area of myRectangle2: "
                        + myRectangle2.area());            //Line 12

        System.out.print("Line 13: myBox1: ");             //Line 13
        myBox1.print();                                    //Line 14
        System.out.println();                              //Line 15
        System.out.println("Line 16: Surface Area of myBox1: "
                        + myBox1.area());                  //Line 16
        System.out.println("Line 17: Volume of myBox1: "
                        + myBox1.volume());                //Line 17

        System.out.print("Line 18: myBox2: ");             //Line 18
        myBox2.print();                                    //Line 19
        System.out.println();                              //Line 20
        System.out.println("Line 21: Surface Area of myBox2: "
                        + myBox2.area());                  //Line 21
        System.out.println("Line 22: Volume of myBox2: "
                        + myBox2.volume());                //Line 22
    }
}
```

Output

```
Line 5: myRectangle1: Length = 0.0; Width = 0.0
Line 8: Area of myRectangle1: 0.0
Line 9: myRectangle2: Length = 8.0; Width = 6.0
```

```
Line 12: Area of myRectangle2: 48.0
Line 13: myBox1: Length = 0.0; Width = 0.0; Height = 0.0
Line 16: Surface Area of myBox1: 0.0
Line 17: Volume of myBox1: 0.0
Line 18: myBox2: Length = 10.0; Width = 7.0; Height = 3.0
Line 21: Surface Area of myBox2: 242.0
Line 22: Volume of myBox2: 210.0
```

The preceding program works as follows: The statement in Line 1 creates the `Rectangle` object `myRectangle1` and initializes its instance variables to 0. The statement in Line 2 creates the `Rectangle` object `myRectangle2` and initializes its instance variables `length` and `width` to `8.0` and `6.0`, respectively.

The statement in Line 3 creates the `Box` object `myBox1` and initializes its instance variables to 0. The statement in Line 4 creates the `Box` object `myBox2` and initializes its instance variables `length`, `width`, and `height` to `10.0`, `7.0`, and `3.0`, respectively.

The statements in Lines 5 through 8 output the length, width, and area of `myRectangle1`. Because the instance variables of `myRectangle1` are initialized to 0 by the default constructor, the area of the rectangle is 0 square units, as shown in the output of Line 8.

The statements in Lines 9 through 12 output the length, width, and area of `myRectangle2`. Because the instance variables `length` and `width` of `myRectangle2` are initialized to `8.0` and `6.0`, respectively, by the constructor with parameters, this rectangle's area is `48.0` square units. See the output of Line 12.

The statements in Lines 13 through 17 output the `length, width, height, surface area,` and `volume` of `myBox1`. Because the instance variables of `myBox1` are initialized to 0 by the default constructor, this box's surface area is `0.0` square units and the volume is `0.0` cubic units. See the output of Lines 16 and 17.

The statements in Lines 18 through 22 output the `length, width, height, surface area,` and `volume` of `myBox2`. Because the instance variables `length, width,` and `height` of `myBox2` are initialized to `10.0, 7.0,` and `3.0`, respectively, by the constructor with parameters, this box's surface area is `242.0` square units and the volume is `210.0` cubic units. See the output of Lines 21 and 22.

From the output of this program, it follows that the redefinition of the methods `print` and `area` in the `class Box` applies only to the object of the type `Box`.

Next we give another example illustrating how to create a subclass.

Example 11-3

Suppose that you want to define a class to group the attributes of an employee. There are full-time employees and part-time employees. Part-time employees are paid based on the number of hours worked and an hourly rate. Suppose that you want to define a class to keep track of a part-time employee's information such as name, pay rate, and hours worked. You can then print the employee's name, together with his or her wages. Recall that Example 8-4 (Chapter 8) defined the class `Person` to store the first name and the last name together with the necessary operations on `name`. Because every employee is a person, we can define a class `PartTimeEmployee` derived from the class `Person`. (See Figure 11-5.) You can also override the method `print` of the class `Person` to print the appropriate information.

The members of the class `PartTimeEmployee` are as follows:

Instance Variables:

```
private double payRate;     //store the pay rate
private double hoursWorked; //store the hours worked
```

Instance Methods:

```
public String toString()
     //Method to return the string consisting of the
     //first name, last name, and the wages in the form:
     //firstName lastName wages are $$$$.$$

public void setNameRateHours(String first, String last,
                              double rate, double hours)
     //Method to set the first name, last name, payRate,
     //and hoursWorked according to the parameters.
     //The parameters first and last are passed to the
     //superclass.
     //Postcondition: firstName = first; lastName = last;
     //               payRate = rate; hoursWorked = hours;

public double getPayRate()
     //Method to return the pay rate
     //Postcondition: The value of payRate is returned

public double getHoursWorked()
     //Method to return the number of hours worked
     //Postcondition: The value of hoursWorked is returned

public double calculatePay()
     //Method to calculate and return the wages

public PartTimeEmployee(String first, String last,
                        double rate, double hours)
     //Constructor with parameters
     //Set the first name, last name, payRate, and
     //hoursWorked according to the parameters.
     //Parameters first and last are passed to the
     //superclass.
```

```
//Postcondition: firstName = first; lastName = last;
//                payRate = rate; hoursWorked = hours;

public PartTimeEmployee()
    //Default constructor
    //Set the first name, last name, payRate, and
    //hoursWorked to the default values.
    //The first name and last name are initialized to an empty
    //string by the default constructor of the superclass.
    //Postcondition: firstName = ""; lastName = "";
    //                payRate = 0; hoursWorked = 0;
```

Figure 11-5   UML diagram of the `class PartTimeEmployee` and the inheritance hierarchy

The definitions of the member methods of the `class PartTimeEmployee` are as follows:

```
public String toString()
{
    return (super.toString() + " wages are: " + calculatePay());
}

public double getPayRate()
{
    return payRate;
}

public double getHoursWorked()
{
    return hoursWorked;
}
```

```
public double calculatePay()
{
    return (payRate * hoursWorked);
}

public void setNameRateHours(String first, String last,
                             double rate, double hours)
{
    setName(first,last);
    payRate = rate;
    hoursWorked = hours;
}
```

The definition of the constructor with parameters is as follows. (Notice that the body contains a call to the superclass's constructor with parameters.)

```
public PartTimeEmployee(String first, String last,
                        double rate, double hours)
{
    super(first, last);
    payRate = rate;
    hoursWorked = hours;
}
```

The definition of the default constructor is:

```
public PartTimeEmployee()
{
    super();
    payRate = 0;
    hoursWorked = 0;
}
```

The definition of the class PartTimeEmployee is:

```
public class PartTimeEmployee extends Person
{
    private double payRate;      //store the pay rate
    private double hoursWorked; //store the hours worked

        //Default constructor
        //Set the first name, last name, payRate, and
        //hoursWorked to the default values.
        //The first name and last name are initialized to an empty
        //string by the default constructor of the superclass.
        //Postcondition: firstName = ""; lastName = "";
        //               payRate = 0; hoursWorked = 0;
    public PartTimeEmployee()
    {
        super();
```

```
        payRate = 0;
        hoursWorked = 0;
   }

      //Constructor with parameters
      //Set the first name, last name, payRate, and
      //hoursWorked according to the parameters.
      //Parameters first and last are passed to the
      //superclass.
      //Postcondition: firstName = first; lastName = last;
      //                payRate = rate; hoursWorked = hours;
   public PartTimeEmployee(String first, String last,
                             double rate, double hours)
   {
        super(first, last);
        payRate = rate;
        hoursWorked = hours;
   }

      //Method to return the string consisting of the
      //first name, last name, and the wages in the form:
      //firstName lastName wages are $$$$.$$
   public String toString()
   {
        return (super.toString() + " wages are: " + calculatePay());
   }

      //Method to calculate and return the wages
   public double calculatePay()
   {
        return (payRate * hoursWorked);
   }

      //Method to set the first name, last name, payRate,
      //and hoursWorked according to the parameters.
      //The parameters first and last are passed to the
      //superclass.
      //Postcondition: firstName = first; lastName = last;
      //                payRate = rate; hoursWorked = hours;
   public void setNameRateHours(String first, String last,
                                  double rate, double hours)

   {
        setName(first,last);
        payRate = rate;
        hoursWorked = hours;
   }

      //Method to return the pay rate
      //Postcondition: The value of payRate is returned
```

11

```
    public double getPayRate()
    {
        return payRate;
    }


    //Method to return the number of hours worked
    //Postcondition: The value of hoursWorked is returned
    public double getHoursWorked()
    {
        return hoursWorked;
    }
}
```

 The definition of the subclass is typically placed in a separate file. Recall that the name of the file must be the same as the name of the class, and the file extension must be `java`.

Protected Members of a Class

The `private` members of a class are `private` to the class and cannot be directly accessed outside the class. Only member methods of that class can access the `private` members. As discussed previously, the subclass cannot access `private` members of the superclass. However, it is sometimes necessary for a subclass to access a `private` member of a superclass. If you make a `private` member become `public`, then anyone can access that member. Recall that the members of a class are classified into three categories: `public`, `private`, and `protected`. So, for a superclass to give a member access to its subclass and still prevent its direct access outside the class, you must declare that member using the modifier `protected`. Thus, the accessibility of a `protected` member of a class falls between `public` and `private`. A subclass can directly access the `protected` member of a superclass.

To summarize, if a member of a superclass needs to be accessed by a subclass, that member is declared using the modifier `protected`.

Example 11-4 illustrates how the methods of the subclass can directly access a `protected` member of the superclass.

Example 11-4

Consider the following definition of the classes `BClass` and `DClass`. (See Figures 11-6 and 11-7.)

```
public class BClass
{
    protected char bCh;
    private double bX;

        //default constructor
```

```java
    public BClass()
    {
        bCh = '*';
        bX = 0.0;
    }

        //constructor with parameters
    public BClass(char ch, double u)
    {
        bCh = ch;
        bX = u;
    }

    public void setData(double u)
    {
        bX = u;
    }

    public void setData(char ch, double u)
    {
        bCh = ch;
        bX = u;
    }

    public String toString()
    {
        return("Superclass: bCh = " + bCh + ", bX = " + bX + '\n');
    }
}
```

11

BClass
#bCh: char -bX: double
+BClass() +BClass(char, double) +setData(double): void +setData(char, double): void +toString(): String

Figure 11-6   UML diagram of the class BClass

The definition of the class BClass contains the protected data member bCh of the type char, and the private data member bX of the type double. It also contains an overloaded method setData; one version of setData is used to set both the data members, and the other version is used to set only the `private` data member. The `class BClass` also has a constructor with default parameters.

Next we derive a `class DClass` from the `class BClass`. The `class DClass` contains a `private` data member `dA` of the type `int`. It also contains a method `setData`, with three parameters, and the method `toString`.

```
public class DClass extends BClass
{
    private int dA;

    public DClass()
    {
        //The definition as shown below
    }

    public DClass(char ch, double v, int a)
    {
        //The definition as shown below
    }

    public void setData(char ch, double v, int a)
    {
        //The definition as shown below
    }

    public String toString()
    {
        //The definition as shown below
    }
}
```

Figure 11-7 UML diagram of the `class DClass`

Let's now write the definition of the method `setData` of the `class DClass`. Because `bCh` is a `protected` data member of the `class BClass`, it can be directly accessed in the definition of the method `setData`. However, because `bX` is a `private` data member of the `class BClass`, the method `setData` of the `class DClass` *cannot* directly access `bX`. Thus, the method `setData` of the `class DClass` must set `bX` by using the method `setData` of the `class BClass`. The definition of the method `setData` of the `class DClass` can be written as follows:

```
public void setData(char ch, double v, int a)
{
    super.setData(v);

    bCh = ch;    //initialize bCh using the assignment
                 //statement
    dA = a;
}
```

Note that the definition of the method `setData` contains the statement

```
super.setData(v);
```

to call the method `setData` with one parameter (of the superclass), to set the data member `bX`, and then directly set the value of `bCh`.

Next let's write the definition of the method `toString` (of the `class DClass`).

```
public String toString()
{
    return (super.toString() + "Subclass dA = " + dA + '\n');
}
```

The constructors' definitions are:

```
public DClass()
{
    super();
    dA = 0;
}

public void DClass(char ch, double v, int a)
{
    super(ch,v);
    dA = a;
}
```

The following program illustrates how the objects of `BClass` and `DClass` work.

```
public class ProtectedMemberProg
{
    public static void main(String[] args)
    {
        BClass bObject = new BClass();              //Line 1

        DClass dObject = new DClass();              //Line 2

        System.out.println("Line 3: " + bObject);   //Line 3
```

```
            System.out.println("Line 4: ***   "
                            + "Subclass object ***");          //Line 4

            dObject.setData('&', 2.5, 7);                      //Line 5

            System.out.println("Line 6: " + dObject);          //Line 6
        }
    }
```

Output

```
Line 3: Superclass: bCh = *, bX = 0.0

Line 4: ***   Subclass object ***
Line 6: Superclass: bCh = &, bX = 2.5
Subclass dA = 7
```

When you write the definitions of the member methods of the `class BClass`, the `protected` data member `bCh` can be accessed directly. However, `DClass` objects *cannot* directly access `bCh`. That is, the following statement is illegal (it is, in fact, a syntax error):

```
dObject.bCh = '&';   //Illegal
```

THE class Object

In Chapter 8, we defined the `class Clock` and later included the method `toString` to return the time as a string. When we included the method `toString`, we noted that every Java class (built-in or user-defined) is automatically provided the method `toString`. If a user-defined class does not provide its own definition of the method `toString`, then the default definition of the method `toString` is invoked. The methods `print` and `println` use the method `toString` to determine what to print. As shown in Chapter 8, the default definition of the method `toString` returns the class name followed by the hash code of the object. You might ask, where is the method `toString` defined?

The method `toString` comes from the Java `class Object`, and is a `public` member of this class. In Java, if you define a class and do not use the reserved word `extends` to derive it from an existing class, then the class you define is automatically considered to be derived from the `class Object`. Therefore, the `class Object` directly or indirectly becomes the superclass of every class in Java. From this, it follows that the definition of the `class Clock` (previously given in Chapter 8)

```
public class Clock
{
    //Declare instance variables as given in Chapter 8
    //Definition of instance methods as given in Chapter 8
    //...
}
```

is, in fact, equivalent to the following:

```
public class Clock extends Object
{
    //Declare instance variables as given in Chapter 8
    //Definition of instance methods as given in Chapter 8
    //...
}
```

Using the mechanism of inheritance, every `public` member of the `class Object` can be overridden and/or can be invoked by every object of any class type. Table 11-1 describes some of the constructors and methods of the `class Object`.

Table 11-1 Some of the Constructors and Methods of the `class Object`

```
public Object()
    //Constructor
```

```
public String toString()
    //Method to return a string to describe the object
```

```
public boolean equals(Object obj)
    //Method to determine if two objects are the same
    //Returns true if the object invoking the method and the object
    //specified by the parameter obj refer to the same memory space;
    //otherwise it returns false
```

```
protected Object clone()
    //Method to return a reference to a copy of the object invoking
    //this method
```

```
protected void finalize()
    //The body of this method is invoked when the object goes out
    //of scope
```

11

Because every Java class is directly or indirectly derived from the `class Object`, it follows from Table 11-1 that the method `toString` becomes a `public` member of every Java class. Therefore, if a class does not override this method, whenever this method is invoked, the method's default definition executes. As indicated previously, the default definition returns the class name followed by the hash code of the object as a string. Usually, every Java class overrides the method `toString`. The `class String` overrides it so that the string stored in the object is returned. The `class Clock` overrides it so that the string containing the time in the form `hh:mm:ss` is returned. Similarly, the `class Person` also overrides it.

The method `equals` is also a very useful method of the `class Object`. This method's definition as given in the `class Object` determines if the object invoking this method and the object passed as a parameter refer to the same memory space, that is, whether they point to data in the same memory space. The method `equals` determines if the two objects are aliases. As in the case of the method `toString`, to implement its own needs, every user-defined `class` also usually overrides the method `equals`. For example, in the `class` `Clock`, the method `equals` was overridden to determine if the instance variables (`hr`, `min`, and `sec`) of two `Clock` objects contained the same value.

As usual, the default constructor is used to initialize an object. The method `clone` makes a copy of the object and returns a reference of the copy. However, the method `clone` only makes a memberwise, that is, field by field, copy of the object.

JAVA STREAM CLASSES

In Chapter 2, we described the classes `InputStreamReader` and `BufferedReader` for inputting data from the standard input device. Chapter 3 described in detail how to perform input/output (I/O) using Java stream classes such as `FileReader`, `FileWriter`, and `PrintWriter`. In Java, stream classes are implemented using the inheritance mechanism, as shown in Figure 11-8.

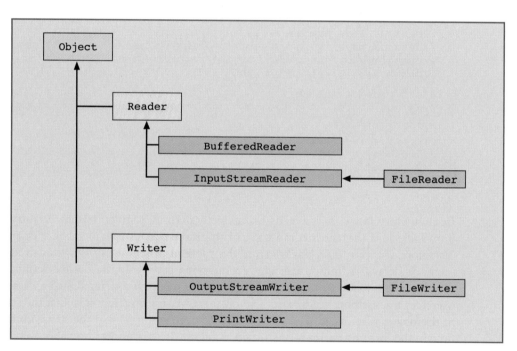

Figure 11-8 Hierarchy of Java stream classes

From Figure 11-8, it follows that the **classes Reader** and **Writer** are derived from the **class Object**. The classes **BufferedReader** and **InputStreamReader** are derived from the **class Reader**, and the **class FileReader** is derived from the **class InputStreamReader**. Similarly, **OutputStreamWriter** and **PrintWriter** are derived from the **class Writer**, and the **class FileWriter** is derived from the **class OutputStreamWriter**. A description of the methods of these classes and other Java stream classes is given in Appendix E.

OBJECTS OF SUPERCLASSES AND SUBCLASSES

Java allows us to treat an object of a subclass as an object of its superclass. In other words, a reference variable of a superclass type can point to an object of its subclass. There are situations when this feature of Java can be used to develop generic code for a variety of applications. However, you cannot automatically consider a superclass object to be an object of a subclass. In other words, you *cannot* automatically make a reference variable of a subclass type point to an object of its superclass.

Suppose that **supRef** is a reference variable of a superclass type. Moreover, suppose that **supRef** points to an object of its subclass. You can use an appropriate cast operator on **supRef** and make a reference variable of the subclass point to the object. On the other hand, if **supRef** does not point to a subclass object and you use a cast operator on **supRef** to make a reference variable of the subclass point to the object, then Java will throw a **ClassCastException**—indicating that the class cast is not allowed. We use examples to illustrate these concepts.

Consider the following statements. (The **classes Person** and **PartTimeEmployee** are as defined before.)

```
Person name, nameRef;                        //Line 1
PartTimeEmployee employee, employeeRef;      //Line 2

name = new Person("John", "Blair");          //Line 3
employee = new PartTimeEmployee("Susan", "Johnson",
                      12.50, 45);            //Line 4
```

The statement in Line 1 declares **name** and **nameRef** to be reference variables of the type **Person**. Similarly, the statement in Line 2 declares **employee** and **employeeRef** to be reference variables of the type **PartTimeEmployee**. The statement in Line 3 instantiates the object **name** and the statement in Line 4 instantiates the object **employee**.

Now consider the following statements:

```
nameRef = employee;                          //Line 5
System.out.println("nameRef: " + nameRef);   //Line 6
```

The statement in Line 5 makes **nameRef** point to the object **employee**. After the execution of the statement in Line 5, the object **nameRef** is treated as an object of the **class**

Person. The statement in Line 6 outputs the value of the object **nameRef**. The output of the statement in Line 6 is:

```
nameRef: Susan Johnson wages are: 562.5
```

Notice that even though **nameRef** is declared as a reference variable of the type **Person**, when the program executes, the statement in Line 6 outputs the first name, the last name, and the wages. This is because when the statement in Line 6 executes to output **nameRef**, the method **toString** of the **class PartTimeEmployee** executes, not the method **toString** of the **class Person**. This is called **dynamic binding** (also called **run-time binding**), that is, the method that gets executed is determined at execution time, not at compile time.

Now consider the following statement:

```
employeeRef = (PartTimeEmployee) name;   //Illegal
```

This statement will throw **ClassCastException** because **name** points to an object of the **class Person**. It does not refer to an object of the **class PartTimeEmployee**. However, the following statement is legal:

```
employeeRef = (PartTimeEmployee) nameRef;
```

Because **nameRef** refers to the object **employee**, (as set by the statement in Line 5), and **employee** is a reference variable of the **PartTimeEmployee** type, this statement would make **employeeRef** point to the object **employee**. Therefore, the output of the statement:

```
System.out.println(employeeRef);
```

is

```
Susan Johnson wages are: 562.5
```

The Operator `instanceof`

As previously described, an object of a subclass type can be considered an object of the superclass type. Moreover, by using an appropriate cast operator, you can treat an object of a superclass type as an object of a subclass type. To determine whether a reference variable that points to an object is of a particular class type, Java provides the operator **instanceof**. Consider the following expression (suppose that **p** is an object of a class type):

```
p instanceof PartTimeEmployee
```

This expression evaluates to **true** if **p** points to an object of the **class PartTimeEmployee**; otherwise it evaluates to **false**.

Example 11-5 further illustrates how the operator **instanceof** works.

Example 11-5

Consider the following classes: (The classes `RectangleShape` and `BoxShape` are the same as the classes `Rectangle` and `Box` given earlier in this chapter. The only difference is that the instance variables of the classes `Rectangle` and `Box` are `private`, while those of the classes `RectangleShape` and `BoxShape` are `protected`. Since the instance variables of the class `RectangleShape` are `protected`, they can be directly accessed in the class `BoxShape`. Therefore, the definition of the methods `area` and `volume` of the class `BoxShape` directly access the instance variables `length` and `width` of the class `RectangleShape`.)

```
public class RectangleShape
{
    protected double length;
    protected double width;

    public RectangleShape()
    {
        length = 0;
        width = 0;
    }

    public RectangleShape(double l, double w)
    {
        setDimension(l, w);
    }

    public void setDimension(double l, double w)
    {
        if(l >= 0)
            length = l;
        else
            length = 0;

        if(w >= 0)
            width = w;
        else
            width = 0;
    }

    public double getLength()
    {
        return length;
    }

    public double getWidth()
    {
        return width;
    }
```

11

```
public double area()
{
    return length * width;
}

public double perimeter()
{
    return 2 * (length + width);
}

public String toString()
{
    return("Length = "  + length
        + ", Width = " + width
        + ", Perimeter = " + perimeter()
        + ", Area = " + area());
}
}
```

The class BoxShape, given next, is derived from the class RectangleShape.

```
public class BoxShape extends RectangleShape
{

    public BoxShape()
    {
        super();
        height = 0;
    }

    public BoxShape(double l, double w, double h)
    {
        super(l, w);
        height = h;
    }

    public void setDimension(double l, double w, double h)
    {
        super.setDimension(l, w);

        if(h >= 0)
            height = h;
        else
            height = 0;
    }

    public double getHeight()
    {
        return height;
    }
```

```java
    public double area()
    {
        return  2 * (length * width + length * height
                    + width * height);
    }

    public double volume()
    {
        return length * width * height;
    }

    public String toString()
    {
        return("Length = "   + length
            + ", Width = " + width
            + ", Height = " + height
            + ", Surface Area = " + area()
            + ", Volume = " + volume());
    }
}
```

Next consider the following application program:

```java
public class SuperSubClassObjects
{

    public static void main(String[] args)
    {
        RectangleShape  rectangle, rectRef;                 //Line 1
        BoxShape box, boxRef;                               //Line 2

        rectangle = new RectangleShape(12, 4);              //Line 3
        System.out.println("Line 4: Rectangle \n"
                        + rectangle + "\n");                //Line 4
        box = new BoxShape(13, 7, 4);                       //Line 5
        System.out.println("Line 6: Box\n"
                        + box + "\n");                      //Line 6
        rectRef = box;                                      //Line 7
        System.out.println("Line 8: Box via rectRef\n"
                        + rectRef + "\n");                  //Line 8

        boxRef = (BoxShape) rectRef;                        //Line 9
        System.out.println("Line 10: Box via boxRef\n"
                        + boxRef + "\n");                   //Line 10

        if(rectRef instanceof BoxShape)                     //Line 11
            System.out.println("Line 12: rectRef is "
                        + "an instance of BoxShape");       //Line 12
        else                                                //Line 13
```

```
            System.out.println("Line 14: rectRef is not "
                      + "an instance of BoxShape");    //Line 14

        if(rectangle instanceof BoxShape)              //Line 15
            System.out.println("Line 16: rectangle is "
                      + "an instance of BoxShape");     //Line 16
        else                                           //Line 17
            System.out.println("Line 18: rectangle is not "
                      + "an instance of BoxShape");     //Line 18
    }
}
```

Output

```
Line 4: Rectangle
Length = 12.0, Width = 4.0, Perimeter = 32.0, Area = 48.0

Line 6: Box
Length = 13.0, Width = 7.0, Height = 4.0, Surface Area = 342.0,
Volume = 364.0

Line 8: Box via rectRef
Length = 13.0, Width = 7.0, Height = 4.0, Surface Area = 342.0,
Volume = 364.0

Line 10: Box via boxRef
Length = 13.0, Width = 7.0, Height = 4.0, Surface Area = 342.0,
Volume = 364.0

Line 12: rectRef is an instance of BoxShape
Line 18: rectangle is not an instance of BoxShape
```

The preceding program works as follows: The statement in Line 1 declares `rectangle` and `rectRef` to be reference variables of the `RectangleShape` type. Similarly, the statement in Line 2 declares `box` and `boxRef` to be reference variables of the `BoxShape` type.

The statement in Line 3 instantiates the object `rectangle` and initializes the instance variables `length` and `width` to `12.0` and `4.0`, respectively. The statement in Line 4 outputs the length, width, and area of `rectangle`.

The statement in Line 5 instantiates the object `box` and initializes the instance variables `length`, `width`, and `height` to `13.0`, `7.0`, and `4.0`, respectively. The statement in Line 6 outputs the length, width, height, surface area, and volume of `box`.

The statement in Line 7 copies the value of `box` into `rectRef`. After this statement executes, `rectRef` points to the object `box`. Notice that `rectRef` is a reference variable of the `RectangleShape` (the superclass) type and `box` is a reference variable of the `BoxShape` (the subclass of `RectangleShape`) type.

The statement in Line 8 outputs the length, width, height, surface area, and volume of **box** via the reference variable **rectRef**. Notice that **rectRef** is a reference variable of the **RectangleShape** type. However, when the statement in Line 8 executes to output **rectRef**, the method **toString** of the **class BoxShape** executes, not the method **toString** of the **class RectangleShape**.

Because the reference variable **rectRef** points to an object of **BoxShape**, the statement in Line 9 uses the cast operator and copies the value of **rectRef** into **boxRef**. (If the reference variable **rectRef** did not point to an object of the type **BoxShape**, then the statement in Line 9 would result in an error.) The statement in Line 10 outputs the length, width, height, surface area, and volume of the object pointed to by **boxRef**.

The statement in Lines 11 through 14 determines if **rectRef** is an instance of **BoxShape**, that is, if **rectRef** points to an object of the **BoxShape** type. Similarly, the statements in Lines 15 through 18 determine if the reference variable **rectangle** is an instance of **BoxShape**.

ABSTRACT METHODS AND CLASSES

An **abstract method** is a method that has only the heading with no body. The heading of an abstract method contains the reserved word **abstract** and ends with a semicolon. The following are examples of abstract methods:

```
public void abstract print();
public abstract object larger(object, object);
void abstract insert(int insertItem);
```

An **abstract class** is a class that is declared with the reserved word **abstract** in its heading. Some facts about abstract classes follow:

- An abstract class can contain instance variables, constructors, finalizer, and nonabstract methods.

- An abstract class can contain abstract method(s).

- If a class contains an abstract method, then the class must be declared abstract.

- You cannot instantiate an object of an abstract class type. You can only declare a reference variable of an abstract class type.

- You can instantiate an object of a subclass of an abstract class, but only if the subclass gives the definitions of *all* the abstract methods of the superclass.

The following is an example of an abstract class:

```
public abstract class AbstractClassExample
{
        protected int x;
```

11

```
public void abstract print();

public void setX(int a)
{
    x = a;
}

public AbstractClassExample()
{
    x = 0;
}
}
```

Abstract classes are used as superclasses from which other subclasses within the same context can be derived. They can be used to force subclasses to provide certain methods, as illustrated in the following example.

Example 11-6

In Chapter 6, we introduced the **class IntClass** so that **int** values can be treated as objects. We also indicated that the **class DoubleClass**, which can be used to treat values of the type **double** as objects, has similar operations. Similarly, you can design the **classes CharClass, LongClass**, and **FloatClass** to treat other values of primitive data types as objects. The three operations that are common to all these classes, and have the same name, are **equals, compareTo**, and **toString**. To ensure that each of these classes provides these three operations, we can create the **abstract class PrimitiveTypeClass** with these operations as **abstract** methods, as follows:

```
public abstract class PrimitiveTypeClass
{
    public abstract boolean equals(PrimitiveTypeClass right);
        //Method to return true if two objects contain the same
        //data

    public abstract int compareTo(PrimitiveTypeClass right);
        //Method to compare two objects

    public abstract String toString();
        //Method to return data as a string
}
```

 In the definition of the **class PrimitiveTypeClass**, notice that the arguments of the methods **equals** and **compareTo** are objects of the type **PrimitiveTypeClass**. We will illustrate how to write the definition of the method for the **class IntClass**.

You can derive the classes IntClass, DoubleClass, and so on, from the class PrimitiveTypeClass. For example, the definition of the class IntClass could be:

```
public class IntClass extends PrimitiveTypeClass
{
    private int x;

    public IntClass()
    {
        x = 0;
    }

    public IntClass(int num)
    {
        x = num;
    }

    public void setNum(int num)
    {
        x = num;
    }

    public int getNum()
    {
        return x;
    }

    public void addToNum(int num)
    {
        x = x + num;
    }

    public void multiplyToNum(int num)
    {
        x = x * num;
    }

    public int compareTo(PrimitiveTypeClass right)
    {
        IntClass temp = (IntClass) right;

        return (x - temp.getNum());
    }

    public boolean equals(PrimitiveTypeClass right)
    {
        IntClass temp = (IntClass) right;

        if(x == temp.getNum())
            return true;
```

11

```
        else
            return false;
    }

    public String toString()
    {
        return (String.valueOf(x));
    }
}
```

 The definition of the **class IntClass** given here is different than the one given in Chapter 6 and used in Chapter 7. The main difference is how the methods **equals** and **compareTo** are implemented. The definition given here is derived from the abstract **class PrimitiveTypeClass**.

INTERFACES

In Chapter 6, you learned that the **class ActionListener** is a special type of class called an **interface**. There are several other classes in Java that are similar to the **interface ActionListener**. For example, window events are handled by the **interface WindowListener**, and mouse events are handled by the **interface MouseListener**. The obvious question is: why does Java have these interfaces? After all, they are also classes. The answer is that Java, in reality, *does not* support multiple inheritance. That is, a class can only extend the definition of one class—a class can be derived *only* from one existing class. However, a Java program might contain a variety of GUI components and thus generate a variety of events such as window events, mouse events, and action events. These events are handled by separate interfaces. Therefore, a program might need to use more than one such interface.

Until now we have handled events by using the mechanism of the inner class. For example, action events were processed by using inner classes. There are two more ways, discussed in Chapter 12, to process events in a Java program—by using anonymous classes and by making the class containing the application program implement the appropriate interface.

When we created an inner class to process an action event, the inner class was built on top of the **interface ActionListener** by using the mechanism of **implements**. Rather than using the inner class mechanism, the class containing the Java program can itself be created on top of an interface, just as we created the GUI program by extending the **class JFrame**. For example, for the **RectangleProgram** in Chapter 6, we could have defined the **class RectangleProgram** as follows:

```
public class RectangleProgram extends JFrame implements
                                    ActionListener
{
   ...
}
```

Of course, doing so would also require us to register the listener using the reference `this`, which was explained in Chapter 8.

To be able to handle a variety of events, Java allows a class to implement more than one interface. This is, in fact, how Java implements multiple inheritance, which is not true multiple inheritance. In the remainder of this section, we provide a few facts about interfaces.

You already know that an interface is a special type of class. How does an interface differ from an actual class?

Interface: An interface is a class that contains only abstract methods and/or named constants.

Interfaces are defined using the reserved word `interface` in place of the reserved word `class`. For example, the definition of the `interface WindowListener` is:

```
public interface WindowListener
{
      public void windowOpened(WindowEvent e);
      public void windowClosing(WindowEvent e);
      public void windowClosed(WindowEvent e);
      public void windowIconified(WindowEvent e);
      public void windowDeiconified(WindowEvent e);
      public void windowActivated(WindowEvent e);
      public void windowDeactivated(WindowEvent e);
}
```

The definition of the `interface ActionListener` is:

```
public interface ActionListener
{
      public void actionPerformed(ActionEvent e);
}
```

11

Example 11-7

The following `class` implements the `interfaces ActionListener` and `WindowListener`:

```
public class ExampleInterfaceImp implements ActionListener,
                                             WindowListener
{
    ...
}
```

 Recall that if a `class` contains an `abstract` method, it must be declared `abstract`. Moreover, you cannot instantiate an object of an `abstract class`. Therefore, if a `class` implements an `interface`, it must provide definitions for each of the methods of the `interface`; otherwise you cannot instantiate an object of that class type.

COMPOSITION

Composition is another way to relate two classes. In **composition**, one or more members of a class are objects of another class type. Composition is a "has-a" relation; for example, "every person has a date of birth."

The **class Person** defined in Chapter 8, Example 8–4 stores a person's first name and last name. Suppose we want to keep track of additional information, such as a personal ID and date of birth. Because every person has a personal ID and a date of birth, we can define a new **class PersonalInfo**, in which one of the members is an object of the type **Person**. We can declare additional members to store the personal ID and date of birth for the **class PersonalInfo**.

First we define another **class**, **Date**, to store only a person's date of birth, and then construct the **class PersonalInfo** from the classes **Person** and **Date**. This way, we can demonstrate how to define a new class using two classes.

To define the **class Date**, we need three data members to store the month, day number, and year. Some of the operations that need to be performed on a date are to set the date and to print the date. The following statements define the **class Date** (see Figure 11-9):

```
public class Date
{
    private int dMonth;      //variable to store the month
    private int dDay;        //variable to store the day
    private int dYear;       //variable to store the year

        //Default constructor
        //Data members dMonth, dDay, and dYear are set to
        //the default values
        //Postcondition: dMonth = 1; dDay = 1; dYear = 1900;
    public Date()
    {
        dMonth = 1;
        dDay = 1;
        dYear = 1900;
    }

        //Constructor to set the date
        //Data members dMonth, dDay, and dYear are set
        //according to the parameters
        //Postcondition: dMonth = month; dDay = day;
        //                dYear = year;
    public Date(int month, int day, int year)
```

```
{
    dMonth = month;
    dDay = day;
    dYear = year;
}

    //Method to set the date
    //Data members dMonth, dDay, and dYear are set
    //according to the parameters
    //Postcondition: dMonth = month; dDay = day;
    //                  dYear = year;
public void setDate(int month, int day, int year)
{
    dMonth = month;
    dDay = day;
    dYear = year;
}

    //Method to return the month
    //Postcondition: The value of dMonth is returned
public int getMonth()
{
    return dMonth;
}

    //Method to return the day
    //Postcondition: The value of dDay is returned
public int getDay()
{
    return dDay;
}
    //Method to return the year
    //Postcondition: The value of dYear is returned
public int getYear()
{
    return dYear;
}

    //Method to return the date in the form mm-dd-yyyy
public String toString()
{
    return (dMonth + "-" + dDay + "-" + dYear);
}
}
```

11

```
                        ┌─────────────────────────────────┐
                        │              Date               │
                        ├─────────────────────────────────┤
                        │ -dMonth: int                    │
                        │ -dDay: int                      │
                        │ -dYear: int                     │
                        ├─────────────────────────────────┤
                        │ +Date()                         │
                        │ +Date(int, int, int)            │
                        │ +setDate(int, int, int): void   │
                        │ +toString(): String             │
                        │ +getMonth(): int                │
                        │ +getDay(): int                  │
                        │ +getYear(): int                 │
                        └─────────────────────────────────┘
```

Figure 11-9   UML diagram of the `class` `Date`

The definition of the method `setDate`, before storing the date into the data members, does not check whether the date is valid. That is, it does not confirm whether `month` is between 1 and 12, `year` is greater than 0, and `day` is valid (for example, for January, `day` should be between 1 and 31). In Programming Exercise 2 at the end of this chapter, you are asked to rewrite the definition of the method `setDate` so that the date is validated before storing it in the data members. Similarly, in Programming Exercise 2, you are asked to rewrite the definition of the constructor with parameters so that it checks for valid values of `month`, `day`, and `year` before storing the date into data members.

Next, we specify the members of the `class` `PersonalInfo` (see Figure 11-10).

Instance Variables:

```
private Person name;
private Date bDay;
private int personID;
```

Instance Methods:

```
public void setPersonalInfo(String first, String last, int month,
                            int day, int year, int ID)
      //Method to set the personal information
      //Instance variables are set according to the parameters
      //Postcondition: firstName = first; lastName = last;
      //        dMonth = month; dDay = day; dYear = year;
      //        personID = ID;

public String toString()
      //Method to return the string containing personal information
```

```
public PersonalInfo(String first, String last, int month,
                    int day, int year, int ID)
    //Constructor with parameters
    //Instance variables are set according to the parameters
    //Postcondition: firstName = first; lastName = last;
    //     dMonth = month; dDay = day; dYear = year;
    //     personID = ID;

public PersonalInfo()
    //Default constructor
    //Instance variables are set to the default values
    //Postcondition: firstName = ""; lastName = "";
    //               dMonth = 1; dDay = 1; dYear = 1900;
    //               personID = 0;
```

```
┌─────────────────────────────────────────────────┐
│        ┌───────────────────────────────┐         │
│        │         PersonalInfo          │         │
│        ├───────────────────────────────┤         │
│        │ -name: Person                 │         │
│        │ -bDay: Date                   │         │
│        │ -personID: int                │         │
│        ├───────────────────────────────┤         │
│        │ +PersonalInfo()               │         │
│        │ +PersonalInfo(String, String, int,      │
│        │           int, int, int)      │         │
│        │ +setPersonalInfo(String, String, int,   │
│        │              int, int, int): void       │
│        │ +toString(): String           │         │
│        └───────────────────────────────┘         │
└─────────────────────────────────────────────────┘
```

Figure 11-10   UML diagram of the class PersonalInfo

The definitions of the methods of the class personalInfo follow:

```
public void setPersonalInfo(String first, String last, int month,
                            int day, int year, int ID)
{
    name.setName(first,last);
    bDay.setDate(month,day,year);
    personID = ID;
}

public String toString()
{
    return ("Name: " + name.toString() + "\n"
        + "Date of birth: " + bDay.toString() + "\n"
        + "Personal ID: " + personID);
}
```

```
public PersonalInfo(String first, String last, int month,
                    int day, int year, int ID)
{
    name = new Person(first,last);   //instantiate and
                                     //initialize the object name
    bDay = new Date(month,day,year);//instantiate and
                                     //initialize the object bDay
    personID = ID;
}

public PersonalInfo()
{
    name = new Person();     //instantiate and initialize
                             //the object name
    bDay = new Date();       //instantiate and initialize
                             //the object bDay
    personID = 0;
}
```

Next, we give the definition of the **class PersonalInfo**:

```
public class PersonalInfo
{
    private Person name;
    private Date bDay;
    private int personID;

        //Default constructor
        //Instance variables are set to the default values
        //Postcondition: firstName = ""; lastName = "";
        //               dMonth = 1; dDay = 1; dYear = 1900;
        //               personID = 0;
    public PersonalInfo()
    {
        name = new Person();
        bDay = new Date();
        personID = 0;
    }

        //Constructor with parameters
        //Instance variables are set according to the parameters
        //Postcondition: firstName = first; lastName = last;
        //               dMonth = month; dDay = day; dYear = year;
        //               personID = ID;
    public PersonalInfo(String first, String last, int month,
                        int day, int year, int ID)
    {
        name = new Person(first,last);
        bDay = new Date(month,day,year);
        personID = ID;
    }
```

```
    //Method to set the personal information
    //Instance variables are set according to the parameters
    //Postcondition: firstName = first; lastName = last;
    //                dMonth = month; dDay = day; dYear = year;
    //                personID = ID;
public void setpersonalInfo(String first, String last,
                            int month, int day, int year,
                            int ID)
{
    name.setName(first,last);
    bDay.setDate(month,day,year);
    personID = ID;
}
    //Method to return the string containing personal
    //information
public String toString()
{
    return ("Name: " + name.toString() + "\n"
        + "Date of birth: " + bDay.toString() + "\n"
        + "Personal ID: " + personID);
}
}
```

PROGRAMMING EXAMPLE: GRADE REPORT

This programming example further illustrates the concepts of inheritance and composition.

The midsemester point at your local university is approaching. The registrar's office wants to prepare the grade reports as soon as the students' grades are recorded. Some of the enrolled students have not yet paid their tuition, however.

If a student has paid their tuition, the grades are shown on the grade report with the grade-point average (GPA).

If a student has not paid the tuition, the grades are not printed. For these students, the grade report contains a message indicating that the grades have been held for nonpayment of the tuition. The grade report also shows the billing amount.

The registrar's office and the business office want you to help write a program that can analyze the students' data and print the appropriate grade reports.

The program is divided into two parts. In the first part, we create the application program that generates the grade report in the window's console environment, as well as stores the output in a file.

In the second part, we create a GUI to display students' grade reports as shown in the section Student Grade Report: GUI Design.

Part I: Student Grade Report: Console Display

For this report, the data is stored in a file in the following form:

```
noOfStudents tuitionRate
studentName studentID isTuitionPaid numberOfCourses
courseName courseNumber creditHours grade
courseName courseNumber creditHours grade
  .
  .
  .
studentName studentID isTuitionPaid numberOfCourses
courseName courseNumber creditHours grade
courseName courseNumber creditHours grade
  .
  .
  .
```

The first line indicates the number of students enrolled and the tuition rate per credit hour. The students' data is given thereafter.

A sample input file follows:

```
3 345
Lisa Miller 890238 Y 4
Mathematics MTH345 4 A
Physics PHY357 3 B
ComputerSci CSC478 3 B
History HIS356 3 A
  .
  .
  .
```

The first line indicates that 3 students are enrolled and the tuition rate is $345 per credit hour. Next, the course data for student **Lisa Miller** is given: Lisa Miller's ID is **890238**, she has paid the tuition, and is taking **4** courses. The course number for the mathematics class she is taking is **MTH345**, the course has **4** credit hours, her mid-semester grade is **A**, and so on. The output of the program is of the following form:

```
Student Name: Lisa Miller
Student ID: 890238
Number of courses enrolled: 4

Course No  Course Name  Credits Grade
CSC478     ComputerSci     3      B
HIS356     History         3      A
```

```
MTH345      Mathematics      4      A
PHY357      Physics          3      B
```

```
Total number of credit hours: 13
Midsemester GPA: 3.54
```

It is clear from this output that the courses must be ordered according to the course number. To calculate the GPA, we assume that the grade A is equivalent to 4 points, B is equivalent to 3 points, C is equivalent to 2 points, D is equivalent to 1 point, and F is equivalent to 0 points.

Input   A file containing the data in the form given previously. For easy reference in the rest of the discussion, let's assume that the name of the input file is stData.txt and this file is on floppy disk A.

Output   A file containing the output of the form given previously.

Problem Analysis and Algorithm Design

We must first identify the main components of the program. The university has students, and every student takes courses. Thus, the two main components are the student and the course.

Let's first describe the component Course.

Course

The main characteristics of a course are the course name, course number, and number of credit hours. Although the grade a student receives is not really a characteristic of a course, to simplify the program, this component also includes the student's grade.

Some of the basic operations that need to be performed on an object of the course type follow:

1. Set the course information.
2. Print the course information.
3. Show the credit hours.
4. Show the course number.
5. Show the grade.

The following defines the members of the class Course (see Figure 11-11).

```
                        Course

        -courseName: String
        -courseNo: String
        -courseGrade: char
        -courseCredits: int

        +Course()
        +Course(String, String, char, int,)
        +setCourseInfo(String, String,
                       char, int): void
        +setCourseName(String): void
        +setCourseNumber(String): void
        +setCourseGrade(char): void
        +setCourseCredits(int): void
        +print(boolean): void
        +print(PrintWriter, boolean): void
        +getCredits(): int
        +getCourseNumber(): String
        +getGrade(): char
        +getCourseInfo(boolean): String
        +copyCourseInfo(Course): void
```

Figure 11-11 UML diagram of the `class` Course

Instance Variables:

```
private String courseName;   //object to store the course name
private String courseNo;     //object to store the course number
private char courseGrade;    //variable to store the grade
private int courseCredits;   //variable to store the
                             //course credits
```

Instance Methods:

```
public void setCourseInfo(String cName, String cNo,
                          char grade, int credits)
   //Method to set the course information
   //The course information is set according to the
   //incoming parameters.
   //Postcondition: courseName = cName; courseNo = cNo;
   //               courseGrade = grade; courseCredits = credits;

public void setCourseName(String cName)
   //Method to set the course name
   //Postcondition: courseName = cName;

public void setCourseNumber(String cNo)
```

```
       //Method to set the course number
       //Postcondition: courseNo = cNo;

public void setCourseGrade(char grade)
       //Method to set the course grade
       //Postcondition: courseGrade = grade;

public void setCourseCredits(int credits)
       //Method to set the course credits
       //Postcondition: courseCredits = credits;

public void print(boolean isGrade)
         //Method to print the course information
         //Postcondition: This method prints the course information
         //on the screen. Furthermore, if the boolean parameter
         //isGrade is true, the grade is shown; otherwise three stars
         //are printed.

public void print(PrintWriter outp, boolean isGrade)
       //Method to print the course information
       //Postcondition: This method sends the course information
       //to a file. Furthermore, if the boolean parameter isGrade
       //is true, the grade is shown, otherwise three stars are
       //shown.

public int getCredits()
       //Method to return the credit hours
       //Postcondition: The value of the instance variable
       //                courseCredits is returned.

public String getCourseNumber()
       //Method to return the course number
       //Postcondition:  The value of the instance variable
       //                courseNo is returned;
public char getGrade()
       //Method to return the grade for the course
       //Postcondition: The value of the instance variable
       //                courseGrade is returned.

public String getCourseInfo(boolean isGrade)
       //Method to return the course information as a string
       //Postcondition: The course no, course name,
       //                course credits, and grade are returned
       //                as a string.
       //      If isGrade is true, the course grade is returned;
```

```
//      otherwise "***" is returned as part of the
//      string.

public Course(String cName, String cNo,
              char grade, int credits)
   //Constructor
   //The object is initialized according to the parameters.
   //Postcondition: courseName = cName; courseNo = cNo;
   //               courseGrade = grade; courseCredits = credits;

public Course()
   //Default Constructor
   //The object is initialized to the default values.
   //Postcondition: courseName = ""; courseNo = "";
   //               courseGrade = '*'; courseCredits = 0;


public void copyCourseInfo(Course otherCourse)
   //otherCourse is copied into this course
   //Postcondition: courseName = otherCourse.courseName;
   //               courseNo = otherCourse.courseNo;
   //               courseGrade = otherCourse.courseGrade;
   //               courseCredits = otherCourse.courseCredits;
```

Next we discuss the definition of the methods to implement the operations of the class `Course`.

The method `setCourseInfo` sets the values of the instance variables according to the values of the parameters. Its definition is:

```
public void setCourseInfo(String cName, String cNo,
                          char grade, int credits)
{
    courseName = cName;
    courseNo = cNo;
    courseGrade = grade;
    courseCredits = credits;
}
```

The definitions of the methods `setCourseName`, `setCourseNumber`, `setCourseGrade`, and `setCourseCredits` are similar to the method `setCourseInfo`. Their definitons are:

```
public void setCourseName(String cName)
{
    courseName = cName;
}
```

```
public void setCourseNumber(String cNo)
{
    courseNo = cNo;
}

public void setCourseGrade(char grade)
{
    courseGrade = grade;
}

public void setCourseCredits(int credits)
{
    courseCredits = credits;
}
```

The method **print** with one parameter prints the course information on the screen. If the **boolean** parameter **isGrade** is **true**, the grade is printed on the screen; otherwise, three stars are shown in place of the grade. The following steps describe this method:

1. Print the course number, the course name, and the credit hours.

2. **if isGrade** is **true**

      Output the grade

   else

      Output three stars.

The definition of the method **print** is:

```
public void print(boolean isGrade)
{
    System.out.print(courseNo + "\t   "
                    + courseName + "\t\t"
                    + courseCredits + "\t");        //Step 1

    if(isGrade)                                      //Step 2
        System.out.println(courseGrade);
    else
        System.out.println("***");
}
```

The method **print**, which has two parameters, sends the course information to a file. Other than sending the output to a file, which is passed as a parameter, this method's definition is exactly the same as the definition of the previous **print** method. The definition of this method is:

```
public void print(PrintWriter outp, boolean isGrade)
{
    outp.print(courseNo + "\t   "
```

```
                     + courseName + "\t\t"
                     + courseCredits + "\t");

    if(isGrade)
       outp.println(courseGrade);
    else
       outp.println("***");
}
```

The constructor with parameters uses the values specified by the formal parameters to initialize the instance variables. The default constructor uses the default values to initialize the instance variables. Their definitions are as follows:

```
public Course(String cName, String cNo,
              char grade, int credits)
{
    courseName = cName;
    courseNo = cNo;
    courseGrade = grade;
    courseCredits = credits;
}

public Course()
{
    courseName = "";
    courseNo = "";
    courseGrade = '*';
    courseCredits = 0;
}
```

The definitions of the remaining methods are as follows.

```
public int getCredits()
{
    return courseCredits;
}

public String getCourseNumber()
{
    return courseNo;
}

public char getGrade()
{
    return courseGrade;
}

public String getCourseInfo(boolean isGrade)
{
    String str;
```

```
        str = courseNo + "\t   "
            + courseName + "\t\t"
            + courseCredits + "\t";

        if(isGrade)
            str = str + courseGrade;
        else
            str = str + "***";

        return str;
}

public void copyCourseInfo(Course otherCourse)
{
        courseName = otherCourse.courseName;
        courseNo = otherCourse.courseNo;
        courseGrade = otherCourse.courseGrade;
        courseCredits = otherCourse.courseCredits;
}
```

The definition of the **class** Course looks like the following. (You can complete the definition of this class as an exercise if you like.)

```
public class Course
{

        private String courseName;    //object to store the course name
        private String courseNo;      //object to store the course
                                      //number
        private char courseGrade;     //variable to store the grade
        private int courseCredits;    //variable to store the
                                      //course credits

        //Place the definitions of the instance methods
        //as discussed here.
        //...
}
```

Next we discuss the component **Student**.

Student

The main characteristics of a student are the student name, student ID, number of courses in which the student is enrolled, courses in which the student is enrolled, and grade for each course. Because every student must pay tuition, we also include a member to indicate whether the student has paid the tuition.

Every student is a person, and every student takes courses. We have already designed a **class** Person to process a person's first name and last name. We have also designed a class to process the course information. Thus, we see that we can derive the **class** **Student** to keep track of a student's information from the **class** Person, and one member of the **class Student** is of the type **Course**. We can add more members as needed.

The basic operations to be performed on an object of the type **Student** are as follows:

1. Set the student information.
2. Print the student information.
3. Calculate the number of credit hours taken.
4. Calculate the GPA.
5. Calculate the billing amount.
6. Because the grade report will print the courses in ascending order, sort the courses according to the course number.

The following defines the members of the **class Student** (see Figure 11-12):

Instance Variables:

```
private int sId;                //variable to store the student ID
private int numberOfCourses;    //variable to store the number
                                //of courses
private boolean isTuitionPaid;    //variable to indicate if
                                  //the tuition is paid
private Course[] coursesEnrolled; //array to store
                                  //the courses
```

Instance Methods:

```
public void setInfo(String fname, String lName, int ID,
                    int nOfCourses, boolean isTPaid,
                    Course[] courses)
   //Method to set a student's information
   //Postcondition: The instance variables are set according
   //               to the parameters

public void setStudentId(int ID)
   //Method to set a student ID
   //Postcondition : sId = ID;

public void setIsTuitionPaid(boolean isTPaid)
   //Method to set whether on not tuition paid
   //Postcondition : isTuitionPaid = isTPaid;

public void setNumberOfCourses(int nOfCourses)
   //Method to set number of courses taken
   //Postcondition : numberOfCourses = nOfCourses;

public void setCoursesEnrolled(Course[] courses)
   //Method to set courses enrolled
   //Postcondition : array courses is copied into the array
   //       coursesEnrolled and the array coursesEnrolled
   //       is sorted.
```

```
public void print(double tuitionRate)
   //Method to print a student's grade report

public void print(PrintWriter outp, double tuitionRate)
   //Method to print a student's grade report
   //The output is stored in a file specified by the
   //parameter outp

public Student()
   //Default constructor
   //Postcondition: Instance variables are initialized

public String getName()
   //Method to return a String with value
   //firstName + " " + lastName
   //Postcondition: returns firstName concatenated
   //       with a space and lastName

public int getStudentId()
   //Method to get a student ID
   //Postcondition: The value of sId is returned

public boolean getIsTuitionPaid()
   //Method to determine if the tuition is paid
   //Postcondition: The value of isTuitionPaid is returned

public int getNumberOfCourses()
   //Method to get the number of courses taken
   //Postcondition: The value of numberOfCourses is returned

public Course getCourse(int i)
   //Method to get a copy of a course taken
   //Postcondition: a copy of coursesEnrolled[i] is returned

public int getHoursEnrolled()
   //Method to return the credit hours in which a
   //student is enrolled
   //Postcondition: Total credits are calculated and returned
public double getGpa()
   //Method to return the grade point average
   //Postcondition: GPA is calculated and returned

public double billingAmount(double tuitionRate)
   //Method to return the tuition fees
   //Postcondition: Billing amount is calculated and returned

private void sortCourses()
   //Method to sort the courses
   //This method sorts the array coursesEnrolled
```

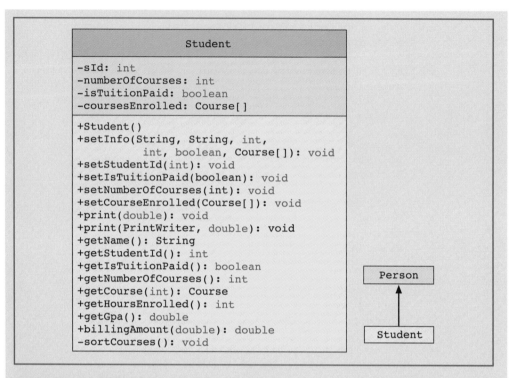

Figure 11-12 UML diagram of the class Student

Note that the method sortCourses to sort the array coursesEnrolled is a private member of the class Student. This is because this method is needed for internal data manipulation and the user of the class does not need to access this member.

Next, we discuss the definitions of the methods to implement the operations of the class Student.

The method setInfo first initializes the private data members according to the incoming parameters. This method then calls the method sortCourses to sort the array coursesEnrolled by course number. The class Student is derived from the class Person, and the variables to store the first name and last name are private members of that class. Therefore, we call the method setName of the class Person, and we pass the appropriate variables to set the first and last names. The definition of the method setInfo is as follows:

```
public void setInfo(String fname, String lName, int ID,
                    int nOfCourses, boolean isTPaid,
                    Course[] courses)
{
    int i;
```

```
        super.setName(fName,lName);   //set the name

        sId = ID;                              //set the student ID
        isTuitionPaid = isTPaid;       //set isTuitionPaid
        numberOfCourses = nOfCourses; //set the number of courses

        for(i = 0; i < numberOfCourses; i++) //set the array
            coursesEnrolled[i].copyCourseInfo(courses[i]);

        sortCourses();          //sort the array coursesEnrolled
}
```

The definitions of the methods `setStudentId`, `setIsTuitionPaid`, `setNumberOfCourses`, and `setCoursesEnrolled` are similar to the definition of the method `setInfo`, and are given next.

```
public void setStudentId(int ID)
{
    sId = ID;
}

public void setIsTuitionPaid(boolean isTPaid)
{
    isTuitionPaid = isTPaid;
}

public void setNumberOfCourses(int nOfCourses)
{
    numberOfCourses = nOfCourses;
}

public void setCoursesEnrolled(Course[] courses)
{
    for(int i = 0; i < numberOfCourses; i++)
        coursesEnrolled[i].copyCourseInfo(courses[i]);

    sortCourses();
}
```

The default constructor initializes the instance variables to the default values.

```
public Student()
{
    super();
    numberOfCourses = 0;
    sId = 0;
    isTuitionPaid = false;
    coursesEnrolled = new Course[6];
```

```
        for(int i = 0; i < 6; i++)
            coursesEnrolled[i] = new Course();
}
```

The method `print`, which has one parameter, prints the grade report on the screen. If the student has paid his or her tuition, the grades and the GPA are shown. Otherwise, three stars are printed in place of each grade, the GPA is not shown, a message indicates that the grades are being held for nonpayment of the tuition, and the amount due is shown. This method has the following steps:

1. To output the GPA and billing amount in a fixed decimal format, declare and instantiate a `DecimalFormat` object.

2. Output the student's name.

3. Output the student's ID.

4. Output the number of courses in which the student is enrolled.

5. Output heading: `Course No   Course Name   Credits   Grade`

6. Print each course's information.

7. Print the total credit hours.

8. `if isTuitionPaid is true`

    Output the GPA

   `else`

    Output the billing amount and a message about withholding the grades.

```
public void print(double tuitionRate)
{
    int i;

    DecimalFormat twoDecimal =
                    new DecimalFormat("0.00");              //Step 1

    System.out.println("Student Name: "
                        + super.toString());                //Step 2

    System.out.println("Student ID: " + sId);               //Step 3

    System.out.println("Number of courses enrolled: "
                        + numberOfCourses);                 //Step 4
    System.out.println("Course No Course Name"
                    + "\t    Credits"
                    + "    Grade");                         //Step 5

    for(i = 0; i < numberOfCourses; i++)                    //Step 6
        coursesEnrolled[i].print(isTuitionPaid);

    System.out.println();
```

```
System.out.println("Total number of credit hours: "
        + twoDecimal.format(getHoursEnrolled())); //Step 7

if(isTuitionPaid)                                  //Step 8
   System.out.println("Midsemester GPA: "
                      + twoDecimal.format(getGpa()));
else
{
   System.out.println("*** Grades are being held for "
                      + "not paying the tuition. ***");
   System.out.println("Amount Due: $"
           + twoDecimal.format(billingAmount(tuitionRate)));
}

System.out.println("-*-*-*-*-*-*-*-*-*-*-*-*-*-"
                   + "*-*-*-*-*-*-*-*-*-*-*-\n");
}
```

The method `print`, which has two parameters, sends the output to a file. For the most part, its definition is the same as the other method `print`, which has one parameter. Because the `class Person` has no method to send the output to a file, we first use the member method `getName` of the `class Person` to retrieve the first and last names. We then print the first and last names. This method's definition is now the same as the definition of the previous method `print`. The definition of this method is:

```
public void print(PrintWriter outp, double tuitionRate)
{
    int i;

    DecimalFormat twoDecimal =
                new DecimalFormat("0.00");

    outp.println("Student Name: "
            + super.toString());

    outp.println("Student ID: " + sId);

    outp.println("Number of courses enrolled: "
            + numberOfCourses);
    outp.println("Course No Course Name"
            + "\t   Credits"
            + "   Grade");

    for(i = 0; i < numberOfCourses; i++)
        coursesEnrolled[i].print(outp, isTuitionPaid);

    outp.println();
```

```
          outp.println("Total number of credit hours: "
                   + twoDecimal.format(getHoursEnrolled()));

       if(isTuitionPaid)
          outp.println("Midsemester GPA: "
                      + twoDecimal.format(getGpa()));
       else
       {
          outp.println("*** Grades are being held for "
                     + "not paying the tuition. ***");
          outp.println("Amount Due: $"
                    + twoDecimal.format(billingAmount(tuitionRate)));
       }

       outp.println("-*-*-*-*-*-*-*-*-*-*-*-*-"
                   + "*-*-*-*-*-*-*-*-*-\n");
}
```

The definitions of the methods getName, getStudentId, getIsTuitionPaid, getNumberOfCourses, and getCourse are given next:

```
public String getName()
{
    return(super.getFirstName() + " " + super.getLastName());
}

public int getStudentId()
{
    return sId;
}

public boolean getIsTuitionPaid()
{
    return isTuitionPaid;
}

public int getNumberOfCourses()
{
    return numberOfCourses;
}

public Course getCourse(int i)
{
    Course temp = new Course();

    temp.copyCourseInfo(coursesEnrolled[i]);

    return temp;
}
```

The method `getHoursEnrolled` calculates and returns the total credit hours that a student is taking. These credit hours are needed to calculate both the GPA and the billing amount. The total credit hours are calculated by adding the credit hours of each course in which the student is enrolled. Because the credit hours for a course are in the `private` data member of an object of type `Course`, we use the member method `getCredits` of the `class Course` to retrieve the credit hours. The definition of this method is:

```java
public int getHoursEnrolled()
{
    int totalCredits = 0;
    int i;

    for(i = 0; i < numberOfCourses; i++)
        totalCredits += coursesEnrolled[i].getCredits();

    return totalCredits;
}
```

If a student has not paid the tuition, the method `billingAmount` calculates and returns the amount due, based on the number of credit hours enrolled. The definition of this method is:

```java
public double billingAmount(double tuitionRate)
{
    return tuitionRate * getHoursEnrolled();
}
```

We now discuss the method `getGpa`. This method calculates a student's GPA. To find the GPA, we find the equivalent points for each grade, add the points, and then divide the sum by the total credit hours the student is taking. The definition of this method is:

```java
public double getGpa()
{
    int i;
    double sum = 0.0;

    for(i = 0; i < numberOfCourses; i++)
    {
        switch(coursesEnrolled[i].getGrade())
        {
        case 'A': sum += coursesEnrolled[i].getCredits() * 4;
                break;
        case 'B': sum += coursesEnrolled[i].getCredits() * 3;
                break;
        case 'C': sum += coursesEnrolled[i].getCredits() * 2;
                break;
        case 'D': sum += coursesEnrolled[i].getCredits() * 1;
                break;
```

```
            case 'F': sum += coursesEnrolled[i].getCredits() * 0;
                     break;
            default: System.out.println("Invalid Course Grade");
            }
     }

     return sum / getHoursEnrolled();
}
```

The method **sortCourses** sorts the array **coursesEnrolled** by course number. To sort the array, we use a selection sort algorithm. Because we will compare the course numbers, which are strings and **private** data members of the **class Course**, we first retrieve and store the course numbers in local variables.

```
private void sortCourses()
{
     int i,j;
     int minIndex;
     Course temp = new Course();     //variable to swap data
     String course1;
     String course2;

     for(i = 0; i < numberOfCourses - 1; i++)
     {
         minIndex = i;

         for(j = i + 1; j < numberOfCourses; j++)
         {
                 //get course numbers
             course1 = coursesEnrolled[minIndex].getCourseNumber();
             course2 = coursesEnrolled[j].getCourseNumber();

             if(course1.compareTo(course2) > 0)
                 minIndex = j;
         }//end for

         temp.copyCourseInfo(coursesEnrolled[minIndex]);
         coursesEnrolled[minIndex].copyCourseInfo(coursesEnrolled[i]);
         coursesEnrolled[i].copyCourseInfo(temp);
     }//end for
}//end sortCourses
```

The definition of the **class Student** looks like the following. (You can complete the definition of this class as an exercise if you like.)

```
import java.io.*;
import java.text.*;
```

```
public class Student extends Person
{
    private int sId;              //variable to store the student ID
    private int numberOfCourses;   //variable to store the number
                                   //of courses
    private boolean isTuitionPaid;  //variable to indicate if
                                    //the tuition is paid
    private Course [] coursesEnrolled; //array to store
                                       //the courses
      //Place the definitions of the instance methods
      //as discussed here.
      //...
}
```

Main Program

Now that we have designed the classes **Course** and **Student**, we will use these classes to complete the program.

We will restrict our program to process a maximum of 10 students. Note that this program can easily be enhanced to process any number of students.

Because the **print** method of the class does the necessary computations to print the final grade report, the main program has very little work to do. In fact, all the main program must do is create the objects to hold the students' data, load the data into these objects, and then print the grade reports. Because the input is in a file and the output will be sent to a file, we declare stream variables to access the input and output files. Essentially, the main algorithm for the program is:

1. Declare the variables.
2. Open the input file.
3. Open the output file.
4. Get the number of students registered and the tuition rate.
5. Load the students' data.
6. Print the grade reports.

Variables   This program processes a maximum of 10 students. Therefore, we must declare an array of 10 components of the type **Student** to hold the students' data. We also need to store the number of students registered and the tuition rate. Because the data will be read from a file, and because the output is sent to a file, we need two stream variables to access the input and output files. Thus, we need the following variables:

```
Student[] studentList = new Student[maxNumberOfStudents];

int noOfStudents;
double tuitionRate;
```

```
BufferedReader infile =
        new BufferedReader(new FileReader("a:\\stData.txt"));
PrintWriter outfile =
        new PrintWriter(new FileWriter("a:\\sDataOut.out"));
```

To simplify the complexity of the method **main**, we write a method, **getStudentData**, to load the students' data.

Method getStudentData   This method has three parameters: a parameter to access the input file, a parameter to access the array **studentList**, and a parameter to know the number of students registered. In pseudocode, the definition of this method is as follows:

For each student in the university:

1. Get the first name, last name, student ID, and **isPaid**.
2. **if isPaid** is 'Y'

   set **isTuitionPaid** to **true**

   else

   set **isTuitionPaid** to **false**
3. Get the number of courses the student is taking.
4. For each course:

   a. Get the course name, course number, credit hours, and grade.

   b. Load the course information into a **Course** object.
5. Load the data into a **Student** object.

We need to declare several local variables to read and store the data. The definition of the method **getStudentData** is:

```
public static void getStudentData(BufferedReader infile,
                                  Student[] sList,
                                  int numberOfStudents)
                                      throws IOException
{
        //Local variables
    String fName;       //variable to store the first name
    String lName;       //variable to store the last name
    int ID;             //variable to store the student ID
    int noOfCourses;    //variable to store the number of courses
    char isPaid;        //variable to store Y/N; that is,
                        //is tuition paid?
    boolean isTuitionPaid;    //variable to store true/false

    String cName; //variable to store the course name
    String cNo;   //variable to store the course number
    int credits;  //variable to store the course credit hours
    char grade;   //variable to store the course grade
```

```
   int count;     //loop control variable
   int i;         //loop control variable

   Course[] courses = new Course[6]; //array of objects to
                                     //store course information
   StringTokenizer tokenizer;

   for(i = 0; i < 6; i++)
      courses[i] = new Course();

   for(count = 0; count < numberOfStudents; count++)
   {
                                                  //Step 1
      tokenizer = new StringTokenizer(infile.readLine());
      fName = tokenizer.nextToken();
      lName = tokenizer.nextToken();
      ID = Integer.parseInt(tokenizer.nextToken());
      isPaid = tokenizer.nextToken().charAt(0);

      if(isPaid == 'Y')                           //Step 2
         isTuitionPaid = true;
      else
         isTuitionPaid = false;

      noOfCourses =
         Integer.parseInt(tokenizer.nextToken());  //Step 3

      for(i = 0; i < noOfCourses; i++)             //Step 4
      {
         tokenizer = new StringTokenizer(infile.readLine());
         cName = tokenizer.nextToken();
         cNo = tokenizer.nextToken();
         credits =
              Integer.parseInt(tokenizer.nextToken());
         grade = tokenizer.nextToken().charAt(0);  //Step 4.a

         courses[i].setCourseInfo(cName, cNo,
                          grade, credits);       //Step 4.b
      }

      sList[count].setInfo(fName, lName, ID,
                       noOfCourses, isTuitionPaid,
                       courses);                  //Step 5
   }//end for
}
```

Method `printGradeReports` This method prints the grade reports. For each student, it calls the method `print` of the `class Student` to print the grade report of each student. The definition of the method `printGradeReports` is:

```
public static void printGradeReports(PrintWriter outfile,
                                     Student[] sList,
                                     int numberOfStudents,
                                     double tuitionRate)
{
    int count;

    for(count = 0; count < numberOfStudents; count++)
        sList[count].print(outfile,tuitionRate);
}
```

Complete Program Listing

```
import java.io.*;
import java.util.*;

public class GradeReportProgram
{
    static final int maxNumberOfStudents = 10;

    public static void main(String[] args) throws IOException,
                                                  FileNotFoundException
    {
        Student[] studentList = new Student[maxNumberOfStudents];

        int noOfStudents;
        double tuitionRate;
        StringTokenizer tokenizer;

        BufferedReader infile =
                new BufferedReader(new FileReader("a:\\stData.txt"));
        PrintWriter outfile =
                new PrintWriter(new FileWriter("a:\\sDataOut.out"));

        for(int i = 0; i < maxNumberOfStudents; i++)
            studentList[i] = new Student();


        tokenizer = new StringTokenizer(infile.readLine());
```

```
        noOfStudents =
            Integer.parseInt(tokenizer.nextToken());   //get the
                                            //number of students
        tuitionRate =
            Double.parseDouble(tokenizer.nextToken()); //get the
                                            //tuition rate

        getStudentData(infile, studentList, noOfStudents);
        printGradeReports(outfile, studentList,
                        noOfStudents, tuitionRate);

        outfile.close();
    }

    //Place the definition of the method getStudentData as
    //described above


    //Place the definition of the method printGradeReports as
    //described above
}
```

Sample Output

```
Student Name: Lisa Miller
Student ID: 890238
Number of courses enrolled: 4
Course No  Course Name  Credits Grade
CSC478     ComputerSci     3      B
HIS356     History         3      A
MTH345     Mathematics     4      A
PHY357     Physics         3      B


Total number of credit hours: 13
Midsemester GPA: 3.54
_-*-_-*-_-*-_-*-_-*-_-*-_-*-_-*-_-*-_-*-_-*-_-*-_-*-_-*-


Student Name: Bill Wilton
Student ID: 798324
Number of courses enrolled: 5
Course No  Course Name  Credits Grade
BIO234     Biology         4      ***
CHM256     Chemistry       4      ***
ENG378     English         3      ***
```

```
MTH346      Mathematics      3      ***
PHL534      Philosophy       3      ***

Total number of credit hours: 17
*** Grades are being held for not paying the tuition. ***
Amount Due: 5865.00
-*-*-*-*-*-*-*-*-*-*-*-*-*-*-*-*-*-*-*-*-*-*-*-*-

Student Name: Dandy Goat
Student ID: 746333
Number of courses enrolled: 6
Course No   Course Name  Credits Grade
BUS128      Business         3       C
CHM348      Chemistry        4       B
CSC201      ComputerSci      3       B
ENG328      English          3       B
HIS101      History          3       A
MTH137      Mathematics      3       A

Total number of credit hours: 19
Midsemester GPA: 3.16
-*-*-*-*-*-*-*-*-*-*-*-*-*-*-*-*-*-*-*-*-*-*-*-*-
```

Input File

```
3 345
Lisa Miller 890238 Y 4
Mathematics MTH345 4 A
Physics PHY357 3 B
ComputerSci CSC478 3 B
History HIS356 3 A
Bill Wilton 798324 N 5
English ENG378 3 B
Philosophy PHL534 3 A
Chemistry CHM256 4 C
Biology BIO234 4 A
Mathematics MTH346 3 C
Dandy Goat 746333 Y 6
History HIS101 3 A
English ENG328 3 B
Mathematics MTH137 3 A
Chemistry CHM348 4 B
ComputerSci CSC201 3 B
Business BUS128 3 C
```

Part II: Student Grade Report: GUI Design

The first part of this programming example illustrated how to display the output in the Windows console environment. In this section, we create the GUI as shown in Figure 11-13 to show the output.

Figure 11-13   GUI to show a student's record

From the desired output, it is clear that the GUI contains various labels, text fields, and buttons. Moreover, when you click one of the buttons on the bottom row, an action event is generated. Therefore, we also need to write the code necessary to handle the events.

The students' records are stored in an array. When the user clicks the button labeled `First`, then the program must display the record of the first student in the list, that is, in the array. Similarly, when the user clicks the `Next` button, the program must display the record of the next student in the list.

An object of the `class JTextField` can display only one line of text. However, the text showing course information contains multiple lines. To display multiline text we make use of the `class JTextArea`. We will create an object of the type `JTextArea` and use appropriate methods of this class to display the courses as desired. We will introduce the methods as we need them. You can refer to Appendix E for a list of methods of the `class JTextArea`.

As in earlier programs, GUI components such as labels are placed in the content pane of the window. Thus, the program contains a window, a container, and various labels, text fields, a text area, and buttons. Let's first declare the reference variables to create labels, text fields, and buttons.

```
//GUI components
//Each of the items to be displayed needs a label and text field.
//Labels end with L, text fields end with TF,
//and buttons end with B.
private JLabel headingL, stNameL, stIDL, noCoursesL,
               courseListL, creditHrsL, gpaL;

private JTextField stNameTF, stIDTF, noCoursesTF,
                   creditHrsTF, gpaTF;

private JTextArea courseListTA; //to display multiline text

private JButton exitB, nextB, prevB, firstB, lastB;
```

The following statements instantiate these objects:

```
      //instantiate labels
headingL = new JLabel("STUDENT RECORD");
stNameL = new JLabel("Student Name ", SwingConstants.RIGHT);
stIDL = new JLabel("Student ID ", SwingConstants.RIGHT);
noCoursesL = new JLabel("Number of Courses ",
                        SwingConstants.RIGHT);
courseListL = new JLabel("Course no          Course name " +
                         "                    Credits " +
                         "               Grade");
creditHrsL = new JLabel("Credit Hours ", SwingConstants.RIGHT);
gpaL =  new JLabel("Midsemester GPA ", SwingConstants.RIGHT);

      //instantiate text fields
stNameTF = new JTextField(10);
stIDTF = new JTextField(10);
noCoursesTF = new JTextField(10);
creditHrsTF = new JTextField(10);
gpaTF =  new JTextField(10);

      //instantiate text area
courseListTA = new JTextArea(6, 20); //6 rows and 20 columns wide
courseListTA.setAutoscrolls(true);   //set scroll bars to show

      //instantiate buttons
exitB = new JButton("Exit");
nextB = new JButton("Next");
prevB = new JButton("Previous");
```

```
firstB = new JButton("First");
lastB = new JButton("Last");
```

We will create a class containing the application program by extending the `class` `JFrame`. We will also create an inner class to handle the action events.

The following statements set the title and the size of the window, and declare a reference variable that points to the content pane of the window.

```
setTitle("Student Information");  //set title of the window
setSize(WIDTH, HEIGHT);          //set size of the window using
                                 //the named constants
                                 //WIDTH and HEIGHT

Container pane  = getContentPane(); //get the container
```

From the GUI design it follows that GUI components are placed at a specific position in the container. To create such an interface, we set the container layout to `null`. The following statement accomplishes this:

```
pane.setLayout(null);         //set container layout to null
```

We use the method **setSize** to specify the size of the GUI components. Recall from Chapter 6 that the heading of the method **setSize** is:

```
public void setSize(int width, int height)
```

The following statements set the size of each component:

```
headingL.setSize(200,30);     //Label headingL is 200 pixels wide
                              //and 30 pixels high
stNameL.setSize(100,30);
stNameTF.setSize(100,30);
stIDL.setSize(100,30);
stIDTF.setSize(100,30);
noCoursesL.setSize(120,30);
noCoursesTF.setSize(100,30);
creditHrsL.setSize(100,30);
creditHrsTF.setSize(100,30);
gpaL.setSize(110,30);
gpaTF.setSize(100,30);
courseListL.setSize(370,30);
courseListTA.setSize(370,120);
firstB.setSize(100,30);
prevB.setSize(100,30);
exitB.setSize(100,30);
nextB.setSize(100,30);
lastB.setSize(100,30);
```

Similarly, we use the method **setLocation** to specify the location of the GUI components in the container. The heading of the method **setLocation** is:

```
public void setLocation(int xCoordinate, int yCoordinate)
```

The following statements set the location of the GUI components in the container:

```
headingL.setLocation(220,10);
stNameL.setLocation(20, 50);
stNameTF.setLocation(120,50);
stIDL.setLocation(20,100);
stIDTF.setLocation(120,100);
noCoursesL.setLocation(300,50);
noCoursesTF.setLocation(420,50);
creditHrsL.setLocation(300,100);
creditHrsTF.setLocation(420,100);
gpaL.setLocation(300,150);
gpaTF.setLocation(420,150);
courseListL.setLocation(70,200);
courseListTA.setLocation(70,230);
firstB.setLocation(20,370);
prevB.setLocation(120,370);
exitB.setLocation(220,370);
nextB.setLocation(320,370);
lastB.setLocation(420,370);
```

We will use the method **add** to put the labels, text fields, text area, and buttons into the container **pane**. The following statements accomplish this:

```
//add labels, text fields, and buttons to the pane
pane.add(headingL);
pane.add(stNameL);
pane.add(stNameTF);
pane.add(stIDL);
pane.add(stIDTF);
pane.add(noCoursesL);
pane.add(noCoursesTF);
pane.add(courseListL);
pane.add(courseListTA);
pane.add(creditHrsL);
pane.add(creditHrsTF);
pane.add(gpaL);
pane.add(gpaTF);
pane.add(firstB);
pane.add(prevB);
pane.add(exitB);
pane.add(nextB);
pane.add(lastB);
```

Method displayGradeReports   Each student's record is stored in the array **studentList**. Therefore, to display a student's grade report, the relevant information is retrieved from the array **studentList** and is displayed in the respective text fields and text area. To simplify displaying a student's record, we write the method `displayGradeReports`. This method takes as its parameter an `int` variable specifying the position (index) in the array where the student's data is stored. Moreover, because the buttons `Next` and `Previous` show the data of the student preceding and following, respectively, the current student, the program must store the index of the current student, which we store in the instance variable `displayedStudentIndex`. Essentially, the definition of the method `displayGradeReports` is:

```
public void displayGradeReports(int stNo)
{
    DecimalFormat twoDecimal =
                      new DecimalFormat("0.00");
    displayedStudentIndex = stNo;
    String CourseListing = "";

    boolean isPaid = studentList[stNo].getIsTuitionPaid();

    stNameTF.setText(studentList[stNo].getName());
    stIDTF.setText(""+studentList[stNo].getStudentId());
    noCoursesTF.setText("" +
                  studentList[stNo].getNumberOfCourses());
    creditHrsTF.setText(""+
          studentList[stNo].getHoursEnrolled());

    if(isPaid)
        gpaTF.setText(""+
              twoDecimal.format(studentList[stNo].getGpa()));
    else
        gpaTF.setText(""+"****");

    for(int count = 0;
            count < studentList[stNo].getNumberOfCourses();
            count++)
    {
        if(count == 0)
            CourseListing =
              studentList[stNo].getCourse(count).getCourseInfo
                                              (isPaid);

        else
            CourseListing = CourseListing + "\n" +
                studentList[stNo].getCourse(count).getCourseInfo
                                              (isPaid);
    }
    if(!isPaid)
        CourseListing = CourseListing + "\n"
                      + "*** Grades are being held for "
```

```
                         + "not paying the tuition. ***\n"
                         + "Amount Due: $" +
              twoDecimal.format(studentList[stNo].billingAmount
              (tuitionRate));

     courseListTA.setText(CourseListing);
}
```

Event Handling The GUI contains five buttons, each generating a specific event. To process these events, we create the `class ButtonHandler` implementing the `interface ActionListener`. Moreover, the method `getActionCommand` of the `class ActionEvent` is used to identify the button generating the event. The definition of the `class ButtonHandler` and the method `actionPerformed` is:

```
private class ButtonHandler implements ActionListener
{
     public void actionPerformed(ActionEvent e)
     {
         if(e.getActionCommand().equals("Previous"))
             if(displayedStudentIndex > 0)
                 displayGradeReports(displayedStudentIndex - 1);
             else
                 displayGradeReports(displayedStudentIndex);
         else if(e.getActionCommand().equals("Next"))
                 if(displayedStudentIndex + 1 < noOfStudents)
                     displayGradeReports(displayedStudentIndex + 1);
                 else
                     displayGradeReports(displayedStudentIndex);
         else if(e.getActionCommand().equals("First"))
                 displayGradeReports(0);
         else if(e.getActionCommand().equals("Last"))
                 displayGradeReports(noOfStudents - 1);
         else
             System.exit(0);
     }
}
```

As usual, we declare and instantiate an object of the type `ButtonHandler` and then register this object to each button. The following statements declare and instantiate the object handler:

```
private ButtonHandler bHandler; //declare the event handler

bHandler = new ButtonHandler(); //instantiate the event handler
```

The following statements register the listener object `bHandler` with the buttons:

```
exitB.addActionListener(bHandler);
nextB.addActionListener(bHandler);
```

```
prevB.addActionListener(bHandler);
firstB.addActionListener(bHandler);
lastB.addActionListener(bHandler);
```

Main Program

As in the first part of this program, this part also processes a maximum of 10 students. Therefore, we must declare an array of 10 components of the type `Student` to hold the students' data. We also must store the number of students registered and the tuition rate. Thus, we need the following variables:

```
Student[] studentList = new Student[maxNumberOfStudents];

int noOfStudents;
double tuitionRate;
```

Because we are creating a GUI, in order to place the data stored in `studentList` in GUI components such as text field and text area, we declare these variables as instance variables of the class containing the application program. Because they will be declared as instance variables, these variables need not be passed as parameters to the method `getStudentData`.

The data will be read from a file, and because the output is sent to a file, we need two stream variables, as declared below, to access the input and output files.

```
BufferedReader infile =
        new BufferedReader(new FileReader("a:\\stData.txt"));
PrintWriter outfile =
        new PrintWriter(new FileWriter("a:\\sDataOut.out"));
```

Method `getStudentData`   Because `studentList` and `noOfStudents` are instance variables, this method can directly access them. Therefore, this method has only one parameter: a parameter to access the input file. In pseudocode, the definition of this method is the same as the definition of this method for the nonGUI application program we designed in the first part. In fact, except for the heading of this method, the body of this method is similar to one given in the first part of this program. Therefore, we give only the heading and leave the body as an exercise for you (see Programming Exercise 11).

```
public static void getStudentData(BufferedReader infile)
                                        throws IOException
{
     //Construct the body of this method.

}
```

In the preceding sections, we defined the necessary algorithms, methods, classes, and GUI components to complete the design of the Java program to create the GUI to display a student's data.

The program listing follows:

```java
//Main program

import java.io.*;
import java.util.*;
import java.text.*;
import javax.swing.*;
import java.awt.*;
import java.awt.event.*;

public class GradeReportProgram extends JFrame
{
    private static final int WIDTH = 550;
    private static final int HEIGHT = 430;

    private static final int maxNumberOfStudents = 10;

        //instance variables
    private Student[] studentList =
                        new Student[maxNumberOfStudents];
    private int noOfStudents;
    private double tuitionRate;
    private int displayedStudentIndex = 0;

        //GUI components
        //Each of the items to be displayed needs a label and
        //text field.
        //Labels end with L and text fields end with TF.
    private JLabel headingL, stNameL, stIDL, noCoursesL,
                courseListL,creditHrsL,gpaL;
    private JTextField stNameTF, stIDTF, noCoursesTF,
                    creditHrsTF, gpaTF;
    private JTextArea courseListTA;
    private JButton exitB, nextB, prevB, firstB, lastB;

    private ButtonHandler bHandler;

    public GradeReportProgram()
    {
      setTitle("Student Information");      //set window title
      setSize(WIDTH,HEIGHT);                //set window size
```

```
Container pane  = getContentPane();   //get container
pane.setLayout(null);   //set container layout to null

bHandler = new ButtonHandler();   //instantiate button
                                  //event handler


    //instantiate labels
headingL = new JLabel("STUDENT RECORD");
stNameL = new JLabel("Student Name ", SwingConstants.RIGHT);
stIDL = new JLabel("Student ID ", SwingConstants.RIGHT);
noCoursesL = new JLabel("Number of Courses ",
                        SwingConstants.RIGHT);
courseListL = new JLabel("Course no          Course name " +
                     "                       Credits " +
                     "              Grade");
creditHrsL = new
     JLabel("Credit Hours ",SwingConstants.RIGHT);
gpaL =  new JLabel("Midsemester GPA ",SwingConstants.RIGHT);

    //instantiate text fields
stNameTF = new JTextField(10);
stIDTF = new JTextField(10);
noCoursesTF = new JTextField(10);
creditHrsTF = new JTextField(10);
gpaTF =  new JTextField(10);

  //instantiate text area
courseListTA = new JTextArea(6, 20);
courseListTA.setAutoscrolls(true);

  //instantiate buttons and register the listener
exitB = new JButton("Exit");
exitB.addActionListener(bHandler);

nextB = new JButton("Next");
nextB.addActionListener(bHandler);

prevB = new JButton("Previous");
prevB.addActionListener(bHandler);

firstB = new JButton("First");
firstB.addActionListener(bHandler);

lastB = new JButton("Last");
lastB.addActionListener(bHandler);
```

```
    //set the size of labels, text fields, and buttons
headingL.setSize(200,30);
stNameL.setSize(100,30);
stNameTF.setSize(100,30);
stIDL.setSize(100,30);
stIDTF.setSize(100,30);
noCoursesL.setSize(120,30);
noCoursesTF.setSize(100,30);
creditHrsL.setSize(100,30);
creditHrsTF.setSize(100,30);
gpaL.setSize(110,30);
gpaTF.setSize(100,30);
courseListL.setSize(370,30);
courseListTA.setSize(370,120);
firstB.setSize(100,30);
prevB.setSize(100,30);
exitB.setSize(100,30);
nextB.setSize(100,30);
lastB.setSize(100,30);

  //set the location of labels, text fields, and buttons
headingL.setLocation(220,10);
stNameL.setLocation(20,50);
stNameTF.setLocation(120,50);
stIDL.setLocation(20,100);
stIDTF.setLocation(120,100);
noCoursesL.setLocation(300,50);
noCoursesTF.setLocation(420,50);
creditHrsL.setLocation(300,100);
creditHrsTF.setLocation(420,100);
gpaL.setLocation(300,150);
gpaTF.setLocation(420,150);
courseListL.setLocation(70,200);
courseListTA.setLocation(70,230);
firstB.setLocation(20,370);
prevB.setLocation(120,370);
exitB.setLocation(220,370);
nextB.setLocation(320,370);
lastB.setLocation(420,370);

  //add labels, text fields, and buttons to the pane
pane.add(headingL);
pane.add(stNameL);
pane.add(stNameTF);
pane.add(stIDL);
pane.add(stIDTF);
pane.add(noCoursesL);
pane.add(noCoursesTF);
```

```
      pane.add(courseListL);
      pane.add(courseListTA);
      pane.add(creditHrsL);
      pane.add(creditHrsTF);
      pane.add(gpaL);
      pane.add(gpaTF);
      pane.add(firstB);
      pane.add(prevB);
      pane.add(exitB);
      pane.add(nextB);
      pane.add(lastB);

      setVisible(true); //show window
  }//end constructor

  public static void main(String[] args) throws IOException,
                                        FileNotFound Exception
  {
      GradeReportProgram gradeProg =
                  new GradeReportProgram();

      StringTokenizer tokenizer;

      BufferedReader infile =
          new BufferedReader(new FileReader("a:\\stData.txt"));

      for(int i = 0; i < maxNumberOfStudents; i++)
          gradeProg.studentList[i] = new Student();

      tokenizer = new StringTokenizer(infile.readLine());
      gradeProg.noOfStudents =
              Integer.parseInt(tokenizer.nextToken());   //get the
                                          //number of students
      gradeProg.tuitionRate =
              Double.parseDouble(tokenizer.nextToken()); //get the
                                                  //tuition rate

      gradeProg.getStudentData(infile);
      gradeProg.displayGradeReports(0);
  }

  //Write and place the definition of the method
  //getStudentData here

  //Place the definition of the class ButtonHandler here

  //Place the definition of the method displayGradeReports here
}
```

Sample Output: (In Programming Exercise 11, at the end of this chapter, you are asked to write the definition of the method `getStudentData`. When you have completed Programming Exercise 11 and execute your program, it should produce the output shown in Figures 11-14 and 11-15.)

Figure 11-14   Sample GUI output of student grade program

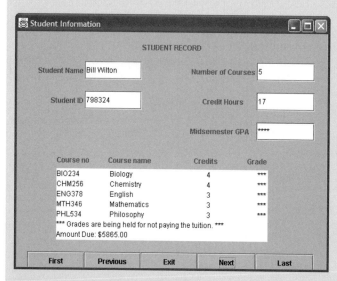

Figure 11-15   Sample output after clicking Next

QUICK REVIEW

1. Inheritance and composition are meaningful ways to relate two or more classes.

2. Inheritance is an "is–a" relationship.

3. Composition is a "has–a" relationship.

4. In single inheritance, the subclass is derived from only one existing class, called the superclass.

5. In multiple inheritance, a subclass is derived from more than one superclass. Java does not support multiple inheritance, that is, in Java a class can only *extend* the definition of one class.

6. The **private** members of a superclass are **private** to the superclass. The subclass cannot directly access them.

7. A subclass can override the method of a superclass, but this redefinition applies only to the objects of the subclass.

8. In general, while writing the definition of the methods of a subclass to specify a call to a **public** method of a superclass, we do the following:

   - If the subclass overrides a **public** method of a superclass, then you specify a call to that **public** method of the superclass by using the reserved word **super** followed by the dot operator followed by the method name with an appropriate parameter list.

   - If the subclass does not override a **public** method of the superclass, you can specify a call to that **public** method by using the name of the method and an appropriate parameter list.

9. While writing the definition of the constructor of a subclass, a call to a constructor of the superclass is specified using the reserved word **super** with an appropriate parameter list. Moreover, the call to a constructor of the superclass must be the first statement.

10. For a superclass to give a member access to its subclass and still prevent its direct access outside the class, you must declare that member using the modifier **protected**.

11. If you define a class and do not use the reserved word **extends** to derive it from an existing class, then the class you define is automatically considered to be derived from the **class Object**.

12. The **class Object** directly or indirectly becomes the superclass of every class in Java.

13. The **classes Reader** and **Writer** are derived from the **class Object**. The classes **BufferedReader** and **InputStreamReader** are derived from the **class Reader**; the **class FileReader** is derived from the **class InputStreamReader**. Similarly, the **classes OutputStreamWriter** and **PrintWriter** are derived from the **class Writer**, and the **class FileWriter** is derived from the **class OutputStreamWriter**.

14. Java allows us to treat an object of a subclass as an object of a superclass, that is, a reference variable of a superclass type can point to an object of a subclass type.

15. You *cannot* automatically consider a superclass object to be an object of a subclass. In other words, you *cannot* automatically make a reference variable of a subclass type point to an object of a superclass type.

16. Suppose that `supRef` is a reference variable of a superclass type. Moreover, suppose that `supRef` points to an object of a subclass. You can use an appropriate cast operator on `supRef` and make a reference variable of the subclass point to the object. On the other hand, if `supRef` does not point to a subclass object, and you use a cast operator on `supRef` to make a reference variable of the subclass point to the object, then Java will throw a `ClassCastException`—indicating that the class cast is not allowed.

17. An abstract method is a method that has only the heading, not the body. Moreover, the heading of an abstract method is terminated with a semicolon.

18. An abstract class is a class that is declared with the reserved word `abstract` in its heading.

19. Following are some of the facts about abstract classes:

   - An abstract class can contain instance variables, constructors, finalizer, and nonabstract methods.

   - An abstract class can contain abstract method(s).

   - If a class contains an abstract method, then the class must be declared abstract.

   - You cannot instantiate an object of an abstract class type. You can only declare a reference variable of an abstract class type.

   - You can instantiate an object of a subclass of an abstract class, but only if the subclass gives the definitions of *all* the abstract methods of the superclass.

20. An `interface` is a class that contains only abstract methods and/or named constants.

21. Java allows a class to implement more than one interface. This is, in fact, the way to implement multiple inheritance in Java.

22. In composition, one or more members of a class are objects of another class type.

EXERCISES

1. Mark the following statements as true or false.

   a. The constructor of a subclass specifies a call to the constructor of the superclass in the heading of the method definition.

   b. The constructor of a subclass specifies a call to the constructor of the superclass using the name of the class.

   c. Suppose that `x` and `y` are classes, one of the data members of `x` is an object of type `y`, and both classes have constructors. The constructor of `x` specifies a call to the constructor of `y` by using the object name of type `y`.

   d. A subclass must have a constructor.

2. Draw a class hierarchy in which several classes are subclasses of a single superclass.

3. Suppose that a `class Employee` is derived from the `class Person` (see Example 8-4, in Chapter 8). Give examples of data and method members that can be added to the `class Employee`.

4. Explain the difference between the `private` and `protected` members of a class.

5. What is the difference between overloading a method name and overriding a method name?

6. Name two situations in which you would use the reserved word `super`.

7. Consider the following class definition:

```
public class AClass
{
    private int u;
    private int v;

    public void print()
    {
    }

    public void set(int x, int y)
    {
    }

    public AClass()
    {
    }

    public AClass(int x, int y)
    {
    }
}
```

What is wrong with the following class definition?

```
class BClass AClass
{
        private int w;

        public void print()
        {
                System.out.println("u + v + w = " +
                (u + v + w);
        }

        public BClass()
        {
                super();
```

11

```
                w = 0;
        }

        public BClass(int x, int y, int z)
        {
                super(x, y);
                w = z;
        }
}
```

8. Consider the following statements:

```
public class YClass
{
        private int a;
        private int b;

        public void one()
        {
        }

        public void two(int x, int y);
        {
        }

        public YClass()
        {
        }
}

class XClass extends YClass
{
        private int z;

        public void one()
        {
        }

        public XClass()
        {
        }
}

YClass yObject;
XClass xObject;
```

a. The private members of YClass are public members of XClass. True or False?

b. Mark the following statements as valid or invalid. If a statement is invalid, explain why.

(i) The following is a valid definition of the method **one** of **YClass**.

```
public void one()
{
      System.out.println(a + b);
}
```

(ii)

```
yObject.a = 15;
xObject.b = 30;
```

(iii) The following is a valid definition of the method **one** of **XClass**.

```
public void one()
{
      a = 10;
      b = 15;
      z = 30;
      System.out.println(a + b + z);
}
```

(iv)

```
System.out.println(yObject.a + " " + yObject.b + " "
                 + xObject.z);
```

9. Assume the declaration of Exercise 8.

a. Write the definition of the default constructor of **YClass** so that the instance variables of **YClass** are initialized to 0.

b. Write the definition of the default constructor of **XClass** so that the instance variables of **XClass** are initialized to 0.

c. Write the definition of the member method **two** of **YClass** so that the instance variable **a** is initialized to the value of the first parameter of **two**, and the instance variable **b** is initialized to the value of the second parameter of **two**.

10. Suppose that you have the following class:

```
public class classA
{
   private int x;                        //Line 1
   protected void setX(int a)            //Line 2
   {                                     //Line 3
      x = a;                             //Line 4
   }
}
```

What is wrong with the following code?

```
public class Exercise10                          //Line 5
{
    public static void main(String[] args) //Line 6
    {
        classA aObject;                          //Line 7

        aObject.setX(4);                         //Line 8
    }
}
```

11. Suppose that you have the following class definition:

```
public class One
{
    private int x;
    private int y;

    public void print()
    {
        System.out.println(x + " " + y);
    }

    protected void setData(int u, int v)
    {
        x = u;
        y = v;
    }
}
```

Consider the following class definition:

```
public class Two extends One
{
    private int z;

    public void setData(int a, int b, int c)
    {
        //Postcondition: x = a; y = b; z = c;
    }

    public void print()
    {
        //Output the values of x, y, and z
    }
}
```

a. Write the definition of the method setData of the class Two as described in the class definition.

b. Write the definition of the method print of the class Two as described in the class definition.

12. Suppose that you have the following class definitions:

```
public class SuperClass
{
    protected int x;

    private String str;

    public void print()
    {
        System.out.println(x + " " + str);
    }

    public SuperClass()
    {
        str = "";
        x = 0;
    }

    public SuperClass(String s, int a)
    {
        str = s;
        x = a;
    }
}


public class SubClass extends SuperClass
{
    private int y;

    public void print()
    {
        System.out.println("SubClass: " + y);
        super.print();
    }

    public SubClass()
    {
        super();
        y = 0;
    }

    public SubClass(String s, int a, int b)
    {
        super("Hello Super", a + b);
        y = b;
    }
}
```

11

What is the output of the following Java code?

```
SuperClass superObject = new SuperClass("This is superclass", 2);
SubClass subObject = new SubClass("DDDDDD", 3, 7);

superObject.print();
subObject.print();
```

13. What does the operator `instanceof` do?

14. What is an abstract method?

15. What is the difference between an abstract class and an interface?

16. Why does Java allow a class to implement more than one interface?

PROGRAMMING EXERCISES

1. In Chapter 8, the `class Clock` was designed to implement the time of day in a program. Certain applications, in addition to hours, minutes, and seconds, might require you to store the time zone. Derive the `class ExtClock` from the `class Clock` by adding a data member to store the time zone. Add the necessary methods and constructors to make the class functional. Also, write the definitions of the methods and the constructors. Finally, write a test program to test your class.

2. In this chapter, the `class Date` was designed to implement the date in a program, but the method `setDate` and the constructor with parameters do not check whether the date is valid before storing the date in the data members. Rewrite the definitions of the method `setDate` and the constructor with parameters so that the values of month, day, and year are checked before storing the date into the data members. Add a method `isLeapYear` to check whether a year is a leap year. Then write a test program to test your class.

3. A point in the x-y plane is represented by its x-coordinate and y-coordinate. Design the `class Point` that can store and process a point in the x-y plane. You should then perform operations on a point, such as showing the point, setting the coordinates of the point, printing the coordinates of the point, returning the x-coordinate, and returning the y-coordinate. Also write a test program to test various operations on a point.

4. Every circle has a center and a radius. Given the radius, we can determine the circle's area and circumference. Given the center, we can determine its position in the x-y plane. The center of a circle is a point in the x-y plane. Design the `class Circle` that can store the radius and center of the circle. Because the center is a point in the x-y plane and you designed the class to capture the properties of a point in Programming Exercise 3, you must derive the `class Circle` from the `class Point`. You should be able to perform the usual operations on a circle, such as setting the radius, printing the radius, calculating and printing the area and circumference, and carrying out the usual operations on the center.

5. Every cylinder has a base and height, where the base is a circle. Design the **class Cylinder** that can capture the properties of a cylinder and perform the usual operations on a cylinder. Derive this class from the **class Circle** designed in Programming Exercise 4. Some of the operations that can be performed on a cylinder are as follows: calculate and print the volume, calculate and print the surface area, set the height, set the radius of the base, and set the center of the base.

6. Using classes, design an online address book to keep track of the names, addresses, phone numbers, and birthdays of family members, close friends, and certain business associates. Your program should be able to handle a maximum of 500 entries.

   a. Define the **class Address** that can store a street address, city, state, and ZIP code. Use the appropriate methods to print and store the address. Also, use constructors to automatically initialize the data members.

   b. Define the **class ExtPerson** using the **class Person** (as defined in Example 8-4, Chapter 8), the **class Date** (as designed in this chapter's Programming Exercise 2), and the **class Address**. Add a data member to this class to classify the person as a family member, friend, or business associate. Also add a data member to store the phone number. Add (or override) methods to print and store the appropriate information. Use constructors to automatically initialize the data members.

   c. Define the **class AddressBook** using previously defined classes. An object of the type **AddressBook** should be able to process a maximum of 500 entries.

   The program should perform the following operations:

   (i)   Load the data into the address book from a disk.

   (ii)   Sort the address book by last name.

   (iii)   Search for a person by last name.

   (iv)   Print the address, phone number, and date of birth (if it exists) of a given person.

   (v)   Print the names of the people whose birthdays are in a given month or between two given dates.

   (vi)   Print the names of all the people between two last names.

   (vii)   For special occasions, such as birthdays, print three different messages: one for family members, one for friends, and one for business associates. Your program should be able to print the names of all family members, friends, or business associates.

7. In Programming Exercise 2, the **class Date** was designed and implemented to keep track of a date, but it has very limited operations. Redefine the **class Date** so that, in addition to the operations already defined, it can perform the following operations on a date:

   a. Set the month.

   b. Set the day.

c. Set the year.

d. Return the month.

e. Return the day.

f. Return the year.

g. Test whether the year is a leap year.

h. Return the number of days in the month. For example, if the date is 3-12-2003, the number of days to be returned is 31 because there are 31 days in March.

i. Return the number of days passed in the year. For example, if the date is 3-18-2003, the number of days passed in the year is 77. Note that the number of days returned also includes the current day.

j. Return the number of days remaining in the year. For example, if the date is 3-18-2003, the number of days remaining in the year is 288.

k. Calculate the new date by adding a fixed number of days to the date. For example, if the date is 3-18-2003 and the days to be added are 25, the new date is 4-12-2003.

l. Return a reference to the object containing a copy of the date.

m. Make a copy of another date. Given a reference to an object containing a date, copy the data members of the object into the corresponding data members of this object.

n. Write the definitions of the methods to implement the operations defined for the class `Date`.

8. The class `Date` defined in Programming Exercise 7 prints the date in numerical form. Some applications might require the date to be printed in another form, such as March 24, 2003. Derive the class `ExtDate` so that the date can be printed in either form.

Add a data member to the class `ExtDate` so that the month can also be stored in string form. Add a method member to output the month in the string format followed by the year—for example, in the form March 2003.

Write the definitions of the method to implement the operations for the class `ExtDate`.

9. Using the classes `ExtDate` (Programming Exercise 8) and `Day` (Chapter 8, Programming Exercise 2), design the class `Calendar` so that, given the month and the year, we can print the calendar for that month. To print a monthly calendar, you must know the first day of the month and the number of days in that month. Thus, you must store the first day of the month, which is of the form `Day`, and the month and the year of the calendar. Clearly, the month and the year can be stored in an object of the form `ExtDate` by setting the day component of the date to 1, and the month and year as specified by the user. Thus, the class `Calendar` has two data members: an object of the type `Day`, and an object of the type `ExtDate`.

Design the class `Calendar` so that the program can print a calendar for any month starting January 1, 1500. Note that the day for January 1 of the year 1500 was a Monday. To calculate the first day of a month, you can add the appropriate days to Monday of January 1, 1500.

For the **class Calendar**, include the following operations:

    a. Determine the first day of the month for which the calendar will be printed. Call this operation **firstDayOfMonth**.

    b. Set the month.

    c. Set the year.

    d. Return the month.

    e. Return the year.

    f. Print the calendar for the particular month.

    g. Add the appropriate constructors to initialize the data members.

10. a. Write the definitions of the methods of the **class Calendar** (designed in Programming Exercise 9) to implement the operations of the **class Calendar**.

    b. Write a test program to print the calendar for either a particular month or a particular year. For example, the calendar for September 2003 is

```
                  September 2003
Sun     Mon     Tue     Wed     Thu     Fri     Sat
         1       2       3       4       5       6
 7       8       9      10      11      12      13
14      15      16      17      18      19      20
21      22      23      24      25      26      27
28      29      30
```

11. Write the definition of the method **getStudentData** of the GUI version of the Programming Example Student Grade Report. Also complete the definition of the main program. When you execute your program, it should produce the output shown in Figures 11-14 and 11-15.

11

12

HANDLING EXCEPTIONS AND EVENTS

In this chapter we go into more detail about what exceptions are in Java and how they are handled. You learn about different kinds of exceptions, and the options that programmers have for dealing with them. You'll also extend what you've learned in Chapters 6 and 11 about event handling.

When we first described the syntax of the method `main` in Chapter 2, we defined an *exception* as an occurrence of an undesirable situation that can be detected during program execution. For example, division by zero is an exception. Similarly, trying to open an input file that does not exist is an exception, as is an array index that goes out of bounds.

Until now our programs have not included code to handle exceptions. If exceptions occurred during program execution, the program terminated with an appropriate error message. However, there are situations when an exception occurs and you don't want the program to simply ignore the exception and terminate. For example, a program that monitors stock performance should not automatically sell if the account balance goes below a certain level. It should inform the stockholder and request an appropriate action.

The code to handle exceptions depends on the type of application you develop. One common way to provide exception-handling code is to add such code at the point where an error might occur. This technique allows the programmer reading the code to see the exception-handling code together with the actual code and determine if the error-checking code is properly implemented. The disadvantage of this approach is that a program can become cluttered with exception-handling code, which can make understanding and maintaining the program difficult, and distract the programmer from ensuring that the program functions correctly.

THE JAVA EXCEPTION HIERARCHY

Chapter 8 discussed how to create your own classes. Every class you design can possibly create its own exceptions. Java provides extensive support for exception handling by providing a number of exception classes. Java also allows users to create and implement their own exception classes to handle exceptions not covered by Java's exception classes. This section discusses the exception classes provided by Java.

The **class Throwable**, which is derived from the **class Object**, is the superclass of the **class Exception**, as shown in Figure 12-1.

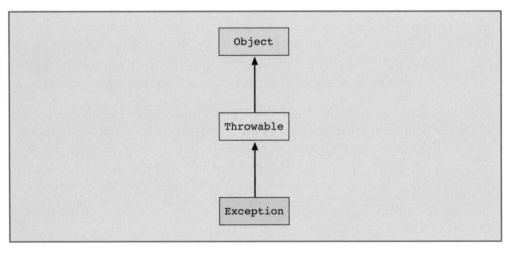

Figure 12-1 The Java exception hierarchy

The **Throwable class** contains various constructors and methods, some of which are described in Table 12-1.

Table 12-1 Some Constructors and Methods of the `class Throwable`

```
public Throwable()
  //Default constructor
  //Creates an instance of Throwable with an empty message string
```

```
public Throwable(String strMessage)
  //Constructor with parameters
  //Creates an instance of Throwable with message string specified
  //by the parameter strMessage
```

```
public String getMessage()
  //Returns the detailed message stored in the object
```

```
public void printStackTrace()
  //Method to print the stack trace showing the sequence of
  //method calls when an exception occurs
```

```
public void printStackTrace(PrintWriter stream)
  //Method to print the stack trace showing the sequence of
  //method calls when an exception occurs
  //Output is sent to the stream specified by the parameter stream.
```

```
public String toString()
  //Returns a string representation of the Throwable object
```

The methods `getMessage`, `printStackTrace`, and `toString` are `public` and are inherited by the subclasses of the `class Throwable`.

The `class Exception` and its subclasses, some of which are shown in Figures 12-2 to 12-4, are designed to catch exceptions that should be caught and processed during program execution, thus making a program more robust. The sections that follow discuss how to use the `class Exception` and its subclasses to handle various types of exceptions, and discuss how to create your own exception classes.

12

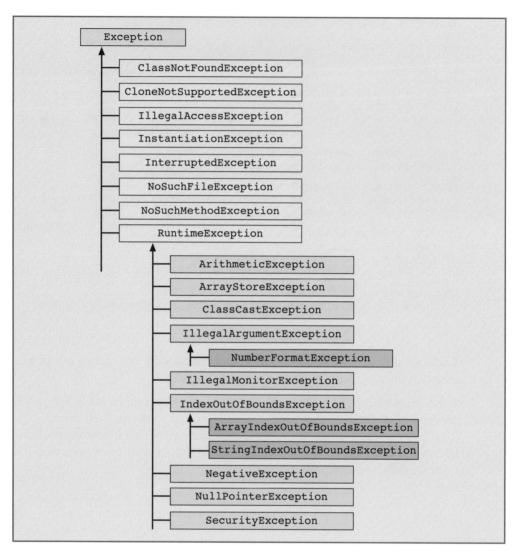

Figure 12-2 The class Exception and some of its subclasses from the package java.lang

Figure 12-3   The `class Exception` and some of its subclasses from the package `java.util` (Notice that the `class RuntimeException` is in the package `java.lang`.)

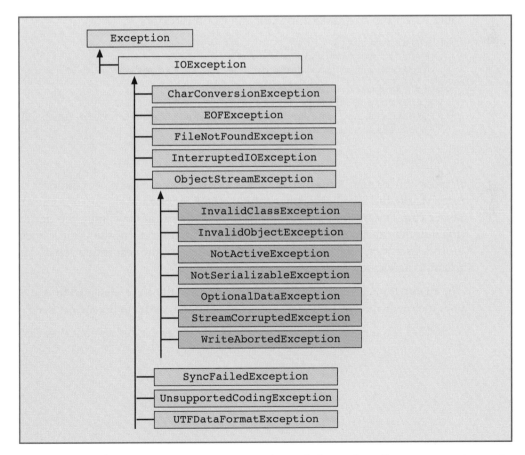

Figure 12-4   The `class IOException` and its subclasses from the `package java.io`

JAVA'S EXCEPTION CLASSES

The **class Exception** is the superclass of the classes designed to handle exceptions. There are various types of exceptions, such as I/O exceptions, number format exceptions, file not found exceptions, and array index out of bounds exceptions. Java categorizes these exceptions into separate classes. Moreover, these predefined exception classes are contained in various packages. The **class Exception** is contained in the **package java.lang**. The classes to deal with I/O exceptions, such as the file not found exception, are contained in the **package java.io**. Similarly, the classes to deal with number format exceptions and arithmetic exceptions, such as division by zero, are contained in the **package java.lang**. Generally, exception classes are placed in the package that contains the methods that throw these exceptions.

The **class Exception** is very simple. It contains only two constructors, as shown in Table 12-2.

Table 12-2 The **class Exception** and its Constructors

```
public Exception()
  //Default constructor
  //Creates a new instance of the class Exception
```

```
public Exception(String str)
  //Constructor with parameters
  //Creates a new instance of the class Exception. The parameter str
  //specifies the message string
```

Because the **class Exception** is a subclass of the **class Throwable**, the **class Exception** and its subclass inherit the methods **getMessage**, **printStackTrace**, and **toString**. The method **getMessage** returns the string containing the detailed message stored in the exception object. The method **toString** returns the detailed message stored in the exception object as well as the name of the exception class. The method **printStackTrace** is discussed later in this chapter.

The **class RuntimeException** is the superclass of the classes designed to deal with exceptions such as division by zero, array index out of bounds, and number format (see Figure 12-2).

Table 12-3 lists some of the exception classes and the type of exceptions they throw.

Table 12-3 Some of Java's Exception Classes

Exception Class	Description
ArithmeticException	Arithmetic errors such as division by 0
ArrayIndexOutOfBoundsException	Array index is either less than 0 or greater than or equal to the length of the array
FileNotFoundException	Reference to a file that cannot be found
IllegalArgumentException	Calling a method with illegal arguments
IndexOutOfBoundsException	An array index is out of bounds
NullPointerException	Reference to an object that has not been instantiated
NumberFormatException	Use of an illegal number format
StringIndexOutOfBoundsException	A string index is either less than 0 or greater than or equal to the length of the string

As we have seen in the previous chapters, Java programs only accept strings as input. Numbers, integer or decimal, are entered as strings. We then use the method `parseInt` of the **class** `Integer` to convert an integer string into the equivalent integer. If the string containing the integer contains only digits, the method `parseInt` will return the integer. However, if the string contains a letter or any other nondigit character, the method `parseInt` throws a `NumberFormatException`. Similarly, the method `parseDouble` also throws this exception if the string does not contain a valid number. The programs that we've written up to this point ignored these exceptions. Later in this chapter we show how to handle these and other exceptions.

Tables 12-4, 12-5, and 12-6 list some of the exceptions thrown by the methods of the **class**es `Integer`, `Double`, `String`, and `StringTokenizer`.

12

Table 12-4 Exceptions Thrown by the Methods of the **class** `Integer`

class Integer		
Method	**Exception Thrown**	**Description**
parseInt(String str)	NumberFormatException	The string str does not contain an int value
valueOf(String str)	NumberFormatException	The string str does not contain an int value

Table 12-5 Exceptions Thrown by the Methods of the `class Double`

class Double		
Method	Exception Thrown	Description
parseDouble(String str)	NumberFormatException	The string str does not contain a double value
valueOf(String str)	NumberFormatException	The string str does not contain a double value

Table 12-6 Exceptions Thrown by the Methods of the `class String`

class String		
Method	Exception Thrown	Description
String(String str)	NullPointerException	str is null
charAt(int a)	StringIndexOutOfBoundsException	The value of a is not a valid index
indexOf(String str)	NullPointerException	str is null
lastIndexOf(String str)	NullPointerException	str is null
substring(int a)	StringIndexOutOfBoundsException	The value of a is not a valid index
substring(int a, int b)	StringIndexOutOfBoundsException	The value of a and/or b is not a valid index

In the preceding chapters, we used the **class StringTokenizer** and its methods to parse a string. Table 12-7 shows the exceptions thrown by some of its methods.

Table 12-7 Exceptions Thrown by the Methods of the `class StringTokenizer`

class StringTokenizer		
Method	Exception Thrown	Description
StringTokenizer(String str)	NullPointerException	str is null
nextToken()	NoSuchElementException	string is null

Appendix E describes various predefined classes as well as the exceptions thrown by the methods of these classes.

CHECKED AND UNCHECKED EXCEPTIONS

In the preceding chapters, whenever we used the methods `readLine` or `read` in the method `main`, we included the `throws IOException` clause. If we did not include this `throws` clause in the heading of the method `main`, the compiler would generate a syntax error. However, we did not worry about situations such as division by zero or even array index out of bounds. If these types of errors occurred during program execution, the program terminated with an appropriate error message. For these types of exceptions we did not need to include any `throws` clause in the heading of any method. So the obvious question is, what type of exceptions need the `throws` clause in a method heading?

Java's predefined exceptions are divided into two categories—checked exceptions and unchecked exceptions. Any exception that can be analyzed by the compiler is called a **checked exception**. For example, `IOException`s are checked exceptions. Since the methods `read` and `readLine` throw `IOException`, these methods throw checked exceptions. When the compiler encounters these method calls, it checks whether the program handles `IOException`s, or reports them by throwing them. Enabling the compiler to check for these types of exceptions reduces the number of exceptions not properly handled by the program. Because our programs so far were not required to handle `IOException`s or other types of predefined exceptions, the programs declared the checked exceptions by throwing them. Later in this chapter we will show an example of how to handle `IOException`s rather than by throwing them.

When a program is being compiled, it may not be possible for the compiler to determine if exceptions such as division by zero or index out of bounds will occur. Therefore, these types of exceptions, called **unchecked exceptions**, are not checked by the compiler. Thus, to significantly improve the correctness of programs, programmers must check for these types of exceptions.

Since the compiler does not check for unchecked exceptions, the program does not need to either declare them using a `throws` clause or provide the code within the program to deal with them. The exceptions belonging to a subclass of the **class RuntimeException** are unchecked exceptions. If a program does not provide code to handle an unchecked exception, then the exception is handled by Java's default exception handler.

In the method heading, the `throws` clause lists the types of exceptions thrown by the method. The syntax of the `throws` clause is:

```
throws ExceptionType1, ExceptionType2, ...
```

where `ExceptionType1`, `ExceptionType2`, and so on are the names of the exception classes.

12

For example, consider the following method:

```
public static void exceptionMethod()
                    throws NumberFormatException, IOException
{
    //statements
}
```

The method `exceptionMethod` throws exceptions of the type `NumberFormatException` and `IOException`.

HANDLING EXCEPTIONS WITHIN A PROGRAM

This section describes how to include the necessary code to handle exceptions within a program.

try/catch/finally Block

Statements that might generate an exception are placed in a `try` block. The `try` block also contains statements that should not be executed if an exception occurs. The `try` block is followed by zero or more `catch` blocks. A `catch` block specifies the type of exception it can catch and contains an exception handler. The last `catch` block may or may not be followed by a `finally` block. Any code contained in a `finally` block always executes, regardless of whether an exception occurs. If a `try` block has no `catch` block, then it *must* have the `finally` block.

Before giving the general syntax of the `try/catch/finally` block, let's observe the following: When an exception occurs, Java creates an object of a specific exception class. For example, if a division by zero exception occurs, then Java creates an object of the `ArithmeticException class`.

The general syntax of the `try/catch/finally` block is:

```
try
{
    //statements
}
catch(ExceptionClassName1 objRef1)
{
    //exception handler code
}
catch(ExceptionClassName2 objRef2)
{
    //exception handler code
}
...
catch(ExceptionClassNameN objRefN)
{
    //exception handler code
}
finally
{
    //statements
}
```

Note the following about `try/catch/finally` blocks:

- If no exception is thrown in a `try` block, all `catch` blocks associated with the `try` block are ignored and program execution resumes after the last `catch` block.

- If an exception is thrown in a `try` block, the remaining statements in the `try` block are ignored. The program searches the `catch` blocks in the order in which they appear after the `try` block and looks for an appropriate exception handler. If the type of the thrown exception matches the parameter type in one of the `catch` blocks, the code of that `catch` block executes and the remaining `catch` blocks after this `catch` block are ignored.

- If there is a `finally` block after the last `catch` block, the `finally` block executes regardless of whether an exception occurs.

As noted, when an exception occurs, an object of a particular exception class type is created. The type of exception handled by a `catch` block is declared in the `catch` block heading, which is the statement between the parentheses after the keyword `catch`.

Consider the following `catch` block:

```
catch(ArithmeticException aeRef)
{
    //exception handler code
}
```

12

This **catch** block catches an exception of the type **ArithmeticException**. The identifier **aeRef** is a reference variable of the type **ArithmeticException**. If an exception of the type **ArithmeticException** is thrown by the **try** block associated with this **catch** block, and control reaches this **catch** block, then the reference parameter **aeRef** contains the address of the exception object thrown by the **try** block. Because **aeRef** contains the address of the exception object, you can access the exception object through the variable **aeRef**. The object **aeRef** stores a detailed description of the thrown exception. You can use the method **getMessage** or the method **toString** to retrieve and print that message containing the description of the thrown exception. We will illustrate this with an example later in the chapter.

Order of **catch** Blocks

A **catch** block can catch all exceptions of a specific type or all types of exceptions. The heading of a **catch** block specifies the type of exception it handles. As discussed in Chapter 11, a reference variable of a superclass type can point to an object of its subclass. Therefore, if in the heading of a **catch** block you declare an exception using the **class Exception**, then that **catch** block can catch all types of exceptions because the **class Exception** is the superclass of all exception classes.

Suppose that an exception occurs in a **try** block and that exception is caught by a **catch** block. Then the remaining **catch** blocks associated with that **try** block are ignored. Therefore, you should be careful about the order in which you list **catch** blocks following a **try** block. For example, consider the following sequence of **try/catch** blocks:

```
try                                     //Line 1
{
    //statements
}
catch(Exception eRef)                   //Line 2
{
    //statements
}
catch(ArithmeticException aeRef)        //Line 3
{
    //statements
}
```

Suppose that an exception is thrown in the **try** block. Because the **catch** block at Line 2 can catch exceptions of all types, the **catch** block at Line 3 cannot be reached. This sequence of **try/catch** blocks would, in fact, result in a compile time error. In a sequence of **catch** blocks following a **try** block, **catch** blocks declaring exceptions of a subclass type should be placed before **catch** blocks declaring exceptions of a superclass type. Often it is useful to make sure that all exceptions thrown by a **try** block are caught. In that case, you should make the **catch** block which declares an exception of the **class Exception** type the last **catch** block.

Using `try/catch` Blocks in a Program

Next we give some examples to illustrate how `try/catch` blocks might appear in a program.

One common error that might occur while inputting numeric data is typing a nonnumeric character such as a letter. Because Java only accepts strings as input, inputting data into a string variable won't cause any problems. However, when we use the methods `parseInt`, `parseFloat`, or `parseDouble` to convert the numeric string into its respective numeric form, the program may terminate with a number format error. This is because each of the methods `parseInt`, `parseFloat`, and `parseDouble` `throw` a number format exception if the numeric string does not contain a number. For example, if the numeric string does not contain an `int` value, then when the method `parseInt` tries to determine the numeric form of the integer string, it throws a `NumberFormatException`.

Another error that might occur when performing numeric calculation is division by zero with integer values. During program execution, if division by zero occurs with integer values and is not addressed by the program, then the program terminates with an error message indicating an attempt to divide by zero. In this case, the program throws an exception of the `class ArithmeticException`.

Example 12-1

This example illustrates how to catch and handle number format and division by zero exceptions. The program in this example also illustrates how a `try/catch` block might appear in a program.

```java
import java.io.*;

public class ExceptionExample1
{
    static BufferedReader keyboard = new
            BufferedReader(new InputStreamReader(System.in));

    public static void main(String[] args)
                    throws IOException                  //Line 1
    {
        int dividend, divisor, quotient;                //Line 2

        try                                             //Line 3
        {
            System.out.print("Line 4: Enter dividend: "); //Line 4
            System.out.flush();                            //Line 5
            dividend =
                    Integer.parseInt(keyboard.readLine()); //Line 6
            System.out.println();                          //Line 7

            System.out.print("Line 8: Enter divisor: ");   //Line 8
```

12

```
        System.out.flush();                        //Line 9
        divisor =
            Integer.parseInt(keyboard.readLine()); //Line 10
        System.out.println();                      //Line 11

        quotient = dividend / divisor;             //Line 12
        System.out.println("Line 13: quotient = "
                            + quotient);           //Line 13
    }
    catch(ArithmeticException aeRef)               //Line 14
    {
        System.out.println("Line 15: Exception "
                        + aeRef.toString());       //Line 15
    }
    catch(NumberFormatException nfeRef)            //Line 16
    {
        System.out.println("Line 17: Exception "
                        + nfeRef.toString());      //Line 17
    }
  }
}
```

Sample Run 1: In this sample run, the user input is shaded.

```
Line 4: Enter dividend: 45

Line 8: Enter divisor: 2

Line 13: quotient = 22
```

Sample Run 2: In this sample run, the user input is shaded.

```
Line 4: Enter dividend: 18

Line 8: Enter divisor: 0

Line 15: Exception java.lang.ArithmeticException: / by zero
```

Sample Run 3: In this sample run, the user input is shaded.

```
Line 4: Enter dividend: 75

Line 8: Enter divisor: f5
Line 17: Exception java.lang.NumberFormatException: f5
```

The program works as follows. The method **main** starts at Line 1, which throws the **IOException**. The statement in Line 2 declares the **int** variables **dividend**, **divisor**, and **quotient**. The **try** block starts at Line 3. The statement in Line 4 prompts the user to enter the value of the dividend. The statement in Line 6 stores the number in the variable **dividend**. The statement in Line 8 prompts the user to enter the value of the divisor, and the statement in Line 10 stores the number in the variable **divisor**. The statement in

Line 12 divides the value of `dividend` by the value of `divisor` and stores the result in `quotient`. The statement in Line 13 outputs the value of `quotient`.

The first `catch` block starts at Line 14 and the second `catch` block starts at Line 16. The `catch` block at Line 14 catches an `ArithmeticException` and the `catch` block at Line 16 catches a `NumberFormatException`.

In Sample Run 1, the program did not throw any exceptions.

In Sample Run 2, the entered value of `divisor` is 0. Therefore, when the `dividend` is divided by the `divisor`, the statement in Line 12 throws the `ArithmeticException`, which is caught by the `catch` block starting at Line 14. The statement in Line 15 outputs the appropriate message.

In Sample Run 3, the value entered at Line 10 for the variable `divisor` contains the letter f, a nondigit character. Because this value cannot be converted to an integer, the statement in Line 10 throws the `NumberFormatException`. Notice that the `NumberFormatException` is thrown by the method `parseInt` of the `class Integer`. The `catch` block starting at Line 16 catches this exception and the statement in Line 17 outputs the appropriate message.

Notice that in Example 12-1 the method `main` still throws the `IOException`. (See Line 1.) This is because we did not include the code to handle this exception. Let's redo the program in Example 12-1 and include a `catch` block for the `IOException`.

Example 12-2

Consider the following code:

```java
import java.io.*;

public class ExceptionExample2
{
    static BufferedReader keyboard = new
            BufferedReader(new InputStreamReader(System.in));

    public static void main(String[] args)          //Line 1
    {
        int dividend, divisor, quotient;            //Line 2

        try                                         //Line 3
        {
            System.out.print("Line 4: Enter dividend: "); //Line 4
            System.out.flush();                     //Line 5
            dividend
                = Integer.parseInt(keyboard.readLine()); //Line 6
            System.out.println();                   //Line 7
```

```
        System.out.print("Line 8: Enter divisor: ");   //Line 8
        System.out.flush();                             //Line 9
        divisor
            = Integer.parseInt(keyboard.readLine());    //Line 10
        System.out.println();                           //Line 11

        quotient = dividend / divisor;                  //Line 12
        System.out.println("Line 13: quotient = "
                           + quotient);                 //Line 13
    }
    catch(ArithmeticException aeRef)                    //Line 14
    {
        System.out.println("Line 15: Exception "
                           + aeRef.toString());         //Line 15
    }
    catch(NumberFormatException nfeRef)                 //Line 16
    {
        System.out.println("Line 17: Exception "
                           + nfeRef.toString());        //Line 17
    }
    catch(IOException ioeRef)                           //Line 18
    {
        System.out.println("Line 19: Exception "
                           + ioeRef.toString());        //Line 19
    }
  }
}
```

This program works the same way as the program in Example 12-1. Here the **IOException** is also handled by the program. (See the statements in Lines 18 and 19.)

The **class Exception** and the Operator **instanceof**

The program in Example 12-2 uses three **catch** blocks to handle three types of exceptions. Recall from Chapter 11 that a reference of a superclass type can point to objects of its subclasses, and using the operator **instanceof**, you can determine if a reference variable points to an object of a particular **class**. You can use this facility to combine the three **catch** blocks of the program of Example 12-2 into one **catch** block as shown by the following program:

```
import java.io.*;

public class ExceptionExample3
{
    static BufferedReader keyboard = new
            BufferedReader(new InputStreamReader(System.in));
```

```
public static void main (String[] args)              //Line 1
{
    int dividend, divisor, quotient;                 //Line 2

    try                                              //Line 3
    {
        System.out.print("Line 4: Enter dividend: ");  //Line 4
        System.out.flush();                          //Line 5
        dividend =
               Integer.parseInt(keyboard.readLine());  //Line 6
        System.out.println();                        //Line 7

        System.out.print("Line 8: Enter divisor: ");  //Line 8
        System.out.flush();                          //Line 9
        divisor
            = Integer.parseInt(keyboard.readLine());  //Line 10
        System.out.println();                        //Line 11

        quotient = dividend / divisor;               //Line 12
        System.out.println("Line 13: quotient = "
                        + quotient);                 //Line 13
    }
    catch(Exception eRef)                            //Line 14
    {
        if(eRef instanceof ArithmeticException)      //Line 15
            System.out.println("Line 16: Exception "
                        + eRef.toString());          //Line 16
        else if(eRef instanceof NumberFormatException) //Line 17
                System.out.println("Line 18: Exception "
                        + eRef.toString());          //Line 18
        else if(eRef instanceof IOException)         //Line 19
                System.out.println("Line 20: Exception "
                        + eRef.toString());          //Line 20
    }
  }
}
```

This program works the same way as the program in Examples 12-1 and 12-2. In this program there is only one **catch** block, which can catch all types of exceptions. (See the statement in Line 14.) This is because, directly or indirectly, the **class Exception** is the superclass of all exception classes and a reference variable of a superclass can point to an object of its subclasses. The parameter, **eRef**, of the **catch** block at Line 14 is a reference variable of the **Exception** type. The statement in Line 15 determines if **eRef** is an instance of the **class ArithmeticException**—that is, if it points to an object of the **class ArithmeticException**. Similarly, the statement in Line 17 determines if **eRef** is an instance of the **class NumberFormatException**, and the statement in Line 19 determines if **eRef** is an instance of the **class IOException**. If **eRef** is an instance of **ArithmeticException**, then the statement in Line 16 executes, and so on.

Example 12-3

The Programming Example Student Grade in Chapter 3 shows a program that calculates a student's grade. The program reads data from a file and writes output to a file. The program given in Chapter 3 throws the `FileNotFoundException` and other exceptions. Now that we know how to handle exceptions in a program, we can rewrite the program and handle the exceptions.

```java
//This program illustrates how to handle FileNotFoundException,
//IOException, or any other exception
//Program: calculate average test score

import java.io.*;
import java.text.DecimalFormat;
import java.util.*;

public class StudentGrade
{
    public static void main (String[] args)
    {

        //Declare and initialize variables              //Step 1
        double test1, test2, test3, test4, test5;
        double average;
        String firstName;
        String lastName;
        StringTokenizer tokenizer;

        try
        {
            BufferedReader inFile = new
                BufferedReader(new FileReader("a:\\test.txt")); //Step 2

            PrintWriter outFile = new
                PrintWriter(new FileWriter("a:\\testavg.out")); //Step 3

            DecimalFormat twoDecimal =
                        new DecimalFormat("0.00");             //Step 4

            tokenizer =
                new StringTokenizer(inFile.readLine());        //Step 5
            firstName = tokenizer.nextToken();                 //Step 6
            lastName = tokenizer.nextToken();                  //Step 6
            outFile.println("Student Name: "
                        + firstName + " " + lastName);         //Step 7

                //Step 8—Retrieve five test scores
            test1 = Double.parseDouble(tokenizer.nextToken());
            test2 = Double.parseDouble(tokenizer.nextToken());
```

```
            test3 = Double.parseDouble(tokenizer.nextToken());
            test4 = Double.parseDouble(tokenizer.nextToken());
            test5 = Double.parseDouble(tokenizer.nextToken());

            outFile.println("Test scores: "
                        + twoDecimal.format(test1) + " "
                        + twoDecimal.format(test2) + " "
                        + twoDecimal.format(test3) + " "
                        + twoDecimal.format(test4) + " "
                        + twoDecimal.format(test5));         //Step 9

            average = (test1 + test2 + test3 + test4
                    + test5) / 5.0;                          //Step 10
            outFile.println("Average test score: "
                        + twoDecimal.format(average));       //Step 11

            outFile.close();                                 //Step 12

        }
        catch(FileNotFoundException fnfeRef)
        {
            System.out.println(fnfeRef.toString());
        }
        catch(IOException ioeRef)
        {
            System.out.println(ioeRef.toString());
        }
        catch(Exception eRef)
        {
            System.out.println(eRef.toString());
        }
    }
}
```

Sample Run: If there is a floppy disk in drive A, but no input file exists, the following message is printed:

```
java.io.FileNotFoundException: a:\test.txt (The system cannot find
the file specified.)
```

The statement to open the input and output file, as well as the input and output statements, are within the **try** block. The first **catch** block catches a **FileNotFoundException**, the second **catch** block catches an **IOException**, and the third **catch** block catches all types of exceptions. As shown in the Sample Run, if the input file does not exist, the statement in Step 2 in the **try** block throws **FileNotFoundException**, which is caught and handled by the first **catch** block.

Rethrowing and Throwing an Exception

When an exception occurs in a `try` block, the control immediately passes to one of the `catch` blocks. Typically, a `catch` block does the following:

- Completely handles the exception.

- Partially processes the exception. In this case the `catch` block either rethrows the same exception or throws another exception for the calling environment to handle the exception.

- Rethrows the same exception for the calling environment to handle the exception.

The `catch` blocks in Examples 12-1 to 12-3 handled the exception. The mechanism of rethrowing or throwing an exception is quite useful in cases when a `catch` block catches the exception, but the `catch` block is unable to handle the exception, or if the `catch` block decides that the exception should be handled by the calling environment. This allows the programmer to provide the exception handling code in one place.

Rethrowing an exception or throwing an exception is accomplished by the `throw` statement. A `throw` statement can throw either a checked or an unchecked exception.

Exceptions are objects of a specific `class` type. Therefore, if you have a reference to an exception object, you can use the reference to throw the exception. In this case, the general syntax to rethrow an exception caught by a `catch` block is:

```
throw exceptionReference;
```

Example 12-4 shows how to rethrow an exception caught by a `catch` block.

Example 12-4

Consider the following Java code:

```
//RethrowExceptionExmp1

import java.io.*;

public class RethrowExceptionExmp1
{
    static BufferedReader keyboard = new
            BufferedReader(new InputStreamReader(System.in));

    public static void main(String[] args)                      //Line 1
    {
        int number;                                             //Line 2

        try                                                     //Line 3
        {
            number = getNumber();                               //Line 4
```

```
        System.out.println("Line 5: number = "
                            + number);                      //Line 5
    }
    catch(NumberFormatException nfeRef)                      //Line 6
    {
        System.out.println("Line 7: Exception "
                            + nfeRef.toString());            //Line 7
    }
    catch(IOException ioeRef)                                //Line 8
    {
        System.out.println("Line 9: Exception "
                            + ioeRef.toString());            //Line 9
    }
}

public static int getNumber()
            throws NumberFormatException, IOException        //Line 10
{
    int num;                                                 //Line 11

    try                                                      //Line 12
    {
        System.out.print("Line 13: Enter an integer: "); //Line 13
        System.out.flush();                                  //Line 14
        num = Integer.parseInt(keyboard.readLine());         //Line 15

        return num;                                          //Line 16
    }
    catch(NumberFormatException nfeRef)                      //Line 17
    {
        throw nfeRef;                                        //Line 18
    }
}
}
```

Sample Run 1: In this sample run, the user input is shaded.

```
Line 13: Enter an integer: 12
Line 5: number = 12
```

Sample Run 2: In this sample run, the user input is shaded.

```
Line 13: Enter an integer: 56t7
Line 7: Exception java.lang.NumberFormatException: 56t7
```

The preceding program contains the method `getNumber`, which reads an integer and returns it to the method `main`. If the number entered by the user contains a nondigit character, the method `getNumber` throws the `NumberFormatException`. This exception is caught by the `catch` block in Line 17. Rather than handle this exception, the method `getNumber` rethrows this exception. (See the statement in Line 18.)

The `catch` block at Line 6 of the method `main` also catches the `NumberFormatException`.

In Sample Run 1, the method `getNumber` successfully reads the number and returns the number to the method `main`. In Sample Run 2, the user enters an illegal number. The statement in Line 15 throws the `NumberFormatException`, which is caught and rethrown by the `catch` block starting at Line 17. After the statement in Line 18 executes, the control goes back to the method `main` (at Line 4), which throws the `NumberFormatException` thrown by the method `getNumber`. The `catch` block at Line 6 catches this exception and the statement in Line 7 outputs the appropriate message.

Notice that the method `getNumber` also throws an `IOException` exception. This is because this method contains an input statement that could throw an `IOException`. Because an `IOException` is a checked exception, the method `getNumber` either should handle this exception or this exception will be implicitly thrown by the system. Therefore, the method `getNumber` throws the exception using the `throws` statement in its heading. This exception is handled in the method `main`.

Example 12-4 illustrates how to rethrow the same exception caught by a `catch` block. When an exception occurs, an object of a specific exception `class` is created by the system. In fact, you can also create your own exception objects and throw them using the `throw` statement. In this case, the general syntax used for the `throw` statement is:

```
throw new ExceptionClassName(messageString);
```

Of course, you could have first created the object and then used the reference of the object in the `throw` statement.

Example 12-5 illustrates how to create and `throw` an exception object.

Example 12-5

```
//RethrowExceptionExmp2

import java.io.*;

public class RethrowExceptionExmp2
{
    static BufferedReader keyboard = new
            BufferedReader(new InputStreamReader(System.in));

    public static void main (String[] args)                    //Line 1
    {
        int number;                                            //Line 2

        try                                                    //Line 3
        {
            number = getNumber();                              //Line 4
```

```
        System.out.println("Line 5: number = "                        //Line 5
                        + number);

    }
    catch(NumberFormatException nfeRef)                                //Line 6
    {
        System.out.println("Line 7: Exception "
                        + nfeRef.toString());                          //Line 7
    }
    catch(IOException ioeRef)                                          //Line 8
    {
        System.out.println("Line 9: Exception "
                        + ioeRef.toString());                          //Line 9
    }
}

public static int getNumber()
            throws NumberFormatException, IOException                 //Line 10
{
    int num;                                                          //Line 11

    try                                                               //Line 12
    {
        System.out.print("Line 13: Enter an integer: ");             //Line 13
        System.out.flush();                                          //Line 14
        num = Integer.parseInt(keyboard.readLine());                 //Line 15

        return num;                                                   //Line 16
    }
    catch(NumberFormatException nfeRef)                               //Line 17
    {
        System.out.println("Line 18: Exception "
                        + nfeRef.toString());                         //Line 18
        throw new NumberFormatException("getNumber");                //Line 19
    }
}
}
```

Sample Run: In this sample run, the user input is shaded.

```
Line 13: Enter an integer: 563r9
Line 18: Exception java.lang.NumberFormatException: 563r9
Line 7: Exception java.lang.NumberFormatException: getNumber
```

The preceding program works similarly to the program in Example 12-4. The difference is in the **catch** block starting at Line 17, in the method **getNumber**. The catch block at Line 17 catches a **NumberFormatException**, outputs an appropriate message at Line 18, and then at Line 19 creates a **NumberFormatException** object with the message string **"getNumber"** and throws the object. The thrown object is caught by the **catch** block at Line 6 in the method **main**. The statement in Line 7 outputs the appropriate message. Notice that the output of the statement in Line 18, the second line of the Sample Run, outputs the number entered by the user, while the statement in Line 7, the third line of the Sample Run, outputs the string getNumber. This is because the statement in Line 19 creates and throws an object that is different from the NumberFormatException object thrown by the statement in Line 15. The object thrown by the statement in Line 19 contains the message string "getNumber".

The programs in Examples 12-4 and 12-5 illustrate how a method can rethrow the same exception object or create an exception object and throw it for the calling method to handle. This mechanism is quite useful; it allows a program to handle exceptions in one location rather than spreading exception-handling code throughout the program.

THE METHOD printStackTrace

Suppose that method A calls method B, method B calls method C, and an exception occurs in method C. Java keeps track of this sequence of method calls. Recall that the class Exception is a subclass of the class Throwable. As shown in Table 12-1, class Throwable contains the public method printStackTrace. Because the method printStackTrace is public, every subclass of the class Throwable inherits this method. When an exception occurs in a method, you can use the method printStackTrace to determine the order in which the methods were called and where the exception was handled.

Example 12-6

This example shows the use of the method printStackTrace to show the order in which methods were called and exceptions handled.

```java
import java.io.*;

public class PrintStackTraceExample1
{
    public static void main (String[] args)
    {
        try
        {
            methodA();
        }
        catch(Exception e)
        {
            System.out.println(e.toString() + " caught in main");
            e.printStackTrace();
        }
    }
}
```

```
public static void methodA() throws Exception
{
    methodB();
}

public static void methodB() throws Exception
{
    methodC();
}

public static void methodC() throws Exception
{
    throw new Exception("Exception generated in method C");
}
}
```

Output

```
java.lang.Exception: Exception generated in method C caught in main
java.lang.Exception: Exception generated in method C
        at PrintStackTraceExample1.methodC
        (PrintStackTraceExample1.java:31)
        at PrintStackTraceExample1.methodB
        (PrintStackTraceExample1.java:26)
        at PrintStackTraceExample1.methodA
        (PrintStackTraceExample1.java:22)
        at PrintStackTraceExample1.main
        (PrintStackTraceExample1.java:11)
```

The preceding program contains the methods methodA, methodB, methodC, and the method main. The method methodC creates and throws an object of the class Exception. The method methodB calls methodC, methodA calls methodB, and the method main calls methodA. The methods methodA and methodB do not handle the exception thrown by methodC, and so contain the throws Exception clause in their heading. The method main handles the exception thrown by methodC, which was propagated first by methodB and then by methodA. The catch block in the method main first outputs the message contained in the exception object and the string " caught in main", then it calls the method printStackTrace to trace the method calls. (See the last four lines of the output.)

The program in Example 12-7 is similar to the program in Example 12-6. The main difference is that the exception thrown by the method C is caught and handled in methodA. Notice that the heading of methodA does not contain any throws clause.

Example 12-7

```java
import java.io.*;

public class PrintStackTraceExample2
{
    public static void main(String[] args)
    {
        methodA();
    }

    public static void methodA()
    {
        try
        {
            methodB();
        }
        catch(Exception e)
        {
            System.out.println(e.toString() + " caught in methodA");
            e.printStackTrace();
        }
    }

    public static void methodB() throws Exception
    {
        methodC();
    }

    public static void methodC() throws Exception
    {
        throw new Exception("Exception generated in method C");
    }
}
```

Output

```
java.lang.Exception: Exception generated in method C caught in methodA
java.lang.Exception: Exception generated in method C
        at PrintStackTraceExample2.methodC
        (PrintStackTraceExample2.java:30)
        at PrintStackTraceExample2.methodB
        (PrintStackTraceExample2.java:25)
        at PrintStackTraceExample2.methodA
        (PrintStackTraceExample2.java:14)
        at PrintStackTraceExample2.main
        (PrintStackTraceExample2.java:7)
```

EXCEPTION-HANDLING TECHNIQUES

When an exception occurs in a program, usually the programmer has three choices—terminate the program, include code in the program to recover from the exception, or log the error and continue. Each of these situations is discussed in the following sections.

Terminate the Program

In some cases, it is best to let the program terminate when an exception occurs. Suppose you have written a program that inputs data from a file. If the input file does not exist when the program executes, then there is no point in continuing with the program. In this case, the program can output an appropriate error message and terminate.

Fix the Error and Continue

In other cases, you will want to handle the exception and let the program continue. Suppose you have a program that takes as input a number. If a user inputs a character in place of a digit, the program will throw a `NumberFormatException`. This is a situation where you can include the necessary code to keep prompting the user to input a number until the entry is valid. For example, you could include the following code in the program. (Assume that all variables are properly declared.)

```
done = false;

do
{
  try
  {
     System.out.print("Enter an integer: ");
     System.out.flush();
     number = Integer.parseInt(keyboard.readLine());
     System.out.println();
     done = true;
  }
  catch(NumberFormatException nfeRef)
  {
     System.out.println("\nException " + nfeRef.toString());
  }
}while(!done);
```

The do...while loop continues to prompt the user until the user inputs a valid integer.

Log the Error and Continue

A program that terminates when an exception occurs usually assumes that termination is reasonably safe. On the other hand, if your program is designed to run a nuclear reactor or continuously monitor a satellite, it cannot be terminated if an exception occurs. These programs should report the exception, but the program must continue to run.

For example, consider a program that analyzes airline-ticketing transactions. Because a large number of ticketing transactions take place each day, a program is run daily to validate that day's transactions. This type of program would take an enormous amount of time to process the transactions. Therefore, when an exception occurs, the program should write the exception into a file and continue to analyze the transactions.

CREATING YOUR OWN EXCEPTION CLASSES

When you create your own classes or write programs, exceptions are likely to occur. As you have seen, Java provides a substantial number of exception classes to deal with these. However, Java does not provide all the exception classes you will ever need. Therefore, Java enables programmers to create exception classes to handle the exceptions not covered by Java's exception classes or to handle their own exceptions. This section describes how to create your own exception classes.

Java's mechanism to process the exceptions you define is the same as that for built-in exceptions. However, you must throw your own exceptions using the **throw** statement.

The exception class that you define extends either the **class Exception** or one of its subclasses. Moreover, the subclass of the **class Exception** is either a predefined class or a user-defined class. In other words, if you have created an exception class, you can define other exception classes extending the definition of the exception class you created.

Typically, constructors are the only methods that you include when you define your own exception class. Because the exception class you define is a subclass of an existing exception class, built-in or user-defined, the exception class that you define inherits the members of the superclass. Therefore, objects of exception classes can use the **public** members of the superclasses.

Because the **class Exception** is derived from the **class Throwable**, it inherits the methods **getMessage** and **toString** of the **class Throwable**. Moreover, because these methods are **public**, they are also inherited by the subclasses of the **class Exception**.

Example 12-8

This example shows how to create your own division by zero exception class:

```
package jpfpatpd.ch12.myExceptionClasses;

public class myDivisionByZeroException extends Exception
{
    public myDivisionByZeroException()
    {
        super("Cannot divide by zero");
    }
```

```
    public myDivisionByZeroException(String strMessage)
    {
        super(strMessage);
    }
}
```

The program in Example 12-9 uses the **class myDivisionByZeroException** designed in Example 12-8.

Example 12-9

```
import java.io.*;

import jpfpatpd.ch12.myExceptionClasses.myDivisionByZeroException;

public class myDivisionByZeroExceptionTestProg
{
    static BufferedReader keyboard
            = new BufferedReader(new InputStreamReader(System.in));

    public static void main(String[] args)
    {
        double numerator;                                           //Line 1
        double denominator;                                         //Line 2

        try                                                         //Line 3
        {
            System.out.print("Line 4: Enter numerator: ");          //Line 4
            System.out.flush();                                     //Line 5
            numerator
                    = Double.parseDouble(keyboard.readLine());     //Line 6
            System.out.println();                                  //Line 7

            System.out.print("Line 8: Enter denominator: ");       //Line 8
            System.out.flush();                                     //Line 9
            denominator
                    = Double.parseDouble(keyboard.readLine());     //Line 10
            System.out.println();                                  //Line 11

            if(denominator == 0.0)                                 //Line 12
                throw new myDivisionByZeroException();             //Line 13

            System.out.println("Line 14: Quotient = "
                            + (numerator / denominator));          //Line 14
        }
```

```
        catch(myDivisionByZeroException mdbzeRef)          //Line 15
        {
           System.out.println("Line 16: "
                           + mdbzeRef.toString());          //Line 16
        }
        catch(Exception eRef)                               //Line 17
        {
           System.out.println("Line 18: "
                           + eRef.toString());              //Line 18
        }
     }
  }
```

Sample Run 1: In this sample run, the user input is shaded.

Line 4: Enter numerator: 25

Line 8: Enter denominator: 4

Line 14: Quotient = 6.25

Sample Run 2: In this sample run, the user input is shaded.

Line 4: Enter numerator: 20

Line 8: Enter denominator: 0

Line 16: jpfpatpd.ch12.myExceptionClasses.myDivisionByZeroException:
Cannot divide by zero

The class myDivisionByZeroException is placed in the package jpfpatpd.ch12.myExceptionClasses, and the program in Example 12-9 imports this class from this package. However, if the class myDivisionByZeroException and the program in Example 12-9 reside in the same subdirectory, then it is not necessary to first create the package and then import the class. For more information see Appendix D.

If the exception class you create is a direct subclass of the class Exception or a direct subclass of an exception class whose exceptions are checked exceptions, then the exceptions of the class you created are checked exceptions.

EVENT HANDLING

In Chapter 6 you learned that when you click on a button, it generates an action event. Similarly, when you press the **Enter** key in a text field, it also generates an action event. In fact, when you press a mouse button to click on a button, in addition to generating an action event, a mouse event is also generated. Similarly, when you press the **Enter** key in a text field, in addition to the action event, it also generates a key event. Therefore, a GUI program can simultaneously generate more than one event.

As described in Chapter 6, Java provides various `interface`s to handle different events. For example, to handle action events, you use the `interface ActionListener`; to handle mouse events, you use the `interface MouseListener`; key events are handled by the `interface KeyListener`; and window events are handled by the `interface WindowListener`. These and other interfaces contain methods that are executed when a particular event occurs. For example, when an action event occurs, the method `actionPerformed` of the `interface ActionListener` is executed.

In order to handle an event, we create an appropriate object and register the object with the GUI component. Recall that the methods of an interface are `abstract`. That is, they only contain the headings of the methods. Therefore, you cannot instantiate an object of an interface. To create an object to handle an event, first you create a class that implements an appropriate interface.

Chapter 6 discussed in detail how to handle action events. Recall that to handle an action event, we do the following:

1. Create a class that implements the `interface ActionListener`. For example, in Chapter 6 for the `JButton calculateB` we created the `class CalculateButtonHandler`.

2. Provide the definition of the method `actionPerformed` within the class that you created in Step 1. The method `actionPerformed` contains the code that the program executes when the specific event is generated. For example, in Chapter 6 when you click on the `JButton calculateB`, the program should calculate and display the area and the perimeter of the rectangle.

3. Create and instantiate an object of the class created in Step 1. For example, in Chapter 6 for the `JButton calculateB`, we created the object `cbHandler`.

4. Register the event handler created in Step 3 with the object that generates an action event using the method `addActionListener`. For example, in Chapter 6 for the `JButton calculateB`, the following statement registers the object `cbHandler` to listen and register the action event.

```
calculateB.addActionListener(cbHandler);
```

Just as you create objects of the class that extends the `interface ActionListener` to handle action events, to handle window events you first create a class that implements the `interface WindowListener` and then create and register objects of that class. You do similar things to handle mouse events.

In Chapter 6, to terminate the program when the close window button is clicked, we used the method `setDefaultCloseOperation` with the predefined named constant `EXIT_ON_CLOSE`. If you want to provide your own code to terminate the program when the window is closed, or if you want the program to take a different action when the window closes, then you use the `interface WindowListener`. That is, first you create a class that implements the `interface WindowListener`, you provide the appropriate definition of the method `windowClosed`, you create an appropriate object of that class, and then you register the object created with the program.

Let's look at the definition of the `interface WindowListener`:

```
public interface WindowListener
{
    void windowActivated(WindowEvent e);
      //This method executes when a window is activated.
    void windowClosed(WindowEvent e);
      //This method executes when a window is closed.
    void windowClosing(WindowEvent e);
      //This method executes when a window is closing; just
      //before a window is closed.
    void windowDeactivated(WindowEvent e);
      //This method executes when a window is deactivated.
    void windowIconified(WindowEvent e);
      //This method executes when a window is iconified.
    void windowOpened(WindowEvent e);
      //This method executes when a window is opened.
}
```

As you can see, the `interface WindowListener` contains several `abstract` methods. Therefore, to instantiate an object of the class that implements the `interface WindowListener`, that class must provide the definition of each method of the `interface WindowListener`, even if a method is not used. Of course, if a method is not used, you could provide an empty body for that method. Recall that if a class contains an `abstract` method, you cannot instantiate an object of that class.

In Chapter 6 we used the mechanism of the inner class to handle events. That is, the class that implemented the interface was defined within the class containing the application program. Chapter 11 noted that rather than create an inner class to implement the interface, the class containing the application program can itself implement the interface. Moreover, because a program can generate various types of events, such as action events and window events, recall from Chapter 11 that Java allows a class to implement more than one interface. However, Java does not allow a class to extend the definition of more than one class; that is, Java does not support multiple inheritance.

For interfaces such as `WindowListener` that contain more than one method, Java provides the `class WindowAdapter`. The `class WindowAdapter` implements the `interface WindowListener` by providing an empty body for each method of the `interface WindowListener`. To be specific, the definition of the `class WindowAdapter` is:

```
public class WindowAdapter implements WindowListener
{
    void windowActivated(WindowEvent e)
    {
    }
    void windowClosed(WindowEvent e)
    {
    }
```

```
    void windowClosing(WindowEvent e)
    {
    }
    void windowDeactivated(WindowEvent e)
    {
    }
    void windowIconified(WindowEvent e)
    {
    }
    void windowOpened(WindowEvent e)
    {
    }
}
```

If you use the mechanism of the inner class to handle a window event, you can create the class by extending the definition of the **class WindowAdapter** and provide the definition of only the methods that the program needs. Similarly, to handle window events, if the class containing the application program does not extend the definition of another class, you can make that class extend the definition of the **class WindowAdapter**.

Chapter 6 discussed in detail how to use the mechanism of the inner class, and Chapter 11 explained how to make the class containing the application program implement more than one interface. As stated in Chapter 11, there is one more way to handle events in a program—using the mechanism of anonymous classes. This mechanism is quite useful to handle events such as window and mouse events since the corresponding interfaces contain more than one method and the program might want to use only one method.

Recall from Chapter 6 that to register an action listener object to a GUI component, you use the method **addActionListener**. To register a **WindowListener** object to a GUI component, you use the method **addWindowListener**. The **WindowListener** object being registered is passed as a parameter to the method **addWindowListener**.

Consider the following code:

```
this.addWindowListener(new WindowAdapter()
            {
                    public void windowClosing(WindowEvent e)
                    {
                        System.exit(0);
                    }
            }
);
```

The preceding statements create an object of the anonymous class, which extends the **class WindowAdapter** and overrides the method **windowClosing**. The object created is passed as an argument to the method **addWindowListener**. The method **addWindowListener** is invoked by explicitly using the reference **this**.

Similarly, you can handle mouse events by using the interface MouseListener. The definition of the interface MouseListener and the class MouseAdapter is:

```
public interface MouseListener
{
    void mouseClicked(MouseEvent e);
      //This method executes when a mouse button is clicked
      //on a component.
    void mouseEntered(MouseEvent e);
      //This method executes when the mouse enters a component.
    void mouseExited(MouseEvent e);
      //This method executes when the mouse exits a component.
    void mousePressed(MouseEvent e);
      //This method executes when a mouse button
      //is pressed on a component.
    void mouseReleased(MouseEvent e);
      //This method executes when a mouse button is released
      //on a component.
}

public class MouseAdapter implements MouseListener
{
    void mouseClicked(MouseEvent e)
    {
    }
    void mouseEntered(MouseEvent e)
    {
    }
    void mouseExited(MouseEvent e)
    {
    }
    void mousePressed(MouseEvent e)
    {
    }
    void mouseReleased(MouseEvent e)
    {
    }
}
```

To register a MouseListener object to a GUI component, you use the method addMouseListener. The MouseListener object being registered is passed as a parameter to the method addMouseListener.

In addition to the GUI components with which you have worked, Chapter 13 introduces other GUI components such as check boxes, option buttons, menu items, and lists. These GUI components also generate events. Table 12-8 summarizes the various events generated by GUI components. Table 12-8 also shows the GUI component, the listener interface, and the name of the method of the interface to handle the event.

Table 12-8 Events Generated by a GUI Component, the Listener Interface, and the Name of the Method of the Interface to Handle the Event

GUI Component	Event Generated	Listener Interface	Listener Method
JButtton	ActionEvent	ActionListener	actionPerformed
JCheckBox	ItemEvent	ItemListener	itemStateChanged
JCheckboxMenuItem	ItemEvent	ItemListener	itemStateChanged
JChoice	ItemEvent	ItemListener	itemStateChanged
JComponent	ComponentEvent	ComponentListener	componentHidden
JComponent	ComponentEvent	ComponentListener	componentMoved
JComponent	ComponentEvent	ComponentListener	componentResized
JComponent	ComponentEvent	ComponentListener	componentShown
JComponent	FocusEvent	FocusListener	focusGained
JComponent	FocusEvent	FocusListener	focusLost
Container	ContainerEvent	ContainerListener	componentAdded
Container	ContainerEvent	ContainerListener	componentRemoved
JList	ActionEvent	ActionListener	actionPerformed
JList	ItemEvent	ItemListener	itemStateChanged
JMenuItem	ActionEvent	ActionListener	actionPerformed
JScrollbar	AdjustmentEvent	AdjustmentListener	adjustmentValueChanged
JTextComponent	TextEvent	TextListener	textValueChanged
JTextField	ActionEvent	ActionListener	actionPerformed
Window	WindowEvent	WindowListener	windowActivated
Window	WindowEvent	WindowListener	windowClosed
Window	WindowEvent	WindowListener	windowClosing
Window	WindowEvent	WindowListener	windowDeactivated
Window	WindowEvent	WindowListener	windowDeiconified
Window	WindowEvent	WindowListener	windowIconified
Window	WindowEvent	WindowListener	windowOpened

12

Even though **key** and **mouse** are not GUI components, they do generate events. Table 12-9 summarizes the events generated by the **key** and **mouse** components.

Table 12-9 Events Generated by key and mouse Components

	Event Generated	Listener Interface	Listener Method
key	KeyEvent	KeyListener	keyPressed
key	KeyEvent	KeyListener	keyReleased
key	KeyEvent	KeyListener	keyTyped
mouse	MouseEvent	MouseListener	mouseClicked

Table 12-9 Events Generated by key and mouse Components (continued)

	Event Generated	Listener Interface	Listener Method
mouse	MouseEvent	MouseListener	mouseEntered
mouse	MouseEvent	MouseListener	mouseExited
mouse	MouseEvent	MouseListener	mousePressed
mouse	MouseEvent	MouseListener	mouseReleased
mouse	MouseEvent	MouseMotionListener	mouseDragged
mouse	MouseEvent	MouseMotionListener	mouseMoved

 The section Key and Mouse Events in Chapter 13 gives examples to show how to handle key and mouse events.

PROGRAMMING EXAMPLE: CALCULATOR

In this programming example, we design a program that simulates a calculator. The program will provide the basic integer arithmetic operations +, −, *, and /. When the program executes, it displays the GUI shown in Figure 12-5.

Figure 12-5 Calculator program GUI

Input Integers via pressing various digit buttons; arithmetic operations via pressing operation buttons; the equals sign via pressing the button containing the symbol = on the calculator panel; and clearing inputs by pressing the "C" button.

Output The result of the operation or an appropriate error message if something goes wrong.

Problem Analysis and GUI and Algorithm Design

As shown in Figure 12-5, the GUI contains 16 buttons, a text field, and a window. The buttons and the text field are placed in the content pane of the window. The user enters the input using the various buttons, and the program displays the result in the text field. To create the 16 buttons, you use 16 reference variables of the type `JButton`, and to create the text field, you use a reference variable of type `JTextField`. You also need a reference variable to access the content pane of the window. As we did in previous GUI programs (in Chapters 6, 8, and 11), we create the class containing the application program by extending the definition of the **class JFrame**, which also allows you to create the necessary window to create the GUI. Thus, we use the following variables to create the GUI components and to access the content pane of the window:

```
private JTextField displayText = new JTextField(30);
private JButton[] button = new JButton[16];

Container pane = getContentPane(); //to access the content pane
```

As you can see from Figure 12-5, the GUI components are nicely organized. To place the GUI components as shown in Figure 12-5, we set the layout of the content pane to `null` and use the methods **setSize** and **setLocation**. The following statement instantiates the **JTextField** object **displayText** and places it in the content pane:

```
displayText.setSize(200, 30);
displayText.setLocation(10, 10);
pane.add(displayText);
```

The size of **displayText** is set to 200 pixels wide and 30 pixels high and it is placed at position (10, 10) in the content pane.

To assign labels to the buttons, rather than write 16 statements, we use an array of strings and a loop. Consider the following statement:

```
private String[] keys = {"7", "8", "9", "/",
                         "4", "5", "6", "*",
                         "1", "2", "3", "-",
                         "0", "C", "=", "+"};
```

Because the size of the **displayText** is 200 pixels wide and there are four **JButton**s in each row, we set the width of each **JButton** to 50 pixels wide. To keep the height of each **JButton** the same as the height of **displayText**, we set the height of each **JButton** to 30 pixels.

The user enters the input via the buttons. Therefore, each button can generate an action event. To respond to the events generated by a button, we will create and register an appropriate object. In Chapters 6, 8, and 11, we used the mechanism of the inner class to create and register a listener object. In this program, we make the class containing the application program implement the `interface ActionListener`. Therefore, we only need to provide the definition of the method `actionPerformed`, which will be described later in this section. Since the class containing the application implements the `interface ActionListener`, we do not need to explicitly instantiate a listener object. We can simply use the reference `this` as an argument to the method `addActionListener` to register the listener.

The following statements instantiate the 16 `JButtons`, place them in the content pane at the proper location, and register the listener object:

```
int x, y;

x = 10;
y = 40;
for(int ind = 0; ind < 16; ind++)
{
    button[ind] = new JButton(keys[ind]); //instantiate the
                                          //JButton and assign it
                                          //a label
    button[ind].addActionListener(this); //register the listener
                                          //object
    button[ind].setSize(50,30);           //set the size
    button[ind].setLocation(x, y);        //set the location
    pane.add(button[ind]);                //place the button
                                          //in the content pane

        //determine the coordinates of the next JButton
    x = x + 50;
    if((ind + 1) % 4 == 0)
    {
        x = 10;
        y = y + 30;
    }
}
```

The inputs to the program are integers, various operations, and the equals symbol. The numbers are entered via the buttons whose labels are digits and the operations are specified via the buttons whose labels are operations. When the user presses the button with the label =, the program displays the results. The user can also press the button with the label C to clear the numbers.

Because Java only accepts strings as inputs to the program, we need two `String` variables to store the number strings. Before performing the operation, the strings will be converted to their numeric form.

In order to input numbers, the user presses various digit buttons, one at a time. For example, to specify that a number is **235**, the user presses the buttons labeled **2**, **3**, and **5** in sequence. After pressing each button, the number is displayed in the text field. Each number is entered as a string and therefore concatenated with the previous string. When the user presses an operation button, it indicates that the user will start entering the second number. Therefore, we use a **boolean** variable which is set to **false** after the first number is input. We will need the following variables:

```
private String numStr1 = "";
private String numStr2 = "";

private char op;
private boolean firstInput = true;
```

When an event is generated by a button, the method **actionPerformed** is executed. Now when the user clicks on the = button, the program must display the result. Similarly, when the user clicks on an operation button, the program should prepare to receive the second number, and so on. We therefore see that the instructions to receive the inputs and operations and display the results will be placed in the method **actionPerformed**. Next we describe this method.

Method **actionPerformed**   As described above, the method **actionPerformed** is executed when the user presses any button. Several things can go wrong while using the calculator. For example, the user might press an operation button without specifying the first number; the user might press the equals button without specifying any number or after inputting the first number. Of course, we must also take care of division by zero. Therefore, the method **actionPerformed** must appropriately respond to the errors.

Suppose that the user wants to add three numbers. After adding the first two numbers, the third number can be added to the sum of the first two numbers. In this case, when the third number is added, the first number is the sum of the first two numbers and the second number becomes the third number. Therefore, after each operation, we will set the first number as the result of the operation. The user can click the **C** button to start a different calculation. This discussion translates into the following algorithm:

1. Declare appropriate variables.
2. Use the method **getActionCommand** to identify the button clicked. Retrieve the label of the button, which is a string.
3. Retrieve the character specifying the button label and store it in the variable **ch**.
4. a. If **ch** is a digit and **firstInput** is **true**, append the character at the end of the first number string; otherwise, append the character at the end of the second number string.

   b. If **ch** is an operation, set the **firstInput** to **false** and set the variable **op** to **ch**.

     c. If ch is = and there is no error, perform the operation, display the result, and set the first number as the result of the operation. If an error occurred, display an appropriate message.

     d. If ch is C, set both number strings to blank and clear the `displayText`.

To perform the operation, we write the method **evaluate**, which is described in the next section.

The definition of the method **actionPerformed** is:

```java
public void actionPerformed(ActionEvent e)
{
    String resultStr;                                    //Step 1

    String str
        = String.valueOf(e.getActionCommand());  //Steps 1 and 2

    char ch = str.charAt(0);                      //Steps 1 and 3

    switch(ch)                                           //Step 4
    {
    case '0': case '1': case '2':                        //Step 4a
    case '3': case '4': case '5':
    case '6': case '7': case '8':
    case '9': if(firstInput)
              {
                  numStr1 = numStr1 + ch;
                  displayText.setText(numStr1);
              }
              else
              {
                  numStr2 = numStr2 + ch;
                  displayText.setText(numStr2);
              }
              break;
    case '+': case '-': case '*':                        //Step 4b
    case '/': op = ch;
              firstInput = false;
              break;
    case '=': resultStr = evaluate();                    //Step 4c
              displayText.setText(resultStr);
              numStr1 = resultStr;
              numStr2 = "";
              firstInput = false;
              break;
    case 'C': displayText.setText("");                   //Step 4d
              numStr1 = "";
              numStr2 = "";
```

```
                            firstInput = true;
        }
    }
```

Method evaluate   The method **evaluate** performs an operation and returns the result of the operation as a string. This method also handles various exceptions such as division by zero and number format error (which occurs if one of the number strings is empty). The definition of this method is:

```java
private String evaluate()
{
    final char beep = '\u0007';

    try
    {
        int A = Integer.parseInt(numStr1);
        int B = Integer.parseInt(numStr2);
        int result = 0;

        switch(op)
        {
        case '+': result = A + B;
                  break;
        case '-': result = A - B;
                  break;
        case '*': result = A * B;
                  break;
        case '/': result = A / B;
        }

        return String.valueOf(result);
    }
    catch(ArithmeticException e)
    {
        System.out.print(beep);
        return "E R R O R: " + e.getMessage();
    }
    catch(NumberFormatException e)
    {
        System.out.print(beep);
        if(numStr1.equals(""))
            return "E R R O R: Invalid First Number" ;
        else
            return "E R R O R: Invalid Second Number" ;
    }
    catch(Exception e)
    {
        System.out.print(beep);
```

```
                return "E R R O R";
        }
}
```

Before writing the complete program, we must do one more thing. When the user clicks the window closing button, the program must terminate. Clicking the window closing button generates a window event. Therefore, we must create a `WindowListener` object and register the object to the class containing the application program because this class extends the definition of the `class JFrame`. The window events are handled by the `interface WindowListener`. To terminate the program when the user clicks the window closing button, we must provide the definition of the method `windowClosing` of the `interface WindowListener`. Because the `interface WindowListener` contains more than one method and we want to use only the method `windowClosing`, we use the mechanism of anonymous class to create and register the window event object. To do so, we make the class containing the application program use the `class WindowAdapter` to create and register the window event object. Creating and registering the window event object is accomplished by the following statements:

```
this.addWindowListener(new WindowAdapter()

            {
                    public void windowClosing(WindowEvent e)
                    {
                            System.exit(0);
                    }
            }
);
```

We can now outline the program listing.

Program Listing

```
//GUI Calculator Program

import javax.swing.*;
import java.awt.*;
import java.awt.event.*;
import java.io.*;

public class Calculator extends JFrame implements ActionListener
{
    private JTextField displayText = new JTextField(30);
    private JButton[] button = new JButton[16];
```

```java
private String[] keys = {"7", "8", "9", "/",
                         "4", "5", "6", "*",
                         "1", "2", "3", "-",
                         "0", "C", "=", "+"};

private String numStr1 = "";
private String numStr2 = "";

private char op;
private boolean firstInput = true;

public Calculator()
{
    setTitle("My Calculator");
    setSize(230, 200);
    Container pane = getContentPane();

    pane.setLayout(null);

    displayText.setSize(200, 30);
    displayText.setLocation(10, 10);
    pane.add(displayText);

    int x, y;

    x = 10;
    y = 40;
    for(int ind = 0; ind < 16; ind++)
    {
        button[ind] = new JButton(keys[ind]);
        button[ind].addActionListener(this);
        button[ind].setSize(50, 30);
        button[ind].setLocation(x, y);
        pane.add(button[ind]);
        x = x + 50;
        if((ind + 1) % 4 == 0)
        {
            x = 10;
            y = y + 30;
        }
    }
}
```

```
        this.addWindowListener(new WindowAdapter()
            {
                public void windowClosing(WindowEvent e)
                {
                    System.exit(0);
                }
            }
        );

        setVisible(true);
    }

    //Place the definition of the method actionPerformed
    //as described here

    //Place the definition of the method evaluate
    //as described here

    public static void main(String[] args)
    {
        Calculator C = new Calculator();
    }
}
```

Sample Run 1: In this sample run (see Figure 12-6), the user entered the numbers **34** and **25** and the operation **+**. The result is shown in the bottom screen.

Figure 12-6 Adding numbers 34 and 25

Sample Run 2: In this sample run (see Figure 12-7), the user attempted to divide by 0, resulting in an error message.

Figure 12-7   An attempt to divide by 0

QUICK REVIEW

1. An exception is an object of a specific exception class. Java provides extensive support for exception handling by providing a number of exception classes. Java also allows users to create and implement their own exception classes.

2. The **class Throwable**, which is derived from the **class object**, is the superclass of the **class Exception**.

3. The methods **getMessage**, **printStackTrace**, and **toString** of the **class Throwable** are **public** and so are inherited by the subclasses of the **class Throwable**.

4. The method **getMessage** returns the string containing the detailed message stored in the exception object.

5. The method **toString** returns the detailed message stored in the exception object as well as the name of the exception class.

6. The **class Exception** and its subclasses are designed to catch exceptions that should be caught and processed during program execution, and thus make a program more robust.

7. The **class Exception** is the superclass of the classes designed to handle exceptions.

8. The **class Exception** is contained in the package **java.lang**.

9. The classes to deal with I/O exceptions, such as the file not found exception, are contained in the **package java.io**.

10. The classes to deal with number format exceptions and arithmetic exceptions, such as division by zero, are contained in the **package java.lang**.

11. Generally, exception classes are placed in the package that contains the methods that throw these exceptions.

12. Java's predefined exceptions are divided into two categories—checked exceptions and unchecked exceptions.

13. Any exception that can be analyzed by the compiler is called a checked exception. For example, **IOExceptions** are checked exceptions.

14. Unchecked exceptions are exceptions that are not checked by the compiler.

15. The **try/catch/finally** block is used to handle exceptions within a program.

16. Statements that may generate an exception are placed in a **try** block. The **try** block also contains statements that should not be executed if an exception occurs.

17. The **try** block is followed by zero or more **catch** blocks.

18. A **catch** block specifies the type of exception it can catch and contains an exception handler.

19. The last **catch** block may or may not be followed by a **finally** block.

20. The code contained in the **finally** block always executes, regardless of whether an exception occurs.

21. If a **try** block has no **catch** block, then it must have the **finally** block.

22. When an exception occurs, an object of a specific exception class is created.

23. A **catch** block can catch all exceptions of a specific type or all types of exceptions.

24. The heading of a **catch** block specifies the type of exception it handles.

25. Typically, a **catch** block does the following:

   - Completely handles the exception.

   - Partially processes the exception. In this case the **catch** block either rethrows the same exception or throws another exception for the calling environment to handle the exception.

   - Rethrows the same exception for the calling environment to handle the exception.

26. The general syntax to rethrow an exception caught by a **catch** block is:

```
throw exceptionReference;
```

27. The general syntax to throw your own exception object is:

    throw new ExceptionClassName(messageString);

28. The method printStackTrace is used to determine the order in which the methods were called and where the exception was handled.

29. The exception class that you define extends the class Exception or one of its subclasses.

30. Action events are handled by appropriately implementing the interface ActionListener.

31. Window events are handled by appropriately implementing the interface WindowListener.

32. The class WindowAdapter implements the interface WindowListener by providing empty bodies to the methods.

33. To register a window listener object to a GUI component, you use the method addWindowListener. The window listener object being registered is passed as a parameter to the method addWindowListener.

34. Mouse events are handled by appropriately implementing the interface MouseListener.

35. The class MouseAdapter implements the interface MouseListener by providing empty bodies to the methods.

36. To register a mouse listener object to a GUI component, you use the method addMouseListener. The mouse listener object being registered is passed as a parameter to the method addMouseListener.

37. Key events are handled by appropriately implementing the interface KeyListener.

12

EXERCISES

1. Mark the following statements as true or false.

   a. The block finally is always executed.

   b. Division by zero is a checked exception.

   c. File not found is an unchecked exception.

   d. Exceptions are thrown in a try block in a method or from a method called directly or indirectly from a try block.

   e. The order in which catch blocks are listed is not important.

   f. An exception can be caught either in the method it occurred or in any one of the methods that led to the invocation of this method.

   g. One way to handle an exception is to print an error message and exit the program.

   h. All exceptions must be reported to avoid compilation errors.

    i. An event handler is a method.

    j. A GUI component can generate only one type of event.

2. Consider the following Java code:

```java
int lowerLimit;

...

try
{
   System.out.println("Entering the try block.");
   if(lowerLimit < 100)
      throw new Exception("Lower limit violation.");
   System.out.println("Exiting the try block.");
}
catch(Exception e)
{
   System.out.println("Exception: " + e.getMessage());
}
System.out.println("After the catch block");
```

What is the output if:

a. The value of `lowerLimit` is 50?

b. The value of `lowerLimit` is 150?

3. Consider the following Java code:

```java
int lowerLimit;
int divisor;
int result;

try
{
   System.out.println("Entering the try block.");
   result = lowerLimit / divisor;
   if(lowerLimit < 100)
      throw new Exception("Lower limit violation.");
   System.out.println("Exiting the try block.");
}
catch(ArithmeticException e)
{
   System.out.println("Exception: " + e.getMessage());
   result = 110;
}
catch(Exception e)
{
   System.out.println("Exception: " + e.getMessage());
}
System.out.println("After the catch block");
```

What is the output if:

a. The value of `lowerLimit` is 50 and the value of `divisor` is 10?

b. The value of `lowerLimit` is 50 and the value of `divisor` is 0?

c. The value of `lowerLimit` is 150 and the value of `divisor` is 10?

d. The value of `lowerLimit` is 150 and the value of `divisor` is 0?

4. Rewrite the Java code given in Exercise 3 so that the new equivalent code has exactly one `catch` block.

5. Correct any compile time errors in the following code:

```java
import java.io.*;
import java.text.DecimalFormat;
import java.util.*;

public class SAverage
{
    public static void main(String[] args)
    {
        //Declare and initialize variables
        double test1, test2, test3, test4;
        double average;
        StringTokenizer tokenizer;

        try
        {
            BufferedReader inFile = new
                BufferedReader(new FileReader("a:\\test.txt"));
            PrintWriter outFile = new
                PrintWriter(new FileWriter("a:\\testavg.out"));
            DecimalFormat twoDecimal =
                        new DecimalFormat("0.00");
            tokenizer =
                new StringTokenizer(inFile.readLine());

            test1 = Double.parseDouble(tokenizer.nextToken());
            test2 = Double.parseDouble(tokenizer.nextToken());
            test3 = Double.parseDouble(tokenizer.nextToken());
            test4 = Double.parseDouble(tokenizer.nextToken());

            outFile.println("Test scores: "
                        + twoDecimal.format(test1) + " "
                        + twoDecimal.format(test2) + " "
                        + twoDecimal.format(test3) + " "
                        + twoDecimal.format(test4));

            average = (test1 + test2 + test3 + test4) / 4.0;
```

12

```
        outFile.println("Average test score: "
                      + twoDecimal.format(average));    //Step 11

        outFile.close();                                //Step 12

    }
    catch(FileNotFoundException e)
    {
        System.out.println(e.toString());
    }
    catch(Exception e)
    {
        System.out.println(e.toString());
    }
    catch(IOException e)
    {
        System.out.println(e.toString());
    }
  }
}
```

6. Define the exception **class TornadoException**. The class should have two constructors, including one default constructor. If the exception is thrown with the default constructor, the method **getMessage** should return

   "Tornado: Take cover immediately!"

   The other constructor has a single parameter, say **m**, of **int** type. If the exception is thrown with this constructor, the method **getMessage** should return

   "Tornado: m miles away; and approaching!"

7. Write a Java program to test the **class TornadoException** specified in Exercise 6.

8. Suppose the exception **class MyException** is defined as follows:

```
public class MyException extends Exception
{
    public MyException()
    {
        super("MyException thrown!");
        System.out.println("Immediate attention required!");
    }
    public MyException(String msg)
    {
        super(msg);
        System.out.println("Attention required!");
    }
}
```

   What output will be produced if the exception is thrown with the default constructor? What output will be produced if the exception is thrown with the non-default constructor with the actual parameter **"May Day, May Day"**?

9. What are the three different ways you can implement an interface?

PROGRAMMING EXERCISES

1. Write a program that prompts the user to enter the length in feet and inches and output the equivalent length in centimeters. If the user enters a negative number or a nondigit number, throw and handle an appropriate exception and prompt the user to enter another set of numbers.

2. Redo Programming Exercise 11 of Chapter 5 so that if the input file does not exist, the program handles the `FileNotFoundException`, outputs an appropriate message, and terminates normally.

3. Redo the Text Processing Programming Example in Chapter 9 so that if the array index goes out of bounds when the program accesses the array `letterCount`, it throws and handles the `ArrayIndexOutOfBoundsException`.

4. Redo Programming Exercise 7 of Chapter 8 so that your program handles exceptions such as division by zero.

5. Extend the Programming Example Calculator of this chapter by adding three buttons with the labels M, R, and E as follows: If the user clicks on the button M, the number currently in the `displayText` field is stored in the variable, say, `memory`; if the user clicks on the button R, the number stored in memory is displayed and also becomes the first number (so that another number can be added, subtracted, multiplied, or divided); and if the user clicks on the button E, the program terminates.

6. The Programming Example Calculator of this chapter is designed to do operations on integers. Write a similar program that can be used to do operations on decimal numbers. (*Note*: If division by zero occurs with values of the `int` data type, the program throws a division by zero exception. However, if you divide a decimal number by zero, Java does not throw the division by zero exception; it returns the answer as `infinity`. However, if division by zero occurs, your calculator program must output the message `ERROR: / by zero`.)

7. In Programming Exercise 7 in Chapter 8, we defined a `class Roman` to implement Roman numerals in a program. In that exercise, we also implemented the method `romanToDecimal` to convert a Roman numeral into its equivalent decimal number.

   a. Modify the definition of the `class Roman` so that the data members are declared as `protected`. Also include the method `decimalToRoman`, which converts the decimal number (the decimal number must be a positive integer) to an equivalent Roman numeral format. Write the definition of the method `decimalToRoman`. Your definition of `class Roman` must contain the method `toString`, which returns the string containing the number in Roman format. For simplicity, we assume that only the letter I can appear in front of another letter and that it appears only in front of the letters V and X. For example, 4 is represented as IV, 9 is represented as IX, 39 is represented as XXXIX, and 49 is represented as XXXXIX. Also, 40 is represented as XXXX, 190 is represented as CLXXXX, and so on.

12

b. Derive the **class** **ExtendedRoman** from the **class** **Roman** to do the following. In the **class** **ExtendedRoman**, add the methods **add**, **subtract**, **multiply**, and **divide** so that arithmetic operations can be performed on Roman numerals.

To add (subtract, multiply, or divide) Roman numerals, add (subtract, multiply, or divide, respectively) their decimal representations and then convert the result to the Roman numeral format. For subtraction, if the first number is smaller than the second number, throw the exception, "**Because the first number is smaller than the second, the numbers cannot be subtracted**". Similarly, for division, the numerator must be larger than the denominator.

c. Write the definitions of the methods **add**, **subtract**, **multiply**, and **divide** as described in part b. Also, your definition of **class** **ExtendedRoman** must contain the method **toString** that returns the string containing the number in Roman format.

d. Write a program to test the various operations on your **class** **ExtendedRoman**.

CHAPTER 13

ADVANCED GUIS AND GRAPHICS

In this chapter, you will:

◆ Learn about applets

◆ Explore the `class Graphics`

◆ Learn about the `class Font`

◆ Explore the `class Color`

◆ Learn to use additional Layout managers

◆ Become familiar with more GUI components

◆ Learn how to create menu-based programs

◆ Explore how to handle key and mouse events

There are two types of Java programs—applications and applets. Up to this point, we have only created application programs. Even the programs we've created that use GUI components are application programs. Java **applets** are small applications that can be embedded in an HTML page. In this chapter, you learn how to create an applet. You will also learn how to convert a GUI application to a Java applet. This chapter also shows you how to use different fonts, colors, and geometric shapes to enhance the output of your programs.

In Chapter 6, you learned how to use GUI components, such as `JFrame`, `JLabel`, `JTextField`, and `JButton`, to make your programs attractive and user friendly. In this chapter, you learn about other commonly used GUI components. The `class JComponent` is the superclass of the classes used to create various GUI components. Figure 13-1 shows the inheritance hierarchy of the GUI classes that you have used in previous chapters, plus the ones you encounter in this chapter. The package containing the definition of the class is also shown.

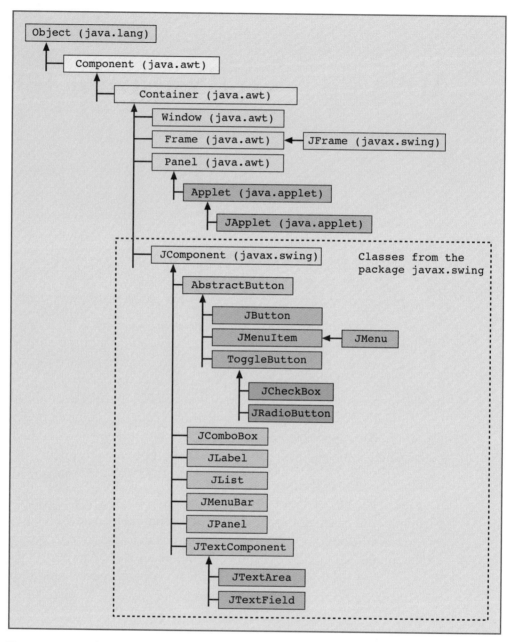

Figure 13-1 Inheritance hierarchy of GUI classes (Classes shown in the dotted rectangle are from the `package javax.swing`)

As shown in Figure 13-1, the class Container, which is a subclass of the class Component, is the superclass of all the classes designed to provide a GUI. Therefore, all public members of these classes are inherited by their subclasses shown in Figure 13-1. Moreover, both the Container and Component classes are abstract.

The class Component contains many methods that are inherited by its subclasses. You have used methods such as setSize and setLocation in various GUI programs. Table 13-1 describes some of the constructors and methods of the class Component.

Table 13-1 Some Constructors and Methods of the class Component

```
protected Component()
  //Constructor
  //Creates a new instance of a component.
```
```
public void addComponentListener(ComponentListener lis)
  //Adds the component listener specified by lis.
```
```
public void addFocusListener(FocusListener lis)
  //Adds the focus listener specified by lis.
```
```
public void addKeyListener(KeyListener lis)
  //Adds the key listener specified by lis.
```
```
public void addMouseListener(MouseListener lis)
  //Adds the mouse listener specified by lis.
```
```
public void addMouseMotionListener(MouseMotionListener lis)
  //Adds the mouse motion listener specified by lis.
```
```
public void removeComponentListener(ComponentListener lis)
  //Removes the component listener specified by lis.
```
```
public void removeFocusListener(FocusListener lis)
  //Removes the focus listener specified by lis.
```
```
public void removeKeyListener(KeyListener lis)
  //Removes the key listener specified by lis.
```
```
public void removeMouseListener(MouseListener lis)
  //Removes the mouse listener specified by lis.
```
```
public void removeMouseMotionListener(MouseMotionListener lis)
  //Removes the mouse motion listener specified by lis.
```
```
public Color getBackground()
  //Returns the background color of this component.
```
```
public Color getForeground()
  //Returns the foreground color of this component.
```
```
public void setBackground(Color c)
  //Sets the background color of this component to color c.
```
```
public void setForeground(Color c)
  //Sets the foreground color of this component to color c.
```
```
public Font getFont()
  //Returns the font of this component.
```

13

Table 13-1 Some Constructors and Methods of the `class Component` (continued)

```
public void setFont(Font ft)
    //Sets the font of this component to ft.
```

```
public void setSize(int w, int h)
    //Sets the size of this component to width w and height h.
```

```
public boolean isVisible()
    //Returns true if the component is visible; false otherwise
```

```
public void setVisible(boolean tog)
    //If tog is true, sets the component to visible;
    //If tog is false, the component is not shown.
```

```
public void paint(Graphics g)
    //Paints the component with the graphic component specified by g.
```

```
public void repaint()
    //Repaints the component.
```

```
public void repaint(int x, int y, int wid, int ht)
    //Repaints the rectangular portion of the component from (x, y)
    //to (x + wid, y + ht).
```

```
public void setLocation(int x, int y)
    //Sets the component at the location (x, y).
```

```
public String toString()
    //Returns a string representation of this component.
```

```
public void update(Graphics g)
    //Invokes the paint method.
```

```
public void validate()
    //Validates this container and all of its subcomponents. The
    //method validate is used to cause a container to lay out its
    //subcomponents once more. Typically called after the components
    //it contains have been added to or modified.
```

The `class Container` inherits all the methods of the `class Component`. In addition to the methods shown in Table 13-1, Table 13-2 shows some commonly used constructors and methods of the `class Container`.

Table 13-2 Some Constructors and Methods of the `class Container`

```
public Component add(Component comp)
    //Appends the specified component to the end of this container.
```

```
public Component add(Component comp, int index)
    //Adds the specified component to this container at the given
    //position specified by index.
```

```
public void paint(Graphics g)
    //Paints the container with the Graphics component specified by g.
```

Table 13-2 Some Constructors and Methods of the `class Container` (continued)

```
public void update(Graphics g)
  //Invokes the paint method.
```

```
public void validate()
  //Validates this container and all of its subcomponents. The
  //method validate is used to cause a container to lay out its
  //subcomponents once more. Typically called after the components
  //it contains have been added to or modified.
```

In the remainder of this chapter, whenever we list the methods of a class, we will not show the methods that are inherited from the `classes Component` and `Container`.

Next we discuss how to create a Java applet. For the most part, the programs in this chapter are Java applets.

APPLETS

The term *applet* refers to a little application. In Java, an **applet** is a Java program that is embedded within a Web page and executed by a Web browser. You create an applet by extending the `class JApplet`, which is contained in the `package javax.swing`.

Table 13-3 describes some commonly used methods of the `class JApplet`.

Table 13-3 Some Members of the `class JApplet` (package `javax.swing`)

```
public void init()
  //Called by the browser or applet viewer to inform this applet
  //that it has been loaded into the system.
```

```
public void start()
  //Called by the browser or applet viewer to inform this applet
  //that it should start its execution. It is called after the init
  //method and each time the applet is revisited in a Web page.
```

```
public void stop()
  //Called by the browser or applet viewer to inform this applet
  //that it should stop its execution. It is called before the
  //method destroy.
```

```
public void destroy()
  //Called by the browser or applet viewer. Informs this applet that
  //it is being reclaimed and that it should destroy any resources
  //that it has allocated. The method stop is called before destroy.
```

```
public void showStatus(String msg)
  //Displays the string msg in the status bar.
```

```
public Container getContentPane()
  //Returns the ContentPane object for this applet.
```

13

Table 13-3 Some Members of the class JApplet (package javax.swing) (continued)

```
public JMenuBar getJMenuBar()
  //Returns the JMenuBar object for this applet.
```

```
public URL getDocumentBase()
  //Returns the URL of the document that contains this applet.
```

```
public URL getCodeBase()
  //Returns the URL of this applet.
```

```
public void update(Graphics g)
  //Calls the paint() method.
```

```
protected String paramString()
  //Returns a string representation of this JApplet; mainly used
  //for debugging.
```

Unlike Java application programs, Java applets do not have the method **main**. Instead, when a browser runs an applet, the methods **init**, **start**, and **paint** are guaranteed to be invoked in sequence. Therefore, as a programmer, to develop an applet, all you have to do is override one or all of the methods **init**, **start**, and **paint**. Of these three methods, the **paint** method has one argument, which is a **Graphics** object. This allows you to use the **class Graphics** without actually creating a **Graphics** object. Later in this chapter, when you see the **class Graphics** in detail, you will notice that the **class Graphics** is an **abstract** class, therefore, you cannot create an instance of this class. For now, all you need to do is import the **package java.awt** so that you can use various methods of the **class Graphics** in the **paint** method. To do so, you need the following two **import** statements:

```
import java.awt.Graphics;
import javax.swing.JApplet;
```

Because you create an applet by extending the **class JApplet**, in skeleton form a Java applet looks something like this:

```
import java.awt.Graphics;
import javax.swing.JApplet;

public class WelcomeApplet extends JApplet
{

}
```

As a general rule, you keep all statements to be executed only once in the **init** method. The **paint** method is used to draw various items, including strings, in the content pane of the applet. Thus, in the applets presented in this chapter, we use **init** to:

- Initialize variables

- Get data from the user

- Place various GUI components

The **paint** method is used to perform output. The **init** and **paint** methods need to share common data items, so these common data items are the data members of the applet.

Let's now create an applet that will display a welcome message. Because there is no initialization required, all you need to do is override the method **paint** so that it draws the welcome message. Whenever you override a method, it is a good idea to invoke the corresponding method of the parent **class**. Thus, whenever you override the **paint** method, the first Java statement is

```
super.paint(g);
```

where **g** is a **Graphics** object. Recall that **super** is a reserved word in Java and refers to the instance of the parent class.

To display the string containing the welcome message, we use the method **drawString** of the **class Graphics**. The method **drawString** is an overloaded method. One of the headings of the method **drawString** is:

```
public abstract void drawString(String str, int x, int y)
```

The method **drawString** displays the string specified by **str** at the horizontal position **x** pixels away from the upper-left corner of the applet, and the vertical position **y** pixels away from the upper-left corner of the applet. In other words, the applet has a coordinate system **XY**, with **X = 0, Y = 0** at the upper-left corner; the **X** value increases from left to right and the **Y** value increases from top to bottom. Thus, the method **drawString** as given previously draws the string **str** starting at the position **(x, y)**.

The following Java applet displays a welcome message:

```
//Welcome Applet

import java.awt.Graphics;
import javax.swing.JApplet;

public class WelcomeApplet extends JApplet
{
    public void paint(Graphics g)
    {
        super.paint(g);                              //Line 1
        g.drawString("Welcome to Java Programming",
                     30, 30);                        //Line 2
    }
}
```

In the preceding applet, the statement in Line 1 invokes the **paint** method of the **class JApplet**. Notice that the method **paint** uses a **Graphics** object **g** as the argument. Recall that the **class Graphics** is an **abstract** class, and for this reason, you cannot create an instance of the **class Graphics**. The system will create a **Graphics** object for you; you need not be concerned about it. The statement in Line 2 draws the string **"Welcome to Java Programming"** at the coordinate position **(30, 30)**.

Up to this point in this book, when we created a GUI application program, we used methods such as `setTitle` and `setSize`. As you can see in the preceding applet, such methods are not used in an applet. Note the following about applets:

- The method `setTitle` is not used in applets because applets do not have titles. An applet is embedded in an HTML document, and the applet itself does not have a title. The HTML document may have a title, which is set by the document.

- The method `setSize` is not used in applets because the applet's size is determined in the HTML document, not by the applet. You do not need to set the size of the applet.

- You need not invoke the method `setVisible`.

- You need not close the applet. When the HTML document containing the applet is closed, the applet is destroyed.

- There is no method `main`.

As with an application, you compile an applet and produce a `.class` file. Once the `.class` file is created, you need to place it in a Web page to run the applet. For example, you can create a file with the `.html` extension, say `WelcomeApplet.html`, with the following lines in the same folder where the `WelcomeApplet.class` file resides:

```
<!DOCTYPE HTML PUBLIC "-//W3C//DTD HTML 4.01 Transitional//EN">

<HTML>
  <HEAD>
    <TITLE>WELCOME APPLET</TITLE>
  </HEAD>
  <BODY>
    <APPLET code = "WelcomeApplet.class" width = "240" height = "60">
    </APPLET>
  </BODY>
</HTML>
```

Once the HTML file is created, you can run your applet either by opening `Welcome.html` with a Web browser, or you can enter

```
appletviewer Welcome.html
```

at a command-line prompt, if you are using the Java Development Kit (JDK).

Sample Run: Figure 13-2 shows the output of the `WelcomeApplet` produced by the Applet Viewer in Windows XP.

Figure 13-2   Output of the WelcomeApplet

You terminate the applet by clicking the close button in the upper-right corner of the Applet Viewer, or by closing the HTML document in which the applet is embedded.

Two ways to make your applets more attractive are to vary the type font and color. Next we introduce the classes Font and Color, contained in the package java.awt.

class Font

The GUI programs we have created so far have used only the default font. To show text in different fonts when the program executes, Java provides the class Font. The class Font is contained in the package java.awt, so you need to use the following import statement in your program:

```
import java.awt.*;
```

The class Font contains various constructors, methods, and constants, some of which are described in Table 13-4.

Table 13-4   Some Constructors and Methods of the class Font

Method

public **Font**(String name, int style, int size)
  //Constructor
  //Creates a new Font from the specified name, style, and point
  //size.

public String **getFamily**()   //Returns the family name of this Font.
public String **getFontName**()   //Returns the font face name of this Font.

13

Typically, you use only the constructor of the **class Font**. As shown in Table 13-4, the constructor of the **class Font** takes the following three arguments:

- A string specifying the **Font** face name (or font name for short)
- An **int** value specifying **Font** style
- An **int** value specifying **Font** size expressed in points, where 72 points equal one inch

Fonts available on a particular system vary widely. However, using the JDK guarantees the following fonts:

- **Serif**
- **SanSerif**
- **Monospaced**
- **Dialog**
- **DialogInput**

If you want to know which fonts are available in your system, you can run the program given next. (This program uses a graphics environment, which is covered later in this chapter.)

```java
import java.awt.*;
public class FontNames
{
    public static void main(String[] args)
    {
        String[] listOfFontNames =
                GraphicsEnvironment.getLocalGraphicsEnvironment()
                    .getAvailableFontFamilyNames();

        for(int i = 0; i < listOfFontNames.length; i++)
            System.out.println(listOfFontNames[i]);
    }
}
```

The **class Font** contains the constants **Font.PLAIN**, **Font.ITALIC**, and **Font.BOLD**, which you can apply to change the style of a font. For example, the Java statement

```java
new Font("Serif", Font.ITALIC, 12)
```

creates a 12-point **Serif** italic font. Likewise, the statement

```java
new Font("Dialog", Font.ITALIC + Font.BOLD, 36)
```

creates a 36-point **Dialog** italic and bold font.

The applet given in Example 13-1 illustrates how to change fonts in text.

```
//FontsDisplayed Applet

import java.awt.*;
import javax.swing.JApplet;

public class FontsDisplayed extends JApplet
{
    public void paint(Graphics g)
    {
        super.paint(g);
        g.setFont(new Font("Courier", Font.BOLD, 24));
        g.drawString("Courier bold 24pt font",30,36);

        g.setFont(new Font("Arial", Font.PLAIN, 30));
        g.drawString("Arial plain 30pt font",30,70);

        g.setFont(new Font("Dialog", Font.BOLD+Font.ITALIC, 36));
        g.drawString("Dialog italic bold 36pt font",30,110);

        g.setFont(new Font("Serif", Font.ITALIC, 30));
        g.drawString("Serif italic 42pt font",30,156);
    }
}
```

The HTML file that invokes this applet contains the following code:

```
<!DOCTYPE HTML PUBLIC "-//W3C//DTD HTML 4.01 Transitional//EN">

<HTML>
  <HEAD>
    <TITLE>Four Fonts</TITLE>
  </HEAD>
  <BODY>
    <APPLET code = "FontsDisplayed.class" width = "500" height = "190">
    </APPLET>
  </BODY>
</HTML>
```

Sample Run: Figure 13-3 shows the output of the `FontsDisplayed` applet in Applet Viewer.

13

Figure 13-3   Output of the FontsDisplayed applet

class Color

So far, we have only used default colors in our GUI programs. For example, text always appeared as black. You may want to show text in different colors or change the background color of a component. Java provides the class Color to accomplish this. Because the class Color is contained in the package java.awt, you need to use the following import statement:

```
import java.awt.*;
```

Table 13-5 shows various constructors and methods of the class Color.

Table 13-5   Some Constructors and Methods of the class Color

```
Color(int r, int g, int b)
  //Constructor
  //Creates an instance of Color with red value r, green value g,
  //and blue value b. In this case, r, g, and b can be
  //between 0 and 255.
  //Example: new  Color(0,255,0)
  //      creates a color with no red or blue component.
Color(int rgb)
  //Constructor
  //Creates an instance of Color with red value r, green
  //value g, and blue value b, choose rgb as
  //r * 65536 + g * 256 + b. In this case, r, g, and b
  //can be between 0 and 255.
  //Example: new  Color(255)
  //      creates a color with no red or green component.
```

Table 13-5 Some Constructors and Methods of the `class` `Color` (continued)

```
Color(float r, float g, float b)
  //Constructor
  //Creates an instance of Color with red value r, green value g,
  //and blue value b. In this case, r, g, and b can be between 0
  //and 1.0.
  //Example: new  Color(1.0,0,0)
  //       creates a color with no green or blue component.
```

```
public Color brighter()
  //Returns a Color that is brighter.
```

```
public Color darker()
  //Returns a Color that is darker.
```

```
public boolean equals(Object o)
  //Returns true if the color of this object is the same as the
  //color of the object o; false otherwise.
```

```
public int getBlue()
  //Returns the value of the blue component.
```

```
public int getGreen()
  //Returns the value of the green component.
```

```
public int getRGB()
  //Returns the RGB value. RGB value is  r * 65536 + g * 256 + b.
```

```
public int getRed()
  //Returns the value of the red component.
```

```
public String toString()
  //Returns a String with information about the color.
```

You can use the methods **setBackground** and **setForeground**, described in Table 13-1, to set the background and foreground color of a component.

Java uses the color scheme known as **RGB**, where **R** stands for red, **G** for green, and **B** for blue, respectively. You create instances of **Color** by mixing red, green, and blue hues in various proportions. The **class** **Color** contains three constructors, as shown in Table 13-5. In the first constructor, an RGB value is represented as three **int** values. The second constructor specifies an RGB value as a single integer. In either form, the closer an **r**, **g**, or **b** value is to 255, the more hue is mixed into the color. For example, if you use the first constructor, pure red is produced by mixing red **255**, green **0**, and blue **0** parts each. To produce the color red, you use the first constructor as follows:

```
Color redColor = new Color(255, 0, 0);
```

Various shades of black, white, and gray can be created by mixing all three colors in the same proportion. For example, the color white has **RGB** values **255**, **255**, **255**, and black has **RGB** values **0**, **0**, **0**. An **RGB** value of **100**, **100**, **100** creates a gray color darker than one with an **RGB** value **200**, **200**, **200**.

13

In addition to the methods shown in Table 13-5, the **class Color** defines a number of standard colors as constants. Table 13-6 shows the color name in bold and its values for easy reference.

Table 13-6 Constants Defined in the **class Color**

Color.black: (0,0,0)	**Color.magenta:** (255,0,255)
Color.blue: (0,0,255)	**Color.orange:** (255,200,0)
Color.cyan: (0,255,255)	**Color.pink:** (255,175,175)
Color.darkGray: (64,64,64)	**Color.red:** (255,0,0)
Color.gray: (128,128,128)	**Color.white:** (255,255,255)
Color.green: (0,255,0)	**Color.yellow:** (255,255,0)
Color.lightGray: (192,192,192)	

A simple applet to illustrate the use of the **class Color** is given in Example 13-2. In Example 13-2, we use the **class GridLayout**, described in Chapter 6, to place the GUI components. Recall that **GridLayout** divides the container into a grid of rows and columns, and so allows you to place the components in rows and columns. Every component placed in a **GridLayout** will have the same width and height. The components are placed from left to right on the first row, followed by left to right on the second row, and so on.

The **class GridLayout** is contained in the **package java.awt**. Appendix E describes various methods of this class. Most often we use the following constructor of the **class GridLayout**:

```
GridLayout(int row, int col)
```

where **row** specifies the number of rows and **col** specifies the number of columns in the grid, respectively. For example, to create a grid with 10 rows and 5 columns, and set it as the layout of the container **c**, you use the following Java statement:

```
c.setLayout(new GridLayout(10,5));
```

In our next applet, we use a grid with 2 rows and 2 columns. Therefore, we use the statement:

```
c.setLayout(new GridLayout(2,2));
```

Example 13-2 uses the method **random** of the **class Math** that returns a random value between 0 and 1. For example, the statement

```
Math.random();
```

returns a random **double** value between 0 and 1. Note that the third constructor of the **Color class** (see Table 13-5) takes three **float** values, each between 0 and 1, as parameters. Therefore, we use the explicit cast operator **(float)** to convert the **double** value returned by the **random** method. Thus, we use the following statements to randomly generate a value for the colors red, green, and blue:

```
red = (float) Math.random();
green = (float) Math.random();
blue = (float) Math.random();
```

These statements assign random **float** values between 0 and 1 to the **float** variables **red**, **green**, and **blue**. Suppose that **bottomrightJL** is a **JLabel**. The statement

```
bottomrightJL.setForeground(new Color(red, green, blue));
```

creates a color and assigns it as the foreground color of the label **bottomrightJL**.

Example 13-2

This example gives the complete program listing and a sample run to show how to set the colors of text and GUI components.

```
//ColorsDisplayed Applet

import java.awt.*;
import javax.swing.*;

public class ColorsDisplayed extends JApplet
{
    JLabel topleftJL, toprightJL, bottomleftJL, bottomrightJL;

    int i;
    float red, green, blue;

    public void init()
    {
        Container c = getContentPane();
        c.setLayout(new GridLayout(2,2));
        c.setBackground(Color.white);
        topleftJL = new JLabel("Red", SwingConstants.CENTER);
        toprightJL = new JLabel("Green", SwingConstants.CENTER);
        bottomleftJL = new JLabel("Blue", SwingConstants.CENTER);
        bottomrightJL = new JLabel("Random", SwingConstants.CENTER);

        topleftJL.setForeground(Color.red);
        toprightJL.setForeground(Color.green);
        bottomleftJL.setForeground(Color.blue);
        red = (float) Math.random();
        green = (float) Math.random();
        blue = (float) Math.random();
        bottomrightJL.setForeground(new Color(red, green, blue));
```

13

```
                    c.add(topleftJL);
                    c.add(toprightJL);
                    c.add(bottomleftJL);
                    c.add(bottomrightJL);
        }
}
```

The HTML file that invokes this applet contains the following code:

```
<!DOCTYPE HTML PUBLIC "-//W3C//DTD HTML 4.01 Transitional//EN">

<HTML>
  <HEAD>
    <TITLE>Four Colors</TITLE>
  </HEAD>
  <BODY>
    <APPLET code = "ColorsDisplayed.class" width = "200" height = "200">
    </APPLET>
  </BODY>
</HTML>
```

Sample Run: Figure 13-4 shows the output of the `ColorsDisplayed` applet.

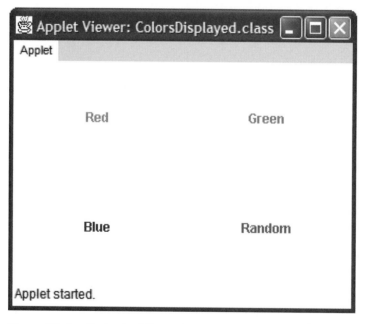

Figure 13-4   Output of the `ColorsDisplayed` applet

You can use both the **class Font** and the **class Color** to enhance your presentation of an applet. For example, consider the **GrandWelcome** applet given in Example 13-3. Since no new ideas are introduced, we give the complete listing followed by the sample run.

Example 13-3

```java
//GrandWelcome Applet

import java.awt.*;
import javax.swing.JApplet;

public class GrandWelcome extends JApplet
{

    public void paint(Graphics g)
    {
        super.paint(g);
        g.setColor(Color.red);
        g.setFont(new Font("Courier", Font.BOLD, 24));
        g.drawString("Welcome to Java Programming",30,30);
    }
}
```

The HTML file for this program contains the following code:

```html
<!DOCTYPE HTML PUBLIC "-//W3C//DTD HTML 4.01 Transitional//EN">
<HTML>
  <HEAD>
    <TITLE>WELCOME</TITLE>
  </HEAD>
  <BODY>
    <APPLET code = "GrandWelcome.class" width = "440" height = "50">
    </APPLET>
  </BODY>
</HTML>
```

Sample Run: Figure 13-5 shows the output of the **GrandWelcome** applet.

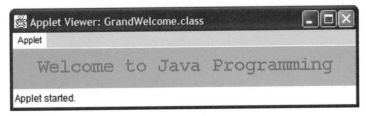

Figure 13-5   Output of the **GrandWelcome** applet

class Graphics

In this section, we present a glimpse of the **class** `Graphics`, which is contained in the **package** `java.awt`. The **class** `Graphics` provides methods for drawing items such as lines, ovals, and rectangles on the screen. Some methods of the **class** `Graphics` draw shapes; others draw bitmap images. This class also contains methods to set the properties of graphic elements including the clipping area, fonts, and colors. Table 13-7 shows some of the constructors and methods of the **class** `Graphics`.

Table 13-7 Some Constructors and Methods of the **class** `Graphics`

```
protected Graphics()
    //Constructs a Graphics object that defines a context in which the
    //user can draw. This constructor cannot be called directly.
```

```
public void draw3Rect(int x, int y, int w, int h, boolean t)
    //Draws a 3D rectangle at (x, y) with width w, height h. If t is
    //true, rectangle will appear raised.
```

```
public abstract void drawArc(int x, int y, int w, int h,
                             int sangle, int aangle)
    //Draws an arc in the rectangle at position (x, y) of width w and
    //height h. The arc starts at angle sangle with an arc angle aangle.
    //Both angles are measured in degrees.
```

```
public abstract boolean drawImage(Image img, int xs1, int ys1,
                int xs2, int ys2, int xd1, int yd1,
                int xd2, int yd2, Color c, ImageObserver ob)
    //Draws the image specified by img from the area defined by
    //bounding rectangle, (xs1, ys1) to (xs2, ys2), in the area defined
    //by the rectangle (xd1, yd1) to (xd2, yd2). Any transparent color
    //pixels are drawn in color c. The ob monitors the progress of
    //the image.
```

```
public abstract void drawLine(int xs, int ys, int xd, int yd)
    //Draws a line from (xs, ys) to (xd, yd).
```

```
public abstract void drawOval(int x, int y, int w, int h)
    //Draws an oval at position (x, y) of width w and height h.
```

```
public abstract void drawPolygon(int[] x, int[] y, int num)
    //Draws a polygon with points (x[0], y[0]), ...,
    //(x[num-1], y[num-1]). Here num is the number of points in
    //the polygon.
```

```
public abstract void drawPolygon(Polygon poly)
    //Draws a polygon as defined by the object poly.
```

```
public abstract void drawRect(int x, int y, int w, int h)
    //Draws a rectangle at position (x, y) having a width w and
    //height h.
```

```
public abstract void drawRoundRect(int x, int y, int w, int h,
                                   int arcw, int arch)
    //Draws a round-cornered rectangle at position (x, y) having a
    //width w and height h. The shape of the rounded corners is
    //determined by arc with width arcw and height arch.
```

Table 13-7 Some Constructors and Methods of the `class` `Graphics` (continued)

```
public abstract void drawString(String s, int x, int y)
    //Draws the string s at (x, y).
```

```
public void fill3Rect(int x, int y, int w, int h, boolean t)
    //Draws a 3D filled rectangle at (x, y) with width w, height h.
    //If t is true, rectangle will appear raised. The rectangle is
    //filled with current color.
```

```
public abstract void fillArc(int x, int y, int w, int h,
                             int sangle, int aangle)
    //Draws a filled arc in the rectangle at position (x, y) of width
    //w and height h starting at angle sangle with an arc
    //angle aangle. Both angles are measured in degrees. The arc is
    //filled with current color.
```

```
public abstract void fillOval(int x, int y, int w, int h)
    //Draws a filled oval at position (x, y) having a width w and
    //height h. The oval is filled with current color.
```

```
public abstract void fillPolygon(int[] x, int[] y, int num)
    //Draws a filled polygon with points (x[0], y[0]), ...,
    //(x[num-1], y[num-1]). Here num is the number of points in
    //the polygon. The polygon is filled with current color.
```

```
public abstract void fillPolygon(Polygon poly)
    //Draws a filled polygon as defined by the object poly. The polygon
    //is filled with current color.
```

```
public abstract void fillRect(int x, int y, int w, int h)
    //Draws a filled rectangle at position (x, y) having a width w
    //and height h. The rectangle is filled with current color.
```

```
public abstract void fillRoundRect(int x, int y, int w, int h,
                                   int arcw, int arch)
    //Draws a filled, round-cornered rectangle at position (x, y)
    //having a width w and height h. The shape of the rounded corners
    //is determined by the arc with width arcw and height arch. The
    //rectangle is filled with current color.
```

```
public abstract Color getColor()
    //Returns the current color for this graphics context.
```

```
public abstract void setColor(Color c)
    //Sets the current color for this graphics context to c.
```

```
public abstract Font getFont()
    //Returns the current font for this graphics context.
```

```
public abstract void setFont(Font f)
    //Sets the current font for this graphics context to f.
```

```
public FontMetrics getFontMetrics()
    //Returns the font metrics associated with this graphics context.
```

```
public FontMetrics getFontMetrics(Font f)
    //Returns the font metrics associated with Font f.
```

```
public void String toString()
    //Returns a string representation of this graphics context.
```

13

You have already used the **drawString** method to output a string. Other **draw** methods are used in a similar manner. For example, to draw a line from (**10, 10**) to (**10, 40**) you use the method **drawLine** as follows:

```
g.drawLine(10,10,10,40);
```

where **g** is a **Graphics** object. Let's draw three more lines, so that our welcome message is inside a box.

```
g.drawLine(10,40,430,40);    //bottom line
g.drawLine(430,40,430,10);   //right line
g.drawLine(430,10,10,10);    //top line
```

Placing these lines in our **GrandWelcome** applet of Example 13-3, we have the program shown in Example 13-4.

Example 13-4

```
//GrandWelcomeLine Applet

import java.awt.*;
import javax.swing.JApplet;

public class GrandWelcomeLine extends JApplet
{
    public void paint(Graphics g)
    {
        super.paint(g);
        g.setColor(Color.red);
        g.setFont(new Font("Courier", Font.BOLD, 24));
        g.drawString("Welcome to Java Programming",30,30);

        g.drawLine(10,10,10,40);     //left line
        g.drawLine(10,40,430,40);    //bottom line
        g.drawLine(430,40,430,10);   //right line
        g.drawLine(430,10,10,10);    //top line
    }
}
```

The HTML file for this program contains the following code:

```
<!DOCTYPE HTML PUBLIC "-//W3C//DTD HTML 4.01 Transitional//EN">

<HTML>
  <HEAD>
    <TITLE>WELCOME</TITLE>
  </HEAD>
  <BODY>
    <APPLET code = "GrandWelcomeLine.class" width = "440" height = "50">
    </APPLET>
```

```
    </BODY>
</HTML>
```

Sample Run: Figure 13-6 shows the output of the `GrandWelcomeLine` applet.

Figure 13-6   Output of the `GrandWelcomeLine` applet

In the applet of Example 13-4, you could have used the method `drawRect` to draw a rectangle rather than four lines. In that case, you could use the following statement.

```
g.drawRect(10,10,430,40);    //draw rectangle
```

The program in Example 13-5 further illustrates how to use various methods of the `Graphics class`. In Example 13-5 we create a random collection of geometric shapes. The program uses the method `random` of the `class Math` to randomly determine the number of figures. We want to have at least 5 and at most 14 figures. Therefore, we declare an `int` variable and initialize it as follows:

```
int noOfFigures;

noOfFigures = 5 + (int)(Math.random()*10); //determine the
                                           //number of figures
```

For each figure, we want a random color, random anchor point, random width, and random height. Further, we want a random shape from a set of possible options. This applies to all figures. Therefore, we need to have a loop similar to the following:

```
for(i = 0; i < noOfFigures; i++)
{
     //...
}
```

Inside the above loop, we determine a random color. We can use the method `random` of the `class Math` to get red, green, and blue values between `0` and `255` and use them to create a random color. Therefore, we need the following statements (assume that `g` is a reference variable of `Graphics` type):

```
int red;
int green;
int blue;
```

```
red = (int)(Math.random() * 256);      //red component
green = (int)(Math.random() * 256);    //green component
blue = (int)(Math.random() * 256);     //blue component

g.setColor(new Color(red, green, blue));   //color for
                                           //this figure
```

We also need to compute four more values for **x**, **y**, and width and height between, say, 0 and 200. Further, to make the program easier to modify, we use the named constant SIZE, initialized to 200. Thus, we need the following Java statements:

```
private final int SIZE = 200;
int x;
int y;
int width;
int height;
int red;

x = (int)(Math.random() * SIZE);          //x value
y = (int)(Math.random() * SIZE);          //y value
width = (int)(Math.random() * SIZE);      //width
height = (int)(Math.random() * SIZE);     //height
```

Now all that is left is to randomly select a shape among, say, rectangle, filled rectangle, oval, and filled oval. So let's assign the values:

- 0 for rectangle

- 1 for filled rectangle

- 2 for oval

- 3 for filled oval

respectively. A switch statement can be used to invoke the appropriate method, as shown in the following:

```
shape = (int)(Math.random() * 4);

switch(shape)
{
case 0 : g.drawRect(x, y, width, height);
         break;
case 1 : g.fillRect(x, y, width, height);
         break;
case 2 : g.drawOval(x, y, width, height);
         break;
case 3 : g.drawOval(x, y, width, height);
         break;
}
```

Putting it all together, we have the Java applet given in Example 13-5.

```
//Java applet to draw ovals and rectangles

import java.awt.*;
import javax.swing.*;

public class OvalRectApplet extends JApplet
{
    private final int SIZE = 200;

    public void paint(Graphics g)
    {
        int shape;
        int noOfFigures;
        int x;
        int y;
        int width;
        int height;
        int red;
        int green;
        int blue;

        int i;

                //determines no. of figures
        noOfFigures = 5 + (int)(Math.random() * 10);

        for(i = 0; i < noOfFigures; i++)
        {
            red = (int)(Math.random() * 256);      //red component
            green = (int)(Math.random() * 256);    //green component
            blue = (int)(Math.random() * 256);     //blue component

            g.setColor(new Color(red, green, blue));  //color for
                                                      //this figure

            x = (int)(Math.random() * SIZE);       //x value
            y = (int)(Math.random() * SIZE);       //y value
            width = (int)(Math.random() * SIZE);   //width
            height = (int)(Math.random() * SIZE);  //height

            shape = (int)(Math.random() * 4);
```

13

```
/**
 *     0 : Rectangle
 *     1 : Filled Rectangle
 *     2 : Oval
 *     3 : Filled Oval
 *
 **/

        switch (shape)
        {
        case 0: g.drawRect(x, y, width, height);
                break;
        case 1: g.fillRect(x, y, width, height);
                break;
        case 2: g.drawOval(x, y, width, height);
                break;
        case 3: g.drawOval(x, y, width, height);
                break;
        }//end switch
    }//end for
  }
}
```

The HTML file for this program contains the following code:

```
<!DOCTYPE HTML PUBLIC "-//W3C//DTD HTML 4.01 Transitional//EN">

<HTML>
  <HEAD>
    <TITLE>OVAL APPLET</TITLE>
  </HEAD>
  <BODY>
    <APPLET code = "OvalRectApplet.class" width = "500" height = "500">
    </APPLET>
  </BODY>
</HTML>
```

Sample Run: Figure 13-7 shows a sample run of OvalRectApplet.

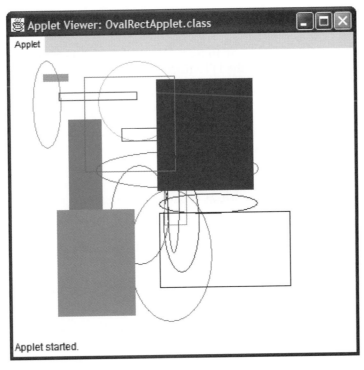

Figure 13-7 Output of the OvalRect applet

Converting an Application Program to an Applet

At this point you might wonder whether there is a simple scheme to convert GUI applications to applets. An applet class shares many features of a GUI application. The main differences are:

- An applet class is derived from the **class JApplet**, whereas a GUI application class is created by extending the **class JFrame**.

- Applets do not have the method **main**. Instead, an applet invokes **init**, **start**, **paint**, **stop**, and **destroy** methods in sequence. Quite often, you place initialization code in **init** and output is produced by the method **paint**.

- Applets do not use constructors. Instead, they use the method **init** to initialize various GUI components and data members.

- Applets do not require methods such as **setVisible**. Applets are embedded in HTML documents, and it is the HTML document that displays the applet.

- Applets do not use the method **setTitle**. The HTML document sets the title.

13

- Applets do not use the method `setSize`. The HTML document specifies the size of the applet.

- Applets do not have to be closed. In particular, there is no `Exit` button. Once again, the applet closes when the HTML document closes.

Therefore, in most cases, you perform the following six steps to convert a GUI application to an applet:

1. Make your `class` extend the definition of the `class JApplet`. In other words, change `JFrame` to `JApplet`.

2. Change the constructor to the method `init`.

3. Remove method calls such as `setVisible`, `setTitle`, and `setSize`.

4. Remove the method `main`.

5. Remove the `Exit` button, if you have one, and all code associated with it, such as the action listener and so on.

As an example, we modify the temperature conversion program presented in Chapter 6 as a GUI application. The statements changed to create an applet are shown as comments.

```
//Java program to convert between Centigrade and Fahrenheit.

import java.awt.*;
import java.awt.event.*;
import javax.swing.*;
import java.text.DecimalFormat;


    //public class TempConversion extends JFrame
    //
    //changed; replace JFrame by JApplet
    //
public class TempConvertApplet extends JApplet
{
    private JLabel centigradeLabel;
    private JLabel  fahrenheitLabel;
    private JTextField centigradeTF;
    private JTextField  fahrenheitTF;
    private CentHandler centigradeHandler;
    private FahrHandler fahrenheitHandler;

    private static final int WIDTH = 500;
    private static final int HEIGHT = 50;
    private static final double FTOC = 5.0/9.0;
    private static final double CTOF = 1.8;          // 9/5
    private static final int OFFSET = 32;

    //public TempConversion()
    //
```

```
 //changed; replace constructor with init method
 //
public void init()
{
        //setTitle("Temperature Conversion");
        //
        //setTitle deleted
        //

    Container c = getContentPane();
    c.setLayout(new GridLayout(1, 4));

    centigradeLabel = new JLabel("Enter Centigrade",
                              SwingConstants.RIGHT);
    fahrenheitLabel = new JLabel("Enter Fahrenheit ",
                              SwingConstants.RIGHT);

    centigradeTF = new JTextField(7);
    fahrenheitTF = new JTextField(7);

    c.add(centigradeLabel);
    c.add(centigradeTF);
    c.add(fahrenheitLabel);
    c.add(fahrenheitTF);

    centigradeHandler = new CentHandler();
    fahrenheitHandler = new FahrHandler();
    centigradeTF.addActionListener(centigradeHandler);
    fahrenheitTF.addActionListener(fahrenheitHandler);

        //setSize(WIDTH,HEIGHT);
        //setSize(WIDTH,HEIGHT) deleted

        //setVisible(true);
        //setVisible(true) deleted
}

private class CentHandler implements ActionListener
{
    public void actionPerformed(ActionEvent e)
    {
        double centigrade, fahrenheit;
        DecimalFormat twoDigits = new DecimalFormat("0.00");

        centigrade = Double.parseDouble(centigradeTF.getText());
        fahrenheit =  centigrade * CTOF + OFFSET;
        fahrenheitTF.setText(""+ twoDigits.format(fahrenheit));
    }
}
```

13

```
        private class FahrHandler implements ActionListener
        {
           public void actionPerformed(ActionEvent e)
           {
              double centigrade, fahrenheit;
              DecimalFormat twoDigits = new DecimalFormat("0.00");

              fahrenheit = Double.parseDouble(fahrenheitTF.getText());
              centigrade = (fahrenheit - OFFSET)*FTOC;
              centigradeTF.setText(""+ twoDigits.format(centigrade));
           }
        }

        //public static void main(String args[] )
        //{
        //TempConversion tempConv = new TempConversion();
        //
        //}
        //
        //method main is deleted
        //
}//end of class
```

The HTML file for this program contains the following code:

```
<!DOCTYPE HTML PUBLIC "-//W3C//DTD HTML 4.01 Transitional//EN">

<HTML>
  <HEAD>
    <TITLE>TEMPERATURE APPLET</TITLE>
  </HEAD>
  <BODY>
    <APPLET code = "TempConvertApplet.class" width = "500" height = "50">
    </APPLET>
  </BODY>
</HTML>
```

ADDITIONAL GUI COMPONENTS

In the remainder of this chapter, we introduce GUI components other than those introduced in Chapter 6. For the most part, these additional GUI components are used in the same way as the ones introduced earlier. For example, you create an instance (or object) using the operator **new**. If the program needs to respond to an event occurring in a GUI component such as **JTextField** or **JButton**, you need to add an event listener and provide the associated method that needs to be invoked, commonly called the event handler. We will also illustrate the use of various methods of the **class Graphics**.

JTextArea

The GUI programs in previous chapters extensively used the **class JTextField** to display a line of text. There are situations when the program must display multiple lines of text. For example, an employee's address is shown in three or more lines. Because an object of the **class JTextField** can display only one line of text, you cannot use an object of this class to display multiple lines of text. Java provides the **class JTextArea** to either collect multiple lines of input from the user or to display multiple lines of output. Using an object of this class, the user can type multiple lines of text, which are separated by pressing the **Enter** key. In Java, each line ends with the newline character '\n'.

The GUI part of the Student Grade Report Programming Example in Chapter 11 uses a **JTextArea** to display multiple lines of text to show the various courses taken by a student and the grade in each course. This section discusses the capabilities of the **class JTextArea** in some detail.

Both **JTextField** and **JTextArea** are derived from the **class JTextComponent** and as such share many common methods. However, you cannot create an instance of the **class JTextComponent** because it is an **abstract** class. Table 13-8 lists some of the constructors and methods of the **class JTextArea**.

Table 13-8 Commonly Used Constructors and Methods of the **class JTextArea**

```
public JTextArea(int r, int c)
   //Constructor
   //Creates a JTextArea instance with r number of rows and
   //c number of columns.
```

```
public JTextArea(String t, int r, int c)
   //Constructor
   //Creates a JTextArea instance with r number of rows, c number
   //of columns, and initial text t.
```

```
public void setColumns(int c)
   //Sets the number of columns to c.
```

```
public void setRows(int r)
   //Sets the number of rows to r.
```

```
public void append(String t)
   //Concatenates the text already in the JTextArea with t.
```

```
public void setLineWrap(boolean b)
   //If b is true, lines are wrapped.
```

```
public void setWrapStyleWord(boolean b)
   //If b is true, lines are wrapped at word boundaries
   //If b is false, word boundaries are not considered.
```

```
public void setTabSize(int c)
   //Sets tab stops every c columns.
```

13

Table 13-9 shows the methods, which you have used with a **JTextField** object, that are inherited by the **class JTextArea** from the parent **class JTextComponent**.

Table 13-9 Methods Inherited by the **class JTextArea** from the Parent **class JTextComponent**

```
public void setText(String t)
   //Changes the text of the text area to t.
```

```
public String getText()
   //Returns the text contained in text area.
```

```
public void setEditable(boolean b)
   //If b is false, user cannot type in the text area. In this case,
   //the text area is used as a tool to display the result.
```

Example 13-6

The program in this example illustrates the usage of **JTextArea**. It creates the GUI shown in Figure 13-8.

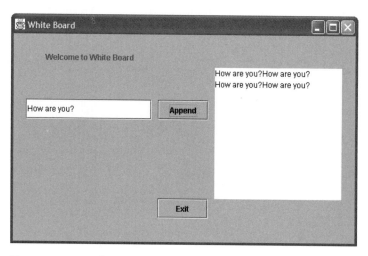

Figure 13-8 White Board GUI

As shown in Figure 13-8, the GUI contains a **JLabel**, two **JButtons**, a text field, and a text area. The user can type a line of text in the text field and when the user clicks on the **Exit** button, the program terminates. Similarly, if the user clicks on the **Append** button, the text in the text field is appended to the text in the text area.

In this example, we write this program as a GUI application. A corresponding applet is left as an exercise for you; see Programming Exercise 8 at the end of this chapter.

As in the previous GUI application program, we create the necessary labels, text fields, and text areas, and place them in the content pane. We also create and place two buttons, `exitB` and `appendB`, in the content pane. The following statements access the content pane, create the GUI components, and place the GUI components in the content pane:

```
private JLabel headingL;
headingL = new JLabel("Welcome to White Board");

private JTextField lineTF;
lineTF =  new JTextField(20);

private JTextArea whiteBoardTA;
whiteBoardTA = new JTextArea(10, 20);

private JButton exitB, appendB;
exitB = new JButton("Exit");
appendB = new JButton("Append");

Container pane = getContentPane();

pane.add(headingL);
pane.add(lineTF);
pane.add(whiteBoardTA);
pane.add(appendB);
pane.add(exitB);
```

We will specify the sizes and the locations of the GUI components when we write the complete program.

In Chapter 6, action listener interfaces are implemented through inner classes. As explained in Chapter 11, any class containing the application can directly implement the `interface` `ActionListener`. The GUI programs of this chapter directly implement the interfaces to handle events. Suppose `WhiteBoard` is the name of the class to implement the application to create the preceding GUI. Then, the heading of this class is:

```
public class WhiteBoard extends JFrame implements ActionListener
```

The method `actionPerformed` is included as a member of the `class WhiteBoard`. To register the action listener with `exitB`, all you need to do is include the following statement in the program:

```
exitB.addActionListener(this);
```

Of course, the necessary code is placed in the method `actionPerformed`.

13

Because action events are generated by the two buttons, the method `actionPerformed` uses the method `getActionCommand` and the method `equals` to identify the source of the event. The definition of this method is:

```
public void actionPerformed(ActionEvent e)
{
    if(e.getActionCommand().equals("Append"))        //Line 1
        whiteBoardTA.append(lineTF.getText());       //Line 2
    else if(e.getActionCommand().equals("Exit"))     //Line 3
            System.exit(0);                          //Line 4
}
```

If the user clicks the **Append** button, then the `if` statement in Line 1 evaluates to `true`. In this case, the statement in Line 2 retrieves the line of text from the text field object `lineTF` and appends it to the text in the text area object `whiteBoardTA`. When the user clicks the **Exit** button, the `if` statement in Line 3 evaluates to `true` and the statement in Line 4 terminates the program.

The complete program listing follows:

```
import java.io.*;
import java.text.*;
import javax.swing.*;
import java.awt.*;
import java.awt.event.*;

public class WhiteBoard extends JFrame implements ActionListener
{
    private static int WIDTH = 550;
    private static int HEIGHT = 350;

    private int row = 10;
    private int col = 20;

        //GUI components
    private JLabel headingL;
    private JTextField lineTF;
    private JTextArea whiteBoardTA;
    private JButton exitB, appendB;

    public WhiteBoard()
    {
        setTitle("White Board");
        Container pane  = getContentPane();
        setSize(WIDTH,HEIGHT);

        headingL = new JLabel("Welcome to White Board");
        lineTF =  new JTextField(20);
```

```
    whiteBoardTA = new JTextArea(row,col);
    exitB = new JButton("Exit");
    exitB.addActionListener(this);

    appendB = new JButton("Append");
    appendB.addActionListener(this);

    pane.setLayout(null);

    headingL.setLocation(50,20);
    lineTF.setLocation(20,100);
    whiteBoardTA.setLocation(320,50);
    appendB.setLocation(230,100);
    exitB.setLocation(230,250);

    headingL.setSize(200,30);
    lineTF.setSize(200,30);
    whiteBoardTA.setSize(200,200);
    appendB.setSize(80,30);
    exitB.setSize(80,30);

    pane.add(headingL);
    pane.add(lineTF);
    pane.add(whiteBoardTA);
    pane.add(appendB);
    pane.add(exitB);

    setVisible(true);
    setDefaultCloseOperation(EXIT_ON_CLOSE);

  } //end of the constructor

public static void main(String[] args) throws IOException
{
    WhiteBoard board = new WhiteBoard();
}

public void actionPerformed(ActionEvent e)
{
    if(e.getActionCommand().equals("Append"))
       whiteBoardTA.append(lineTF.getText());
    else if(e.getActionCommand().equals("Exit"))
            System.exit(0);
  }
}
```

13

Sample Run: Figure 13-9 shows a sample run of this program. (Note that to get the new line in the text area, click the mouse to position the insertion point in the text area, and then press the Enter key. The next append should now be in the next line.)

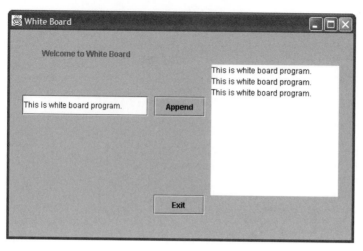

Figure 13-9 Sample run of White Board program

JCheckBox

In the previous section you learned how to use text fields and text areas to collect input from the user. When you use a text field or a text area to input data, users can type anything they want. However, sometimes you want the user to select from a set of predefined values. For example, to specify gender, the user would select either male or female; similarly, a student would select either undergraduate or graduate. In addition to freeing the user from typing in such values, to get precise input, you want the user to select a value from a set of given values.

The `JCheckBox` and `JRadioButton` classes allow a user to select a value from a set of given values. Both of these classes are subclasses of the **abstract class ToggleButton**. This section describes the **class JCheckBox**. The **class JRadioButton** is discussed in the next section.

Table 13-10 shows some of the constructors and methods of the **class JCheckBox**.

Table 13-10 Some Constructors and Methods of the **class JCheckBox**

```
public JCheckBox()
   //Constructor: Creates an initially unselected check box
   //with no label and no icon.
   //Example: JCheckBox myJCheckBox = new JCheckBox()
   //         myJCheckBox points to a check box with no label and no
   //         icon.
public JCheckBox(Icon icon)
   //Constructor: Creates an initially unselected check box with
   //the specified icon and no label.
   //Example: JCheckBox myJCheckBox = new JCheckBox(anIcon);
   //         myJCheckBox points to a check box with icon "anIcon".
```

Table 13-10 Some Constructors and Methods of the `class JCheckBox` (continued)

```
public JCheckBox(Icon icon, boolean selected)
  //Constructor: Creates a check box with the specified
  //image and selection state, but without label.
  //Example: JCheckBox myJCheckBox = new JCheckBox(anIcon, true);
  //        myJCheckBox points to a selected check box with
  //        anIcon as icon.
```

```
public JCheckBox(String text)
  //Constructor: Creates an unselected check box with
  //the specified label.
  //Example: JCheckBox myJCheckBox = new JCheckBox("Box");
  //    myJCheckBox points to an unselected check box with
  //    label "Box".
```

```
public JCheckBox(String text, boolean selected)
  //Constructor: Creates a check box with the specified
  //label and selection state.
  //Example: JCheckBox myJCheckBox = new JCheckBox("Box", false);
  //        myJCheckBox points to an unselected check box with
  //        label "Box".
```

```
public JCheckBox(String text, Icon icon)
  //Constructor: Creates a check box with the specified image
  //and with specified label.
  //Example: JCheckBox myJCheckBox = new JCheckBox("Box", anIcon,);
  //        myJCheckBox points to an unselected check box with label
  //        "Box" and anIcon as icon.
```

```
public JCheckBox(String text, Icon icon, boolean selected)
  //Constructor: Creates a check box with the specified image
  //and selection state, and with the specified text.
  //Example: JCheckBox myJCheckBox =
  //                        new JCheckBox("Box",anIcon, true);
  //        myJCheckBox points to a selected check box with label "Box"
  //        and anIcon as icon.
```

```
public boolean isSelected()
  //This method is inherited from the AbstractButton class and is
  //used to retrieve the state of a button.
  //Example: if(myJCheckBox.isSelected() == true)
  //        The "if" block will be executed provided myJCheckBox
  //        is checked.
```

```
public boolean setSelected(boolean b)
  //This method is inherited from the AbstractButton class and is
  //used to set the state of a button.
  //Example: myJCheckBox.setSelected(true);
  //        myJcheckBox gets checked.
```

Similar to buttons, check boxes also come with their own identifying labels. Consider the following statements:

```
JCheckBox italicCB;                        //Line 1
italicCB = new JCheckBox("Italic");        //Line 2
```

The statement in Line 1 declares `italicCB` to be a reference variable of the `JCheckBox` type. The statement in Line 2 creates the object `italicCB` and assigns it the label `Italic`. After the statement in Line 2 executes, the figure shown in Figure 13-10 results.

Figure 13-10   Check box with label

In Figure 13-10, the box to the left of the label `Italic` is a check box. The user clicks on it to select or deselect it. For example, clicking on the check box in Figure 13-10 produces the result shown in Figure 13-11.

Figure 13-11   Result of clicking the check box

If you click on the check box of Figure 13-11, the check mark disappears. A check box is an example of a toggle button. If it is not selected and you click on it, then the box is selected and a check mark appears. If it is selected and you click on it, the check mark disappears.

When you click on a `JCheckBox`, it generates an **item event**. Item events are handled by the `interface ItemListener`. The `interface ItemListener` contains only the `abstract` method `itemStateChanged`. The heading of the method is:

```
public void itemStateChanged(ItemEvent e)
```

To make the program respond to the event generated by clicking a check box, you write the code that needs to be executed in the body of the method `itemStateChanged`, and register an item listener object to the check box.

Next we write an applet that has two check boxes and also displays a line of text. The first check box is used to indicate the selection of bold style and the second to indicate the selection of italic style. The user can click the check boxes to change the font and style of the text.

We create two check boxes with the labels `"Bold"` and `"Italic"` and place them in the content pane of the applet. The method `init` contains the necessary statements for these initializations. Therefore, the `init` method can be written as follows:

```
public void init()
{
    Container c = getContentPane();    //get the container
    c.setLayout(null);                 //set the layout to null

        //create the check boxes with appropriate labels
    boldCB = new JCheckBox("Bold");
    italicCB = new JCheckBox("Italic");

        //set the sizes of the check boxes
    boldCB.setSize(100,30);
    italicCB.setSize(100,30);

        //set the location of the check boxes
    boldCB.setLocation(100,100);
    italicCB.setLocation(300,100);

        //register item listener to the check boxes
    boldCB.addItemListener(this);
    italicCB.addItemListener(this);

        //add the check boxes to the pane
    c.add(boldCB);
    c.add(italicCB);
}
```

To specify the font and style of the text, we use two `int` variables, `intBold` and `intItalic`. These variables are set to `Font.PLAIN` when the check boxes are not checked. They are set to `Font.BOLD` and `Font.ITALIC`, respectively, if the corresponding check boxes are checked. To create bold and italic fonts, you simply add the values of the variables `bold` and `italic`. In other words, you can create desired fonts by just using `intBold + intItalic` as the style value. Note that because `Font.PLAIN` has value zero, `Font.PLAIN + Font.PLAIN` remains `Font.PLAIN`. The `paint` method can be used to set the color and font, and to display the welcome message. The definition of the method `paint` can be written as follows:

```
public void paint(Graphics g)
{
    super.paint(g);
    g.setColor(Color.red);
    g.setFont(new Font("Courier", intBold + intItalic, 24));
    g.drawString("Welcome to Java Programming",30,30);
}
```

To make the program respond to the events generated by the check boxes, next we write the definition of the method `itemStateChanged`. As shown earlier, the method `itemStateChanged` has one parameter, e, which is of the type `ItemEvent`. Because there are two check boxes, we use the method `getSource` to identify the box generating the event.

13

The expression

```
e.getSource() == boldCB
```

is `true` if the check box associated with `boldCB` generated the event. Similarly, the expression

```
e.getSource() == italicCB
```

is `true` if the check box associated with `italicCB` generated the event.

After identifying the check box that generated the event, we determine whether the user selected or deselected the check box. For this, we use the method `getStateChange` of the class `ItemEvent` that returns either the constant `ItemEvent.SELECTED` or the constant `ItemEvent.DESELECTED`, which are defined in the class `ItemEvent`. For example, the expression

```
e.getStateChange() == ItemEvent.SELECTED
```

is `true` if the event `e` corresponds to selecting the check box.

Finally, every time an event happens, you want to change the font accordingly. This can be achieved by invoking the `paint` method. To call the `paint` method, you need a `Graphics` object. So, you invoke the `repaint` method, which in turn invokes the `paint` method. Therefore, you need to call the `repaint` method before leaving the event handler method.

The definition of the method `itemStateChanged` is:

```
public void itemStateChanged(ItemEvent e)
{
    if(e.getSource() == boldCB)
    {
        if(e.getStateChange() == ItemEvent.SELECTED)
            intBold = Font.BOLD;
        if(e.getStateChange() == ItemEvent.DESELECTED)
            intBold = Font.PLAIN;
    }

    if(e.getSource() == italicCB)
    {
        if(e.getStateChange() == ItemEvent.SELECTED)
            intItalic = Font.ITALIC;
        if(e.getStateChange() == ItemEvent.DESELECTED)
            intItalic = Font.PLAIN;
    }

    repaint();
}
```

Now that the necessary components are written, we can write the complete program.

```java
//Welcome Applet with check boxes

import java.awt.*;
import java.awt.event.*;
import javax.swing.*;

public class GrandWelcomeCheckBox extends JApplet implements
                                                    ItemListener
{
    private int intBold = Font.PLAIN;
    private int intItalic = Font.PLAIN;
    private JCheckBox boldCB, italicCB;

    public void init()
    {
        Container c = getContentPane();
        c.setLayout(null);
        boldCB = new JCheckBox( "Bold");
        italicCB = new JCheckBox( "Italic");

        boldCB.setSize(100,30);
        italicCB.setSize(100,30);

        boldCB.setLocation(100,100);
        italicCB.setLocation(300,100);

        boldCB.addItemListener(this);
        italicCB.addItemListener(this);

        c.add(boldCB);
        c.add(italicCB);
    }

    public void paint( Graphics g)
    {
        super.paint(g);
        g.setColor(Color.red);
        g.setFont(new Font("Courier", intBold + intItalic, 24));
        g.drawString("Welcome to Java Programming",30,30);
    }

    public void itemStateChanged(ItemEvent e)
    {
        if(e.getSource() == boldCB)
        {
            if(e.getStateChange() == ItemEvent.SELECTED)
                intBold = Font.BOLD;
```

13

```
        if(e.getStateChange() == ItemEvent.DESELECTED)
           intBold = Font.PLAIN;
     }

     if(e.getSource() == italicCB)
     {
        if(e.getStateChange() == ItemEvent.SELECTED)
           intItalic = Font.ITALIC;
        if(e.getStateChange() == ItemEvent.DESELECTED)
           intItalic = Font.PLAIN;
     }

     repaint();
   }
}
```

The HTML file for this program contains the following code:

```
<!DOCTYPE HTML PUBLIC "-//W3C//DTD HTML 4.01 Transitional//EN">

<HTML>
  <HEAD>
    <TITLE>WELCOME</TITLE>
  </HEAD>
  <BODY>
    <APPLET code = "GrandWelcomeCheckBox.class" width = "440" height = "200">
    </APPLET>
  </BODY>
</HTML>
```

Sample Run: Figure 13-12 shows a sample run of the applet with check boxes.

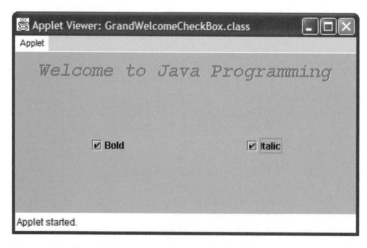

Figure 13-12   Welcome applet with check boxes

JRadioButton

Check boxes allow the user to select a value from a set of values. The program in the previous section used two check boxes. The user could select or deselect one or both check boxes. However, there are situations in which you want the user to make only one selection from a set of values. For example, if the user needs to select the gender of a person, the user selects either female or male, but not both. If you want the user to select exactly one, and only one, of the options presented, you use radio buttons. To make such selections possible, Java provides the class JRadioButton.

Table 13-11 shows some of the constructors and methods of the class JRadioButton.

Table 13-11 Some Constructors and Methods of the class JRadioButton

```
public JRadioButton()
  //Constructor: Creates an initially unselected radio button
  //with no label and no icon.
  //Example: JRadioButton myJRadioButton = new JRadioButton();
  //    myJRadioButton points to a radio button with no label
  //    and no icon.
```

```
public JRadioButton(Icon icon)
  //Constructor: Creates an initially unselected radio button
  //with the specified icon and no label.
  //Example: JRadioButton myJRadioButton = new JRadioButton(anIcon);
  //    myJRadioButton points to a radio button with icon "anIcon".
```

```
public JRadioButton(Icon icon, boolean selected)
  //Constructor: Creates a radio button with the specified
  //icon and selection state, but without label.
  //Example:JRadioButton myJRadioButton =
  //                      new JRadioButton(anIcon, true);
  //    myJRadioButton points to a selected radio button with
  //    anIcon as icon.
```

```
public JRadioButton(String text)
  //Constructor: Creates an unselected radio button with the
  //specified text as label.
  //Example: JRadioButton myJRadioButton = new JRadioButton("Box");
  //    myJRadioButton points to an unselected radio button
  //    with label "Box".
```

```
public JRadioButton(String text, boolean selected)
  //Constructor: Creates a radio button with the specified
  //text as label and selection state.
  //Example:
  //    JRadioButton myJRadioButton = new JRadioButton("Box",false);
  //        myJRadioButton points to an unselected radio button
  //        with label "Box".
```

13

Table 13-11 Some Constructors and Methods of the `class JRadioButton` (continued)

```
public JRadioButton(String text, Icon icon)
  //Constructor: Creates a radio button with the specified
  //icon and with specified text as label.
  //Example:
  //  JRadioButton myJRadioButton = new JRadioButton("Box", anIcon);
  //    myJRadioButton points to an unselected radio button
  //    with label "Box" and icon anIcon.
```

```
public JRadioButton(String text, Icon icon, boolean selected)
  //Constructor: Creates a radio button with the specified
  //icon and selection state, and with the specified text as label.
  //Example: JRadioButton myJRadioButton =
  //                  new JRadioButton("Box", anIcon, true);
  //    myJRadioButton points to a selected radio button with
  //    label "Box" and anIcon as icon.
```

```
public boolean isSelected()
  //This method is inherited from the AbstractButton class and is
  //used to retrieve the state of a button.
  //Example: if(myJRadioButton.isSelected() == true)
  //      The "if" block will be executed provided myJRadioButton
  //      is checked.
```

```
public boolean setSelected(boolean b)
  //This method is inherited from the AbstractButton class and is
  //used to set the state of a button.
  //Example: myJRadioButton.setSelected(true);
  //         myJRadioButton gets checked.
```

Radio buttons are created the same way check boxes are created. Consider the following statements:

```
private JRadioButton redRB, greenRB, blueRB;        //Line 1
redRB = new JRadioButton("Red");                    //Line 2
greenRB = new JRadioButton("Green");                //Line 3
blueRB = new JRadioButton("Blue");                  //Line 4
```

The statement in Line 1 declares `redRB`, `greenRB`, and `blueRB` to be reference variables of the `JRadioButton` type. The statement in Line 2 instantiates the object `redRB` and assigns it the label `"Red"`. Similarly, the statements in Lines 3 and 4 instantiate the objects `greenRB` and `blueRB` and with the labels `"Green"` and `"Blue"`, respectively.

As with check boxes, we create and place radio buttons in the content pane of the applet. However, in this case, to force the user to select only one radion button at a time, we create a button group and group these radio buttons. Consider the following statements:

```
private ButtonGroup ColorSelectBGroup;              //Line 5

ColorSelectBGroup = new ButtonGroup();              //Line 6
ColorSelectBGroup.add(redRB);                       //Line 7
```

```
ColorSelectBGroup.add(greenRB);                //Line 8
ColorSelectBGroup.add(blueRB);                 //Line 9
```

The statement in Lines 5 and 6 creates the object `ColorSelectBGroup` and the statements in Lines 7, 8, and 9 add the radio buttons `redRB`, `greenRB`, and `blueRB` to this object. The statements in Lines 1 to 9 create and group the radio buttons shown in Figure 13-13.

Figure 13-13   Radio buttons

Because the radio buttons `redRB`, `greenRB`, and `blueRB` are grouped, the user can select only one of these buttons. Similar to `JCheckBox`, `JRadioButton` also generates an `ItemEvent`. So we use the `interface ItemListener` and its method `itemStateChanged` to handle the events.

In the following example, we start with the applet we created in the section `JCheckBox` and add three radio buttons so that the text color can be selected from the list: red, green, blue.

Grouping buttons enforces the constraint that only one radio button can be selected at any time. This also affects how you write the event handler. Since only one button can be selected, once you know the source of the event, you can conclude that the associated radio button is selected. Thus, the relevant code for handling the events generated by these radio buttons can be written as follows:

```
if(e.getSource() == redRB)
   currentColor = Color.red;
else if(e.getSource() == greenRB)
      currentColor = Color.green;
else if(e.getSource() == blueRB)
      currentColor = Color.blue;
```

13

The complete program along with the sample run follows:

```java
import java.awt.*;
import java.awt.event.*;
import javax.swing.*;

public class GrandWelcomeRButton extends JApplet implements
                                                    ItemListener
{
    private int intBold = Font.PLAIN;
    private int intItalic = Font.PLAIN;
    private Color currentColor = Color.black;
    private JCheckBox boldCB, italicCB;
    private JRadioButton redRB, greenRB, blueRB;
    private ButtonGroup ColorSelectBGroup;

    public void init()
    {
        Container c = getContentPane();
        c.setLayout(null);
        boldCB = new JCheckBox("Bold");
        italicCB = new JCheckBox("Italic");
        redRB = new JRadioButton("Red");
        greenRB = new JRadioButton("Green");
        blueRB = new JRadioButton("Blue");

        boldCB.setSize(100,30);
        italicCB.setSize(100,30);
        redRB.setSize(100,30);
        greenRB.setSize(100,30);
        blueRB.setSize(100,30);

        boldCB.setLocation(100,70);
        italicCB.setLocation(100,150);
        redRB.setLocation(300,70);
        greenRB.setLocation(300,110);
        blueRB.setLocation(300,150);

        boldCB.addItemListener(this);
        italicCB.addItemListener(this);
        redRB.addItemListener(this);
        greenRB.addItemListener(this);
        blueRB.addItemListener(this);

        c.add(boldCB);
        c.add(italicCB);
        c.add(redRB);
        c.add(greenRB);
        c.add(blueRB);
```

```
        ColorSelectBGroup = new ButtonGroup();
        ColorSelectBGroup.add(redRB);
        ColorSelectBGroup.add(greenRB);
        ColorSelectBGroup.add(blueRB);
    }

    public void paint(Graphics g)
    {
        super.paint(g);
        g.setColor(Color.orange);
        g.drawRoundRect(75,50,125,140,10,10);
        g.drawRoundRect(275,50,125,140,10,10);
        g.setColor(currentColor);
        g.setFont(new Font("Courier", intBold + intItalic, 24));
        g.drawString("Welcome to Java Programming",30,30);
    }

    public void itemStateChanged(ItemEvent e)
    {
        if(e.getSource() == boldCB)
        {
           if(e.getStateChange() == ItemEvent.SELECTED)
              intBold = Font.BOLD;
           if(e.getStateChange() == ItemEvent.DESELECTED)
              intBold = Font.PLAIN;
        }

        if(e.getSource() == italicCB)
        {
           if(e.getStateChange() == ItemEvent.SELECTED)
              intItalic = Font.ITALIC;
           if(e.getStateChange() == ItemEvent.DESELECTED)
              intItalic = Font.PLAIN;
        }

        if(e.getSource() == redRB)
           currentColor = Color.red;
        else if(e.getSource() == greenRB)
              currentColor = Color.green;
        else if(e.getSource() == blueRB)
              currentColor = Color.blue;

        repaint();
    }
}
```

13

The HTML file for this program contains the following code:

```
<!DOCTYPE HTML PUBLIC "-//W3C//DTD HTML 4.01 Transitional//EN">

<HTML>
  <HEAD>
    <TITLE>WELCOME</TITLE>
  </HEAD>
  <BODY>
    <APPLET code = "GrandWelcomeRButton.class" width = "440" height = "200">
    </APPLET>
  </BODY>
</HTML>
```

Sample Run: Figure 13-14 is a sample run showing check boxes and radio buttons.

Figure 13-14 Sample run showing check boxes and radio buttons

JComboBox

A **combo box**, commonly known as a drop-down list, is used to select an item from a list of possibilities. A JComboBox generates an ItemEvent monitored by an ItemListener, which invokes the method itemStateChanged exactly as in JCheckBox or JRadioButton.

Table 13-12 lists some constructors of the class JComboBox.

Table 13-12 Some Constructors of the `class JComboBox`

```
public JComboBox()
   //Constructor: Creates a new JComboBox with no items to select.
   //Example: JComboBox selectionList = new JComboBox();
   //          "selectionList" is created but has no selectable items.
```

```
public JComboBox(Vector v)
   //Constructor: Creates a new combo box to display elements
   //in the vector provided as an input parameter.
   //Example: JComboBox selectionList = new JComboBox(v);
   //          selectionList points to a combo box that lists the
   //          elements contained in Vector v.
```

```
public JComboBox(Object[] o)
   //Constructor:  Creates a new combo box for selection that displays
   //elements in the object array provided as an input parameter.
   //Example: JComboBox selectionList = new JComboBox(o);
   //     creates the new combo box called selectionList and
   //     displays the selections.For an object
   //     list, would display o.tostring() values.
```

In the previous two sections, we created an applet that uses check boxes and radio buttons to change the font and style of text. In this section, we add a `JComboBox` to the program so that the user can select a font from a list of font names, and apply that font to the text.

To create a combo box, we first declare a reference variable as follows:

```
private JComboBox fontFaceDD;                              //Line 1
```

Next we create an array of strings and initialize it with the list of font names. The corresponding Java statement is:

```
private String fontNames[] = {"Dialog", "Century Gothic",
                      "Courier","Serif"};        //Line 2
```

Next we use the variable `fontFaceDD`, declared in Line 1, and the array of strings `fontNames`, created in Line 2, to create a combo box. Consider the following statement:

```
fontFaceDD = new JComboBox(fontNames);                   //Line 3
```

This statement creates the object `fontFaceDD` and initializes this object using the strings in the array `fontNames`.

There are four items in the object `fontFaceDD`. When you click on the combo box it shows you these four choices. You can control the number of choices shown by using the method `setMaximumRowCount`. For example, the statement

```
fontFaceDD.setMaximumRowCount(3);
```

sets the number of choices to be shown to 3. Because there are four choices in the combo box `fontFaceDD`, a vertical scroll bar appears to the right of the box. You can scroll this bar to see and select other choices.

13

When you click on an item in the combo box, it generates an item event. To process item events, we use the **interface ItemListener**. As described in the previous section, the item event handler code is placed in the body of the method **itemStateChanged**.

When the user selects an item from a combo box, the index of the selected item can be obtained by using the method **getSelectedIndex()**. For example, the statement

```
currentFontName = fontNames[fontFaceDD.getSelectedIndex()];
```

assigns the current font name to the string variable **currentFontName**.

The complete program listing for this **JComboBox** example is given in Example 13-7.

Example 13-7

```
//Welcome program with check boxes, radio buttons, and combo box

import java.awt.*;
import java.awt.event.*;
import javax.swing.*;

public class GrandWelcomeFinal extends JApplet implements
                                                ItemListener
{
    private int intBold = Font.PLAIN;
    private int intItalic = Font.PLAIN;
    private Color currentColor = Color.black;
    private String currentFontName ="Courier";
    private JCheckBox boldCB, italicCB;
    private JRadioButton redRB, greenRB, blueRB;
    private ButtonGroup ColorSelectBGroup;
    private JComboBox fontFaceDD;
    private String[] fontNames
                = {"Dialog","Century Gothic","Courier","Serif"};

    public void init()
    {
        Container c = getContentPane();
        c.setLayout(null);
        boldCB = new JCheckBox("Bold");
        italicCB = new JCheckBox("Italic");
        redRB = new JRadioButton("Red");
        greenRB = new JRadioButton("Green");
        blueRB = new JRadioButton("Blue");
        fontFaceDD = new JComboBox(fontNames);
        fontFaceDD.setMaximumRowCount(3);
```

```
        boldCB.setSize(80,30);
        italicCB.setSize(80,30);
        redRB.setSize(80,30);
        greenRB.setSize(80,30);
        blueRB.setSize(80,30);
        fontFaceDD.setSize(80,30);

        boldCB.setLocation(100,70);
        italicCB.setLocation(100,150);
        redRB.setLocation(300,70);
        greenRB.setLocation(300,110);
        blueRB.setLocation(300,150);
        fontFaceDD.setLocation(200,70);

        boldCB.addItemListener(this);
        italicCB.addItemListener(this);
        redRB.addItemListener(this);
        greenRB.addItemListener(this);
        blueRB.addItemListener(this);
        fontFaceDD.addItemListener(this);

        c.add(boldCB);
        c.add(italicCB);
        c.add(redRB);
        c.add(greenRB);
        c.add(blueRB);
        c.add(fontFaceDD);
        ColorSelectBGroup = new ButtonGroup();
        ColorSelectBGroup.add(redRB);
        ColorSelectBGroup.add(greenRB);
        ColorSelectBGroup.add(blueRB);
    }

public void paint(Graphics g)
{
        super.paint(g);
        g.setColor(Color.orange);
        g.drawRoundRect(75,50,324,140,10,10);
        g.drawLine(183,50,183,190);
        g.drawLine(291,50,291,190);

        g.setColor(currentColor);
        g.setFont(new Font(currentFontName, intBold + intItalic, 24));
        g.drawString("Welcome to Java Programming",30,30);
    }
```

13

```
    public void itemStateChanged(ItemEvent e)
    {
        if(e.getSource() == boldCB)
        {
            if(e.getStateChange() == ItemEvent.SELECTED)
                intBold = Font.BOLD;
            if(e.getStateChange() == ItemEvent.DESELECTED)
                intBold = Font.PLAIN;
        }

        if(e.getSource() == italicCB)
        {
            if(e.getStateChange() == ItemEvent.SELECTED)
                intItalic = Font.ITALIC;
            if(e.getStateChange() == ItemEvent.DESELECTED)
                intItalic = Font.PLAIN;
        }

        if(e.getSource() == redRB)
            currentColor = Color.red;
        else if(e.getSource() == greenRB)
                currentColor = Color.green;
        else if(e.getSource() == blueRB)
                currentColor = Color.blue;

        if(e.getSource() == fontFaceDD)
            currentFontName =
                        fontNames[fontFaceDD.getSelectedIndex()];

        repaint();
    }
}
```

The HTML file for this program contains the following code:

```
<!DOCTYPE HTML PUBLIC "-//W3C//DTD HTML 4.01 Transitional//EN">

<HTML>
  <HEAD>
    <TITLE>WELCOME</TITLE>
  </HEAD>
  <BODY>
    <APPLET code = "GrandWelcomeFinal.class" width = "440" height = "200">
    </APPLET>
  </BODY>
</HTML>
```

Sample Run: Figure 13-15 shows a sample run for the Welcome applet with check boxes, combo box, and radio buttons.

Figure 13-15   Welcome applet with check boxes, combo box, and radio buttons

JList

A **list** displays a number of items from which the user can select one or more items. In this section, we illustrate the use of a single selection list. The programming example at the end of this chapter uses a multiple selection list. Table 13-13 shows some constructors and methods of the `class JList`.

Table 13-13   Some Constructors and Methods of the `class JList`

```
public JList()
  //Constructor: Creates a new JList with no items to select.
  //Example: JList selectionList = new JList();
  //         "selectionList" is created but has no selectable items.

public JList(Vector v)
  //Constructor: Creates a new list to display elements in the
  //vector provided as an input parameter.
  //Example: JList selectionList = new JList(v);
  //         selectionList is a new list that lists the elements
  //         contained in Vector v.

public JList(Object[] o)
  //Constructor:  Creates a new list for selection that displays
  //elements in the object array provided as an input parameter.
  //Example: JList selectionList = new JList(o);
  //      creates the new list called selectionList and displays
  //      the selections. For an object
  //      list, would display o.toString() values.
```

13

Table 13-13 Some Constructors and Methods of the `class JList` (continued)

```
public void setSelectionMode(ListSelectionModel listselectionmodel)
   //Method to set the model for managing list selections. Allows
   //only one item to be selected or a range of contiguous or
   //noncontiguous items to be selected.
   //Example: pictureList.setSelectionMode
   //                  (ListSelectionModel.SINGLE_SELECTION);
   //      limits pictureList to allow only a single selection
   //      at a time.
```

```
public void setSelectionBackground(Color sbColor)
   //Method to set the color of the background of a selected item
   //Example: myList.setSelectionBackground(myCustomColor);
   //   This statement sets the color that appears in the background
   //   of a selected item in myList to the color represented by the
   //   Color object myCustomColor.
```

```
public void addListSelectionListener(ListSelectionListener lsl)
   //Method to add a listener class to take action when an item
   //in the list is selected.
   //Example: pictureList.addListSelectionListener(handler)
   //   This statement adds a new ListSelectionListener object,
   //   named handler, to the pictureList to process events related to
   //   selection of a list item.
```

```
public int getSelectedIndex()
   //When an item in the list is selected, this method returns the
   //index of that item (0 to # of items - 1). Returns -1 if
   //nothing is selected.
   //Example: myLabel.setIcon
   //                  (pictures[ pictureList.getSelectedIndex() ]);
   //   This statement sets an icon for a label to the item in an
   //   array of image icons specified by the index of the selected
   //   item in the list.
```

Let's write a program that uses a `JList` and `JLabel`s to create the GUI as shown in Figure 13-16.

Figure 13-16   GUI using `JList` and `JLabel`

The GUI in Figure 13-16 contains four GUI components—a `JList` and three `JLabels`. The `JList` object contains the list of items, such as `Pie Diagram`, `Line Graph`, and `Bar Graph`. The first `JLabel` contains the string `"Select an Image"`. Below this label is the `JList` object, and below the `JList` object is a `JLabel` that displays an image. For example, if the user selects Normal Curve, this `JLabel` object shows the image of a normal curve. Below the label showing an image is a `JLabel` that displays the name of the image. For example, in Figure 13-16, this label displays the text `Normal Curve`.

The top and the bottom labels display a line of text, so they are manipulated using strings as labels. The label showing an image is manipulated using images. For this program we include five JPEG images. The following statement creates the `JLabel` object `promptJL` with `Select an Image` as its label and sets the justification of the label to center:

```
private JLabel promptJL = new JLabel("Select an Image",
                             SwingConstants.CENTER);
```

13

The following statements declare `displayPicJL` and `infoJL` to be reference variables of the `JLabel` type:

```
private JLabel displayPicJL;
private JLabel infoJL;
```

We use `displayPicJL` to display the image and `infoJL` to display the name of the image as shown in Figure 13-16. We explain in the following paragraphs how to change the text and image of these labels during program execution.

We now discuss how to create the `JList` with five items. For the most part, creating a `JList` is similar to creating a `JComboBox`. To create a `JList`, we first declare a reference variable as follows:

```
private JList pictureJList;
```

Next we create an array of strings consisting of the names of the images. The following statement creates the array `pictureNames` of five components:

```
private String[] pictureNames = {"Pie Diagram",
                                 "Line Graph",
                                 "Bar Graph",
                                 "Table",
                                 "Normal Curve"};
```

Next we use the array `pictureNames` to create the `JList` object `pictureJList` as follows:

```
pictureJList = new JList(pictureNames);
```

As in the case of combo boxes, you can use the method `setVisibleRowCount` to set the number of visible rows of a `JList`. For example, the following statement sets the number of visible rows of `pictureJList` to 3:

```
pictureJList.setVisibleRowCount(3);
```

In the program we are writing we want the user to select only one item at a time from `pictureJList`, so we set `pictureJList` to single selection mode by using the method `setSelectionMode` together with the constant `ListSelectionModel.SINGLE_SELECTION` as follows:

```
pictureJList.setSelectionMode(ListSelectionModel.SINGLE_SELECTION);
```

When the user selects an image from `pictureJList`, the program displays the corresponding image using the `JLabel` object `displayPicJL`. We use the **class ImageIcon** and create an array of images as follows:

```
private ImageIcon[] pictures = {new ImageIcon("pieDiagram.jpg"),
                                new ImageIcon("lineGraph.jpg"),
                                new ImageIcon("barGraph.jpg"),
                                new ImageIcon("table.jpg"),
                                new ImageIcon("normalCurve.jpg")};
```

When the user clicks to select an item from the JList object pictureJList, ListSelectionEvent is generated. To process ListSelectionEvent we use the interface ListSelectionListener. This interface has the method valueChanged, which is executed when a ListSelectionEvent occurs. The heading of this method is:

```
public void valueChanged(ListSelectionEvent e)
```

We can put the code to display the required image and its name in this method. When the user clicks on an item in the JList, we can determine the index of the selected item by using the method getSelectedIndex. We then use this index to select the corresponding image from the array pictures and the name of the image from the array pictureNames. We can now use the method repaint to repaint the pane. The definition of the method valueChanged is:

```
public void valueChanged(ListSelectionEvent e)
{
    displayPicJL.setIcon(
             pictures[pictureJList.getSelectedIndex()]);
    infoJL.setText(
             pictureNames[pictureJList.getSelectedIndex()]);
    repaint();
}
```

Of course, we must register the list selection listener to the JList. This is accomplished by the following statement:

```
pictureJList.addListSelectionListener(this);
```

There are five items in the JList. When the program executes, it displays only three of these items in the list at a time. Therefore, we want to attach a vertical scroll bar to the JList object pictureJList, so that the user can scroll to select an item not currently shown in the list. To do so, we use the class JScrollPane as follows. First we create the JScrollPane object selectionJS and initialize this object using the object pictureJList. We then add the object to the pane selectionJS. The following statements illustrate this concept:

```
selectionJS = new JScrollPane(pictureJList);
pane.add(selectionJS);
```

We will set the pane layout to null and specify the size and the location of the GUI components. These statements are provided in the complete program listing given next.

```
//Program to demonstrate JLIST

import java.awt.*;
import javax.swing.*;
import javax.swing.event.*;

public class JListPictureViewer extends JFrame implements
                                ListSelectionListener
```

13

```
{
    private String[] pictureNames = {"Pie Diagram",
                                     "Line Graph",
                                     "Bar Graph",
                                     "Table",
                                     "Normal Curve"};

    private ImageIcon[] pictures =
                {new ImageIcon("pieDiagram.jpg"),
                 new ImageIcon("lineGraph.jpg"),
                 new ImageIcon("barGraph.jpg"),
                 new ImageIcon("table.jpg"),
                 new ImageIcon("normalCurve.jpg")};

    private BorderLayout layoutBL;
    private JList pictureJList;
    private JScrollPane selectionJS;
    private JLabel promptJL;
    private JLabel displayPicJL;
    private JLabel infoJL;

    public JListPictureViewer()
    {
        super("Photo Viewer");

        Container pane = getContentPane();
        pane.setLayout(null);

        promptJL = new JLabel("Select an Image",
                              SwingConstants.CENTER);
        promptJL.setSize(350,20);
        promptJL.setLocation(10,0);
        pane.add(promptJL);

        pictureJList = new JList(pictureNames);
        pictureJList.setVisibleRowCount(3);
        pictureJList.setSelectionMode
                (ListSelectionModel.SINGLE_SELECTION);
        pictureJList.addListSelectionListener(this);

        selectionJS = new JScrollPane(pictureJList);
        selectionJS.setSize(350,60);
        selectionJS.setLocation(10,20);
        pane.add(selectionJS);

        displayPicJL = new JLabel(pictures[4]);
        displayPicJL.setSize(350,350);
        displayPicJL.setLocation(10,50);
```

```
        pane.add(displayPicJL);

        infoJL = new JLabel(pictureNames[4],
                            SwingConstants.CENTER);
        infoJL.setSize(350, 20);
        infoJL.setLocation(10, 380);
        pane.add(infoJL);

        setSize(380, 440);
        setVisible(true);
        setDefaultCloseOperation(EXIT_ON_CLOSE);
    }

    public static void main(String args[])
    {
        JListPictureViewer picViewer = new JListPictureViewer();
    }

    public void valueChanged(ListSelectionEvent e)
    {
        displayPicJL.setIcon(
            pictures[pictureJList.getSelectedIndex() ]);
        infoJL.setText(
            pictureNames[pictureJList.getSelectedIndex() ]);
        repaint();
    }
}
```

Sample Run: Figure 13-17 shows a sample run of the `JListPictureViewer` program.

13

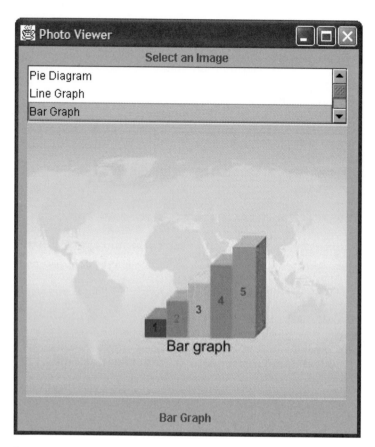

Figure 13-17 Sample run of the `JListPictureViewer` program

LAYOUT MANAGERS

In earlier chapters, you have seen two layout managers, `GridLayout` and `null`. For `GridLayout`, you specify the number of rows and columns you want, and you can place your components from left to right, row by row, from top to bottom. If you choose `null` layout, you have to specify the size and the location of each component. Java provides many layout managers. In this section we briefly introduce two more layout managers.

FlowLayout

`FlowLayout` is the default layout manager for a Java application. Creating a `FlowLayout` manager is similar to creating a `GridLayout` manager. For example, suppose that you have the following declaration:

```
Container pane = getContentPane();
```

The statement

```
pane.setLayout(new FlowLayout());
```

or

```
FlowLayout flowLayoutMgr = new FlowLayout();
pane.setLayout(flowLayoutMgr);
```

sets the layout of the container pane to `FlowLayout`. `FlowLayout` places the components from left to right until no more items can be placed. The next item will be placed in the second line. Thus, a `FlowLayout` manager works similarly to a `GridLayout` manager. The main difference between these two layouts is that in a `GridLayout`, all rows (columns) have the same number of components and all components have the same size. However, in a `FlowLayout`, there is no such guarantee. Moreover, in a `FlowLayout`, you can align each line left, center, or right using a statement such as

```
flowLayoutMgr.setAlignment(FlowLayout.RIGHT);
```

Note that the default alignment is `LEFT`.

The following Java application program illustrates the use of the `FlowLayout` manager.

```
//Program to illustrate FlowLayout

import javax.swing.*;
import java.awt.*;

public class FlowLayoutExample extends JFrame
{
    private static int WIDTH = 350;
    private static int HEIGHT = 350;

        //Variables to create GUI components
    private JLabel labelJL;
    private JTextField textFieldTF;
    private JButton buttonJB;
    private JCheckBox checkboxCB;
    private JRadioButton radioButtonRB;
    private JTextArea textAreaTA;

    private FlowLayout flowLayoutMgr;

    public FlowLayoutExample()
    {
        setTitle("FlowLayout Manager");              //Line 1
        Container pane = getContentPane();           //Line 2
        setSize(WIDTH,HEIGHT);                       //Line 3

        flowLayoutMgr = new FlowLayout();            //Line 4
        pane.setLayout(flowLayoutMgr);               //Line 5
```

13

```
        flowLayoutMgr.setAlignment(FlowLayout.CENTER);   //Line 6

        labelJL = new JLabel("First Component");         //Line 7
        textFieldTF = new JTextField(15);                //Line 8
        textFieldTF.setText("Second Component");         //Line 9
        buttonJB = new JButton("Third Component");       //Line 10

        checkboxCB = new JCheckBox("Fourth Component");  //Line 11

        radioButtonRB =
              new JRadioButton("Fifth Component");       //Line 12

        textAreaTA = new JTextArea(10,20);               //Line 13

        textAreaTA.setText("Sixth Component.\n");        //Line 14

        textAreaTA.append(
            "Use the mouse to resize the window.");      //Line 15

            //place the GUI components into the pane
        pane.add(labelJL);                               //Line 16
        pane.add(textFieldTF);                           //Line 17
        pane.add(buttonJB);                              //Line 18
        pane.add(checkboxCB);                            //Line 19
        pane.add(radioButtonRB);                         //Line 20
        pane.add(textAreaTA);                            //Line 21

        setVisible(true);                                //Line 22
        setDefaultCloseOperation(EXIT_ON_CLOSE);         //Line 23
    }

    public static void main(String[] args)               //Line 24
    {
        FlowLayoutExample flow =
                  new FlowLayoutExample();                //Line 25
    }
}
```

Sample Run: Figure 13-18 shows a sample run of the `FlowLayoutExample` program.

Figure 13-18   Sample run of the `FlowLayoutExample` program

The preceding program works as follows. The statement in Line 1 sets the title of the window and the statement in Line 2 accesses the content pane. The statement in Line 3 sets the size of the window. The statement in Line 4 creates the `FlowLayout` object `flowLayoutMgr`, and the statement in Line 5 uses this object to set the layout of the pane to `FlowLayout`. The statement in Line 6 sets the GUI alignment to centered. The statement in Line 7 instantiates the `JLabel` object `labelJL`. The statement in Line 8 instantiates the `text` object `textFieldTF` and the statement in Line 9 sets the text of the object `textFieldTF`. The statement in Line 10 instantiates the `JButton` object `buttonJB`, and the statement in Line 11 instantiates the `JCheckBox` object `checkboxCB`. The statement in Line 12 instantiates the `JRadioButton` object `radioButtonRB`. The statement in Line 13 instantiates the `JTextArea` object `textAreaTA` with 10 rows and 20 columns. The statement in Line 14 places the text `Sixth Component` into the text area, and the statement in Line 15 appends the text

`Use the mouse to resize the window.`

The statements in Lines 16 through 21 place the GUI components in the pane. The statement in Line 22 sets the visibility of the window to `true`, and the statement in Line 23 sets the window closing option to close when the program terminates. When the program executes, the statement in Line 25 creates the window with the GUI components shown in the sample run.

BorderLayout

The `BorderLayout` manager allows you to place items in specific regions. This layout manager divides the container into five regions: `NORTH`, `SOUTH`, `EAST`, `WEST`, and `CENTER`. Components placed in the `NORTH` and `SOUTH` regions extend horizontally, completely spanning one edge to the other. However, `EAST` and `WEST` components extend vertically between the components in the `NORTH` and `SOUTH` regions. The component placed at the `CENTER` expands to occupy any unused regions.

In the following example, we create five components and place them in the content pane using the `BorderLayout` manager.

```
//Program to illustrate BorderLayout

import javax.swing.*;
import java.awt.*;

public class BorderLayoutExample extends JFrame
{
    private static int WIDTH = 350;
    private static int HEIGHT = 300;

        //GUI components
    private JLabel labelJL;
    private JTextField textFieldTF;
    private JButton buttonJB;
    private JCheckBox checkboxCB;
    private JRadioButton radioButtonRB;
    private JTextArea textAreaTA;

    private BorderLayout borderLayoutMgr;

    public BorderLayoutExample()
    {
        setTitle("BorderLayout Manager");
        Container pane = getContentPane();
        setSize(WIDTH, HEIGHT);

        borderLayoutMgr = new BorderLayout(10,10);
        pane.setLayout(borderLayoutMgr);
        labelJL = new JLabel("North Component");
        textAreaTA = new JTextArea(10,20);
        textAreaTA.setText("South Component.\n");
```

```
        textAreaTA.append(
           "Use the mouse to change the size of the window.");
        buttonJB = new JButton("West Component");
        checkboxCB = new JCheckBox("East Component");
        radioButtonRB = new JRadioButton("Center Component");

        pane.add(labelJL,BorderLayout.NORTH);
        pane.add(textAreaTA,BorderLayout.SOUTH);
        pane.add(buttonJB,BorderLayout.EAST);
        pane.add(checkboxCB,BorderLayout.WEST);
        pane.add(radioButtonRB, BorderLayout.CENTER);

        setVisible(true);
        setDefaultCloseOperation(EXIT_ON_CLOSE);
    }

    public static void main(String[] args)
    {
        BorderLayoutExample flow = new BorderLayoutExample();
    }
}
```

Sample Run: A sample run of the BorderLayoutExample program is shown in Figure 13-19.

Figure 13-19   Sample run of the BorderLayoutExample program

MENUS

Menus allow you to provide various functions without cluttering the GUI with too many components. Menus can be attached to objects such as `JFrame` and `JApplet`.

The `classes JFrame` and `JApplet` both have a method `setJMenuBar` that allows you to set a menu bar. To set a menu bar, say `menuMB`, you need the following statements:

```
private JMenuBar menuMB = new JMenuBar();   //creates a menu bar

setJMenuBar(menuMB);                        //sets the menu bar
```

Once you have created a menu bar, you can add menus, and in each menu you can add menu items. For instance, to create an `Edit` menu and add it to the menu bar created above, you need the following two statements:

```
JMenu editM = new JMenu("Edit");   //creates a menu "Edit"
menuMB.add(editM);                 //adds the menu to menu bar
                                   //menuMB created above
```

Likewise, if you need to create a `File` menu, you may do so by adding the following lines of code:

```
JMenu fileM = new JMenu("File");

menuMB.add(fileM);
```

Notice that the order in which you add menus to the menu bar determines the order in which they appear. For example, if you want the `File` menu to appear first, you must add it first.

The following program illustrates the use of menus.

```
import java.awt.*;
import java.awt.event.*;
import javax.swing.*;

public class TextEditor extends JFrame implements ActionListener
{
    private JMenuBar menuMB = new JMenuBar(); //creates the menu bar
    private JMenu fileM, editM, optionM;
    private JMenuItem exitI;
    private JMenuItem cutI, copyI, pasteI, selectI;
    private JTextArea pageTA = new JTextArea();
    private String scratchpad = "";

    public TextEditor()
    {
        setTitle("Simple Text Editor");
        Container pane = getContentPane();
        pane.setLayout(new BorderLayout());
        pane.add(pageTA,BorderLayout.CENTER);
        pane.add(new JScrollPane(pageTA));
```

```java
        pageTA.setLineWrap(true);
        setJMenuBar(menuMB);
        setFileMenu();
        setEditMenu();
        setSize(300,200);
        setVisible(true);
        setDefaultCloseOperation(EXIT_ON_CLOSE);
    }

    private void setFileMenu()
    {
        fileM = new JMenu("File");
        menuMB.add(fileM);
        exitI = new JMenuItem("Exit");
        fileM.add(exitI);
        exitI.addActionListener(this);
    }

    private void setEditMenu()
    {
        editM = new JMenu("Edit");
        menuMB.add(editM);
        cutI = new JMenuItem("Cut");
        editM.add(cutI);
        cutI.addActionListener(this);
        copyI = new JMenuItem("Copy");
        editM.add(copyI);
        copyI.addActionListener(this);
        pasteI = new JMenuItem("Paste");
        editM.add(pasteI);
        pasteI.addActionListener(this);
        selectI = new JMenuItem("Select All");
        editM.add(selectI);
        selectI.addActionListener(this);
    }

    public void actionPerformed(ActionEvent e)
    {
        JMenuItem mItem = (JMenuItem) e.getSource();
        if(mItem == exitI)
        {
            System.exit(0);
        }
        else if(mItem == cutI)
        {
                scratchpad = pageTA.getSelectedText();
                pageTA.replaceRange("",
                        pageTA.getSelectionStart(),
                        pageTA.getSelectionEnd());
        }
```

13

```
            else if(mItem == copyI)
            {
                    scratchpad = pageTA.getSelectedText();
            }
            else if(mItem == pasteI)
            {
                    pageTA.insert(scratchpad, pageTA.getCaretPosition());
            }
            else if(mItem == selectI)
            {
                    pageTA.selectAll();
            }
    }

    public static void main(String args[])
    {
        TextEditor texted = new TextEditor();
    }
}
```

Sample Run: A sample run of the program with menus is shown in Figure 13-20.

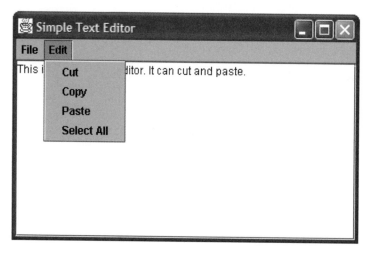

Figure 13-20   Sample run of the TextEditor program

KEY AND MOUSE EVENTS

In this and the preceding chapters, you learned how to handle action events when you click a button. Moreover, Chapter 12 noted that when you press the **Enter** key in a text field, an action event is generated. Also recall that when you press a mouse button to click a button, in addition to generating an action event, a mouse event is generated. Likewise, when you press the `Enter` key in a text field, in addition to the action event, a key event is generated. Therefore, a GUI program can simultaneously generate more than one event. In this section, we give various programs to show how to handle key and mouse events.

Recall from Chapter 12 that key events are handled by the `interface KeyListener`, and mouse events are handled by the `interfaces MouseListener` and `MouseMotionListener`. The key and mouse events and the corresponding event handler were shown in Table 12-9, which is reproduced in Table 13-14.

Table 13-14 Events Generated by the Keyboard and Mouse

	Event Generated	Listener Interface	Listener Method
key	KeyEvent	KeyListener	keyPressed
key	KeyEvent	KeyListener	keyReleased
key	KeyEvent	KeyListener	keyTyped
mouse	MouseEvent	MouseListener	mouseClicked
mouse	MouseEvent	MouseListener	mouseEntered
mouse	MouseEvent	MouseListener	mouseExited
mouse	MouseEvent	MouseListener	mousePressed
mouse	MouseEvent	MouseListener	mouseReleased
mouse	MouseEvent	MouseMotionListener	mouseDragged
mouse	MouseEvent	MouseMotionListener	mouseMoved

Key Events

This section describes how to handle key events. As shown in Table 13-14, there are three types of key events. The `interface KeyListener` contains the methods—`keyPressed`, `keyReleased`, and `keyTyped`—that correspond to these events. The action that needs to be taken when a key event occurs is specified by these methods. When you press a meta key (such as Control, Shift, or Alt), the method `keyPressed` is executed; when you type a regular alphanumeric key, the method `keyTyped` is executed. When you release any key, the method `keyReleased` is executed. The program in Example 13-8 shows how to handle key events.

Example 13-8

This program displays the character which corresponds to the key typed by the user. For example, if the user presses the key **A**, the program displays **A**. We use a `JTextField` object to display the character.

When you type an alphanumeric key, a key event is generated. The key event is handled by the method `keyTyped`. The necessary code to display the key is placed in the body of the method **keyTyped**. Before displaying the key typed by the user, the previous character is removed from the **JTextField** object. In other words, the program displays only one character at a time, corresponding to the key typed. In this program, the font of the character is set to **Courier** and the color of the character is randomly selected.

Because the interface **keyListener** contains three methods and we want to implement only one of these methods, we use the anonymous class mechanism to register a listener object. The complete program listing follows. (Notice that the program uses a message dialog box to inform the user what to do.)

```
//Key Event

import java.awt.*;
import java.awt.event.*;
import javax.swing.*;

public class OneChar extends JApplet
{
    JTextField oneLetter = new JTextField(1);

    public void init()
    {
        Container c = getContentPane();

            //register the listener object
        oneLetter.addKeyListener(new KeyAdapter()
        {
            public void keyTyped(KeyEvent e)
            {
                float red, green, blue;
                Color fg, bg;

                oneLetter.setText(" ");
                red = (float) Math.random();
                green = (float) Math.random();
                blue = (float) Math.random();
                fg = new Color(red, green, blue);
                bg = Color.white;
                oneLetter.setForeground(fg);
                oneLetter.setBackground(bg);
                oneLetter.setCaretColor(bg);
                oneLetter.setFont(new Font("Courier", Font.BOLD, 200));
            }
        });

        c.setLayout(new GridLayout(1,1));
        c.setBackground(Color.white);
        c.add(oneLetter);
        JOptionPane.showMessageDialog
```

```
                    (null, "Click on the applet; then type a key ",
                    "Information", JOptionPane.PLAIN_MESSAGE );
        }
}
```

The HTML file for this program contains the following code:

```
<!DOCTYPE HTML PUBLIC "-//W3C//DTD HTML 4.01 Transitional//EN">

<HTML>
  <HEAD>
    <TITLE>ONECHAR APPLET</TITLE>
  </HEAD>
  <BODY>
    <APPLET code = "OneChar.class" width = "350" height = "300">
    </APPLET>
  </BODY>
</HTML>
```

Sample Run: Figure 13-21 shows a sample run of the `OneChar` applet. (Notice that Figure 13-21 does not show the message dialog box. However, when you execute this program, it first shows the message dialog box.)

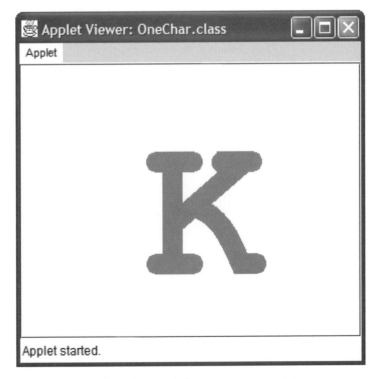

Figure 13-21   Sample run of the `OneChar` applet

Mouse Events

This section describes how to handle mouse events. A mouse can generate seven different types of events, as shown earlier in Table 13-14. As you see in Table 13-14, some mouse events are handled by the **interface MouseListener** and others are handled by the **interface MouseMotionListener**. Table 13-14 also shows which listener method is executed when a particular mouse event occurs. Example 13-9 illustrates how to handle mouse events.

Example 13-9

This example shows how to handle the following mouse events: mouse clicked, mouse entered, mouse exited, mouse pressed, and mouse released. To handle these events, we use the methods of the **interface MouseListener**. The **MouseExample** program contains six labels corresponding to the five mouse events and one label to display the mouse location. When you run this program and use the mouse, the foreground color of the label corresponding to the generated mouse event changes, and the mouse location where the event occurred is displayed.

```
//Program to illustrate mouse events

import javax.swing.*;
import java.awt.*;
import java.awt.event.*;

public class MouseExample extends JFrame
                          implements MouseListener
{
    private static int WIDTH = 350;
    private static int HEIGHT = 250;

        //GUI components
    private JLabel[] labelJL;

    public MouseExample()
    {
        setTitle("Mouse Events");
        Container pane  = getContentPane();
        setSize(WIDTH,HEIGHT);

        GridLayout gridMgr = new GridLayout(6,1,10,10);
        pane.setLayout(gridMgr);

        labelJL = new JLabel[6];

        labelJL[0] = new JLabel("Mouse Clicked",
                            SwingConstants.CENTER);
        labelJL[1] = new JLabel("Mouse Entered",
                            SwingConstants.CENTER);
```

```
         labelJL[2] = new JLabel("Mouse Exited",
                              SwingConstants.CENTER);
         labelJL[3] = new JLabel("Mouse Pressed",
                              SwingConstants.CENTER);
         labelJL[4] = new JLabel("Mouse Released",
                              SwingConstants.CENTER);
         labelJL[5] = new JLabel("",SwingConstants.CENTER);

         for(int i = 0; i < labelJL.length; i++)
         {
             labelJL[i].setForeground(Color.gray);
             pane.add(labelJL[i]);
         }

         pane.addMouseListener(this);

         setVisible(true);
         setDefaultCloseOperation(EXIT_ON_CLOSE);
    }

    public void mouseClicked(MouseEvent event)
    {
        for(int i = 0; i < labelJL.length; i++)
        {
            if(i == 0)
                labelJL[i].setForeground(Color.yellow);
            else
                labelJL[i].setForeground(Color.gray);
        }

        labelJL[5].setText("["+ event.getX() + ","
                        + event.getY()+"]");

    }

    public void mouseEntered(MouseEvent event)
    {
        for(int i = 0; i < labelJL.length; i++)
        {
            if(i == 1)
                labelJL[i].setForeground(Color.green);
            else
                labelJL[i].setForeground(Color.gray);
        }

        labelJL[5].setText("["+ event.getX() + ","
                        + event.getY()+"]");
    }
```

13

```java
    public void mouseExited(MouseEvent event)
    {
       for(int i = 0; i < labelJL.length; i++)
       {
          if(i == 2)
             labelJL[i].setForeground(Color.red);
          else
             labelJL[i].setForeground(Color.gray);
       }

       labelJL[5].setText("["+ event.getX() + ","
                             + event.getY()+"]");
    }

    public void mousePressed(MouseEvent event)
    {
       for(int i = 0; i < labelJL.length; i++)
       {
          if(i == 3)
             labelJL[i].setForeground(Color.blue);
          else
             labelJL[i].setForeground(Color.gray);
       }

       labelJL[5].setText("["+ event.getX() + ","
                             + event.getY()+"]");
    }

    public void mouseReleased(MouseEvent event)
    {
       for(int i = 0; i < labelJL.length; i++)
       {
          if(i == 4)
             labelJL[i].setForeground(Color.pink);
          else
             labelJL[i].setForeground(Color.gray);
       }

       labelJL[5].setText("["+ event.getX() + ","
                             + event.getY()+"]");
    }

    public static void main(String[] args)
    {
       MouseExample flow = new MouseExample();
    }
}
```

Sample Run: Figure 13-22 shows a sample run of the MouseExample program.

Figure 13-22 Sample run of the `MouseExample` program

Example 13-10

The `FreeDrawApplet` in this example shows how to handle the mouse event, mouse dragged. You can handle the event mouse moved in a similar way. These events are handled by the `interface MouseMotionListener`, which contains the methods `mouseDragged` and `mouseMoved`, which, in turn, are used to handle mouse dragged and mouse moved events, respectively.

The program starts with some colored dots. If you drag a dot with the mouse, the dot turns into a line. In this way, you can "freehand draw" different pictures. What is really happening is that we created small circle objects. The program contains the method `selected` to check whether or not the mouse is on the circle. If you drag the circle, the method `mouseDragged` is invoked and it paints a new circle. The sequence of circles gives the impression of drawing a line. The complete program listing follows.

```java
//MouseMotionListener applet

import javax.swing.*;
import java.awt.event.*;
import java.applet.*;
import java.awt.*;

public class FreeDrawApplet extends JApplet implements
                                    MouseMotionListener
```

```
{
        //instance variables
    ColorCircle[] myGraph;

    final int NUM_CIRCLES = 7;
    final int WIDTH = 400;
    final int HEIGHT = 400;

    public class ColorCircle
    {
        private int x;
        private int y;

        public void setX(int iNewX)
        {
            x = iNewX;
        }

        public void setY(int iNewY)
        {
            y = iNewY;
        }

        public void paint (Graphics g)
        {
            g.fillOval(x - 10,y - 10,20,20);
        }

        public boolean selected(int iXcoord, int iYcoord)
        {
            if((iXcoord >=x - 10) && (iXcoord <= x + 10)
                && (iYcoord >= y - 10) && (iYcoord <= y + 10))
                return true;
            else
                return false;
        }
    }

    public void init()
    {
        addMouseMotionListener(this);
        myGraph = new ColorCircle[NUM_CIRCLES];

        for(int i = 0; i < NUM_CIRCLES; i++)
        {
            ColorCircle myVertex = new ColorCircle();
            myVertex.setX((int) (Math.random() * (WIDTH - 50) ));
            myVertex.setY((int) (Math.random() * (HEIGHT - 100)));
            myGraph[i] = myVertex;
        }
```

```
        JOptionPane.showMessageDialog(null,
            "Try to drag any one of the colored circles ",
            "Information", JOptionPane.PLAIN_MESSAGE );

    }

    public void paint(Graphics g)
    {
        Color[] myColor = {Color.black, Color.red, Color.blue,
                            Color.green, Color.cyan,
                            Color.orange, Color.yellow};

        if(NUM_CIRCLES > 0)
            for(int i = 0; i < NUM_CIRCLES; i++)
            {
                g.setColor(myColor[i]);
                myGraph[i].paint(g);
            }
    }

    public void mouseDragged(MouseEvent event)
    {
        int iX = event.getX();
        int iY = event.getY();

        for(int i = 0; i < NUM_CIRCLES; i++)
            if(myGraph[i].selected(iX, iY))
            {
                myGraph[i].setX(iX);
                myGraph[i].setY(iY);
                break;
            }

        repaint();
    }

    public void mouseMoved(MouseEvent p1)
    {
    }
}
```

The HTML file for this program contains the following code:

```
<!DOCTYPE HTML PUBLIC "-//W3C//DTD HTML 4.01 Transitional//EN">

<HTML>
  <HEAD>
    <TITLE>Drawing Board</TITLE>
  </HEAD>
  <BODY>
```

13

```
        <APPLET code = "FreeDrawApplet.class" width = "400" height = "400">
        </APPLET>
    </BODY>
</HTML>
```

Sample Run: Figure 13-23 shows a sample run of the `FreeDrawApplet`.

Figure 13-23   Sample run of the `FreeDrawApplet`

In the program `FreeDrawApplet`, we use small circles to draw lines. Because there is no GUI component we can use, we created the `class ColorCircle`. This class has two `private` members `x` and `y` of the type `int`. The point (`x`, `y`) specifies the center of the circle, and the radius of the circle is fixed at 10 pixels. In addition to the methods to set the values of `x` and `y`, there are only two other methods, `paint` and `isSelected`, in the `class ColorCircle`. The `paint` method draws a filled circle of radius 10 at the point (`x`, `y`). The method `isSelected` returns `true` if and only if (`iXcoord`, `iYcoord`) lies inside a 20 by 20 square with the point (`x`, `y`) as the center. We use this method to check whether the mouse is at, say, (`iXcoord`, `iYcoord`) on the circle with center (`x`, `y`). Note that because `ColorCircle` is not a GUI component, it can generate any event. Therefore, any time a `mouseDragged` event is generated, we must check whether the mouse is on any of the circles. We do so using the following `for` loop:

```
for(int i = 0; i < NUM_CIRCLES; i++)
    if(myGraph[i].selected(iX, iY))
    {
        myGraph[i].setX(iX);
        myGraph[i].setY(iY);
        break;
    }
```

Note that if a `mouseDragged` event occurs on a `ColorCircle` object, the preceding `for` loop sets the current mouse position as the new center of the `ColorCircle` object. This, in effect, moves the `ColorCircle` object. By continually moving a `ColorCircle` object, we create a line.

PROGRAMMING EXAMPLE: JAVA KIOSK

In this programming example, we design a program that simulates a fast food kiosk. The program displays a menu similar to one you might find in a fast food restaurant. The user makes a selection and then presses a `JButton` to mark the end of the selection process. The program then calculates and displays the bill. The sample output is shown in Figure 13-24.

Figure 13-24   Sample output of the Java Kiosk program

Input Input to the program is a list of selected items from the menu shown on the left in Figure 13-24.

Output Output of the program is the bill shown on the right in Figure 13-24.

Problem Analysis and GUI and Algorithm Design

As shown in Figure 13-24, there are five GUI components: a frame, a label, a list, a text area, and a button. All components other than the frame are placed in the content pane of the window. The user selects various list items and then presses the `Selection Completed` button. Recall that when you click on a button it generates an action event, which is processed by using the `interface ActionListener`. Therefore, we will create and register an action listener object with the button.

When the event is generated, the event handler computes the subtotal, tax, and total. The program then displays the result in the text area. To create the label, list, text area, and button, you use reference variables of the types `JLabel`, `JList`, `JTextArea`, and `JButton`, respectively. You also need a reference variable to access the content pane of the window. As in the GUI programs in previous chapters, we create the class containing the application program by extending the definition of the `class JFrame`; this also allows you to create the necessary window to create the GUI. Thus, we use the following reference variables to create GUI components and to access the content pane of the window:

```
private JList yourChoices;
private JTextArea bill;

private Container pane;
JLabel yourChoicesJLabel;
JButton button;
```

The next step is to instantiate four GUI components and initialize the pane using the method `getContentPane`. Recall that, to create a list, you first create an array of strings, and then use the array as the argument in the constructor of the `JList`. Instantiate other GUI components the same way you have done previously. This program uses the `BorderLayout` to neatly place all four GUI components. We place the label in the NORTH region, the list in the WEST region, the text area in the EAST region, and the button in the SOUTH region.

The following statement creates the array of strings to create the menu:

```
static String[] yourChoicesItems =
                    {"Blueberry Muffins   0.85",
                     "Strawberry Bagels   0.80",
                     "Lite Yogurt         0.75",
                     "Vanilla Ice Cream   2.75",
                     "Hash Browns         2.50",
                     "Toast               2.00",
                     "French Fries        1.50",
                     "Onion Soup          3.00",
```

```
                              "Coffee              0.90",
                              "Iced Tea            1.00",
                              "Hot Chocolate       1.75"};
```

The following statements create the necessary GUI components and place them in the container:

```
private JList yourChoices;
private JTextArea bill;

private Container pane;

pane = getContentPane();
pane.setBackground(new Color(0, 200, 200));
pane.setLayout(new BorderLayout(5, 5));

        //Create a label and place it in the NORTH region
        //and set the font of this label
JLabel yourChoicesJLabel = new JLabel("A LA CARTE MENU");
pane.add(yourChoicesJLabel,BorderLayout.NORTH);
yourChoicesJLabel.setFont(new Font("Dialog",Font.BOLD,20));

        //Create a list and place it in the WEST region
        //and set the font of this list
yourChoices = new JList(yourChoicesItems);
pane.add(new JScrollPane (yourChoices),BorderLayout.WEST);
yourChoices.setFont(new Font("Courier",Font.BOLD,14));

        //Create a text area and place it in the EAST region
        //and set the font of this text area
bill = new JTextArea();
pane.add(bill,BorderLayout.EAST);
bill.setFont(new Font("Courier",Font.PLAIN,10));

        //Create a button and place it in the SOUTH region and
        //add an action listener.
JButton button = new JButton("Selection Completed");
pane.add(button,BorderLayout.SOUTH);
button.addActionListener(this);
```

You need another array to keep track of the prices of various items.

```
static double[] yourChoicesPrices = {0.85, 0.80, 0.75, 2.75,
                                     2.50, 2.00, 1.50, 3.00,
                                     0.90, 1.00, 1.75};
```

The following statements set the size of the window and set its visibility to true:

```
setSize(500, 360);
setVisible(true);
```

Recall that when an action event is generated by a button, the method `actionPerformed` is invoked. When the user clicks on the button, the program must compute the subtotal, tax, and total, and display the result in a text area. The instructions to perform those tasks are placed in the method `actionPerformed`, which is described next.

Method `actionPerformed`   As noted previously, the method `actionPerformed` is executed when the user clicks the button. The method `actionPerformed` calculates and displays the bill. We write the method `displayBill` that computes the bill and displays it using a text area. The method `actionPerformed` invokes the method `displayBill` to display the bill. The definition of the method `actionPerformed` is:

```
public void actionPerformed(ActionEvent event)
{
    if(event.getActionCommand().equals("Selection Completed"))
    {
        displayBill();
    }
}
```

Method `displayBill`   The method `displayBill` first needs to identify the items selected by the user. The method `getSelectedIndices` of the `JList` will return an array of indices. Because you need an integer array to hold these indices, you might need the following Java statements:

```
int[] listArray = yourChoices.getSelectedIndices();
double localTax = 0.065;
double tax;
double subtotal = 0;
double total;
```

Note that `listArray[0], listArray[1],...,` `listArray[listArray.length - 1]` contains the indices of the items selected from the menu list. Therefore, the following `for` loop computes the total cost of the items selected from the menu:

```
for(int index = 0; index < listArray.length; index++)
    subTotal = subTotal + yourChoicesPrices[listArray[index]];
```

Next we compute the tax and add it to `subTotal` to get the billing amount.

```
tax = localTax * subTotal;
total = subTotal + tax;
```

To display the bill, we append the necessary statements to the **JTextArea** and invoke the **repaint** method to redraw the GUI components. To place another order, we unselect the selected items. The definition of the method **displayBill** is:

```java
    // method to display order and total cost
private void displayBill()
{
    int[] listArray = yourChoices.getSelectedIndices();
    double localTax = 0.065;
    double tax;
    double subtotal = 0;
    double total;

        //set the text area to non-edit mode
        //and start with an empty string
    bill.setEditable(false);
    bill.setText("");

        //calculate cost of items ordered
    for(int index = 0; index < listArray.length; index++)
        subTotal = subTotal + yourChoicesPrices[listArray[index]];

    tax = localTax * subTotal;
    total = subTotal + tax;

        //display costs
    bill.append("            JAVA KIOSK A LA CARTE\n\n");
    bill.append("--------------- Welcome ----------------\n\n");
    for(int index = 0; index < listArray.length; index++)
    {
        bill.append(yourChoicesItems[listArray[index]] + "\n");
    }

    bill.append("\n");
    bill.append("SUB TOTAL\t\t$"+twoDigits.format(subTotal)+"\n");
    bill.append("TAX      \t\t$"+twoDigits.format(tax)+"\n");
    bill.append("TOTAL    \t\t$"+twoDigits.format(total)+"\n\n");
    bill.append("Thank you - Have a Nice Day\n\n");

        //reset list array
    yourChoices.clearSelection();

    repaint();
}
```

The program listing is as follows.

```
//A la Carte

import java.awt.*;
import java.awt.event.*;
import javax.swing.*;
import javax.swing.event.*;
import java.text.DecimalFormat;

public class AlaCarte extends JFrame implements ActionListener
{
    static DecimalFormat twoDigits = new DecimalFormat("0.00");

    static String[] yourChoicesItems =
                        {"Blueberry Muffins   0.85",
                         "Strawberry Bagels   0.80",
                         "Lite Yogurt         0.75",
                         "Vanilla Ice Cream   2.75",
                         "Hash Browns         2.50",
                         "Toast               2.00",
                         "French Fries        1.50",
                         "Onion Soup          3.00",
                         "Coffee              0.90",
                         "Iced Tea            1.00",
                         "Hot Chocolate       1.75"};

    static double[] yourChoicesPrices = {0.85, 0.80, 0.75, 2.75,
                                         2.50, 2.00, 1.50, 3.00,
                                         0.90, 1.00, 1.75};
    private JList yourChoices;
    private JTextArea  bill;

    private Container pane;

    public AlaCarte()
    {
        super("Welcome to Java Kiosk");

            //Get the content pane and set its background color
            //and layout manager.
        pane = getContentPane();
        pane.setBackground(new Color(0, 200, 200));
        pane.setLayout(new BorderLayout(5, 5));
```

```java
                //Create a label and place it at NORTH. Also
                //set the font of this label.
        JLabel yourChoicesJLabel = new JLabel("A LA CARTE MENU");
        pane.add(yourChoicesJLabel,BorderLayout.NORTH);
        yourChoicesJLabel.setFont(new Font("Dialog",Font.BOLD,20));

                //Create a list and place it at WEST. Also
                //set the font of this list.
        yourChoices = new JList(yourChoicesItems);
        pane.add(new JScrollPane (yourChoices),BorderLayout.WEST);
        yourChoices.setFont(new Font("Courier",Font.BOLD,14));

                //Create a text area and place it at EAST. Also
                //set the font of this text area.
        bill = new JTextArea();
        pane.add(bill,BorderLayout.EAST);
        bill.setFont(new Font("Courier",Font.PLAIN,12));

                //Create a button and place it in the SOUTH region and
                //add an action listener.
        JButton button = new JButton("Selection Completed");
        pane.add(button,BorderLayout.SOUTH);
        button.addActionListener(this);

        setSize(500,360);
        setVisible(true);
        setDefaultCloseOperation(EXIT_ON_CLOSE);
    }

                //Method to display the order and the total cost
    private void displayBill()
    {
        int[] listArray = yourChoices.getSelectedIndices();
        double localTax = 0.065;
        double tax;
        double subTotal = 0;
        double total;

            //Set the text area to non-edit mode and start
            //with an empty string.
        bill.setEditable(false);
        bill.setText("");

                //Calculate cost of the items ordered.
        for(int index = 0; index < listArray.length; index++)
            subTotal = subTotal
                        + yourChoicesPrices[listArray[index]];
```

```
        tax = localTax * subTotal;
        total = subTotal + tax;

            //Display the costs.
        bill.append("            JAVA KIOSK A LA CARTE\n\n");
        bill.append("-------------- Welcome ----------------\n\n");

        for(int index = 0; index < listArray.length; index++)
        {
            bill.append(yourChoicesItems[listArray[index]] + "\n");
        }

        bill.append("\n");
        bill.append("SUB TOTAL\t\t$"
                    + twoDigits.format(subTotal)+"\n");
        bill.append("TAX      \t\t$"
                    + twoDigits.format(tax)+"\n");
        bill.append("TOTAL    \t\t$"
                    + twoDigits.format(total)+"\n\n");
        bill.append("Thank you - Have a Nice Day\n\n");

            //Reset list array.
        yourChoices.clearSelection();

        repaint();
    }

    public void actionPerformed(ActionEvent event)
    {
        if(event.getActionCommand().equals("Selection Completed"))
            displayBill();
    }

    public static void main(String[] args)
    {
        AlaCarte alc = new AlaCarte();
    }
}
```

Sample Run: Figure 13-25 shows a sample run of the program. (To make more than one selection, click the first selection, hold the Ctrl key, and then click the left mouse button on other selections. To make contiguous selections, click the first item, hold the Shift key, and then click the last item you want to select.)

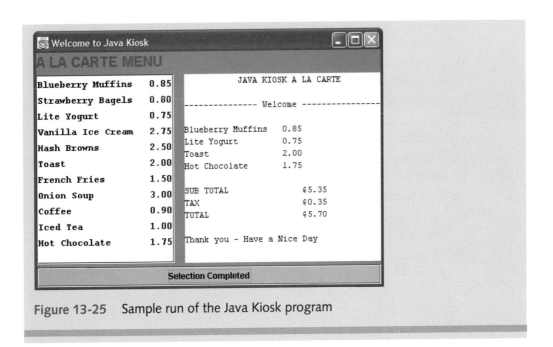

Figure 13-25   Sample run of the Java Kiosk program

QUICK REVIEW

1. The term applet means a little application.

2. An applet is a Java program that is embedded within a Web page and executed by a Web browser.

3. You create an applet by extending the `class JApplet`, which is contained in the `package javax.swing`.

4. Unlike a Java application program, Java applets do not have the `main` method.

5. When a browser runs an applet, the methods `init`, `start`, and `paint` are guaranteed to be invoked in sequence.

6. All statements to be executed only once are kept in the `init` method of an applet.

7. An applet does not have a title.

8. The `classes Font` and `Color` are contained in the `package java.awt`.

9. Java uses the color scheme known as **RGB**, where **R** stands for red, **G** for green, and **B** for blue, respectively.

10. You create instances of the `class Color` by mixing red, green, and blue hues in various proportions.

11. An applet class is derived from the `class JApplet`, whereas a GUI application class is created by extending the `class JFrame`.

12. Applets do not use constructors.

13

13. Java provides the **class JTextArea** either to collect multiple lines of input from the user or to display multiple lines of output.

14. Java provides the **classes JCheckBox** and **JRadioButton** to allow a user to select a value from a set of given values.

15. A check box is also called a toggle button.

16. To force the user to select only one radio button at a time, you create a button group and add radio buttons to the group.

17. A combo box, commonly known as a drop-down list, is used to select an item from a list of possibilities.

18. A **JList** displays a number of items from which the user can select one or more items.

19. The **FlowLayout** manager places GUI components from left to right until no more items can be placed in a line. Then the next item is placed in the following line.

20. In the case of **BorderLayout** manager, the component placed at the center expands to occupy any unused regions.

21. Menus allow you to provide various functions without cluttering the GUI with components.

22. Menus can be attached to objects such as **JFrame** and **JApplet**.

23. Key events are handled by the **interface KeyListener**; mouse events are handled by the **interfaces MouseListener** and **MouseMotionListener**.

EXERCISES

1. Mark the following statements as true or false.

   a. An applet's width and height are specified in the HTML file.

   b. In Java, **JApplet** is a class.

   c. To display an applet, you need not invoke a method such as **setVisible( )**.

   d. You must include an exit button in all Java applets.

   e. When an applet is loaded, the method **start** is invoked before the method **init**.

   f. Check boxes are used to display the output of a program.

   g. A radio button comes with a label.

   h. You use **JList** to create a combo box.

   i. **JTextField** can be used to output multiple lines of text.

2. Name four GUI components that can be used for input only.

3. Name two GUI components that can be used for both input and output.

4. Name a GUI component that can be used for output only.

5. Why do you need check boxes in a GUI program?

6. Fill in the blanks in each of the following:

   a. The _____ method of the **class Graphics** draws a rectangle.

   b. RGB is short for _____, _____, and _____.

   c. The method _____ is invoked when an item is selected from a combo box and a(n) _____ is registered to handle the event.

   d. The _____ method of the **class Graphics** can be used to draw a circle.

   e. Font sizes are specified in units called _____.

   f. Both **JTextField** and **JTextArea** inherit directly from the **class** _____.

   g. The method **Random** returns a value between _____ and _____.

   h. The method _____ gets the string in the **JTextArea**, and the method _____ changes the string displayed in a **JTextArea**.

   i. The **BorderLayout** manager divides the container into five regions: _____, _____, _____, _____, and _____.

   j. The _____ class is used to create a slider for _____.

   k. You cannot use **System.out.println** inside a(n) _____ method.

7. Write the necessary statements to create the following:

   a. A **JList** with the list items **orange, apple, banana, grape,** and **pineapple**

   b. A check box with the label **draft**

   c. A group of three radio buttons with the labels **home, visitor,** and **neutral**

   d. A menu bar

   e. A Courier bold 32-point font

   f. A new color that is not already defined in the **class Color**

8. Correct any syntax errors in the following program.

```
//Grand Welcome Problem Applet

import java.awt.*;
import javax.swing.JApplet;

public class GrandWelcomeProblem extends JApplet
{
    public int()
    {
            JLabel myLabel = new JLabel("");
    }
```

13

```
public void paint( Graphics g)
{
    super.paint(g);
    Container pane = g.getContentPane( );
    pane.setLayout(BORDER_LAYOUT);
    pane.add(BORDER_LAYOUT.CENTER);

    myLabel.setText("A Grand Welcome to Java Programming!");
}
}
```

PROGRAMMING EXERCISES

1. Create an applet to draw a digit using the method **drawLine** of the **class Graphics**.
   For instance, if the input is 4, the applet will display as shown in Figure 13-26.

Figure 13-26   Figure for Programming Exercise 1

2. Modify the applet created in Programming Exercise 1 by adding eight radio buttons so the user can change the color of the digit drawn.

3. Modify the applet created in Programming Exercise 1 by adding a color menu to change the color of the digit drawn.

4. Modify the applet created in Programming Exercise 1 by adding a **JList** of eight items so the user can change the background color of the applet.

5. Create an applet that will draw a set of ovals similar to that shown in Figure 13-27. The user can specify the number of ovals.

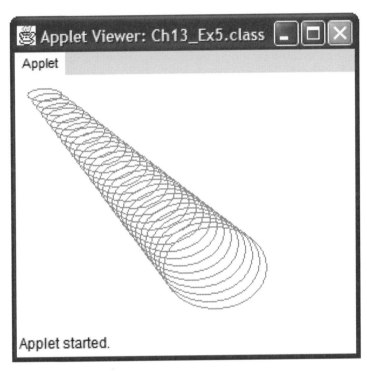

Figure 13-27   Figure for Programming Exercise 5

6. Modify the applet in Programming Exercise 5 by adding three different types of GUI components so the user can select:

   a. Number of figures: 1, 2, 4, 8, 16 or various combinations of these numbers

   b. Type of figures: circle, oval, rectangle, or square

   c. Color: red, blue, green, yellow, pink, black, cyan, or magenta

7. Modify the applet in Programming Exercise 5 by adding the necessary menus so the user can select:

   a. Number of figures: 1, 10, 20, 30, or 40

   b. Type of figures: circle, oval, rectangle, or square

   c. Color: red, blue, green, yellow, pink, black, cyan, or magenta

8. Convert the `WhiteBoard` program (given earlier in this chapter) from an application to an applet.

9. Redo `JListPictureViewer` (given earlier in this chapter) using one of the layout managers. For this exercise, just use a `JList` and one `JLabel` to display the image.

10. Create an applet to draw lines. The user can choose the start and end points of the line to be drawn by clicking the mouse.

11. Create an application to illustrate mouse events, mouse motion events, and keyboard events. The user interface is shown in Figure 13-28. The key code corresponding to a key event or position of the mouse is displayed just above the text field.

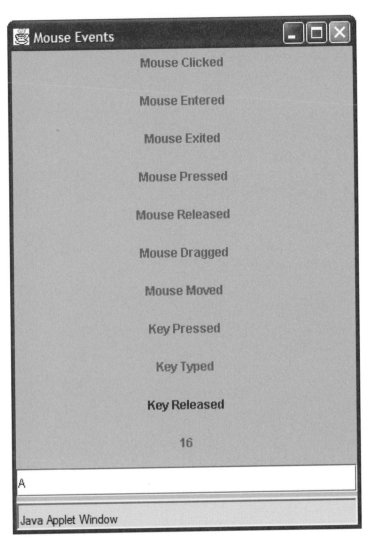

Figure 13-28   Figure for Programming Exercise 11

12. Create an applet to draw lines, rectangles, squares, circles, and ovals. The user can select any one of these through a menu. The user also can choose the start and end points of the line to be drawn by clicking the mouse. For other geometric figures, the user chooses the upper-left corner and lower-right corner by clicking the mouse.

13. Convert the Java Kiosk Programming Example from an application to an applet.

14. Create an applet that starts with displaying several colored circles which can be moved to different places in the applet by dragging a mouse.

13

RECURSION

In previous chapters, to devise problem solutions we used the most common technique, called iteration. For certain problems, however, using the iterative technique to obtain the solution is quite complicated. This chapter introduces another problem-solving technique, called recursion, and provides several examples demonstrating how recursion works.

RECURSIVE DEFINITIONS

The process of solving a problem by reducing it to smaller versions of itself is called **recursion**. Recursion is a powerful way to solve certain problems for which the solution would otherwise be very complicated. Let's consider a familiar problem.

In mathematics, the factorial of an integer is defined as follows:

$$0! = 1 \qquad\qquad\qquad (14\text{-}1)$$
$$n! = n \times (n - 1)! \quad \text{if} \quad n > 0 \qquad (14\text{-}2)$$

In this definition, 0! is defined to be 1, and if n is an integer greater than 0, first we find $(n - 1)!$ and then multiply it by n. To find $(n - 1)!$, we apply the definition again. If $(n - 1) > 0$, then we use Equation 14-2; otherwise, we use Equation 14-1. Thus, for an integer n greater than 0, $n!$ is obtained by first finding $(n - 1)!$ (that is, $n!$ is reduced to a smaller version of itself) and then multiplying $(n - 1)!$ by n.

Let's apply this definition to find 3!. Here $n = 3$. Because $n > 0$, we use Equation 14-2 to obtain

$$3! = 3 \times 2!$$

Next we find 2!. Here $n = 2$. Because $n > 0$, we use Equation 14-2 to obtain

$$2! = 2 \times 1!$$

Now to find 1!, we again use Equation 14-2 because $n = 1 > 0$. Thus:

$$1! = 1 \times 0!$$

Finally, we use Equation 14-1 to find 0!, which is 1. Substituting 0! into 1! gives 1! = 1. This gives $2! = 2 \times 1! = 2 \times 1 = 2$, which in turn gives $3! = 3 \times 2! = 3 \times 2 = 6$.

Note that the solution in Equation 14-1 is direct—that is, the right side of the equation contains no factorial notation. The solution in Equation 14-2 is given in terms of a smaller version of itself. The definition of the factorial as given in Equations 14-1 and 14-2 is called a **recursive definition**. Equation 14-1 is called the **base case**, the case for which the solution is obtained directly; Equation 14-2 is called the **general case** or **recursive case**.

Recursive definition: A definition in which something is defined in terms of a smaller version of itself.

From the previous example, it is clear that:

1. Every recursive definition must have one (or more) base cases.

2. The general case must eventually be reduced to a base case.

3. The base case stops the recursion.

The concept of recursion in computer science works in a similar fashion. Here we talk about recursive algorithms and recursive methods. An algorithm that finds the solution to a given problem by reducing the problem to smaller versions of itself is called a **recursive algorithm**. The recursive algorithm must have one or more base cases, and the general solution must eventually be reduced to a base case.

A method that calls itself is called a **recursive method**. That is, the body of the recursive method contains a statement that causes the same method to execute before completing the current call. Recursive algorithms are implemented using recursive methods.

Next let's write the recursive method that implements the factorial definition.

```
public static int fact(int num)
{
    if(num == 0)
        return 1;
    else
        return num * fact(num - 1);
}
```

Figure 14-1 traces the execution of the following statement:

```
System.out.println(fact(4));
```

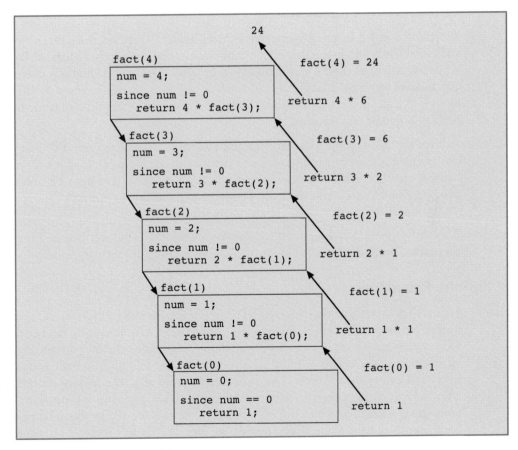

Figure 14-1 Execution of the expression `fact(4)`

The output of the preceding statement is

24

In Figure 14-1, the downward arrows represent the successive calls to the method `fact`, and the upward arrows represent the values returned to the caller, that is, the calling method.

While tracing the execution of the recursive method `fact`, note the following:

- Logically, you can think of a recursive method as having unlimited copies of itself.

- Every call to a recursive method—that is, every recursive call—has its own code and its own set of parameters and local variables.

- After completing a particular recursive call, the control goes back to the calling environment, which is the previous call. The current (recursive) call must execute completely before the control goes back to the previous call. The execution in the previous call begins from the point immediately following the recursive call.

Direct and Indirect Recursion

A method is called **directly recursive** if it calls itself. A method that calls another method and eventually results in the original method call is called **indirectly recursive**. For example, if method A calls method B and method B calls method A, then method A is indirectly recursive. Indirect recursion could be several layers deep. For example, if method A calls method B, method B calls method C, method C calls method D, and method D calls method A, then method A is indirectly recursive.

Indirect recursion requires the same careful analysis as direct recursion. The base cases must be identified and appropriate solutions to them must be provided. However, tracing through indirect recursion can be a tedious process. Therefore, extra care must be exercised when designing indirect recursive methods. For simplicity, this book considers only problems that involve direct recursion.

A recursive method in which the last statement executed is the recursive call is called a **tail recursive method**. The method `fact` is an example of a tail recursive method.

Infinite Recursion

Figure 14-1 shows that the sequence of recursive calls reached a call that did not make any further recursive calls. That is, the sequence of recursive calls eventually reached a base case. However, if every recursive call results in another recursive call, then the recursive method (algorithm) is said to have infinite recursion. In theory, infinite recursion executes forever. Every call to a recursive method requires the system to allocate memory for the local variables and formal parameters. In addition to this, the system also saves information so that after completing a call the control can be transferred back to the right caller. Therefore, because computer memory is finite, if you execute an infinite recursive method on a computer, the method will execute until the system runs out of memory, which results in abnormal termination of the program.

Recursive methods (algorithms) must be carefully designed and analyzed. You must make sure that every recursive call eventually reduces to a base case. In what follows, we give various examples illustrating how to design and implement recursive algorithms.

To design a recursive method, you must:

1. Understand the problem requirements.

2. Determine the limiting conditions. For example, for a list, the limiting condition is determined by the number of elements in the list.

3. Identify the base cases and provide a direct solution to each base case.

4. Identify the general cases and provide a solution to each general case in terms of a smaller version of itself.

PROBLEM SOLVING USING RECURSION

Examples 14-1 through 14-3 illustrate how recursive algorithms are developed and implemented in Java using recursive methods.

Example 14-1: Largest Element in the Array

In Chapter 9, we used a loop to find the largest element in an array. In this example, we use a recursive algorithm to find the largest element in an array. Consider the list given in Figure 14-2.

Figure 14-2   List with six elements

14

The largest element in the list given in Figure 14-2 is 10.

Suppose list is the name of the array containing the list elements. Also suppose that list[a]...list[b] stands for the array elements list[a], list[a + 1], ..., list[b]. For example, list[0]...list[5] represents the array elements list[0], list[1], list[2], list[3], list[4], and list[5]. In a similar way, list[1]...list[5] represents the array elements list[1], list[2], list[3], list[4], and list[5]. To write a recursive algorithm to find the largest element in list, let's think in terms of recursion.

If list is of length 1, then list has only one element, which is the largest element. Suppose the length of list is greater than 1. To find the largest element in list[a]...list[b], we first find the largest element in list[a + 1]...list[b] and then compare this largest element with list[a]. That is, the largest element in list[a]...list[b] is given by

```
maximum(list[a], largest(list[a + 1]...list[b]))
```

Let's apply this formula to find the largest element in the list shown in Figure 14-2. This list has six elements, given by list[0]...list[5]. Now the largest element in list is

```
maximum(list[0], largest(list[1]...list[5]))
```

That is, the largest element in list is the maximum of list[0] and the largest element in list[1]...list[5]. To find the largest element in list[1]...list[5], we use the same formula again because the length of this list is greater than 1. The largest element in list[1]...list[5] is then

```
maximum(list[1], largest(list[2]...list[5]))
```

and so on. Note that every time we use the preceding formula to find the largest element in a sublist, the length of the sublist in the next call is reduced by one. Eventually, the sublist is of length 1, in which case the sublist contains only one element, which in turn is the largest element in the sublist. From this point onward, we backtrack through the recursive calls. This discussion translates into the following recursive algorithm, which is presented in pseudocode:

```
if the size of the list is 1
    the only element in the list is the largest element
else
    to find the largest element in list[a]...list[b]
        a. find the largest element in list[a + 1]...list[b] and call
           it max
        b. compare the elements list[a] and max
            if(list[a] >= max)
                the largest element in list[a]...list[b] is list[a]
            else
                the largest element in list[a]...list[b] is max
```

This algorithm translates into the following Java method to find the largest element in an array:

```
public static int largest(int[] list,
                          int lowerIndex, int upperIndex)
{
    int max;

    if(lowerIndex == upperIndex)    //size of the sublist is 1
        return list[lowerIndex];
    else
    {
        max = largest(list, lowerIndex + 1, upperIndex);
        if(list[lowerIndex] >= max)
            return list[lowerIndex];
        else
            return max;
    }
}
```

Consider the list given in Figure 14–3.

```
                          [0] [1] [2] [3]
                    list | 5 | 10 | 12 | 8 |
```

Figure 14-3   List with four elements

Let's trace the execution of the following statement:

`System.out.println(largest(list,0,3));`

Here `upperIndex = 3` and the list has four elements. Figure 14-4 traces the execution of `largest(list,0,3)`.

14

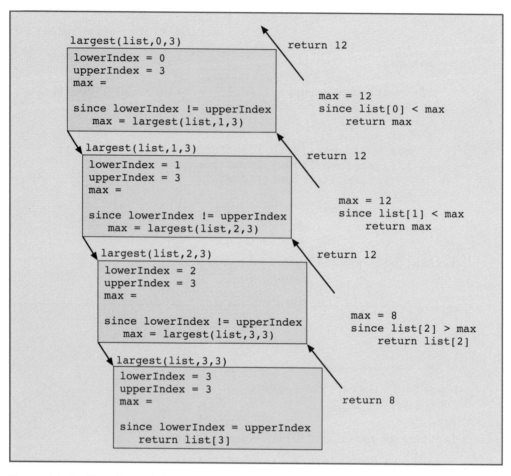

Figure 14-4 Execution of the expression `largest(list,0,3)`

The value returned by the expression `largest(list,0,3)` is 12, which is the largest element in `list`.

The following Java program uses the method `largest` to determine the largest element in the list:

```
//Recursion: Largest Element in an Array

import java.io.*;

public class  largestElementInAnArray
{
```

```java
public static void main(String[] args)
{
    int[] intArray = {23, 43, 35, 38, 67, 12, 76, 10, 34, 8};

    System.out.println("The largest element in intArray: "
                  + largest(intArray, 0, intArray.length - 1));
}

public static int largest(int[] list,
                          int lowerIndex, int upperIndex)
{
    int max;

    if(lowerIndex == upperIndex)    //size of the sublist is 1
        return list[lowerIndex];
    else
    {
        max = largest(list, lowerIndex + 1, upperIndex);
        if(list[lowerIndex] >= max)
            return list[lowerIndex];
        else
            return max;
    }
}
}
```

Sample Run:

```
The largest element in intArray: 76
```

Example 14-2: Fibonacci Number

In Chapter 5, we designed a program to determine the desired Fibonacci number. In this example, we write a recursive method, rFibNum, to determine the desired Fibonacci number. The method rFibNum takes as parameters three numbers representing the first two numbers of the Fibonacci sequence and a number n, the desired nth Fibonacci number. The method rFibNum returns the nth Fibonacci number in the sequence.

Recall that the third Fibonacci number is the sum of the first two Fibonacci numbers. The fourth Fibonacci number in a sequence is the sum of the second and third Fibonacci numbers. Therefore, to calculate the fourth Fibonacci number, we add the second Fibonacci number and the third Fibonacci number (which itself is the sum of the first two Fibonacci numbers). The following recursive algorithm calculates the nth Fibonacci number, where a denotes the first Fibonacci number, b the second Fibonacci number, and n the nth Fibonacci number:

$$\text{rFibNum}(a,b,n) = \begin{cases} a & \text{if } n = 1 \\ b & \text{if } n = 2 \\ \text{rFibNum}(a,b,n-1) + \text{rFibNum}(a,b,n-2) & \text{if } n > 2. \end{cases} \quad (14\text{-}3)$$

14

Suppose that we want to determine:

   1. `rFibNum(2,5,4)`

Here a = 2, b = 5, and n = 4. That is, we want to determine the fourth Fibonacci number of the sequence whose first number is 2 and whose second number is 5. Because n is 4 > 2,

`rFibNum(2,5,4) = rFibNum(2,5,3) + rFibNum(2,5,2)`

Next we determine `rFibNum(2,5,3)` and `rFibNum(2,5,2)`. Let's first determine `rFibNum(2,5,3)`. Here, a = 2, b = 5, and n is 3. Since n is 3,

   1.a `rFibNum(2,5,3) = rFibNum(2,5,2)+ rFibNum(2,5,1)`

This statement requires that we determine `rFibNum(2,5,2)` and `rFibNum(2,5,1)`. In `rFibNum(2,5,2)`, a = 2, b = 5, and n = 2. Therefore, from the definition given in Equation 14-3, it follows that:

   1.a.1 `rFibNum(2,5,2) = 5`

To find `rFibNum(2,5,1)`, note that a = 2, b = 5, and n = 1. Therefore, by the definition given in Equation 14-3:

   1.a.2 `rFibNum(2,5,1) = 2`

We substitute the values of `rFibNum(2,5,2)` and `rFibNum(2,5,1)` into (1.a) to get:

`rFibNum(2,5,3) = 5 + 2 = 7`

Next we determine `rFibNum(2,5,2)`. As in (1.a.1), `rFibNum(2,5,2) = 5`. We can substitute the values of `rFibNum(2,5,3)` and `rFibNum(2,5,2)` into (1) to get:

`rFibNum(2,5,4) = 7 + 5 = 12`

The following recursive method implements this algorithm:

```
public static int rFibNum(int a, int b, int n)
{
  if(n == 1)
     return a;
  else if(n == 2)
          return b;
  else
     return rFibNum(a, b, n - 1) + rFibNum(a, b, n - 2);
}
```

Let's trace the execution of the following statement:

`System.out.println(rFibNum(2, 3, 5));`

In this statement, the first number is 2, the second number is 3, and we want to determine the 5th Fibonacci number of the sequence. Figure 14-5 traces the execution of the expression `rFibNum(2,3,5)`. The value returned is 13, which is the 5th Fibonacci number of the sequence whose first number is 2 and whose second number is 3.

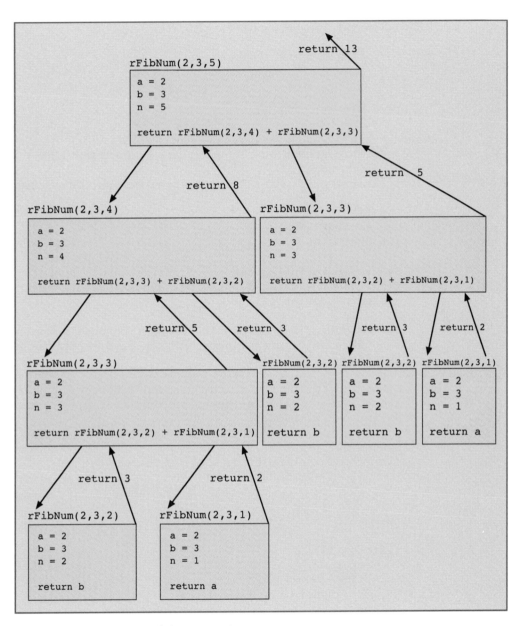

Figure 14-5   Execution of the expression rFibNumber(2,3,5)

14

The following Java program uses the method `rFibNum`:

```java
//Recursion: Fibonacci Number

import java.io.*;

public class FibonacciNumber
{
    static BufferedReader keyboard = new
            BufferedReader(new InputStreamReader(System.in));

    public static void main(String[] args) throws IOException
    {
        int firstFibNum;
        int secondFibNum;
        int nth;

        System.out.print("Enter the first Fibonacci number: ");
        firstFibNum = Integer.parseInt(keyboard.readLine());
        System.out.println();

        System.out.print("Enter the second Fibonacci number: ");
        secondFibNum = Integer.parseInt(keyboard.readLine());
        System.out.println();

        System.out.print("Enter the desired Fibonacci number: ");
        nth = Integer.parseInt(keyboard.readLine());
        System.out.println();

        System.out.println("The Fibonacci number at position "
                    + nth + " is: "
                    + rFibNum(firstFibNum, secondFibNum, nth));
    }

    public static int rFibNum(int a, int b, int n)
    {
        if(n == 1)
            return a;
        else if(n == 2)
                return b;
        else
            return rFibNum(a, b, n - 1) + rFibNum(a, b, n - 2);
    }
}
```

Sample Runs: In these sample runs, the user input is shaded.

Sample Run 1:

```
Enter the first Fibonacci number: 2

Enter the second Fibonacci number: 5

Enter the desired Fibonacci number: 6

The Fibonacci number at position 6 is: 31
```

Sample Run 2:

```
Enter the first Fibonacci number: 3

Enter the second Fibonacci number: 4

Enter the desired Fibonacci number: 6

The Fibonacci number at position 6 is: 29
```

Sample Run 3:

```
Enter the first Fibonacci number: 12

Enter the second Fibonacci number: 18

Enter the desired Fibonacci number: 15

The Fibonacci number at position 15 is: 9582
```

Example 14-3: Tower of Hanoi

In the nineteenth century, a game called the Tower of Hanoi was popular in Europe. This game is based on a legend regarding the construction of the temple of Brahma. According to this legend, at the creation of the universe, priests in the temple of Brahma were given three diamond needles, with one needle containing 64 golden disks. Each golden disk is slightly smaller than the disk below it. The priests' task was to move all 64 disks from the first needle to the third needle. The rules for moving the disks are as follows:

1. Only one disk can be moved at a time.

2. The removed disk must be placed on one of the needles.

3. A larger disk cannot be placed on top of a smaller disk.

14

The priests were told that once they had moved all the disks from the first needle to the third needle, the universe would come to an end.

Our objective is to write a program that prints the sequence of moves needed to transfer the disks from the first needle to the third needle. Figure 14-6 shows the Tower of Hanoi problem with three disks.

Figure 14-6 Tower of Hanoi problem with three disks

As before, we think in terms of recursion. Let's first consider the case when the first needle contains only one disk. In this case, the disk can be moved directly from needle 1 to needle 3. Now let's consider the case when the first needle contains only two disks. In this case, first we move the first disk from needle 1 to needle 2, and then we move the second disk from needle 1 to needle 3. Finally, we move the first disk from needle 2 to needle 3. Next, we consider the case when the first needle contains three disks, and then generalize this to the case of 64 disks (in fact, to an arbitrary number of disks).

Suppose that needle 1 contains three disks. To move disk number 3 to needle 3, the top two disks must first be moved to needle 2. Disk number 3 can then be moved from needle 1 to needle 3. To move the top two disks from needle 2 to needle 3, we use the same strategy as before. This time we use needle 1 as the intermediate needle. Figure 14-7 shows a solution to the Tower of Hanoi problem with three disks.

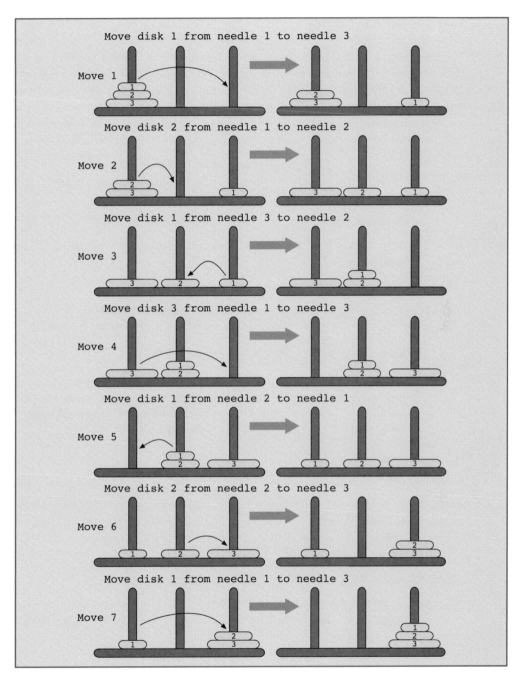

Figure 14-7   Solution to Tower of Hanoi problem with three disks

Let's now generalize this problem to the case of 64 disks. To begin, the first needle contains all 64 disks. Disk number 64 cannot be moved from needle 1 to needle 3 unless the top 63 disks are on the second needle. So first we move the top 63 disks from needle 1 to needle 2, and then we move disk number 64 from needle 1 to needle 3. Now the top 63 disks are all on needle 2. To move disk number 63 from needle 2 to needle 3, we first move the top 62 disks from needle 2 to needle 1, and then we move disk number 63 from needle 2 to needle 3. To move the remaining 62 disks, we use a similar procedure. This discussion translates into the following recursive algorithm given in pseudocode. Suppose that needle 1 contains n disks, where $n \geq 1$.

1. Move the top $n - 1$ disks from needle 1 to needle 2 using needle 3 as the intermediate needle.

2. Move disk number n from needle 1 to needle 3.

3. Move the top $n - 1$ disks from needle 2 to needle 3 using needle 1 as the intermediate needle.

This recursive algorithm translates into the following Java method:

```java
public static void moveDisks(int count, int needle1,
                             int needle3, int needle2)
{
    if(count > 0)
    {
        moveDisks(count-1, needle1, needle2, needle3);
        System.out.println("Move disk " + count + " from needle "
                        + needle1 + " to needle " + needle3 + ".");
        moveDisks(count-1, needle2, needle3, needle1);
    }
}
```

Next let's determine how long it would take to move all the disks from needle 1 to needle 2.

If needle 1 contains 3 disks, then the number of moves required to move all 3 disks from needle 1 to needle 3 is $2^3 - 1 = 7$. Similarly, if needle 1 contains 64 disks, then the number of moves required to move all 64 disks from needle 1 to needle 3 is $2^{64} - 1$. Since $2^{10} = 1024 \approx 1000 = 10^3$,

$$2^{64} = 2^4 * 2^{60} \approx 2^4 * 10^{18} = 1.6 * 10^{19}$$

Here, the symbol $\approx$ denotes "approximately equal to." The number of seconds in one year is approximately $3.2 * 10^7$. Suppose the priests move one disk per second and they do not rest. Now

$$1.6 * 10^{19} = 5 * 3.2 * 10^{18} = 5 * (3.2 * 10^7) * 10^{11}$$
$$= (3.2 * 10^7) * (5 * 10^{11})$$

Thus, the time required to move all 64 disks from needle 1 to needle 3 is roughly $5 * 10^{11}$ years. It is estimated that our universe is about 15 billion $= 1.5 * 10^{10}$ years old.

Also, $5 * 10^{11} = 50 * 10^{10} \approx 33 *(1.5 * 10^{10})$. This calculation shows that our universe would last about 33 times as long as it already has.

Assume that a computer can generate 1 billion or 10^9 moves per second. Then the number of moves that the computer can generate in one year is:

$(3.2 * 10^7) * 10^9 = 3.2 * 10^{16}$

So the computer time required to generate 2^{64} moves is:

$2^{64} \approx 1.6 * 10^{19} = 1.6 * 10^{16} * 10^3 = (3.2 * 10^{16}) * 500$

Thus, it would take about 500 years for the computer to generate 2^{64} moves at the rate of 1 billion moves per second.

RECURSION OR ITERATION?

In Chapter 5, we designed a program to determine a desired Fibonacci number. That program used a loop to perform the calculation. In other words, the programs in Chapter 5 used an iterative control structure to repeat a set of statements. More formally, **iterative control structures** use a looping structure, such as `while`, `for`, or `do...while`, to repeat a set of statements. In Example 14-2, we designed a recursive method to calculate a Fibonacci number. From the examples in this chapter, it follows that in recursion, a set of statements is repeated by having the method call itself. Moreover, a selection control structure is used to control the repeated calls in recursion.

Similarly, in Chapter 9, we used an iterative control structure (a `for` loop) to determine the largest element in a list. In this chapter, we use recursion to determine the largest element in a list. In addition, this chapter began by designing a recursive method to find the factorial of a non-negative integer. Using an iterative control structure, we can also write an algorithm to find the factorial of a non-negative integer. The only reason we gave a recursive solution to a factorial problem is to illustrate how recursion works.

We thus see that there are usually two ways to solve a particular problem—iteration and recursion. The obvious question is, which method is better—iteration or recursion? There is no simple answer. In addition to the nature of the problem, the other key factor in determining the best solution method is efficiency.

When we traced the execution of the program in Example 7-11 (Chapter 7), we saw that whenever a method is called, memory space for its formal parameters and (automatic) local variables is allocated. When the method terminates, that memory space is then deallocated.

In this chapter, while tracing the execution of recursive methods, we see that every (recursive) call also has its own set of parameters and local variables. That is, every (recursive) call requires that the system allocate memory space for its formal parameters and local variables, and then deallocate the memory space when the method exits. Thus, there is overhead associated with executing a (recursive) method, both in terms of memory space and computer

14

time. Therefore, a recursive method executes more slowly than its iterative counterpart. On slower computers, especially those with limited memory space, the (slow) execution of a recursive method would be noticeable.

Today's computers, however, are fast and have inexpensive memory. Therefore, the execution of a recursive method is not so noticeable. Keeping in mind the power of today's computers, the choice between iteration or recursion depends on the nature of the problem. Of course, for problems such as mission control systems, efficiency is absolutely critical and, therefore, the efficiency factor dictates the solution method.

As a general rule, if you think an iterative solution is more obvious and easier to understand than a recursive solution, use the iterative solution, which is more efficient. On the other hand, problems exist for which the recursive solution is more obvious or easier to construct, such as the Tower of Hanoi problem. (In fact, it turns out that it is difficult to construct an iterative solution for the Tower of Hanoi problem.) Keeping in mind the power of recursion, if the definition of a problem is inherently recursive, then you should consider a recursive solution.

PROGRAMMING EXAMPLE: CONVERTING A NUMBER FROM DECIMAL TO BINARY

This programming example discusses and designs a program that uses recursion to convert a non-negative integer in decimal format—that is, base 10—into the equivalent binary number—that is, base 2. First we define some terms.

Let **x** be a non-negative integer. We call the remainder of **x** after division by 2 the **rightmost bit** of x.

Thus, the rightmost bit of 33 is 1 because 33 % 2 is 1, and the rightmost bit of 28 is 0 because 28 % 2 is 0.

We first use an example to illustrate the algorithm to convert an integer in base 10 to the equivalent number in binary format.

Suppose we want to find the binary representation of 35. First, we divide 35 by 2. The quotient is 17 and the remainder—that is, the rightmost bit of 35—is 1. Next we divide 17 by 2. The quotient is 8 and the remainder—that is, the rightmost bit of 17—is 1. Next we divide 8 by 2. The quotient is 4 and the remainder—that is, the rightmost bit of 8—is 0. We continue this process until the quotient becomes 0.

The rightmost bit of 35 cannot be printed until we have printed the rightmost bit of 17. The rightmost bit of 17 cannot be printed until we have printed the rightmost bit of 8, and so on. Thus, the binary representation of 35 is the binary representation of 17 (that is, the quotient of 35 after division by 2), followed by the rightmost bit of 35.

Thus, to convert a non-negative integer num in base 10 into the equivalent binary number, we first convert the quotient num / 2 into an equivalent binary number, and then append the rightmost bit of num to the binary representation of num / 2.

This discussion translates into the following recursive algorithm, where binary(num) denotes the binary representation of num:

  1. binary(num) = num if num = 0.
  2. binary(num) = binary(num / 2) followed by num % 2 if num > 0.

The following recursive method implements this algorithm:

```java
public static void decToBin(int num, int base)
{
    if(num > 0)
    {
        decToBin(num/base, base);
        System.out.print(num % base);
    }
}
```

Figure 14-8 traces the execution of the following statement:

```java
decToBin(13,2);
```

where num is 13 and base is 2.

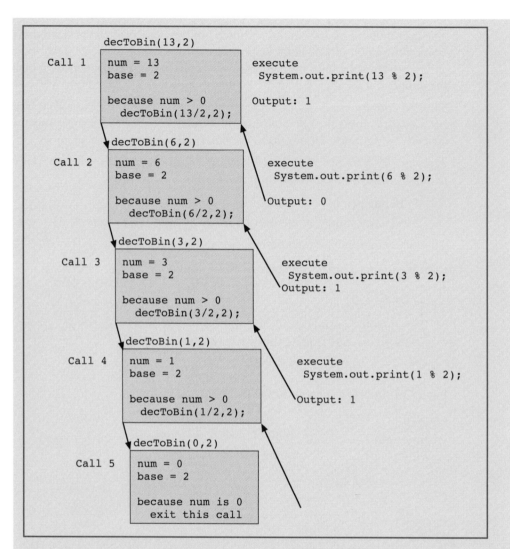

Figure 14-8   Execution of the statement `decToBin(13,2);`

Since the `if` statement in Call 5 fails, this call does not print anything. The first output is produced by Call 4, which prints 1; the second output is produced by Call 3, which prints 1; the third output is produced by Call 2, which prints 0; and the fourth output is produced by Call 1, which prints 1. Thus, the output of the statement

`decToBin(13, 2);`

is

1101

The following Java program tests the method `decToBin`:

```java
//Recursion: Program - Decimal to Binary

import java.io.*;

public class DecimalToBinary
{
    static BufferedReader keyboard = new
           BufferedReader(new InputStreamReader(System.in));

    public static void main(String[] args) throws IOException
    {
        int decimalNum;
        int base;

        base = 2;

        System.out.print("Enter number in decimal: ");
        decimalNum = Integer.parseInt(keyboard.readLine());
        System.out.println("");
        System.out.print("Decimal " + decimalNum + " = ");
        decToBin(decimalNum, base);
        System.out.println(" binary");
    }

    public static void decToBin(int num, int base)
    {
        if(num > 0)
        {
            decToBin(num/base, base);
            System.out.print(num % base);
        }
    }
}
```

Sample Run: In this sample run, the user input is shaded.

```
Enter number in decimal: 57

Decimal 57 = 111001 binary
```

PROGRAMMING EXAMPLE: SIERPINSKI GASKET

To draw the shapes of natural scenes such as mountains, trees, and clouds, graphic programmers typically use special mathematical tools, called **fractals**, related to fractal geometry. Fractal geometry is a major area of research in mathematics in its own right. The term fractal was introduced by the mathematician Benoit Mandelbrot in the late 1970s. Roughly speaking, a fractal is a geometric shape in which certain patterns repeat, perhaps at a different scale and orientation. Mandelbrot is credited to be the first person to demonstrate that fractals occur in various places in mathematics and nature.

Because in a fractal certain patterns occur at various places, a convenient and effective way to write programs to draw fractals is to use recursion. In this section, we describe a special type of fractal called a **Sierpinski gasket**.

Suppose that you have the triangle ABC given in Figure 14-9(a). Now determine the midpoints P, Q, and R of the sides AB, AC, and BC, respectively. Next draw the lines PQ, QR, and PR. This creates three triangles, APQ, BPR, and CRQ, as shown in Figure 14-9(b), of similar shape as in the triangle ABC. The process of finding the midpoints of the sides and then drawing the lines through those midpoints is now repeated on each of the triangles APQ, BPR, and CRQ, as shown in Figure 14-9(c). Figure 14-9(a) is called a Sierpinski gasket of order or level 0; Figure 14-9(b) is called a Sierpinski gasket of order or level 1; Figure 14-9(c) is called a Sierpinski gasket of order or level 2; and Figure14-9(d) shows a Sierpinski gasket of order or level 3.

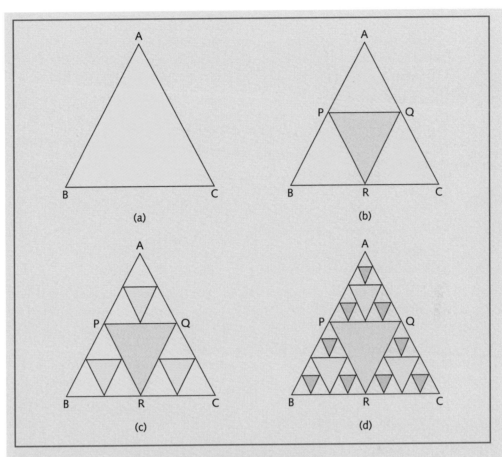

Figure 14-9   Sierpinski gaskets of various orders (levels)

Input   The input to the program is a non-negative integer indicating the level of the Sierpinski gasket.

Output   A triangle shape displaying a Sierpinski gasket of the given order.

Problem Analysis and Algorithm Design

The problem is as described previously. Initially, we specify the coordinate of the first triangle and then draw the triangle. We use the **class Point**, as described in Appendix E, to store the *x-y* coordinates of a point. We also use the method **drawLine**, as described in Chapter 13, to draw a line between two points.

For each triangle, we need three objects of the **class Point** to store the vertices of a triangle, and three more objects to store the midpoints of a side. Because we frequently need to find the midpoints of a line, we write the method **midPoint**, which returns the coordinates of the midpoint of a line. Its definition is:

```
private Point midPoint(Point pOne, Point pTwo)
{
  Point mid = new Point((pOne.x + pTwo.x) / 2,
                        (pOne.y + pTwo.y) / 2 );

        return mid;
}
```

The recursive algorithm to draw a Sierpinski gasket is as follows:

Base case: If level is 0, draw the first triangle.

Recursive case: If level is greater than 0, for each triangle in the Sierpinski gasket, find the midpoints of the sides and draw lines through those points.

Suppose that **p1, p2,** and **p3** are the three vertices of a triangle, and **lev** denotes the number of levels of the Sierpinski gasket to be drawn. The following method implements the recursive algorithm to draw a Sierpinski gasket:

```
private void drawSierpinski(Graphics   g, int lev,
                            Point p1, Point p2, Point p3)
{
    Point midP1P2;
    Point midP2P3;
    Point midP3P1;

    if(lev > 0)
    {
       g.drawLine(p1.x, p1.y, p2.x, p2.y);
       g.drawLine(p2.x, p2.y, p3.x, p3.y);
       g.drawLine(p3.x, p3.y, p1.x, p1.y);

       midP1P2 = midPoint(p1, p2);
       midP2P3 = midPoint(p2, p3);
       midP3P1 = midPoint(p3, p1);

       drawSierpinski(g, lev - 1, p1, midP1P2, midP3P1);
       drawSierpinski(g, lev - 1, p2, midP2P3, midP1P2);
       drawSierpinski(g, lev - 1, p3, midP3P1, midP2P3);
    }
}
```

The complete algorithm to draw a Sierpinski gasket of a given order is provided in the following program listing. Notice that the program uses an input dialog box to get the user's input.

Complete Program Listing

```java
//Java program to draw SierpinskiGasket

import java.awt.*;
import javax.swing.*;

public class SierpinskiGasket extends JApplet
{
    int level = 0;

    public void init()
    {
        String levelStr = JOptionPane.showInputDialog
                          ("Enter the depth of recursion: ");

        level = Integer.parseInt(levelStr);
    }

    public void paint(Graphics g)
    {
        Point pointOne = new Point(20, 280);
        Point pointTwo = new Point(280, 280);
        Point pointThree = new Point(150,20);

        drawSierpinski(g, level, pointOne, pointTwo, pointThree);
    }

    private void drawSierpinski(Graphics  g, int lev,
                                Point p1, Point p2, Point p3)
    {
        Point midP1P2;
        Point midP2P3;
        Point midP3P1;

        if(lev > 0)
        {
            g.drawLine(p1.x, p1.y, p2.x, p2.y);
            g.drawLine(p2.x, p2.y, p3.x, p3.y);
            g.drawLine(p3.x, p3.y, p1.x, p1.y);

            midP1P2 = midPoint(p1, p2);
            midP2P3 = midPoint(p2, p3);
            midP3P1 = midPoint(p3, p1);

            drawSierpinski(g, lev - 1, p1, midP1P2, midP3P1);
            drawSierpinski(g, lev - 1, p2, midP2P3, midP1P2);
```

```
            drawSierpinski(g, lev - 1, p3, midP3P1, midP2P3);
        }
    }

    private Point midPoint(Point pOne, Point pTwo)
    {
        Point mid = new Point((pOne.x + pTwo.x) / 2,
                              (pOne.y + pTwo.y) / 2 );

        return mid;
    }
}
```

Sample Run: In these sample runs, the user input is entered in input dialog boxes.

Sample Run 1: Figure 14–10 shows Sample Run 1.

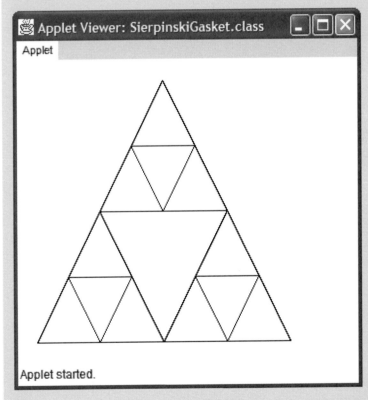

Figure 14-10   Recursion depth of 3 produces a Sierpinski gasket of order 2

Sample Run 2: Figure 14–11 shows Sample Run 2.

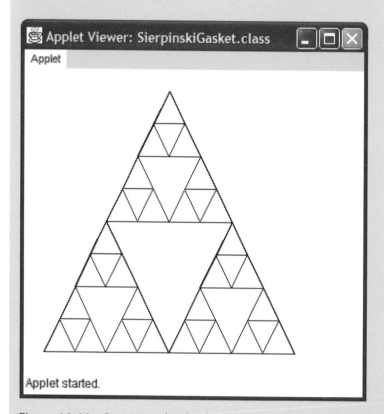

Figure 14-11 Recursion depth of 4 produces a Sierpinski gasket of order 3

QUICK REVIEW

1. The process of solving a problem by reducing it to smaller versions of itself is called recursion.

2. A recursive definition defines the problem in terms of smaller versions of itself.

3. Every recursive definition has one or more base cases.

4. A recursive algorithm solves a problem by reducing it to smaller versions of itself.

5. Every recursive algorithm has one or more base cases.

6. The solution to the problem in a base case is obtained directly.

7. A method is called recursive if it calls itself.

8. Recursive algorithms are implemented using recursive methods.

9. Every recursive method must have one or more base cases.

10. The general solution breaks the problem into smaller versions of itself.

11. The general case must eventually be reduced to a base case.

12. The base case stops the recursion.

13. While tracing a recursive method:

    a. Logically, you can think of a recursive method as having unlimited copies of itself.

    b. Every call to a recursive method—that is, every recursive call—has its own code and its own set of parameters and local variables.

    c. After completing a particular recursive call, the control goes back to the calling environment, which is the previous call. The current (recursive) call must execute completely before the control goes back to the previous call. The execution in the previous call begins from the point immediately following the recursive call.

14. A method is called directly recursive if it calls itself.

15. A method that calls another method and eventually results in the original method call is said to be indirectly recursive.

16. A recursive method in which the last statement executed is the recursive call is called a tail recursive method.

17. To design a recursive method, you must do the following:

    a. Understand the problem requirements.

    b. Determine the limiting conditions. For example, for a list, the limiting condition is determined by the number of elements in the list.

    c. Identify the base cases and provide a direct solution to each base case.

    d. Identify the general case(s) and provide a solution to each general case in terms of smaller versions of itself.

18. A recursive method in which the last statement executed is the recursive call is called a tail recursive method.

14

1. Mark the following statements as true or false.

   a. Every recursive definition must have one or more base cases.

   b. Every recursive method must have one or more base cases.

   c. The general case stops the recursion.

   d. In the general case, the solution to the problem is obtained directly.

   e. A recursive method always returns a value.

2. What is a base case?

3. What is a recursive case?

4. What is direct recursion?

5. What is indirect recursion?

6. What is tail recursion?

7. Consider the following recursive method:

```
public static int mystery(int number)          //Line 1
{
    if(number == 0)                             //Line 2
        return number;                          //Line 3
    else                                        //Line 4
        return(number + mystery(number - 1));   //Line 5
}
```

   a. Identify the base case.

   b. Identify the general case.

   c. What valid values can be passed as parameters to the method `mystery`?

   d. If `mystery(0)` is a valid call, what is its value? If not, explain why.

   e. If `mystery(5)` is a valid call, what is its value? If not, explain why.

   f. If `mystery(-3)` is a valid call, what is its value? If not, explain why?

8. Consider the following recursive method:

```
public static void funcRec(int u, char v)               //Line 1
{
    if(u == 0)                                          //Line 2
        System.out.print(v);                            //Line 3
    else if(u == 1)                                     //Line 4
            System.out.print((char)((int)(v) + 1);     //Line 5
    else                                                //Line 6
        funcRec(u - 1, v);                              //Line 7
}
```

Answer the following questions:

a. Identify the base case.

b. Identify the general case.

c. What is the output of the following statement?

```
funcRec(5,'A');
```

9. Consider the following recursive method:

```
void exercise(int x)
{
    if(x > 0 && x < 10)
    {
        System.out.print(x + " ");
        exercise(x + 1);
    }
}
```

What is the output of the following statements?

a. `exercise(0);`

b. `exercise(5);`

c. `exercise(10);`

d. `exercise(-5);`

10. Consider the following method:

```
int test(int x, int y)
{
    if(x == y)
        return x;
    else if(x > y)
            return (x + y);
    else
        return test(x + 1, y - 1);
}
```

What is the output of the following statements?

a. `System.out.println(test(5,10));`

b. `System.out.println(test(3,9));`

11. Consider the following method:

```
int Func(int x)
{
    if(x == 0)
        return 2;
    else if(x == 1)
            return 3;
    else
        return (Func(x - 1) + Func(x - 2));
}
```

What is the output of the following statements?

a. `System.out.println(Func(0));`

b. `System.out.println(Func(1));`

c. `System.out.println(Func(2));`

d. `System.out.println(Func(5));`

12. Suppose that `intArray` is an array of integers and `length` specifies the number of elements in `intArray`. Also suppose that `low` and `high` are to integers such that `0 <= low < length, 0 <= high < length` and `low < high`. That is, `low` and `high` are two indices in `intArray`. Write a recursive definition that reverses the elements in `intArray` between `low` and `high`.

13. Write a recursive definition to multiply two positive integers m and n using repeated addition.

PROGRAMMING EXERCISES

1. Write a recursive method that takes as a parameter a non-negative integer and generates the following pattern of stars. If the non-negative integer is 4, then the pattern generated is:

```
****
***
**
*
*
**
***
****
```

Also write a program that prompts the user to enter the number of lines in the pattern and uses the recursive method to generate the pattern. For example, specifying the number of lines to be 4 generates the above pattern.

2. Write a recursive method to generate a pattern of stars such as the following:

```
*
**
***
****
****
***
**
*
```

Also write a program that prompts the user to enter the number of lines in the pattern and uses the recursive method to generate the pattern. For example, specifying the number of lines to be 4 generates the above pattern.

3. Write a recursive method to generate the following pattern of stars:

Also write a program that prompts the user to enter the number of lines in the pattern and uses the recursive method to generate the pattern. For example, specifying the number of lines to be 4 generates the above pattern.

4. Write a recursive method, vowels, that returns the number of vowels in a string. Also write a program to test your method.

5. Write a recursive method that finds and returns the sum of the elements of an int array. Also write a program to test your method.

6. A palindrome is a string that reads the same both forward and backward. For example, the string "madam" is a palindrome. Write a program that uses a recursive method to check whether a string is a palindrome. Your program must contain a value–returning recursive method that returns true if the string is a palindrome and false otherwise. Use appropriate parameters in your method.

7. Write a program that uses a recursive method to print a string backward. Your program must contain a recursive method that prints the string backward. Use appropriate parameters in your method.

8. Write a recursive method, reverseDigits, that takes an integer as a parameter and returns the number with the digits reversed. Also write a program to test your method.

9. Write a recursive method, power, that takes as parameters two integers x and y such that x is nonzero and returns x^y. You can use the following recursive definition to calculate x^y. If $y \geq 0$,

$$power(x, y) = \begin{cases} 1 & \text{if } y = 0 \\ x & \text{if } y = 1 \\ x * power(x, y - 1) & \text{if } y > 1. \end{cases}$$

If $y < 0$,

$$power(x, y) = \frac{1}{power(x, -y)}.$$

Also write a program to test your method.

14

10. **Greatest Common Divisor.** Given two integers x and y, the following recursive definition determines the greatest common divisor of x and y, written $gcd(x,y)$:

$$gcd(x, y) = \begin{cases} x & \text{if } y = 0 \\ gcd(y, x\%y) & \text{if } y \neq 0 \end{cases}$$

(*Note:* In this definition, % is the mod operator.)

Write a recursive method, **gcd**, that takes as parameters two integers and returns the greatest common divisor of the numbers. Also write a program to test your method.

11. Write a recursive method to implement the recursive definition of Exercise 12 (reversing the elements of an array between two indices). Also write a program to test your method.

12. Write a recursive method to implement the recursive definition of Exercise 13 (multiply two positive integers using repeated addition). Also write a program to test your method.

13. In the Programming Example, Converting a Number from Decimal to Binary, given in this chapter, you learned how to convert a decimal number into its equivalent binary number. Two more number systems, octal (base 8) and hexadecimal (base 16), are of interest to computer scientists.

The digits in the octal number system are 0, 1, 2, 3, 4, 5, 6, and 7. The digits in the hexadecimal number system are 0, 1, 2, 3, 4, 5, 6, 7, 8, 9, A, B, C, D, E, and F. So A in hexadecimal is 10 in decimal, B in hexadecimal is 11 in decimal, and so on.

The algorithm to convert a positive decimal number into an equivalent number in octal (or hexadecimal) is the same as that discussed for binary numbers. Here we divide the decimal number by 8 (for octal) and by 16 (for hexadecimal). Suppose a_b represents the number a to the base b. For example, 75_{10} means 75 to the base 10 (that is decimal), and 83_{16} means 83 to the base 16 (that is, hexadecimal). Then

$$753_{10} = 1361_8$$
$$753_{10} = 2F1_{16}$$

The method of converting a decimal number to base 2, or 8, or 16 can be extended to any arbitrary base. Suppose you want to convert a decimal number n into an equivalent number in base b, where b is between 2 and 36. You then divide the decimal number n by b as in the algorithm for converting decimal to binary.

Note that the digits in, say base 20, are 0, 1, 2, 3, 4, 5, 6, 7, 8, 9, A, B, C, D, E, F, G, H, I, and J.

Write a program that uses a recursive method to convert a number in decimal to a given base b, where b is between 2 and 36. Your program should prompt the user to enter the number in decimal and in the desired base.

Test your program on the following data:

9098 and base 20

692 and base 2

753 and base 16

14. **Converting a Number from Binary to Decimal.** The language of a computer, called machine language, is a sequence of 0s and 1s. When you press the A key on the keyboard, 01000001 is stored in the computer. Note that the collating sequence of A in the Unicode character set is 65. In fact, the binary representation of A is 01000001 and the decimal representation of A is 65.

The numbering system we use is called the decimal system, or base 10 system. The numbering system that the computer uses is called the binary system, or base 2 system. This chapter described how to convert a decimal number into an equivalent binary number. The purpose of this exercise is to write a program to convert a number from base 2 to base 10.

To convert a number from base 2 to base 10, we first find the weight of each bit in the binary number. The weight of each bit in the binary number is assigned from right to left. The weight of the rightmost bit is 0. The weight of the bit immediately to the left of the rightmost bit is 1, the weight of the bit immediately to the left of it is 2, and so on. Consider the binary number 1001101. The weight of each bit is as follows:

```
weight   6   5   4   3   2   1   0
         1   0   0   1   1   0   1
```

We use the weight of each bit to find the equivalent decimal number. For each bit, we multiply the bit by 2 to the power of its weight and then we add all of the numbers. For the above binary number, the equivalent decimal number is

$$1 * 2^6 + 0 * 2^5 + 0 * 2^4 + 1 * 2^3 + 1 * 2^2 + 0 * 2^1 + 1 * 2^0$$

$$= 64 + 0 + 0 + 8 + 4 + 0 + 1$$

$$= 77$$

To write a program that converts a binary number into the equivalent decimal number, we note two things: (1) the weight of each bit in the binary number must be known; and (2) the weight is assigned from right to left. Because we do not know in advance how many bits are in the binary number, we must process the bits from right to left. After processing a bit, we can add 1 to its weight, giving the weight of the bit immediately to the left to it. Also, each bit must be extracted from the binary number and multiplied by 2 to the power of its weight. To extract a bit, you can use the mod operator. Write a method that converts a binary number into an equivalent decimal number. Moreover, write a program and test your method for the following values: 11000101, 10101010, 11111111, 10000000, and 1111100000.

15. Write a program that uses recursion to draw a Koch snowflake fractal of any given order. A Koch snowflake of order 0 is an equilateral triangle. To create the next-higher-order fractal, each line segment in the shape is modified by replacing its middle third with a sharp protrusion made of two line segments, each having the same length as the replaced one, as shown in Figure 14-12.

14

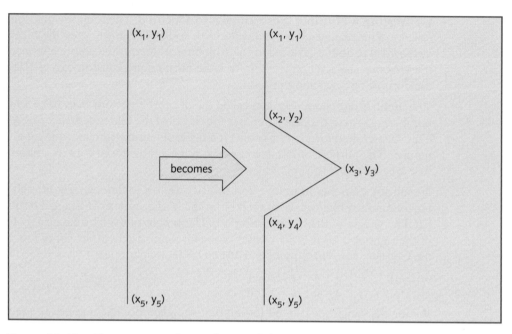

Figure 14-12   Line segments for Koch snowflakes

Here is the necessary information to compute the three new points (x_2, y_2), (x_3, y_3), and (x_4, y_4) in terms of (x_1, y_1) and (x_5, y_5).

Let

```
deltaX = x₅ - x₁
deltaY = y₅ - y₁
```

Then

```
x₂ = x₁ + deltaX / 3,
y₂ = y₁ + deltaY / 3,

x₃ = 0.5 * (x₁ + x₅) + √3 * (y₁ - y₅) / 6,
y₃ = 0.5 * (y₁ + y₅) + √3 * (x₅ - x₁) / 6,

x₄ = x₁ + 2 * deltaX / 3,
y₄ = y₁ + 2 * deltaY / 3,
```

The first three Koch snowflakes produced by the program might look like Figure 14-13.

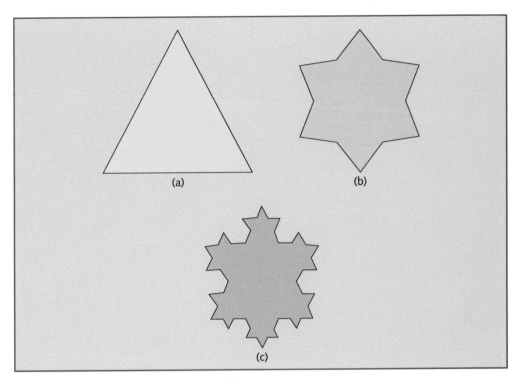

(a)

(b)

(c)

Figure 14-13   First three Koch snowflakes

14

APPENDIX

A

JAVA RESERVED WORDS

The following table lists Java reserved words in alphabetical order.

abstract	else	interface	super
boolean	extends	long	switch
break	false	native	synchronized
byte	final	new	this
case	finally	null	throw
catch	float	package	throws
char	for	private	translate
class	goto	protected	true
const	if	public	try
continue	import	return	void
default	implements	short	volatile
do	instanceof	static	while
double	int	strictfp	

B

OPERATOR PRECEDENCE

The following table shows the precedence of operators in Java from highest to lowest, and their associativity.

Operator	Description	Precedence Level	Associativity
.	Object member access	1	Left to right
[ ]	Array subscripting	1	Left to right
(parameters)	Method call	1	Left to right
++	Post increment	1	Left to right
--	Post decrement	1	Left to right
++	Pre increment	2	Right to left
--	Pre decrement	2	Right to left
+	Unary plus	2	Right to left
-	Unary minus	2	Right to left
!	Logical not	2	Right to left
~	Bitwise not	2	Right to left
new	Object instantiation	3	Right to left
(type)	Type conversion	3	Right to left
*	Multiplication	4	Left to right
/	Division	4	Left to right
%	Remainder (modulus)	4	Left to right
+	Addition	5	Left to right
-	Subtraction	5	Left to right
+	String concatenation	5	Left to right
<<	Left shift	6	Left to right
>>	Right shift with sign extension	6	Left to right
>>>	Right shift with zero extension	6	Left to right
<	Less than	7	Left to right
<=	Less than or equal to	7	Left to right
>	Greater than	7	Left to right
>=	Greater than or equal to	7	Left to right
instanceof	Type comparison	7	Left to right
==	Equal to	8	Left to right
!=	Not equal to	8	Left to right
&	Bitwise AND	9	Left to right
&	Logical AND	9	Left to right
^	Bitwise XOR	10	Left to right
^	Logical XOR	10	Left to right

Operator	Description	Precedence Level	Associativity
|	Bitwise OR	11	Left to right
|	Logical OR	11	Left to right
&&	Logical AND	12	Left to right
||	Logical OR	13	Left to right
? :	Conditional operator	14	Right to left
=	Assignment	15	Right to left
	Compound Operators		
+=	Addition, then assignment	15	Right to left
+=	String concatenation, then assignment	15	Right to left
−=	Subtraction, then assignment	15	Right to left
*=	Multiplication, then assignment	15	Right to left
/=	Division, then assignment	15	Right to left
%=	Remainder, then assignment	15	Right to left
<<=	Left shift, then assignment	15	Right to left
>>=	Right shift, then assignment	15	Right to left
&=	Bitwise AND, then assignment	15	Right to left
&=	Logical AND, then assignment	15	Right to left
|=	Bitwise OR, then assignment	15	Right to left
|=	Logical OR, then assignment	15	Right to left
^=	Bitwise XOR, then assignment	15	Right to left
^=	Logical XOR, then assignment	15	Right to left

C

CHARACTER SETS

This appendix lists and describes the character sets for ASCII (American Standard Code for Information Exchange, which also comprises the first 128 characters of the Unicode character set) and EBCDIC (Extended Binary Coded Decimal Interchange Code).

ASCII (American Standard Code for Information Interchange), the first 128 characters of the Unicode character set

The following table shows the first 128 characters of the Unicode (ASCII) character set.

	ASCII									
	0	1	2	3	4	5	6	7	8	9
0	NUL	SOH	STX	ETX	EOT	ENQ	ACK	BEL	BS	HT
1	LF	VT	FF	CR	SO	SI	DLE	DC1	DC2	DC3
2	DC4	NAK	SYN	ETB	CAN	EM	SUB	ESC	FS	GS
3	RS	US	b	!	"	#	$	%	&	'
4	(	)	*	+	,	-	.	/	0	1
5	2	3	4	5	6	7	8	9	:	;
6	<	=	>	?	@	A	B	C	D	E
7	F	G	H	I	J	K	L	M	N	O
8	P	Q	R	S	T	U	V	W	X	Y
9	Z	[	\	]	^	_	`	a	b	c
10	d	e	f	g	h	i	j	k	l	m
11	n	o	p	q	r	s	t	u	v	w
12	x	y	z	{	|	}	~	DEL		

The numbers 0–12 in the first column specify the left digit(s) and the numbers 0–9 at the head of the remaining columns specify the right digit of each character in the ASCII data set. For example, the character in the row marked 6 (the number in the leftmost) and the column marked 5 (the number in the second row) is A. Therefore, the character at position 65 (which is the 66th character) is A. The character **b** at position 32 represents the blank character.

For more information on Unicode/ASCII character set, visit the *http://www.unicode.org* Web site.

The first 32 characters, that is, the characters at positions 00–31 and at position 127, are non-printable characters. The previous table shows the abbreviations of these characters. The meaning of these abbreviations is as follows:

NUL	Null character	VT	Vertical tab	SYN	Synchronous idle
SOH	Start of header	FF	Form feed	ETB	End of transmitted block
STX	Start of text	CR	Carriage return	CAN	Cancel
ETX	End of text	SO	Shift out	EM	End of medium
EOT	End of transmission	SI	Shift in	SUB	Substitute
ENQ	Enquiry	DLE	Data link escape	ESC	Escape
ACK	Acknowledge	DC1	Device control 1	FS	File separator
BEL	Bell character (beep)	DC2	Device control 2	GS	Group separator
BS	Back Space	DC3	Device control 3	RS	Record separator
HT	Horizontal tab	DC4	Device control 4	US	Unit separator
LF	Line feed	NAK	Negative acknowledge	DEL	Delete

EBCDIC (Extended Binary Coded Decimal Interchange Code)

The following table shows some of the characters of the EBCDIC character set.

EBCDIC										
	0	1	2	3	4	5	6	7	8	9
6					b̲					
7						.	<	(	+	|
8	&									
9	!	$	*	)	;	¬	-	/		
10							^	,	%	_
11	>	?								
12		`	:	#	@	`	=	"		a
13	b	c	d	e	f	g	h	i		
14						j	k	l	m	n
15	o	p	q	r						
16		~	s	t	u	v	w	x	y	z
17								\	{	}
18	[	]								
19				A	B	C	D	E	F	G
20	H	I								J
21	K	L	M	N	O	P	Q	R		
22							S	T	U	V
23	W	X	Y	Z						
24	0	1	2	3	4	5	6	7	8	9

The numbers 6–24 in the first column specify the left digit(s) and the numbers 0–9 at the head of the remaining columns specify the right digit of the characters in the EBCDIC data set. For example, the character in the row marked 19 (the number in the first column) and column marked 3 (the number in the second row) is A. Therefore, the character at position 193 (which is the 194th character) is A. The character b̲ at position 64 represents the blank character. The preceding table does not show all characters in the EBCDIC character set. In fact, the characters at positions 00–63 and 250–255 are nonprintable control characters.

D

PACKAGES AND
USER-DEFINED CLASSES

Chapter 7 discusses user-defined methods, in particular methods with parameters. As explained in Chapter 3, there are two types of variables in Java—primitive and reference. The program in Example 7-7 illustrates if a formal parameter is of the primitive type and the corresponding actual parameter is a variable, then the formal parameter cannot change the value of the actual parameter. In other words, changing the value of a formal parameter of a primitive data type has no effect on the actual parameter. However, if a formal parameter is a reference variable, then both the actual and the formal parameter refer to the same object. That is, only formal parameters that are reference variables are capable of passing values outside the function.

Java provides classes corresponding to each primitive data type, so values of primitive data types can be considered objects. For example, you can use the `class Integer` to treat `int` values as objects, `class Double` to treat `double` values as objects, and so on. These classes, called wrapper classes, were described in Chapter 6.

As discussed in Chapter 3, even though you can use the wrapper `class Integer` to treat `int` values as objects, the `class Integer` does not provide any method to change the value of an existing `Integer` object. The same is true for other wrapper classes. In Chapter 6, we introduced the `class IntClass` so that values of the `int` type can be wrapped in an object. The `class IntClass` also provides methods to change the value of an `IntClass` object. We use reference variables of the `IntClass` type to pass `int` values outside a method.

In addition to the `class IntClass`, we created the `class DoubleClass` to treat values of the type `double` as objects, the `class CharClass` to treat values of the type `char` as objects, and so on. In the next section, we give the complete definition of these classes and explain how to use these classes.

PRIMITIVETYPE CLASSES

This section gives the definitions of the `classes IntClass`, `LongClass`, `CharClass`, `FloatClass`, `DoubleClass`, and `BooleanClass` that we introduced in Chapter 6.

Class: `IntClass`

```java
public class IntClass
{
    private int x;     //variable to store the number

        //default constructor
        //Postcondition: x = 0
    public IntClass()
    {
        x = 0;
    }
        //constructor with parameter
        //Postcondition: x = num
    public IntClass(int num)
    {
        x = num;
    }

        //Method to set the data member x
        //Postcondition: x = num
    public void setNum(int num)
    {
        x = num;
    }

        //Method to return the value of x
        //Postcondition: The value of x is returned
    public int getNum()
    {
        return x;
    }

        //Method to update the value of x by adding
        //the value of num
        //Postcondition:x = x + num;
    public void addToNum(int num)
    {
        x = x + num;
    }
```

```
    //Method to update the value of x by multiplying
    //the value of x by num
    //Postcondition: x = x * num;
public void multiplyToNum(int num)
{
    x = x * num;
}

    //Method to compare the value of x with the value of num
    //Postcondition: Returns a value < 0 if x < num
    //               Returns 0 if x == num
    //               Returns a value > 0 if x > num
public int compareTo(int num)
{
    return (x - num);
}

    //Method to compare x with num for equality
    //Postcondition: Returns true if x == num;
    //               otherwise it returns false
public boolean equals(int num)
{
    if(x == num)
        return true;
    else
        return false;
}

    //Method to return the value of x as a string
public String toString()
{
    return (String.valueOf(x));
}
}
```

Consider the following statements:

```
IntClass firstNum = new IntClass();        //Line 1
IntClass secondNum = new IntClass(5);      //Line 2
int num;                                   //Line 3
```

The statement in Line 1 creates the object **firstNum** and initializes it to **0**. The statement in Line 2 creates the object **secondNum** and initializes it to **5**. The statement in Line 3 declares **num** to be an **int** variable. Now consider the following statements:

```
firstNum.setNum(24);                       //Line 4
secondNum.addToNum(6);                     //Line 5
num = firstNum.getNum();                   //Line 6
```

The statement in Line 4 sets the value of `firstNum` (in fact, the value of the data member `x` of `firstNum`) to 24. The statement in Line 5 updates the value of `secondNum` to 11 (the previous value 5 is updated by adding 6 to it.) The statement in Line 6 retrieves the value of the object `firstNum`, (the value of the data member `x`), and assigns it to `num`. After this statement executes, the value of `num` is 24.

The following statements output the values of `firstNum` and `secondNum` (in fact, the values of their data members).

```
System.out.println("firstNum = " + firstNum);
System.out.println("secondNum = " + secondNum);
```

The following table shows how variables of `int` type and the corresponding reference variables of `IntClass` type work.

	int	IntClass

Declaration without or with initialization	`int x, y = 5;`	`IntClass x, y;`
		`x = new IntClass();`
		`y = new IntClass(5);`

Assignment	`x = 24;`	`x.setNum(24);`
	`y = x;`	`y.setNum(x.getNum());`
Addition	`x = x + 10;` `x = x + y;`	`x.addToNum(10);` `x.addToNum(y.getNum());`
Multiplication	`x = x * 10;` `x = x * y;`	`x.multiplyToNum(10);` `x.multiplyToNum(y.getNum());`
Comparison	`if(x < 10)` `if(x < y)`	`if(x.compareTo(10) < 0)` `if(x.compareTo(y.getNum()) < 0)`
	`if(x <= 10)` `if(x <= y)`	`if(x.compareTo(10) <= 0)` `if(x.compareTo(y.getNum()) <= 0)`

	`if(x == 10)`
	`if(x == y)`
		`if(x.compareTo(10) == 0)`
		`if(x.compareTo(y.getNum()) == 0)`
		or
		`if(x.equals(10))`
		`if(x.equals(y.getNum()))`

	`if(x > 10)` `if(x > y)`	`if(x.compareTo(10) > 0)` `if(x.compareTo(y.getNum()) > 0)`
	`if(x >= 10)` `if(x >= y)`	`if(x.compareTo(10) >= 0)` `if(x.compareTo(y.getNum()) >= 0)`

	`if(x != 10)`
	`if(x != y)`
		`if(x.compareTo(10) != 0)`
		`if(x.compareTo(y.getNum()) != 0)`
		or
		`if(!x.equals(10))`
		`if(!x.equals(y.getNum()))`

Output	`System.out.println(x);`	`System.out.println(x);`

Class: LongClass

```
public class LongClass
{
    private long x;

    public LongClass()
    {
        x = 0;
    }

    public LongClass(long num)
    {
        x = num;
    }

    public void setNum(long num)
    {
        x = num;
    }

    public long getNum()
    {
        return x;
    }

    public void addToNum(long num)
    {
        x = x + num;
    }

    public void multiplyToNum(long num)
    {
        x = x * num;
    }

    public long compareTo(long num)
    {
        return (x - num);
    }

    public boolean equals(long num)
    {
        if(x == num)
            return true;
        else
            return false;
    }
```

```
    public String toString()
    {
        return (String.valueOf(x));
    }
}
```

Class: CharClass

```
public class CharClass
{
    private char ch;

    public CharClass()
    {
        ch = ' ';
    }

    public CharClass(char c)
    {
        ch = c;
    }

    public void setChar(char c)
    {
        ch = c;
    }

    public int getChar()
    {
        return ch;
    }

    public char nextChar()
    {
        return (char)((int)ch + 1);
    }

    public char prevChar()
    {
        return (char)((int)ch - 1);
    }

    public String toString()
    {
        return (String.valueOf(ch));
    }
}
```

Class: FloatClass

```
public class FloatClass
{
    private float x;

    public FloatClass()
    {
        x = 0;
    }

    public FloatClass(float num)
    {
        x = num;
    }

    public void setNum(float num)
    {
        x = num;
    }

    public float getNum()
    {
        return x;
    }

    public void addToNum(float num)
    {
        x = x + num;
    }

    public void multiplyToNum(float num)
    {
        x = x * num;
    }

    public float compareTo(float num)
    {
        return (x - num);
    }

    public boolean equals(float num)
    {
        if(x == num)
            return true;
        else
            return false;
    }
```

D

```
    public String toString()
    {
        return (String.valueOf(x));
    }
}
```

Class: DoubleClass

```
public class DoubleClass
{
    private double x;

    public DoubleClass()
    {
        x = 0;
    }

    public DoubleClass(double num)
    {
        x = num;
    }

    public void setNum(double num)
    {
        x = num;
    }

    public double getNum()
    {
        return x;
    }

    public void addToNum(double num)
    {
        x = x + num;
    }

    public void multiplyToNum(double num)
    {
        x = x * num;
    }

    public double compareTo(double num)
    {
        return (x - num);
    }
```

```java
    public boolean equals(double num)
    {
        if(x == num)
            return true;
        else
            return false;
    }

    public String toString()
    {
        return (String.valueOf(x));
    }
}
```

Class: `BooleanClass`

```java
public class BooleanClass
{
    private boolean flag;

    public BooleanClass()
    {
        flag = false;
    }

    public BooleanClass(boolean f)
    {
        flag = f;
    }

    public boolean get()
    {
        return flag;
    }

    public void set(boolean f)
    {
        flag = f;
    }

    public String toString()
    {
        return (String.valueOf(flag));
    }

}
```

Using PrimitiveType Classes in a Program

This section describes how to use the classes introduced in the previous section.

There are two ways to use the **class IntClass** provided by the text. One way to use this class is to first create a package and put this class in that package. For example, you can create the package:

`jpfpatpd.ch07.primitiveTypeClasses`

and put the class in this package.

In this case, you place the statement

`package jpfpatpd.ch07.primitiveTypeClasses;`

before the definition of the **class IntClass**.

The definition of the **class IntClass** is in the file **IntClass.java**. We need to compile this file and place this in the directory:

`jpfpatpd.ch07.primitiveTypeClasses`

To do so, we issue the following command at the command line:

`javac -d c:\j2sdk1.4.0-rc\jre\lib IntClass.java`

The **class IntClass** is now placed in the appropriate subdirectory of **j2sdk1.4.0-rc**.

 On our computer, we placed JDK in the directory `C:\j2sdk1.4.0.-rc`.

You can now import this class in a program using the **import** statement. For example, you can use either of the following statements to use the **class IntClass** in your program:

`import jpfpatpd.ch07.primitiveTypeClasses.*;`

or

`import jpfpatpd.ch07.primitiveTypeClasses.IntClass;`

The second way to use primitive type classes in a program is to keep the file **IntClass.java** and the program in the same directory. Remove the **package** command

`package jpfpatpd.ch07.primitiveTypeClasses;`

before the definition of the **class IntClass**.

First compile the file **IntClass.java** and then compile the program. In this case, you add the following statements in the **autoexec.bat** file.

```
SET PATH = %PATH%;c:\j2sdk1.4.0-rc\bin;
SET CLASSPATH =.; c:\j2sdk1.4.0-rc\jre\lib;
```

Using a Software Development Kit (SDK)

If you are using an SDK such as CodeWarrior, Forte for Java, or J++ Builder, then you can place the file containing the definition of the class in the same directory that contains your program. You do not need to create any package. However, you can also create a package using the SDK. In this case, place the appropriate `package` statement before the definition of the class and use the compile command provided by the SDK. (In most cases, you do not need to specify any subdirectory.) The compiled file will be placed in the appropriate directory. You can now import the class without adding it to the project.

 If you have created a package for your classes, to avoid compilation errors, do not add the file containing the definition of the class to the project.

APPENDIX

E

Java Classes

This appendix describes various Java classes and some of their commonly used members that are used or mentioned in this text. For a detailed description of all Java classes, visit the Web site *http://java.sun.com*.

Class: Boolean (Package `java.lang`)

Constructors

```
public Boolean(boolean param)
  //Creates an object initialized with the value specified
  //by param
public Boolean(String str)
  //Creates a Boolean object initialized to true if the string
  //specified by str is not null and is equal, ignoring case,
  //to the string "true".
```

Methods

```
public boolean booleanValue()
  //Return true if the value of the object is true;
  //otherwise it returns false.
public int hashCode()
  //Returns the hash code of this object.
public String toString()
  //If the state of the object is true, returns the String
  //object with the value "true"; Otherwise returns the String
  //object with the value "false".
public static Boolean valueOf(String str)
  //Returns a Boolean object initialized to the value
  //specified by str.
```

Class: BorderLayout (Package `java.awt`)

Constructors

```
public BorderLayout()
  //Creates a border layout with 0 horizontal
  //and 0 vertical gaps between components.
```

```
public BorderLayout(int hgap, int vgap)
  //Creates a border layout with the specified
  //horizontal and vertical gaps between components.
  //The horizontal gap is specified by hgap
  //and the vertical gap is specified by vgap.
```

Methods

```
public int getHgap()
  //Returns the horizontal gap between components.
public void setHgap(int hgap)
  //Sets the horizontal gap between components.
public int getVgap()
  //Returns the vertical gap between components.
public void setVgap(int vgap)
  //Sets the vertical gap between components.
```

Class: BufferedReader (Package java.io)

Constructors

```
public BufferedReader(Reader rd)
  //Creates a BufferedReader object. The object is initialized
  //using rd.
public BufferedReader(Reader rd, int size)
  //Creates a BufferedReader object. The object is initialized
  //using rd and to the size specified by size. The default size
  //is 8192 characters.
```

Methods

```
public void close() throws IOException
  //Closes the BufferedReader object.
public int read() throws IOException
  //Returns a single character as an int from the
  //BufferedReader stream. Returns -1 if the end of stream
  //is reached.
public String readLine() throws IOException
  //Returns a line of character as a string.
  //The line of characters ends with \r, \n, or \r\n.
  //Returns null if the end of stream is reached.
public boolean ready() throws IOException
  //Returns true if the object is read to be read. If the object
  //is nonempty, the state is true.
public void reset() throws IOException
  //Resets the BufferedReader object.
```

```
public long skip(long num) throws IOException
    //Skips the next number of characters specified by num. The
    //number of characters skipped are returned.
```

CLASS: Character (PACKAGE java.lang)

Constructors

```
public Character(char ch)
    //Creates an object with value specified by ch.
```

E

Methods

```
public static int digit(char ch, int base)
    //Returns the numeric value of ch in radix base
    //specified by base
public static int forDigit(int digit, int base)
    //Returns the numeric value of digit in radix base
    //specified by base
public boolean equals(Object obj)
    //Returns true if this object is equal to the object
    //specified by obj; otherwise it returns false
public static int getNumericValue(char ch)
    //Returns the Unicode representation, as a nonnegative integer
    //of the character specified by ch. If ch has no
    //numeric representation -1 is returned; If ch cannot be
    //represented as a nonnegative integer -2 is returned.
public int hashCode()
    //Returns the hash code of this object.
public static boolean isDigit(char ch)
    //Returns true if ch is a digit; false otherwise.
public static boolean isLetter(char ch)
    //Returns true if ch is a letter; false otherwise.
public static boolean isLowerCase(char ch)
    //Returns true if ch is a lowercase letter; false otherwise.
public static boolean isUpperCase(char ch)
    //Returns true if ch is an uppercase letter; false otherwise.
public static boolean isSpaceChar(char ch)
    //Returns true if ch is the space character; false otherwise.
public static boolean isWhitespace(char ch)
    //Returns true if ch is a white space character;
    //false otherwise.
public static char toLowerCase(char ch)
    //Returns the character that is the lowercase equivalent of ch.
    //If ch does not have a corresponding lowercase letter,
    //it returns ch.
```

```
public static char toUpperCase(char ch)
  //Returns the character that is the uppercase equivalent of ch.
  //If ch does not have a corresponding uppercase letter,
  //it returns ch.
public String toString()
  //Returns a string representation of the object.
```

CLASS: Color (PACKAGE java.awt)

Named Constants

```
public static final Color black =   new Color(0,0,0);
public static final Color blue =   new Color(0,0,255);
public static final Color cyan =   new Color(0,255,255);
public static final Color darkGray =   new Color(64,64,64);
public static final Color gray =   new Color(128,128,128);
public static final Color green =   new Color(0,255,0);
public static final Color lightGray =   new Color(192,192,192);
public static final Color magenta =   new Color(255,0,255);
public static final Color orange =   new Color(255,200,0);
public static final Color pink =   new Color(255,175,175);
public static final Color red =   new Color(255,0,0);
public static final Color white =   new Color (255,255,255);
public static final Color yellow =   new Color(255,255,0);
```

Constructors

```
public Color(int r, int g, int b)
  //Creates an instance of Color with red value r, green value g,
  //and blue value b. In this case, r, g, and b can be
  //between 0 and 255.
public Color(int rgb)
  //Creates an instance of Color with red value r, green
  //value g, and blue value b, choose rgb as
  //r * 65536 + g * 256 + b. In this case, r, g, and b
  //can be between 0 and 255.
public Color(float r, float g, float b)
  //Creates an instance of Color with red value r, green value g,
  //and blue value b. In this case, r, g, and b can be between 0
  //and 1.0.
```

Methods

```
public Color brighter()
  //Returns a Color that is brighter
public Color darker()
  //Returns a Color that is darker
```

```
public boolean equals(Object o)
   //Checks whether Color objects have identical RGB values
public int getBlue()
   //Returns the value of the blue component
public static Color getColor(String str)
   //Returns the color specified by str. The string specified by
   //str contains an int value.
public static Color getColor(String str, Color cl)
   //Returns the color specified by str. The string specified by
   //str contains an int value. If the color cannot be
   //determined, the color cl is returned.
public static Color getColor(String str, int cl)
   //Returns the color specified by str. The string specified by
   //str contains an int value. If the color cannot be
   //determined, the color cl is returned.
public int getGreen()
   //Returns the value of the green component
public int getRGB()
   //Returns the RGB value. RGB value is r * 65536 + g * 256 + b
public int getRed()
   //Returns the value of the red component
public static  Color getColor(String nm)
   //Finds a color in the system properties.
public String toString()
   //Returns a String with information about the color
```

CLASS: Component (PACKAGE java.awt)

Constructors

```
protected Component()
   //Creates a new instance of a component
```

Methods

```
public String getName()
   //Returns the name of the component.
public void setName(String name)
   //Sets the name of the component.
public Container getParent()
   //Returns the parent of this component.
public boolean isValid()
   //Returns true if this component is valid.
   //A component is valid if it is correctly sized and placed
   //within its parent container and all its children are also
   //valid.
```

```
public boolean isDisplayable()
  //Returns true if this component is displayable.
public boolean isVisible()
  //Returns true if this component is visible.
public void setVisible(boolean tog)
  //If tog is true, sets the component to visible;
  //If tog is false, the component is not shown.
public boolean isShowing()
  //Returns true if this component is showing on screen.
public boolean isEnabled()
  //Returns true if this component is enabled.
public void setEnabled(boolean b)
  //Component is enabled if b is true.
  //Component is disabled if b is false.
public Color getBackground()
  //Returns the background color of this component
public Color getForeground()
  //Returns the foreground color of this component.
public void setBackground(Color c)
  //Sets the background color of this component to color c.
public void setForeground(Color c)
  //Sets the foreground color of this component to color c.
public Font getFont()
  //Returns the font of this component.
public void setFont(Font ft)
  //Sets the font of this component to ft.
public void setSize(int w, int h)
  //Sets the size of this component.
public boolean isVisible()
  //Returns true if the component is visible.
public void setVisible(boolean tog)
  //If tog is true, sets the component to visible;
  //If tog is false, the component is not shown.
public void paint(Graphics g)
  //Paints the component with the graphic component specified by g.
public void repaint()
  //Repaints the component.
public void repaint(int x, int y, int wid, int ht)
  //Repaints the rectangular portion of the component from (x, y) to
  //(x + wid, y + ht)
public void setLocation(int x, int y)
  //Sets the component at the location (x, y).
public String toString()
  //Returns a string representation of this component.
public void update(Graphics g)
  //Invokes the paint method.
public void validate()
  //Validates this container and all of its subcomponents. The
  //method validate is used to cause a container to lay out its
```

```
//subcomponents once more. Typically called after the components
//it contains have been added to or modified.
public void addFocusListener(FocusListener lis)
  //Adds the focus listener specified by lis.
public void addKeyListener(KeyListener lis)
  //Adds the key listener specified by lis.
public void addMouseListener(MouseListener lis)
  //Adds the mouse listener specified by lis.
public void addMouseMotionListener(MouseMotionListener lis)
  //Adds the mouse motion listener specified by lis.
public void removeFocusListener(FocusListener lis)
  //Removes the focus listener specified by lis.
public void removeKeyListener(KeyListener lis)
  //Removes the key listener specified by lis.
public void removeMouseListener(MouseListener lis)
  //Removes the mouse listener specified by lis.
public void removeMouseMotionListener(MouseMotionListener lis)
  //Removes the mouse motion listener specified by lis.
```

E

CLASS: Container (PACKAGE java.awt)

Constructor

```
public Container()
//Creates a new Container.
```

Methods

```
public void add(Object obj)
  //Method to add an object to the pane.
public Component add(Component comp)
  //Appends the specified component to the end of this container.
public Component add(Component comp, int index)
  //Adds the specified component to this container at the
  //given position.
public void setLayout(LayoutManager ob)
  //Method to set the layout of the pane.
public LayoutManager getLayout()
  //Returns the layout manager for this container.
public void setFont(Font ft)
  //Sets the font of this component to ft.
public void validate()
  //Validates this container and all of its subcomponents. The
  //method validate is used to cause a container to lay out its
  //subcomponents once more. Typically called after the
  //components it contains have been added to or modified.
```

```
public void remove(int index)
    //Removes the specified component from the container.
public void remove(Component comp)
    //Removes the specified component from this container.
public void removeAll()
    //Removes every component from this container.
public void paint(Graphics g)
    //Paints the container.
public void update(Graphics g)
    //Updates the container.
```

CLASS: DecimalFormat (PACKAGE java.text)

Constructors

```
public DecimalFormat()
    //Creates an object with default pattern.
public DecimalFormat(String str)
    //Creates an object with the pattern specified by str.
public DecimalFormat(String str, DecimalFormatSymbols symbols)
    //Creates an object with the pattern specified by symbols.
```

Methods

```
public void applyPattern(String str)
    //Sets the pattern of the object.
public String toPattern()
    //Returns the pattern of the object as a string.
public object clone()
    //Returns a copy of the object.
public boolean equals(Object obj)
    //Returns true if this object is equal to the object
    //specified by obj; otherwise returns false.
public String format(double num)
    //Returns a string containing the formatted num.
public String format(long num)
    //Returns a string containing the formatted num.
public DecimalFormatSymbols getDecimalFormatSymbols()
    //Returns the decimal number format symbols of the object.
public void setDecimalFormatSymbols(DecimalFormatSymbols symbols)
    //Sets the decimal number format symbols of this object.
public int hashCode()
    //Returns the hash code of the object.
```

CLASS: Double (PACKAGE java.lang)

Named Constants

```
public static final double MAX_VALUE = 1.7976931348623157E308;
public static final double MIN_VALUE = 4.9E-324;

public static final double NEGATIVE_INFINITY = -1.0/0.0;
public static final double POSITIVE_INFINITY = 1.0/0.0;
```

Constructors

```
public Double(double num)
   //Creates an object initialized to the value specified
   //by num.
public Double(String str) throws NumberFormatException
   //Creates an object initialized to the value specified
   //by the num contained in str.
```

Methods

```
public byte byteValue()
   //Returns the value of the object as a byte value.
public short shortValue()
   //Returns the value of the object as a short value.
public int intValue()
   //Returns the value of the object as an int value.
public long longValue()
   //Returns the value of the object as a long value.
public double doubleValue()
   //Returns the value of the object as a double value.
public float floatValue()
   //Returns the value of the object as a float value.
public int hashCode()
   //Returns the hash code of the object.
public boolean equals(Object obj)
   //Returns true if the value of this object is equal
   //to the value of the object specified by obj;
   //otherwise returns false.
public boolean isInfinity()
   //Returns true if the value of this object is positive
   //or negative infinity; otherwise returns false.
public static boolean isInfinity(double num)
   //Returns true if the value of num is positive
   //or negative infinity; otherwise returns false.
public static double parseDouble(String str) throws
                                       NumberFormatException
   //Returns the value of the number contained in str.
```

E

```
public String toString()
   //Returns the double value, of the object, as a string.
public static String toString(double num)
   //Returns the value of num as a string.
public static Double valueOf(String str) throws
                                        NumberFormatException
   //Returns a Double object initialized to the value
   //specified by str.
```

Class: Exception (Package java.lang)

Constructors

```
public Exception()
   //Creates a new instance of the class Exception.
public Exception(String str)
   //Creates a new instance of the class Exception. The
   //parameter str specifies the message string.
```

Class: FileReader (Package java.io)

Constructors

```
public FileReader(FileDescriptor fd)
                  throws FileNotFoundException
   //Creates a FileReader object from a file descriptor.
public FileReader(String fileName) throws FileNotFoundException
   //Creates a FileReader object from a file name.
```

Methods

```
public void close() throws IOException
   //Closes the FileReader.
public int read() throws IOException
   //Returns a single character as an int from the FileReader.
   //Returns -1 if the end of stream is reached.
public boolean ready() throws IOException
   //Returns true if the object is ready to be read. If the
   //object is nonempty, the state is true.
public void reset() throws IOException
   //Resets the object.
```

CLASS: FileWriter (PACKAGE java.io)

Constructors

```
public FileWriter(String fileName) throws IOException
  //Creates a FileWriter object from a filename.
public FileWriter(String fileName, boolean a)
                                    throws IOException
  //Creates a FileWriter object from a filename.
  //The boolean a indicating whether or not to append to
  //the file.
public FileWriter(FileDescriptor fd)
  //Creates a FileWriter object from a file descriptor.
```

Methods

```
public String getEncoding()
  //Returns the name of the character encoding being used.
public void write(int c) throws IOException
  //Writes a single character.
public void write(char[] cbuf, int off, int len)
                                throws IOException
  //Writes a part of an array of characters.
public void write(String str, int off, int len)
                                throws IOException
  //Writes a part of a string.
public void flush() throws IOException
  //Empty the stream.
public void close() throws IOException
  //Closes the stream.
```

CLASS: Float (PACKAGE java.lang)

Named Constants

```
public static final float MAX_VALUE = 3.4028235E38;
public static final float MIN_VALUE = 1.4E-45;

public static final float NEGATIVE_INFINITY = -1.0f/0.0f;
public static final float POSITIVE_INFINITY = 1.0f/0.0f;
```

Constructors

```
public Float(float num)
  //Creates an object initialized to the value specified
  //by num.
```

```
public Float(double num)
  //Creates an object initialized to the value specified
  //by num.
public Float(String str) throws NumberFormatException
  //Creates an object initialized to the value specified
  //by the num contained in str.
```

Methods

```
public byte byteValue()
  //Returns the value of the object as a byte value.
public short shortValue()
  //Returns the value of the object as a short value.
public int intValue()
  //Returns the value of the object as an int value.
public long longValue()
  //Returns the value of the object as a long value.
public double doubleValue()
  //Returns the value of the object as a double value.
public float floatValue()
  //Returns the value of the object as a float value.
public int hashCode()
  //Returns the hash code of the object.
public boolean equals(Object obj)
  //Returns true if the value of this object is equal
  //to the value of the object specified by obj;
  //otherwise returns false.
public boolean isInfinity()
  //Returns true if the value of this object is positive
  //or negative infinity; otherwise returns false.
public static boolean isInfinity(float num)
  //Returns true if the value of num is positive
  //or negative infinity; otherwise returns false.
public static float parseFloat(String str) throws
                                     NumberFormatException
  //Returns the value of the number contained in str.
public String toString()
  //Returns the float value, of the object, as a string
public static String toString(float num)
  //Returns the value of num as a string
public static Float valueOf(String str) throws
                                     NumberFormatException
  //Returns a Float object initialized to the value
  //specified by str.
```

CLASS: FlowLayout (PACKAGE java.awt)

Constructors

```
public FlowLayout()
  //Creates a flow layout with a centered alignment.
  //Both vertical and horizontal gaps are set as
  //5 units (default).
public FlowLayout(int alignment)
  //Creates a flow layout with the specified alignment.
  //Both vertical and horizontal gaps are set as
  //5 units (default).
  //The possible values of the alignment argument are
  //FlowLayout.LEFT, FlowLayout.RIGHT, or FlowLayout.CENTER.
public FlowLayout(int alignment, int hgap, int vgap)
  //Creates a flow layout with the specified alignment
  //and the given horizontal and vertical gaps.
  //The possible values of the alignment argument are
  //FlowLayout.LEFT, FlowLayout.RIGHT, or FlowLayout.CENTER.
```

Methods

```
public int getAlignment()
  //Gets the alignment. Possible values are
  //FlowLayout.LEFT, FlowLayout.RIGHT, FlowLayout.CENTER,
  //FlowLayout.LEADING, or FlowLayout.TRAILING.
public void setAlignment(int alignment)
  //Sets the alignment. Possible values are
  //FlowLayout.LEFT, FlowLayout.RIGHT, FlowLayout.CENTER,
  //FlowLayout.LEADING, or FlowLayout.TRAILING.
public int getHgap()
  //Gets the horizontal gap between components.
public void setHgap(int hgap)
  //Sets the horizontal gap between components.
public int getVgap()
  //Gets the vertical gap between components.
public void setVgap(int vgap)
  //Sets the vertical gap between components.
```

CLASS: Font (PACKAGE java.awt)

Named Constants

```
int PLAIN: 0
int BOLD: 1
int ITALIC: 2
```

Constructors

```
public Font(String name, int style, int size)
  //Creates a new Font from the specified name, style,
  //and point size.
```

Methods

```
public String getFamily()
  //Returns the family name of this font.
public String getFontName()
  //Returns the font face name of this font.
public static Font getFont(Map attributes)
  //Returns a Font appropriate to this attribute set.
public static Font createFont(int fontFormat,
                              InputStream fontStream)
                   throws FontFormatException,
                          IOException
  //Creates a new Font with the specified font type and
  //input data.
public String getPSName()
  //Returns the Postscript name of this font.
public String getName()
  //Returns the logical name of this font.
public int getStyle()
  //Returns the style of this font.
  //The possible values are: PLAIN, BOLD, ITALIC,
  //or BOLD+ITALIC.
public int getSize()
  //Returns the point size of this font.
public boolean isPlain()
  //Returns true if font style is PLAIN; false otherwise.
public boolean isBold()
  //Returns true if font style is BOLD; false otherwise.
public boolean isItalic()
  //Returns true if font style is ITALIC; false otherwise.
public static Font getFont(String nm)
  //Returns a Font object from the system properties list.
public static Font getFont(String nm, Font font)
  //Gets the specified font from the system properties list.
```

Class: Graphics (Package java.awt)

Constructors

```
protected Graphics()
  //Constructs a Graphics object that defines a context in which
  //user can draw. This constructor can not be called directly.
```

Methods

public abstract void **clearRect**(int x, int y, int w, int h)
  //Draws a rectangle with no fill pattern in the current
  //background color at position (x, y) having a width w and
  //height h.
public abstract void **clipRect**(int x, int y, int w, int h)
  //Sets a clipping rectangle area at position (x, y) of
  //width w and height h.
public abstract void **copyArea**(int x, int y, int w, int h,
                                  int newx, int newy)
  //Copies rectangular area at (x, y) with width w and
  //height h to new position (newx, newy).
public abstract Graphics **create**()
  //Returns a copy of the entire graphics context.
public abstract Graphics **create**(int x, int y, int w, int h)
  //Returns a copy of the rectangular graphics context at
  //position (x, y) having width w and height h to
  //new position (newx, newy).
public abstract void **dispose**()
  //Draws a rectangle with no fill pattern in the current
  //background color at position (x, y) having a width w and
  //height h.
public void **draw3Rect**(int x, int y, int w, int h, boolean t)
  //Draws a 3D rectangle at (x, y) with width w, height h. If t is
  //true, rectangle will appear raised.
public abstract void **drawArc**(int x, int y, int w, int h,
                                 int sangle, int aangle)
  //Draws an arc starting at position (x, y) having a width w and
  //height h, starting at angle sangle with an arc angle aangle.
  //Both angles are measured in degrees.
public void **drawBytes**(byte[] str, int i, int n, int x, int y)
  //Draws n bytes of array str, starting with array index i, n
  //characters, at (x, y).
public void **drawChars**(char[] str, int i, int n, int x, int y)
  //Draws n characters of array str, starting with array index i,
  //n characters, at (x, y).
public abstract boolean **drawImage**(Image img, int x, int y,
                                       Color c, ImageObserver ob)
  //Draws the image specified by img at (x, y). Any transparent
  //color pixels are drawn in color c, and ob monitors the
  //progress of the image.
public abstract boolean **drawImage**(Image img, int x, int y,
                                       ImageObserver ob)
  //Draws the image specified by img at (x, y). The ob monitors
  //the progress of the image.

```
public abstract boolean drawImage(Image img, int x, int w, int h,
                                  int y, Color c, ImageObserver ob)
   //Draws the image specified by img at (x, y) having width w and
   //height h. Any transparent color pixels are drawn in color c,
   //and ob monitors the progress of the image.
public abstract boolean drawImage(Image img, int x, int w, int h,
                                  int y, ImageObserver ob)
   //Draws the image specified by img at (x, y) having width w and
   //height h. The ob monitors the progress of the image.
public abstract boolean drawImage(Image img, int xs1, int ys1,
                     int xs2, int ys2, int xd1, int yd1,
                     int xd2, int yd2, Color c, ImageObserver ob)
   //Draws the image specified by img from the area defined by
   //bounding rectangle, (xs1, ys1) to (xs2, ys2) in the area
   //defined by the rectangle (xd1, yd1) to (xd2, yd2). Any
   //transparent color pixels are drawn in color c.
   //The ob monitors the progress of the image.
public abstract boolean drawImage(Image img, int xs1, int ys1,
                        int xs2, int ys2, int xd1, int yd1,
                        int xd2, int yd2, ImageObserver ob)
   //Draws the image specified by img from the area defined by
   //bounding rectangle, (xs1, ys1) to (xs2, ys2) in the area
   //defined by the rectangle (xd1, yd1) to (xd2, yd2). The ob
   //monitors the progress of the image.
public abstract void drawLine(int xs, int ys, int xd, int yd)
   //Draws a line from (xs, ys) to (xd, yd).
public abstract void drawOval(int x, int y, int w, int h)
   //Draws an oval at position (x, y) of width w and height h.
public abstract void drawPolygon(int[] x, int[] y, int num)
   //Draws a polygon with points (x[0], y[0]), ...,
   //(x[num-1], y[num-1]). Here num is the number of points in
   //the polygon.
public abstract void drawPolygon(Polygon poly)
   //Draws a polygon as defined by the object poly.
public abstract void drawRect(int x, int y, int w, int h)
   //Draws a rectangle at position (x, y) having a width w and
   //height h.
public abstract void drawRoundRect(int x, int y, int w, int h,
                                   int arcw, int arch)
   //Draws a round-cornered rectangle at position (x, y)
   //having a width w and height h. The shape of the rounded
   //corners are determined by arc with width arcw and
   //height arch.
public abstract void drawString(String s, int x, int y)
   //Draws the string s at (x, y).
public void fill3Rect(int x, int y, int w, int h, boolean t)
   //Draws a 3D filled rectangle at (x, y) with width w,
   //height h. If t is true, rectangle will appear raised.
   //The rectangle is filled with current color.
```

```
public abstract void fillArc(int x, int y, int w, int h,
                             int sangle, int aangle)
  //Draws a filled arc starting at position (x, y) having a
  //width w and height h. The starting at angle sangle with
  //an arc angle aangle. Both angles are measured in degrees.
  //The arc is filled with current color.
public abstract void fillOval(int x, int y, int w, int h)
  //Draws a filled oval at position (x, y) having a width w and
  //height h. The oval is filled with current color.
public abstract void fillPolygon(int[] x, int[] y, int num)
  //Draws a filled polygon with points (x[0], y[0]), ...,
  //(x[num-1], y[num-1]). Here num is the number of points in
  //the polygon. The polygon is filled with current color.
public abstract void fillPolygon(Polygon poly)
  //Draws a filled polygon as defined the by object poly.
  //The polygon is filled with current color.
public abstract void fillRect(int x, int y, int w, int h)
  //Draws a filled rectangle at position (x, y) having a
  //width w and height h. The rectangle is filled with
  //current color.
public abstract void fillRoundRect(int x, int y, int w, int h,
                                   int arcw, int arch)
  //Draws a filled round-cornered rectangle at position (x, y)
  //having a width w and height h. The shape of the rounded
  //corners are determined by arc with width arcw and height
  //arch. The rectangle is filled with current color.
public abstract Shape getClip()
  //Returns a shape object of the current clipping area for
  //this graphics context.
public abstract Rectangle getClipBounds()
  //Returns the rectangle describing the bounds of the current
  //clipping area for this graphics context.
public abstract Color getColor()
  //Returns the current color for this graphics context.
public abstract void setColor(Color c)
  //Sets the current color for this graphics context.
public abstract Font getFont()
  //Returns the current font for this graphics context.
public abstract void setFont(Font f)
  //Sets the current font for this graphics context.
public FontMetrics getFontMetrics()
  //Returns the font metrics associated with this
  //graphics context.
public FontMetrics getFontMetrics(Font f)
  //Returns the font metrics associated with Font f.
public abstract void setClip(int x, int y, int w, int h)
  //Sets the clipping area as the rectangle at (x, y)
  //with width w and height h.
public abstract void setClip(Shape s)
  //Sets the clipping area to be a specified shape s.
```

```
public abstract void setXORmode(Color c)
   //Sets the current graphics context's paint mode to
   //overwrite any subsequent destinations with alternating
   //current color and color c.
public void String toString()
   //Returns a string representation of this graphics context.
```

CLASS: GridLayout (PACKAGE java.awt)

Constructors

```
public GridLayout()
   //Creates a one row, one column grid layout.
public GridLayout(int rows, int cols)
   //Creates a grid layout with the specified number
   //of rows and columns. All grids are given equal size.
public GridLayout(int rows, int cols, int hgap, int vgap)
   //Creates a grid layout with the specified number of
   //rows and columns; and given vertical and horizontal gaps.
   //All grids are given equal size.
```

Methods

```
public int getRows()
   //Gets the number of rows.
public void setRows(int rows)
   //Sets the number of rows.
public int getColumns()
   //Gets the number of columns.
public void setColumns(int cols)
   //Sets the number of columns.
public int getHgap()
   //Gets the horizontal gap between components.
public void setHgap(int hgap)
   //Sets the horizontal gap between components.
public int getVgap()
   //Gets the vertical gap between components.
public void setVgap(int vgap)
   //Sets the vertical gap between components.
```

CLASS: InputStreamReader (PACKAGE java.io)

Constructors

```
public InputStreamReader(Reader rd)
   //Creates a InputStreamReader object. The object is
   //initialized using rd.
```

```
public InputStreamReader(Reader rd, int size)
  //Creates a InputStreamReader object. The object is
  //initialized using rd and to the size specified by size.
  //The default size is 8192 characters.
```

Methods

```
public void close() throws IOException
  //Closes the InputStreamReader.
public int read() throws IOException
  //Returns a single character as an int from the
  //InputStreamReader. Returns -1 if the end of stream
  //is reached.
public boolean ready() throws IOException
  //Returns true if the object is ready to be read. If the
  //object is nonempty, the state is true.
public void reset() throws IOException
  //Resets the object.
```

CLASS: Integer (PACKAGE java.lang)

Named Constants

```
public static final int MAX_VALUE = 2147483647;
public static final int MIN_VALUE = -2147483648;
```

Constructors

```
public Integer(int num)
  //Creates an object initialized to the value specified
  //by num.
public Integer(String str) throws NumberFormatException
  //Creates an object initialized to the value specified
  //by the num contained in str.
```

Methods

```
public byte byteValue()
  //Returns the value of the object as a byte value.
public short shortValue()
  //Returns the value of the object as a short value.
public int intValue()
  //Returns the value of the object as an int value.
public long longValue()
  //Returns the value of the object as a long value.
public double doubleValue()
  //Returns the value of the object as a double value.
```

```
public float floatValue()
   //Returns the value of the object as a float value.
public int hashCode()
   //Returns the hash code of the object.
public boolean equals(Object obj)
   //Returns true if the value of this object is equal
   //to the value of the object specified by obj;
   //otherwise returns false.
public static int parseInt(String str) throws
                                 NumberFormatException
   //Returns the value of the number contained in str.
public static int parseInt(String str, int base) throws
                                 NumberFormatException
   //Returns the value, in radix base, of the int
   //contained in str.
public static String toBinaryString(int num)
   //Returns the string representation of num in
   //binary (base 2).
public static String toHexString(int num)
   //Returns the string representation of num in
   //hexadecimal (base 16).
public static String toOctalString(int num)
   //Returns the string representation of num in octal
   //(base 8).
public String toString()
   //Returns the int value, of the object, as a string.
public static String toString(int num)
   //Returns the value of num as a string.
public static String toString(int num, int base)
   //Returns the value of num, in radix base, as a string.
public static Integer valueOf(String str) throws
                                 NumberFormatException
   //Returns an Integer object initialized to the value
   //specified by str.
public static Integer valueOf(String str, int base) throws
                                 NumberFormatException
   //Returns an Integer object initialized to the value,
   //in radix base, specified by str.
```

CLASS: JApplet (PACKAGE javax.swing)

Constructors

Methods

```
public void init()
   //Called by the browser or applet viewer to inform this applet
   //that it has been loaded into the system.
```

```
public void start()
   //Called by the browser or applet viewer to inform this
   //applet that it should start its execution. It is
   //called after the init method and each time the applet is
   //revisited in a Web page.
public void stop()
   //Called by the browser or applet viewer to inform this
   //applet that it should stop its execution. It is called
   //before the method destroy.
public void destroy()
   //Called by the browser or applet viewer. Informs this
   //applet that it is being reclaimed and that it should
   //destroy any resources that it has allocated. The method
   //stop is called before destroy.
public void showStatus(String msg)
   //Displays the string msg in the status bar.
public Container getContentPane()
   //Returns the contentPane object for this applet.
public void setContentPane(Container contentPane)
   //Sets the contentPane object for this applet.
public JLayeredPane getLayeredPane()
   //Returns the layeredPane object for this applet.
public void setLayeredPane(JLayeredPane layeredPane)
   //Sets the layeredPane for this applet.
public JMenuBar getJMenuBar()
   //Returns the JMenuBar object for this applet.
public void setJMenuBar(JMenuBar menuBar)
   //Sets the JMenuBar object for this applet.
public URL getDocumentBase()
   //Returns the URL of the document that contains this applet.
public URL getCodeBase()
   //Returns the URL of this applet.
public void update(Graphics g)
   //Calls the paint() method.
protected String paramString()
   //Returns a string representation of this applet;
   //mainly used for debugging.
```

CLASS: JButton (PACKAGE javax.swing)

Constructors

```
public JButton()
   //Creates the Jbutton object with no text or icon.
public JButton(Icon ic)
   //Creates the Jbutton object with the icon specified by ic.
```

```
public JButton(String str)
   //Creates the Jbutton object to the text specified by str.
public JButton(String str, Icon ic)
   //Creates the Jbutton object to the text specified
   //by str and icon specified by ic.
```

Methods

```
public String getText()
   //Method to return the text contained in button.
public void setText(String str)
   //Method to set the text of button to the string specified
   //by str.
public boolean isSelected()
   //Returns true if the button is selected, false otherwise.
public void setSelected(boolean b)
   //Sets the state of the button to b. This method does not
   //trigger an actionEvent. For that, call doClick.
public void addActionListener(ActionListener obj)
   //Method to register a listener object to the button object.
public void doClick()
   //Programmatically perform a "click."
public void doClick(int msec)
   //Programmatically perform a "click." Button appears pressed
   //for msec milliseconds.
public Icon getIcon()
   //Returns the default icon.
public void setIcon(Icon icon)
   //Sets the default icon.
public Icon getPressedIcon()
   //Returns the pressed icon.
public Icon setPressedIcon()
   //Sets the pressed icon.
public Icon getSelectedIcon()
   //Returns the selected icon.
public void setSelectedIcon(Icon icon)
   //Sets the selected icon.
public Icon getDisabledIcon()
   //Returns the icon used when the button is disabled.
   //If there is no disabled icon, one from the default
   //icon is constructed.
public void setDisabledIcon(Icon icon)
   //Sets the disabled icon.
public int getVerticalTextPosition()
   //Returns the vertical position of the text.
   //Returns one of the following constant values:
   //SwingConstants.CENTER (the default)
   //SwingConstants.TOP
   //SwingConstants.BOTTOM
```

```
public void setVerticalTextPosition(int pos)
  //Sets the vertical position of the text.
  //possible values are:
  //SwingConstants.CENTER (the default)
  //SwingConstants.TOP
  //SwingConstants.BOTTOM
public int getHorizontalTextPosition()
  //Returns the horizontal position of text.
  //Returns one of the following constant values:
  //SwingConstants.RIGHT
  //SwingConstants.LEFT
  //SwingConstants.CENTER
  //SwingConstants.LEADING
  //SwingConstants.TRAILING (the default)
public void setHorizontalTextPosition(int pos)
  //Sets the horizontal position of the text.
  //Possible values are:
  //SwingConstants.RIGHT
  //SwingConstants.LEFT
  //SwingConstants.CENTER
  //SwingConstants.LEADING
  //SwingConstants.TRAILING (the default)
public void setActionCommand(String actionCommand)
  //Sets the action command.
public String getActionCommand()
  //Returns the action command.
public int getMnemonic()
  //Returns the keyboard mnemonic. The mnemonic is the key
  //which when combined with the meta key (usually Alt) will
  //"click" this button if focus is within the button's
  //ancestor window.
public void setMnemonic(int mnemonic)
  //Sets the keyboard mnemonic. The mnemonic is the key
  //which when combined with the meta key (usually Alt) will
  //"click" this button if focus is within the button's
  //ancestor window.
public void setEnabled(boolean b)
  //Sets the button enabled if b is true;
  //disabled if b is false.
```

CLASS: JCheckBox (PACKAGE javax.swing)

Constructors

```
public JCheckBox()
  //Creates an initially unselected check box
  //with no label and no icon.
```

```
public JCheckBox(Icon icon)
  //Creates an initially unselected check box
  //with the specified icon and no label.
public JCheckBox(Icon icon, boolean selected)
  //Creates a check box with the specified
  //icon and selection state, but without label.
public JCheckBox(String text)
  //Creates an unselected check box with
  //the specified label.
public JCheckBox(String text, boolean selected)
  //Creates a check box with the specified
  //label and selection state.
public JCheckBox(String text, Icon icon)
  //Creates a check box with the specified image
  //and with specified label.
public JCheckBox(String text, Icon icon, boolean selected)
  //Creates a check box with the specified image
  //and selection state, and with the specified text.
```

Methods

```
public String getText()
  //Returns the text contained in checkbox.
public void setText(String str)
  //Sets the text of checkbox to the string specified by str.
public boolean isSelected()
  //Returns true if the checkbox is selected, false otherwise.
public void setSelected(boolean b)
  //Sets the state of the checkbox to b. This method does not
  //trigger an actionEvent. For that, call doClick.
public void addActionListener(ActionListener obj)
  //Method to register a listener object to the checkbox
  //object
public void doClick()
  //Programmatically perform a "click."
public int getVerticalTextPosition()
  //Returns the vertical position of the text.
  //Returns one of the following constant values:
  //SwingConstants.CENTER (the default)
  //SwingConstants.TOP
  //SwingConstants.BOTTOM
public void setVerticalTextPosition(int pos)
  //Sets the vertical position of the text.
  //Possible values are:
  //SwingConstants.CENTER (the default)
  //SwingConstants.TOP
  //SwingConstants.BOTTOM
public int getHorizontalTextPosition()
  //Returns the horizontal position of text.
  //Returns one of the following constant values:
```

```
//SwingConstants.RIGHT
//SwingConstants.LEFT
//SwingConstants.CENTER
//SwingConstants.LEADING
//SwingConstants.TRAILING (the default)
```
public void **setHorizontalTextPosition**(int pos)
```
//Sets the horizontal position of the text.
//Possible values are:
//SwingConstants.RIGHT
//SwingConstants.LEFT
//SwingConstants.CENTER
//SwingConstants.LEADING
//SwingConstants.TRAILING (the default)
```
public void **setActionCommand**(String actionCommand)
```
//Sets the action command.
```
public String **getActionCommand**()
```
//Returns the action command.
```
public int **getMnemonic**()
```
//Returns the keyboard mnemonic. The mnemonic is the key
//which when combined with meta key (usually Alt) will
//"click" this checkbox if focus is within the checkbox's
//ancestor window.
```
public void **setMnemonic**(int mnemonic)
```
//Sets the keyboard mnemonic. The mnemonic is the key
//which when combined with meta key (usually Alt) will
//"click" this checkbox if focus is within the checkbox's
//ancestor window.
```
public void **setEnabled**(boolean b)
```
//Sets the checkbox enabled if b is true;
//disabled if b is false.
```

CLASS: JComboBox (PACKAGE javax.swing)

Constructors

public **JComboBox**()
```
//Creates a new JComboBox with no items to select.
```
public **JComboBox**(Vector v)
```
//Creates a new combo box to display elements
//in the vector provided as an input parameter.
```
public **JComboBox**(Object[] o)
```
//Creates a new combo box for selection that displays
//elements in the object array provided as an input parameter.
```

Methods

public void **addItem**(Object ob)
```
//Adds an item to the list of items. In order for this
```

```
    //method to work, the JComboBox must use a mutable
    //data model.
public void insertItemAt(Object ob, int index)
    //Inserts an item at a given index in the list of items.
    //In order for this method to work, the JComboBox
    //must use a mutable data model.
public void removeItem(Object ob)
    //Removes an item from the list of items.
    //In order for this method to work, the JComboBox
    //must use a mutable data model.
public void removeItemAt(int index)
    //Removes the item at index from the list of items.
    //This method works only if the JComboBox uses a mutable
    //data model.
public void removeAllItems()
    //Removes all items from the item list.
    //This method works only if the JComboBox uses a mutable
    //data model.
public void addItemListener(ItemListener aListener)
    //Adds an ItemListener.
    //aListener will receive one or two ItemEvents when the
    //selected item changes.
public void setEnabled(boolean b)
    //If b is true, the combo box is enabled; thus items can
    //be selected.
public int getItemCount()
    //Returns the number of items in the list.
public Object getItemAt(int index)
    //Returns the list item at index. If index is out of range
    //a null value is returned.
public void setEditable(boolean b)
    //JComboBox field is editable if b is true. An editable
    //JComboBox allows the user to type into the field or
    //select an item from the list to initialize the field.
    //By default, a combo box is not editable.
public boolean isEditable()
    //Returns false if the JComboBox is not editable.
    //By default, a combo box is not editable.
public void setMaximumRowCount(int count)
    //Sets the maximum number of rows to be displayed.
    //If the number of items is greater than count, scrollbar
    //is used.
public int getMaximumRowCount()
    //Returns the maximum number of items that can
    //display without a scrollbar.
```

CLASS: JFrame (PACKAGE javax.swing)

Constructors

```
public JFrame()
  //Creates a JFrame object without any title.
public JFrame(String s)
  //Creates a JFrame object with the title specified by s.
public JFrame(GraphicsConfiguration gc)
  //Creates a JFrame object in the specified
  //GraphicsConfiguration of a screen device with no title.
public JFrame(String t, GraphicsConfiguration gc)
  //Creates an object JFrame in the specified
  //GraphicsConfiguration of a screen device and title.
```

Methods

```
public void setSize(int w, int h)
  //Sets the size of the window.
public void setTitle(String s)
  //Sets the title of the window.
public void setVisible(boolean b)
  //Method to display window in the program. If the value of
  //b is true the window will be displayed on the screen.
public int getDefaultCloseOperation()
  //Returns the operation that occurs when the user closes
  //this frame.
public void setDefaultCloseOperation(int operation)
  //Method to determine the action to be taken when the user
  //clicks on the window closing button to close the
  //window. Choices for the parameter operation are the named
  //constants — EXIT_ON_CLOSE, HIDE_ON_CLOSE, DISPOSE_ON_CLOSE,
  //and DO_NOTHING_ON_CLOSE. The named constant EXIT_ON_CLOSE
  //is defined in the class JFrame. The last three named
  //constants are defined in javax.swing.WindowConstants.
public void addWindowListener(WindowEvent e)
  //Method to register a window listener object to a JFrame.
public void update(Graphics g)
  //Invokes the method paint(g).
public void setJMenuBar(JMenuBar mbar)
  //Sets the menubar for this JFrame.
public JMenuBar getJMenuBar()
  //Returns the menubar set on this JFrame.
public JRootPane getRootPane()
  //Returns the rootPane object for this JFrame.
protected void setRootPane(JRootPane r)
  //Sets the rootPane property.
```

E

```
public Container getContentPane()
  //Returns the contentPane object for this JFrame.
public void setContentPane(Container pane)
  //Sets the contentPane  for this JFrame.
public JLayeredPane getLayeredPane()
  //Returns the layeredPane object for this JFrame.
public void setLayeredPane(JLayeredPane layeredPane)
  //Sets the layeredPane for this JFrame.
```

CLASS: JLabel (PACKAGE javax.swing)

Constructors

```
public JLabel()
  //Creates a JLabel object with no text or icon.
public JLabel(String str)
  //Creates a JLabel object with left-aligned text specified
  //by str.
public JLabel(String str, int align)
  //Creates a JLabel object with text specified by str.
  //The value of align can be any one of the following:
  //    SwingConstants.LEFT,
  //    SwingConstants.RIGHT,
  //    SwingConstants.CENTER
  //These constants are defined in the class SwingConstants.
public JLabel(Icon icon)
  //Constructs a JLabel with an icon.
public JLabel(Icon icon, int align)
  //Creates a JLabel object with an icon.
  //The value of align can be any one of the following:
  //    SwingConstants.LEFT,
  //    SwingConstants.RIGHT,
  //    SwingConstants.CENTER
  //These constants are defined in the class SwingConstants.
public JLabel(String t, Icon icon, int align)
  //Constructs a JLabel with both text and an icon.
  //The icon is to the left of text.
  //The value of align can be any one of the following:
  //    SwingConstants.LEFT,
  //    SwingConstants.RIGHT,
  //    SwingConstants.CENTER
  //These constants are defined in the class SwingConstants.
```

Methods

```
public Icon getIcon()
  //Returns the graphic image (glyph, icon) that
  //the label displays.
```

```
public void setIconTextGap(int IconTextGap)
  //Sets the gap between icon and text properties if
  //both are set.
public int getIconTextGap()
  //Returns the gap between icon and text properties
  //if both are set.
public void setVerticalAlignment(int Align)
  //Sets the label's alignment along the Y-axis.
  //The value of align can be any one of the following:
  //    SwingConstants.TOP,
  //    SwingConstants.CENTER (default),
  //    SwingConstants.BOTTOM.
  //These constants are defined in the class SwingConstants.
public int getVerticalAlignment()
  //Returns the label's alignment along the Y-axis.
public void setHorizontalAlignment(int Align)
  //Sets the label's alignment along the X-axis.
  //The value of align can be any one of the following:
  //    SwingConstants.LEFT,
  //    SwingConstants.RIGHT,
  //    SwingConstants.CENTER
  //These constants are defined in the class SwingConstants.
public int getHorizontalAlignment()
  //Returns the label's alignment along the X-axis.
public void setVerticalTextPosition(int TextPos)
  //Sets the vertical text position relative to the
  //icon. The value of align can be any one of the following:
  //    SwingConstants.TOP,
  //    SwingConstants.CENTER (default),
  //    SwingConstants.BOTTOM.
  //These constants are defined in the class SwingConstants.
public int getVerticalTextPosition()
  //Returns the vertical text position.
public void setHorizontalTextPosition(int TextPos)
  //Sets the horizontal text position relative to the
  //icon. The value of align can be any one of the following:
  //    SwingConstants.LEFT,
  //    SwingConstants.RIGHT,
  //    SwingConstants.CENTER
  //These constants are defined in the class SwingConstants.
public int getHorizontalTextPosition()
  //Returns the horizontal text position.
```

CLASS: JList (PACKAGE javax.swing)

Constructors

```
public JList()
   //Creates a new JList with no items to select.
public JList(Vector v)
   //Creates a new list to display elements in the
   //vector provided as an input parameter.
public JList(Object[] o)
   //Creates a new list for selection that displays elements
   //in the object array provided as an input parameter.
```

Methods

```
public void setSelectionBackground(Color sbColor)
   //Sets the color of the background of a
   //selected item.
public void addListSelectionListener(ListSelectionListener lsl)
   //Adds a listener class to take action when an
   //item in the list is selected.
public void removeListSelectionListener
                          (ListSelectionListener lsnr)
   //Removes a listener of the list that is notified every
   //time change to the selection occurs.
public void setSelectionMode(int selectionMode)
   //Sets the selection mode. The selectionMode values are:
   //ListSelectionModel.SINGLE_SELECTION - Only one list index
   //can be selected.
   //ListSelectionModel.SINGLE_INTERVAL_SELECTION - One contiguous
   //index interval can be selected.
   //ListSelectionModel.MULTIPLE_INTERVAL_SELECTION - There's no
   //restriction on what can be selected (default).
public int getSelectionMode()
   //Returns the current selectionMode.
public int getAnchorSelectionIndex()
   //Returns the first index argument from the most recent
   //addSelectionModel orsetSelectionInterval method invocation.
public int getLeadSelectionIndex()
   //Returns the second index argument from the most recent
   //addSelectionInterval or setSelectionInterval method
   //invocation.
public int getMinSelectionIndex()
   //Returns the smallest selected index.
public int getMaxSelectionIndex()
   //Returns the largest selected index.
public boolean isSelectedIndex(int index)
   //Returns true if the specified index is selected.
```

```
public boolean isSelectionEmpty()
    //Returns true if selected list is empty.
public void clearSelection()
    //Clears the selection list.
public int[] getSelectedIndices()
    //Returns an array of all of the selected indices in
    //increasing order.
public void setSelectedIndex(int index)
    //Selects a single item.
public void setSelectedIndices(int[] indices)
    //Selects a set of items.
public Object[] getSelectedValues()
    //Returns an array of the values for the selected items.
public int getSelectedIndex()
    //When an item in the list is selected, this method returns
    //the index of the first item (0 to # of items - 1).
    //Returns -1 if nothing is selected.
public Object getSelectedValue()
    //Returns the first selected value, or null if there is no
    //selected item.
```

CLASS: JMenu (PACKAGE java.swing)

Constructors

```
public JMenu()
    //Creates a new JMenu with no text.
public JMenu(String t)
    //Creates a new JMenu with specified text.
public boolean isSelected()
    //Returns true if the menu is currently selected
    //(highlighted).
public void setSelected(boolean b)
    //Sets the menu selected or not selected as specified.
public boolean isPopupMenuVisible()
    //Returns the visibility status of a popup menu. The value
    //returned is true if the menu's popup window is visible.
public void setPopupMenuVisible(boolean b)
    //Sets the visibility status of a popup menu.
protected Point getPopupMenuOrigin()
    //Returns the origin for the JMenu's popup menu.
public int getDelay()
    //Returns the time, in milliseconds, delay before submenus
    //are displayed.
public void setDelay(int dtime)
    //Sets the time, in milliseconds, delay before submenus
    //are displayed.
```

```
public void setMenuLocation(int x, int y)
  //Sets the location of the popup component.
public JMenuItem add(JMenuItem menuItem)
  //Adds a menu item to the end of this menu.
public Component add(Component c)
  //Adds a component to the end of this menu.
public Component add(Component c, int index)
  //Adds a component at specified position of this menu.
public JMenuItem add(String s)
  //Creates a new menu item with the specified text and adds
  //it to the end of this menu.
public void addSeparator()
  //Adds a new separator to the end of the menu.
public void insert(String s, int pos)
  //Creates and inserts a new menu item with the specified text
  //at a given position.
public JMenuItem insert(JMenuItem mi, int pos)
  //Inserts the specified JMenuItem at a given position of
  //this menu.
public void insertSeparator(int index)
  //Inserts a menu separator at the specified position.
public JMenuItem getItem(int pos)
  //Returns the JMenuItem at the specified position.
public int getItemCount()
  //Returns the number of items on this menu. The count
  //includes separators.
public void remove(JMenuItem item)
  //Deletes the specified menu item from this menu.
public void remove(int pos)
  //Deletes the menu item at the specified index from
  //this menu.
public void remove(Component c)
  //Deletes the specified component from this menu.
public void removeAll()
  //Deletes all menu items from this menu.
public int getMenuComponentCount()
  //Returns the number of components on this menu.
public Component getMenuComponent(int n)
  //Returns the component at a specified position
public Component[] getMenuComponents()
  //Returns an array of Components of the menu's subcomponents
  //including separators.
public boolean isTopLevelMenu()
  //Returns true if the menu is a top-level menu.
public boolean isMenuComponent(Component c)
  //Returns true if the specified component is part of this
  //menu's submenu hierarchy.
public JPopupMenu getPopupMenu()
  //Returns the popup menu of this menu. If no popup menu exists,
  //it will create one.
```

```
public void addMenuListener(MenuListener l)
   //Adds a listener for menu events.
public void removeMenuListener(MenuListener l)
   //Removes a listener for menu events.
public void doClick(int pressTime)
   //Programmatically performs a "click". This method overrides
   //the one in the class AbstractButton.
```

CLASS: JMenuBar (PACKAGE javax.swing)

Constructor

```
public JMenuBar()
   //Creates a new menu bar.
```

Methods

```
public JMenu add(JMenu c)
   //Appends the specified menu to the end of the menu bar.
public JMenu getMenu(int index)
   //Returns the menu at the specified position in the menu bar.
public int getMenuCount()
   //Returns the number of items in the menu bar.
public void setHelpMenu(JMenu menu)
   //Sets the help menu for the menu bar.
public JMenu getHelpMenu()
   //Gets the help menu for the menu bar.
public int getComponentIndex(Component c)
   //Returns the index of the specified component.
public void setSelected(Component sel)
   //Sets the currently selected component.
public boolean isSelected()
   //Returns true if a component of the menu bar is selected.
public boolean isBorderPainted()
   //Returns true if the menu bar's border is painted.
public void setBorderPainted(boolean b)
   //Border is painted if b is true.
protected void paintBorder(Graphics g)
   //Method that paints the menu bar's border if BorderPainted
   //property is true.
public void setMargin(Insets m)
   //Sets the margin between the menu bar's border and its menus.
   //To get the default margin, set it to null.
public Insets getMargin()
   //Returns the margin between the menu bar's border and its
   //menus.
```

E

CLASS: JMenuItem (PACKAGE javax.swing)

Constructors

```
public JMenuItem()
    //Constructs a new JMenuItem with no set text or icon.
public JMenuItem(Icon icon)
    //Constructs a new JMenuItem with the specified icon.
public JMenuItem(String t)
    //Constructs a new JMenuItem with the specified text.
public JMenuItem(String t, Icon icon)
    //Constructs a new JMenuItem with the specified text and
    //icon.
public JMenuItem(String t, int mnemonic)
    //Constructs a new JMenuItem with the specified text and
    //keyboard mnemonic.
```

Methods

```
protected void init(String t, Icon icon)
    //Initializes the menu item with the specified text and icon.
public void setEnabled(boolean b)
    //Enables or disables this menu item as specified.
public void setAccelerator(KeyStroke keyStroke)
    //Sets the accelerator key, that is, the key combination
    //that invokes the menu item's action listeners without
    //navigating the menu hierarchy using a mouse.
public KeyStroke getAccelerator()
    //Returns the KeyStroke which serves as an accelerator
    //for the menu item.
```

CLASS: JRadioButton (PACKAGE javax.swing)

Constructors

```
public JRadioButton()
    //Creates an initially unselected radio button
    //with no label and no icon.
public JRadioButton(Icon icon)
    //Creates an initially unselected radio button
    //with the specified icon and no label.
public JRadioButton(Icon icon, boolean selected)
    //Creates a radio button with the specified
    //image and selection state, but without label.
public JRadioButton(String text)
    //Creates an unselected radio button with the
    //specified label.
```

```
public JRadioButton(String text, boolean selected)
  //Creates a radio button with the specified
  //label and selection state.
public JRadioButton(String text, Icon icon)
  //Creates a radio button with the specified image and
  //with specified label.
public JRadioButton(String text, Icon icon, boolean selected)
//Creates a radio button with the specified
//image and selection state, and with the specified text.
```

Methods

```
public String getText()
  //Returns the text contained in radio button.
public void setText(String str)
  //Sets the text of radio button to the string
  //specified by str.
public boolean isSelected()
  //Returns true if the radio button is selected, false
  //otherwise.
public void setSelected(boolean b)
  //Sets the state of the radio button to b. This method does
  //not trigger an actionEvent. For that, call doClick.
public void addActionListener(ActionListener obj)
  //Registers a listener object to the radio button
  //object.
public void doClick()
  //Programmatically performs a "click."
public int getVerticalTextPosition()
  //Returns the vertical position of the text.
  //Returns one of the following constant values:
  //    SwingConstants.CENTER (the default)
  //    SwingConstants.TOP
  //    SwingConstants.BOTTOM
public void setVerticalTextPosition(int pos)
  //Sets the vertical position of the text.
  //Possible values are:
  //    SwingConstants.CENTER (the default)
  //    SwingConstants.TOP
  //    SwingConstants.BOTTOM
public int getHorizontalTextPosition()
  //Returns the horizontal position of text.
  //Returns one of the following constant values:
  //    SwingConstants.RIGHT
  //    SwingConstants.LEFT
  //    SwingConstants.CENTER
  //    SwingConstants.LEADING
  //    SwingConstants.TRAILING (the default)
```

```
public void setHorizontalTextPosition(int pos)
   //Sets the horizontal position of the text.
   //Possible values are:
   //    SwingConstants.RIGHT
   //    SwingConstants.LEFT
   //    SwingConstants.CENTER
   //    SwingConstants.LEADING
   //    SwingConstants.TRAILING (the default)
public void setActionCommand(String actionCommand)
   //Sets the action command.
public String getActionCommand()
   //Returns the action command.
public int getMnemonic()
   //Returns the keyboard mnemonic. The mnemonic is the key which
   //when combined with the meta key (usually Alt) will "click"
   //this radio button if focus is within the radio button's
   //ancestor window.
public void setMnemonic(int mnemonic)
   //Sets the keyboard mnemonic. The mnemonic is the key which
   //when combined with the meta key (usually Alt) will "click"
   //this radio button if focus is within the radio button's
   //ancestor window.
public void setEnabled(boolean b)
   //Sets the radio button enabled if b is true;
   //disabled if b is false.
```

CLASS: JTextArea (PACKAGE javax.swing)

Constructors

```
public JTextArea()
   //Creates a JTextArea instance with 0 number of rows and
   //0 number of columns.
public JTextArea(int r, int c)
   //Creates a JTextArea instance with r number of rows and
   //c number of columns.
public JTextArea(String t)
   //Creates a JTextArea instance with 0 number of rows,
   //0 number of columns and initial text t.
public JTextArea(String t, int r, int c)
   //Creates a JTextArea instance with r number of rows,
   //c number of columns and initial text t.
```

Methods

```
public void setColumns(int c)
   //Sets the number of columns to c.
```

```
public int getColumns()
    //Returns the number of columns.
public void setRows(int r)
    //Sets the number of rows to r.
public int getRows()
    //Returns the number of rows.
public void append(String t)
    //Concatenates the text already in the JTextArea with t.
public void setLineWrap(boolean b)
    //If b is true, lines are wrapped.
public boolean getLineWrap()
    //Returns true if line wrapping is set.
public void setWrapStyleWord(boolean b)
    //If b is true, lines are wrapped at word boundaries.
    //If b is false, word boundaries are not considered.
public void getWrapStyleWord()
    //Returns true if lines are wrapped at word boundaries.
    //Returns false if word boundaries are not considered.
public void setTabSize(int c)
    //Sets tab stops every c columns.
public int getTabSize()
    //Returns number of characters used to expand a tab stop.
public void setText(String t)
    //Changes the text of the text area to t.
public String getText()
    //Returns the text contained in text area.
public void setEditable(boolean b)
    //If b is false, user can not type in the text area. In this
    //case, the text area is used as a tool to display the result.
public int getLineCount()
    //Determines the number of lines contained in the text area.
public void insert(String str, int p)
    //Inserts the specified text at a given position.
public void replaceRange(String str, int start, int end)
    //Replaces text from the specified start to end position
    //with the new text given.
public void setFont(Font font)
    //Sets the current font.
```

CLASS: JTextField (PACKAGE javax.swing)

Constructors

```
public JTextField()
    //Creates a JTextField object with 0 columns.
    //Initial text is set to null.
```

```
public JTextField(int columns)
   //Creates a JTextField object with number of columns
   //specified by columns.
public JTextField(String str)
   //Creates a JTextField object with the text
   //specified by str
public JTextField(String str, int columns)
   //Creates a JTextField object with the text specified by
   //str and sets the size of the text field
```

Methods

```
public void setColumns(int c)
   //Sets the number of columns to c.
public int getColumns()
   //Returns the number of columns.
public void setText(String str)
   //Sets the text of the text field to string
   //specified by str.
public String getText()
   //Returns the text contained in text field.
public void setEditable(boolean b)
   //If the value of the Boolean variable b is false, user can
   //not type in the text field.
   //In this case, the text field is used as a tool to
   //display the result.
public void addActionListener(ActionListener obj)
   //Registers a listener object to a JTextField.
public void removeActionListener(ActionListener obj)
   //Removes a registered listener object.
public int getHorizontalAlignment()
   //Returns the horizontal alignment of the text.
   //Valid values are:
   //    JTextField.LEFT
   //    JTextField.CENTER
   //    JTextField.RIGHT
   //    JTextField.LEADING
   //    JTextField.TRAILING
public void setHorizontalAlignment(int a)
   //Sets the horizontal alignment of the text.
   //Valid values are:
   //    JTextField.LEFT
   //    JTextField.CENTER
   //    JTextField.RIGHT
   //    JTextField.LEADING
   //    JTextField.TRAILING
public void setFont(Font font)
   //Sets the current font.
```

CLASS: Long (PACKAGE java.lang)

Named Constants

```
public static final long MAX_VALUE = 9223372036854775807;
public static final long MIN_VALUE = -9223372036854775808;
```

Constructors

```
public Long(long num)
  //Creates an object initialized to the value specified
  //by num.
public Long(String str) throws NumberFormatException
  //Creates an object initialized to the value specified
  //by the num contained in str.
```

Methods

```
public byte byteValue()
  //Returns the value of the object as a byte value.
public short shortValue()
  //Returns the value of the object as a short value.
public int intValue()
  //Returns the value of the object as an int value.
public long longValue()
  //Returns the value of the object as a long value.
public double doubleValue()
  //Returns the value of the object as a double value.
public float floatValue()
  //Returns the value of the object as a float value.
public int hashCode()
  //Returns the hash code of the object.
public boolean equals(Object obj)
  //Returns true if the value of this object is equal
  //to the value of the object specified by obj;
  //otherwise returns false.
public static long parseLong(String str) throws
                                     NumberFormatException
  //Returns the value of the number contained in str.
public static long parseLong(String str, int base) throws
                                     NumberFormatException
  //Returns the value, in radix base, of the long value
  //contained in str.
public static String toBinaryString(long num)
  //Returns the string representation of num in binary (base 2).
public static String toHexString(long num)
  //Returns the string representation of num in
  //hexadecimal (base 16).
```

E

```
public static String toOctalString(long num)
    //Returns the string representation of num in octal (base 8).
public String toString()
    //Returns the long value of the object as a string.
public static String toString(long num)
    //Returns the value of num as a string.
public static String toString(long num, int base)
    //Returns the value of num, in radix base, as a string.
public static Long valueOf(String str) throws
                                    NumberFormatException
    //Returns a Long object initialized to the value
    //specified by str.
public static Long valueOf(String str, int base) throws
                                    NumberFormatException
    //Returns a Long object initialized to the value,
    //in radix base, specified by str.
```

CLASS: Math (PACKAGE java.lang)

Methods

```
public static int abs(int x)
    //Returns the absolute value of x.
public static long abs(long x)
    //Returns the absolute value of x.
public static double abs(double x)
    //Returns the absolute value of x.
public static float abs(float x)
    //Returns the absolute value of x.
public static double ceil(double x)
    //Returns a value of the type double, which is the
    //smallest integer value that is not less than x.
public static double exp(double x)
    //Returns e^x, where e is approximately 2.7182818284590455.
public static double floor(double x)
    //Returns a value of the type double, which is the
    //largest integer value less than x.
public static double log(double x) throws ArithmeticException
    //Returns a value of the type double, which is
    //the natural logarithm of x.
public static int max(int x, int y)
    //Returns the larger of x and y.
public static long max(long x, long y)
    //Returns the larger of x and y.
public static double max(double x, double y)
    //Returns the larger of x and y.
```

```
public static float max(float x, float y)
   //Returns the larger of x and y.
public static int min(int x, int y)
   //Returns the smaller of x and y.
public static long min(long x, long y)
   //Returns the smaller of x and y.
public static double min(double x, double y)
   //Returns the smaller of x and y.
public static float min(float x, float y)
   //Returns the smaller of x and y.
public static double pow(double x, double y)
   //Returns x^y.
public static double random()
   //Returns a random number between 0.0 and 1.0.
public static int round(float x)
   //Returns a value which is the integer closest to x.
public static long round(double x)
   //Returns a value which is the integer closest to x.
public static double sqrt(double x)
   //Returns the positive square root of x; x must be
   //nonnegative.
public static double cos(double x)
   //Returns the cosine of x measured in radians.
public static double sin(double x)
   //Returns the sine of x measured in radians.
public static double tan(double x)
   //Returns the tangent of x measured in radians.
public static double acos(double x)
   //Returns the arc cosine of x measured in radians.
public static double asin(double x)
   //Returns the arc sine of x measured in radians.
public static double atan(double x)
   //Returns the arc tangent of x measured in radians.
```

E

CLASS: Point (PACKAGE java.awt)

Variables

```
public int x;
public int y;
```

Constructors

```
public Point()
   //Creates an object and initializes x and y to 0.
public Point(int a, int b)
   //Creates an object and initializes x to a and y to b.
```

```
public Point(Point p)
   //Creates an object and initializes it using the object p.
```

Methods

```
public boolean equals(Object ob)
   //Returns true if this object is same as the object ob;
   //otherwise returns false.
public Point getLocation()
   //Returns the location of the object.
public void move(int a, int b)
   //Moves the object at the location (a, b).
public void setLocation(int a, int b)
   //Sets the location of object at (a, b).
public void setLocation(Point p)
   //Sets the location of object at p.
public int hashCode()
   //Returns the hash code of the object.
public String toString()
   //Returns a string representation of the object.
```

CLASS: PrintWriter (PACKAGE java.io)

Constructors

```
public PrintWriter(Writer out)
   //Creates a new PrintWriter. No automatic line flushing.
public PrintWriter(Writer out, boolean af)
   //Create a new PrintWriter.
   //boolean af determines whether or not automatic
   //line flushing is enabled.
public PrintWriter(OutputStream out)
   //Creates a PrintWriter from an OutputStream.
   //No automatic line flushing.
public PrintWriter(OutputStream out, boolean autoFlush)
   //Create a new PrintWriter from an existing OutputStream.
```

Methods

```
public void flush()
   //Flushes the stream.
public void close()
   //Closes the stream.
public boolean checkError()
   //Flushes the stream and checks its error state.
protected void setError()
   //Sets an error state.
```

```java
public void write(int c)
    //Writes a single character.
public void write(char[] b, int offset, int length)
    //Writes a part of an array of characters.
public void write(char[] buf)
    //Writes an array of characters.
public void write(String s, int offset, int length)
    //Writes a part of a string.
public void write(String s)
    //Writes a string.
public void print(boolean b)
    //Prints a boolean value.
public void print(char c)
    //Prints a character.
public void print(int i)
    //Prints an integer.
public void print(long l)
    //Prints a long integer.
public void print(float f)
    //Prints a floating-point number.
public void print(double d)
    //Prints a double-precision floating-point number.
public void print(char[] s)
    //Prints an array of characters.
public void print(String s)
    //Prints a string.
public void print(Object obj)
    //Prints an object.
public void println()
    //Terminates the current line by printing the line
    //separator string.
public void println(boolean x)
    //Prints a boolean value followed by the line separator string.
public void println(char x)
    //Prints a character followed by the line separator string.
public void println(int x)
    //Prints an integer followed by the line separator string.
public void println(long x)
    //Prints a long integer followed by the line separator string.
public void println(float x)
    //Prints a floating-point number followed by the line
    //separator string.
public void println(double x)
    //Prints a double-precision floating-point number
    //followed by the line separator string.
public void println(char[] x)
    //Prints an array of characters followed by the line
    //separator string.
```

E

```
public void println(String x)
   //Prints a String followed by the line separator string.
public void println(Object x)
   //Prints an Object followed by the line separator string.
```

CLASS: String (PACKAGE java.lang)

Constructors

```
public String()
   //Creates a String object with no characters.
public String(char[] arg)
   //Creates a String object with the character array specified
   //by arg.
public String(char[] arg, int index, int length) throws
                         StringIndexOutOfBoundsException
   //Creates a String object with the character array specified
   //by arg, starting at index and of length
   //specified by length.
public String(String str)
   //Creates a String object and initializes the string
   //object with characters specified by str.
public String(StringBuffer str)
   //Creates a String object and initializes the string
   //object with characters specified by str.
```

Methods

```
public char charAt(int index) throws
                         StringIndexOutOfBoundsException
   //Returns the character at the position specified by index.
public int compareTo(String str)
   //Compares two strings character by character.
   //Returns a negative value if this string is less than str.
   //Returns 0 if this string is same as str.
   //Returns a positive value if this string is greater
   //than str.
public String concat(String str)
   //Returns the string that is this string concatenated
   //with str.
public static String copyValueOf(char[] arg)
   //Returns the string containing the characters of arg.
public static String copyValueOf(char[] arg, int index,
                         int length)
   //Returns the string containing the characters, starting
   //at index and of length specified by length, of arg.
public boolean endsWith(String str)
   //Returns true if the string ends with the string specified
   //by str. Otherwise, returns false.
```

```
public boolean equals(String str)
   //Returns true if this string is same as str.
   //Otherwise returns false.
public boolean equalsIgnoreCase(String str)
   //Returns true if this string is same as str; case of the
   //letters are ignored. Otherwise it returns false.
public int indexOf(char ch)
   //Returns the index of the first occurrence of the character
   //specified by ch; if the character specified by ch does not
   //appear in the string, it returns -1.
public int indexOf(char ch, int pos)
   //Returns the index of the first occurrence of the character
   //specified by ch; the parameter pos specifies from where to
   //begin the search. If the character specified by ch does not
   //appear in the string, it returns -1.
public int indexOf(String str)
   //Returns the index of the first occurrence of the string
   //specified by str; if the string specified by str does not
   //appear in the string, it returns -1.
public int indexOf(String str, int pos)
   //Returns the index of the first occurrence of the string
   //specified by str. The parameter pos specifies where to
   //begin the search; if the string specified by str does not
   //appear in the string, it returns -1.
public int length()
    //Returns the length of the string.
public boolean regionMatches(int ind, String str, int strIndex,
                             int len)
   //Returns true if the substring of str starting at strIndex
   //and length specified by len is the same as the substring
   //of this String object starting at ind and having the
   //same length.
public boolean regionMatches(boolean ignoreCase, int ind,
                  String str, int strIndex, int len)
   //Returns true if the substring of str starting at strIndex
   //and length specified by len is the same as the substring of
   //this String object starting at ind and having the same
   //length.If ignoreCase is true, then during character
   //comparison case is ignored.
public String replace(char charToBeReplaced,
                  char charReplacedWith)
   //Returns the string in which every occurrence of
   //charToBeReplaced is replaced with charReplacedWith.
public boolean startsWith(String str)
   //Returns true if the string begins with the string
   //specified by str; otherwise returns false.
public String substring(int startIndex)
            throws StringIndexOutOfBoundsException
```

E

```
                //Returns the string which is a substring of this string
                //starting at startIndex until the end of the string.
        public String substring(int startIndex, int endIndex)
                        throws StringIndexOutOfBoundsException
                //Returns the string which is a substring of this string
                //starting at startIndex until endIndex - 1.
        public String toLowerCase()
                //Returns the string that is same as this string except that
                //all uppercase letters of this string are replaced with
                //their equivalent lowercase letters.
        public String toUpperCase()
                //Returns the string that is same as this string except
                //that all lowercase letters of this string are replaced
                //with their equivalent uppercase letters.
        public char[] toCharArray()
                //Returns the object as an array of characters.
        public String toString()
                //Returns the object as a string.
        public static String valueOf(boolean b)
                //Returns a string representation of b.
        public static String valueOf(char ch)
                //Returns a string representation of ch.
        public static String valueOf(int num)
                //Returns a string representation of num.
        public static String valueOf(Long num)
                //Returns a string representation of num.
        public static String valueOf(double decNum)
                //Returns a string representation of decNum.
        public static String valueOf(float decNum)
                //Returns a string representation of decNum.
```

CLASS: StringBuffer (PACKAGE java.lang)

Constructors

```
        public StringBuffer()
                //Creates a StringBuffer object with no characters.
        public StringBuffer(int length) throws NegativeArraySizeException
                //Creates an empty StringBuffer object with initial capacity
                //specified by length.
        public StringBuffer(String str)
                //Creates a StringBuffer object and initializes the
                //object with characters specified by str.
```

Methods

```
public StringBuffer append(boolean b)
  //Appends the string specified by b to the string of
  //this object.
public StringBuffer append(char ch)
  //Appends the string specified by ch to the string of
  //this object.
public StringBuffer append(char[] arg)
  //Appends the character array specified by arg to the
  //string of this object.
public StringBuffer append(char[] arg, int index, int length)
  //Appends the character array specified by arg, starting at
  //index and of length specified by length, to the
  //string of this object.
public StringBuffer append(double num)
  //Appends the string representation of num to the string of
  //this object.
public StringBuffer append(float num)
  //Appends the string representation of num to the string of
  //this object.
public StringBuffer append(int num)
  //Appends the string representation of num to the string of
  //this object.
public StringBuffer append(long num)
  //Appends the string representation of num to the string of
  //this object.
public StringBuffer append(Object ob)
  //Appends the string representation of ob to the string of
  //this object.
public StringBuffer append(String str)
  //Appends the string representation of str to the string of
  //this object.
public int capacity()
  //Returns the capacity of the object.
public char charAt(int index) throws
                          StringIndexOutOfBoundsException
  //Returns the character at the position specified by index.
public void ensureCapacity(int m)
  //Sets the minimum capacity of the object to m. The new
  //capacity may be greater than m.
public void getChars(int st, int end, char[] chArray,
            int index) throws StringIndexOutOfBoundsException
  //Copies the characters of this object starting at st until
  //end into chArray starting at index.
public StringBuffer insert(int index, boolean b)
                  throws StringIndexOutOfBoundsException
  //Inserts the string representation of b into this object
  //starting at index.
```

```
public StringBuffer insert(int index, char ch)
                    throws StringIndexOutOfBoundsException
   //Inserts the string representation of ch into this object
   //starting at index.
public StringBuffer insert(int index, char[] chArray)
                    throws StringIndexOutOfBoundsException
   //Inserts the string representation of chArray into this
   //object starting at index.
public StringBuffer insert(int index, double num)
                    throws StringIndexOutOfBoundsException
   //Inserts the string representation of num into this object
   //starting at index.
public StringBuffer insert(int index, float num)
                    throws StringIndexOutOfBoundsException
   //Inserts the string representation of num into this object
   //starting at index.
public StringBuffer insert(int index, int num)
                    throws StringIndexOutOfBoundsException
   //Inserts the string representation of num into this object
   //starting at index.
public StringBuffer insert(int index, long num)
                    throws StringIndexOutOfBoundsException
   //Inserts the string representation of num into this object
   //starting at index.
public StringBuffer insert(int index, Object ob)
                    throws StringIndexOutOfBoundsException
   //Inserts the string representation of ob into this object
   //starting at index.
public StringBuffer insert(int index, String str)
                    throws StringIndexOutOfBoundsException
   //Inserts the string representation of str into this object
   //starting at index.
public int length()
   //Returns the length of the string.
public StringBuffer reverse()
   //Returns a StringBuffer object with characters of the
   //string of this object reversed.
public void setCharAt(int index, char ch)
   //Sets the character at index to the character specified
   //by ch.
public void setLength(int length) throws
                            StringIndexOutOfBoundsException
   //Sets length of the string of this object to length; may
   //truncate the string.
public String toString()
   //Returns the object as a string.
```

CLASS: StringTokenizer (PACKAGE java.util)

Constructors

```
public StringTokenizer(String str)
  //Creates a StringTokenizer object. The object is initialized
  //using the string specified by str. The delimiting characters
  //are the default characters.
public StringTokenizer(String str, String delimits)
  //Creates a StringTokenizer object. The object is initialized
  //using the string specified by str. The string specified by
  //delimits specifies the delimiters.
public StringTokenizer(String str, String delimits, boolean tok)
  //Creates a StringTokenizer object. The object is initialized
  //using the string specified by str. The string delimits
  //specifies the delimiters. If the boolean variable tok
  //is true, the delimiters are treated as words.
```

Methods

```
public int countTokens()
  //Returns the number of tokens in the string.
public boolean hasMoreElements()
  //Returns the value true if there are tokens left in the string;
  //otherwise returns false.
public boolean hasMoreTokens()
  //Returns the value true if there are tokens left in the string;
  //otherwise returns false.
public String nextElement() throws NoSuchElementException
  //Returns the next token in the string.
public String nextToken() throws NoSuchElementException
  //Returns the next token in the string.
public String nextToken(String delimits) throws
                                    NoSuchElementException
  //Returns the next token in the string.
  //The string delimits specifies the delimiters.
```

CLASS: Throwable (PACKAGE java.lang)

Constructors

```
public Throwable()
//Default constructor.
//Creates an instance of Throwable with an empty message string.
```

```
public Throwable(String strMessage)
//Constructor with parameters.
//Creates an instance of Throwable with message string
//specified by the parameter strMessage.
```

Variables

```
public String getMessage()
  //Returns the detailed message stored in the object.
public void printStackTrace()
  //Prints the stack trace showing the sequence of
  //method calls when an exception occurs.
public void printStackTrace(PrintStream stream)
  //Prints the stack trace showing the sequence of
  //method calls when an exception occurs. Output is sent
  //to the stream specified by the parameter stream.
public void printStackTrace(PrintWriter stream)
  //Prints the stack trace showing the sequence of
  //method calls when an exception occurs.
  //Output is sent to the stream specified by the parameter stream.
public String toString()
  //Returns a string representation of the Throwable object.
```

CLASS: Vector (PACKAGE java.util)

Variables

```
protected int capacityIncrement;
protected int elementCount;
protected Object[] elementData; //Array of references
```

Constructors

```
public Vector()
  //Creates an empty vector of 10 components.
public Vector(int size)
  //Creates an empty vector of the length specified by size.
public Vector(int size, int increm)
 //Creates an empty vector of the length specified by size and
 //capacity increment specified by increm.
```

Methods

```
public void addElement(Object insertObj)
  //Adds the object insertObj at the end.
```

```
public int capacity()
  //Returns the capacity of the vector.
public Object clone()
  //Returns a copy of the vector
public boolean contains(Object obj)
  //Returns true if the Vector object contains the specified
  //by obj; otherwise it returns false.
public void copyInto(Object[] dest)
  //Copies the elements of this vector into the array dest.
public Object elementAt(int index) throws
                           ArrayIndexOutOfBoundsException
  //Returns the element of the vector at location specified
  //by index.
public void ensureCapacity(int size)
  //Sets the capacity of this vector to size.
public Object firstElement() throws NoSuchElementException
  //Returns the first element of the vector.
public int indexOf(Object obj)
  //Returns the position of the first occurrence of the element
  //specified obj in the vector.
  //If item is not in the vector, it returns -1.
public int indexOf(Object obj, int index)
  //Starting at index, the method returns the position of the
  //first occurrence of the element specified by obj in the
  //vector. If item is not in the vector, it returns -1.
public void insertElementAt(Object insertObj, int index)
                      throws ArrayIndexOutOfBoundsException
  //Inserts the object insertObj at the position specified
  //by index.
public boolean isEmpty()
  //Returns true if the vector is empty; otherwise it
  //returns false.
public Object lastElement() throws NoSuchElementException
  //Returns the last element of the vector.
public int lastIndexOf(Object obj)
  //Starting at the last element, using a backward search, this
  //method returns the position of the first occurrence of the
  //element specified by obj in the vector.
  //If obj is not in the vector, it returns -1.
public int lastIndexOf(Object item, int index)
  //Starting at the position specified by index and using a
  //backward search, this method returns the position of the
  //first occurrence of the element specified obj in the vector.
  //If item is not in the vector, the method returns -1.
public void removeAllElements()
  //Removes all elements of the vector.
public boolean removeElement(Object obj)
  //If an element specified by obj exists in the list, the
  //element is removed and true is returned; otherwise
  //false is returned.
```

E

```
public void removeElementAt(int index) throws
                                ArrayIndexOutOfBoundsException
   //If an element at position specified by index exists, it is
   //removed from the vector.
public void setElementAt(Object obj, int index) throws
                                ArrayIndexOutOfBoundsException
   //The element specified by obj is stored at position specified
   //by index.
public int size()
   //Returns the number of elements in the vector.
public void trimToSize()
   //Reduces the length of the vector to the number of elements
   //currently in the vector.
public String toString()
   //Returns a string representation of this vector.
```

APPENDIX

F

ANSWERS TO SELECTED EXERCISES

Chapter 1

1. a. True; b. False; c. True; d. True; e. False; f; False; g. True; h. True; i. True;

2. Control unit, instruction register, program counter, arithmetic logic unit, and accumulator.

4. Keyboard and mouse.

5. Monitor and printer.

8. Instructions in a high level language are closer to the natural language, such as English, and therefore, are easier to understand and learn than the machine language.

Chapter 2

1. a. False; b. False; c. False; d. True; e. True; f. True; g. True; h. False; i. True; j. False.

3. a

5. a. `3`; b. not possible; c. not possible; d. `38.5`; e. `1`; f. `2`; g. `2`; h. `420.0`.

6. a, b, c, e, h, j, and k are valid; d, f, g, and i are invalid.

8. Only the variable declarations in Lines 3 and 4 are correct.

9. a and c are valid.

11. a. `-10 * a`

    b. `'8'`

    c. `(b * b - 4 * a * c) / 2 * a`

    d. `(-b + (b * b - 4 * a * c)) / 2 * a`

12. `x = 5`

    `y = 2`

    `z = 3`

    `w = 9`

14. `x = 875, y = 374.98`

15. a. `x = 2, y = 5, z = 6`

b. `x + y = 7`

c. `Sum of 2 and 6 is 8`

d. `z / x = 3`

e. `2 times 2 = 4`

17. `System.out.println(); or System.out.print("\n"); or System.out.print('\n');`

18. a and c are correct.

20. a. `x *= 2;`

b. `x += y-2;`

c. `sum += num;`

d. `z *= x + 2;`

e. `y /= x + 5;`

21. a. `x = x + 5 - z;`

b. `y = y * (2 * x + 5 - z);`

c. `w = w + 2 * z + 4;`

d. `x = x - (z + y - t);`

e. `sum = sum + num;`

f. `x = x / (y - 2);`

23.

	a	b	c	sum
`sum = a + b + c;`	3	5	14.1	22
`c /= a;`	3	5	4.7	22
`b += c - a;`	3	6	4.7	22
`a *= 2 * b + c;`	50	6	4.7	22

Chapter 3

1. a. False; b. True; c. True; d. True.

3. An object is an instance of a specific class.

5. `str = new String("Java Programming");`

6.

a. The value stored in ch is `'G'`.

   b. The value stored in `ch` is `'h'`.

   c. The value stored in `len` is `28`.

   d. The value stored in `position` is 7.

   e. The value stored in `position` is 23.

11.

```
JOptionPane.showMessageDialog(null,
            "Current Temperature: 70 degrees",
            "Temperature", JOptionPane.QUESTION_MESSAGE);
```

12.

   a. `75.40`

   b. `982.90`

   c. `75.399`

   d. `982.898`

15. a. Same as before.

   b. The file contains the output produced by the program.

   c. The file contains the output produced by the program. Old contents are erased.

   d. The program would prepare the file and store the output in the file.

Chapter 4

1. a. True; b. False; c. False; d. False; e. False; f. False; g. False; h. False; i. True.

2. a. i; b. i; c. ii; d. i; e. iii.

5. Omit the semicolon after `else`.

```
if(score >= 60)
   System.out.println("You pass.");
else
    System.out.println("You fail.");
```

8. `15`

11.

```
import java.io.*;

public class Errors
{
     static BufferedReader keyboard =
```

```
                new BufferedReader(new
                        InputStreamReader(System.in));

    public static void main(String[] args) throws IOException
    {
        int a, b;
        int c;
        boolean found;

        System.out.print("Enter the first integers: ");
        a = Integer.parseInt(keyboard.readLine());
        System.out.println();

        System.out.print("Enter the second integers: ");
        b = Integer.parseInt(keyboard.readLine());

        if(a > a * b  &&  10 < b)
            found = 2 * a > b;
        else
        {
            found = 2 * a < b;
            if(found)
                a = 3;
            c = 15;
            if(b > 0)
            {
                b = 0;
                a = 1;
            }
        }
    }
}
```

Chapter 5

1. a. False; b. True; c. False; d. True; e. True; f. True; g. True; h. False.

2. y = 1 and count = 100

3. 5

5. when ch > 'Z'

6. Sum = 112

8. Sum = 157

12. 8   23   21   0   23   0   12   1   20

14. 0 10 30 60

15. 2 7 17 37 77 157

17. a. *

   b. `infinite loop`

   c. `infinite loop`

   d. `****`

   e. `******`

   f. `***`

20. 11   19   30   49

23. a. `Both`

   b. `do...while`

   c. `while`

   d. `while`

26.

   (i)

```
number = Integer.parseInt(keyboard.readLine());

while(number != -1)
{
    total =  total + number;
    number = Integer.parseInt(keyboard.readLine());
}
```

27. a.

```
number = 1;
while(number <= 10)
{
    System.out.print(number + " ");
    number++;
}

System.out.println();
```

Chapter 6

1. a. True; b. True; c. False; d. True; e. False; f. False; g. True; h. True; i. True; j. False; k. False; l. False.

3. `JTextField`.

5. To identify other GUI components such as a `JTextField`.

6. Quite often you need to type less in a GUI program compared to its non-GUI version. Further, interface is easy to use and understand. For example, it is the GUI that made Internet popular!

7. Through the process outlined, you have methodology which will allow you to critically think and plan you problem solving approach. You may be able to identify the flaws involved in your thinking before you implement it. A well-analyzed problem leads to a well designed algorithm. Moreover, a program that is well-analyzed is easier to modify and spot and fix errors. No one will build a house without a blueprint.

10. a. method `add`; b. action event; c. `actionPerformed`; d. `new`; e. data, method; f. `JFrame`; g. event-driven h. `getText`, `setText`; i. superclass, subclass; j. `java.awt.event`; k. pixel.

14. Some of the methods are: `play`, `fastForward`, `fastBackward`, `stop`, `record`. There can be other methods such as `setTime`, `setDate`, `setRecordTime`, `setRecordDuration`, `setChannel`, `setSpeed`, and so on.

17. `Patron`: data members include `patronID`, `firstName`, `lastName`, `phone`, `email`, `address`, `status`, `noOfitemsOnLoan`; and methods include `set` and `get` methods for data members, `list itemsOnHand`, `calculateFine`.

   `Book`: data members include `bookID`, `title`, `author`, `ISBN`, `published`; and methods include `set` and `get` methods for data members.

   `LendRecord`: `patronID`, `bookID`, `dateOfLending`, `returnDate`, `fine`; and method include `set` and `get` methods for data members, `computeFine`.

Chapter 7

1. a. True; b. True; c. True; d. True; e. False; f. True; g. False; h. False.

3. a. Invalid; Method type is missing.

   b. Valid.

   c. Invalid; Data type for the parameter **b** is missing.

   d. Invalid; Missing parentheses after the method name.

5. a. `4`; b. `26`; c. `10 4 0`; d. `0`

8. a. (i) `125`; (ii) `432`

   b. The method computes x^3, where **x** is the argument of the function.

14.
```
3    4    6    7
3    15   6    19
3    14   6    9
```

Chapter 8

1. a. False ; b. False; c. True; d. False; e. False.

3. a. (i) Constructor at Line 1.

   (ii) Constructor at Line 3.

   (iii) Constructor at Line 4.

d.

```
public CC(int a, int b)
{
    u = a;
    v = b;
    w = 0;
}

public CC(int a, int b, double d)
{
    u = a;
    v = b;
    w = d;
}
```

5.

```
06:23:17
06:23:17
```

6.

   a. 6;

   b. 2;

   c. 2;

9. Both aa and bb point to the object bb.

10. `06:23:17`

11. The purpose of the copy constructor is to initialize an object, when the object is instantiated, using an existing object of the same type.

13. `package jpfpatpd.ch08.strangeClasses;`

Chapter 9

1. a. True; b. True; c. True; d. True; e. False; f. False; g. True.

3.

   a. `funcOne(list,50);`

   b. `System.out.print(funcSum(50,list[3]));`

   c. `System.out.print(funcSum(list[29],list[9]));`

   d. `funcTwo(list,Alist);`

5. `Array components are: 5, 6, 9, 19, 23, 37`

6. `List elements: 11 16 21 26 30`

8. a. 30

   b. 5

   c. 6

   d. row

   e. column

9. a. `int[][] alpha = new int[10][20];`

   b.

```
for(j = 0; j < alpha.length; j++)
   for(k = 0; k < alpha[0].length; k++)
       alpha[j][k] = 0;
```

Chapter 10

1. a. False; b. True; c. False; d. False; e. False; f. True.

2. a. 8; b. 6; c. 1; d. 8.

4.

   a.

Iteration	first	last	mid	list[mid]	No. of comparisons
1	0	10	5	55	2
2	0	4	2	17	2
3	0	1	0	2	2
4	1	1	1	10	2
5	2	1	the loop stops unsuccessful search		

This is an unsuccessful search. The total number of comparisons is 8.

6. `list = ["One", "Six", "Two", "Three", "Four", "Five"];`

8.

```
[Hello, 10, Happy, 20, Sunny, 30]
[Hello, 10, Joy, Happy, Sunny, 30]
```

Chapter 11

1. a. True; b. False; c. True; d. False.

4. The private members of a **class** are **private**; they cannot be directly accessed by the member functions of the derived class. The **protected** members of the base class can be directly accessed by the member function of the derived class

6. In a constructor of a subclass and during the overriding of a method in a subclass.

7. a. The statement

   ```
   class BClass AClass
   ```

   should be

   ```
   class BClass extends AClass
   ```

   b. Missing) in **System.out.println** statement.

   c. Variables u and v are private in **class AClass** and cannot be accessed directly accessed in **class BClass**.

9.

a.
```
public YClass()
{
    a = 0;
    b = 0;
}
```

b.
```
public XClass()
{
    super(0,0);
    z = 0;
}
```

c.
```
public void two(int u, int v)
{
    a = u;
    b = v;
}
```

10. **aObject** need to be initilized.

14. An abstract method is a method that only has the heading with no body. Moreover, the heading of an abstract method contains the reserved word **abstract** and ends with a semicolon.

15. An interface is a class that contains only abstract methods and/or named constants. It has no instance variables. An abstract class on the other hand can have instance variables. Further, an abstract class need not have any abstract methods.

Chapter 12

1. a. True; b. False; c. False; d. True; e. False; f. True; g. True; h. False; i. True; j. False.

2. (a) `Entering the try block.`
      `Exception: Lower limit violation.`
      `After the catch block`

3. (a) `Entering the try block.`
      `Exception: Lower limit violation.`
      `After the catch block`

   (c) `Entering the try block.`
      `Exiting the try block.`
      `After the catch block`

6.
```
public class TornadoException extends Exception
{
    public TornadoException()
    {
        super("Tornado: Take cover immediately");
    }

    public TornadoException(int m)
    {
        super("Tornado: " + m + "miles away; and approaching!");
    }
}
```

9. Any class can implement an interface. The three different options are to use an inner class, or an anonymous inner class or the application (the applet) program class itself to implement an interface.

Chapter 13

1. a. True; b. True; c. True; d. False; e. False; f. False; g. True; h. False; i. False.

2. `JCheckBox`, `JRadioButton`, `JComboBox` and `JList`.

5. Sometimes you want the user to select from a set of predefined values. In addition to freeing the user from typing in such values, to get a precise input you want the user to select a value from a set of given values.

7. b.

```
JCheckBox qualityCB;
qualityCB = new JCheckBox("draft");
```

d. `private JMenuBar menuMB = new JMenuBar();`

Chapter 14

1. a. True; b. True; c. False; d. False; e. False.

4. A function is called directly recursive if it calls itself.

5. A function that calls another function and eventually results in the original function call is said to be indirectly recursive.

7. a. The statements in Lines 2 and 3.

c. Any nonnegative integer.

e. It is a valid call. The value of `mystery(5)` is `10`.

9. a. It does not produce any output.

b. `5  6  7  8  9`

11. a. `2`

b. `3`

c. `5`

d. `21`

12. Suppose that `low` specifies the starting index and `high` specifies the ending index in the array. The elements of the array between `low` and `high` are to be reversed.

```
if(low < high)
{
     a. swap(list[low], list[high])
     b. reverse elements between low + 1 and high - 1)
}
```

Index